THE IRISH JACOBITE ARMY

The Irish Jacobite Army
Anatomy of the force

HARMAN MURTAGH
&
DIARMUID MURTAGH

FOUR COURTS PRESS

Typeset in 10.5 pt on 13.5 pt CaslonPro by
Carrigboy Typesetting Services for
FOUR COURTS PRESS LTD
7 Malpas Street, Dublin 8, Ireland
www.fourcourtspress.ie
and in North America for
FOUR COURTS PRESS
c/o IPG, 814 N. Franklin St, Chicago, IL 60610.

© Harman Murtagh and Four Courts Press 2024

A catalogue record for this title is available from the British Library.

ISBN 978-1-80151-121-6

All rights reserved.
Without limiting the rights under copyright reserved alone, no part of this publication may be reproduced, stored in or introduced into a retrieval system, or transmitted, in any form or by any means (electronic, mechanical, photocopying, recording or otherwise), without the prior written permission of both the copyright owner and publisher of this book.

SPECIAL ACKNOWLEDGMENT

The author and publisher would like to thank

The Technological University of the Shannon

and

The Military History Society of Ireland

for their generous support.

Printed in England
by CPI Antony Rowe, Chippenham, Wilts.

Contents

LIST OF ILLUSTRATIONS, MAPS AND TABLES ... ix

INTRODUCTION ... 1

1. *The peacetime armed forces, 1685–8* ... 7
    The Irish standing army ... 7
    Developments under the restoration ... 9
    The restoration militia ... 14
    Ordnance and engineering ... 15
    James II's reforms ... 16
    Tyrconnell's purge of the army ... 18
    The Catholic officers ... 24
    Training and equipment ... 25
    The Irish army in 1688 ... 27

2. *The Irish army and the English revolution, 1688–9* ... 31
    The overthrow of King James ... 31
    The loss of the Irish regiments in England ... 33
    Tyrconnell enlarges the Irish army ... 35
    Irish Protestants and William ... 38
    French involvement ... 40
    The reorganization of the army ... 42
    The summer campaign ... 44
    Scottish interlude ... 47

3. *The campaigns of 1690–1* ... 49
    Preliminaries to the Boyne ... 49
    The Boyne battle ... 51
    The defence of Limerick ... 55
    Cork and Kinsale ... 57
    The winter offensive and the rapparee campaign ... 58
    Saint-Ruth takes command ... 60
    Ballymore and Athlone ... 60
    The battle of Aughrim ... 61
    The end of the Irish war ... 66

CONTENTS

4. *Infantry* — 68
- Infantry numbers and units — 68
- Infantry regiments — 69
- Regimental organization and personnel — 73
- Recruitment and desertion — 85
- Camp followers — 90
- Clothing — 91
- Weapons and equipment — 95
- Infantry drill, training and tactics — 102

5. *Cavalry and dragoons* — 111
- Role and numbers — 111
- The cavalry regiments — 112
- Regimental organization and personnel of the cavalry — 113
- Horseguards and mounted grenadiers — 117
- 'The priding cavalry' — 119
- The dragoon regiments — 120
- Regimental organization and personnel of the dragoons — 122
- Clothing, equipment and weaponry — 124
- Cavalry and dragoon horses — 128
- Cavalry drill, tactics and training — 131

6. *Artillery and engineering* — 134
- The new professions — 134

  ARTILLERY — 134
- Organization and command — 134
- Personnel — 136
- Weapons — 138
- Transport — 144
- Ammunition — 146
- Deployment — 147

  ENGINEERING — 152
- Organization and personnel — 152
- Fortress warfare — 155

7. *Command and staff* — 161
- King and council — 161
- Tyrconnell's position — 162
- Marshal Rosen — 164

Comte de Lauzun   166
Marquis de Saint-Ruth   166
Patrick Sarsfield   168
Subordinate generals   169
Order of battle   170
Civilian administrators   174
Staff appointments   177
Battle control   178

8. *Support services: law, medicine and chaplaincy*   180
Law   180
Medicine   186
Chaplaincy   192

9. *The French dimension*   195
French policy   195
The French generals, 1689–90   200
Regimental officers, 1689–90   202
The French expeditionary force, 1690   205
Saint-Ruth's involvement, 1691   208
Technical officers   210
The supply of *matériel* and money   213
Irish soldiers for France   219

10. *Finance and logistics*   225
The financial challenge   225
The copper coinage   228
Food supply   231
Bread supply   233
Meat and dairy food   240
Drink   242
Transport   245
Fodder   247
Accommodation   250
Wartime industry   251

11. *Auxiliary forces*   256
The militia   256
Balldearg O'Donnell's army   258
The rapparees   268

CONTENTS

12. *Backgrounds and beliefs* — 281
   - Composition of the officer corps — 281
   - BACKGROUNDS — 282
   - Peers and gentry — 282
   - Merchants, lawyers and officials — 286
   - Junior officers — 287
   - Prewar military experience — 289
   - Protestant officers — 293
   - Gael and Norman — 294
   - Financial and property resources — 298
   - Jacobite houses — 301
   - BELIEFS — 303
   - Motives for enlistment — 303
   - King James's legitimacy — 304
   - Kingdom or colony — 306
   - Defence of country — 309
   - Recovery of land — 310
   - Restoration of Catholicism — 311
   - Will to resist — 313

13. *The army's fate* — 314
   - The surrender terms — 314
   - Offers and counter-offers — 315
   - Re-forming the army in France — 317
   - The position of the officers — 322
   - Deployments in the nine years war — 323
   - Full integration into the French army — 323
   - Recruitment — 327
   - Irish regiments in Spain — 330
   - The 'wild geese' and the Jacobite cause — 332

EPILOGUE — 336

ABBREVIATIONS AND BIBLIOGRAPHY — 340

INDEX — 369

Illustrations, Maps and Tables

PLATES
appear between pages 182 and 183

1. Richard Talbot, duke of Tyrconnell, captain general
2. King James II
3. Conrad Von Rosen, marshal
4. Patrick Sarsfield, earl of Lucan, major general
5. James FitzJames, duke of Berwick, lieutenant general
6. Antonin-Nompar de Caumont, comte Lauzun, captain general of the French
7. Anthony Hamilton, major general
8. Justin MacCarthy, Viscount Mountcashel, lieutenant general
9. Henry Luttrell, brigadier general
10. Marquis d'Usson, lieutenant general
11. Thomas Maxwell, major general
12. Battle of Bantry Bay, 1689
13. Battle of the Boyne, 1690
14. Siege of Limerick, 1690
15. Battle of Aughrim, 1691
16. Portumna Castle, Co. Galway
17. Loughmoe Castle, Co. Tipperary

FIGURES

1. A cavalry kettledrummer	6
2. A cavalry officer	30
3. A dragoon sergeant	48
4. An infantry musketeer	67
5. Infantry officers	110
6. Baron de Pointis, French artillerist	160
7. Colour of earl of Antrim's infantry regiment	194
8. 6-pounder field gun	224
9. 'Gun-money' from the Limerick mint, 1691	255
10. Matchlock musket	280
11. Seventeenth-century sword	335
12. Trooper, FitzJames's cavalry, France, 1760	339

MAPS

1. Ireland, 1689–91 — 8
2. The battle of the Boyne, 1690 — 52
3. The battle of Aughrim, 1691 — 63

TABLES

1. The Irish military establishment and its cost, 1688 — 27
2. The infantry establishment, 1689 — 70
3. The exercise of the musketeers — 105
4. The cavalry establishment, 1689 — 112
5. The dragoon establishment, 1689 — 121
6. French regiments in Ireland, 1690 — 206
7. Daily rates of pay, July 1689 — 227
8. Balldearg O'Donnell's forces, 1691 — 262
9. Irish regiments in France, 1692 — 321

CREDITS

Figures Anne Murtagh; *Maps* Sarah Gearty; *Plates* 1, 3, 4, 6, 7, 11, 12 Alamy; 2 National Army Museum, London; 5 Casa de Alba Foundation, Madrid; 13 Photo © National Gallery of Ireland.

Introduction

For three years, from 1689 to 1691, Ireland was a significant theatre in the early stages of a major European war. Multi-national armies, led by generals of European reputation, were involved across the island in a series of military operations – sieges, pitched battles and other manoeuvres. The forces involved were immense: in 1690 over 60,000 soldiers were present at the battle of the Boyne and a year later perhaps 40,000 at the battle of Aughrim. George Story's contemporary estimate of the loss of life in the war was 'at least one hundred thousand, young and old', of whom just over a quarter were combatants and the rest civilian victims of wartime hardship and privation. He computed that 617 Jacobite army officers and 12,676 other ranks were killed in action, together with 2,650 rapparees or partisans whom the Williamites killed or hanged. The accompanying destruction of property, loss of livestock and other goods, and general economic disruption further meant, he wrote, that treble the number of casualties were 'ruined and undone'. The war led to the migration of 20,000 Irish soldiers to France, accompanied by numbers of women and children, and they were followed by a stream of migratory Irishmen to continental armies for much of the eighteenth century. The war enjoys a variety of titles. In Ireland it is known as the Williamite/Jacobite war, the war of the (two) kings (in Irish: *cogadh an dá rí*) and, more recently, the war of the three kings. It was also a theatre of the major European conflict variously known as the nine years war, the war of the grand alliance or the war of the league of Augsburg. By any standards, it was a major crisis in Irish history, releasing shockwaves that have yet to fully subside.

Three distinct but intertwined issues underlay the war in Ireland. First, it was a dynastic dispute precipitated by the Dutch *stadhouder* William of Orange's seizure of the English throne from his Catholic father-in-law, King James II, in the coup of late 1688 known in Britain as the glorious revolution. Those who continued to support James came to be called Jacobites from *Jacobus*, the Latin version of his name. The term dates from 1690. Second, William was largely motivated by his desire to include England's military and financial potential in the alliance forming on the Continent against his *bête noire*, King Louis XIV's France, the pre-eminent European power. Louis countered the setback of William's coup by sending James to Ireland, to use the island as a stepping stone to re-establish himself in Britain, or at the very least distract William and his resources from the coming continental war. The arrival of James, with French military support of both personnel and *matériel*, compelled William to pursue a military solution in Ireland. Third, Ireland was chosen for the French intervention because at least three-quarters of its two million or so inhabitants were Catholics – Gaelic Irish and Old English – who could be counted on to support their co-religionist, James. During his short reign, the Irish Catholics had already recovered much of the power and position they had lost over the preceding century, and they now contributed a substantial army to back James. While they sought a better accommodation for the practice of their religion, the principal price they demanded for their support was the reversal of the property confiscations that had transferred ownership of almost 80 per cent of Irish land to immigrants from Britain. These New English and Scots were Protestants who formed perhaps a quarter of the population, and were especially numerous in Ulster. The antagonism between the old inhabitants and the new flared into civil war when Protestants sided with William in response to the threat Catholic support for James posed to their property and security. Contemporaries also noticed the strong hatred the Irish Catholics bore towards the English. They were '*ennemis irréconciliables*' in the opinion of the astute French ambassador, the comte d'Avaux. After King James and the French departed in the autumn of 1690, the nationalistic character of the war became more transparent with the resolution of the leading Irish army officers 'to defend their country', and their disposition to bypass James and deal directly with the French government.

As befitted a leader of the grand alliance, William was able to bring into the Irish war a multi-national army of English, Dutch, Danish, German, Huguenot and Protestant Irish soldiers, led by generals of similar international backgrounds. James's army largely comprised Catholic Irish, although he had the assistance of several hundred French and British officers, together with seven battalions of French infantry in 1690. The Irish Jacobite army was not a rabble, but a properly organized force, admittedly handicapped by the rapidity of its expansion, inexperience, indifferent leadership and shortages of arms and *matériel*. These deficiencies were most obvious the first two years of the war. With combat experience, better supplies of arms and ammunition and more professional leadership, the army grew in capability and confidence, and its morale was good, if fragile, as it embarked on its third year of campaigning in 1691. Although it never matched the firepower of its opponents, the army had its successes, not least in maintaining resistance as long as it did. Its pertinacity made all the more dramatic the pathos of its defeat. Colonel Charles O'Kelly lamented the 'public calamity of my countrymen, my unfortunate countrymen' and wrote of his tears at the 'frequent remembrance of the slaughter of Aughrim and the sad separation at Limerick'.

There are already several authoritative accounts of the war, such as those of Demetrius Charles Boulger (1911), J.G. Simms (1969), Richard Doherty (1998) and John Childs (2007), together with descriptions of the major engagements, notably G.A. Hayes-McCoy on the battles of the Boyne and Aughrim, J.G. Simms on the first siege of Limerick, Pádraig Lenihan on the battle of the Boyne, Michael McNally on the battles of the Boyne and Aughrim, and Piers Wauchope and others on the siege of Derry. However, the main focus of this study is to describe and analyse the army's formation, composition, character and capability. Opening chapters on its background and combat record are followed by description and analysis of the army's infantry, cavalry, dragoons, weaponry, tactical disposition, artillery, engineering, command and staff, finance, logistics and other supports, and the backgrounds and beliefs of its personnel. French military involvement is examined, as are the roles of various Irish auxiliaries. A final chapter outlines the army's fate and explores the degree to which its personnel, formations and ethos endured in exile on the Continent. Developments in other armies of the late seventeenth century are not disregarded, and the analysis is set in the context of Irish and European history. What is presented is largely a micro-historic study, focussed on a relatively well-documented, if obscure, corner of Irish and European history. But then, as Simon Schama observes, it is the historian's duty to wage war on forgetfulness.

Much source material has been made available by the Irish Manuscripts Commission, particularly the d'Avaux *Négociations* and three detailed volumes of *Franco-Irish correspondence, 1688–92*. Also very valuable are the commission's publications *The proclamations of Ireland*, *The acts of James II's Irish parliament of 1689* and *Poema de Hibernia*, together with the 'Letter book of Richard Talbot', 'Lists of Irish Jacobites' and other contributions in *Analecta Hibernica*. Most of the army's Irish records are lost or destroyed, but Manuscript 181 of the Carte collection in the Bodleian Library, Oxford, has details of the army's administration over the summer of 1689, some of which is published with other material in Macpherson's *Original papers*. The National Library of Ireland holds small collections of Tyrconnell and Kilmallock papers, and Trinity College Dublin further Kilmallock papers. There are regimental and officer lists in the Bodleian, TCD and the British Library. Published eye-witness accounts from the Jacobite side include the memoirs of King James and those of John Stevens, Charles O'Kelly, Nicholas(?) Plunkett, Charles Leslie and the duke of Berwick. The poetry of Dáibhidh Uí Bhruadair contributes a Gaelic perspective. The *Calendar of state papers, domestic series*, and the *Clarendon and Rochester correspondence* are useful sources for James II's reign. Much information on the Jacobite army is also found in the numerous

Williamite sources. These include the Clarke papers in TCD, the Reduction of Ireland papers in the Royal Irish Academy, and such publications as *Dublin Intelligence, London Gazette,* George Story's *An impartial history of the wars of Ireland* and *A continuation of the impartial history,* and William King's *The state of the Protestants under the late King James's government,* which has valuable appendices, as has Walter Harris's eighteenth-century biography of William III. There are numerous Williamite pamphlets and soldiers' memoirs, such as those of Parker, Kane, Mackay, Dumont de Bostaquet and Claudianus. The Historical Manuscripts Commission's *Ormonde, Finch* and other collections and the Irish Manuscript Commission's *The Danish force in Ireland* are also valuable.

Among secondary contributions to have influenced this study are the numerous and ever-perceptive works of J.G. Simms, especially his monograph *Jacobite Ireland 1685–91,* the ground-breaking *Jacobite movement* by Sir Charles Petrie, John Childs's study, *The army, James II and the glorious revolution,* Éamonn Ó Ciardha's *Ireland and the Jacobite cause,* which adds a fresh dimension to Jacobite studies by utilizing the perceptions of the Irish Gaelic poets, and *Kings in conflict* edited by W.A. Maguire. The army lists, English and Irish, of Charles Dalton are monumental works of scholarship. James Dalton's *King James's Irish army list* has long been relied upon by researchers. In recent years scholars such as Micheline Kerney-Walsh, Eoghan Ó hAnnracháin, Nathalie Genet-Rouffiac and others have greatly informed our knowledge of Irish soldiers on the Continent, although after 150 years John Cornelius O'Callaghan's *History of the Irish brigades* still remains the best overview. There are full-scale modern biographies of leading Jacobite army leaders: Tyrconnell by Pádraig Lenihan, Sarsfield by Piers Wauchope, Berwick by Sir Charles Petrie, Mountcashel by Darren Graham and King James by John Miller. Accounts of these and numerous lesser figures are to be found in the *Oxford dictionary of national biography,* the *Dictionary of Irish biography,* Richard Hayes's *Biographical dictionary of Irishmen in France* and John Childs's *Biographical dictionary of British army officers on foreign service.* There is much material in the thirty-three volumes of the Military History Society of Ireland's authoritative journal *The Irish Sword. The Irish Genealogist* and the journals of Ireland's many local historical societies have also been useful. I have profited greatly from such comparative studies as David Chandler's *The art of war in the age of Marlborough,* C.H. Firth's *Cromwell's army,* Christopher Duffy's *The fortress in the age of Vauban and Frederick the Great,* David Parrott's *The business of war,* John Childs's *The army of Charles II,* R.E. Scouller's *The armies of Queen Anne,* John Lynn's monumental study of the French army *Giant of the grand siècle,* Guy Rowlands's *The dynastic state and the army under*

Louis XIV and by no means least Kenneth Ferguson's unpublished PhD thesis 'The army in Ireland from the restoration to the act of union'. Many other sources and secondary authorities have been used, as the footnotes and bibliography make clear. The final chapter outlining the survival of the Irish army's traditions on the Continent is largely based on the work of others.

This study has a lengthy history of its own. It started life as doctoral dissertation of my father Diarmuid Murtagh, incomplete at the time of his premature death in 1956. While respecting his basic scheme and utilizing much of his research and ideas, I have now revised and rewritten the work, utilizing newly available sources, reworking his sources and adding new chapters, such as those on logistics, the French dimension, the auxiliaries and the army's subsequent fate. The outcome, I believe, is a genuine joint work. I know my father was greatly encouraged by his friends in the Military History Society of Ireland, such as Sir Charles Petrie, Professor G.A. Hayes-McCoy, Colonel Dan Bryan and Dr J.G. Simms. The last named was my own inspiring and rigorous teacher, both at undergraduate and postgraduate level, in the history school of Trinity College Dublin. I have benefitted from the encouragement and guidance of many friends and fellow-scholars. Sadly, some such as N.W. English, Sheila Mulloy, Rolf Loeber, Micheline Kerney-Walsh, T.P O'Neill and Raymond Gillespie are now deceased. I think also of my late mother, who stoically bore the time-consuming and unremunerative historiographical activities of both a husband and a son. I too have been sustained by the friendship and encouragement of the present council and members of the Military History Society, not least that of Anthony Cudmore, Donal O'Carroll, Kenneth Ferguson, Pat MacCarthy, Don Bigger and Tony Kinsella, and the late Kevin Danaher and Pat Hogan. Others who have guided or encouraged me at various stages include Patrick Melvin, Pádraig Lenihan, Magda Loeber, Gearoid O'Brien and Michael Byrne. Darren Laye and the other participants in the Jacobite Studies Trust virtual workshop have helped me to realize that the path of Jacobite studies is less lonely than I had thought. Bill Runacre in particular has been particularly generous with information from sources of which I was unaware. I am particularly indebted to Jennie Strevens for her translations of Fumeron's dispatches. The in-text drawings are by Anne Murtagh and the maps by Sarah Gearty. I am very grateful to both. My special thanks go also to Mary Shine Thompson who has critically read the manuscript from a literary perspective. However, none but its authors bear responsibility for any errors or shortcomings the work may contain. I am grateful to the staffs of the various libraries and archive repositories that have facilitated my research: in Dublin, the TCD Library, the National Library of Ireland, the Royal Irish Academy Library and Dublin City Library and

Archive; in Oxford, the Bodleian Library; and in Athlone the Aidan Heavey Library and the library of the Technological University of the Shannon. Finally, my wife Anne, and my children Vanessa and Harman, deserve my deep thanks for tolerating my long absences in libraries, at conferences or in my study, as I strove to bring this work to fruition.

I plan to follow this study with a companion volume, which will list the regiments of the army, briefly outline the history and record of each, and list their officers with, as far as possible, their biographical details.

This work has been published with the generous support of the Military History Society of Ireland and the Technological University of the Shannon, which is greatly appreciated.

Dates are given in the Julian style, still used in Britain and Ireland in 1689–91, and at that time ten days behind the Gregorian calendar that was widely followed on the Continent. However, the year has been treated as beginning on 1 January.

Footnote references are given in an abbreviated form, the key to which has been incorporated in the bibliography.

Harman Murtagh

Figure 1. A cavalry kettledrummer

CHAPTER 1

The peacetime armed forces, 1685–8

The Irish standing army

THE CONCEPT OF A permanent standing army in Ireland dated from the suppression of Silken Thomas FitzGerald's revolt against King Henry VIII in 1537. Although most of the government's soldiers were paid off, 340 men were retained as a retinue for the Irish lord deputy and treasurer, and to provide garrisons for a dozen castles. The military offices of marshal, master of the ordnance and clerk of the checks dated from *circa* 1540. In 1641 the army was about 3,000 strong; it grew to 15,000 in the late 1650s, but contracted again after King Charles II's restoration in 1660. In 1685, at the time of King James II's accession, the army had a peacetime establishment of seven regiments of infantry, three of cavalry and a single troop of mounted grenadiers, the latter a recent innovation in England, copied from France. In addition, to attend the lord lieutenant there were two ceremonial units of negligible military value: a troop of horseguards formed from gentlemen's sons to escort the viceroy, and a company of footguards composed of elderly soldiers, dressed like the English yeomen of the guard and equipped with battle-axes. The establishment strength of the Irish army at that time was 7–8,000 men. For much of Charles II's reign, its size exceeded that of the English establishment, until the latter's numbers were boosted by the return of the 3,000-strong Tangier garrison in 1684 and subsequent further enlargement by King James. The peacetime Irish army absorbed 85 per cent of the local revenue, placing it at the centre of the government's priorities and concerns.[1]

Under Charles II, the army's primary purpose was to act as a Protestant police force to protect and maintain the post-restoration settlement from both the aggrieved Catholic Irish and disaffected Protestant sectarian extremists. Its subsidiary role was the more obvious military function of protecting the country against invasion in time of war. It also provided personnel to support the British army and navy in wartime, and for the Tangier garrison. James II

---

[1] Ferguson, 'Army in Ireland', pp 1, 9, 15–17; Beckett, 'Irish armed forces', pp 42–3; Parker, *Memoirs*, 3; *Ormonde MSS*, i, pp 400–7; *IALKC*, pp 147–53; Dalton, i, pp 254–5; *CTB*, pp 1742–6; *CSPD 1685*, pp 76–9; Miller, 'Catholic officers', p. 39.

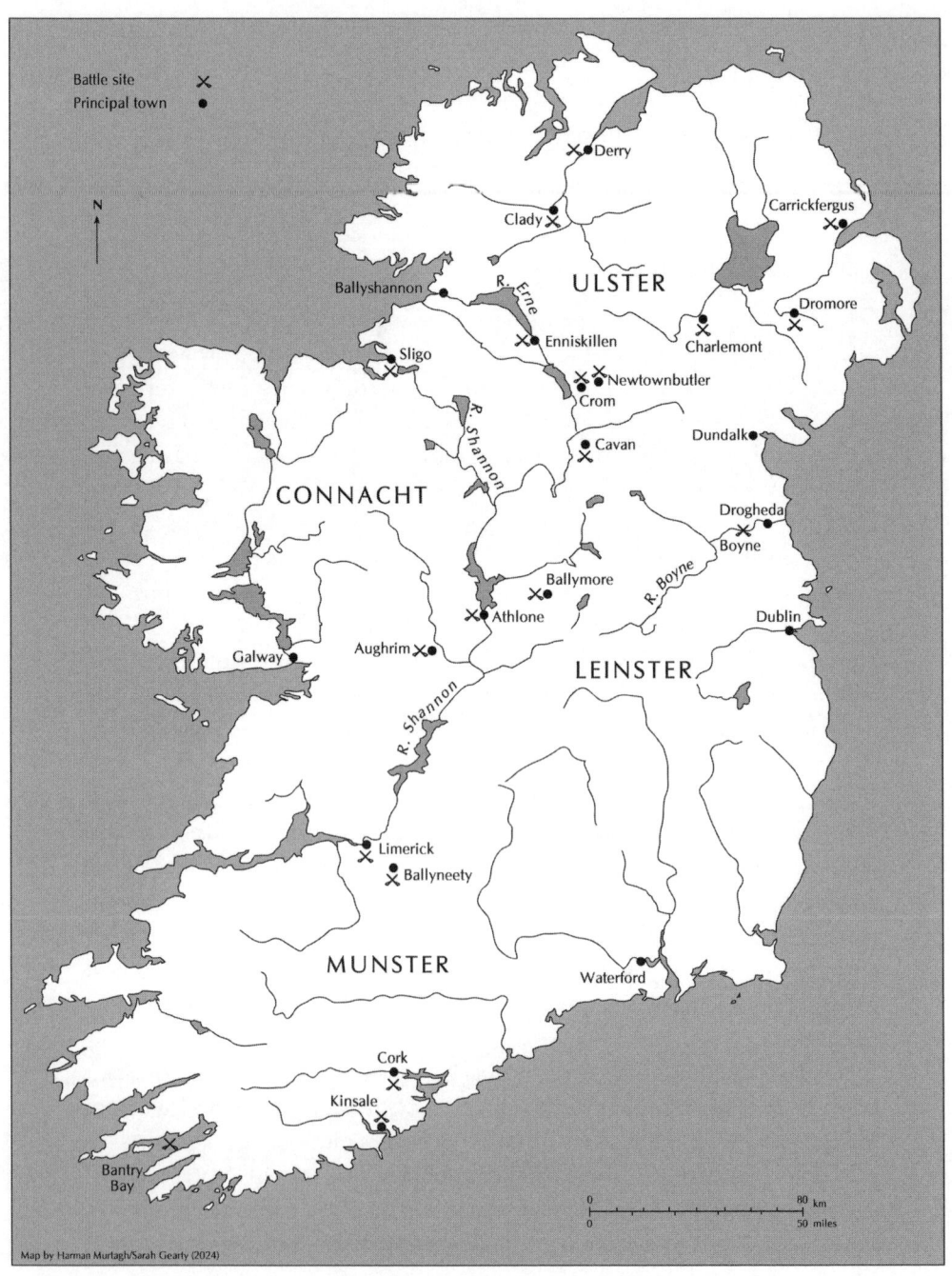

Map 1. Ireland, 1689–91

regarded the Irish army as a reserve force available for deployment in England in the event of a crisis. Like its English and Scottish equivalents, the Irish army was no more than a local organization of the land forces of the crown, and subject to royal control. Nevertheless, its insularity, functions, funding, system of appointments and continuity of personnel combined to infuse it with much of the character of a distinctive force, sometimes indeed referred to as the army *of* Ireland. In social terms, a commission in the army offered an employment outlet for younger sons and those of military disposition, as well as adding to the status, security and incomes of those officers who were members of the post-restoration Irish elite. Appointments were generally the prerogative of the lord lieutenant, who was the army's commander-in-chief. The great figure of restoration Ireland was the 1st duke of Ormond, but his viceroyalty ended in 1685. He had taken a particular interest in the army, many of whose officers benefitted from his patronage. At James's accession the senior officer was the aged 1st earl of Granard, newly promoted to lieutenant general. This made way for the appointment of the earl of Arran, Ormond's fourth son, to the prestigious, if empty, post of marshal. Granard's active military service was gained in Scotland in the 1640s under Montrose. Subsequently, as a tried and trusted royalist, he had risen steadily in the post-restoration Irish army. The other staff officers were the muster-master general and clerk of the checks (one office), the advocate and surgeon generals, and the senior ordnance officers.[2]

Developments under the restoration

The restoration Irish army had evolved from the Cromwellian army of occupation, whose personnel continued to form the bulk of its rank and file, which differed from the practice in England. Room was found for Protestant royalists, especially among the commissioned officers. Ormond continued to harbour concerns about the reliability of so many ex-Cromwellian soldiers. In 1663 Captain Blood's abortive attempt to seize Dublin Castle and take Ormond hostage confirmed the viceroy's suspicions of the army, which he retained into the 1680s. To strengthen security, Ormond recruited a new twelve-company regiment in England, known as the Irish footguards, which embarked for Ireland in 1662 and was quartered in Dublin. The regiment was dressed in red coats, and Richard Butler, later earl of Arran, was its first colonel. The rest of the army continued to be organized in troops and

---

2 *CSPD 1684–5*, pp 108–9; *1685*, p. 144; Beckett, 'Irish armed forces', p. 45; Miller, 'Catholic officers', p. 42; Hand, 'Constitutional position', p. 331; *IALKC*, pp 87–8; *DIB*, iii, pp 1046–7; Ferguson, 'Army in Ireland', p. 17.

companies, the pre-commonwealth structures to which it had reverted in 1660, and it was distributed in garrisons throughout the island. It was poorly equipped: in 1676 it had only 500 good muskets and 300 barrels of powder. Half its pikes were broken. The number of troops and companies varied from time to time: in 1682 the army comprised twenty-four troops of horse and seventy companies of foot in addition to the footguards regiment. Eight companies of the returned Tangier garrison were added in 1684. The independent-company model was distinctly old-fashioned, but in Ireland it suited the policing role of the army, which necessitated its distribution in small units throughout the island.[3]

Any possibility that the army might pose a threat to the security of the regime was lessened by its dispersal in over fifty garrisons and the absence of a command structure of regimental field officers. Furthermore, organization in companies and troops cost the government less, as no regimental establishments had to be provided and paid for. In any case, in the absence of barracks, dispersal in small units was necessary to facilitate the billeting of the army in inns and private houses. The latter type of accommodation was of doubtful legality, but a practical necessity. Since arrears in pay left soldiers dependent on local credit, it was difficult to transfer units from one location to another. In 1676, with pay nine months in arrears, company commanders were permitted to allow their men to take on labouring work, while cavalry troopers were allowed to go home to live off their farms. Indeed, particularly in the case of the cavalry, if a commander had an estate, it was common for his troop to be stationed conveniently close by to supplement his labour needs at harvest time. Local recruiting facilitated part-time soldiering, with troopers combining modest military duties with farming activities, sometimes only turning up for the former on muster days. Such a system was inimical to the army's professionalism, as it militated against the maintenance of discipline, proficiency in drill, exposure to new weapons, ways and ideas, and the honing of the skills required to conduct combined manoeuvres. Nevertheless, a review at the Curragh in 1670, for which the army was temporarily regimented, impressed observers. Tentative proposals to 'new-model' the army on a permanent basis by regimenting the cavalry (1662) and later the whole army (1670) came to nothing until the mid-1680s.[4]

The Irish government's finances improved sufficiently in the last decade of Charles II's reign to provide a surplus that was used to fund the Tangier

---

3 Ferguson, 'Army in Ireland', p. 10; Carte, *Ormond*, iv, pp 118–19, 123–5; Beckett, *Cavalier duke*, pp 85–7; Beckett, 'Irish armed forces', pp 42–3; Falkiner, 'Regiment of guards', pp 79–80, 88; *IALKC*, pp 131, 140–3; Childs, *Charles II*, p. 207.   4 Beckett, 'Irish armed forces', pp 46–8; *IALKC*, pp 131–5; Guy, 'Irish military establishment', pp 212–13; Childs, *Charles II*, 206.

garrison and, after its closure, to allow the remission of £30,000 annually to England to help pay for the army there, a practice that continued until 1688. At the beginning of that year the army accounted for 85 per cent of the Irish revenue. Funds also became available for the erection of the Royal Hospital for old soldiers at Kilmainham. In 1684 the increased revenue finally allowed the troops and companies of the Irish army to be grouped together in regiments similar in size and structure to those in England. Three new cavalry regiments were formed, each of nine troops, one being of dragoons. The regimental establishment was 39 officers and 441 other ranks. (There were no lieutenant colonels in the cavalry at this stage.) The footguards and six new infantry regiments each comprised thirteen companies, of which one was a company of grenadiers – assault troops – a new concept at the time, introduced from France. The strength of the other ranks of each company in the footguards was 98, providing for an establishment of 44 officers and 1,274 other ranks. In the rest of the infantry regiments, the equivalent strength was only 66 per company, giving each regiment an establishment of 44 officers and 858 other ranks. However, in practice units were seldom, if ever, at their nominal establishment strength. As early as 1685 King James, an old soldier himself, sought to curb 'that great abuse of officers in mustering servants, tenants, townsmen and other uncertain persons to complete the number of their regiments, companies and troops' for inspection by the muster master or his agent. Payment to a regiment was based on the number mustered. A false return, achieved by adding to unit strength on inspection day, represented a straight, but of course dishonest gain by the officers. Two officials, the muster-master general and the controller of the musters, oversaw the musters, which were supposed to take place regularly to ensure that units were up to strength, and properly armed and equipped. The growth in revenue ensured that the army was paid more promptly: in 1686 the earl of Clarendon, while viceroy, claimed to have reduced the period of arrears from six months to two. However, by 1688 the flight of so many Protestants had damaged the Irish economy, causing revenue to fall again, with a consequent increase of arrears in military pay.[5]

Overall, the commissioned officers numbered 465. In 1685 all but one of the colonels were peers or knights, as were several of the troop and company commanders, with many of the remainder being their relatives. In each regiment the colonel, lieutenant colonel (or major in the cavalry) were also

---

[5] Beckett, 'Irish armed forces', pp 52–3; Ferguson, 'Army in Ireland', pp 16–17; *CTB*, pp 1742–6; *Ormonde MSS*, i, pp 400–6; *CSPD 1685*, p. 111; *1686–7*, p. 25; Childs, *Charles II*, pp 104–9; *Clarendon*, ii, p. 97; Melvin, 'Irish troop movements', p. 91.

company or troop commanders, drawing thereby the pay of both ranks. An infantry colonel, for example, was paid £201 per annum in 1688 together with an additional £134 4s. for his captaincy. Although not officially sanctioned, an officer's commission was generally regarded as his proprietorial right, forfeited only by his death. If, before that, he disposed of it by passing it on to a kinsman, or more likely selling it, a new commission was invariably granted to the donee or purchaser. Henry Pargiter, for example, reputedly purchased a lieutenancy in the footguards for £800 in 1677, while Thomas Brooke spent 'most of his fortune' purchasing a cavalry captaincy in 1680, presumably at much the same figure as his namesake, George Brooke, who spent £1,600 on a similar commission the same year. The pay of a cavalry captain was £235 per annum, so in straight financial terms the Brookes' investment would have yielded an annual return of approximately 14.5 per cent. King James was opposed to the sale of commissions, but the practice was too deep-seated to be stopped. In any case he was prepared to make exceptions, as in the case of Captain Robert Forbes, who was allowed to sell his captaincy in his father's regiment and purchase the lieutenant colonelcy from Robert Salkeld, who was 'aged and willing to retire and live in Yorkshire'. In fact, Salkeld did not retire immediately, but instead secured command of the troop of mounted grenadiers, which he then sold to Lord Ikerrin, who in turn sold his newly granted captaincy in Justin MacCarthy's foot to John Rothe. Thus, military office was not only a place of trust in the king's service, but also a valuable item of capital that brought both respectability and profit to its holder. Many officers were English in background, and most of the remainder came from the New English section of Irish society, the descendants of Elizabethan and early-Stuart settlers. In the earl of Granard's foot, for example, Granard himself and six of the captains were New English, two company commanders were Old English, the descendants of the medieval immigrants, and the remaining four, including the lieutenant colonel, were English. The junior officers are harder to classify, but were probably in much the same proportion. Purchase and influence, rather than seniority, were the ladders to promotion, with the consequence that subalterns were often quite elderly, whereas more senior officers could be comparatively youthful. Ormond, with his son the earl of Arran and his grandson the earl of Ossory (aged twenty), commanded the three cavalry regiments in 1685, as well as the footguards and another infantry regiment. Technically they were Old English, but by culture and inclination differed little from the New English, although when it suited him Ormond, an Irish speaker, would maintain that 'he was the most Irish Irishman of all'.[6]

6 *Clarendon*, i, p. 437; *CSPD 1684–5*, p. 211; *1687–9*, 145; Ohlmeyer, *Making Ireland English*, pp 6–8; *IALKC*, p. 150; *CSPD 1686–7*, pp 12, 181, 192; Miller, 'Catholic officers', p. 37.

For other ranks (non-commissioned officers and private soldiers) the establishment figure was variously estimated at 7,736 in 1686 and 8,242 in 1688. These numbers were not achieved in practice: in 1686 actual strength was more than 2,000 below the establishment figure. Throughout Charles II's reign, a Protestant monopoly of the army was maintained by enforcement of the Elizabethan oath of supremacy, which the muster-master general's officials administered as required. Although the oath could be suspended under the royal prerogative, and there was no Irish equivalent to the English test acts, nonetheless conformity in the Irish Caroline army was tightly maintained. No Catholics were commissioned, with the short-lived exception of Richard Talbot in 1672, and none appear to have served in the lower ranks before 1685. The rank and file may have been predominantly English: whole companies disbanded in 1686 were reported 'for the most part English'.[7]

Some Catholics with military inclinations were able to serve in British units overseas, specifically the Anglo-Dutch brigade (1674–85), the Tangier colony (1661–84), the British brigade in Portugal (1662–8), and most notably in the British brigade sent by Charles II to support France in the war against the Dutch (1672–8). The latter involvement included a fifteen-company Irish regiment raised and commanded by the duke of Ormond's nephew, Sir George Hamilton, until his death in 1676, and thereafter by Thomas Dungan, both Catholics. A second short-lived regiment for France, raised and commanded by the Old English Protestant Wentworth Dillon, 4th earl of Roscommon, was incorporated into Hamilton's in 1672. Irishmen also served in the duke of Monmouth's foot in the same force. These units were an important training ground for Catholic officers who later served in James II's army, such as Richard Hamilton, Patrick Sarsfield, Justin MacCarthy and several others. Dungan, prior to his appointment as lieutenant governor of Tangier, and then MacCarthy attempted to revive the regiment in Ireland in 1678–9, employing a mixture of officers who had already served in France and others wishing to do so, but the project was abandoned amid the turbulence surrounding the 'popish plot'. The list of officers at that time is a pointer to future senior Jacobite army leaders. Some Irish officers and other personnel remained on in the French service after 1678, apparently retaining a collective identity as companies within at least three Franco-German regiments, probably supplemented by quiet recruitment in Ireland. There was also a complement of Irish mercenary officers in the Habsburg armies and those of smaller Catholic states, although their number had decreased after the end of the thirty years war. These exceptions qualify, but do not substantially alter, the

---

7 *Ormonde MSS*, i, p. 435; *IALKC*, p. 85; Childs, *Charles II*, pp 25–8, 104–5; 'Rycaut letters', p. 158.

fact that Charles II's Irish army was a Protestant force closed to Catholics, whose primary role was to provide security for the Protestant population.[8]

The restoration militia

A second military force available to the restoration government was the militia. This was a part-time military force raised from the civil population and organized on a county basis. It was trained and armed to supplement the regular army in time of emergency. In Ireland, the concept was first introduced in the 1620s, but confined at that time to the Ulster-plantation counties. Indeed, Protestant communities were prone to make *ad hoc* defensive arrangements whenever they felt threatened. The outbreak of the Dutch war was the background to the successful formation by the government of a national militia in 1666. Its role was envisaged as a police force to keep the country quiet, while the army confronted any possible invasion. The project was supported by the Munster president, the earl of Orrery, who had a strong interest in military affairs (on which he had written a manual), but Ormond was wary of a militia, fearing that its membership would be a means of re-arming ex-Cromwellians, whom he distrusted. For this reason, the militia was not placed on a statutory basis, allowing the government to call it into being only when it was required, which in practice was confined to three occasions: 1666; 1672 during the war with the Dutch; and 1678 at the time of the 'popish plot', when the militia disarmed the Catholic population. In 1672 its strength was put at 10,000 cavalry and 14,000 infantry. Information survives on its organization in King's County, showing an array of two troops of horse and three companies of foot, amounting to just over 400 men in all. Its administration was in the charge of the commissioners of array, comprised of the sheriffs and some other prominent landowners. The captains were drawn from the same class. The imposition of the oath of supremacy ensured that the personnel were entirely Protestant. However, funding for pay and for the purchase of arms and ammunition was raised locally from all landowners, including Catholics, rated at 600 acres per horseman and 300 acres for each foot soldier. The weaponry and other military accoutrements purchased were the property of the troop or company. Captains were expected to muster their men for training and inspection for a day every two months, but this only occurred at times of militia activity.[9]

---

[8] Childs, *Charles II*, pp 105, 237–9, 242–3, 245–6, 249–50; Dalton, i, pp 209, 245; *CSPD 1685*, p. 111; Wauchope, *Sarsfield*, pp 14–16; Ó Ciosáin, 'Irish migration to France', p. 102.
[9] Ferguson, 'Army in Ireland', pp 12–14; Miller, 'Non-professional soldiery', pp 317–23; Loeber, 'Irish militia documents', passim; *A new history of Ireland*, iii, p. 441.

Ordnance and engineering

Artillery, engineering and all armaments matters fell within the provenance of a separate government department called the ordnance office. In 1685 it was headed by Lord Mountjoy, an army colonel, who was promoted to brigadier in 1687. As ordnance master, he drew a salary of £500 per annum and was a member of the privy council. The rest of the ordnance staff numbered fifty-eight, more than two-thirds of whom were gunners. A return of 1688 shows thirty gunners based in Dublin, together with the master gunner and his mate. The rest were posted singly at the principal coastal garrisons and inland at Athlone. Their capability is unknown, but in 1689 Marshal Schomberg described their English equivalents as 'ignorant, lazy and cowardly', and it is unlikely that the gunners in Ireland were any better. An account of the ordnance in 1684 returned almost 700 guns of all calibres and types in the Dublin stores and the various garrisons. They were largely fortress cannon, with so many described as 'unserviceable', 'broke', 'cut', 'unmounted', 'scaled' or 'buried in the ground' that it is clear the ordnance was in very poor condition. There was scarcely any equipment to furnish an artillery train, and to draw it only two wagons and ten carts without any horses. The ordnance office was responsible for the supply and repair of the army's weapons. It carried some limited stocks in 1684, including almost 3,000 each of serviceable muskets, pikes and bandoliers, 640 carbines and 800 cases of pistols. In 1686 the earl of Clarendon, the lord lieutenant, reported complaints from all the officers about the condition of their arms, which he confirmed as being 'very bad'. Arms were generally supplied from the English ordnance, but Clarendon recommended having them made in Dublin, presumably using civilian gunsmiths. Whether anything was done to further this proposal is unknown. However, repairable arms were sent for mending to England a few months later.[10]

The ordnance included a chief engineer and fire officer at a salary of £50 per annum. This appointment was held by a Danish engineer, Captain Frederick Fieffe, until 1688, when, accompanied by Mountjoy's son, he took service with the emperor against the Turks. No major work appears to have been carried out on Irish fortifications in his time. Although there were many small forts and walled towns with *trace Italienne* features, especially around the coast, Ireland lacked major artillery fortresses. The most significant fortress constructed in the restoration period was Charles Fort at Kinsale, albeit to a much smaller scale than the massive pentagonal structure originally conceived, so that it was little more than a gun battery overlooking the seaward approach

---

10 *CSPD 1685*, pp 59, 165; *1686–7*, pp 31, 130–1, 397; *1689–90*, p. 231; *CTB 1685–9*, p. 1744; *Ormonde MSS*, i, pp 358–97.

and very poorly located to resist a land attack. Charles Fort's curtailment was due to lack of money. The enormous expense involved in fortress construction inhibited any implementation of the 1673 recommendations of Sir Bernard de Gomme, chief engineer to King Charles II, for the construction of a star fort at Dublin, or those of Captain Thomas Phillips, third engineer of the English ordnance, in 1685 for the construction of fourteen new forts and the repair of five others, which he estimated would cost £554,000, nearly twice the total Irish annual budget. Indeed, such was the indifference of the Irish government to the poor state of its ordnance and fortifications that of £5,500 unspent by the ordnance office in 1687, £2,000 was gifted by King James to Mountjoy.[11]

James II's reforms

The decision to end Ormond's viceroyalty had been taken prior to Charles II's death, but was only implemented after James's accession. The lords justices who then took temporary control of the Irish government were told that the grant of military commissions would henceforth be reserved to the king. Although most commissions were confirmed, a tentative start was made at introducing Catholic officers into the army. Initially the royal prerogative was used to dispense with the oath of supremacy in each case, but the need for this was soon obviated by the substitution in its place of a simple oath of fidelity. Richard Talbot, the leading Irish Catholic figure who was soon to be earl of Tyrconnell, became colonel of Arran's cavalry regiment, and Justin MacCarthy, an experienced professional soldier who was a Catholic nephew of Ormond, was given the latter's infantry regiment. The ceremonial horseguard troop and battle-axe company were both abolished. A new dragoon regiment was formed under Richard Hamilton, another Catholic nephew of Ormond and a brother-in-law of Tyrconnell's wife. Each of the three existing cavalry regiments lost its dragoon troop to the new regiment, bringing its strength to ten troops or companies, numbering 635 officers and men, but with a corresponding reduction of cavalry troops to eight per regiment. From the outset the new regiment's composition was predominantly Catholic; more than three-quarters of its personnel were so estimated in 1686. A small number of other Catholic officers received lesser appointments in 1685. They included Anthony Hamilton, elder brother of Richard, who was made lieutenant colonel of Newcomen's foot. The rank of cavalry lieutenant colonel was introduced in

---

11 *CSPD 1686–7*, pp 369, 397; Worthington, *Central Europe*, p. 123; Murtagh, 'Thomas Phillips', pp 106–9; *ODNB*, vol. 44, pp 142–3; Loeber, 'Engineers', pp 231, 236, 283; Kerrigan, *Fortifications*, pp 104–28; Loeber & Murtagh, 'Artillery fortifications', pp 234–5.

1688. These changes left the full establishment strength of the peacetime army at 466 officers and 8,242 other ranks. In practice, it was never achieved, certainly where rank and file were concerned.[12]

Tyrconnell played a central role in the army's history under King James. He was a cadet of an Old English family in the Pale, who as a youth had fought for the royalists in Ireland, where he had been one of the very few soldier-survivors of Cromwell's siege of Drogheda in 1649. Exiled during the commonwealth period, he had risen to the rank of lieutenant colonel in James's regiment in the Spanish service. Since then, apart from briefly holding a commission in the Irish army in 1672 and serving in 1673 as a gentleman volunteer during the Solebay naval battle, he had had no active military involvement. In the Irish army after 1685, his role was as an administrator rather than a field commander: according to Clarendon, he was incapable of even drawing up a regiment in formation. Intelligent, forceful and energetic, he had remained close to James after the restoration, using his influence to become the principal agent of Irish Catholics at court, a role that gained him considerable importance and wealth. By 1690, he is estimated to have built up an estate of 9–15,000 acres in Dublin, Kildare and Wicklow. After his accession, James's policy in England was probably no more than to give Catholics a share of civil and military appointments: for example, by late 1687 about 11 per cent of the officers appointed to the English army were Catholics. But in Ireland, where Catholics formed three-quarters of the population, Tyrconnell's policy ran well ahead of James's intentions. Tyrconnell's principal political objective was to reverse the post-commonwealth land settlement, which had left people of his background, the Old English, largely dispossessed. This would have been of little benefit to the Gaelic Irish, whose property losses mainly occurred in the wake of earlier conflicts. Tyrconnell was thought to have had little affinity with them, although common adversity was to drive both traditions closer together when the war came. He also sought to overturn the Protestant monopoly of places in government and in the army.[13]

To achieve and sustain a Catholic ascendancy, Tyrconnell realized that control of the army was essential. Following his appointment in 1685, the lords justices were instructed to consult him on all matters relating to the army, which they appear to have done. He was given authority to inspect the force and to appoint subalterns. The changes made in 1685 were relatively small.

---

12 *CSPD 1685*, pp 59, 76–9, 149, 216, 236, 258–9, 352, 397; *CTB*, pp 2048–9; Dalton, ii, p. 13; *Ormonde MSS*, i, pp 400, 406, 432, 436–9.   13 Lenihan, *Last cavalier*, passim; Miller, 'Tyrconnell and James II', passim; Miller, 'Catholic officers', p. 47.

Excluding the new dragoon regiment, only eighteen Catholic officers and 522 other ranks had displaced Protestants before 1686. However, the Argyle and Monmouth rebellions against James in Britain provided a pretext for disarming the Irish Protestant militia and securing their weapons in the king's stores. The process took over a year, but it diminished the potential for Protestant resistance to the radical changes Tyrconnell had in mind. In addition, the rebellions made it easier for him to persuade James of the need to purge the Irish army of the 'dross' of those perceived to be 'much inclined to presbytery, even of the Cromwellian stamp'.[14]

Tyrconnell was disappointed that Clarendon rather than himself was made lord lieutenant of Ireland at the end of 1685. He hastened to London, where he used his influence with James to undermine Clarendon. According to Thomas Sheridan, his estranged secretary, Tyrconnell told James that the Irish army was full of Cromwellians and disaffected officers, and could not be trusted unless Catholics replaced them. Clarendon was excluded from patronage over the army, which he viewed as a diminution of his authority and very much resented, while in 1686 Tyrconnell replaced Granard as lieutenant general in Ireland. Other senior army appointments made at the time were of Justin MacCarthy to major general and three brigadiers: Richard Hamilton, Sir Thomas Newcomen and Lord Mountjoy. Newcomen was Tyrconnell's Protestant brother-in-law. Both he and Mountjoy, also a Protestant and the master of the ordnance, had been infantry colonels since the regimentation of the army in 1684. Early in 1686 Ossory was transferred to command of the footguards in place of his deceased brother, Arran. Ossory's former major, the Protestant earl of Ardglass, succeeded to the command of his cavalry regiment. Ormond's influence was in visible decline: the five regimental commands that he and his sons had enjoyed at James's accession were now reduced to two. Critically, James gave Tyrconnell 'power to regulate the troops [including] to place and displace whom he pleased'.[15]

Tyrconnell's purge of the army

On his return to Ireland in June 1686, Tyrconnell commenced a thorough replacement of the army's Protestant personnel of all ranks with Catholics. Nevertheless, in the early stages in particular, he justified the changes on the grounds that the men purged were unsuitable by reason of age, physical disability, Cromwellian sympathies, or 'servants of someone or other and no

---

14 *CSPD 1685*, pp 59, 76–9, 149, 153, 187–8, 249, 252, 275, 397; *1686–7*, p. 139; Simms, *Jacobite Ireland*, pp 20–2; *James II*, ii, p. 60.   15 *Clarendon*, i, p. 288; 'Sheridan's narrative', pp 4–5; *CSPD 1686–7*, pp 20, 123, 173, 376; *James II*, ii, pp 60–1.

officers, and good for nothing, as most of the lieutenants and cornets of this army are at present'. In the footguards, he told Clarendon: 'we have here a great many old men, and of different statures: they must all be turned out, for the king would have all his men, young and old, of one size'. There was a modicum of truth in the defects alleged by Tyrconnell. In Ossory's horse, for example, although three-quarters of the officers post-dated 1670, seven first appeared in the 1660s and two served prior to that. Ormond put the army's surviving ex-commonwealth officers at no more than ten, of whom only the surgeon general, the aged James Fountain, ranked above captain. Tyrconnell identified some of the subalterns he sought to discharge as servants of named officers. In this, he had some support from Granard, who gave the king a list of officers unsuited for their employments. Allegedly this was done in connivance with Tyrconnell, but it may also have been a valid estimate. That some men were no longer fit for duty seems to be supported by Clarendon's concern to have them admitted to the Royal Hospital at Kilmainham after their discharge. He thought 350 of the 500 men turned out of the footguards in June 1686 'all in appearance very able and lusty', itself an implication that 150 were not. His statement that 'it is said they are too little', which he did not refute, is perhaps an admission that this too was so. Tyrconnell decreed 'two certain sizes one for musketeers and another for pikemen' in the footguards, 'and those that were too short or long for his standard ... must trip off.'[16]

At this time, Tyrconnell secured commissions for almost 150 new officers. They would, of course, replace existing officers, who were to be dismissed without compensation. He was also authorized to replace all non-commissioned officers and common soldiers that he judged unfit for the king's service. When he returned to Ireland in June, the changes were implemented at all rank levels, despite Clarendon's misgivings and pleadings on behalf of those 'in the common calamity of being put out'. He complained that 'a great many good men, who had bought their employments will be ruined', citing the case of Captain Collier, the son of an old royalist, who was left with only £50 to support a wife and five children. Another hard case was that of Captain Twistleton, whose royalist father had been killed in the civil war and who had used what little remained of the family wealth to purchase the commission from which he was now cashiered. Lord Blayney's brother, who had laid out all his younger son's patrimony to purchase a captaincy in Mountjoy's foot, was in a similar position. Clarendon's interventions met with no success. Tyrconnell told him that 'the king who is a Roman Catholic is resolved to employ his

16 *CSPD 1685*, p. 433; *1686–7*, p. 162; *Ormonde MSS*, i, pp 398–9; *Clarendon*, i, p. 469; *IALKC*, p. 148; Childs, *James II*, pp 56–79; *Ireland's lamentation*, pp 9–11; Riegler, 'Anglo-Irish Catholics', passim.

subjects of that religion ... and therefore some must be put out to make room for such as the king likes'.[17]

In reality little mercy was shown to Protestants who fell within Ormond's sphere of patronage, whereas others who had distanced themselves from him, such as Newcomen, Granard and those under their protection, fared better. A small number were able to secure some compensation, such as the pensions given to Lord Roscommon, dismissed from a lieutenant colonelcy of horse, and Sir Albert Conyngham, replaced as lieutenant general of the ordnance. Sir Charles Fielding, another displaced lieutenant colonel, was compensated with the governorship of Culmore Fort. Most, however, appear to have received nothing. Requests for commissions in the English army, such as that by Captain Thomas Brooke – 'turned out without any cause known to him' – appear to have fallen on deaf ears. Swift Nix, a former highwayman who had been pardoned by Charles II, was reported to have been killed when he refused to surrender his commission as a captain in Newcomen's foot. In fact, he appears to have survived whatever altercation occurred, but lost his command. The displaced officers were naturally antagonistic to James and his regime. In the region of a hundred eventually turned up in Holland, where some were immediately employed in the Dutch service, although the rest had to await William's expedition to England to resume their military careers. Others, such as Gustavus Hamilton, Chidley Coote and Thomas Lloyd, remained in Ireland. They subsequently provided leadership to William's supporters or, like Lord Kingston, the 5th and 6th earls of Roscommon and Thomas Brooke, joined his army in England after 1688.[18]

The three new colonels in 1686, Ossory, Ardglass and Lord Arthur Forbes, successor to his father Granard, were all Irish Protestants. However, Forbes's appointment cleared the way for the English Catholic, Dominic Sheldon, to become lieutenant colonel and *de facto* commander of Tyrconnell's cavalry regiment. As Ossory, who succeeded his grandfather as 2nd duke of Ormond in 1688, was an absentee, *de facto* command of the footguards rested with the regiment's lieutenant colonel, the English Catholic, William Dorrington, appointed in 1686. Three more Catholic colonels were appointed in 1687: Anthony Hamilton, a brother-in-law of Tyrconnell, to Theodore Russell's regiment; Viscount Galmoy to Ardglass's cavalry; and the wealthy young earl of Clancarty, nephew of Justin MacCarthy and son-in-law of the earl of Sunderland, the English secretary of state, to Fairfax's regiment. Russell, a German professional soldier and a Protestant, retained his rank on a brevet

---

17 *CSPD 1686–7*, pp 154, 158; *Clarendon*, i, pp 401, 431; *James II*, ii, pp 60–1; 'Rycaut letters', p. 148.   18 *CSPD 1686–7*, pp 161, 173; *1687–9*, pp 92, 145; 'Sheridan's narrative', p. 21; Childs, *James II*, p. 74; *CTB 1685–9*, pp 1942–3, 2062–3; *Clarendon*, i, p. 437; Harris, 'Swift Nix', pp 20–1.

basis and was appointed lieutenant colonel of Ormond's horse with the right of succession to the colonelcy, which he duly secured when the old duke died in early 1688. Alexander MacDonnell, a veteran Catholic officer, was commissioned major in the same regiment. Thus, by early 1688, of eleven colonelcies in the Irish army only five were retained by Protestants: Russell, Newcomen, Forbes, Mountjoy and the absentee 2nd duke of Ormond. Lawrence Dempsey, an experienced Catholic veteran of continental warfare, transferred from the horse grenadiers to become lieutenant colonel of Ardglass's. Two other Catholic lieutenant colonels were Sir John FitzGerald in MacCarthy's foot and John Butler, yet another nephew of Ormond, in Hamilton's dragoons. By the end of 1686 Catholic lieutenant colonels numbered six out of eight, and Catholic majors seven out of eleven. However, the bulk of the new appointments were at subaltern level. Altogether, by September 1686 nearly 40 per cent of the army's officers had been replaced by Catholics. The new officers were drawn from Catholic 'establishment' families. More than a dozen were peers or their sons. Tyrconnell's many relatives and connections were well represented, but the Gaelic Irish, with only 25 per cent of the new appointments, less so. This may have been more on account of their reduced circumstances than Tyrconnell's alleged antipathy to 'the Os and the Macs', asserted by Sheridan and subsequently repeated by the anonymous author of 'The groans of Ireland'. However, Tyrconnell had no difficulty in appointing Felix O'Neill advocate general in place of the Protestant Sir John Topham.[19]

A parallel turnover of personnel was implemented in relation to non-commissioned officers and other ranks. There was an influx of Catholic rank and file in 1685, followed by a pause and then a sharp rise after Tyrconnell became lieutenant general. Officers drew up lists of men in their troops and companies that they proposed to disband and simultaneously prepared lists of Catholic replacements. The changes were then made, frequently on Tyrconnell's personal order. Initially some effort was made to justify the dismissals on grounds of age or other unsuitability, and there may have been some validity to this, but the true reason in most cases, and apparent to all, was that the army was being Catholicized. Yet when Tyrconnell said as much at a review in Kilkenny, the resulting furore forced him to deny it. Others were less discreet: Captain Nicholas d'Arcy of Russell's foot, for example, paraded his company and asked were there any men that did not go to Mass. The forty that answered in the affirmative were forthwith discharged and forty men,

---

19 *CSPD 1686–7*, pp 20, 51–2, 339, 421; *1687–9*, pp 77, 124, 291; Dalton, ii, p. 13; 'Sheridan's narrative', p. 17; 'The groans of Ireland', p. 131.

reputedly kept by d'Arcy for a week in his private house, replaced them. The displaced men of all ranks received their arrears of pay. In the case of discharged cavalry troopers, the horses that were properly theirs were retained to mount their replacements. Tyrconnell agreed that the animals should be valued, but then declared that the new men lacked the means to pay for them other than by instalments. Clarendon subsequently countered that if the horses were not paid for, the dismissed troopers should be entitled to take them. By the end of September 1686, of 96 cavalry corporals and trumpeters, 30 were Catholics. In the new dragoon regiment, 37 of 40 non-commissioned officers, together with 32 hautboys and drummers, were Catholics. In the infantry 60 of 195 sergeants and 85 of 273 corporals were Catholics, but there were only 2 Catholic drummers. In all, at 39 per cent the proportion of new NCOs was similar to that of commissioned officers, the retention rate being related to the need to train the new soldiers. The 5,043 Catholic private men represented 67 per cent of the army's strength at that rank. In one day, 400 men were dismissed from the footguards. The purge moved more slowly in regiments commanded by Protestant colonels, such as Ardglass's cavalry and the infantry regiments of Mountjoy and Granard. Newcomen's was the exception, with almost 85 per cent of the private soldiers Catholic as well as half the officers.[20]

    Returns for two infantry companies in the summer of 1686 show the process in detail. In Lord Enniskillen's company in Fairfax's infantry regiment, 43 men, largely with English surnames, were discharged to be replaced by Irishmen, of whom almost half shared Enniskillen's surname of Maguire. In Captain Nix's company of Newcomen's regiment 45 men were similarly replaced, possibly at the instance of Nix's ensign, Luke Reilly, as 11 of the new intake shared his surname. Catholic company commanders generally accelerated the process, which Clarendon complained frequently involved junior officers issuing commands to their superiors. While some of the new men may have been found through family or seigneurial influence, there were also reports of recruiting at fairs and at the St John's Day pattern at Kilmainham holy well. The dismissals were naturally unpopular with the Protestant population, whose spokesmen depicted the new army personnel in derogatory terms. Clarendon described the new recruits as 'strange wretches', many of whom were unable to speak English. According to the Williamite author, Dean William King, the purge left 2–300 Protestant officers 'not worth anything', and 5–6,000 soldiers made beggars, while 'the scum and rascality' of the kingdom – 'cowherds, horseboys or footmen' – were now made officers, and

---

20 *Ormonde MSS*, i, pp 430–5; ibid., n.s., vii, pp 433, 454–5; viii, p. 346; 'Rycaut letters', pp 161–2; *Clarendon*, i, pp 476, 501, 512; ii, pp 26–7, 35.

they behaved themselves with the greatest insolence towards Protestants without fear of retribution. Another commentator alleged the new soldiers were 'the very scum of the people', selected by the priests 'for some bloody end'. It was alleged that they neglected sanitation, and were so ignorant that on enlistment each soldier tied a string around one wrist to distinguish right from left. When they were jeered in Dublin, however, they reacted forcefully, and one or two people were killed. A handful of other acts of violence were reported. Clarendon wrote that 'some of their officers being young and unexperienced [sic] did not keep them in good discipline'; on the whole, however, the transition was peaceable.[21]

Tyrconnell finally secured full control of the Irish government in 1687, when he succeeded the hapless Clarendon as viceroy, although with the lesser title of lord deputy. He seized the opportunity to drive his reform of the Irish army to the desired conclusion. He brought sixty-nine further military commissions with him when he arrived in February. An additional twenty-four new commissions were sent over in March, together with a number of 'changes' to existing appointments. Between then and November 1688 over 200 new commissions were issued. Some were to new officers, although many were merely promotions and transfers. Remaining Protestant officers were advised to sell their commissions, and many did so very cheaply for fear of losing all by being dismissed. A small number of new commissions and appointments went to Protestants, but they numbered less than a score, and it was alleged, with some exaggeration, that by 1688 the only Protestant officers left were those of the best quality and interest. Certainly, by then both officers and other ranks were predominantly Catholic. Remaining Protestants were mainly in the regiments of Forbes and Mountjoy, but even there they numbered less than half the total. More than a score of Protestant (or possibly ex-Protestant) officers remained in the army in 1689, although several subsequently defected. Robert Parker, a private soldier in Mountjoy's regiment at this time, related that following Tyrconnell's review of the army at the Curragh camp in 1687, the Protestant officers and soldiers, including himself, were cashiered on the regiment's return to its quarters. This was not entirely true as regards Mountjoy's regiment, which retained six Protestant, or partly Protestant, companies that defected to the Williamites in early 1689. Forbes's regiment had 130 Protestant soldiers when it landed in England in 1688, and a small number of Protestants were retained in other regiments too, if only to discipline and train the new recruits. The remaining Protestants continued to

21 *Ormonde MSS*, i, pp 416–18; ibid., n.s., viii, p. 346; *Clarendon*, i, p. 479; ii, p. 2; *CSPD 1686–7*, pp 209, 245; King, pp 25–6, 61.

be purged in 1689, although as late as October two Protestant troopers were reported to have deserted from Galmoy's horse.[22]

The Catholic officers

Most of the new officers, especially those of subaltern rank, lacked previous military experience. However, the field officers – colonels, lieutenant colonels and majors – were frequently military professionals who were veterans of overseas warfare. Most had been in the French or Anglo-French service, but some came from the Anglo-Dutch brigade, the Tangier garrison or elsewhere. Thus, for example, Tyrconnell had served as a lieutenant colonel in Flanders in the late 1650s. Justin MacCarthy, Dominic Sheldon, Lawrence Dempsey, William Dorrington, Anthony and Richard Hamilton, and possibly their brother John, were among three dozen who were veterans of the French service. Another French veteran was John Butler, the Catholic nephew of the 1st duke of Ormond, who succeeded Hamilton as colonel of the dragoon regiment in 1687. Marmaduke Pudsey had served in the Anglo-Dutch brigade; Philip Meagher, George Talbot, John Pinkney and Toby Caulfield in Tangier; and Alexander MacDonnell 'in considerable stations for forty years in Germany'. Both Forbes and Mountjoy took leave to visit the imperial theatre of operations against the Turks. By 1688 about fifty officers, constituting almost 11 per cent of the peacetime officer corps, can be identified as having had military service on the Continent, or, in a few cases, in England. Although little is known of the detail, these officers must have infused a degree of professionalism into the reformed army. That helped to compensate for the loss of so many veterans, who in any case were often aged, given to lackadaisical ways and generally deficient in modern combat experience. Clarendon, after an inspection in Cork, was forced to admit that he saw Justin MacCarthy's foot 'all drawn out and exercise; which they perform as well as can be expected from men who have been no longer in the service'. At Limerick he viewed Hamilton's dragoons 'at exercise, at which they are as adroit, as it is possible for new men to be; it is indeed a very fine regiment and need not be afraid to appear before the king, if there were occasion'.[23]

22 *CSPD 1686–7*, pp 332, 335, 339–40, 399; *1687–9*, p. 215; 'Sheridan's narrative', p. 21; Milligan, *Londonderry*, p. 28; Childs, *James II*, pp 65–6; Parker, *Memoirs*, p. 5; *F-I corr.*, iii, p. 85.
23 Clarendon, i, p. 506; ii, p. 1; Childs, *James II*, p. 78; Simms, *Jacobite Ireland*, p. 46; Lenihan, *Last cavalier*, pp 30–1; Dalton, i, pp 203, 207, 209, 302; Childs, *BD*, pp 12, 41; *ODNB*, vol. 24, pp 766–7; *IALKC*, p. 143; *Ormonde MSS*, n.s., vii, p. 472; de Corthuy, f. 15; *CP*, vi, p. 55; ix, p. 350; Riley, *Tangier*, passim.

A dozen of the new pre-war officers were Englishmen, maintaining the tradition of the Caroline army, except of course that they were Catholics. King James justified their appointment to commands in the Irish army by reminding Tyrconnell they were more than matched by the number of Irishmen serving in England. The latter group numbered about two dozen, mostly Catholics. Many of them were later prominent in the wartime Irish army, such as Patrick Sarsfield, Henry Luttrell, Edward Scott and the 4th earl of Abercorn. Richard Hamilton became colonel of an English cavalry regiment in 1687, while retaining his rank of brigadier in Ireland. There were certainly a substantial number of English-born Protestant officers in the Irish army at James's accession. Most were subsequently weeded out, but a small number still remained up to 1688 or later. A dozen English officers were new appointments by James. They included the Catholics Dominic Sheldon to *de facto* command of Tyrconnell's Horse, William Dorrington to *de facto* command of the footguards and William Barker to the majority in the same regiment.[24]

A regimental chaplaincy was quite a lucrative appointment, with pay at £112 per annum, equivalent to a cavalry cornet and not far below that of an infantry captain. As early as 1685 MacCarthy had insisted that the chaplain of his regiment share his salary with a priest he had brought in, but in general chaplains were Protestant clergymen until 1686, when Tyrconnell ordered the admission of Catholic chaplains to three regiments, including the footguards. In 1687 Archbishop Dominic Maguire, the Catholic primate, was appointed chaplain general of the army with a supervisory role over the appointment and conduct of regimental chaplains. This was a prelude to excluding Protestants altogether, although Protestant colonels, such as Forbes and Mountjoy, probably delayed the change in their regiments.[25]

Training and equipment

Regiments were brought together for summer exercises, with month-long training camps, similar to those held in England, organized at the Curragh in 1687 and 1688. One of the training sessions involved an imitation of the siege of Buda and other feats of arms. Some attempt was also made to address the army's deficiencies in weaponry and *matériel*, a persistent problem in Charles II's time that the lords justices raised again in 1685. The English ordnance

---

24 Dalton, ii, passim; *CSPD 1685*, p. 76; *1687–9*, pp 77, 215, 530; Melvin, 'Revolution of 1688', p. 290. **25** *CTB*, p. 1746; *Ormond MSS*, n.s., viii, p. 344; *CSPD 1686–7*, pp 254, 353; *Ireland's lamentation*, p. 13.

supplied muskets, carbines, pistols, hatchets, some halberds and bayonets, together with other equipment to arm the new grenadier companies and dragoon troops in May of that year, but Granard complained of the poor quality of the weapons sent. At least one dragoon captain purchased flintlocks for his troop. Mountjoy sought new arms for an Irish army of 7,800 men; instead, 7,000 firearms, mostly matchlocks but also snaphances, carbines and pistols, were sent over to London in 1687 to be fitted with new stocks and locks. This work was completed before the end of the year, when the weapons were returned, and the Irish exchequer ordered to pay for it. 500 barrels of 'good, new and serviceable powder' were also supplied. The Irish ordnance was furnished with six mortars. A thousand bayonets had been requested in 1687, which were clearly intended for the grenadier companies. Whether they were ever supplied is unknown, and certainly they were not on general issue, as Dorrington complained that the footguards had none when they landed in England in 1688. At that time, he also lamented the 'illness of our arms' and expressed his shame at the soldiers' 'abominably ill' hats. Nevertheless, when reviewed by James in London, the king was pleased that most of the guardsmen were six-footers, and they were described as 'tall sprightly young men, their clothes also very fresh and fashionably made, each man having a frock to keep him clean'.[26]

Two proclamations of July 1688 'for the good government of the army' set out the rates of pay and deductions for private soldiers in the infantry and mounted corps. An infantry private's annual pay of £7 18s. 4d., after deductions for poundage (a shilling in the pound for the paymaster), the Royal Hospital and the regimental agent, apparently went entirely on clothing, accoutrements and subsistence. Cavalry and dragoons fared somewhat better: after similar deductions, privates were left respectively with £5 6s. 7d. and £3 19s. 3d., with a further reduction allowed to pay for a horse, if they did not furnish their own mount. An infantry soldier was to receive annually a coat, hat, breeches, three pairs of shoes, two pairs of stockings, two shirts, two cravats, a sash, garters with buckles and a pair of shoe buckles. The corresponding clothing allowance for cavalry and dragoons is not stated; it was likely to have been similar but with boots instead of shoes. Officers were enjoined to keep the soldiers in good order, to secure billets through the local magistrates, and to refrain from pressing recruits or seizing livestock or goods without consent or payment. Officers were allowed three months' leave while their unit was in winter quarters, but with one field officer per regiment and

26 *CSPD 1685*, pp 155, 165, 293, 317; *1686–7*, pp 46, 81, 121, 130–1; *1687–9*, pp 4, 140, 185; *Proclamations*, pp 54–5; *Ormonde MSS*, n.s., viii, pp 6–7; Simms, *Jacobite Ireland*, p. 46.

two subalterns per troop or company always present. Other ranks might be granted one month's leave between musters, but no more than one NCO and four other ranks were to be absent at any one time. The Articles of War, which were the regulations for the soldiers' conduct, were to be read to the regiment every three months.[27]

The Irish army in 1688

The effect of the radical peacetime changes was to transform the Irish army into a force that was loyal to King James, but with weakened capability due to the enormous turnover of officers and other ranks. These changes left it poorly led, especially at subaltern level, and inadequately trained when the crisis of late 1688 occurred. Its weaponry, clothing and other equipment appear to have been mediocre. Its artillery was weak and its train virtually non-existent. Had the army been afforded further time, these shortcomings might have been addressed: the Curragh training camps were an obvious effort to do so. Its problems were accentuated by the loss of a third of its strength in England in a vain attempt to prop up James's ailing regime, and its subsequent enormous expansion in response to the Williamite threat, which further strained its limited resources, diluted its meagre levels of professionalism and exposed its inadequacies.

TABLE 1 *The Irish military establishment and its cost, 1688* [28]

Command and staff:
- 1   lieutenant general (earl of Tyrconnell)
- 1   major general (Justin MacCarthy)
- 3   brigadiers (Richard Hamilton, Sir Robert Newcomen & Viscount Mountjoy)
- 1   quartermaster general (Sir Charles Murray)
- 1   master general of the ordnance (Viscount Mountjoy)
- 1   muster-master general and commissioner for accounts (Abraham Yarner)
- 6   commissaries of the musters
- 1   advocate general (Felix O'Neill)
- 1   surgeon general (Charles Thompson)
- 1   chaplain general (Archbishop Dominic Maguire)

  Total: 17
  Annual cost: £5,186

27 *Proclamations*, pp 56–63.   28 *CTB*, pp 1742–6.

Regimental establishment:
  1 troop of horse grenadiers (Lord Ikerrin), comprising 3 officers (1 captain and 2 lieutenants), 2 sergeants, 3 corporals, 2 drummers, 2 hautboys and 50 soldiers.
  Total: 3 officers, 59 other ranks
Annual cost: £2,217 8s.

  earl of Tyrconnell's horse, comprising 8 troops, each with 4 officers (1 captain, 1 lieutenant, 1 cornet, 1 quartermaster), 3 corporals, 1 trumpeter and 45 soldiers; the colonel's troop with 1 kettledrummer in place of a trumpeter; the major's troop to have 3 trumpeters and 50 soldiers; *staff:* 1 adjutant, 1 quartermaster, 1 chaplain and 1 surgeon.
  Total: 36 officers, 399 other ranks
Annual cost: £15,878 16s.

  Viscount Galmoy's horse, comprising 8 troops, each with 4 officers (1 captain, 1 lieutenant, 1 cornet, 1 quartermaster), 3 corporals, 1 trumpeter and 45 soldiers; the colonel's troop with 1 kettledrummer in place of a trumpeter; *staff:* 1 adjutant, 1 quartermaster, 1 chaplain and 1 surgeon.
  Total: 36 officers, 392 other ranks
Annual cost: £15,626 16s.

  Theodore Russell's horse, comprising 8 troops, each with 4 officers (1 captain, 1 lieutenant, 1 cornet, 1 quartermaster), 3 corporals, 1 trumpeter and 45 soldiers; the colonel's troop with 1 kettledrummer in place of a trumpeter; *staff:* 1 adjutant, 1 quartermaster, 1 chaplain and 1 surgeon.
  Total: 36 officers, 392 other ranks
Annual cost: £15,626 16s.

  John Butler's dragoons, comprising 10 troops, each with 4 officers (1 captain, 1 lieutenant, 1 cornet, 1 quartermaster), 2 sergeants, 3 corporals, 2 drummers, 2 hautboys and 50 soldiers; *staff:* 1 major (no troop), 1 adjutant, 1 quartermaster, 1 chaplain, 1 surgeon, 1 gunsmith.
  Total: 46 officers, 590 other ranks
Annual cost: £17,191 2s. 8d.

  Royal regiment of footguards (duke of Ormond), comprising 13 companies, each with 3 officers (1 captain, 1 lieutenant, 1 ensign), 3 sergeants, 3 corporals, 1 drummer and 90 soldiers; *staff:* 1 major, 1 adjutant, 1 quartermaster, 1 surgeon, 1 chaplain. (The establishment probably also included 1 drum major and 1 piper, as it did in 1686. Then also each company had two drummers.)
  Total: 45 officers, 1,262 other ranks
Annual cost: £19,443 4s.

earl of Clancarty's foot, comprising 13 companies, each with 3 officers (1 captain, 1 lieutenant, 1 ensign), 2 sergeants, 3 corporals, 1 drummer and 60 soldiers; *staff*: 1 major, 1 adjutant, 1 quartermaster, 1 surgeon, 1 chaplain.

Total: 44 officers, 858 other ranks
Annual cost: £12,073 5s. 4d.

Lord Forbes's foot, comprising 13 companies, each with 3 officers (1 captain, 1 lieutenant, 1 ensign), 2 sergeants, 3 corporals, 1 drummer and 60 soldiers; *staff*: 1 major, 1 adjutant, 1 quartermaster, 1 surgeon, 1 chaplain.

Total: 44 officers, 858 other ranks
Annual cost: £12,073 5s. 4d.

Anthony Hamilton's foot, comprising 13 companies, each with 3 officers (1 captain, 1 lieutenant, 1 ensign), 2 sergeants, 3 corporals, 1 drummer and 60 soldiers; *staff*: 1 major, 1 adjutant, 1 quartermaster, 1 surgeon, 1 chaplain.

Total: 44 officers, 858 other ranks
Annual cost: £12,073 5s. 4d.

Justin MacCarthy's foot, comprising 13 companies, each with 3 officers (1 captain, 1 lieutenant, 1 ensign), 2 sergeants, 3 corporals, 1 drummer and 60 soldiers; *staff*: 1 major, 1 adjutant, 1 quartermaster, 1 surgeon, 1 chaplain.

Total: 44 officers, 858 other ranks
Annual cost: £12,073 5s. 4d.

Viscount Mountjoy's foot, comprising 13 companies, each with 3 officers (1 captain, 1 lieutenant, 1 ensign), 2 sergeants, 3 corporals, 1 drummer and 60 soldiers; *staff*: 1 major, 1 adjutant, 1 quartermaster, 1 surgeon, 1 chaplain.

Total: 44 officers, 858 other ranks
Annual cost: £12,073 5s. 4d.

Sir Thomas Newcomen's foot, comprising 13 companies, each with 3 officers (1 captain, 1 lieutenant, 1 ensign), 2 sergeants, 3 corporals, 1 drummer and 60 soldiers; *staff*: 1 major, 1 adjutant, 1 quartermaster, 1 surgeon, 1 chaplain.

Total: 44 officers,
Annual cost: £12,073 5s. 4d.

Total regimental establishment strength: 466 officers
8,242 other ranks

Ordnance personnel:
- 1 master of the ordnance
- 1 lieutenant of the ordnance
- 1 surveyor/comptroller
- 1 clerk of the ordnance and deliveries
- 1 storekeeper
- 1 chief engineer
- 1 master gunner
- 1 master gunner's mate
- 1 armourer
- 41 gunners
- 2 gunner's mates
- 7 clerks of the stores

Total ordnance personnel: 59
Annual cost: £2,268

Total cost, including command & staff salaries
and Dublin allowance: £178,016 16s. 10d.
Subvention to support English army: £30,000
Total of Irish military list: £208,016 16s.

Figure 2. A cavalry officer

CHAPTER 2

The Irish army and the English revolution, 1688–9

The overthrow of King James

AT THE END OF 1688 England was invaded by a Dutch army, to which the English army offered no resistance, and King James II was overthrown. The coup was led by James's nephew and son-in-law, William of Orange, who was *stadhouder* (chief executive and captain general) of most of the provinces of the wealthy Dutch Republic, a polity that was a commercial rival of France. William was nervous of an Anglo-French alliance, probably unnecessarily, as James was disposed to favour neutrality. William also wanted to bring the growing economic power of England into the European alliance forming against France, his lifelong enemy. Up to the early summer of 1688 this would naturally have happened in the course of time, as William's wife, Mary, was James's heir. But with the birth of a son to James by his second wife, Queen Mary of Modena, the prospect of Mary of Orange's succession faded, and this prompted William to make his strike. He did so in the knowledge that James was in deep political trouble in England, brought about by his Catholic religion, the threat of a Catholic succession through his new-born son, fear of his authoritarianism based on his absolute belief in the divine rights of kings, and his general political ineptitude. Within the English political establishment, including crucially the upper echelons of the royal army, these factors combined to create considerable support for James's deposition and replacement by William and Mary. Their joint sovereignty was promulgated in February 1689, but William, with Mary's acquiescence, took charge of the government from 24 December 1688, following James's flight to France the day before.[1]

Earlier, in March 1688, the growing estrangement between William and James had led the latter to recall the six-regiment British brigade from the Dutch army. About a hundred officers, Catholics and some others, responded, and three new regiments were formed for them in England. One, commanded by Colonel Roger MacElligott, was Irish. Not many of the rank and file in

---

[1] Vallance, *Glorious Revolution*, passim; Harris, *Revolution*, pp 182–272; Miller, *James II*, pp 188–99; Troost, *William III*, pp 173–94.

Holland obeyed James's recall order, so MacElligott's regiment was made up by taking ten men from each infantry company of the Irish army: about 720 men in all, presuming the grenadier companies were left intact. They were brought over to England in May. MacElligott's soldiers soon earned a bad reputation: in Portsmouth they robbed, drank and beat up the inhabitants. In a *cause célèbre*, five captains in the duke of Berwick's English regiment were cashiered for refusing to enlist Irishmen surplus to MacElligott's needs. Louis XIV had undertaken to pay the three new regiments, but after two months he ended this arrangement when he realized that the operation had led to very little net reduction in the strength of the Anglo-Dutch brigade. MacElligott and some of the English and Scottish officers who returned from Holland at this time subsequently found their way into the Irish Jacobite army.[2]

Despite intense preparations in the Netherlands, James had been slow to grasp the enormity of the threat to his regime. This was partly due to the ineptitude of his ambassador to The Hague, the Irishman Ignatius White, marquis d'Albeville, who warned him only in mid-September that the Dutch were ready to sail within a week. As late as 8 September the earl of Sunderland, James's secretary of state, acknowledged a message from Tyrconnell 'about the noise and preparations of our neighbours [the Dutch]', but complacently added that King James was very well assured that whatever the design might have been, it was not against him. Earlier the French had warned James of the impending threat, and they expressed surprise at his lethargy about defending himself. D'Albeville's September dispatch caused panic in Whitehall. To support James's regime, Tyrconnell was ordered on 25 September to send over to Chester or Liverpool 'with all diligence and speed possible' a battalion of the Irish footguards, Butler's dragoons, Forbes's foot and another infantry battalion, which turned out to be Anthony Hamilton's. Subsequently a further infantry regiment was requested. Mountjoy's was chosen for the role, but it was never actually sent. The Irish soldiers were to be paid in England from 1 November and were strictly prohibited from bringing their wives or children with them. The footguards 'battalion' comprised seven companies, amounting to 700 officers and men. The other two infantry battalions were complete, but with company strength at 50 rather than 60 soldiers, they amounted to about 1,500 all ranks. The dragoon regiment at full strength numbered 650 all ranks. The total therefore was 2,850. Adding the 720 men previously supplied to form the rank and file of MacElligott's regiment, and assuming actual unit strengths to have approximated to the above figures, almost 3,600 Irish soldiers were in England to support King

2 Childs, *James II*, chapter v; Garland, 'MacElligott', pp 121–7; *CSPD 1687–9*, pp 181, 187; Dalton, ii, pp 151–3; Simms, *Jacobite Ireland*, p. 46.

James in the November crisis. In England, Forbes's regiment was noted as being expert at their arms and well disciplined. Initially the soldiers from Ireland were posted to the London area. Subsequently the infantry accompanied James to Salisbury, with the dragoons providing an escort for the king and his family. As James's resistance disintegrated and the remnants of his forces fell back towards London, the Irish were involved in a number of skirmishes, notably at Reading where three dragoon troops under Major George Mathew incurred fifty casualties in a sharp exchange with the pursuing Williamites. That the Irish were a sinister presence formed part of Williamite propaganda, and the Reading skirmish was consequently magnified into a blow against popery. Elsewhere, false reports that the Irish troops were 'killing, burning and destroying all before them' provoked widespread panic.[3]

The loss of the Irish regiments in England

Before he finally left London for exile in France, James ordered the Irish soldiers in England to lay down their arms. The footguards were disarmed when they evacuated Tilbury Fort. Hamilton's, MacElligott's and Butler's regiments were disarmed at East Grinstead on 31 December. About 1,800 personnel from these four disbanded regiments, together with the Catholic personnel from Forbes's regiment, were then interned on the Isle of Wight. William arranged with his ally, Emperor Leopold I, to take them into the imperial service, and in the spring of 1689 1,200 Irish soldiers were shipped to Hamburg under the command of Denis MacGillycuddy, an Anglo-Dutch veteran and former lieutenant colonel of MacElligott's regiment. There, many deserted, including MacGillycuddy and a number of officers, who made their way back to Ireland through France. Only 930 of the original party were eventually rounded up to travel on to central Hungary, where they were to be deployed. Their progress was marked by complaints from the various towns they plundered along the way. In Hungary they continued to give trouble, probably with the encouragement of the Jacobite envoy in Poland, so that in 1690 their unit was broken up and the remaining personnel dispersed among other regiments. Some light is thrown on their attitude and level of political awareness by an imperial war council report that they had never wished to enter the imperial service because they were bound to King James, and the emperor was waging war against the king of France, who was James's ally. About a third of the Irish troops in England succeeded in escaping after being

---

3 *CSPD 1687–9*, p. 283; Vallance, *Glorious Revolution*, pp 109, 114–15; Melvin, 'Irish troop movements', passim; *James II*, ii, pp 257–8; Simms, *Jacobite Ireland*, p. 46.

disbanded. They made their way to Ireland or France, despite William's orders to the port authorities to prevent this. This group included Colonels Anthony Hamilton and Roger MacElligott, together with William Dorrington, commander of the footguards battalion. Colonel John Butler, however, was taken into custody at Whitehaven and incarcerated in the Tower of London for the rest of the war.[4]

Lord Forbes had been promoted brigadier on his arrival in England. He urged James to use the Irish and Scots to attack William and warned him of the conspiracy in the army against him. After James's flight, he resigned his commission, telling William that he felt unable to enter the service of another prince during James II's lifetime. He was sent to the Tower in May 1689, but released on bail the following October. Meanwhile the Protestant portion of his regiment, which had been excluded from disbandment, was given to Sir John Edgeworth, Forbes's major, who was soon dismissed on grounds of peculation and replaced by the earl of Meath. The regiment was recruited up to strength in England, and served with the Williamite army in Ireland throughout the war. It was the only pre-war Irish unit to survive the revolution in British service, later becoming the Royal Irish Regiment, ranking eighteenth in the line, until its disbandment in 1922. Butler's, Hamilton's and Forbes's regiments all disappeared from the Irish army. Dorrington, however, was given command of the remaining Irish footguards on his return to Ireland, and Roger MacElligott raised a new regiment in west Munster in the summer of 1689. A number of officers in the English army who were loyal to James resigned their commissions or were dismissed by William. They were allowed to follow James to France. This group included Patrick Sarsfield, an Irish officer in the horseguards, who had distinguished himself in a skirmish with the Williamites at Wincanton soon after the invasion.[5]

Militarily, the Irish soldiers had proved of little value to James, although they were hardly to blame for this. In propaganda and political terms their presence in England was a great mistake. There were already suspicions about James's motives in introducing Catholic officers, some of them Irish, into the army in England, although until 1688 they amounted to only just over 10 per cent of the total. The introduction of Irish regiments that were predominantly Catholic alarmed and antagonized English opinion, and raised concerns that they were the forerunner of a policy of coercion by James. The move also offended his English army and undermined its loyalty to him, as well as

4 Melvin, 'Irish troop movements', pp 100–2; Melvin, 'Revolution of 1688', p. 305; 'Longford letters', p. 60; Childs, *William III*, pp 10–12; O'Neill, 'Conflicting loyalties', p. 117; Garland, 'MacElligott', p. 124; Simms, *Jacobite Ireland*, p. 47.   5 Ferguson, 'Army in Ireland', p. 21; Parker, *Memoirs*, p. 13; Gretton, *Royal Irish Regiment*, pp 2–4; Wauchope, *Sarsfield*, pp 37–9, 43.

adding to the perception that his regime was near collapse. Rumour, fuelled by Williamite propaganda, generated widespread fears of burnings and massacres by the Irish, opening the way for William and his Dutch army to pose as deliverers rather than invaders. Even though many of the Irish officers and men eventually succeeded in returning home, the immediate military impact of the whole episode was the loss of almost half of Tyrconnell's army at a time when he needed as many established units and experienced personnel as possible to train and organize the large number of new soldiers that he was mobilizing to uphold James's regime in Ireland.[6]

Tyrconnell enlarges the Irish army

On 12 October 1688 James empowered Tyrconnell to raise three new regiments of foot and a 500-strong dragoon regiment to replace the units sent to England. The viceroy responded by issuing commissions for new regiments to five Catholic peers: the earls of Clanricard, Limerick, Tyrone and Antrim, and Viscount Clare. He also restored the footguards to full strength, adding a company of grenadiers and subsequently enlarging the regiment with the addition of a second battalion. It took time to commission, raise, organize and equip these new units. Antrim's regiment, which was without uniforms and armed only with skeans (daggers) and clubs, was ready to garrison Derry by early December. Limerick's commission seems only to have been implemented after March 1689, when his son, Walter Lord Dungan, an ex-cornet of James's English horseguards, arrived in Ireland from France and raised a dragoon regiment. The other three peers all raised regiments; indeed, Lord Clare and his sons were eventually to contribute three to the Irish army. Preparations for further enlargement of the army probably lay behind the postings of Justin MacCarthy to Cork and Anthony Hamilton to Limerick. In late November James also authorized Tyrconnell to re-establish an Irish militia and appoint its officers, although this body only came into being in July 1689.[7]

News of the English revolution and James's overthrow left Tyrconnell in a very uncertain situation. Externally he faced a threat from William, and internally from the Irish Protestants who for the most part supported William's accession. Over the next few months, he skilfully managed a difficult situation by appearing to negotiate with William while simultaneously enlarging his army and seeking French support. A letter from James, written on 26 November, had informed him of events in England and given him instructions. What they were is unknown, but at a subsequent meeting of the

---

6 Melvin, 'Revolution of 1688', passim; Miller, 'Catholic officers', pp 47, 49.

Irish privy council Tyrconnell was reported to have been 'altogether for war and [he] showed plausible reasons for success, which opinion had the ascendant'. Orders were given to the secretaries 'to draw commissions speedily for the levying of regiments, horse, foot and dragoons', and on 8 December the lord deputy was reported 'all day very busy in giving out commissions for raising 20,000 men'. 'Nobility and gentry from all parts of the realm' flocked to Dublin, possessed of 'so gallant an ardour' for King James's cause, it was said, but presumably also to defend and extend the recent gains made by Catholics, and to stake their own claim to a commission, which was seen as a prestigious and valuable asset that yielded an income and carried a potential resale value. Tyrconnell was obliged to issue a proclamation forbidding non-commissioned officers and soldiers from deserting the old regiments to seek a higher rank in the new. According to the comte d'Avaux, who came as French ambassador, Tyrconnell issued commissions indiscriminately, many to colonels and captains who were ignorant or incapable. Over the next three months the army's size steadily increased. One source put the figure in early January 1689 at 34,000 men; less than a month later Tyrconnell himself confirmed that 40,000 men had enlisted for the new regiments, to which can be added the remnants of the old army, amounting to a force approaching 45,000 strong. Other estimates went as high as 50,000 and 60,000, but were probably an exaggeration. The Catholic population of Ireland in the 1680s probably approached two million, so the manpower was there for a substantial force. The Irish Williamite, Sir Robert Southwell, estimated that 120,000 men were fit for war. However, sufficient labour had to be held back to service the needs of the agricultural economy, and the army's size had to be consistent with what the country could support and in harmony with its command, staff and logistical capability. It is instructive that contemporary French field armies had a median strength of about 33,000 and an average strength of 39,000. Anything much larger became difficult for a single general to control effectively. Many of Tyrconnell's new regiments had numerous companies, far in excess of the standard thirteen: Lord Galway, who had already raised twenty-seven, was reported to be seeking commissions for another thirteen.[8]

Tyrconnell had no money to pay or clothe the new soldiers, so in lieu of purchase or other payment for their commissions, the officers were required to

7 *CSPD 1687–9*, pp. 312, 356; Dalton, ii, p. 116; *d'Avaux*, pp 18–19; Simms, *Jacobite Ireland*, p. 49; King, p. 116; Tyrconnell letters, no. 8; *Proclamations*, pp 111–14; Tyrconnell to treasury commissioners, 4 November 1689 (Clarke collection, item 2.1); Boulger, p. 77. 8 *Proclamations*, pp 74–5; Simms, *Jacobite Ireland*, pp 50, 53; Lenihan, *Last cavalier*, pp 122–32; *James II*, ii, p. 20; *JN*, pp 36–8, 47; BL, Add. MS 28,053; *d'Avaux*, pp 26–7, 182; 'Longford letters', pp 48, 54, 57; *Ireland's lamentation*, pp 16–17; *Ormonde MSS*, n.s., viii, pp 357, 359; *CSPD 1689–90*, p. 440;

subsist their troop or company for the first three months of 1689, which, in fact, most lacked the means to do. Consequently, until a regular system of pay was established in May, disorder was widespread, as the soldiers survived by looting, stealing and what amounted to free quartering. These abuses appear to have borne particularly heavily on Protestants, who were targeted because of their wealth, perceived disloyalty and history of antagonism to Catholics. Certainly, they were loud in their complaints. William King, for example, alleged that many were burned out of their houses, citing several instances. Tyrconnell had sought to allay Protestant fears in early December by promising protection for all who remained firm in their allegiance to James. He issued a proclamation in February threatening to cashier officers who failed to prevent waste, spoil, violence, or the exaction of provisions, victuals or money from civilians without due payment. It had little effect: by the end of March, Protestants were reporting that all their livestock had been stolen, rents due to them were unpaid, their houses violated and their goods robbed. Many had fled the country, and protection money was being exacted from those that remained. Conrad von Rosen, the French general sent to command in Ireland, observed that the disorder would continue until the troops were paid. 18,000 weapons were available in the stores to arm the new regiments. This fell well short of what was needed, especially as many firearms were in very poor condition: King James's memoirs recalled that not above a thousand were of any use. It was reported that on Tyrconnell's orders all the gunsmiths, carpenters and joiners were employed cleaning, stocking and locking the old firearms, and the cutlers at cleaning and sheathing the swords. These measures, together with the army's enlargement, clearly strengthened Tyrconnell's ability to resist a Williamite takeover of Ireland and to suppress local Protestant opposition. A bellicose attitude also strengthened his hand for any negotiations with William, an option he seems to have genuinely considered, although it was later claimed that his tentative moves in this respect were no more than 'a feigned disposition of submitting' that bought time for his military build-up. However, it was a contingency he appears to have kept in mind, until he was sure that James was coming to Ireland with large-scale French support. Indeed, fears that his negotiations with William were genuine led to reports of the people loudly declaring that if Tyrconnell thought of making such a treaty, they would burn him in his palace and give themselves up to the French.[9]

A new history of Ireland, iii, p. 389; Connolly, *Religion, law and power*, p. 43; Lynn, *Giant of the grand siècle*, pp 526–7; *An account of the present state Ireland is in*.   **9** *Proclamations*, pp 77–8; 'A journal of what passed since his majesty's arrival' (Bodl., Carte MS 181), ff 30–1; King, pp 134–5, 139–44; *James II*, ii, p. 328; *AH*, 21, p. 137; *d'Avaux*, p. 50; *An account of the present state Ireland is in*.

Irish Protestants and William

Irish Protestants were alarmed at the breakdown in law and the threat they perceived to their property and even their lives from 'the papists ... now grown so intolerably insolent that we dreaded the fatal scene of forty-one might be repeated'. This was a reference to the Irish rising of 1641 when it was vividly remembered that many Protestant settlers were robbed, abused and even murdered. Protestants began to form armed associations in areas where they were numerous. Initially these bodies were defensive, but Tyrconnell viewed them as a threat to his authority. This proved correct, for where the associations survived, they openly declared for William and Mary and sought their military support. Protestant resistance in Munster was ended in late February, when Justin MacCarthy was sent there with six companies from his own regiment. He suppressed groups holding out in Bandon and Castlemartyr, and disarmed a force being formed by Lord Inchiquin. In Dublin, Protestants formed about half the city's pre-crisis population of 60,000. Although their numbers were eroded by subsequent migration to England, those that remained were nevertheless a substantial group and, given their location, capable of posing a threat to Tyrconnell's regime. An early plan to seize Dublin Castle was defused by the Protestant peers, Granard and Mountjoy, who were still loyal to James. Tyrconnell threatened to punish those who met at 'unseasonable times with firearms in great numbers'. He brought more troops into the city environs, billeting them in the Royal Hospital, from which the old soldiers were ejected, and in Chichester House, the parliament building in College Green. When parties of the remaining Protestant soldiers deserted from the footguards, the horse grenadiers, Mountjoy's and MacCarthy's regiments, Tyrconnell dismissed others and offered the Protestant officers that were left the opportunity to resign, which over a score in Dublin accepted. The enlarged army was then almost entirely Catholic, although some Protestants were still to be found among the rank and file of the old cavalry regiments, such as Galmoy's. They were finally removed in October, on account of their tendency to desert to the enemy with their mounts, arms and equipment. In February Tyrconnell ordered the seizure of all privately held arms in Dublin, a measure that successfully disarmed the city's Protestants. In Sligo and throughout Ulster, formidable Protestant groupings assembled to defend themselves. They set up separate commands for the different regions of Ulster and established a council of five to coordinate defence measures. Military units were formed and drilled, with purged Protestant ex-officers, such as Lords Kingston and Mountalexander, the two Gustavus Hamiltons and Sir Arthur Rawdon, playing a prominent part. Derry and Enniskillen resisted the introduction of Catholic garrisons. An envoy sent to apprise William of developments returned in February bearing commissions for the associations' officers, but nothing else. William and Mary were proclaimed in Derry and Enniskillen, and their accession was generally accepted by the northern Protestants. However, Tyrconnell contained the situation by agreeing to Derry being garrisoned by Protestant soldiers from Mountjoy's regiment and promising to take no action against the north pending instructions from King James.[10]

William himself was preoccupied with the consolidation of his position in Britain; his uncertain constitutional situation was only finally settled by the convention 'parliament' on 6 February 1689. A week later William and his wife Mary were proclaimed joint sovereigns of England, Scotland and Ireland. The legality of this operation was of course open to question, especially as far as Ireland was concerned, not only because of the constitutional novelty of an English 'convention' substituting one king of Ireland for another, but also because James's arrival in Ireland in March clearly contradicted the premise that he had vacated his Irish throne. Ireland initially was not at the centre of William's concerns. But in the early days of January 1689, in response to indications that Tyrconnell was prepared to surrender his authority, William released the Irish general, Richard Hamilton, from the Tower of London, where he had been confined since the revolution, and sent him to Dublin to treat with Tyrconnell. Because of Irish Protestant lobbying in London, little seems to have been on offer save a return to the *status quo* in 1684, which would have reversed the gains made by Catholics in the interim. A proclamation of William and Mary in February called on the Irish to lay down their arms, but again offered little in return except very vague assurances on the 'private exercise of their religion' and the enjoyment of their estates 'according to law'. In any case, on arrival in Dublin Hamilton promptly disavowed his mission and bolstered Tyrconnell's will to resist. He was promoted to lieutenant general, as it seems was Justin MacCarthy about the same time. In mid-January Tyrconnell sent Judge Stephen Rice and Viscount Mountjoy to France. Mountjoy was still a brigadier in the army and a potential military leader of Protestant resistance in Ireland. Ostensibly the mission was to persuade James to allow Tyrconnell to surrender to William, an explanation that was partly a ruse to gain time, for Rice had secret instructions to assure James of Tyrconnell's utmost commitment to him, and to recommend

10 Parker, *Memoirs*, p. 6; *JN*, pp 41–2; Murphy, *Mountcashel*, p. 16; *PI*, ii, p. 57; Childs, *Williamite wars*, pp 13, 52–3; Simms, *Jacobite Ireland*, pp 55–7; Connolly, *Religion, law and power*, p. 147; 'Longford letters', pp 50–2, 54–6, 58; *AH*, pp 21, 99; *Proclamations*, pp 68–70, 79–80; *F-I corr.*, iii, p. 85.

Mountjoy's detention. Accordingly, Mountjoy was imprisoned in the Bastille, where he remained until exchanged in 1692.[11]

French involvement

In mid-January two officers arrived in Ireland from France. One was Michael Rothe, a captain in the Irish footguards who had escaped from England in 1688. He brought a letter from James encouraging Tyrconnell to hold out at least until the summer, although the only assistance on offer at that stage was 7–8,000 muskets that King Louis had agreed to send. Rothe's companion was the baron de Pointis, a French naval officer sent by the marquis de Seignelay, the navy minister, to report on the Irish situation. Pointis was impressed by the enthusiasm of the Irish, observing that they were resolved to perish rather than submit to Protestant domination. He reported that Tyrconnell could have raised 100,000 men if he wished. The new soldiers were paying great attention to arms and drill, but lacked uniforms and adequate supplies of weapons. About half had muskets or pikes, the rest only sticks tipped with nails. His conclusion was that in their present situation, the Irish Catholics would be unable to hold out against William. However, if supplied with arms, officers and money, they could easily repel an invasion and even carry the fight into England. Acting on Pointis's report, Seignelay overcame the opposition of the marquis de Louvois, the French war minister, and persuaded Louis to intervene in Ireland. Tyrconnell appears to have placed great store on the psychological and indeed constitutional importance of James's personal presence. He told Pointis, what he had originally told Rice and was later to confirm to the French ambassador, d'Avaux, that if James refused to come, the Irish would seek the protection of the king of France. Tyrconnell's demand for James's presence probably influenced the French decision to send the exiled king to Ireland. Tyrconnell also extended a formal invitation to James to come. As Marshal Vauban put it to Louvois: 'when a man plays his last card, he ought to play it himself, or be on the spot'. A consequence of James's direct involvement was that Major General Maumont, the original ranking French officer chosen for Ireland, was subordinated to the higher-ranking Lieutenant General Conrad von Rosen.[12]

A French fleet under Admiral Gabaret carried James to Ireland, and he disembarked at Kinsale on 22 March 1689, accompanied by Rosen, Maumont

11 Beddard, *Revolutions*, pp 91–4, 163–4; *CSPD 1689–90*, p. 6; 'Longford letters', p. 47; *James II*, ii, pp 320–1, 327; *d'Avaux*, pp 105, 182; Simms, *Jacobite Ireland*, p. 51.   12 Simms, *Jacobite Ireland*, pp 53, 59–61; *d'Avaux*, pp 6 et seq., 87–8; *James II*, ii, p. 319; Turner, *James II*, p. 463; *AH* 21, 23; BL Add. MS 28,053.

and the accomplished French diplomat, the comte d'Avaux, together with approximately a hundred French, English and Irish officers, and some supplies. In May a second and larger convoy, commanded by Admiral Châteaurenault, arrived at Bantry to land more officers and supplies, together with 3,000 Irish, English and Scottish personnel. It included 120 French regimental officers, forty cadets and a number of generals, artillerists and engineers, tasked with injecting a degree of professionalism into James's forces. The general officers certainly made an important contribution, although two of them were killed at an early stage during the siege of Derry. The regimental officers were of mixed quality, and their involvement with the army was beset by language difficulties and Irish reluctance to admit them to regimental establishments. Nevertheless, their input must have had an impact. D'Avaux was uncomfortable with the task of army administration, and he was greatly relieved by the arrival in May of François de Fumeron, an experienced and capable *commissaire* from Louvois's team, who played a key role in preparing the Irish army for war both in 1689 and 1691. The 1689 fleets also brought *matériel*, consisting of 3,000 swords, 16,000 sabres, 1,000 pairs of pistols, 500 carbines, 500 muskets, 500 flintlocks, 100,000 pounds of gunpowder and about a million *livres* (c.£60,000). A further 4,600 muskets followed in August. Although the number of muskets was insufficient and much of the other weaponry in poor condition, it went some considerable way towards arming the new regiments. An English fleet under Admiral Herbert attempting to intercept Châteaurenault's ships at the mouth of Bantry Bay had the worst of an inconclusive naval battle, the largest ever fought in Irish waters. This engagement marked the opening of hostilities between Williamite England and France, although war was not formally declared until 17 May.[13]

Tyrconnell met King James at Cork and was rewarded for his loyalty with a dukedom. He was also promoted to captain general of the Irish army. Subsequently James made a splendid ceremonial entry into Dublin, a pageant that included the garrison under arms and the firing of cannon. Direction of affairs now passed to King James and the triumvirate of d'Avaux, Tyrconnell and James's secretary of state, the Scottish earl of Melfort. Differences arose straight away. Neither James nor Melfort was interested in Tyrconnell's objective of overthrowing the post-Cromwellian land settlement. Their aim was to use the Irish army to invade Britain, via either Scotland or England, but d'Avaux and Tyrconnell took the view that an essential prerequisite was that the entire island of Ireland must first be completely secured. Tyrconnell deeply

---

[13] *F-I corr.*, i, xlii; *AH*, 21, pp 98, 101, 128, 137; *JN*, pp 201–41, 315–16; *d'Avaux, suppl.*, pp 9–12; Le Fevre, 'Battle of Bantry Bay', pp 1–16.

resented Melfort's influence; pleading ill-health, he frequently absented himself from proceedings. The French accused Melfort of incompetence and lack of attention to duty. A campaign to suppress William's Protestant supporters in the north had commenced even before James's arrival. It was triggered by Mountalexander's attempt to dislodge the poorly armed Irish garrison from Carrickfergus, the stronghold of the earl of the Antrim and Cormac O'Neill, the leading Antrim Jacobites. In response, Richard Hamilton and Dominic Sheldon led a force of 2,500 men into Ulster. It was largely drawn from the old regiments and accompanied by a few field guns. Having routed the east-Ulster Protestants at the break of Dromore, the Jacobite force moved westwards, forcing a passage across the river crossings at Clady and Strabane against Williamite opposition. A force assembled by the Sligo Protestants disintegrated, with many of the personnel making their way to Enniskillen. At the end of April, a second gathering of pro-Williamite forces in east Down was easily routed by a force led by the veteran Scottish officer, Thomas Buchan, in an engagement near Newtownards, known as the break of Killyleagh. Thus, by the early summer, the Jacobite army had performed well, confining the pro-Williamite enclave in the north to the region covered by the last-remaining Protestant strongholds of Derry and Enniskillen.[14]

The reorganization of the army

Meanwhile in Dublin, the decision was taken to re-order and reduce the ungainly military force newly raised by Tyrconnell. The army was the cause of widespread disorder, with too little discipline, too few arms, too many regiments with too many companies and very poor administration. Some of the new regiments had as many as thirty-five, forty and forty-four companies, whereas James's goal was the standard thirteen-company, single-battalion unit. Tyrconnell proposed a force of 30,000, but James wanted 35,000 infantry alone, together with 2,600 cavalry and 3,800 dragoons. A complication was that in the midst of administrative chaos, the actual number enlisted remained unknown for many months. Tyrconnell put it at 50,000, a figure that d'Avaux seems to have accepted, but as late as mid-June Fumeron reported that he still did not know the exact number, and doubted if it amounted to more than two-thirds of the 40,000 that were claimed. By September 1689, in the wake of the summer campaign, Fumeron could account for only 21,700 men. Eventually a total strength of around 35,000 was settled upon to serve both the needs of the

14 *D'Avaux*, pp 6, 483, 507 *et seq.*, 545; *AH*, 21, pp 23, 131–2, 136, 200; *JN*, 47; Tyrconnell letters, nos 8, 18; Simms, 'Sligo', pp 126–7; Childs, *Williamite wars*, pp 51–74; Wauchope, *Londonderry*, passim.

garrisons and the field army. This remained the standard into 1691, when *Commissaire* Fumeron reported that while it might not be met, he expected to have a minimum of 30,500 under arms. The French view was that this was the most that could be maintained, armed and disciplined, although d'Avaux recognized how difficult it would be to sustain a force of even this size. The unpleasant task of managing the reductions fell to Tyrconnell, who had opposed them. In April he travelled to the various garrisons to implement the cuts. One review was at the Curragh. According to Colonel Charles O'Kelly, whose own regiment was one of those disbanded, the reductions fell mainly on the Old Irish, for whom Tyrconnell 'seemed to have no inclination, believing them more dangerous than William himself'. Tyrconnell's mission may have laid the foundation for his later unpopularity with much of the army, as well as contributing to growing Irish disenchantment with King James. Sarsfield and possibly other senior officers apparently assisted him. At Birr, Oxburgh's regiment was reviewed by Sarsfield, who then disbanded nine companies before proceeding to Portumna to disband numerous companies of Lord Galway's regiment. In at least one case a company was transferred from one regiment to another, and there may have been other instances of this.[15]

The disbanded officers were reported to have been 'struck to the very heart' by the decision because of their 'uncommon zeal for the cause', the money they had spent supporting their men over four or five months, and the prospect of honour, which was now denied them. All Tyrconnell could offer was the king's thanks and a vague assurance of preferment in the future. The plan was to retain twenty-five of the new infantry regiments and disband fifteen. But in practice Tyrconnell failed to implement such a drastic contraction of regimental numbers, probably because of the opposition he encountered on the ground, although his explanation was that he had 'found amongst the infantry so many good men that he could not think of disbanding them'. Five regiments were certainly discontinued at this time. The number of companies in the remainder was reduced, but less radically than planned: at the end of June there were still seven regiments with twenty companies or more, five of whom were under review for retention as two-battalion units. In addition, at that time more than forty detached companies were still in being, not as yet disbanded. The disbanded soldiers were so disorderly that James was obliged to appoint local gentlemen as provost marshals in each county to restrain and punish the malefactors without delay. A return from May 1689 lists the

15 *D'Avaux*, pp 29, 37, 78, 182–4, 414; *AH*, 21, pp 115, 136–7; *JN*, p. 52; 'A journal of what passed since his majesty's arrival' (Bodl., Carte MS 181), f. 10; *Poema*, pp 156–8; *Rosse papers*, p. 230; O'Kelly, xiii, p. 47; 'Gafney', pp 162, 166–7.

strength of the re-ordered army as seven regiments each of horse and dragoons, and forty-one of infantry. By November d'Avaux accounted for forty-five infantry regiments, including five at two-battalion strength, together with four additional regiments provisionally destined for France.[16]

The summer campaign

After its strong start in Munster and east Ulster, the Irish army performed poorly in the subsequent summer campaign of 1689. The central event was the siege of Derry lasting from mid-April to the end of July. Although the city twice came close to submitting, in the end the siege was a failure. The French general officers, Maumont and Pusignan, who might have conducted operations efficiently, were both killed at the outset. After this, direction of the siege was left to Richard Hamilton, who had no experience of siege warfare and was regarded by the French as a thoroughly incompetent commander. The Jacobite artillery was far too weak and badly managed to breach the fortifications, or even guard the seaward approach up the Foyle, when the relief ships finally broke through the boom that supposedly blocked the deep-water channel. The logistical supply line was long and tortuous, while its supporting Dublin administration was irresolute and chaotic. There was much rain, but insufficient tents to shelter the troops. Pay was withheld, and food was in short supply. Lack of trench tools prevented the construction of any serious siege works. But, above all, the army was ill-prepared for such a contest. As late as 6 June its strength at Derry was less than 4,000 men, of which two-thirds were drawn from the new-raised regiments. Most contingents consisted of detachments rather than full battalions. Even after reinforcements arrived, army strength continued to be eroded by sickness and desertion, both of which were widespread. In early July the besiegers did not exceed 5,000. The French reported the Irish officers as ignorant and useless. It was a bad example to their men that some absented themselves without leave, while many failed to attend the siege at all. The soldiers were poorly armed: some had only pointed sticks, others lacked bandoliers or swords. Many muskets were damaged or broken, and those that were serviceable were prone to deteriorate in the hands of men ignorant of both their use and their maintenance. Looting and theft were endemic and morale low. *Commissaire* Fumeron described it as an army of gypsies and mutineers in which the efforts of honourable men were undermined. Chaos was reported when the siege was finally raised. The camp was abandoned amid scenes of disorder. Frequently deserted by their officers,

16 *JN*, p. 53; *d'Avaux*, pp 233, 285, 569–71; Tyrconnell letters, no. 12; Story, p. 98; 'A journal of what passed since his majesty's arrival' (Bodl., Carte MS 181), f. 26.

many of whom had gone home, the soldiers moved off in disorganized bands that were very vulnerable to attack had the garrison shown any initiative. Abandoned weapons and equipment were left behind in heaps. There were no transport wagons and thus no means of evacuating the sick and wounded, many of whom were left behind. Four of the withdrawing regiments halted at Drogheda, where they found quarters or pitched camp, while nine that were reported 'extremely shattered and thin' went on to Dublin.[17]

The army's inadequacy at this time was clearly demonstrated by its unsuccessful combat operations over the summer, which exposed its shortcomings at all levels. At Derry, Hamilton's men seized a strategic point called Windmill Hill, only to be driven from it with heavy losses by a sally from the city the next day. A later assault on the wall near Butcher's Gate by Clancarty's regiment was driven back by heavy fire from the defenders, which caused more than a hundred casualties. A sally by the Williamites in early August caught the besiegers unawares, and they suffered thirty-five casualties. Operations against Enniskillen were even more disastrous. In March an attempt by Viscount Galmoy to capture the outlying stronghold of Crom Castle was unsuccessful. The Jacobites were unable to prevent the Enniskillen cavalry from raiding their quarters and thwarting Sarsfield's attempt to disrupt the Enniskilleners' communications on the Erne to Ballyshannon. A substantial Jacobite force under Justin MacCarthy and Anthony Hamilton was sent to deal with Enniskillen. Crom was again besieged, but the operation had to be abandoned, when Hamilton was badly defeated near Lisnaskea in an unsuccessful attempt to block a relief force approaching from Enniskillen. When MacCarthy gave battle outside Newtownbutler, his troops, described as 'raw and newly raised' although they included his own 'old' regiment, fled before the determined assault of the Enniskilleners, only to be trapped in the watery wilderness of the Erne where many were drowned or massacred. MacCarthy himself was badly wounded and made prisoner. Another regiment involved was Lord Clare's dragoons, although the colonel himself was absent in command of Munster. The Derry and Enniskillen defeats led to a precipitate Jacobite abandonment of Sligo, which the Enniskilleners occupied before pressing south across the Curlew mountains to eject the Jacobite garrison from Boyle. A final casualty of the unsuccessful Ulster campaign was the withdrawal to France of Melfort, James's unpopular secretary of state, who was distrusted by the French and detested by the Irish, especially Tyrconnell. His role was now divided between civil and military affairs, with Sir Richard

17 *D'Avaux*, pp 189–90, 280, 295–6, 509; *d'Avaux suppl.*, p. 39; *F-I corr.*, iii, pp 31, 41; *AH*, 21, pp 115, 130, 136, 140–1, 146–9, 154–5, 165, 200; Simms, *Jacobite Ireland*, pp 100–13; *Proclamations*, pp 111–12; *James II*, ii, p. 372; *Ormonde MSS*, n.s., viii, p. 369.

Nagle, a leading Irish lawyer and close associate of Tyrconnell, filling the office of secretary for war.[18]

These setbacks left the Jacobite army in serious disarray; for one thing, more than 12,000 muskets had been lost at Derry and Newtownbutler. Then at the end of August it faced a grave new threat from the arrival in Ulster of the experienced veteran, the duke of Schomberg, with 10,000 men, sent by William to establish his authority in Ireland. No opposition to their disembarkation came from a mounted Jacobite force in the locality under the Scottish brigadier, Thomas Maxwell, which withdrew south. Schomberg's first target was the Jacobite garrison at Carrickfergus, which was drawn from two new regiments of Gaels: Charles MacCarthy More's from Munster and nine companies of Cormac O'Neill's Ulstermen. Although bombarded and heavily outnumbered, they put up a spirited resistance. This seems to have been driven by Lieutenant Colonel Owen MacCarthy, an officer who had served in England and possibly on the Continent, and who was later to command a regiment of his own. After a week, with their powder virtually exhausted, the defenders surrendered on honourable terms that allowed them to march out with their weapons to the nearest Jacobite garrison. A detailed return in late August put the whole Irish army, including garrisons, at just over 20,000 men, with most units substantially below strength and nearly half the soldiers unarmed.[19]

There was alarm in Dublin at Schomberg's arrival. The French counselled a withdrawal of the Jacobite forces behind the Shannon, but James, resolute for once, refused 'to be tamely walked out of Ireland, but to have one blow for it at least' and insisted instead on advancing with all available troops to Drogheda to confront Schomberg. He was supported by Tyrconnell, who resumed a much more active role after Melfort's departure and strongly opposed any abandonment of Dublin and Leinster to the Williamites. Accompanied by only 300 cavalry, James rode north as far as Drogheda on 26 August, leaving Tyrconnell behind in Dublin to put together an army. To d'Avaux's surprise, Tyrconnell threw himself into the task with enthusiasm and drive, supported by the Irish officers. By mid-September the Jacobites had twenty-eight cavalry squadrons and twenty-seven infantry battalions in the field against Schomberg, a total of 13,600 men, supported by eleven mixed-calibre artillery pieces. The soldiers were short of swords and sabres, few had

---

18 Simms, *Jacobite Ireland*, pp 104, 107, 113–19; *AH*, 21, p. 164; *d'Avaux*, pp 384–6, 429, 452; *JN*, p. 82; O'Kelly, pp 37–8; Simms, 'Sligo', pp 127–8; Doherty, *Williamite war*, pp 46–71; Hamilton, *Inniskillingmen*; McCarmick, *Inniskillingmen*; *Great news of a bloody fight in Newton*; Graham, *Mountcashel*, pp 115–53.   **19** *AH*, 21, p. 167; *JN*, p. 87; Story, pp 7–10; Simms, *Jacobite Ireland*, pp 122–3; *d'Avaux*, pp 443, 451–4; Dalton, i, p. 209; ii, p. 143.

bayonets and some muskets were unserviceable. Nevertheless, morale seems to have been high: an officer recorded the army's 'great alacrity and readiness to march towards the enemy, though many of the men were very raw and undisciplined, and the generality almost naked or at least ragged and ill-shod'. Although somewhat smaller than Schomberg's forces, which had been supplemented by the Ulster Protestant regiments, the challenge mounted by James's army was enough to bring Schomberg's progress to a halt at Dundalk. The Jacobites set up camp at Ardee, and at one point advanced towards Schomberg's camp 'to offer battle to the enemy and provoke them, if possible, to come out and fight him', as King James's memoirs claimed. But Schomberg did not respond. Beset by logistical problems, the outbreak of disease in his army and his own inertia, he never advanced beyond Dundalk, and in October withdrew his forces into winter quarters in Ulster. In the west, Sarsfield recovered Sligo, Jamestown and Boyle. Thus, after a summer of defeats, the Jacobite position had stabilized. Their confidence was restored, and there was even criticism of James for not attacking Schomberg, or at least harrying his retreat. However, the reality was that the Williamites had established a solid bridgehead in Ulster, where most of the province was under their control, and the only remaining Jacobite garrison was at Charlemont. James, although pleased that his autumn campaign had ended 'much to his honour and advantage', lapsed back into passivity. Rosen, thoroughly disillusioned by his disagreements with James, resigned his command in November. After this, the opportunity to use the winter to train the army was largely squandered, with the officers absent from their units, and their time 'idly spent in revels and gaming, and other debauches unfit for a Catholic court'. Whatever its shortcomings, the Irish army by the end of its 1689 campaign was substantially in the form that it would retain until the end of the war.[20]

Scottish interlude

After his energetic resistance to Schomberg, James became increasingly disillusioned with Ireland, as his objective of returning to Britain to secure his restoration seemed further than ever from realization. The only assistance he had been able to send to his Scottish supporters was 400 men from a new regiment formed by Colonel James Purcell, largely officered by Scots and Englishmen, with some 'dragoons' recruited in east Ulster by the Scottish Jacobite, Sir Alexander MacLean. Seven companies of Lord Bophin's infantry were also scheduled for Scotland, but there is no evidence that they actually

20 *D'Avaux*, pp 443, 479; *James II*, ii, p. 373; *F-I corr.*, iii, pp 71–3, 105–6; *Stevens*, pp 79, 92; O'Kelly, p. 41.

went. In July 1689 this force was carried from Carrickfergus to Scotland on board French frigates. It was led by Colonel Alexander Cannon, a Scottish veteran of the Anglo-Dutch brigade. Seventy-five unattached officers, presumably also Scots, accompanied him. The Irish soldiers soon fought at the battle of Killiecrankie, where the Jacobites were victorious, but lost their charismatic leader, Viscount Dundee, who was mortally wounded. From his deathbed, he praised the Irish contribution and sought a reinforcement of horse and dragoons, but no more soldiers were sent from Ireland. After wintering on Mull, Purcell returned to Ireland, leaving his men to serve under Scottish commanders. Cannon succeeded Dundee but was decisively defeated at Cromdale in 1690, where his force included 120 Irishmen, serving in Thomas Buchan's regiment. A further 170 remained on Mull, where Sir John MacLean held out until 1692. Meanwhile, both Louis and Louvois made clear to James that at least until Schomberg was crushed and Ulster subdued they ruled out any further intervention in Britain. Tyrconnell took a different view on the grounds that Ireland could not endure a protracted war. As late as November 1689 fruitless plans for a 7,800-strong invasion force were drawn up. But the army's focus was on specifically Irish objectives, and there was little Irish enthusiasm for an invasion of Britain.[21]

Figure 3. A dragoon sergeant

[21] *D'Avaux*, pp 252, 400, 562, 655; 'Talbot letter-book', pp 108, 120; Maclean-Bristol, *Castor & Pollux*, p. 117; Hopkins, *Glencoe*, pp 154, 212–13; *James II*, ii, p. 352; Powley, *Naval war*, p. 242; Young, 'Scotland and Ireland', pp 76–83.

CHAPTER 3

The campaigns of 1690–1

Preliminaries to the Boyne

THE WINTER SEASON OF 1689–90 was marked by skirmishes and seizures of livestock from enemy quarters. In November a Jacobite force briefly occupied Newry, but then withdrew. Mosstown House, an isolated Williamite garrison in County Longford, surrendered to the Jacobites in January. A substantial engagement occurred at Cavan the following month. Berwick confronted a Williamite force to the north of the town. Reports vary as to the numbers engaged, but there appear to have been at least a thousand men on each side. Although the Williamite horse were driven back, a musket volley from the Irish infantry was ineffectual because they fired too high, whereas a Williamite counter volley drove the Irish back to the protection of an earthwork fort. A counterattack on the Williamites engaged in plundering the town was repulsed. Stores, provisions and ammunition were looted or destroyed before the Williamites withdrew. The Jacobites suffered a number of casualties, including Brigadier William Nugent, who was killed. The defeat was a blow to morale, the English Jacobite, John Stevens, calling it an 'inexcusable shame'. Another Jacobite setback was the surrender of Charlemont Fort, their last Ulster stronghold. But this was only after a stubborn defence by its governor, the veteran Teague O'Regan, who held out until food supplies were exhausted and only then capitulated on honourable terms. James was pleased with O'Regan's performance, knighted him and sent him to command in Sligo, where he again proved a stubborn and proficient governor.[1]

Disappointed by Schomberg's performance in 1689 (for which William bore considerable responsibility) the king determined to come to Ireland himself to conduct the campaign in 1690. Unchallenged by the French navy, he built up his forces in advance to 37,000, taking care to remedy the defects that had beset Schomberg: poor logistics, inadequate medical services and weak artillery. As befitted an army of the grand alliance against France, William's force was multi-national, comprising English, Ulster-Irish, Dutch, Huguenot and Danish units, the latter including many Germans. More than

1 *JN*, pp 91–3; Story, pp 51–2, 54–5; *Stevens*, pp 99–100; Berwick, *Memoirs*, pp 60–2; Simms, 'Sligo', pp 130–5.

a third was cavalry or dragoons. The continental troops, amounting to between a third and a half of the army's strength, were regarded as its superior component. A number of Irish Protestants, including ex-Irish army officers, served in English regiments newly raised for the war. Landing at Belfast Lough in mid-June, William declared that he had not come to let the grass grow under his feet and without delay gathered his forces and commenced to march south to confront James preferably in a pitched battle.[2]

The Jacobite army had been reinforced by seven French battalions in 1690, but had lost over 5,000 officers and men sent to France in return. Partly for this reason, but also because of the need to garrison the port towns in the south and west, and some inland strongholds, and also because some units still lacked arms, it could place no more than 25,000 men in the field, including the French. Opinion on the Jacobite side was divided on strategy. The French had long advocated falling back behind the natural barrier of the Shannon to conduct a defensive war, which would play to their objective of tying William and his army down in Ireland for as long as possible. It would also minimize the risk to the Jacobite army, especially its French contingent, in accordance with the instructions given by the French war minister, the marquis de Louvois, to the French expedition's commander, Comte de Lauzun. Tyrconnell, too, favoured avoiding battle, while conceding that abandonment of Dublin and Leinster was also unpalatable. Faced with this choice, James opted to make a stand when William took the offensive. After all, it had worked against Schomberg the year before, and the River Boyne offered an 'indifferent good' defensive position. He was conscious that to abandon the east of the island, including the capital and the homes and estates of many of his principal supporters, for the poor province of Connacht would disillusion and dishearten the army in which 'his men seemed desirous to fight'. His rather desultory conduct of events at the Boyne suggests that there may have been an element of fatalism in the decision. His Irish sojourn had brought James no closer to returning to England; his relations with the Irish had deteriorated and he may have preferred to put matters to the test, whatever the outcome, in order to bring his situation to a resolution. The initial Jacobite advance went well north of the Boyne some distance beyond Dundalk to eat up the fodder and thwart the expected Williamite offensive. The army then fell back on Ardee. From there on 29 June it withdrew across the Boyne in two columns, one over the bridge at Drogheda and the other five kilometres upstream across the ford at Oldbridge. The army camped on the northern slopes of Donore Hill. Next day William's army arrived at Tullyallen, north of the river.[3]

2 Story, pp 95–7; Ferguson, 'Army in Ireland', pp 39–41; Childs, *Williamite wars*, p. 206.   3 *F-I corr.*, iii, p. 82; *AH*, 4, pp 126–7, 130, 132–3; 'Lauzun's reports', pp 113, 117–18; *James II*, ii, pp 393–4.

The Boyne battle

The Jacobites detached 1,300 men from their field army to garrison Drogheda, and destroyed the next bridge about twelve kilometres upstream at Slane. However, the Boyne in between was fordable in many places, especially at low tide. A strength of the position was the precipitous ridge immediately south of the river, which offered good defensive possibilities and made it difficult for any substantial Williamite force to deploy on the south bank, except on two wider plains. One was at Oldbridge and the second further west between Rossnaree and Slane. Lauzun considered the position weak, but another French general, Léry-Girardin, thought it favourable and the most advantageous location to give battle between Dundalk and Dublin. A major weakness of posting the army at Oldbridge was that immediately to its west the Boyne bent south, opening up the possibility of a Williamite force moving upstream to outflank the Oldbridge position. Both sides recognized this. William declined Schomberg's advice to concentrate his main attack upstream and decided instead to make it at Oldbridge. He did, however, agree to send Schomberg's son, Meinhard, to probe upstream with a strong party of mounted troops followed by a force of infantry. Dawn reports of Meinhard Schomberg's force moving west on 1 July confirmed James's apprehensions about the Oldbridge position, and he ordered the left wing and the centre of his army to do likewise. This left only a third of his smaller army to confront two-thirds of the larger Williamite army when it attacked across the Boyne at Oldbridge. This was at low tide, shortly after 10.00 a.m. William's artillery had kept the Jacobites on the ridge well back from the river bank, except for Clanricard's regiment, which occupied some houses in the hamlet of Oldbridge, where they took up position both there and behind a barrier they erected on the path leading up from the ford. Little else had been done to fortify the river bank. Shortly before the Williamite assault the Jacobite position at Oldbridge was further weakened when James ordered the removal of the French artillery, much to the surprise of its commander, Laisné. Had the French guns remained, they would surely have troubled the Williamite infantry, but in the event only the half dozen cannon on the Jacobite left played any part in the battle.[4]

---

4 'Lauzun's reports', p. 118; Barbe, 'Battle of the Boyne', pp 21–3; Story, pp 78–9; *JN*, p. 99; *F-I corr.*, i, pp 447, 452–3; ii, pp 75, 77; iii, pp 125, 130. Modern accounts of the battle of the Boyne include Hayes-McCoy, *Irish battles*, pp 214–37; Simms, 'Eye-witnesses of the Boyne'; Berresford Ellis, *Boyne water*; O'Carroll, 'Battlefield of the Boyne'; Lenihan, *Boyne*; McNally, *Boyne*; Murtagh, *Boyne guide*.

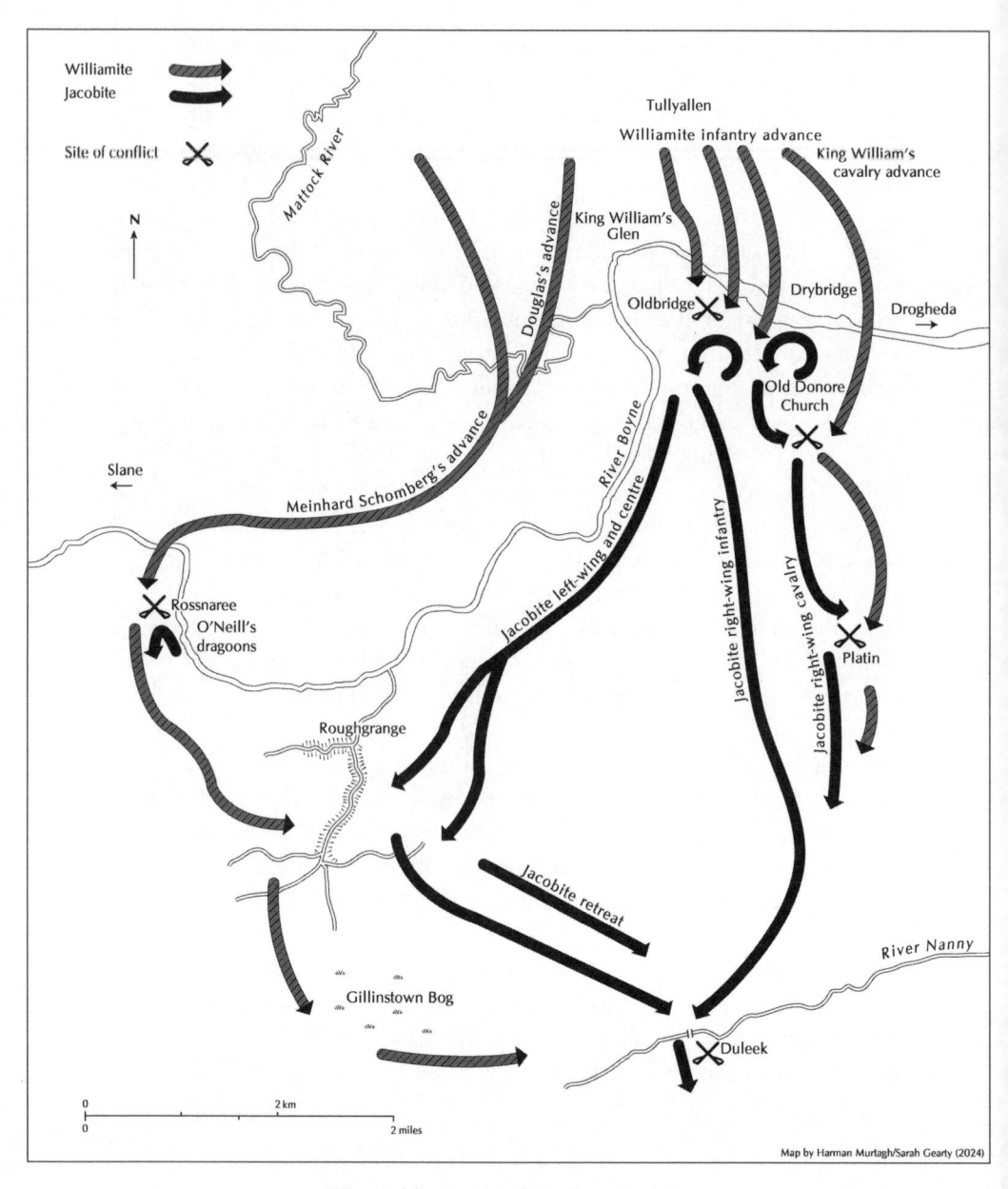

Map 2. The battle of the Boyne, 1690

Three battalions of Dutch guards commenced the Williamite attack. They advanced down the defile known today as King William's Glen, waded across the Oldbridge ford and easily ejected Clanricard's men from Oldbridge village, before taking up position in a wheatfield on the adjoining plain. Successive waves of Williamite infantry then advanced down the steep slope from Tullyallen to cross the Boyne immediately east of Oldbridge on a two-kilometre front. They were challenged by the remaining Irish infantry – five regiments, including the footguards – which moved down from their position on the ridge to engage them. But the Irish musketry was poor. The Williamite infantry could not be dislodged from their position on the south bank, and their fire soon drove off the Jacobite infantry. Lord Dungan's dragoons, who engaged the Danish infantry on the Williamite left, withdrew after their colonel was killed. The only real threat came from the four Jacobite cavalry regiments remaining in the Oldbridge sector. With no Williamite cavalry to oppose them, Tyrconnell's, Parker's and the horseguards, perhaps a thousand sabres in all, staged a number of effective charges into the infantry, while Sutherland's was held in reserve. The Dutch guards met the cavalry with tight formation, volley fire and fixed bayonets, but the neighbouring Huguenot battalions, less experienced and without bayonets, pikes or *chevaux-de-frise,* suffered severely. Marshal Schomberg crossed the river to encourage them, only to be killed in the *mêlée*. The Jacobite cavalry contained the Williamite infantry, but at a heavy cost to themselves. Parker was wounded, his lieutenant colonel and major were both killed, and only thirty troopers of his regiment came off unscathed. Tyrconnell's and the horseguards must have suffered similar attrition.[5]

The turning point came when William himself led the left wing of his cavalry, perhaps 2,000 men, across the most easterly and difficult ford opposite Drybridge. This was guarded by Lord Clare's dragoons, but after firing an ineffectual volley, they withdrew, leaving William's cavalry to ascend unopposed through a narrow defile to open ground, where they deployed and advanced towards the Jacobite flank. This threat compelled the Jacobite cavalry, probably nearing exhaustion in any case, to break off the engagement on the south river bank, and withdraw to the high ground at Donore (the original village beside the churchyard) where, with the remaining dragoons, they successfully held off William's cavalry. Retiring south to nearby Platin, they again resisted the Williamites. There was sharp fighting at both locations. At Platin, Richard Hamilton was wounded and captured and James's bastard son, the duke of Berwick, had to be rescued when his horse was killed under

5 *JN*, p. 99; Story, pp 79–82; *James II*, ii, pp 398–400; *Danish force*, pp 42–3, 45–6.

him. These holding actions enabled the Jacobite infantry to make good their withdrawal from the Oldbridge sector, and they were followed by the cavalry.⁶

Meanwhile on the west side of the battlefield, Meinhard Schomberg's cavalry had crossed the Boyne between Rossnaree and Slane, overcoming determined opposition from a Jacobite dragoon regiment, which retired only when their colonel, Sir Neil O'Neill, was badly wounded. South of the river, the Williamite cavalry then deployed on the 'very fine plain', and Schomberg advanced eastwards towards the Jacobite left flank. This was exactly the manoeuvre James had feared, but better Jacobite reconnaissance would have revealed that the flank was well protected by a deep ravine at Roughgrange, stretching south-west from the Boyne for two kilometres. The ravine prevented any engagement between the two armies on the west side of the battlefield. With the arrival of infantry support, perhaps a third of the Williamite army was now deployed on their right wing. Schomberg began to move south, but his progress was slow. 'Great ditches' enclosing cornfields obstructed the cavalry, and the infantry became immersed in a 'damned deep bog'. Nevertheless, the Jacobite army was now threatened by a pincer trap as both wings of the Williamite army threatened to converge on it. The escape route was across the stone bridge that traversed the River Nanny at Duleek. James and Lauzun led the way, followed by the army's left wing and centre. The withdrawal was orderly until the fleeing cavalry from the right wing collided with the forces retiring from the left. Chaos followed, and the withdrawal degenerated into a rout. Weapons were discarded and baggage abandoned as the army fled in panic across the Nanny bridge. It was saved from destruction by the French infantry who drew up with the cannon of the left wing on the high ground south of the bridge. They held off the pursuing Williamite cavalry, before retreating in good order to stand again to similar effect at The Neale.⁷

More than 60,000 soldiers were at the Boyne, but the majority were never engaged, and casualties amounted to only about a thousand Jacobites and 500 Williamites. William had displayed great personal courage on the battlefield, but his failure to take old Schomberg's advice probably denied him an overwhelming victory. Ironically, the Jacobite army was saved from annihilation by James's blundering generalship. The general feeling was that the Irish cavalry had done well on the day, and they certainly won the respect of their opponents. The infantry was judged to have performed badly, which

---

6 Story, pp 82–4; *Finch MSS*, ii, pp 329–30; *Dumont de Bostaquet*, p. 230; *JN*, pp 101–2.   **7** Story, pp 78, 84–5; *JN*, pp 99–100; 'Diaries of the Boyne', p. 81; Lord Meath's letter; *Stevens*, pp 122–4; *F-I corr.*, i, p. 449; iii, p. 131.

insofar as it was true, was probably accounted for by their inexperience and lack of musketry practice. But there was a general feeling of bewilderment as to how the army could have been so easily routed in circumstances where the majority of soldiers were never engaged and never discharged a shot. James immediately returned to France. He saw no further hope of achieving his restoration through Ireland and was as disillusioned with the Irish as they were with him. Before departing he told his Irish followers to make what terms they could for themselves.[8]

The defence of Limerick

In great disarray, the Jacobite troops fell back on Limerick where they regrouped. Tyrconnell and Lauzun urged an attempt to come to terms with the Williamites, but all that was on offer in William's ill-advised, post-Boyne Finglas declaration was protection for the common soldiers who submitted, while 'the desperate leaders of the present rebellion' (the army officers) were to be left to the event of war, or at best to William's mercy. With little to gain by surrender, their army intact and a sense that the Boyne defeat was due to 'several defects of military management', the senior officers, led by Sarsfield, 'the darling of the army', ignored Tyrconnell's defeatist advice and decided to fight on from fortress Connacht, 'the citadel of Ireland', relatively secure behind the broad River Shannon. An attack on Athlone, the key mid-Shannon crossing, by a 7,500-strong Williamite force was repulsed by Colonel Richard Grace, the veteran Jacobite governor, who broke down the bridge and defied the Williamites from the west riverbank. An immediate reaction to the violent depredations of the Williamite soldiers on this expedition was an upsurge in partisan warfare by Irish rapparees, which caused the Williamites considerable trouble for the rest of the war. Meanwhile, a large force of Gaelic Irish, led by Balldearg O'Donnell, an Irish officer returned from Spain, guarded the upper Shannon crossings, while the Sligo garrison secured the approach from the north.[9]

William's pursuit of the Jacobite army was delayed by concerns that England would be invaded, following the French naval victory off Beachy Head. In the interim, by securing Waterford and the fort guarding the approach to Waterford Harbour at Duncannon, which both capitulated to a show of force, William gained a port on the south coast through which to

---

[8] *JN*, pp 102, 104; Story, pp 80, 85, 88; *F-I corr.*, i, p. 445; *Stevens*, p. 121; *Danish force*, p. 45.
[9] *Proclamations*, ii, pp 195–6; O'Kelly, pp 57–9, 60–1; Story, pp 99–104: *James II*, ii, p. 414; *JN*, pp 109–13, 270; 'O'Donnells in exile', p. 54; Simms, 'Sligo', pp 130–1.

supply his army. The slowness of his advance gave the Jacobites time to rally and re-organize their army at Limerick. According to Berwick, it now comprised 3,500 cavalry and 20,000 infantry, but with only half of the latter armed. Lauzun was disparaging about the possibility of defending Limerick and withdrew the French infantry to Galway. However, the capable French officer, Major General Boisseleau, remained at Limerick to command the city's defence for which he had a garrison, variously estimated at 8–12,000 men drawn from twenty-eight infantry regiments, together with a regiment each of horse and dragoons. William finally reached Limerick in the second week of August. Much of the city was built on an island in the Shannon, but the Irishtown was situated on the mainland to the east. Irish cavalry guarded the difficult river crossings to the north. It was towards the walled Irishtown, therefore, that William directed his attack. The conventional parallels and zig-zag trenches were dug to provide cover for his men to approach the walls. Before they could be stormed, an artillery bombardment was needed to create a breach. The slow-moving Williamite siege train followed well behind the main army. On the night of 11 August, while encamped at Ballyneety, it was surprised by 600 cavalry and dragoons, led by Sarsfield and guided by rapparees, which had crossed the Shannon at Killaloe. The Irish troopers killed about sixty of the personnel accompanying the train, sabotaged the ten heavy siege guns, blew up 12,000 pounds of gunpowder and 120 wagons, together with quantities of match, grenades and bombs, and killed or drove off 500 horses. The raiding party evaded interception by recrossing the Shannon at Portumna. The attack was a humiliation for William. It crippled his capacity to besiege Limerick effectively, while greatly boosting Jacobite morale and further enhancing Sarsfield's reputation. Some of the Williamite guns were repaired and ships' cannon were brought up from Waterford, but the bombardment was delayed and the shortage of ammunition diminished the firepower of the siege batteries. As a result, when William ordered an assault, only a narrow breach had been made in the Irishtown wall. It was stoutly defended when the Williamite infantry attacked on 27 August, and they were driven back with 2,300 casualties. The weather was deteriorating and naval support that was expected had not arrived. On 29 August William raised the siege and returned to England. For the remainder of the war, his army in Ireland was commanded by the capable Dutch general, Godard de Ginkel.[10]

10 Story, *Continuation*, p. 35; Story, pp 112–30; Berwick, *Memoirs*, i, p. 69; *F-I corr.*, ii, pp 82–3, 96–7, 99, 103, 106–7; iii, p. 139; *JN*, pp 113–17; *Stevens*, pp 166–84; *Danish force*, pp 54–9, 67–75; Simms, 'Limerick'; Lenihan, 'Boisseleau and the "battle of the breach"'.

Cork and Kinsale

Towards the end of September, the earl of Marlborough landed at Cork Harbour with 5–6,000 fresh infantry and was joined by a further 5,000 drawn from the continental contingent of the Williamite forces in Ireland. His first objective was Cork city, garrisoned by 4–5,000 men commanded by Colonel Roger MacElligott, an experienced veteran of the Anglo-Dutch brigade, who had impressed the French. Cork was a walled town, but overlooked by high ground, from which the Williamite artillery bombarded the city. Berwick was said to have counselled the city's abandonment, although his memoirs are silent on this point. MacElligott's position was weak, but he hoped for relief from the Jacobite army. However, this was blocked by the Williamites, leaving him with no option but to surrender unconditionally. The whole garrison became prisoners of war, depriving the Jacobite army of the regiments of MacElligott, Clancarty, Tyrone, Cavenagh, Owen MacCarthy and Barrett, with their colonels. Marlborough then proceeded to Kinsale, where the Jacobites occupied James Fort and Charles Fort on either side of Kinsale Harbour. James Fort was overrun in a sharp fight in which its governor, Lieutenant Colonel Cornelius O'Driscoll, was killed with half the garrison, and the 200 survivors made prisoner. Charles Fort was a modern fortress, but overlooked by high ground on its landward side. The governor, the veteran Sir Edward Scott, initially rejected Marlborough's summons to surrender. His garrison had been depleted to reinforce Cork, but was still 1,200-strong and well supplied. Again, no relief came, so when the fortress had been under fire from Marlborough's batteries for two days, terms were agreed that allowed the garrison to march off with their arms to Limerick. The need to end the campaign because of a deterioration in the weather seems to have motivated Marlborough to concede terms to Kinsale denied to the Cork garrison. Scott's actions won praise, and he was subsequently appointed to the vacant colonelcy of an infantry regiment. The loss of Cork and Kinsale meant that the campaign of 1690 ended badly for the Jacobites. These ports were probably no longer useful for communications with France, and it might have been wiser to vacate them. Instead, their capture was damaging to morale, and the loss of so many regiments in Cork was a serious blow that could have been avoided by a major relief column or, failing that, an early withdrawal. MacElligott was criticized: his forces were insufficient to defend Cork, and indeed had he initially negotiated with Marlborough, the garrison might have been saved from capture. For the Williamites, Marlborough's efficient Munster campaign made an embarrassing contrast to William's own failure at Limerick.[11]

11 *CSPD 1690–1*, p. 106; *Finch MSS*, ii, p. 459; *Danish force*, pp 79–80, 86–7; Story, pp 140–5;

The winter offensive and the rapparee campaign

The decision to continue the struggle after the Boyne had divided the Jacobite high command. Tyrconnell and his closest supporters were defeatist and argued in favour of trying to achieve terms. Against them were ranged Sarsfield and most of the leading army officers, including Henry Luttrell, Gordon O'Neill, Nicholas Purcell, John Wauchope and William Dorrington, whose stance was much more belligerent. Even after the successful defence of Limerick and Athlone, the peace party, chiefly civilian landowners, argued that these successes only strengthened the case for negotiation. The division was bitter, with Tyrconnell and his supporters calling his opponents 'caballists', 'intriguers' and 'mutineers', while they asserted that his supporters were 'traitors', and that he was 'a perfidious and ungrateful man' who was not only militarily incompetent but designed 'to bring them again under the English yoke'. It came as a surprise to the Irish Jacobites that, despite their success in defending Limerick, Lauzun persisted in withdrawing the French troops from Ireland, sailing from Galway aboard Admiral d'Amfreville's fleet in late September, and taking with him all but thirty of the French officers that had come to strengthen the Jacobite army. Tyrconnell, whose credit with the army was now very low, also went to France, anxious to shore up his authority with James and Louis before the army sent a deputation there to discredit him. In his absence he left Berwick in charge of the army with an advisory council of officers, evenly divided between Tyrconnellites and supporters of Sarsfield. An abortive attack on Birr Castle and the failure to relieve Cork or Kinsale weakened Berwick's authority, and the leading colonels insisted on other arrangements. These left Berwick nominally in command, but placed real power in the hands of Sarsfield and the militants. An army deputation was sent to France. Their representations ensured that a French general would replace Tyrconnell as commander-in-chief for the 1691 campaign. Louis would not send troops again, but he would supply arms and *matériel*. Louvois's strong insistence on recruits for the Mountcashel brigade from Ireland placed Tyrconnell in an awkward position with the army after his return in January 1691, but he managed to fend off this French demand until the end of the war.[12]

Meanwhile, the peace party were in contact with the Williamites through John Grady, a County Clare Catholic barrister, who travelled back and forth between the quarters of the two armies. Tyrconnell was aware of these contacts

---

James II, ii, p. 419; Berwick, *Memoirs*, i, p. 78; *F-I corr.*, iii, p. 214; *JN*, pp 119–21; Simms, 'Cork'; Ó Murchada, 'Cork'; Kerrigan, 'Charles Fort, Kinsale', pp 330–2; Churchill, *Marlborough*, i, pp 288–93. **12** *JN*, pp 110–11; *F-I corr.*, i, p. 121; ii, pp 96, 210, 230–2, 257; *AH*, 21, pp 214–15; Cooke, *Birr*, pp 81–4; O'Kelly, pp 83–95, 102–6; *James II*, ii, pp 420–5.

before his departure. However, it was only after the failure of the siege of Limerick that the Williamites showed interest in Grady's overtures, allowing serious negotiations to begin. There appears to have been very considerable Jacobite support for the negotiations. According to an Irish source, 'a great many began to hearken willingly to the proposal ... some out of solid avarice, preferring their private interest to the public ... and some really believing that there was a necessity for it'. However, although agreement was close, the army leaders were unconvinced of either Williamite good faith or the sufficiency of the terms on offer, and they remained intransigent. Matters came to a head in December 1690, when the Williamite army, supported by a naval squadron, launched a four-pronged attack on the Jacobite quarters 'in the midst of winter, when the earth was all covered with snow ... [and] no part of the river [Shannon] was fordable'. The successful Jacobite response was managed by Sarsfield, and the Williamites admitted that 'all we have got by it is the fatiguing of our army, the discouragement of our men and the encouragement of the enemy'. Sarsfield believed that the offensive was encouraged by 'some traitors amongst us', who were in a correspondence with the enemy 'to deliver to him our strongest posts'. He insisted on the dismissal of Lord Riverston, the acting Jacobite secretary of state, and his brother-in-law, Colonel Alexander MacDonnell, the governor of Galway. Judge Denis Daly was imprisoned, and others who seem to have come under suspicion were Colonels John Hamilton, Lord Galway and Richard Grace, the governor of Athlone. Some confirmation of Sarsfield's view came from the Williamite writer George Story, according to whom the winter offensive had been occasioned by correspondence with Daly and some others on the Irish side proposing the surrender of Galway. Although relatively little known, Sarsfield's containment of the Williamite winter offensive was a considerable military success, which consolidated the ascendancy of the Jacobite resistance party at least for the time being.[13]

The Irish infantry and dismounted dragoons had fought well at Limerick, behind the protection afforded by the city's defences and conscious that the survival of Jacobite Ireland depended on their resolution. The army had also contained the Williamite winter offensive. The Ballyneety raid demonstrated yet again the formidable calibre of the cavalry, but thereafter the mounted troops were under-used by the high command. Neither Tyrconnell in 1690 nor the marquis de Saint-Ruth, the army commander in 1691, deployed them in raids into the enemy's rear. Not only would this strategy have troubled the Williamites but, if visited by success, it might have arrested the deterioration

---

13 *F-I corr.*, ii, pp 96, 143, 230–2; *JN*, p. 111; O'Kelly, p. 90; Murtagh, '"Some traitors amongst us"', pp 144–7; Simms, 'Williamite peace tactics'.

in cavalry morale that surfaced in 1691. Instead, it was left to the rapparees, with some input of army personnel, to mount an effective partisan campaign against the Williamite quarters during the winter of 1690–1, and rapparee activity continued up to the end of the war.

Saint-Ruth takes command

The Jacobite army survived the winter of 1690–1, but only in conditions of great privation, with the garrisons coming close to starvation. Tyrconnell brought little in terms of money and supplies when he returned to Ireland in January 1691, and he remained unpopular with the army. His formal authority over it ceased in early May with the arrival at Limerick, amid scenes of jubilation, of a French fleet, bringing a new army commander, the marquis de Saint-Ruth, accompanied by three other French generals, some technical officers and a considerable supply of arms, ammunition, *matériel*, clothing and food. Saint-Ruth's presence raised Jacobite morale: not only was he a competent soldier, but he was empathetic towards the Irish, and energetic in preparing the army and improving the fortifications of key strongholds for the coming summer campaign. He was careful to keep a neutral stance between the different Jacobite factions and attempted to reconcile them, but he was probably not displeased by the consolidation of his authority when the army officers drove Tyrconnell from the camp. For his part, Tyrconnell felt that Saint-Ruth ignored his advice, or even acted contrary to it, but neither is there much evidence that the French general paid particular attention to the views of the Sarsfield faction.[14]

Ballymore and Athlone

For the 1691 campaign, the Williamite army mustered at Mullingar, and it was clear that Ginkel planned to open his campaign with an attack on Athlone. He first easily overcame the advanced Jacobite garrison at mid-way Ballymore. Saint-Ruth had ignored it, and over 800 soldiers were needlessly lost. Ginkel was then joined by his continental troops before advancing on Athlone with 18,000 men, and a siege train of thirty-six heavy guns and six mortars, 'such a one as had never before been seen in that kingdom'. By 20 June the Williamite army was in position outside the east town of Athlone. The Shannon divided Athlone, and the Williamites easily stormed the east town. It was only lightly defended in order to buy time for Saint-Ruth to bring up the main Jacobite army of about 21,000 men to support the defence

---

[14] *AH*, 21, pp 216–17, 219–21; O'Kelly, p. 117; *F-I corr.*, ii, pp 331–4, 354.

of the west town, where he arrived the next day. He placed the French lieutenant general, the marquis d'Usson, in charge of the town's defence. The Williamite siege artillery bombarded the west town, reducing it and the east side of the castle to rubble, as well as breaching Jacobite earthwork defences on the river bank. However, the river presented a formidable obstacle to any Williamite assault. It was traversed by a narrow stone bridge. A number of arches had been broken down by the Jacobites, who with great courage and determination overthrew repair works put in place by Ginkel's pioneers. Jacobite fire then thwarted an attempt to erect a pontoon bridge to the south of the town. Ginkel's final assault was across the old ford that had given Athlone its name, and it met with unexpected success. Only three regiments could form the Jacobite garrison at any one time. Saint-Ruth, with the idea of exposing his soldiers to fire, had insisted on their rotation. D'Usson was absent in the camp when the attack occurred, and it caught the defending regiments by surprise. They seem to have been inexperienced. Their musket fire failed to stop the Williamite grenadiers who led the van of the attack, and the defences were easily overrun. The Williamites quickly repaired the bridge, which opened the way for their troops to pour into the west town. The west-town fortifications had been left intact, contrary to Saint-Ruth's orders, preventing him from mounting a counterattack. The loss of Athlone was a severe blow to the Jacobite army. Stevens noted 'manifest tokens of fear on most men's faces'. A Jacobite officer recorded 'general consternation all over Ireland that a gate should be opened into Connacht which was the last refuge of the nation'. Another wrote: 'never was a town, which was so well held before, so basely lost'.[15]

The battle of Aughrim

Athlone had been carelessly lost, with the disastrous consequence of giving the Williamite army *entrée* into fortress Connacht. It was reported that 'none was more sensibly afflicted than brave Saint-Ruth', who was said to be 'in a sensible of grief … after such a concatenation of errors', for which he publicly blamed d'Usson. The army withdrew west. A council of war was held at Ballinasloe, at which the consensus view, advocated by Sarsfield and others, was reported to be to put the infantry into Limerick and Galway, while sending the cavalry and dragoons across the Shannon to raid into Munster and Leinster as far as Dublin. Saint-Ruth may have been open to this strategy.

15 Story, *Continuation*, pp 80, 87–91; *F-I* corr., ii, p. 375; *Inchiquin MSS*, p. 30; O'Kelly, p. 124; *Danish force*, pp 114–18; *Stevens*, pp 204–11; Murtagh, 'Ballymore', pp 242–6; Murtagh (D.), 'Siege of Athlone'; Murtagh, *Athlone history and settlement*, pp 150–62.

However, unless it forced Ginkel out of Connacht to protect his rear, it did not meet the problem of how the Jacobite army was to be sustained without full control of the province and its adjoining territories. So instead, when the Williamite army advanced west, Saint-Ruth, having found a good defensive position at Aughrim west of Ballinasloe, decided to offer battle, hoping thereby to redeem his reputation. Kilcommadan Hill, a long eminence just south of Aughrim village, was fronted by a small river and marsh that made it impassable to cavalry and presented a significant obstacle to infantry. Narrow causeways provided access on either flank, which were otherwise guarded by small rivers and an extensive bog to the north. The Jacobite army was drawn up on the eastern slopes of the hill, with the infantry in the centre and the cavalry and dragoons on the flanks. Initially it was deployed in two lines, but according to one source it became necessary to draw both lines into one to protect the flanks. Good use had been made of earthen field boundaries, which were converted into breastwork defences.[16]

Ginkel advanced from Ballinasloe on 12 July. Although impressed by the strength of Saint-Ruth's position, he resolved on an immediate attack. Like Saint-Ruth he adopted the conventional deployment of infantry in the centre with cavalry on the flanks. The sun and breeze were in the faces of his men when, at about 5.00 p.m., his left wing, comprising his continental troops and reinforced by field artillery, advanced towards Urraghry, the southernmost of the two passes leading into the Jacobite position. A sharp struggle developed as the Williamites engaged the Jacobite right, where Sarsfield commanded the cavalry. The Jacobites resisted with great determination. Before the battle, Saint-Ruth and the Catholic chaplains had done what they could to raise Irish morale, and there was a widespread realization that the army was making its last stand. As Saint-Ruth declared, 'all and the all of the nation lay at stake'. The Irish infantry made skilful use of their improvised breastworks for a system of defence in depth. An eyewitness wrote:

> Here we fired upon one another for a considerable time. The Irish behaved like men of another nation, defending their ditches stoutly, till our men put their pieces over at the other and then having lines of communication from one ditch to another, they would presently post themselves again and flank us. This occasioned great firing on both sides.

---

16 *JN*, p. 136; O'Kelly, pp 129–31; Story, *Continuation*, pp 121–37; *Danish force*, pp 119–24; *F-I corr.*, ii, p. 375; Account of Aughrim (Westminster Diocesan Archives, B6, 258). Modern accounts of the battle include Murtagh (D.), 'Aughrim'; Simms, *Jacobite Ireland*, pp 216–29; Hayes-McCoy, *Irish battles*, pp 238–72; Doherty, *Williamite war*, pp 167–83; Childs, *Williamite wars*, pp 329–39; McNally, *Aughrim*.

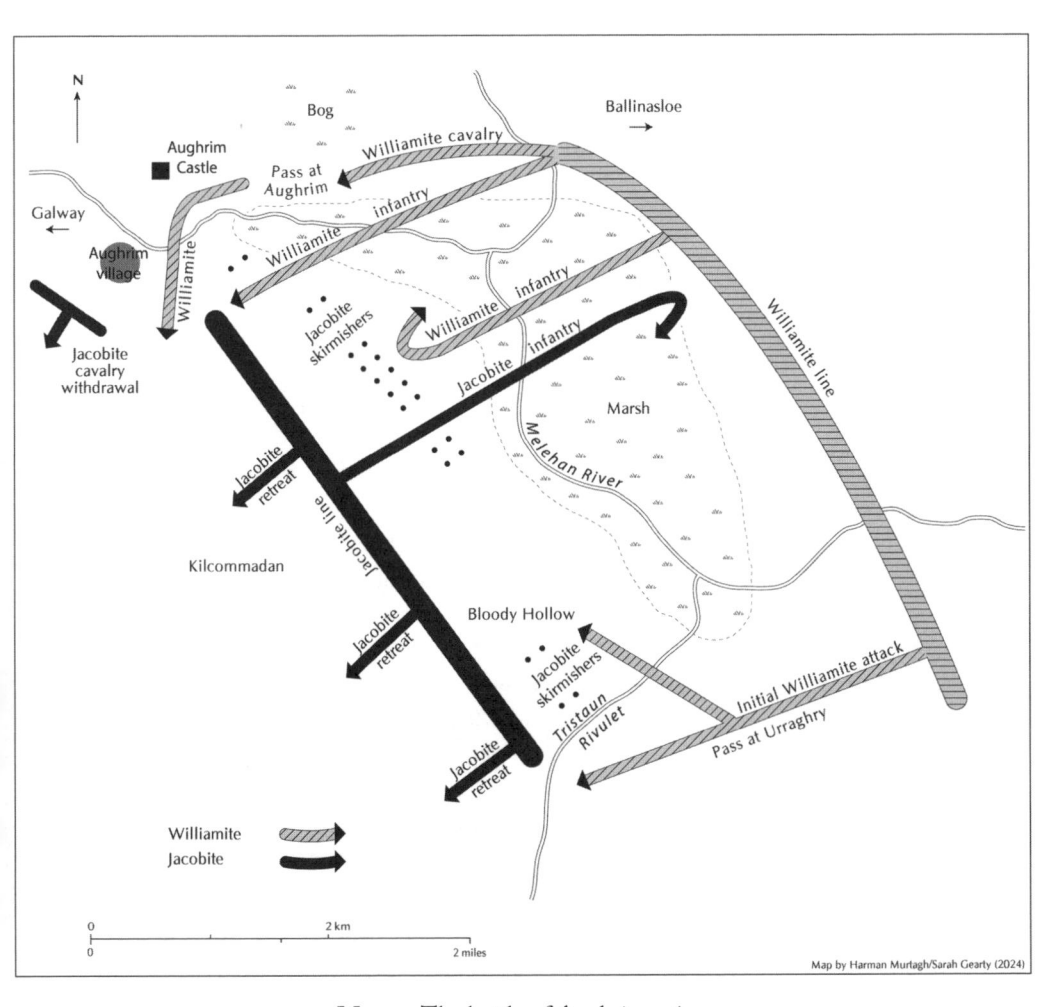

Map 3. The battle of Aughrim, 1691

Ginkel's Urraghry attack made slow progress, and after an hour and a half the fighting in the southern sector subsided.[17]

To strengthen his embattled right wing, Saint-Ruth switched troops across from his left, including a battalion taken out of the front line. This encouraged Ginkel to mount a major attack on the Irish centre with his British battalions. Ten regiments waded through the swamp up to their waists in mud and water, only to be routed by volleys of musket fire, discharged 'so near as to burn their clothes', followed by a determined Irish counterattack in which the Jacobite footguards and Gordon O'Neill's Ulstermen plied pike and musket butt until 'the blood ran into their shoes'. The Williamite troops were rallied, but it was clear that the attack had largely failed. Williamite observers were now pessimistic, whereas Saint-Ruth was jubilant, calling out that the day was won and that he would drive the enemy back to the gates of Dublin. However, two Williamite regiments managed to hold their ground on the extreme right of their attack, possibly taking advantage of a gap in the Jacobite line caused by the earlier transfer of troops to strengthen the Jacobite right at Urraghry. To support these infantry units, Williamite cavalry started to advance along the narrow causeway leading into Aughrim village on the Jacobite left. This was covered by Walter Burke's infantry battalion posted in Aughrim Castle, but to little effect, as allegedly their musket balls were of the wrong calibre. The exact sequence of events is unclear, but it seems that Saint-Ruth, noticing the activity on his left wing, was riding across the battlefield to take control of the situation when he was killed instantly by a chance Williamite cannon shot, 'a cursed ball that carried such a measure of woe'. It was surely the job of the Irish cavalry and dragoons on the left wing to respond to the developing Williamite attack. Instead, they offered no resistance and tamely rode off to the west. Perhaps Sheldon, who commanded on the left, was awaiting orders. One officer alleged that Saint-Ruth was keeping the left part of his horse as a *corps de reserve* to sustain the foot, of which he was a little dubious. However, the real explanation seems to be that news of Saint-Ruth's death brought the low morale and war weariness of the cavalry to a head. Ginkel had taken the opportunity after the fall of Athlone to publish a proclamation offering pardons and the retention of their estates to those who submitted, and this may have had an impact on the cavalry once Saint-Ruth's grip was no more.[18]

The decisive point in the battle had now arrived. Caught on their unprotected left flank by the Williamite cavalry, the Irish centre crumbled. In

---

17 Story, *Continuation*, p. 122; Account of Aughrim (Westminster Diocesan Archives, B6, 258); *Danish force*, p. 121; *JN*, p. 140. **18** *James II*, ii, pp 457–8; *JN*, pp 141–7; Account of Aughrim (Westminster Diocesan Archives, B6, 258); *Proclamations*, pp 253–5.

the centre, the Williamite infantry renewed their offensive across the swamp. To the south, the Irish right came under renewed pressure and began to give ground. In dismay and increasing disarray, the Jacobite army fell back across Kilcommadan Hill. There was no one to take control. The French general, the comte de Tessé, who was Saint-Ruth's second-in-command, was wounded while attempting to oppose the Williamite cavalry and left the battlefield without making provision for a successor. Sarsfield had remained, or been kept, in the background while Saint-Ruth was in command. With a force of cavalry, he and Galmoy now did what they could to cover the retreat, but they were unable to save the infantry from near massacre. The scene was vividly described by the Danish soldier, Andreas Claudianus:

> The Irish fled all over the fields ... not knowing what to do or where to turn, since from all sides the inescapable violence meets them ... throwing away their arms and finding no place to make a stand within a distance of seven miles. The women, children [and] waggoners filled every road with lamentation and weeping. Worse was the sight of the battle when many men and horses pierced by wounds could have neither flight nor rest. Sometimes trying to rise they fell suddenly, weighed down by the mass of their bodies. Some with mutilated limbs and weighed down by pain asked for the sword as a remedy, but the conqueror would not even fulfil with the sword or the musket the desire of him who implored him. Others spewed forth their breath mixed with blood and threats, grasping their bloodstained arms in an icy embrace, as if in readiness for some future battle ... From the bodies of all blood ... flowed over the ground and so inundated the fields that you could hardly take a step without slipping ... O horrible sight!

Only dusk, and the descent of a misty rain brought the slaughter to an end and allowed the survivors to escape towards Galway and Limerick. Estimates of the Irish casualties varied from the *Jacobite narrative*'s 2,000 killed and 600 wounded to the 7,000 killed, according to some Williamite sources. The truth probably lies somewhere in between. King James's memoirs put the Irish loss at 'near four thousand men'. Williamite casualties were 1,744 killed and wounded, perhaps a pointer towards the accuracy of the higher estimates of Jacobite casualties. The Williamites took 450 prisoners. Apart from Saint-Ruth, the Jacobite losses, killed or captured, included both infantry major generals, William Dorrington and John Hamilton, two brigadiers and at least sixteen infantry colonels. Ninety-eight junior officers were said to have been killed, and 500 captains and subalterns made prisoner. If these figures are correct, they represented a quarter of the officer corps. All the Jacobite artillery and baggage was captured, together with thirty-two infantry colours and fourteen cavalry standards. It was the bloodiest battle in Irish history and the decisive engagement of the war. Ginkel had won an overwhelming victory. The defeat was all the more bitter for the Jacobites because success had been within their grasp, as the Williamite general Würtemburg conceded: 'their [Jacobite] infantry did wonders; if their cavalry had done the same, we should have been utterly defeated'.[19]

The end of the Irish war

It was clear that an ultimate Williamite victory in the war was now all but inevitable. Galway capitulated a week later. Jacobite defeatism and defections grew: an estimated 1,500 of the Galway garrison and many officers deserted *en route* to Limerick. Balldearg O'Donnell defected to the Williamites. Tyrconnell, now in bellicose mode, resumed control of the army and required officers to take an oath not to submit individually to the Williamites. Not all consented. Two brigadiers, Henry Luttrell and Robert Clifford, were arrested, the former when found to be in correspondence with the enemy, and the latter for failure to defend the Shannon crossing north of Limerick. The French believed that Clifford was part of a wider group anxious for terms. Colonel Edward Wilson was also arrested. By August, there was already talk of the Irish army capitulating and going to France. Sligo, which had put up a brave resistance in the north-west, surrendered in September. Once again, the Jacobite forces concentrated on Limerick, their last major stronghold, with the infantry deployed in the city and the cavalry camped nearby in County Clare. Measures were taken to rebuild the army, but the French generals were pessimistic. The veterans lost at Aughrim could not be quickly replaced, or morale easily revived. D'Usson, now the senior French general, was an uninspiring successor to Saint-Ruth, and chiefly motivated to secure as many Irish soldiers as he could for France. When Tyrconnell suddenly died, Sarsfield re-emerged as the key Jacobite leader.[20]

Jacobite hopes were pinned on an expected convoy of arms, food and *matériel* from France. The Williamite army recrossed the Shannon at Banagher, investing Limerick on the south and east at the end of August. There was naval support from an English squadron off the west coast.

---

19 Jordan, 'Aughrim', pp 6–7; Story, *Continuation*, pp 134–7; *JN*, pp 147–8; *Danish force*, pp 123–4.   **20** Story, *Continuation*, pp 164–73, 182–3, 235; *F-I corr.*, ii, pp 386, 392–4, 401–2, 502–3, 506, 522; *JN*, pp 149–50, 152, 155; O'Kelly, p. 147.

Compared to that of the previous year, the 1691 Williamite siege of Limerick was conducted on a low key. There was an artillery bombardment, but Ginkel made no attempt to storm the city by a full-scale assault. Instead, he concentrated on bringing the Irish to negotiate, threatening 'blood and destruction' if they 'continued obstinate'. At first, Jacobite resistance seemed firm, but the failure of the promised French supply fleet to arrive, and anxiety about the dwindling food supply sapped their resolve. It seemed prudent to make terms before it was too late. The cavalry was cut off from Limerick, when the Williamites extended the city's investment to the west of the city on 22 September. This was the occasion of sharp fighting in the vicinity of Thomond Bridge. The next day the Jacobites asked for terms, and the subsequent ceasefire brought hostilities to an end.[21]

Figure 4. An infantry musketeer

21 Story, *Continuation*, pp 179, 188–233; *Danish force*, pp 130–5; *F-I corr.*, i, p. 143; ii, pp 400, 513–14; *James II*, ii, pp 462–5.

CHAPTER 4

Infantry

Infantry numbers and units

IN THE LATTER HALF of the seventeenth century, as indeed throughout most of military history, infantry soldiers were the backbone of every army, constituting two-thirds of the French, Spanish and imperial forces of the period, a proportion that had risen to almost 84 per cent in France by 1696. About three-quarters of the restoration English army were infantry, a substantial increase on the mid-century civil wars, when the cavalry component of both royalist and parliamentary forces was particularly strong. In Ireland, the peacetime infantry establishment of 6,719 in 1686 amounted to 80 per cent of the army's total strength. The new standing armies were designed to expand in wartime. In May 1689 Melfort claimed to Louvois that the enlarged Irish army was 50,000 strong, a number repeated by d'Avaux, but probably no more than a paper figure at best. More credible figures for the infantry in the enlarged wartime Irish army were returns of 29,248 in 1689, 23,000 towards the end of 1690 and 25,000 in 1691, numbers that represented four to five times peacetime strength. In each case the infantry figure amounted to 80 per cent or more of the total force, possibly implying that this was its predetermined proportion, although a French estimate at the end of 1689 put the infantry component as high as 90 per cent. Foot soldiers were much cheaper and easier to equip and maintain than mounted men. Their combat role was enhanced by the development of firearms and other weaponry. Improvements to deployment and drill maximized battlefield order and discipline, as well as musketry effectiveness. In siege warfare, which was central to late-seventeenth-century campaigns, foot soldiers were pre-eminent both in attack and defence.[1]

Infantry fought as battalions, but the administrative unit throughout Europe was the regiment comprising one, two or even three battalions. In Britain and Ireland, the regiment generally equated with a single battalion, although there were exceptions to this. In the Irish army of 1689, after the

---

[1] Chandler, *Art of war*, p. 30; Lynn, *Giant of the grand siècle*, p. 47; *Ormonde MSS*, i, p. 447; *AH*, 21, p. 104; d'Avaux, pp 29, 451–4; *F-I corr.*, i, p. 218; ii, pp 223, 336–7; iii, pp 71–2, 181, 183, 215–17.

chaos of the initial expansion was sorted out and the army reorganized, four of the forty-five regiments still retained a second battalion. For the campaign of 1690 the second battalions of Gordon O'Neill's and Henry Dillon's went out of existence, the former apparently furnishing the personnel for Felix O'Neill's new regiment and the latter for the new regiments of Arthur Dillon and Walter Burke. Boisseleau's lost its second battalion, the ranks having thinned, it was alleged, because of the colonel's failure to pay the men. Thus in 1690–1 virtually all regiments were single-battalion units, the sole exception being the footguards, which retained two battalions and indeed for a time in 1690–1 apparently expanded to three. In keeping with the European norm, almost all the regiments in the Irish army were named after their colonels. The only exceptions in the infantry were the footguards, nominally the king's personal bodyguard, and two regiments, Clancarty's and Lacy's, that were successively designated as the Prince of Wales's foot. In all the other units, if the colonel changed, then so too did the regimental title, thereby complicating the task today of establishing regimental lineages. Writing from Limerick in November 1691, a Jacobite commentator recognized that authority lay with the colonels, who 'give no obedience to orders, but to such as themselves have a mind to execute, and such as are under colonels value no commands, but such as come from their colonels'.[2]

Infantry regiments

The seven infantry regiments of the peacetime army in 1688 were the footguards, and those of the earl of Clancarty, Lord Forbes, Anthony Hamilton, Justin MacCarthy, Viscount Mountjoy and Sir Thomas Newcomen. Of these, Forbes's and Hamilton's regiments, together with a battalion of the footguards, were lost in England in the revolution. To replace them, in late 1688 a new battalion was added to the footguards, and four new infantry regiments were raised by Catholic peers: the earls of Antrim, Tyrone and Clanricard, and Viscount Clare. Soon afterwards, the army was greatly enlarged by the addition of thirty-two new regiments, raised by Tyrconnell in the wake of the English revolution, together with four further regiments raised over the summer. (This figure discounts a number of short-lived regiments culled in April 1689.) The net result was that the Irish infantry establishment in 1689 amounted to forty-five regiments.

---

2 *F-I corr.*, ii, p. 239; 'Journal 1/6 to 18/7 1689' (Carte MS 181), f. 7; *Finch MSS*, ii, p. 476.

TABLE 2 *The infantry establishment, 1689***

footguards	Viscount Clare	Roger MacElligott
earl of Antrim	Sir Michael Creagh	Brian MacMahon
Dudley Bagenal	Henry Dillon	Charles Moore
John Barrett	Sir Maurice Eustace	Viscount Mountcashel
Baron Bellew	Iriel Farrell	William Nugent
marquis de Boisseleau	Sir John FitzGerald	Charles O'Brien
Baron Bophin	Viscount Galway	Daniel O'Donovan
Dominic Browne	Viscount Gormanston	Cormac O'Neill
Nicholas Browne	John Grace	Gordon O'Neill
Edward Butler	John Hamilton	Edmund O'Reilly
Richard Butler	Viscount Iveagh	Heward Oxburgh
Walter Butler	Viscount Kenmare	Robert Ramsay
Charles Cavenagh	Viscount Kilmallock	Baron Slane
earl of Clancarty	Baron Louth	duke of Tyrconnell
earl of Clanricard	Charles MacCarthy More	earl of Tyrone

Note
* The new regiments are listed under the names of their original colonels; the surviving old regiments are listed under the names of their colonels in 1689.

The new colonels appointed by James to replace the Protestant colonels, Mountjoy and Newcomen, were John Hamilton, a younger brother of Anthony and Richard and a brother-in-law of Lady Tyrconnell, and Robert Ramsay, a Scottish Catholic officer who had followed James to Ireland. After Ramsay was killed at the siege of Derry, command of his regiment went to Henry FitzJames, an illegitimate son of the king, whose title of grand prior of the Knights of Saint John of Jerusalem in England provided the name of his regiment in 1689–90. The sole French colonel was Alexandre Rainier, marquis de Boisseleau, an officer of the *gardes françaises*, whom James had made governor of Cork. His colonelcy of a new regiment may have been intended to compensate him for his disappointment with his initial rank of brigadier. Boisseleau's 1,600-strong two-battalion regiment was initially formed largely from 'foreigners', probably some of the 3,000 Jacobites that were landed at Bantry in May 1689. Several changes took place during the year. The young earl of Westmeath was appointed to command the regiment raised in the name of Tyrconnell, of which Lieutenant Colonel Francis Toole had been *de facto* commander. The experienced Roger O'Gara replaced Iriel Farrel. Thomas Butler replaced his elderly father, Walter Butler. Art MacMahon, a continental veteran, replaced Brian MacMahon. The regiment of Daniel MacCarthy Reagh, which had been scheduled for disbandment, was instead amalgamated with that of Charles MacCarthy More. Each was ordered to provide six and a half companies to form a single battalion unit, known for a time as the regiment of the 'two MacCarthys'. The other disbanded regiments (not included in the establishment list above) were those of Viscount Clanmalier, Sir Henry Lynch, Henry MacTool O'Neill and MacThomas O'Reilly.[3]

The number of regiments increased to forty-nine in 1690 and, in addition, several changes of name occurred. Five regiments were sent to France. Of these, two, Robert Fielding's and Arthur Dillon's, were new units, but three, Mountcashel's, Richard Butler's and Lord Clare's, now commanded by his son, Daniel O'Brien, were existing regiments, which were transferred from the Irish to the French army. They were more than compensated for by the addition of seven new regiments to the 1690 establishment. These were those of Viscount Kingsland, Baron Enniskillen, Felix O'Neill, Walter Burke, Hugh MacMahon, Denis MacGillycuddy and Cúconnacht Maguire. Owen MacCarthy took over as colonel from Charles MacCarthy More. Later in the year, on the death of John Grace, his son, Robert, succeeded him as colonel. Six regiments were lost to the army in the surrender of Cork: those of Clancarty, Tyrone, Owen MacCarthy, MacElligott, Cavenagh and Barrett. A further eleven regiments – 'all mere Irish' – appear to have been raised in late 1689 or early 1690, but were never taken into pay and ordered to be disbanded. These included the regiments of John Browne of Westport, Baron Castleconnel, James Butler, James Talbot, Edmund Nugent and Charles O'Kelly, later the author of *Macariae excidium*, an important account of the war. Browne's was merged into Fielding's prior to the latter's departure for France. Four other regiments of this group – Charles Geoghegan's, Roger O'Connor's, Roger O'Cahan's and Brian MacDermott's – survived as units in Balldearg O'Donnell's auxiliary force. The fate of Manus O'Donnell's, the remaining regiment of the group scheduled for disbandment, is less clear: although his regiment was reported to have been disbanded apparently in early 1690, he is the likely colonel of the O'Donnell regiment that is listed on the establishment in March 1691, suggesting that his unit may have maintained some kind of existence or at least been capable of revival for the final campaign.[4]

---

3 *Ormonde MSS*, n.s., viii, p. 354; Officer list (Bodl., Carte MS 181), ff 15–56; 'Journal 1/6 to 18/7 1689' (ibid.), ff 10, 20, 71; *JN*, pp 56, 201–33; *d'Avaux*, pp 42, 95, 119, 160; Tyrconnell letters, no. 12; *AH*, 21, p. 142; *F-I corr.*, ii, p. 337; 'Clann Carthaigh', i, pp 367–8. 4 King, appendix, p. 70; *Memoirs of the family of Grace*, pp 42–3; *F-I corr.*, i, pp 363–70; ii, p. 336; iii, pp 182, 216; Story, p. 98; *Stevens*, pp 141–2; Ó Murchada, 'Cork', pp 3, 12; Kinsella, *Catholic survival*, p. 44.

Many more changes occurred in 1691, and some of the detail is confusing, as indeed *Commissaire* Fumeron found even at the time. The number of regiments in March that year stood at forty-seven (excluding Clancarty's, which is listed, although it had been captured at Cork). The following appears to have been the outcome of the changes. Henry Oxburgh succeeded his father. Gormanston's regiment went to Richard Eustace, its veteran lieutenant colonel. Kilmallock's likewise went to its lieutenant colonel, John Moone Power. William Tuite took command of Boisseleau's. Francis Toole resumed command of Westmeath's. Charles O'Brien was succeeded by William Saxby, a veteran who had been the regiment's major. Mark Talbot, a natural son of Tyrconnell and a veteran of the French army who was already a brigadier, became colonel of the former grand prior regiment. Sir Edward Scott, the defender of Kinsale, replaced James Purcell, who had apparently raised a new regiment before being killed at Limerick. Sir Nicholas Browne was probably succeeded by Nicholas FitzGerald and Dudley Bagenal by James Power. The Prince of Wales's regiment, commanded by Colonel James Lacy, and the regiments of Edward FitzGerald, Maurice Connell and (Manus?) O'Donnell seem to have been new, although O'Donnell's, as explained above, was possibly a revived unit. In March or later, seven of Balldearg O'Donnell's regiments were absorbed into the army for garrison duty: the regiments of Brian O'Neill, Roger O'Cahan, Conor O'Rourke, Brian MacDermott and Conor O'Connor were in Limerick, while Brian MacArt O'Neill's and (Daniel?) O'Doherty's were in Galway. In the catastrophic Aughrim defeat fifteen infantry regiments lost their commanders, who were either killed or captured: Viscounts Galway and Kenmare; Barons Bellew, Bophin and Slane; John Hamilton, Gordon O'Neill, Felix O'Neill, Charles Moore, Cúconnacht Maguire, Walter Burke, Robert Grace, Thomas Butler, Maurice Connell and William Tuite. This brought further changes to a confused situation.[5]

Some of the lost colonels were replaced, and the names of their regiments duly changed: thus, John Hamilton was succeeded by his lieutenant colonel James Nugent. Alexander Maguire likewise replaced his colonel, Cúconnacht Maguire. Edward Wilson seems to have replaced Maurice Connell and Dermot or Daniel O'Mahony succeeded William Tuite. William Burke succeeded Lord Bophin. James Power's regiment appears to have merged with Lord Galway's, which henceforth was called Power Galway. Some regiments, such as those of Baron Bellew, Felix O'Neill and Walter Burke, continued to be listed under the names of their lost colonels. Other new names to appear

---

[5] *F-I corr.*, ii, pp 220–1, 335–6, 391; iii, pp 213–16; *Stevens*, p. 199; Story, *Continuation*, pp 137–8; *KJIL*, ii, p. 784.

were John Wauchope, Edward Hussey, – Murphy, B. FitzGerald, Michael Burke and William Burke. Several of the latter group probably replaced lost colonels, but of which regiments is unclear, and some indeed may have commanded new-raised units, formed in response to Tyrconnell's order for a general mobilization. On 22 September James Skelton, another new colonel, was captured, mortally wounded, during the attack on Thomond Bridge, but a regiment was still listed under his name on 8 October. Charles MacCarthy More reappears as a regimental commander, but whether of an existing regiment or a new one is unclear; certainly, it was not his original regiment, which had been captured at Cork, when commanded by his successor, Owen MacCarthy. There is also mention of a shadowy second MacCarthy regiment in 1691. Both formed part of the Limerick garrison in August.[6]

There were also a number of independent companies. Jean Dully's fusilier company was formed in 1689 to escort the artillery. Darby Keefe had a dragoon troop in 1689, and Francis Toole a fusilier company in 1690 to support their role as provosts marshal. Colonel Garrett Moore's company was formed for the defence of Banagher and later served with Balldearg O'Donnell's force, before joining the Limerick garrison in 1691. Other garrison companies in 1689 were the Limerick mayor's and Michael Burke's, which was raised for the defence of Dungannon. Arthur French's was raised for the defence of Galway, where he was mayor. Other short-lived companies on the army list were those of Miles Costello, Charles White and James Lacy. In addition to Moore's, three other independent companies, hitherto listed as army units, served with Balldearg O'Donnell's force in 1691: those of Patrick Burke, Michael Cormack and Henry O'Neill.[7]

Regimental organization and personnel

As well as being the usual regimental unit, the battalion was the standard infantry combat formation. On active service it was common for badly below-strength regiments to be temporarily united to form a single battalion. In the campaign against Schomberg, for example, the grand prior's and Thomas Butler's were joined. At the first siege of Limerick, when most regiments were depleted by desertion after the Boyne, a prisoner told the Williamites that the Irish had formed thirty-nine regiments into thirteen battalions. John Stevens gives examples: 'the grand prior [was] joined by Slane's and Boisseleau's; Butler [was] joined by Sir Michael Creagh, Westmeath and Grace; the two

---

6 *F-I corr.*, ii, pp 388, 391, 404–7; *JN*, p. 152; Clarke corr., no. 1132; Story, *Continuation*, p. 225.
7 *D'Avaux*, p. 570; TCD MS 670, f. 1; Officer list (Bodl., Carte MS 181), ff 11, 57; 'Journal 1/6 to 18/7 1689' (ibid.), f. 11; *F-I corr.*, ii, pp 222, 338.

MacMahons and Iveagh composed the third battalion; Gordon and Felix O'Neill the fourth'. In the line of battle two, three or four battalions/regiments were generally grouped as a brigade. As yet brigades were largely temporary formations, although the permanent rank of brigadier general had emerged for colonels qualified for such a command. The field officers in overall command of a regiment were the colonel, lieutenant colonel and major. They bore general responsibility for the unit's discipline, good order and state of readiness. The colonel was the regiment's commander. Appointments to this rank were heavily dependent on the assets and status of the incumbent. In 1672, for example, the purchase of Sir Edward Scott's colonelcy cost the duke of Buckingham £1,500.[8]

Peers and baronets constituted 40 per cent of the colonels in 1689, and almost all the remainder were men of substance and prestige, whose wealth and seigneurial influence were central to raising the regiment and the subsequent maintenance of its strength, welfare and cohesion. However, colonels were not necessarily possessed of military knowledge or skill. Two-thirds of the original colonels had no military experience outside the pre-war Irish army, and a number were entirely new to military life. Such unseasoned commanders generally depended on the advice of a professional soldier, who held the rank of lieutenant colonel or major in the regiment. Among several examples of the latter were John Skelton in Clancarty's, John Power in Creagh's, John Binns in FitzGerald's and Oliver O'Gara in Farrell's. As the war went on, there was a tendency for more experienced officers to be promoted to colonelcies; among them O'Gara, Richard Eustace, James Lacy, Sir Edward Scott, Mark Talbot and Francis Carroll. Where the colonel was a professional soldier like Mountcashel, he sometimes held a higher appointment that necessitated his frequent or permanent absence from his regiment, which the lieutenant colonel would then command. A similar situation prevailed where the titular colonel was simply absent, apparently a not-infrequent occurrence. The lieutenant colonel would in any case command the second battalion of a two-battalion regiment. The major was usually responsible for training, musters, the day-to-day management of the regiment and its finances. Thus, following the panic in the aftermath of the fall of Athlone, every major reviewed his regiment. In an impending combat situation, the major posted the men, drew up the regiment and attended on the major generals, when they marked out the ground for battle formation. It

---

8 *CTB, 1687–8*, part 3, p. 1745; Story, pp 97–8; Tyrconnell letters, no. 8; Officer list (Bodl., Carte MS 181), f. 15; *F-I corr.*, i, pp 237–40; iii, pp 49, 71–2, 215; 'Gafney', p. 170; *Stevens*, pp 86, 186–7; *Danish force*, p. 71; *d'Avaux*, pp 569–70; *IALKC*, pp xx–xxi.

is clear from Captain George Gafney's memorandum book that his monies for his company came from his major. Other members of the regimental staff were the adjutant, quartermaster, chaplain (sometimes two) and surgeon. The adjutant's role was to assist the major (as his French title *aide-major* implies) with the regiment's administration. The quartermaster was responsible for billeting, an important and potentially fraught responsibility in the absence of barracks, and the selection of campsites. He may also have acted as the regimental provost with responsibility for confining and maintaining prisoners. All four ranked as officers, although their pay rates indicate a fairly low position in the army's hierarchy. The adjutant received the pay of a lieutenant (probably supplementing his existing pay, if he also held a subaltern's appointment in the regiment, as many did). The quartermaster and the surgeon had two-thirds of a lieutenant's pay and the chaplain half it.[9]

In line with contemporary French and English practice, the standard battalion comprised thirteen companies. Musketeers and pikemen formed twelve and grenadiers one. The latter were specially armed assault troops, drawn from the tallest and strongest men in the regiment. The company was an administrative sub-unit of the regiment, but it had little relevance or identity on the battlefield, where regiments formed up as battalions, with only the grenadiers standing apart. The other-ranks establishment of a company at the start of hostilities in 1689 was two sergeants, three corporals, a drummer and sixty-two private soldiers. The twenty-two footguards companies were larger, each with three sergeants, a drummer and ninety other ranks. However, these numbers were difficult to sustain in wartime. Referring to 1689, John Stevens observed:

> I am eyewitness that regiments that mustered 700 and upwards at home came not into the field or even to Dublin 400 strong ... What was worst of all, the people, greedy of novelties and ignorant of the dangers and hardships attending the military life, flocked to be soldiers ... but when they perceived how dear they were to buy their bread and liberty, rather than expose their lives or undergo the labours and wants a soldier is often exposed to, they deserted in vast numbers, returning to their former security.

Thus, the twelve battalions stationed around Dublin in August 1689 averaged only 360 men each. In September the total infantry strength was returned at

---

9 Officer list (Bodl., Carte MS 181), ff 17, 51, 52; *Stevens*, p. 212; Lynn, *Giant of the grand siècle*, pp 225–6; *d'Avaux*, pp 124–5; 'Gafney', pp 166–7.

16,273, an average of twenty-seven men per company. However, the October muster, which omitted three regiments, put the strength of the forty-seven battalions included at 28,543, an average of just over 600 each, although there was considerable variation between regiments. Nevertheless, this was a remarkable recovery from September, if either figure is accurate. For the Boyne campaign of 1690, the first-line regiments, such as the footguards, Bellew's, Gordon O'Neill's, Louth's and the grand prior's, were at full strength. Others, such as Tyrone's, MacElligott's, Westmeath's and Antrim's, had contracted to 50-man companies, the French standard at the time, reducing them to 650-strong battalions, which was recognized as the standard strength thereafter, although not necessarily consistently achieved by individual units. In March 1691 for example, the infantry numbered 25,000, which was a sixth below 50-man company establishment strength. The old problem of 'great abuses in the musters' was referred to by General Richard Hamilton in 1689.[10]

Each company was commanded by a captain, supported by two other commissioned officers: a lieutenant and an ensign. Administration of his company was central to a captain's role. He was responsible for the distribution of uniforms, pay, weapons and powder to his men. To prepare his men for combat, his duty was to 'drill his soldiers very accurately, showing them all the postures of the pike and musket, then how to march, counter-march ... to advance forwards and to retreat backwards at the sound of the drum'. He was expected to be familiar with his men and 'to stir up their valours to undergo pain and peril'. He was to lead them into battle, and to bring up the rear when they left the field. In combat, as the basic unit was the battalion, his duty was to obey orders and eschew any exercise of tactical discretion. The colonel and lieutenant colonel were also company commanders (drawing the appropriate additional pay), although the major was not. The lieutenant was the second-ranking company officer, the captain's deputy and assistant in all respects. Command of the colonel's company was frequently delegated to his lieutenant, sometimes styled captain lieutenant. The third and junior commissioned officer was the ensign. Grenadier companies had two lieutenants and no ensign. In the autumn of 1689, the footguards had two lieutenants per company, probably because their companies were larger than those of other regiments.[11]

Prior to regimentation, each company in the army would have had its own colour, a square-shaped flag (2.1 metres to 2.25 metres in France), borne by

---

10 *D'Avaux*, pp 124–5, 451–4; Officer list (Bodl., Carte MS 181), passim; *JN*, pp 201–33; *F-I corr.*, iii, pp 59–61, 215–16; *Stevens*, pp 62–3, 86, 113, 215–16; Westport papers (MS 40,899/4 [6–8]).   11 Chandler, *Art of war*, pp 94–5; TCD MS 670, passim; *Animadversions of warre*, pp 201–3; BL, Add. MS 9763, f. 44.

the ensign. At the formation of the Irish footguards in 1662, each of the twelve companies had a colour, all apparently a yellow field with a crimson cross and an identifying badge. However, by the time of the war in Ireland, although the rank of ensign was retained for a company's junior commissioned officer, battalions were limited to three actual colours, as in France. This, for example, was the case in the grand priors' regiment, which comprised a single battalion in 1690. On the march the ensign carried the colour, half-furled up, on his shoulder. When closing with the enemy, he unfurled the colour and let it fly, holding it aloft with an extended arm, or resting the staff against his waste if he grew tired or the wind was strong. The colours indicated the location of the battalion's commander and served as a rallying point for the unit's personnel. During the disorderly retreat from the Boyne, for example, the colours of each regiment were fixed on high ground for stragglers to be more easily reunited with their regiments. Preserving its colours was regarded as a matter of honour for a unit. In the closing stages of the Boyne battle, French officers removed the colours of their regiments from their staffs and put them into their pockets to prevent them falling into Williamite hands.[12]

The colours of six Irish infantry regiments were described by Stevens. In his own unit, the grand prior's, the colonel's colour was white, as was the general practice in France. The other two colours depicted a flaming city, with the motto *The fruits of rebellion*. The footguards' colours were no longer the post-restoration design, but depicted the royal arms: St George's cross with the four quadrants filled respectively by the passant guardant lions of England; the rampant lion of Scotland; the Irish harp; and the *fleur-de-lis* of France to which the English monarchy still laid claim. The earl of Antrim's comprised a red cross on a green field, in each quarter of which was a hand proper coming out of the clouds, holding a gold cross of Jerusalem (a cross-crosslet), and in the centre an Irish harp with a crown imperial, and the motto associated with the Emperor Constantine *In hoc signo vinces* (In this sign [of the cross] thou shalt conquer). The colours of Lord Bellew's regiment were made up of a diagonal field of black and tawny stripes. On the top next the spear was a crown imperial, encircled by the Bellew family motto *Tout d'en haut* (All from above [i.e., God]), and in the centre the Irish harp and crown imperial. The colonel's colour was distinguished by a small, red cross *pattée* (narrow arms at the centre, flared in a curve or straight-line shape, to be broader at the perimeter). Gordon O'Neill's colours were white, with a bloody hand in the centre, surrounded by the motto *Pro rege at patria pugno* (I fight for king and

12 Lawson, *Uniforms*, p. 128; Chartrand, *Louis XIV's army*, p. 39; *Stevens*, pp 130, 216; Hayes-McCoy, *Irish flags*, pp 63–5; *F-I corr.*, i, pp 450, 453.

country), with again the colonel's colour distinguished by a red cross *pattée*. The colours in Lord Louth's regiment were filamot (meaning the colour of dead leaf or *feuille morte*), the colonel's plain and the others with a blue cross, a crown imperial in the centre and the motto *Festina lente* (Hasten slowly). Two colours captured from the Irish at Derry are said to have been yellow, with the phoenix symbol and the motto *Dum spiro spero* (While I breathe, I hope). Hayes-McCoy suggests they may have belonged to the Eustace regiment or to one of the Butler units. Kilmallock's regiment appears to have carried the colonel's coat of arms on its colours. Thirty-one Irish infantry colours captured at Aughrim were afterwards displayed in St James's Park, London. Some bore the motto *Un Dieu, un roi, une foi* (One God, one king, one faith).[13]

An officer's authority came from a written commission from the king. That appointing Cornelius MacGillycuddy to a captaincy in Lord Slane's regiment is an example:

> To our trusty and well-beloved Cornelius MacGillycuddy, captain, greeting. We, reposing special trust and confidence as well in the care and diligence, and circumspection, as in the loyalty, courage and readiness, of you to'ds His Majesty's good and faithful service – have nominated, constituted and appointed – and we do by virtue of the power and authority unto us given by His Majesty under the great seal of England, hereby nominate, constitute and appoint you the said Cornelius MacGillycuddy, captain of Lord Slane's regiment, which company you are to take into your charge and care as captain thereof, and duly exercise both officers and soldiers in arms; and as they are hereby commanded to obey you as their captain, so you are likewise to observe and follow such orders and directions as you shall, from time to time, receive from us or other superior officer or officers according to the discipline of war in pursuance of the trust reposed in you. And for so doing this shall be your sufficient warrant and commission. Given under our hand and seal of arms at His Majesty's Castle of Dublin, the [ ] day of December in the fourth year of His Majesty's reign.
> Entered in the muster-master general's office 24 Dec. 1688, Abraham Yarner. Tyrconnell.

Somewhat reduced wording was used for the commission promoting George Aylmer to a lieutenant colonelcy in the footguards in 1690:

---

13 *Stevens*, pp 214–16; Hayes-McCoy, *Irish flags*, pp 60–3; Le Fleming MSS, p. 327.

James, by the grace of God, king of England, Scotland, France and Ireland, Defender of the Faith, to our trusty and well-beloved George Aylmer, captain of our Regiment of Guards, greeting. Our will and pleasure is that you take place and command upon occasion in our army, as younger lieutenant colonel therein, and we command all our officers and soldiers to acknowledge you as youngest lieutenant colonel and you to observe and follow such orders and directions as you shall from time to time receive from me or any of your superior officers, according to the rules and discipline of King James, and in pursuance of the trust we have hereby reposed in you. Given at our court in Dublin castle, the 4th day of April in the fifth year of our reign. By his majesty's command, R'd Nagle, Kt.

In Ireland, army commissions, although issued in the king's name, were normally in the gift of the viceroy, Clarendon being the exception. Tyrconnell retained the power to do so until superseded by General Saint-Ruth in 1691. In the army expansion after the revolution, Tyrconnell was reported to have given blank commissions to the new colonels, who in effect therefore appointed their own officers, drawing on relatives, and on those connections and neighbours possessing the means and influence to raise and support new troops. This was also the basis of much of the officer selection for the Mountcashel brigade, sent to France. The senior officers were drawn from the remaining leaders of a very traditional society in which descendants of dispossessed landed families – often commissioned as junior officers – also continued to enjoy influence and respect. In some ways a regiment resembled a business partnership managed by the colonel, in which the officers invested their service, resources and recruiting power in return for their (marketable) commissions and the accompanying status of military rank, prestige, pay and whatever other pickings were to be had. The new regiments possessed especially strong regional associations. The subalterns, it was said, were for the most part relatives of their colonels. In the earl of Antrim's regiment, for example, fully a quarter of the officers were Macdonnells like himself, and included the earl's illegitimate son, his two teenage grandsons and his brother-in-law. Most of his other officers bore familiar Ulster Gaelic names, such as O'Neill, O'Donnell, Magill, MacSweeney and O'Cahan. The company commanders of Sir Michael Creagh's 'Dublin' regiment were drawn largely from Catholic merchant, business and propertied families of the city and its environs.[14]

14 *McGillycuddy papers*, pp 163–4; original commission in possession of Sir Richard Aylmer of Dublin, who in 1986 kindly furnished the writer with a transcription; 'A journal of what has

In the confusion surrounding the expansion of the army in early 1689, existing officers frequently transferred to new regiments and some were recorded as holding commissions in more than one. Sir Thomas Crosbie, for example, was simultaneously returned as a captain in three different regiments in the summer. But thereafter officers do not appear to have held more than one appointment at a time, except of course for general officers who retained their colonelcies, where they had them, and the regimental field officers, who were also company or troop commanders. There was considerable movement within regiments, and some movement between them, with casualties, resignations and submissions to the enemy providing internal promotion and transfer opportunities. Family connections were also exploited. There appear to have been numerous promotions towards the end of the war, partly to fill gaps after the Aughrim losses, but possibly also to strengthen officers' future career prospects as hostilities drew to a close. About 40 per cent of the infantry colonels changed during the war, mostly due to casualties, a few on age grounds or, in the case of Kilmallock and Westmeath, because of their transfer to the cavalry. Bagenal and the grand prior went to France. Some were succeeded by family members; others by a veteran soldier or their lieutenant colonel. In general, as time went on, the high command showed a preference for replacing inexperienced colonels with veteran officers. Age was not as decisive a factor as it is in a modern army. There were youthful colonels, such as Berwick, Westmeath, Clancarty and the grand prior, and many middle-aged or even elderly subalterns.[15]

Stevens had a low opinion of the competence or application of his fellow officers. He complained:

> [they] had seen and knew no more than their men ... The commanders ... not only wanted valour to lead on, or conduct to post their men to advantage, but through ignorance have run themselves into dangers and then cowardly and basely been the first that betook themselves to a shameful flight.

A similarly jaundiced view was taken by the French. They had little confidence in the quality or ability of the Irish officers, and their correspondence, especially in 1689, is loud in its criticism. They accused the Irish officers of neglecting their duties. The colonels and captains, they said, were ignorant and

---

passed since his majesty's arrival' (Carte MS 181), f. 29; *James II*, ii, p. 452; McDonnell, *Wild geese*, pp 121–2; Officer list (Bodl., Carte MS 181), ff 5, 21; Scouller, *Armies of Queen Anne*, p. 127; *F-I corr.*, i, p. 360. **15** *F-I corr.*, ii, p. 544.

incapable, and the subalterns particularly bad. Outside the campaigning season, which was the time continental armies concentrated on training and drill, instead of recruiting and disciplining the army, the Irish officers went home, or else spent their time in idleness and in 'the fooleries of gaming, drinking and whoring'. Dublin, according to the censorious Stevens, became 'a sink of corruption and living emblem of sodom'. It rankled the elitist French that many of the captains seemed of inferior birth – tailors, butchers and shoemakers, according to d'Avaux – whose low social status would have barred them from commissioning in France. They maintained poor discipline, and their supervision of weapon-care was especially remiss. Boisseleau complained of the pilfering, ignorance and sloth of the officers. He was critical too of their poor performance at the Boyne, as were other French, as well as King James and Stevens. In fact, many of the faults must have stemmed from inexperience. But the Irish were said to have been reluctant to take guidance from French and English officers, who were generally accepted into the regiments only into positions of shared command or with supernumerary *reformé*-officer status, the fate also of many disbanded Irish officers. In Stevens's regiment, at one time more than half the complement of officers were *reformés*. In June 1691, after almost all the French *reformés* had gone home, 427 *reformé*-officers and officers *en second* still remained in the army, including forty-seven of field rank.[16]

Rosen complained that most of the Irish officers were professionally ignorant and useless. He called them a wretched lot, lacking courage or pride, who would throw themselves to the ground at the sound of a cannon shot. When he came to Derry, he discovered that many were absent from their commands. It was found necessary to issue a proclamation in November 1689 ordering officers to stay with the regiments to which they were assigned. Such criticisms noticeably lessened as the war proceeded. Presumably the Irish officers were learning 'on the job', and their rough demeanour (to French and British eyes) and fellowship with their men may not have been disadvantageous on the battlefield. The main problems recorded by Fumeron during the build-up to the 1691 campaign concerned the officers' financial poverty and related low morale. He added that Saint-Ruth and the other French generals were unimpressed with the Irish concept of service, but this opinion was in relation to the hostility of much of the army leadership to Tyrconnell. General de Tessé reported that the infantry officers in particular became so defeatist after Aughrim that Tyrconnell felt it necessary to obtain

---

16 *Stevens*, pp 64, 67, 92, 124; *AH*, 21, p. 154; *d'Avaux*, pp 119, 182, 389, 459, 470; *JN*, p. 90; *F-I corr.*, i, pp 246, 268, 447; ii, pp 82, 220, 347.

a written promise from each not to surrender on an individual basis and without permission. While well intentioned, this step did nothing in his view to improve overall morale. Nevertheless, despite its defeats, the Irish infantry fought better in 1691 than in the earlier campaigns, suggesting that experience had improved the leadership qualities and professionalism of the officer corps.[17]

Sergeants and corporals were generally appointed from the ranks by their company commanders, allegedly often from their own relatives. Some sergeants may have been officers who lost their commands with the army's contraction. The ideal sergeant, according to a seventeenth-century commentator, was a valiant, active and experienced man, who was knowledgeable about the standard martial exercises and fit to be the 'eye, ear, mouth, hand and feet' of his superior officers. A corporal 'ought to be a man of stayed years, of no less wisdom, valour and experience, than a sergeant', and an exemplar to his men. Non-commissioned officers played a role in instruction, drill and weapons training. They were expected to show example to their soldiers by being 'resolute and forward' in low-level combat leadership. Two instances of the latter occurred in 1691: a sergeant inspired the Jacobite resistance at Ballymore Castle, and soon afterwards during the siege of Athlone Sergeant Custume played a key role in the brave defence of the bridge. Both men paid with their lives. In the French army, companies were divided into three squads, each commanded by a corporal, in which the personnel did duty together, and shared tents and mess facilities. Possibly a similar arrangement pertained in Ireland.[18]

Every company had a drummer. Although two are listed in Captain Gafney's, only one appears to have been paid at the appropriate corporal's rate. An infantry drum of the period was a painted wooden cylinder, generally of chestnut, over which a skin of parchment was stretched, and tensioned by zig-zag cords. Resonance was enhanced by three fine cords stretched across the bottom, which formed the 'snare' that gave this type of drum its name. The drum was suspended by a strap over the left shoulder and played with two drumsticks. Captain Gafney purchased a drum for his company in Dublin for a pound, had it fitted with a new drum skin for an additional shilling and six pence, and obtained a set of drumsticks for a further shilling and sixpence. The footguards alone had a drum major on their establishment, but some colonels may have followed the English practice of hiring a drum major at their own

---

[17] *AH*, 21, pp 99, 145, 173–4; *Proclamations*, ii, p. 132; *F-I corr.*, ii, pp 249, 334, 411; iii, pp 57, 66.
[18] *Animadversions of warre*, pp 196–8; *James II*, ii, p. 454; Story, *Continuation*, pp 88–9, 102; Lynn, *Giant of the grand siècle*, p. 441; *Stevens*, p. 64.

expense. Nicholas Browne's and Lord Tyrone's certainly had one, and Lord Kilmallock may have had a drum major in mind when he sought fourteen drums and fourteen drummer's uniforms – 'blue cloth coats embroidered' – for the thirteen companies in his regiment. The drum major's function was to instruct and lead the drummers. The drummer's primary function was to convey the commander's orders by signals upon his drum, which was audible above the din of battle or at a distance. On several occasions, both Stevens and Gafney record *reveille* being beaten at the generals' orders. On another occasion, according to Stevens, 'the *alarm* beat furiously'. At Aughrim a drummer beat the *charge*, and at Galway the garrison marched out with drums beating and colours flying. Brigadier Kane, a Williamite veteran of the war, records other drumbeats such as a *ruffle* (take care), *march, halt, a preparative, a flam* (fire!) and *retreat*. The *tattoo* set the evening watch. Drummers were used to draw attention to recruiting parties. Another function was to negotiate with the enemy. Drummers signalled this intention by beating a *parley*. At Athlone in 1690 James Douglas, the Williamite general, sent a drummer to summon the town, to which the governor, old Colonel Richard Grace, responded somewhat unchivalrously by firing his pistol over the messenger's head. At Cork and Kinsale, the Irish beat a *parley* prior to negotiating their surrender, as they did at Ballymore in 1691. While the Williamites were at Galway, a drummer came from Limerick to negotiate an exchange of prisoners. When in contact with the enemy, a drummer was enjoined to observe and take notice of everything in order to bring back intelligence to his officers, but equally to be 'very wary that nothing be screwed from him, neither by fair nor foul means; wherefore he must be wary of the enemies' friendship in bestowing courtesies upon him especially in giving him drink'.[19]

Bagpipes or war pipes had been used in Ireland since at least late-medieval times, and the footguards had a piper on their establishment. His instrument was almost certainly a set of mouth-blown war pipes, which by then had three drones, according to the poet, Dáibhí Ó Bruadair. These instruments may have been widely used: in 1689 pipers from several companies played 'The king enjoys his own again' as part of the reception for James in Dublin. In 1691 O'Donovan's regiment went into action with its bagpipe playing.[20]

Earlier in the seventeenth century, rank and file soldiers had been referred to as common men or common soldiers, but in the English civil war the soldiers of the parliamentary army had insisted on the substitution of the word

---

[19] 'Gafney', pp 165, 168–9; *Ormonde MSS*, n.s., viii, pp 346, 368; BL, Add. MS 9763, ff 32, 44; Kilmallock papers, carton 2; Kane, *Campaigns*, p. 116 *et seq*.; Story, pp 101, 142, 145; *JN*, p. 232; *Ormonde MSS*, i, p. 423; *Animadversions of warre*, pp 195–6.   [20] *Ormonde MSS*, i, p. 423; Ó Bruadair, iii, p. 181; *Ireland's lamentation*, p. 29; *DI*, 20–27 January 1691.

'private' for 'common', so that rank and file personnel were known as 'private soldiers', or later in the century as 'private sentinels'. Contemporary sources for the Irish army describe the rank and file as 'private men' or simply 'men'. First impressions of them were unfavourable. Stevens described them as 'the rabble of the country' and 'the most rude and useless sort of mountaineers'. He associated the men with slavery and beggary, alleging that they found it difficult to understand the words of command, much less obey them. Fumeron thought the army before Derry in 1689 was little more than a disorderly force of gypsies, with only a few committed to the cause. The men had no experience of musketry. Winter absenteeism inhibited training and many went into battle without ever having fired a shot, although a shortage of powder for instruction also underlay this deficiency. The close relationship between officers and men was thought to undermine discipline. Stevens complained 'the commissioned officer could not punish his sergeant or corporal because he was his cousin or foster brother, and they durst not correct the soldier, lest he fly in their face or run away'. He held that Irish soldiers needed to be governed with rigour and severity. In contrast, Fumeron thought that more was to be had from them by being gentle and pleasant rather than severe. In time, as the army grew in experience and its critics became more familiar with it, their initial adverse opinions mellowed. Fumeron had no criticism to make of the men in the last year of the war, while Stevens came to admire their stoicism in the face of hardship and adversity, and he praised the 'utmost bravery' they displayed at the battle of Aughrim. In that engagement, another officer wrote of the infantry: 'all the world must allow that since the Creation, never men fought better even to a miracle, for ... during the whole action, I could neither see nor hear of one soldier that went away, nor seemed even to look back'. A characteristic of the Irish soldiers was their fondness for shouting and hallowing before an engagement.[21]

Physical size and strength were significant factors in the warfare of the time. A contemporary Irish account described the men of Kildare as 'very hardy, laborious and industrious, of healthful bodies and constitutions, able and inured to bear labour and live to a great age, generally to seventy or eighty'. D'Avaux was impressed by the physique of the Irish soldiers. He observed that they were well built and taller than the French soldiers of the period. He also commented on the hardiness of the Irish. Fumeron noted that the Irish soldiers were big and strong, and he found their general disposition very positive. They were enthusiastic for battle, and he thought that with more skill

---

[21] Story, p. 75; *AH*, 21, pp 144–5, 149; *Stevens*, pp 62, 63, 70, 192–3; Account of Aughrim (Westminster Diocesan Archives, B6, 258).

and improved discipline, it would be hard to find better soldiers. D'Esgrigny, the *intendant* in 1690, likewise noted that Irishmen were tall and well built. He thought they were well suited for military life because they were sturdy and dogged, and could survive on very little. Lauzun considered the Irish men as good as could be found anywhere in the world. Boisseleau's opinion was that proper training, better discipline and professional leadership would make them into excellent soldiers. Their attitude was good, and they would be fine in battle. Brigadier Famechon judged that if they were under better leadership, serving outside Ireland and properly trained, the Irish had the qualities to make good soldiers. In 1691 Cormac O'Neill's 900 Ulstermen were noted as being 'as likely, clever, lusty well-shaped fellows, as ever eyes beheld'. Earlier, a Williamite observer described MacCarthy More's Munster regiment as 'lusty, strong fellows'. The Danish soldier Andreas Claudianus observed that the Irish soldiers were young and strong, but more used to farming than warfare. The favourable impression made by the Irish soldiers encouraged the French to seek more Irish recruits to serve in France. Louvois pursued this policy during the war, and it became a core French objective as hostilities neared their end.[22]

Recruitment and desertion

To enlarge the standing army, Tyrconnell was reported in December 1688 to have given out commissions to raise 20,000 men, a figure increased to 50,000 the next month. Irish society was predominantly rural, and the army's manpower must largely have been drawn from the underclass of tenant farmers, artisans, farm workers, other labourers and vagrants, supplemented by their equivalents in the cities and towns, which at that time were far less significant centres of population. The 3–4,000 professional soldiers that remained from the pre-war Irish army were of similar background.

There is no doubting the initial enthusiasm of the Irish populace for the war effort. Soon after his arrival, d'Avaux observed that nearly all the peasantry had taken up arms. In the first two months of recruiting, over 50,000 were reported to have enlisted. There was even anxiety that the flood of men to the colours would leave a shortage of labour to gather in the harvest and threaten the food supply. Several incentives were in play. An officer noted 'the greatness of affection which the poor people showed to the royal cause'. Seigneurial

---

22 'Account of Co. Kildare in 1682', p. 343; *d'Avaux*, pp 26, 29, 52; *F-I corr.*, i, pp 143, 268, 348; ii, p. 386; iii, pp 28, 80, 132–3; *Stevens*, p. 199; *AH*, 21, pp 137, 139; *Proclamations*, pp 218, 223; *CSPD 1689–90*, p. 437; 'Lauzun's reports', p. 125; Lynn, *Giant of the grand siècle*, p. 323; Story, p. 10; Claudianus, pp 283–5.

influence encouraged both recruitment and commitment to the war effort. No doubt, peer pressure also played a role. Moreover, the war had the backing of the influential Catholic clergy. Schomberg reported that the 'Romish priests' had been active in exhorting people to give their lives for their church. Another Williamite commentator related that 'the priests all over the country tell them they must go and serve King James, or else it is a mortal sin'. Reports that possession of a half-pike, skean or bayonet was a precondition for attendance at Mass receive some confirmation from the poet, Ó Bruadair, who wrote of 'hundreds marching to Mass with their bandoliers'. Anti-English sentiment was another factor: the perceptive d'Avaux observed that the Irish were 'irreconcilable enemies' of the English and, if allowed to, would slaughter them all. Fumeron reported the enthusiasm of the Irish soldiers for battle. More cynically, the English Jacobite, John Stevens, attributed their ardour for enlistment to the promise of better diet, clothing and pay, observing that 'no people have more encouragement to be soldiers ... for they live not at home so well at best, as they do at worst in the army'. Drummers were employed to draw attention to recruiting parties at such gathering points as fairs and holy wells. It was perhaps a compliment to the new recruits that Williamite sources referred to them in derogatory terms, such as 'the scum' of the country, 'thieves, robbers and tories' and 'all the rascality of Ireland'. Admittedly, in 1689 Lord Clare ordered his son to take what serviceable men he could find from the prisons. Stevens noted the reluctance of the estated men to release the 'better sort of people' to the army. But, in general, as the pro-Jacobite Protestant clergyman Charles Leslie pointed out, for want of the men he desired, James took the best he could get and gave them time and opportunity to accomplish themselves. After the 1689 setbacks in the north, when troop numbers were low, the French thought that finding new recruits was easy enough, but they criticized the inactivity of the Irish officers to do so.[23]

Responsibility for filling their companies generally lay with the captains, and commissions were given upon condition of furnishing a given number of men for the service. Few had much wealth, but recruitment was strongly localized, where officers could call on traditional local or family loyalties and connections: the residue of their seigneurial influence. As William King observed, the descendants of former Irish landowners 'by their pretended title and gentility ... have such an influence on the poor tenants of their own nation and religion ... that these tenants look on them still ... as a kind of

---

23 *Ormonde MSS*, n.s., viii, pp 346, 357, 359; *JN*, pp 38, 152; *An account of the present state Ireland is in*; Ó Bruadair, iii, p. 129; d'Avaux, pp 42, 51; *F-I corr.*, iii, pp 57, 66, 70; Stevens, pp 70, 140; *CSPD 1689–90*, p. 369; *Inchiquin MSS*, p. 17; King, p. 623; Leslie, pp 187–8.

landlords, maintain them after a fashion of idleness and entertain them in their coshering manner'. John Stevens, an English Jacobite who served in the Irish army, recorded that 'the muster rolls run high, every officer being quartered near home the better to enable him to raise his men or rather to put it into his power to enable him to muster all the rabble of the country'. Infantry regiments had particularly strong regional or even local associations, as the four extant rank-and-file rolls show. Almost half of Lord Enniskillen's company in 1686 consisted of fellow Maguires, and most of the remainder bore clearly identifiable Ulster Gaelic surnames, such as O'Neill, O'Cahan, MacQuillan and O'Sheil. Likewise, Swift Nix's reformed company bore largely Gaelic surnames, mostly associated with south and east Ulster, as well as County Louth, where the unit was billeted at the time. In 1689 George Gafney's company in Edward Butler's foot, although less homogenous, had a majority of names that can be linked to Kilkenny and the adjoining counties. Most were Gaelic, but about a third were Old English. Lord Kilmallock's company had many Cork names, but others that were more varied. About half were of Gaelic origin and most of the remainder were Old English, including five named Welsh or Welshman. In Dublin, its home city, Sir Michael Creagh's regiment recruited 950 men in a week in July 1689. Other recruits to the army came from the 3,000 Irish, English and Scottish soldiers that landed at Bantry in 1689. They were refugees from the revolution in England, who had made their way to France.[24]

Brian MacMahon's regiment was reported to have been entirely raised from Ulster creaghts, the itinerant cattle drovers who fled with their families and livestock from the Williamites. The creaghts also supplied much of the personnel of Balldearg O'Donnell's force. Only a third of the new regiments brought onto the establishment in 1689 were from Ulster and Connacht, which were the most Gaelic provinces. Stressing the fighting qualities of the Ulster Gaels, Balldearg alleged they were being discriminated against. However, against this there was the fact that few substantial Catholic landowners remained in Ulster, and those with the capacity to raise a regiment did so. After the Boyne, many soldiers in the regiments recruited in Leinster and Munster appear to have deserted their units to seek protection under William's Finglas declaration. According to Balldearg O'Donnell, Ulstermen replaced them in such numbers as to constitute half the rank and file of the regiments from the southern provinces. Possibly this influx of Ulstermen lay behind Berwick's report in the autumn of 1690 that recruiting was going very

---

24 *Stevens*, p. 62; King, p. 37; *Ormonde MSS*, i, pp 416–18; Gafney, pp 162–3; Kilmallock papers, carton 2; *Ormonde MSS*, n.s., viii, pp 368–9; *JN*, p. 270; *F-I corr.*, i, p. xlii.

well. He was optimistic that an early training camp could be organized the following spring involving at least twenty battalions of the field army, not counting those in garrison.[25]

Soldiers frequently regarded their engagement as being only to their immediate officers. Stevens complained they 'will follow none but their own leaders'. At Cavan, early in 1690, when Colonel William Nugent was killed, his regiment abandoned the engagement, as did Dungan's dragoons in similar circumstances at the Boyne. Earlier, at the siege of Derry, after their captain was killed, a dragoon troop refused to serve further, maintaining their engagement had been to him personally and was terminated by his death, a defence that cut little ice with Marshal Rosen, who complained that the practice was widespread. Nevertheless, the French generally respected the preference of the rank and file to be commanded by Irishmen. They observed that the Irish more willingly followed the old nobility, and the five colonels selected for the Mountcashel brigade were all connected to the peerage. Early thoughts about replacing the regimental officers in Mountcashel's brigade with more qualified Frenchmen were soon discarded. Rosen, noting the deference of the rank and file to their colonels, believed the men would desert if their leaders were replaced by Frenchmen. Indeed, both officers and soldiers of the O'Brien regiment loudly declared that they would refuse to go to France unless led by an O'Brien. While the war continued, soldiers in Ireland were reluctant to go to France. Mountcashel brought his own regiment up to strength by forcefully recruiting some of the Jacobite militia. Robert Fielding, one of Mountcashel's designated colonels, paid Colonel John Browne, the Mayo barrister and entrepreneur, £3,000 to raise men. When none were forthcoming, the ranks had to be filled by merging Browne's own recently raised regiment with Fielding's, against the wishes of Browne and some of his officers.[26]

Aversion to French service could be used as a recruiting ploy. In 1690, when Lord Kilmallock was experiencing recruiting difficulties, his brother suggested getting the parish priests to announce that men should join Irish regiments voluntarily as an alternative to being conscripted into the newly arrived French battalions, where they would not be well treated. Detachments of Cormac O'Neill's Ulster regiment were assigned to fill vacancies in the French regiments that landed in 1690, but they had to be accompanied by their officers to prevent their desertion. When it became clear that the French

---

25 *D'Avaux*, p. 632; *Stevens*, pp 63, 140, 192–3; *JN*, pp 269–70; Account of Aughrim (Westminster Diocesan Archives, B6, 258).   **26** *JN*, pp 100–1; *Stevens*, pp 63, 100; *F-I corr.*, i, pp 265, 423; Macpherson, *Original papers*, i, p. 211; *AH*, 21, pp 145–6; *d'Avaux*, pp 78–9, 683; Kinsella, *Catholic survival*, pp 44–5.

regiments were returning to France, all their Irish personnel deserted rather than accompany them. Strong demands from Louvois for more Irish recruits for the French service met with little positive response until the war ended. Large numbers of James Lacy's regiment deserted in 1691 on learning that their colonel had offered to lead them to France. This attitude changed after the treaty of Limerick was concluded later that year when some 16,000 soldiers agreed to follow Sarsfield to France despite Williamite inducements to remain in Ireland. Even then, General d'Usson stressed the importance of retaining regional identity for the re-formed units, when the Jacobite soldiers arrived in France.[27]

Desertion was a common factor in seventeenth-century armies, and commanders frequently offered financial incentives and other inducements to persuade their opponent's soldiers to change sides. In August 1689 d'Avaux promised a pardon to all former soldiers of the French army serving with the Williamites if they deserted. There was a steady trickle of French deserters throughout the war. They were not employed in the Jacobite army, however, but sent back to France. King James made a similar offer to British soldiers in the Williamite service. It met with little response, although a small number of English, Scots and Irish who deserted in early 1691 were incorporated into the Jacobite forces. There were substantial defections from the Jacobite army by the remaining Protestant officers and soldiers in the wake of the 1688 revolution and some were still deserting as late as the autumn of 1689. However, with the exception of Balldearg O'Donnell, there is little evidence of Jacobite soldiers deserting to serve in the Williamite army, at least until the war had ended. Nevertheless, there was plenty of desertion and absenteeism. According to John Stevens, the soldiers deserted in large numbers on being exposed to the rigours of military life. During the siege of Derry, hardship, lack of food and the absenteeism of officers contributed to widespread desertion. When the siege was lifted, Rosen complained that the colonels and many officers simply abandoned their commands and headed to Dublin, followed by their men in a stampede. Subsequent desertions occurred in the wake of military setbacks. After the Boyne, William's Finglas declaration encouraged soldiers from Leinster and east Munster to go home and some officers also submitted. In the winter of 1690–1 few seem to have deserted despite their hardship and Williamite threats to their families, where the latter remained in the Williamite quarters. Two Jacobite officers who deserted by swimming across the Shannon informed Ginkel of the underwater ford at Athlone by

27 *F-I corr.*, i, p. 410; ii, pp 95, 330, 455, 512; Simms, 'Sarsfield of Kilmallock', p. 208.

which the Williamites ultimately crossed the Shannon to capture the town. After Athlone fell in 1691, 'the Connacht regiments grew very thin, so that the foot by desertion and marauding was reduced from 17,000 to about 11,000 men'. But the soldiers' absences were not necessarily permanent, and shortly after the army seems to have quickly returned again to full strength for the battle of Aughrim. Subsequent desertions and submissions to the Williamites obliged Tyrconnell to seek an assurance from each army officer not to submit individually. Deserters were sometimes shot in front of the troops to discourage others. In 1690 two deserters from Zurlauben's French regiment were recaptured and executed by having their heads smashed in as an example to the rest.[28]

Camp followers

The soldiers went to war accompanied by their wives and children. Rosen recorded a thousand women at the Derry camp in 1689. The Williamites were told that the 200 women and children in Charlemont, when it surrendered in 1690, were there because the soldiers would not stay in the garrison without them, prompting Schomberg to observe 'that there was more love than policy in it'. Huts had to be provided for women camp followers at Killaloe in 1691. When Ballymore capitulated in June of that year, 645 women were found with the garrison of about 1,100 men. In the wake of the Irish defeat at Aughrim, wailing women and children filled the adjoining roads, and after the capitulation of Galway women and small children clung to the soldiers of the garrison, as they marched out of the city. Balldearg O'Donnell's creaghts were accompanied by their families, and the rapparees sheltered their families in their hideouts. After the war many wives and children of Irish soldiers accompanied their breadwinner to France, where dismayed officials reported officers disembarking with families of ten and twelve and ordinary soldiers coming with their wives and four or five children, although many were left behind. Presumably women and children accompanying the army in Ireland during the war were similarly numerous. Typically soldiers' wives would have washed, sewed, nursed, cooked and even acted as servants. An instance of women in combat occurred during the 1690 siege of Limerick when 'they boldly stood in the breach' and hurled broken bottles to help check the Williamite assault on the Irishtown.[29]

28 *D'Avaux*, pp 455–6; *Proclamations*, pp 123–4; *F-I corr.*, i, pp 202, 233, 246, 404, 433; ii, pp 68, 240, 252, 256, 357, 411; iii, p. 85; 'Longford letters', pp 50, 52; Story, *Continuation*, pp 106, 182–3, 234; *Stevens*, p. 63; *JN*, pp 269–70; *AH*, 21, p. 160.   **29** *F-I corr.*, ii, pp 332, 475; O'Kelly, pp 156–8; Story, pp 62, 129; *Stevens*, pp 199–200; *AH*, 21, p. 144; *Claudianus*, pp 149, 257–9, 285.

The army had many other camp followers. They included sutlers and pedlars who accompanied it to supplement the soldiers' material needs, officers' servants, spectators of all sorts who came to observe the army's operations and waggoners to provide its transport. A seigneurial strand was added to the mix where a chieftain was accompanied by his followers. Although unmentioned, prostitutes were probably present to provide sexual services where desired. Camp followers, especially the soldiers' dependent families, had to be fed, clothed, transported, housed and guarded. They were not specifically included in Fumeron's ration quotas, although officers, depending on rank, received extra rations. However, other ranks were allotted only a single ration. Possibly their families were fed through the device of issuing rations to a battalion on the basis that it was at full strength, when this was seldom so. They were likely to have been inveterate scavengers and looters after battles and while on the march, as the Ulster camp followers of the Williamite army certainly were at the Boyne. In the Williamite quarters, the sheriffs were ordered to drive the families of Jacobite soldiers killed in rebellion across the Shannon. The parents of Jacobite soldiers were denied Williamite protections, unless they persuaded their sons to desert. A French officer reported in December 1690 that multitudes of women and children driven from the Williamite quarters faced famine if not supplied from the Jacobite stores. The lot of non-combatants trapped in the no-man's-land between the armies was particularly harsh. The Williamite, Robert Parker, recorded that near Ballymore in 1691:

> the miserable effects of war appeared in a very melancholy manner; for the enemy, to prevent a famine amongst themselves, had drove all useless mouths from among them the last winter. And we, for the same reason, would not suffer them to come within our frontiers. So, between both, they lay in a miserable condition. These wretches came flocking in great numbers about our camp, devouring all the filth they could meet with. Our dead horses crawling with vermin, as the sun had parched them, were very delicious food to them, while their infants sucked those carcasses with as much eagerness as if they were at their mothers' breasts.[30]

Clothing

While some degree of uniformity in military dress had long been in existence, especially for sovereign's escorts and ceremonial purposes, the attiring of

---

30 *F-I corr.*, ii, pp 166, 343–7; Story, p. 82; *Proclamations*, pp 211, 218, 223; Parker, pp 25–6.

ordinary infantry units uniformly was a product of mid-seventeenth-century reforms that most European armies had adopted by the 1680s. A standardized uniform distinguished friend from foe and could be refined to identify individual regiments. By diminishing individuality, it fostered obedience and sharpened drill. It also strengthened unit cohesion, facilitated battlefield deployment, lifted *esprit de corps*, presented a show to observers, attracted recruits and cost less if purchased in bulk. As early as 1645, it was stipulated that the English New Model army should wear red coats, and this colour was generally retained after the restoration. In France it was only in 1685 that an ordinance prescribed grey-white for regular French infantry. At its creation in 1662, the Irish footguards regiment wore scarlet coats. The rest of the post-restoration Irish army seems generally to have followed suit, although it was not until 1686 that Tyrconnell imposed strict uniformity in apparel. Red remained the preferred colour of the soldiers' coats, each regiment being differentiated by its facings – the supposed colour of the lining exposed in generous turned-back cuffs. Stevens recounted that 'everyone had liberty to take up red cloth, white lining and pewter buttons to make regimental coats'. His own regiment, the grand prior's, wore red lined with white, except for the drummers who word blue with white loops (fasteners instead of buttons). The footguards were 'clad in red lined with blue'. Lord Bellew's regiment wore red lined with orange tawny, and Gordon O'Neill's red lined white but with red facings. However, the heavy demands of the new regiments on the available clothing supply meant that insufficient red cloth was available, and some units were clothed in material of other colours. D'Avaux refers to red, blue and grey cloth being used, and when 300 Irish soldiers were captured by Colonel Lloyd near Belturbet, he 'got only as many red coats as would serve two companies, many of their men being new levies, wearing grey'. Antrim's and Louth's regiments had white coats with, respectively, red and filamot facings. The coats of Colonel MacCarthy More's foot were lined with green and Lord Bophin's with yellow. Captured Jacobite uniforms were donned by some of the Derry defenders, who were said to 'strut in scarlet laced with silver and gold, and others in buff'. No contemporary image of the Irish infantry exists, but like other European soldiers of the period, their coats would have been full-skirted garments, reaching to just above the knee, and fastened by pewter buttons.[31]

The clothing order for Viscount Kilmallock's regiment provides a proposed inventory of a new soldier's full apparel. Each man was to have a blue coat,

---

[31] Childs, *Warfare*, pp 102–3; Lawson, *Uniforms*, p. 11, Chandler, *Art of war*, pp 84–6; Lynn, *Giant of the grand siècle*, pp 173–6; *Stevens*, pp 106–8, 215–16; *d'Avaux*, p. 211; Hamilton, *Inniskillingmen*, p. 27; *Ormonde MSS*, n.s., viii, p. 367; 'Gafney', p. 164; *A true and impartial account of the most material passages in Ireland*, p. 25.

lined with red, except for sergeants who were to have red coats, fastened with loops extended across the chest, which would have given their coats a distinctive appearance. The sixty-five men of the grenadier company likewise were to have coats fastened with loops. The drummers were to have embroidered caps and coats, the latter fastened with loops. All were to have red breeches, which on the contemporary European model would have reached to just below the knee, together with red stockings, buckle shoes, gloves, two shirts, two cravats and a haversack. The estimated cost of clothing the regiment was £1,118. Unfortunately for Kilmallock's plans, the Jacobite high command halted clothing purchases by individual colonels and decreed instead that central stores in Dublin acquire and issue uniforms. These were duller, cheaper and with fewer items than Kilmallock wanted. 862 sets of clothing were eventually provided, each comprising an overcoat 'of very good frieze', a waistcoat, stockings, breeches and a single shirt. Sergeants had to make do with the same coats as privates. Waist belts had supplanted baldrics, but were in short supply in 1689. Colonel Daniel O'Donovan's regiment was similarly apparelled: each soldier had a lined frieze coat, breeches, a hat and hat band, a pair of shoes with buckles, a shirt, a cravat, a sash, a pair of stockings and a waistcoat, all costing one pound and four shillings, a rather less generous clothing allocation than that in peacetime. It was common for campaign casualties, including enemy dead and prisoners, to be stripped of their clothing to meet the clothing needs of soldiers.[32]

Most soldiers wore a hat, wide-brimmed with a low crown. Ó Bruadair wrote of soldiers whose hatbands were gaily bedecked with ribbons. The exceptions were the grenadiers and drummers, who wore caps to facilitate slinging muskets or drums. These caps appear to have resembled an old-fashioned nightcap, with a bag hanging at the back, but probably with a stiffened front. Certainly, in the grand prior's regiment the grenadiers' caps bore on the front the image of a flaming city with the motto: *The fruits of rebellion*. Richard Nugent's regiment was nicknamed 'the Caps', 'because they all wore them like grenadiers, as being more easily to be had than hats'. The exigencies of supplying the expanded wartime army caused a reduction of the soldiers' peacetime clothing allocation, which Tyrconnell had decreed in 1687 as 'a coat and breeches lined, and after ten months to be turned without charge; a hat, four pairs of shoes, three pairs of stockings, three shirts, three cravats and a sash, all very good in their kind, according to the patterns of the several particulars shown and lodged with us'. Clearly, in 1689, to meet the

---

32 Kilmallock papers, carton 2; Hamilton, *Inniskillingmen*, p. 27; Simms, 'Sarsfield of Kilmallock', pp 205–6; *KJIL*, ii, p. 713.

clothing needs of the expanded army took time, and as late as June the process was far from complete. Furthermore, active service quickly wore out clothing. The siege of Derry left many soldiers in rags. In early September the force mustered to resist Schomberg was initially 'very ragged and ill shod', with only half the troops in uniforms. The emergency brought about improvement, and at last by 1690 the field army seems to have been adequately clothed. The grand prior's regiment had whatever cloth it needed out of the stores to make regimental coats before the campaign. MacElligott's was described as well armed and clothed. The footguards had new clothes that 'made a fine show'.[33]

Officers adopted a degree of finery, with uniforms that were generally of better material and cut, and with added embellishments such as lace, gold buttons and sashes. Captain Gafney paid for muslin cravats for himself, a hat with the brim edged in lace and a scarlet ribbon round the crown, together with a silk-lined red waistcoat, gold buttons and a belt with a silver buckle. In Kilmallock's regiment the officers' uniforms, including Kilmallock's own red coat, were supplied by Dublin tailors, who subsequently complained of being unpaid. Sir Teague O'Regan, who defended Charlemont in 1689–90, was described on its surrender as wearing 'a plain red coat, an old weather-beaten wig hanging down at full length, a little narrow white beaver [hat] cocked up, a yellow cravat string … [and] boots with a thousand wrinkles'. Gorgets, which were crescent-shaped metal plates suspended from the neck by a ribbon, were worn by officers in England. There is no mention of their use in Ireland, but it is likely that they were worn at least by officers of the pre-war army.[34]

The peacetime army was re-clothed every eighteen months, but this timescale could not be met during the war: by late 1690 the clothes of the Limerick garrison 'were worn to rags, insomuch that many could scare hide their nakedness in the daytime'. However, the arrival of 20,000 grey uniform coats from France alleviated the problem for the 1691 campaign, although the number was 10,000 less than needed and, when distributed, the coats were found to be rather short and tight fitting on the big frames of the Irish men. In December 1690 an order was issued for clothiers and weavers to come to Galway, and this may have had some effect, for Fumeron was able to report that garments were being sourced locally, including trousers, stockings, shoes and woollen caps in the absence of hats. Shoes and stockings were part of the standard attire of a soldier and very necessary in the damp Irish climate, but prone to wear out. In 1689 there were concerns that many of the Irish soldiers

---

33 Lawson, *Uniforms*, pp 20, 29; *Ó Bruadair*, iii, p. 131; *Stevens*, pp 79, 189, 216; *d'Avaux*, pp 459, 468; *Ormonde MSS*, n.s., viii, p. 382.   34 Lawson, *Uniforms*, p. 22; 'Gafney', pp 163–4; Kilmallock papers, carton 3; Story, p. 62.

lacked shoes, especially during and after the autumn campaign against Schomberg. Attempts were made to increase local manufacture and to secure supplies from France. 20,000 pairs accompanied the French invasion force in 1690, although these may have been mainly for their own use. By the winter of 1690–1, Stevens reported that 'abundance of the soldiers were barefoot or at least so near it that their wretched shoes and stockings could scarce be made to hang on their feet and legs'. Fumeron confirmed this picture, but was able to report that shoes were being locally sourced for the 1691 campaign. It is possible that many of these may have been the heal-less brogues of untreated leather, normally worn by the Irish peasants. Certainly '750 pairs of brogues' were distributed to Sir John FitzGerald's regiment of foot in 1689. Stevens himself had a pair of proper shoes made in Limerick. By the start of the 1691 campaign, every soldier had been supplied with two pairs of locally-made shoes, stockings and breeches. Shoes in large quantities were among the needs of the Irish soldiers when they arrived in France. Soldiers carried food and personal possessions in knapsacks.[35]

Weapons and equipment

The field officers of infantry regiments were mounted, at least when on the march, and company officers too, where they could afford it. Prior to the siege of Limerick, for example, the horses of the garrison officers were taken up for the cavalry, and in the course of the siege two infantry colonels had their horses shot under them in a skirmish outside the wall. In 1691 Stevens bemoaned the fact that *en route* to join the main field army, due to the shortage of horses, the officers of his regiment were all afoot, leaving him 'quite spent with fatigue'. While their apparel to some extent differentiated officers and sergeants from other ranks, their primary distinguishing feature was the weapons they bore. Officers carried swords and short half-pikes or spontoons, known as leading staffs. In one of the attacks on Windmill Hill during the siege of Derry, 'a line of colonels with their pikes in hand' led the infantry advance. The regulation length of French spontoons of the period was 2.27m to 2.6m, and they had a pear-shaped, pointed, iron head above a twisted crossbar. 5,000 came from France in 1689, although in 1690 Captain Gafney supplied his own at a cost of six shillings. A lead staff was a thrust weapon, and on one occasion at least John Stevens used his as such. However, when vertical,

---

35 *Stevens*, pp 120, 139, 193; 'Journal 1/6 to 18/7 1689' (Carte MS 181), f. 6; *F-I corr.*, i, pp 132, 147; ii, pp 214, 268; iii, p. 95; *Proclamations*, p. 179; *AH*, 21, p. 215; *James II*, ii, p. 451; *d'Avaux*, pp 532–3, 540, 558.

lead staffs had a degree of visibility on a battlefield, and were also used to 'dress' or arrange the ranks and files, and to force down musket barrels that were too highly elevated. Ideally sergeants carried halberds, which were also staff weapons that had a metal head, which combined a spear point with a cleaver-like blade and a hooked fluke. The complex head was challenging to forge, and halberds may have been a rarity, with half-pikes – as often in France – being substituted in their place: a French return of 1691 refers to 'halberds or spontoons'. A return of 1685 seems to imply that the halberds at that time were reserved to the sergeants of the then sole regiment of dragoons. Nevertheless, in 1689 Kilmallock ordered twenty-six halberds for the sergeants of his infantry regiment. The halberds were used to dress the ranks and files. For the corporals and private soldiers, the basic infantry weapons were pikes, swords and muskets, the latter with bayonets, if available.[36]

The army's shortage of weapons at the beginning of hostilities is exemplified by Antrim's new regiment, which arrived before Derry in December 1688, allegedly armed with only skeans and clubs. Over three years France supplied just enough arms to equip the army, but never enough to fully equip it at one time. This was not due to bad will: it was a heavy logistical demand for the French war ministry to source and supply hand-made weaponry sufficient to equip a whole army in Ireland. On the eve of the Boyne in 1690, over half the infantry in the field army lacked swords, pikes or bayonets, and their muskets were reported to be in a very poor state. However, the cumulative effect of the supplies sent from France, especially for the infantry, was to maximize firepower by 1691. This may partly explain their improved performance in the last campaign, in which the Williamites said the Irish fought 'like men of another nation', which was intended as a compliment. However, 10,000 arms needed for the new men conscripted after Aughrim were unavailable.[37]

The standard infantry firearm was the matchlock musket, so-called because of its firing mechanism, in which ignition came from a smouldering match, made of hempen cord, soaked in a nitrate solution. To load the weapon the musketeer rammed into the barrel a charge of powder and a lead ball, followed by a wad to stop the ball rolling forward. Fine powder was then piled onto a shallow pan beside a small vent in the side of the barrel, called a touch hole. The smouldering match was then inserted into a clamp, which was released when the musketeer pulled the trigger, plunging the match into the pan to

---

36 *CSPD 1685*, p. 165; *Stevens*, pp 124, 134; 'Gafney', p. 165; *F-I corr.*, i, p. 235; *JN*, p. 76; Kemp, *Weapons*, pp 32–3; Chartrand, *Louis XIV's army*, pp 20, 23; Kilmallock papers, carton 2.
37 King, p. 116; *F-I corr.*, i, p. 436; ii, p. 386; Story, *Continuation*, p. 129.

ignite the fine powder there, which in turn sent a flash through the touch hole, exploding the main charge to eject the lead ball from the barrel. The considerable 'kick' from the discharge of a musket meant that it was best held under rather than against the soldier's shoulder, although in France Louvois insisted that musketeers support the weapons on their shoulders for better sighting and greater accuracy. Originally muskets had required a stand, but by the late seventeenth century a standard British weapon had reduced in weight to $c.5.7$ kilograms, and the stand was no longer necessary. French muskets were slightly heavier, but fired a smaller ball. The mixture of calibres caused problems for the Irish army, as Irish ball was too large for the French muskets. Problems arose over this in 1689, but by early 1691 the issue had been addressed to the extent of ensuring that each regiment was supplied with one calibre of musket. The disparity could still cause difficulties: at Aughrim, at a critical point in the engagement, a supply of wrong-calibre ball prevented Walter Burke's regiment, which garrisoned the castle guarding the causeway on the Jacobite left wing, from firing their muskets, thus facilitating the advance of the Williamite cavalry. Accompanying equipment for a musket included a ramrod; a small powder flask containing better-quality priming powder; a bandolier of twelve small flasks ('the twelve apostles'), each containing a measure of coarser powder sufficient for the main charge to fire a single shot; a pouch to hold musket balls; and, ideally, a set of tools to clean and repair the musket. The bandolier was worn across the chest.[38]

A typical British musket of the late seventeenth century was $c.158$ centimetres in length and had an 18-millimetre calibre, although the barrel diameter was measured in bore – the number of musket balls made from a pound of lead that it would fit, which was twenty in France, with the qualification that the French pound was slightly lighter than its English counterpart. Matchlock reloading drill took an experienced soldier at least a minute. The effective killing range was little more than a hundred metres. Misfires were of the order of one in two. Due to their inaccuracy, smooth-bore muskets were best discharged in volleys against massed opponents, especially after visibility was reduced by gunsmoke from earlier firing. The matchlocks had a number of disadvantages: the smouldering matches were very hazardous with so much powder around; they had to be constantly adjusted in the clamp and kept free of ash; their glow exposed night operations to discovery; the matches were prone to extinguishment in the wet weather common in Ireland; and large quantities of match were needed to keep an army supplied.

38 Roberts & Tinsey, 'Matchlock musket', pp 16–20; Holmes (ed.), *Weapon*, pp 148–55; *Ormonde MSS*, n.s., viii, p. 365; *AH*, 21, p. 136; *F-I corr.*, ii, p. 203; *JN*, pp 146–7.

Nevertheless, the matchlock was simple to operate, and possessed a consistent, close-range killing power, making it a very effective weapon. Matchlock muskets were standard, and were sourced from the regiments of the original standing army, the Dublin stores, confiscations from Protestants, including the disarming of the militia in 1685 and, above all, from France, which sent more than 13,000 over a period of time, together with bandoliers, powder and match. Powder and match were in short supply, especially in 1689.[39]

The demands on available supplies of muskets and their frequent bad condition led to shortages, particularly in 1689. Soon after his arrival, King James reviewed Cavenagh's infantry regiment at Dungannon, which was 'armed half with pikes and half with muskets'. To his surprise, the condition of the muskets was so bad and so much out of order that he found not one in a hundred of them could be fired. D'Avaux was told that an inspection had shown not one in ten of the muskets in Creagh's regiment was serviceable. When he reviewed a detachment of infantry bound for Derry, the ambassador noticed that they possessed only useless, old or broken muskets, without powder, match or ball. In June Fumeron reported that the besiegers of Derry had only 1,800 serviceable muskets. The seventeen infantry regiments present there in July lacked more than a thousand, and of those they had, 2,770 were in need of repair. The following month d'Avaux reported that only 3,000 of the locally sourced muskets were serviceable. The initial consignments sent from France comprised many old or broken weapons, although following his complaints subsequent deliveries were of better quality. The poor state of many weapons was compounded by the neglect of the Irish soldiers who were unused to the care of firearms and even abandoned them on the march, or made off with them if they deserted. D'Avaux declared that if 50,000 muskets came from France, only 10,000 would still be serviceable after six months in the hands of Irish soldiers. He repeatedly blamed the poor supervision of the Irish officers for this neglect. However, King James refused to countenance his suggested remedy that the officers in default should be made to pay for the repairs. Large numbers of muskets were abandoned when the army withdrew from Derry in 1689, and again in 1690 during the retreat from the Boyne. There was only one Catholic gunsmith in Dublin; the rest were Protestants and reportedly uncooperative in effecting repairs. It was alleged that they used iron fragments to block the touch holes of the muskets. Nevertheless, by the autumn of 1689 the situation had improved: in the force that confronted Schomberg, over 10,000 muskets were serviceable, with only 1,600 lacking or

---

39 O'Carroll, 'Change and continuity in weapons', p. 246; *F-I corr.*, i, p. xlii; ii, p. 369; iii, p. 76; *d'Avaux*, pp 335–6, 388–9, 445–6, 459, 471.

broken. France supplied over 5,000 muskets in 1689. For the 1690 campaign 15–20,000 more were sought, but only 3,000 matchlocks appear to have come with Lauzun. From this consignment 499 muskets were sent to equip Lord Kilmallock's regiment at Limerick, but once more their quality was poor: 'the most part of them unfixed, some wanting triggers, cocks, screw pins, rammers, and some with their stocks broken'. A return of the army's needs at the end of 1690 stated that of the 23,000 infantry, 5,750 were armed with pikes and 8,000 had firearms, but 9,252 weapons of all sorts were needed for the rest. This deficit was met by 5,000 muskets and 4,000 pike heads sent from France in 1691. Fumeron was satisfied with their condition, but shortages still remained, and not all the soldiers could be armed. When Galway surrendered in July, a Williamite observer commented that the rusty muskets of the garrison were hardly fit for war.[40]

A modification of the matchlock musket was the fusil or flintlock/firelock, which substituted a flint held in a cock for the smouldering match. When the trigger was pulled, the flint struck a steel cover over the firing pan, knocking it back to expose the priming powder, which was simultaneously ignited by the spark generated from the impact of the flint on the steel. The absence of smouldering matches and the practice of carrying the charges of powder for the fusil in a *cartouche* or leather cartridge box made the weapon generally safer to use, and particularly so for grenadiers or for tasks such as guarding the train with its large stock of powder. It could also be primed and made ready to fire in advance. The fusil was more reliable in damp weather and probably quicker to reload, but in other respects it was similar to the matchlock and no more effective. Indeed, its delicate firing mechanism was more prone to breakage. Flintlock technology was known since the 1630s, but the introduction of fusils to armies was slow, partly because they were about 50 per cent more expensive to make. Fusils became widespread in the French army only in the 1690s, and some matchlocks were still in use as late as 1704. Although the Irish infantry remained largely dependent on the matchlock, at least 3,500 fusils were sent from France, and some others were manufactured in Dublin. In January 1690 Lord Kilmallock sought Dublin-made firelocks for his regiment. Both James and Tyrconnell requested the inclusion of as many firelocks as possible in the consignments of firearms from France.[41]

---

40 *D'Avaux*, pp 100, 232, 334–6, 389, 459, 468, 470–1, 499, 524, 562; *AH*, 21, pp 136–7, 140, 154, 165, 176; Story, p. 84; *F-I corr.*, i, pp xlii, 132, 218; ii, pp 289, 331; iii, pp 10, 49, 58, 183, 187, 190; 'Talbot letter-book', pp 112, 116; Macpherson, *Original papers*, i, p. 309; *Stevens*, p. 119; 'A journal of what has passed since his majesty's arrival' (Carte MS 181), f. 12; Simms, 'Sarsfield of Kilmallock', p. 208; Claudianus, p. 285. 41 Chandler, *Art of war*, pp 75–80; Lynn, *Giant of the grand siècle*, pp 458–64; *CSPD 1685*, p. 165; *F-I corr.*, i, p. xlii; ii, pp 368–9; 'Talbot letter-book',

Grenadiers and dragoons were issued with fusils because they were safer and could be slung ready primed. The arms to be issued to both Dominic Browne's and Cormac O'Neill's regiments in June 1689 included sixty-five firelocks, which were primarily for the grenadier companies. Surplus firelocks went to ordinary musketeers. Stevens, for example, mentioned 'a strong detachment of firelocks' sent out to guard the road to Newry in the manoeuvres before the Boyne. At the siege of Limerick, in relation to both fusils and swords, he lamented that 'we had but few of these sorts of arms'. Burke's independent company of 200 fusiliers is mentioned in 1689 and 1691. At Aughrim, the Irish swopped their muskets for the firelocks of fallen Williamite soldiers. Infantry officers frequently carried pistols in their belts. These short-barrelled weapons operated with a flintlock firing mechanism, although some with the older wheellock firing system may still have been in use. The characteristic weapon of the grenadier was the hand grenade, primarily intended for use in siege warfare. The grenade was a hollow iron ball, filled with gunpowder and primed with a fuse. Each grenadier carried a pouch of twelve to fifteen grenades, with the match to ignite the fuses in an attached box. Grenades were among the many shortages of the army during the siege of Derry in 1689. Later, in the autumn campaign of that year, only 780 were available. It is not clear whether any grenades were supplied from France in 1690 beyond those that came with the French troops, who utilized more than 750. However, an on-going shortage is suggested by the sending of more than 14,000 with Saint-Ruth in 1691, together with 18,000 fuses. Another item of grenadier equipment was a hatchet, used as an assault weapon and as a means of cutting through the fascines that typically obstructed a breach in a fortification. 3,000 were sought for the grenadiers and dragoons at the end of 1690, but none were recorded as sent.[42]

A pike was a pole weapon, supposedly at least sixteen feet long, although frequently less, with a shaft of ash or spruce, on which was mounted a pointed flat or triangular steel head that was held in place by long metal cheeks, and with an iron-shod butt. Pikemen tended to be taller and stronger than musketeers. The standard ratio of pikemen to musketeers was one to three, but the proportion of pikes was dropping in most armies. In the Jacobite force fielded against Schomberg in 1689, pikes formed about a quarter of the weaponry. Captain Gafney acquired sixteen 'spearheads' and steel spuds for the

pp 103, 107; 'Journal 1/6 to 18/7 1689' (Carte MS 181), f. 11; Kilmallock papers, carton 3; Macpherson, *Original papers*, i, p. 309; *An account of the present state Ireland is in*; *d'Avaux*, pp 322, 562.   **42** 'Journal 19/5 to 18/6 1689' (Carte MS 181), f. 70; 'Segrave papers', p. 387; *Stevens*, pp 117, 171, 197; Childs, *Warfare*, pp 154–5; Chandler, *Art of war*, p. 81; *F-I corr.*, i, pp 183, 240; ii, p. 368; iii, pp 75, 204.

fifty-two private men in his company, which represented a pike quota of between a third and a quarter. The proportion of pikes in the army may have approached a third in 1691. With insufficient weapons to go around, especially in 1689, scythes – ten to a company – with their blades mounted upright, were also employed. One regiment sent to Derry had only shillelaghs, and two had pikes without metal points. This may have been due to administrative failure, however, as d'Avaux complained that 8,000 pike heads that had been sent from France lay unmounted on shafts in the Dublin stores. A further 4,000 pike heads were sent from France for the 1691 campaign. By the late seventeenth century, the morions (pot helmets) and upper-body armour previously worn by pikemen had been abandoned. So too had their original offensive role, and by 1689–91 their task was largely confined to protecting the musketeers, who were especially vulnerable to cavalry attack during the reloading process.[43]

Pikes were unwieldy and bayonets, which made a pikeman out of every musketeer, were coming into use. However, early bayonets suffered from the drawback of being plugged into the muzzle of the gun barrel, thereby disabling the weapon from being fired. The ring bayonet, which overcame this problem, had also been conceived, but as yet was little used due to the difficulty of securing it firmly to the barrel. Plug bayonets were about 30cms long. They consisted of a double-edged knife blade, with a tapered wooden haft terminating in a brass ferrule. From 1685 a small number of bayonets were in service in the Irish army, and a further 500 were issued in 1689, probably to the grenadier companies, which lacked pikes, but were armed with firelocks/ fusils, the firearms initially most associated with the introduction of the bayonet. Fumeron proposed the manufacture of 20,000 bayonets in Dublin for issue to the soldiers without swords, but this was not done. For the 1690 campaign Captain Gafney had his own bayonet made at a cost, with its belt, of twenty-four shillings. More bayonets came from France in 1691, but their distribution was confined to the grenadiers. In Ireland, for the final campaign Fumeron gave an allowance of iron and steel to each company to manufacture its own bayonets. The outcome is unknown, but it seems unlikely that the distribution of bayonets ever extended much beyond the soldiers armed with flintlocks, and perhaps not even to all of them.[44]

A sword was standard equipment for pikemen and musketeers. It was both an offensive and defensive weapon. The older practice of slinging a sword from

---

43 Chandler, *Art of war*, pp 81–4; 'Gafney', p. 165; *d'Avaux*, pp 468, 470; *F-I corr.*, ii, p. 369; iii, pp 47, 49, 90; *AH*, 21, p. 115. **44** Childs, *Warfare*, pp 153–4; Chandler, *Art of war*, pp 82–4; 'Gafney', pp 164–5; *d'Avaux*, p. 140; *F-I corr.*, ii, p. 331; iii, p. 94; *CSPD 1685*, p. 165.

a baldric had been abandoned in favour of suspending it in a leather scabbard from a belt. Swords were in short supply in Ireland, 'there being an extreme want of them among the forces'. The shortage was aggravated by the scarcity of sword cutlers. In the summer of 1689 King James sought 13,000 swords from France – 'more if possible, and preferably sabres' – with a proportionate quantity of belts. Sabres were curved swords. Although primarily a cavalry weapon, they were sometimes used by infantry also. Captain Gafney had two backswords, a much-favoured infantry weapon with a single-edged, straight blade that facilitated both thrusting and slashing movements. He also owned a couple of rapiers, which were slender, sharply pointed thrusting weapons. The French fleets brought 3,000 swords (in addition to sabres) in 1689, leaving many infantrymen short. The swords in the first 1689 consignment were of very bad quality – old and broken, according to Fumeron – but following complaints, those sent subsequently were better. The infantry was short more than 10,000 swords in September 1689. At the Boyne in 1690 only half the infantry had swords, and later Stevens noted that very few soldiers had swords at Limerick. 5,000 sent in 1691 went first to the grenadiers. A want of belts in 1689 meant that many of those who had swords were obliged to carry them in their hands. Without swords, once they had discharged their weapons, musketeers resorted to 'club musket', if they engaged the enemy at close quarters.[45]

Infantry drill, training and tactics

An infantry recruit was taught weapon handling, drill and the proper responses to orders, and instructed in the performance of collective unit operations. These skills, which were vital to maximize firepower, were more readily available in the permanent standing armies of the later seventeenth century than in the more *ad hoc* mercenary or temporary formations of earlier eras, when soldiers and indeed officers had to learn on the job. Manuals of instruction were available, such as Louis de Gaya's, *L'art de guerre* (1677) (English edition published in London, 1678), Allain Mallet's, *Les travaux de Mars* (Amsterdam, 1672) and *Military discipline or the art of shewing directions for the postures in exercising of the pike and musket ... by Capt JS* (London, 1689). An early Irish contribution to the field of military thought was Gerat Barry's *A discourse of military discipline*, published in Brussels in 1634. Another Irish military theorist was the earl of Orrery, author of *A treatise on the art of war* (1677). Orders from senior commanders and ordinances of sovereigns or their

---

45 Chandler, *Art of war*, p. 81; 'Gafney', p. 165; *Stevens*, pp 171, 186; Macpherson, *Original papers*, i, p. 309; *AH*, 21, p. 137; *F-I corr.*, i, p. xlii; iii, p. 49.

representatives also influenced instruction and training practice. Attention was paid to developments in continental armies. In 1686–7 King James had sent an observer to the French, Dutch and imperial armies 'to view the method of their encamping, embattling, exercising and what else may occur observable and thereon to make a true and exact representation'. Several officers, including some from the Irish army, gained experience of combat and military practices in the imperial forces, campaigning successfully against the Turks during the 1680s. The most influential manual in Charles II's restoration armies was the detailed *An abridgement of English military discipline*, first published in 1675–6, which the king specifically appointed for use by his forces in Scotland and Ireland as well as England. It was also adopted by James II in a new and more up-to-date edition in 1686, despite its original compiler being his executed rebel nephew, the duke of Monmouth.[46]

In Ireland, Tyrconnell's army faced particular training challenges due to a number of factors: the dismissal of the old personnel, the loss of a third of the peacetime army in England, the exclusion of a generation of Catholics from military service during Charles II's reign, the army's large and rapid expansion, and an on-going shortage of weapons and powder. There was a want of skilled instructors, a gap that 150 French officers were brought in to fill in 1689. No doubt their presence was beneficial, but their impact was blunted by language difficulties and by hostility from the Irish officers, who resented the French presence and attitude. A cadre of Irish, English and Scottish Catholic officers had experience of military service abroad or in James's English army. Tyrconnell had sought to engage such veterans for his peacetime army, and their number grew with the influx of British Jacobites in 1689. In the infantry, officers with overseas or even British experience numbered less than a hundred, an average of about two per unit. These veterans tended to take their duties seriously, and many held field rank in their regiments. For example, in the footguards Dorrington and Barker, colonel and lieutenant colonel respectively, were both Englishmen who had served previously on the Continent, as apparently had Arundel, the captain of the grenadier company. In a line regiment, such as Thomas Butler's, the colonel had fought with the imperial forces against the Turks, and had subsequently served in King James's English army, as had Watson and Price, the lieutenant colonel and major, while Coulouvray, the grenadier captain, was French. More typical perhaps was Sir Heward Oxburghs's regiment, where only Lieutenant Colonel Edward Scott and Major Lawrence Delahunty had experience, which they had gained

---

46 Lynn, *Giant of the grand siècle*, pp 478–9; Chandler, *Art of war*, pp 102–8; Childs, *Charles II*, pp 63–5; *CSPD 1686–7*, pp 212, 400.

in the pre-war English army. Undoubtedly these veterans were an important influence in readying the army for war. They were familiar with up-to-date military practice and must have been versed in the military manuals of the time. They spoke English, and in the case of two dozen or so probably Irish as well. However, even with the addition of the French, those already possessed with military skills were a small minority of the officer corps, perhaps 10 per cent, and the vast majority of officers, especially those commissioned for the war, entered service quite ignorant of military practice, having never been in any army before. Stevens observed that most Irish officers knew no more than their men, and consequently had little understanding of how to exercise or train them. The majority of the soldiers confronting Schomberg at Dundalk were raw and undisciplined, and Stevens lamented that when there was time and opportunity for training during the winter of 1689–90, the officers neglected their commands and ignored their main business of recruiting and disciplining the army. There were numerous French complaints about the shortcomings of the Irish officers, especially in the first year of the war, when they were variously described by a litany of uncomplimentary terms, such as bad, dishonest, idle, absent, low-born, neglectful of discipline, negligent in their duty, and lacking spirit or honour. This was not a promising setting for the inculcation of basic military skills, such as instilling discipline, drilling for marching and battle, and learning the thirty-six evolutions needed by a pikeman, the thirty-two exercises of a matchlock musketeer, the twenty-seven of a fusilier or the forty-eight 'movements' of a grenadier. The formalized loading exercise for firearms was in part a safety measure to avoid accidents. Soldiers also needed to be able to recognize the words and drumbeats of command and know the proper responses to them.[47]

Most of the soldiers had never before owned or fired a musket. One solution was to set up training camps, with a programme of drilling, musketry, inspection and mock battles, an arrangement adopted both in France and England, and widely regarded as beneficial to the maintenance of an army's efficiency and readiness. Tyrconnell had formed such camps at the Curragh before the war. Wartime training camps were mooted as early as May 1689, with three initially planned, adjoined by magazines. But there were delays in their formation, despite French enthusiasm for the project. Timber and straw were gathered to make huts for the Dublin camp at Loughlinstown, south of the city, but its completion was deferred for a time, allegedly out of fears of disorder in the capital from the concentration of so many raw soldiers nearby.

47 *Stevens*, pp 64, 79, 92; *F-I corr.*, ii, p. 81; iii, p. 59.

TABLE 3 *The exercise of the musketeers**

flintlock	common	matchlock
	join your right hand to your musket	
	poise your musket	
	rest your musket	
	cock your musket	
		try your match
		blow your match
		cock and try your musket
guard your musket		guard your pan
		blow your match
	present	and open your pan
	fire	
	recover your arms	
half bend your musket		return your match
	clean your pan	
	handle your pricker	
	prime	
	shut your pan	
	blow off the loose corns	
	cast about to charge	
	handle your charge	
	open it with your teeth	
	charge with powder	
	draw forth your scourer	
	shorten it to an inch	
	charge it with bullet	
	ram down your powder and ball	
	withdraw/recover your scourer	
	shorten it to a handful	
	return your scourer	
	poise your musket	
	shoulder/order your musket.[48]	

Note
*The column on the left relates to the flintlock; that on the right to the matchlock; the centre column is common to both.

48 *Abridgement of English military discipline*, pp 11–12, 18–19.

Eventually in August, in face of the impending threat from Schomberg, the capable French officer, the marquis de Boisseleau, was brought up from the south, where he had already formed two small training camps in Cork, and was authorized to form the Louglinstown camp. By the end of the month, ten battalions were encamped there. About the same time the grand prior's regiment exercised at its own camp outside Drogheda. In France, weapons drill was normally done within companies and under the supervision of sergeants; probably the same practice applied in Ireland. The office of inspector general of infantry, successively held by the chevalier de Banqué and Colonel Edward Wilson, was intended to supervise weapons training and the standardization of drill. In France, inspectors were empowered to discharge old and unfit soldiers and veto subaltern or NCO appointments, but it is unlikely that in Ireland they could have challenged the colonels in this way. For want of muskets, much of the initial training was done with sticks. According to Stevens, when the soldiers came to handle a pike or a musket, they had to begin again. Where muskets were available, shortage of powder severely compromised practice firing, and soldiers often went into action without any musketry experience. Tyrconnell complained to Queen Mary in February 1690:

> How is it possible to make our foot fit for any service when we have not any ammunition to inure them to fire, two-thirds of our musketeers never having fired one shot because we have no powder to give them?

His concerns appear to have been borne out that same month by the Jacobite defeat at Cavan, when a volley from their musketeers 'scarce killed a man, for they shot over them', a typical error of untrained men. Just before the Boyne the grand prior's regiment spent two days 'teaching the men to fire, which many of them had never been accustomed to before'. The poor performance of the Irish infantry at Oldbridge may have been due, at least in part, to their inadequate musketry skills. A volley from the Irish infantry in Oldbridge village 'at something too great a distance' only caused two casualties to the Dutch guards, as they waded across the Boyne, and a little later the Danes reported that 'an enemy salvo ... did us no harm at all except that three men of the guards were wounded'. The training deficit of units equipped only with pointed sticks or shillelaghs was even more pronounced.[49]

It is noticeable that these criticisms lessened as the war went on. They were not, for example, repeated by Fumeron in his detailed factual reports of 1691.

---

49 Lynn, *Giant of the grand siècle*, pp 522–3; *Story*, pp 54, 80; *d'Avaux*, pp 140, 325–6, 387, 459, 470; *Stevens*, p. 63; 'Talbot letter-book', pp 110–11; *F-I corr.*, iii, pp 28, 63; *AH*, 21, p. 115; 'A journal of what has passed since his majesty's arrival' (Carte MS, 181), ff 37–8; Rowlands,

A training camp at Killaloe preceded the 1691 campaign. Fifteen battalions of foot were already there when Stevens's regiment arrived. At the exercises that followed he found 'our old men as imperfect, through the want of use as the new'. In the ensuing battle of Aughrim, the musket fire of 'the Irish slew numbers from their little old ditches', while a Williamite eyewitness referred to 'great firing on *both* sides', adding that 'exposed to the enemy's shot from the adjacent ditches, our men were forced to quit their ground'. While the training camps may have had an impact, probably the most significant factor in the improvement of infantry firepower was simply that the skills of officers and soldiers had grown with combat experience, and that by 1691 muskets and powder were more readily available than before.[50]

As well as individual training, soldiers needed to be prepared for the collective skills required of their unit: marching, camping, battlefield deployment and combat. On the march, the units of an army proceeded, where possible, in two or sometimes three columns, the station of each regiment corresponding to its position in the order of battle. On the battlefield it was customary for the most senior regiment to take the place of honour on the right of the front line, the second most senior on the left of that line, the third in seniority on the right of the second line and the fourth on the left of that line, leaving the more junior regiments in the centre. This was the order of battle of the Irish army in 1689. In 1690 the large Williamite army approached the Boyne in three lines. Generally marching columns were from eight to twenty files wide, necessitating movement 'over the green fields', which the widespread lack of enclosure in Ireland facilitated, although the uneven and watery nature of the countryside, coupled with the absence of any attempt to march in cadenced step, must have slowed progress and disrupted formation. Within each battalion, companies took their place according to the seniority of their commanders, but with the grenadiers in the van. Pikemen marched with their company. The same order was observed in camp, which was arrayed in two lines, divided by a 'street'. This marching and camping order was observed by the Jacobite army during the autumn campaign against Schomberg in 1689.[51]

Once on the battlefield, the columns swung into two lines to confront the enemy. The battalions were the tactical units, with under-strength battalions grouped together to maintain a minimum strength of 600 or so in combat situations. To form for battle, each battalion broke into its constituent parts. A standard formation was for the pikemen to unite in a solid phalanx, five or six

---

Dynastic state, p. 192.   50 Story, *Continuation*, pp 129–30; *JN*, p. 100; *Danish force*, p. 45; *Stevens*, pp 199–200; *F-I corr.*, ii, p. 331.   51 Childs, *Charles II*, p. 100; *Stevens*, pp 80–2; *F-I corr.*, iii, facing p. 49, pp 71–2; Story, p. 73.

ranks deep, at the centre of their battalion. The musketeers, likewise abandoning company formation, came together in two groups, again five or six ranks deep, which flanked the pikemen on either side. A French refinement was to position a quarter of the pikemen in the midst of each block of musketeers or on their flanks, leaving only half the pikemen in the middle. Both dispositions were intended to facilitate the pikemen's primary role, which was to ward off any threat from enemy cavalry by fanning out in front of the musketeers to present a hedge of spear points for their protection. The grenadier company retained its formation and guarded the right flank of the battalion. Ideally fusiliers guarded the left flank, but if the battalion had none, the grenadiers were divided between both flanks. The musketeers provided the firepower on which armies increasingly relied and which was maximized by the more linear deployments that had become the norm during the course of the seventeenth century. The musketeers were deployed five or six ranks deep, each rank two halberd lengths (four metres) apart. At the head of each file stood the best soldier in the file. A sergeant was posted at the flank end of each rank of musketeers, with the remaining sergeants forming a rank in the rear, presumably to discourage waverers from among the main body. Allowing an average shoulder width of each man to be half a metre, a 650-strong battalion, arrayed in six ranks spaced at the standard order of a metre apart, would have occupied a front of *circa* 150 metres, but less if its files were drawn up in close order of half a metre between each man, or more if drawn up in open order of two metres between each. Indeed, under artillery fire, to lessen casualties, a battalion could be drawn up at a distance of three metres between files. As the battalion went forward in battle formation, the officers divided up between the front and rear according to a set plan determined by rank and seniority. The colours were posted in the centre of the pikes. The officers marched in line until the battalion came within the range of the enemy. As the musketeers made ready, the officers in front then fell back towards the intervals between the files directly behind them. Their new position, 'neither without the battalion nor within it', cleared the field of fire for the musketeers, while allowing the officers to retain visibility right and left across the battalion's front rank. Initially the colonel on horseback led the battalion from the front, but before it engaged he dismounted to take up his position at the centre of the pikemen.[52]

Firing commenced when the battalion came to within thirty paces of the enemy. The inaccuracy of the musketeers' weapons, whether matchlocks or

---

52 Chandler, *Art of war*, p. 110; Lynn, *Giant of the grand siècle*, pp 479–80; *Abridgement of English military discipline*, pp 5–9, 143, 149–54; Faulkner, 'An Irish diary of 1689', p. 28.

fusils, meant that fire was most effective when discharged in repeated volleys. This was achieved by the front four or five ranks all kneeling, with only the rearmost rank standing to discharge their volley and commence reloading; then the rank in front of them would stand and fire and so on until all ranks had discharged their weapons. With the front four or five ranks kneeling once more, the whole process was repeated. This method of sustaining fire was developed in France and adopted in the 1685 version of the *Abridgement of English military discipline*, published in Dublin as well as London and republished in 1686. It replaced the earlier practice, whereby each rank stepped forward to fire and then withdrew through the other ranks to reload, a complex manoeuvre that was a recipe for confusion in open battle even in the best-drilled armies. However, the older practice, or a form of it, was possibly retained when a battalion lined breastworks, such as the Irish army utilized at Aughrim, or when it was defending fortifications as at Athlone and Limerick. Platoon firing, introduced to England by William's Dutch, put out a higher volume of fire per salvo than the older system, but the French influence would have ensured that it was not employed by the Jacobite musketeers, probably to their detriment in the preliminary infantry engagement at Oldbridge during the battle of the Boyne. Infantry engaged with their opponents largely by exchanging volleys of musket fire. Hand-to-hand combat was uncommon, except perhaps in the later stages of a battle. But it certainly occurred at Aughrim, when the Irish infantry counter-attacked in the centre 'making use of club musket ... [and] performed uncommon execution'.[53]

On the battlefield, an army as a whole was deployed in two lines, with a reserve to the rear. The *Abridgement* recommended a distance of 300 paces between the lines. The infantry was in the centre, flanked by the cavalry. The dragoons were posted on the extremities of each wing, or initially to skirmish in advance of the army. Of course, battlefield exigencies sometimes prevented this standard deployment or forced its adjustment. As the *Abridgement* put it: 'there can be no certain rules for any order of battle, which depend chiefly on the circumstances of place and other accidents that may happen'. Nevertheless, the standard deployment was broadly adopted by both armies in the three major field battles of the Irish war: Newtownbutler, the Boyne and Aughrim. Fifty to sixty metres was the recommended distance between the battalions in each line. It was best practice to post the battalions of the second line opposite the open spaces in the front line, which seems also to have been the case in Ireland, as suggested in the 1689 Jacobite order of battle and depicted in

[53] Lynn, *Giant of the grand siècle*, pp 485–6; Blackmore, 'British military firepower', pp 59–62 and chapter 3; Story, p. 26; *Abridgement of English military discipline*, p. 103; Story, *Continuation*, pp 129–30; *JN*, p. 141.

Story's plan of Aughrim (1691). The *Abridgement* also provided for battalions to form into defensive hollow or solid squares, where necessary. The purpose of drill was directly related to enabling an army, battalion by battalion, to undertake the battlefield formations, manoeuvres and combat operations described above, a process that would have been facilitated by exercises in the training camps of 1689 and 1691. However, their impact should not be overestimated: Louis XIV's military adviser, the marquis de Chamlay, considered that five or six years were necessary to create an infantry regiment. In any case, it was challenging for all but the most disciplined and experienced infantry to stand in formation or manoeuvre successfully on an open battlefield while subject to sustained enemy fire. The Irish infantry performed poorly in this respect at Newtownbutler, and during the battle of the Boyne it was ineffectual in challenging the Williamites on the open ground south of the river at Oldbridge. At Aughrim, on the other hand, where the musketeers had the protection of a great many small enclosures bounded by hedges and 'ditches' (in this case meaning low banks of earth or stone), the Irish infantry offered much more successful and determined resistance, for 'they naturally loved a breastwork between them and bullets'.[54]

Figure 5. Infantry officers

---

[54] Lynn, *Giant of the grand siècle*, 516; *Abridgement of English military discipline*, 154; *F-I corr.*, iii, facing p. 49; Story, *Continuation*, 122, facing p. 135.

CHAPTER 5

Cavalry and dragoons

Role and numbers

CAVALRY WERE SOLDIERS mounted and equipped for combat on horseback. Strictly speaking, in the late seventeenth century dragoons were infantry mounted on horseback for mobility, who dismounted for combat. This seems to have been the practice in the Irish Jacobite army, but already dragoons were also performing a number of cavalry roles that eventually were to make them indistinguishable from cavalry proper. Although the growth of firepower had somewhat circumscribed the role of mounted soldiers on the battlefield, their mobility ensured that they remained a vital component of every army. They guarded the train and infantry on the march, patrolled roads and countryside in the vicinity of the army's encampment, made foraging forays, and destroyed crops and shelter to deny them to an advancing enemy. They conducted reconnaissance, threatened their opponents' communications and engaged in ambushes and raids, such as Sarsfield's destruction of the Williamite siege train at Ballyneety in 1690. In battle, they were normally posted on the wings to protect the flanks of the infantry from the enemy horse. Outside the cavalry, at the extremity of each wing of the front line, or sometimes skirmishing in advance of the main body, were the dragoons. The Jacobite army's order of battle in 1689 followed the standard convention of deploying the cavalry on the wings of each of its three lines, with the dragoons at the extremities. In practice, this deployment, although probably in two lines, was used in the major field engagements of the Boyne and Aughrim. At both engagements the immediate cause of the Jacobite defeat was the penetration respectively of their army's right and left flanks by the Williamite cavalry. Where a defeated army broke and its formation collapsed, the opposing cavalry was particularly valuable in exploiting the victory by pursuing and harrying the fleeing soldiers. In this situation, the role of the defeated army's own cavalry was to defend its infantry against this pursuit, as Sarsfield and Galmoy tried to do with their regiments at Aughrim. At the Boyne, even the Williamites admitted that the Irish cavalry had performed extremely well. Dragoons used their mobility to counter advance parties of the enemy, harry the main body of the opposing field army, or skirmish on the fringes of their own. They also fought as infantry in the defence of fortresses. The maintenance of mounted regiments presented particular logistical challenges in terms of securing horses, finding stabling and procuring feed. The immense forage requirements of the cavalry horses, together with those of the train and infantry officers, determined the length of an army's stay in a locality. An inspector, apparently equivalent to that in the infantry, reviewed the condition of cavalry and dragoons in June 1690.[1]

In the late seventeenth century, the mounted troops of most armies formed a quarter to a third of their numerical strength. The 2,317 officers and other ranks of mounted regiments of the Irish peacetime army formed a quarter of its establishment, a proportion that was replicated in King William's army in Ireland in 1690. On his arrival in 1689, King James sought an army of 41,400, of which the mounted element was to be 6,400 or just over 15 per cent of the total. At an autumn review that year, when army strength was well below James's earlier ideal, the cavalry and dragoons formed 18.5 per cent of the army. By 1691 that proportion had risen only slightly to 20 per cent.[2]

The cavalry regiments

The pre-war Irish army comprised three cavalry regiments (not including the single dragoon regiment) together with a troop of mounted grenadiers. In late 1688 the regiments respectively were commanded by Tyrconnell himself, Viscount Galmoy and the German mercenary, Theodore Russell. As in the infantry, cavalry regiments took the name of their colonel, changing it when he changed. On Patrick Sarsfield's return to Ireland with King James, he was made colonel of the regiment commanded by Russell, who then defected to the Williamites. Tyrconnell and Galmoy retained their commands. In 1689 four new cavalry regiments were raised, commanded respectively by John Parker, Hugh Sutherland, the earl of Abercorn and Henry Luttrell. A troop of horseguards, commanded by Lord Dover, was also added to the army.

TABLE 4 *The cavalry establishment, 1689**

Tyrconnell	Galmoy	Sarsfield
Parker	Sutherland	Abercorn
Luttrell	1 horseguard troop	1 mounted-grenadier troop.[3]

Note
* The new regiments are listed under the names of their original colonels; the old regiments are listed under the names of their colonels in 1689.

1 Chandler, *Art of war*, p. 27; Childs, *Warfare*, pp 155–8; *Danish force*, p. 43; *Stevens*, p. 178; Story, *Continuation*, p. 102; *F-I corr.*, i, p. 421; iii, facing p. 49.   2 Chandler, *Art of war*, pp 29–30; Lynn, *Giant of the grand siècle*, p. 528; *CTB*, pp 1742–6; Story, p. 97; *F-I corr.*, ii, pp 213, 336–7; iii, pp 91–2, 182–3; *Ormonde MSS*, i, p. 447.   3 *CTB*, pp 1742–6; Wauchope, *Sarsfield*, p. 49; Officer

For the 1690 campaign, the dragoon regiment of Nicholas Purcell converted into a six-troop cavalry regiment. A second troop of horseguards was also raised in 1690, and its command was given to James's illegitimate son, the duke of Berwick. With the addition of the mounted grenadiers, the two horseguard troops equated numerically to a regiment, so that the total number of cavalry regiments in 1690 can be put at nine. In 1691 it was increased to eleven by the addition of the regiments of Charles O'Brien and Viscount Merrion. O'Brien's had been the dragoon regiment of his elder brother, Daniel O'Brien, until he went to France with the Mountcashel Brigade. Their father, Viscount Clare, then commanded the regiment until his death in late 1690. Under his younger son, Charles O'Brien, it converted to a cavalry regiment in March 1691. Merrion's was a new unit, first mentioned in early 1691. It was listed as part of Balldearg O'Donnell's auxiliary army in the summer, and included with the rest of the cavalry in an August return. Prior to then, O'Donnell's cavalry strength was limited to Conor O'Connor's single troop 'in a very bad state'. Early in 1691 the young earl of Westmeath, formerly commander of an infantry regiment, took over from the Englishman John Parker, who had been wounded at the Boyne, although mention of two colonels in the regiment after Aughrim suggests that Parker may have been retained in a supernumerary role. Sarsfield's transfer to succeed Lord Dover in command of the 1st troop of horseguards opened the way for his brother-in-law, Viscount Kilmallock, formerly an infantry colonel, to secure the colonelcy of his cavalry regiment prior to the 1691 campaign. Thus, only two of the cavalry regiments changed colonels during the war, together with one of the horseguard troops. In 1689 a short-lived independent troop of horse called Grace's is mentioned, together with another independent cavalry troop in Limerick. The independent unit commanded in early 1690 by Charles White of Leixlip, a cavalry officer, may also have been a cavalry troop.[4]

Regimental organization and personnel of the cavalry

The administrative unit of a cavalry regiment was the troop, which corresponded to the infantry company. By 1689 the three original regiments, who had lost their dragoon troops to the new dragoon regiment in 1685, had been restored to nine-troop strength, and indeed Tyrconnell's was briefly increased to ten. Initially the four new regiments had only six troops, although in some cases this number was subsequently increased. In 1690 Parker's

list (Bodl., Carte MS 181), ff 1–7, 11; *F-I corr.*, i, pp 237–40.   **4** *F-I corr.*, i, pp 237–40, 257; ii, pp 222, 249, 338, 389; iii, pp 61–2, 179, 198, 216; Story, p. 97; TCD MS 670, ff 1, 8.

regiment comprised eight troops, although only 300 strong. In the Boyne campaign the two horseguard troops each numbered '200 private gentlemen' plus a score of officers. By June 1691 five regiments were comprised of nine troops, while Kilmallock's appears to have been increased to twelve, whereas four – Sutherland's, Abercorn's, O'Brien's and Merrion's – remained at six-troop strength. There were still also two troops of horseguards and the mounted grenadiers. In 1689 the establishment strength of a cavalry troop increased to fifty troopers from the pre-war figure of forty-five. On this basis the sixty troops listed in September 1689 should have numbered 3,000, whereas in fact they were returned at 1,832, an average of thirty troopers per troop. However, by then the three pre-war regiments had suffered considerable attrition, having campaigned in the north for almost five months throughout the summer. A return from the following month gives 1,949 troopers, of whom 1,664 were mounted, together with 227 officers and 43 trumpeters. For 1690 there is little statistical information, beyond Berwick's statement that the horse numbered 3,500. Parker's horse averaged thirty-seven per troop that year.[5]

Berwick was hopeful of having 6,000 horse and dragoons in the field in 1691. In March of that year Fumeron's projected strength of the cavalry for the coming campaign was 3,000, an average of just over forty per troop. The figure does not include Merrion's regiment of six troops reported 'in a very bad state', which probably added another 300 or more to the total. (In August Merrion's mustered 315 all ranks.) However, by June Fumeron estimated that the seventy-two troops of cavalry would number 3,600 – fifty per troop – to which could be added the 300 personnel of the horseguards and Merrion's men. This would have brought cavalry numbers for the final campaign to well over 4,000, assuming, as Fumeron did, that all troops were at full strength. The August return of 3,697 that was well into the vicissitudes of the summer campaign suggests that the figure of 4,000 or more for the cavalry strength at its outset may be close to the truth. To this total can be added over 300 commissioned officers. Thus in 1691, the final year of the war, the cavalry appears to have achieved its greatest numerical strength, perhaps because of the faith placed in it after its achievements at the Boyne and Ballyneety the previous year. In the general *levée* after Aughrim, a deserter told the Williamites, possibly with some exaggeration, that 2,000 new-raised men had joined the army's mounted corps.[6]

---

5 *D'Avaux*, pp 125–6; *Story*, p. 97; *F-I corr.*, iii, pp 61, 92, 179; *Stevens*, pp 111, 214; 'Journal 19/5 to 18/6 1689' (Carte MS 181), ff 67, 68; Berwick, *Memoirs*, i, p. 69.   6 *Finch MSS*, ii, p. 480; *F-I corr.*, ii, pp 336–8, 391, 405–6, 459; iii, p. 216; Clarke corr., no. 995.

Each troop had four commissioned officers: a captain, a lieutenant, a cornet and a quartermaster. All three regimental field officers, the colonel, lieutenant colonel and major, were also troop commanders. In addition to the field officers, the regimental staff comprised the adjutant, chaplain, surgeon and regimental quartermaster. The extant evidence, omitting the regiments that converted from dragoon units, suggests that in round terms about three-quarters of the cavalry officers on the establishment in 1689–90 were Irish, and the remainder English and French, the latter numbering only eighteen, which was 7 per cent of the total. About 9 per cent of the officers had experienced military service on the Continent, 14 per cent had served in England and a further 10 per cent in the pre-war Irish army. This suggests that almost two-thirds were new to military life. They were mainly Irish, but mostly of Old English ancestry (less than 20 per cent had Gaelic names), and they held the lower-ranking appointments. The senior cavalry officers were generally of high quality. Many of the field officers possessed continental or English experience. This was true of most of the colonels: Berwick, Dover, Sarsfield, Abercorn, Kilmallock, Henry Luttrell, Parker, Sutherland and the *de facto* commander of Tyrconnel's regiment, Dominic Sheldon. Lieutenant colonels with continental experience included Lawrence Dempsey of Galmoy's and Edmund Prendergast of Sutherland's, together with several majors, such as Roger McGilligan of Sarsfield's, and Charles MacDonnell of Purcell's. Galmoy, who had not served outside Ireland, proved an able commander, but initially could rely on the support of Dempsey, his veteran lieutenant colonel. Westmeath and O'Brien were young aristocrats, who had two years' experience of regimental command in the infantry before joining the cavalry. Two cavalry regiments had French lieutenant colonels and majors, generally sharing their rank with an Irish counterpart. More than half of Parker's officers were English, of whom most had held pre-war commissions in England. In general, this weight of military experience gave the cavalry a degree of professionalism in the first years of the war that was lacking in the infantry, and they were the corps of the Irish army most respected by their Williamite opponents.[7]

The role of the different commissioned ranks was similar to their infantry counterparts. The captain led the troop from the front both on the march and in battle, with the cornet at his side, while the lieutenant brought up the rear. However, because of the importance of billeting, including finding stabling and feed for the horses, and ensuring that they were shod and in good condition, each troop had its own quartermaster. This was in addition to the

---

7 *D'Avaux*, pp 125–6; Childs, *BD*, passim; Dalton, ii, passim; TCD MS 670, ff 1–7; *A particular and full account of ... Aghrim*, p. 3; Bodl., Carte MS 181, ff 1–7; BL, Add. MS 9763, ff 35–43.

regimental quartermaster, who presumably oversaw all. According to a contemporary authority, a quartermaster 'ought to know to read, write and cast account ... for he ought to keep the roll of all the troopers'. His duties included regular inspection of horses, arms and accoutrements. Some of the cavalry and dragoon quartermasters had a mercantile background or can be identified as men of business. The cavalry equivalent of the ensign was the cornet, whose role was to carry the troop standard. This was an embroidered rectangular flag, mounted on a lance that identified the troop and acted as a focus for it to re-group around its commander. No record of any Irish standard survives, but it is likely that the design of the horseguard troop standards would have followed their English counterparts: a crimson background, emblazoned with two silver angels sustaining a gold crown surmounting the royal cypher *JR*, with the royal motto *Dieu et mon droit* and three small crowns beneath it. In England, uniquely among the cavalry, the horseguard troops also carried a swallow-tailed guidon, but it is not known if this practice was followed in Ireland. Cavalry regiments were frequently dispersed in individual troops, each of which seems to have retained its own standard, which probably explains the capture of as many as eleven standards at Aughrim, where much of the cavalry was not heavily engaged. The colour of the mounted grenadiers was most likely a guidon, which was the case in England. Some cavalry and dragoon regiments had two chaplains, or even three as in the case of Tyrconnell's in 1689. Virtually all included a number of *reformé* (supernumerary) officers, French and Irish.[8]

The other ranks in a cavalry troop comprised three corporals, a trumpeter and an establishment of fifty troopers. The trumpeter was the cavalry equivalent of the infantry drummer. Primarily his role was to sound commands and signals to the troop, that were audible above the din of battle or in situations where its personnel were dispersed, but he also communicated with the enemy on such matters as a summons to surrender or an offer to negotiate. King James, for example, in 1689 sent a trumpeter to summon Derry to surrender. The trumpet of the time was a brass tube *c.*750mm long. Lacking keys or valves, it depended on the player's embouchure to vary its sounds and form its calls. It was the common practice in England and France to embellish trumpets with a decorative banner, and it is likely that this was also adopted in Ireland. The status of the trumpeters is indicated by the fact that their pay was the same as that of cavalry corporals and more than double that of an infantry

---

[8] *Military duties of officers of cavalry*, pp 36–42; Lawson, *Uniforms*, p. 149 *et seq.*; *Ormonde MSS*, n.s., viii, p. 15; Harris, appendix, p. ix; Officer list (Bodl., Carte MS 181), ff 1, 2, 6; BL, Add. MS 9763, f. 42.

drummer. In the colonel's troop of the three original cavalry regiments, a kettledrummer replaced a trumpeter. Kettledrums were copper bowls with a drumhead of animal skin. Adorned with banners, they were slung in pairs immediately in front of the saddle on either side of the drummer's horse. Whether kettledrums formed part of the equipment of the new regiments is unknown, but if so, the horseguard troops were the most likely candidates. The Irish cavalry was reported to have ridden into Dublin after the Boyne, defiantly sounding kettledrums and trumpets. Among the booty captured by the Williamites at Aughrim was a kettledrum. Surprisingly, the only reference to farriers is in a French report of 1689 which stated that carts were necessary to transport them. A farrier to accompany each troop was mentioned in James II's Scottish army in 1685. In Ireland, selected troopers with appropriate skills may have fulfilled the role as, without doubt, the provision of shoeing, teeth-filing, hair-clipping and veterinary services for as many as sixty horses was a demanding necessity to sustain a troop's combat readiness. The desirability of troopers to possess riding skills, together with expertise in horse care and management, and, if possible, to supply their own horse, probably meant that the rank and file of the cavalry were largely recruited from the stronger-farmer class. General Léry-Girardin noted that in contrast to other regiments, Galmoy's and Tyrconnell's horse were actively recruiting in the autumn of 1689. In January 1691 the cavalry was reported to be recruiting actively for the coming summer campaign.[9]

Horseguards and mounted grenadiers

The two troops of horseguards, with the mounted grenadiers, equated numerically to another cavalry regiment. The first troop was formed in 1689, shortly after King James's arrival in Ireland. A special unit or units to guard the king's person was a common concept at the time. Louis XIV, for example, had the *maison militaire du roi*, a mixture of cavalry, infantry and horse grenadiers. In England, the horseguards had evolved from a group of gentlemen formed to protect the king's person during the civil war to become a unit of the establishment there in 1661. The Irish restoration army's equivalent unit was abolished in 1685 to help fund the formation of its new dragoon regiment. The horseguard troop of 1689 was therefore a new unit, but modelled on its English counterpart, and commanded by Lord Dover, an English aristocrat who had accompanied James to Ireland, but who had formerly commanded

---

9 *D'Avaux*, pp 125–6, 711; *CTB*, pp 1742–6; *James II*, p. 333; *A true and perfect journal*, p. 7; Le Fleming MSS, 327; Lawson, *Uniforms*, p. 92; *F-I corr.*, iii, pp 66, 212.

the 4th troop of horseguards in England, where Patrick Sarsfield had been his lieutenant. In 1691 Sarsfield succeeded Dover in command of the 1st troop of Irish horseguards, suggesting an element of continuity with the original English troop. A second troop 'in all respects answerable to the first' was added at the start of 1690 with the duke of Berwick as commander. The horseguard troops were different in structure to the regular cavalry. The establishment in each comprised a captain (who ranked as a colonel), two lieutenants (lieutenant colonels), a cornet (major), a guidon (major), four exempts/exangs (a rank peculiar to horseguards, but effectively captains), eight brigadiers (lieutenants) and eight sub-brigadiers (cornets), together with 200 gentlemen 'troopers'. By 1691 the number of troopers had dropped to 150. Four 'staff' were listed: presumably they comprised each troop's quartermaster, chaplain, surgeon and adjutant. At the Boyne, the horseguards fought with 'unspeakable bravery'. Although the names of some individuals are known, no full list of horseguard officers or personnel during their time in Ireland is extant. According to d'Usson and de Tessé, the unit was filled with many good men who had served in England. A third of Sarsfield's troop, presumably Irishmen, were dissuaded from going to France, but 150 horseguards sailed in December 1691. A list of the two troops re-formed there seems to contradict the French generals' assertion that they were comprised of Englishmen. Sarsfield's troop certainly was, but two-thirds of Berwick's personnel had Irish names, including about a fifth that were Gaelic in origin. The single troop of mounted grenadiers, extant since 1684, was attached to the horseguards. Mounted grenadiers carried hand grenades in addition to their other weapons. They were classed as dragoons, as they would normally have dismounted to ignite and throw their grenades. Their troop commander in 1689 was Piers Butler, brother and successor to the unit's former commander, Lord Ikerrin, who had died at the end of 1688. The pre-war establishment comprised the captain, a lieutenant, a cornet, two sergeants, three corporals, two drummers and two hautboys (oboists), and fifty private soldiers. Fumeron listed it with the horseguards in September 1689, and subsequently it was mentioned in a Jacobite pamphlet as being with King James's forces at Ardee, after which its winter quarters were in Dublin. Thereafter, apart from a single and unreliable listing in August 1691, the mounted grenadiers were absent from Irish wartime army lists, although a Williamite source listed the unit in April 1690.[10]

10 Rowlands, *Dynastic state*, pp 346–7; Childs, *Charles II*, p 16; Dalton, ii, pp 75, 118; *F-I corr.*, i, pp 238, 453; ii, pp 450, 459, 520–1; iii, pp 63, 198, 218; *Stevens*, p. 214; List of 1st horseguards (SHAD, AG, A1 1241), f. 112; List of 2nd horseguards (BS-G, MS 3537), ff 58–61; *CTB*, p. 1744; *A journal of the most remarkable occurrences*, p. 6; Story, p. 97; Clarke corr., no. 995.

'The priding cavalry'

The traditional social eminence of the cavalry meant that its officers tended to be drawn from the upper ranks of society. In the wartime army more than half the colonels were peers or their sons. The junior officers came frequently from the Jacobite elite or their kinsmen. Six were impecunious peers, and there was a handful of baronets and knights. As in the infantry, peacetime cavalry commissions were generally purchased at considerable cost – £800 for an Irish lieutenancy and twice that for a captaincy – but this was probably cheaper than in England. In any case, a commission was an investment that could be resold provided the holder did not die in service. Presumably this practice continued in wartime, although probably in a very depressed market due to the large number of new commissions that were being issued. The sense of superiority enjoyed by 'the priding cavalry' extended to the rank and file, who were expected to supply their own horses and accoutrements, although these could also be paid for out of regimental funds that were reimbursed by deductions from the individual trooper's pay. Certainly, at the end of the war most of the cavalrymen and dragoons went home with their mounts, implying an assumption of proprietorship. The three original cavalry regiments had impressed even Clarendon, who rated them 'as adroit in their exercise as any men could be' and 'generally better mounted than the light horse in England'. King James rated the Irish cavalry 'extreme good' and in September 1689 d'Avaux declared:

> One may be confident in the cavalry, which for the most part is good enough; one could not see a better regiment than Tyrconnell's and Galmoy's. Parker's, which is newly formed, is also good. Colonel Sarsfield is at the head of some good enough cavalry.

The other regiments, he reported, were less satisfactory, but they of course were new. Fumeron observed that one of the old regiments was very fine, both as regards men and horses, later praising the excellence of both Galmoy's and Tyrconnell's. On the other hand, he rated Purcell's worthless as a dragoon unit and doubted that it would be any better as cavalry. Stevens regarded the cavalry as the best part of the army, being 'for the most part good men, well-armed and mounted, but their number not very great', while an Irish view was that some of their horse 'might vie with the best in Europe'. Famechon, who was generally critical of the Irish army, praised some cavalry regiments as very fine and smart.[11]

11 *CSPD 1686–7*, p. 215; *Clarendon*, i, pp 436–7, 499–500; *James II*, ii, p. 457; *d'Avaux*, pp 464,

The cavalry did not disappoint its admirers. In 1689 the old regiments did well at Dromore and Cladyford, although the cavalry – possibly Abercorn's new regiment – performed badly at Newtownbutler. In 1690 the cavalry gave a very good account of themselves at the Boyne and in the Ballyneety raid. Their heavy casualties that year, especially at the Boyne, may have reduced their effectiveness in 1691. At the Boyne, for example, Tyrconnell's and Parker's suffered the most, only thirty of the latter's troopers remaining unscathed. Fumeron found the cavalry in poor condition in early 1691: clothing, arms and boots were all needed, and he thought it would be difficult to make up the shortage of 1,400 troopers and their horses, although this was in fact achieved. Kilmallock experienced considerable difficulty in equipping three new troops that were added to his cavalry regiment for the final campaign. But by then the morale of the cavalry had declined. They came mainly from the part of Ireland occupied by the Williamites. Their will to continue resistance after the fall of Athlone was probably further weakened by the well-timed publication of a Williamite proclamation promising their estates to officers who submitted within three weeks. Soon afterwards at Aughrim, the withdrawal of the cavalry on the army's left wing, under Sheldon and Henry Luttrell, exposed the infantry to massacre and was a major factor in the heavy Irish defeat. Possibly their failure to engage the enemy was because they awaited orders from Saint-Ruth, but this was little excuse for their conduct. However, the right wing fought well early in the battle, and in the final stage Sarsfield and Galmoy did what they could to cover the retreat. To a considerable degree Ginkel's strategy in 1691 was dictated by his fear that the Irish cavalry would debouch against his lines of communication. Before Aughrim, Saint-Ruth was reported to have had such a move in contemplation, which Tyrconnell by then also advocated in contrast to his earlier negative reaction when Berwick had suggested it in 1690.[12]

The dragoon regiments

Dragoon regiments had been employed in the thirty years war, during which, for example, the assassins of the great Wallenstein were drawn from the Irish imperial dragoon regiment of Colonel Walter Butler. The term 'dragoon' emanated from their early weapon, the *dragon*, which was a type of blunderbuss. In 1635 dragoons were introduced in France. In England, a

468; *AH*, 21, p. 128, 149; *F-I corr.*, i, p. 257; ii, pp 522, 526; iii, pp 132–3; *JN*, p. 47; *Stevens*, p. 79; *Clarendon*, ii, p. 17. **12** *D'Avaux*, p. 385; Simms, 'Sarsfield of Kilmallock', pp 209–10; *James II*, ii, pp 399–400; *F-I corr.*, ii, pp 213–14; Simms, *Jacobite Ireland*, pp 97–8, 225–6; Account of Aughrim (Westminster Diocesan Archives, B6 258); Lenihan, *Last cavalier*, p. 172.

dragoon regiment formed part of parliament's New Model army from its creation in 1645. Later, James II's English army included three dragoon regiments. In Ireland the dragoon troops attached to the three cavalry regiments helped to form Richard Hamilton's new dragoon regiment in 1685, but the unit's loss in England during the revolution meant that the wartime dragoon regiments in the Irish army were all new. In 1689 d'Avaux originally planned for seven regiments of dragoons, but by August their number had grown to eight. They took their names from their colonels, as was customary.

TABLE 5 *The dragoon establishment, 1689**

| Clifford | O'Neill | Cotter | Purcell |
| O'Brien | Luttrell | Dungan | Maxwell |

Note
* The regiments are listed under the names of their original colonels.

Three of the colonels, Robert Clifford, Walter Lord Dungan and Sir James Cotter, were Irish professional soldiers who had overseas experience, as had the Scot, Thomas Maxwell. Cotter in fact had taken over from Thomas Trant, who had briefly commanded the regiment when it was first raised and was a son of the wealthy Jacobite, Sir Patrick Trant. Neil O'Neill, Nicholas Purcell and Simon Luttrell were substantial Irish Catholic landowners, while Daniel O'Brien was the eldest son of Lord Clare, another continental veteran, who had actually raised the regiment.[13]

There were several changes in 1690. The conversion of Purcell's regiment to cavalry reduced the number of dragoon regiments to seven, which remained the establishment number thereafter. Francis Carroll, another continental veteran, replaced Cotter. Daniel O'Brien's regiment reverted to his father, Lord Clare. On the latter's death in November 1690, his younger son, Charles O'Brien, succeeded to its command. When O'Neill and Dungan were killed at the Boyne, their regiments went respectively to O'Neill's brother, Sir Daniel O'Neill, and to Walter Nugent, an Irish officer who was a first cousin of Dungan. Nugent was killed at Aughrim, after which Captain Richard Bellew, later 3rd Baron Bellew of Duleek, seems to have commanded this regiment through the final months of the war, although he is not recorded as holding the rank of colonel. In 1691 the O'Brien regiment converted to cavalry and

---

13 Wilson, *Europe's tragedy*, pp 538–40; Lynn, *Giant of the grand siècle*, p. 494; Childs, *James II*, p. xi; *Ormonde MSS*, i, pp 400, 422; *d'Avaux*, pp 126–7, 452–4; TCD MS 670, f. 14; *F-I corr.*, i, pp 237–40; iii, p. 91.

was replaced by a new dragoon regiment, raised by Edmund O'Reilly. As O'Reilly was also colonel of an infantry regiment, *de facto* command of the dragoon unit may have been exercised by Owen/John O'Reilly, who was ranked lieutenant colonel after the war. Although Maxwell was captured at the siege of Athlone, his regiment appears to have retained his name, but in practice Daniel Magennis, its lieutenant colonel, must have commanded it thereafter. Clifford presumably forfeited command of his regiment when he was arrested on suspicion of treachery during the 1691 siege of Limerick. In all, six of the dragoon regiments lost their colonels during the war: killed, captured or replaced. There is an isolated reference to an independent dragoon troop, probably short-lived, raised by Colonel Hugh MacMahon in 1690.[14]

Regimental organization and personnel of the dragoons

The regimental organization of the dragoons fell between that of infantry and cavalry, a reflection of their hybrid character as mounted infantry. Each regiment consisted of ten or twelve companies, resembling the infantry in both number and nomenclature (although they were sometimes called troops). The company establishment provided for four commissioned officers: a captain, a lieutenant, a cornet and a quartermaster, the latter two ranks being peculiar to cavalry. The role of the cornet was to carry his unit's guidon, the swallow-tailed dragoon colour of the period. Although it is very likely that the Irish dragoons carried guidons, there is no specific reference to them. In England each dragoon troop/company had its own guidon, but it is not known whether this was the practice with the new wartime regiments in Ireland. Assuming their use, it is possible to speculate that their design may have resembled that of their English counterparts, which consisted of the royal cypher *JR* above a crown embroidered in gold, all on a crimson background, with perhaps an additional device to distinguish the particular unit. The other ranks comprised fifty dragoons, three corporals, two sergeants and two drummers. Sergeants and drummers were infantry ranks. It is likely that the second drummer was in fact a hautboy, whose role was to sound a primitive oboe of the same name. This instrument was particularly associated with dragoons and mounted grenadiers. It was introduced to Britain from France in 1678, and the pre-war Irish army included two hautboys, as well as two drummers per troop in the dragoon establishment. The clear, piercing sound of the hautboy was both audible and distinctive for the communication of signals on the battlefield. A

14 *F-I corr.*, i, pp 237–40, 257; ii, pp 208, 223, 249, 337, 376, 405, 510; iii, pp 212–13, 216; *PI*, i, p. 220; Officer list (Bodl., Carte MS 181), f. 14; *KJIL*, i, p. 296; *JN*, pp 102–3; *AH*, 22, p. 102; Hopkins, *Glencoe*, p. 212; *A particular and full account of ... Aghrim*, p. 4.

drum, however small, must have been awkward to manage on horseback. Hautboys, presumably of the dragoons, were among the instruments reportedly played by the Irish mounted troops when they rode into Dublin 'in very good order' after the Boyne defeat. The eight dragoon regiments of 1689 totalled eighty-one companies. A return of August that year showed them with a total strength of 2,485 men, or just over thirty per company, which was well short of the establishment figure of fifty. Stevens's description of 'Brigadier Maxwell's dragoons ... making up twelve complete troops [*sic*] and near 600 men, well accoutred and disciplined' suggests an improvement in 1690. Dungan's regiment, he reported as 400 strong in eight troops of 50 men. There is no further information for that year. At the start of the 1691 campaign, the dragoon regiments appear to have been up to full strength. The seven regiments comprised seventy-four companies at establishment strength, totalling 3,700 men plus approximately 300 officers. In August, after Aughrim, the dragoons mustered 2,679 officers and men.[15]

The regimental staff comprised colonel, lieutenant colonel and major, together with chaplain, adjutant, surgeon and regimental quartermaster. Service in the dragoons was not as prestigious as the cavalry, but more so than an infantry appointment, and this was reflected in the rates of pay. Military professionals were well represented in the higher commissioned ranks. Five of the colonels had served abroad, as had Major Conly Geoghegan of Dungan's. Lieutenant Colonel Alexander Mackenzie of Clifford's was a Tangier veteran. Four regiments had French lieutenant colonels. In all, only 10 per cent of the total dragoon officer corps are known to have had pre-war military experience, in either Ireland, England or on the Continent. Seven peers or their sons are listed as officers, with a similar number of baronets and knights. Dungan complained that his officers were awkward and ignorant, alleging that men of service, such as Toby Byrne who had served in Hamilton's regiment, were passed over 'to make room for some young country schoolboy', adding 'I have some lieutenants that are not worth one pin'. However, officers who were veterans of the Hamilton/Butler dragoon regiment and who had managed to escape from England after its demise were generally re-employed. As in the cavalry, those most suited to be dragoon troopers were likely to have possessed riding and horse-care skills.[16]

The officer lists suggest that the dragoon regiments, like the infantry, had a strong regional flavour. Most of the company commanders in the O'Brien

---

15 *D'Avaux*, pp 123–8; Haynes, *History of the hautboy*, pp 148, 161; *CTB*, p. 1746; *A true and perfect journal*, p. 7; Lawson, *Uniforms*, pp 106, 149 *et seq.*; *F-I corr.*, ii, pp 337–40, 405; iii, pp 63, 181; Stevens, pp 115, 214.   **16** *D'Avaux*, p. 127; Macpherson, *Original papers*, i, p. 309; Childs, *BD*, passim; Dalton, i, p. 191; Tyrconnell letters, no. 72.

regiment, for example, were from County Clare, except for the Knight of Kerry and Roger O'Shaughnessy of Gort, who were from neighbouring counties, but were both kinsmen of the colonel. Many of the regiment's subalterns appear to have been small Catholic landowners, although Florence MacNamara was a chancery barrister and James MacDonnell was Lord Clare's attorney. The junior officers for the most part bore other well-known Clare names, such as Neylan, Lysaght and Hurley, or names associated with the adjoining counties. Other dragoon regiments presented a similar picture: Clifford's was linked to the midlands; Dungan's and Luttrell's to east Leinster; Cotter's to Cork and its neighbouring counties; Purcell's to Tipperary and Kilkenny; Maxwell's to east Ulster; and O'Neill's largely to Leinster, but with some Ulster input also. All four known officers in O'Reilly's bore the same surname as their colonel. At least two quartermasters were former merchants, and it is likely that several of the rest were also men of business. Irishmen comprised 95 per cent of the dragoon officers, with English and a handful of French forming only 5 per cent of the total. The surnames of just over 40 per cent were of Gaelic origin, which was more than twice that of the cavalry. The bond between officers and other ranks was close: on the death of their captain during the siege of Derry, twenty-five of Sir Neil O'Neill's regiment deserted with their horses. The rest of the company also sought to go home, claiming that their engagement was to their captain alone. The high command rejected their contention, and they were forced to cast lots to select one of them to be shot.[17]

Clothing, equipment and weaponry

Cavalrymen wore wide-brimmed hats, cravats, coats, shirts and waistcoats similar to infantry, with different coloured facings distinguishing each regiment. In most respects the dragoons were similarly apparelled, except that they are likely to have worn grenadier caps like their English and French counterparts to better facilitate the slinging of their muskets over their shoulders. Similar caps were probably worn by the mounted grenadiers, as was the case in England. The leather coats of the mid-century wars had given away to woollen cloth, usually dyed red, the colour Ormond's horse was required to adopt in 1686, when it was found to be clothed in buff. The facings of his regiment's new coats were blue. It was the unit later commanded by Sarsfield.

17 Bodl., Carte MS 181, ff 8–18 and passim; *KJIL*, i, p. 368; *AH*, 21, p. 189; *PI*, ii, p. 33; *BPB 1988*, i, p. 1436; TCD MS 670, ff 9–14 and passim; *JN*, pp 233–9; Maynard, 'Legal profession', p. 37; 'Survey of Catholic estates', pp 126–7; information on MacDonnell from M. Haugh.

In 1690 the Williamites encountered an Irish cavalry regiment 'of red lined with white'. However, certainly up to 1688 Galmoy's troopers were wearing light grey coats, lined red. Red was probably also the preferred colour of dragoon coats, but Clare's regiment was nicknamed the Yellow Dragoons, most likely because its coats were of yellow cloth, or perhaps leather, although possibly the sobriquet may have referred to its facings. Presumably in 1691 both cavalry and dragoons were clothed with the grey coats that came from France. Cavalry and dragoon coats were wide-skirted, pleated garments to facilitate the needs of the mounted soldier. They were without collars, and a stock, sometimes referred to as a cravat, was worn around the throat not only as a protection against inclement weather but as a safety measure to stiffen support for the rider's neck in the event of a fall. Stocks could also be used as temporary bandages for rider or horse. They were secured in place by a pin; among the items Kilmallock sought for his regiment in 1691 were 600 stockpins. Leather was retained for cavalry waistcoats, certainly in France and the Netherlands, and possibly in Ireland and England too. As in France and England, officers tended to dress extravagantly, their hats adorned with feathers and their coats embellished with gold buttons and lace. Many would have worn shoulder-length wigs. In 1688 Galmoy's troopers wore 'black hats, laced galloon' (decorative woven gold or silver braid). Each trooper had a cloak, which was carried rolled up and attached to his saddle with straps.[18]

A distinguishing feature of cavalrymen was their massive, heavy leather boots, worn as a leg protection against crushing in impacts or hostile weapon thrusts. Wide bucket tops that provided protection above the knee could be turned down when they dismounted. High heels helped secure the rider's feet in his stirrups. Such boots were not easy to walk in, and in 1691 Kilmallock sought 500 pairs of shoes, in addition to boots, for his regiment. Dragoon boots, costing far less, were shorter and made of lighter, more pliable leather to facilitate movement on foot. Spurs, secured by broad 'butterfly' spur leathers, were generally of the rowel type, with a toothed wheel at the end. In contemporary portraiture, it was conventional for officers to be depicted in full body armour, but in practice, this was no longer much worn on the battlefield, except by east-European heavy cavalry. Lobster-pot helmets seem largely to have fallen out of use. In combat, cavalrymen commonly wore a 'skull', which was an iron cap beneath their hats that provided head protection against sword cuts. Until 1697 English cavalry wore cuirasses, which were iron breast and

18 *LG*, 24–27 September 1688; Lawson, *Uniforms*, pp 83–112; Chartrand, *Louis XIV's army*, pp 35, 37; d'Avaux, p. 211; *DI*, no. 14, 22–30 December 1690; *Ormonde MSS*, n.s., vii, pp 451, 480; Stevens, p. 129.

back plates to protect the torso. In Ireland, while they may have been available to the older regiments, the horseguards were the only cavalrymen known to have worn them, and their cuirasses were reported to have protected them well at Aughrim. These may have come from the Limerick stores, where 260 serviceable cuirasses were held at the end of 1689. Custume's party of dragoons wore body armour when demolishing the works on the bridge of Athlone, probably only issued to them because of the operation's hazards. However, it is significant that such protection was available, when required.[19]

The Irish cavalry was in French terminology *cavalerie légère*, or light cavalry. In 1688 Galmoy's regiment was recorded as being armed with swords, carbines and pistols, and this appears to have remained the standard for the war. Thus, in May 1689 carbines, cases of pistols, sabres and belts were supplied to the 320 men of Henry Luttrell's new cavalry regiment. Consignments of weaponry came from France, but fell short of what was necessary, and it took time to equip the new units adequately. In the cavalry, the sword was the primary weapon of both officers and other ranks. British cavalry swords of the period were straight-bladed weapons, designed more for thrusting than slashing. However, cavalry sabres had been introduced in France in 1679, and these curved, slashing weapons probably constituted a proportion of the Irish cavalry swords. Swords were housed in leather scabbards, hung from a waist belt, according to modern French practice, rather than the outmoded shoulder baldric. The belt could also support a small cartridge box. Kilmallock sought 600 cartridge boxes for his regiment in 1691. In 1689 swords and belts were issued to the O'Brien dragoon regiment and presumably were standard equipment for the other dragoon regiments also. Ideally, a brace of flintlock pistols, with barrels at least 35cms long, fitted into holsters resting on the horse's withers. This standard may not have been fully met: the 1,484 pistols held by the cavalry regiments in August 1691 would have averaged less than one for every two troopers. A carbine was a short-barrel, light, flintlock musket intended to keep enemy skirmishers at a distance until the cavalry was ready to close. Carbines were hooked to a shoulder belt by a bar and swivel, but carried, muzzle down, in a bucket holster. Musketoons are also mentioned. Strictly speaking these were wide-muzzled blunderbusses, but in practice often of the same calibre as a musket and therefore in reality little different from a carbine. The number of carbines held by the cavalry in August 1691 was 1,754, which was only a little more than one for every two troopers, although the inclusion of pistols brought the number of firearms up

---

[19] Chandler, *Art of war*, p. 34; Kilmallock papers, carton 2; Lawson, *Uniforms*, pp 83–4; *Danish force*, p. 123; Story, *Continuation*, p. 102; *F-I corr.*, i, p. 254.

to one per trooper. Some carbines may have been discarded at Aughrim, but possibly this may have been all they ever had, with of course their swords.[20]

Initially the dragoons were equipped like grenadiers. Muskets with slings, some large carbines, pistols, bayonets, hatchets, grenade pouches, cartouche boxes with girdles and a small quantity of halberds were sent to Ireland in 1685, earmarked for the dragoon and grenadier units introduced that year. In 1689 d'Avaux sought from France flintlocks for the grenadiers and dragoons, and there was disappointment when an expected consignment of 2,000 from Portugal turned out to be a mere forty-seven that were serviceable. 16,000 sabres sent from France with the 1689 convoys were probably adequate, but 1,000 pairs of pistols with holsters and 500 carbines/musketoons clearly were not. A dozen companies of new dragoons that paraded in Dublin in September lacked uniforms and arms, and the dragoons as a whole were reported to be without bayonets. Nevertheless, by the autumn less than 200 cavalry troopers were without carbines, although a fifth of the dragoons were returned as still lacking arms. Some additional cavalry weapons came in 1690, when 1,000 carbines/musketoons, 3,000 sabres or swords and 500 pairs of pistols were listed for sending with the fleet carrying Lauzun's expedition. Maxwell's dragoon regiment was subsequently described as 'well armed' for the campaign that year. Sabres, pistols and carbines/musketoons with leather holsters to arm 500 troopers came with Saint-Ruth. For the 1691 campaign the dragoons were armed with flintlock muskets, although in the wake of Aughrim 30 per cent lacked them.[21]

Horse furniture included high-backed saddles, bridles, bits, stirrup irons and leathers, holsters, carbine buckets, blankets and leather straps. Such items were available in Ireland, but not in the quantity the army urgently required. In 1689 it was estimated that 2,500 saddles and bridles were needed for the mounted corps. A thousand sets of tack were sent from France that year, together with 500 pistol holsters. More may have come in 1690. A thousand saddles, bridles, bits and stirrups, together with a dozen barrels of horse-nails, accompanied Saint-Ruth in 1691. Fumeron thought the saddles sent then were old, and he complained of the absence of saddlebags, which meant that items, which the cavalry were obliged to carry with them, were likely to injure their horses. Horseshoes were supplied by Colonel John Browne's ironworks.

20 *LG*, 24–27 September 1688; 'Journal 19/5 to 18/6 1689' (Carte MS 181), ff 68, 69; Lynn, *Giant of the grand siècle*, pp 489–91; Chartrand, *Louis XIV's army*, pp 18, 33; *Ormonde MSS*, n.s., viii, p. 371; Blackmore, *Arms and armour*, pp 24–52; Kilmallock papers, carton 2. **21** *CSPD 1685*, p. 165; *d'Avaux*, pp 296, 311; *F-I corr.*, i, p. xlii; ii, pp 369, 390, 405; iii, pp 91, 94, 189; Lawson, *Uniforms*, p. 105; Chartrand, *Louis XIV's army*, p. 37; *Stevens*, p. 112.

Finally, it should be noted that troopers were expected to pay for their tack and weapons, the cost of which was included in the 'off-reckonings' deducted from their pay.[22]

Cavalry and dragoon horses

An essential component of any mounted corps was a supply of suitable horses. It is likely that the quality of horses in the Anglo-Norman east of Ireland, where most of the cavalry was recruited, was generally superior to that in the more remote parts of the island. But horse-breeding in any case was a developing industry in late seventeenth-century Ireland, and horses, the engines of transport and tillage, were not in short supply. According to Sir William Petty, Ireland contained 100,000 horses. Ownership was extensive: he thought a third of the Irish cabins possessed a small horse and that every man kept a pony to ride. A French contractor reported that almost all the native horses were small, and better fitted for riding than for drawing loads, to which they were unused. Sir William Temple observed in 1673 that 'horses in Ireland are a drug', their greatest defect being in their casual breeding, but he added:

> In the studs of persons of quality in Ireland, where care is taken and cost is not spared, we see horses bred of excellent shape and vigour, and size, so as to reach great prices at home, and encourage strangers to find the market here; among whom I met with one this summer that came over on that errand, and bought about twenty horses to carry over into the French army, from twenty to three score pounds price at the first hand.

A pioneer in importing quality horses for breeding was Samuel Winter, the commonwealth provost of Trinity College, who had extensive property in Co. Meath. Breeding generally improved as horse farming became more commercialized, with premium prices obtainable for better quality animals in demand for racing, hunting, riding and drawing coaches. Racing was already established at the Curragh, Downpatrick and Youghal. Aristocrats built modern stables and imported breeding stock from England. The duke of Ormond sent over several stallions. Lord Cork had an 'Arabian' at his stud farm outside Youghal, while his brother, Lord Orrery, was memorialized for 'His care to breed brave horses thou would'st ride / In peace for pleasure and in war for fight'. Three animals sold by Cork in the 1660s realized prices

---

22 *F-I corr.*, i, pp 6, 89, 119, 132–3, 219; ii, pp 267, 288, 368–9; iii, pp 18, 173, 183; *d'Avaux*, p. 711; *Clarendon*, ii, p. 23; Westport papers, 40,900/6 (1) & (7).

ranging from £25 to £60. In County Down, Lord Mountalexander was keenly interested in horse breeding and racing. Seven Irish horses selected for the dauphin were captured aboard a French ship in the Shannon estuary in 1691. Parallel to this, the native Irish garrons and hobbies sold at country markets for as little as a half crown. Most horses were employed in working roles of ploughing, cart-pulling and mundane transport.[23]

Horse breeding was not confined to the new Protestant elite. In 1670 Colonel Daniel O'Brien, later 3rd Viscount Clare, strove to become 'the greatest breeder of horses in the king's dominions, for I keep about my house 16,000 acres for my mares, colts and deer'. He sent a gift to Lord Arlington of 'a gelding that I have some tried after the hounds, and though he be of an Irish breed, I think he will not be left behind by any company that hunts in England'. Francis Eustace, a captain in O'Neill's dragoons, maintained a stud farm on his 2,300-acre Kildare estate. Awareness of the breeding quality of Arabian stallions lay behind a letter sent by Colonel Francis Taaffe to his brother, the earl of Carlingford, after the relief of Vienna in 1683, in which the writer apologized for failing to meet Carlingford's request 'to find out a couple of fine Turkish horses for you … for all that were better than ordinary were taken by the Poles and other of our generals, who were more eager after plunder than myself'. Quality horses remained a minority and were reported to be as expensive in Ireland as in France. The cavalry was mounted on the better animals, which were expected to be at least fourteen and a half hands in height – cob size in modern terminology. In 1686 Clarendon had observed two of the Irish cavalry regiments that he inspected to be 'generally better mounted than the light horse in England'. Prior to his departure for France, Mountcashel sought to acquire a couple of geldings from County Clare, and 'had rather of Lord Thomond's breed than any other'. For the 1691 campaign, Lord Kilmallock, by then a cavalry colonel, had three horses, described as a stone horse, a black gelding and a grey mare, which were rated as 'fitting for the best monarch in Christendom'. Lord Clare's stud farm must have provided the foundation for mounting his regiment. Possibly Maxwell's dragoons owed something to the output of the Corporation of horse breeders of County Down, patented by James II in 1686. In general, dragoon horses of the period were smaller and less expensive than their cavalry counterparts. The hardy and nimble Irish garrons and hobbies fulfilled their needs.[24]

23 Temple, *Works*, pp 20–1; MacLysaght, *Irish life*, p. 144; Mahaffy, *Trinity*, p. 301; *A new history of Ireland*, iii, p. 401; Barnard, *Making the grand figure*, pp 226–34; *F-I corr.*, i, p. 219; ii, pp 322, 325; *Ormonde MSS*, n.s., vii, pp 155; *CP*, ix, p. 307; Kelly, *Sport in Ireland*, pp 31–3. **24** *Taaffe letters*, p. 33; *Proclamations*, p. 154; Lawson, *Uniforms*, p. 106; 'Eustace family', pp 377; *Inchiquin MSS*, p. 21; Simms, 'Sarsfield of Kilmallock', p. 210; *Clarendon*, i, pp 499–500.

The three original cavalry regiments came into the war mounted, but saddle horses had to be found for the four new units, together with the horseguards, all the dragoons and the infantry officers, as well as draught animals for the train. With the expansion of the army, the seizure of horses became widespread and enjoyed official sanction, following a proclamation of 1 March 1689. The animals taken were to be handed over to the regimental colonels, who were supposed to account for them to the county lieutenants and sheriffs. However, plough and draught horses, to which were later added those of the Dublin brewers, were exempted from seizure, probably to little effect. King alleged that Protestants alone lost 10,000 horses, which were taken with little regard for their serviceability to the military. Another complained:

> It was usual for any soldier to stop a gentleman and take his horse, and make him go on foot through on the road, and though he had a pass or protection in his pocket, which if produced they would tear up and scorn at it, and carry away the horse which would fall to the share of some Irish officer, so that horses grew scarce; and many [were] sold for forty shillings which cost ten pounds.

Certainly, as a later Jacobite proclamation confirmed, widespread misappropriation occurred. Troopers in the new cavalry and dragoon regiments procured mounts wherever they could, even stealing them from the old regiments or from each other. Sarsfield was licensed to seize horses in Connacht to replace those of Captain Roger Farrell's troop 'ruined in the king's arrival'. The seizure of horses for the army was eventually forbidden because it led to 'great disorders', and because the loss of so many ploughgarrons threatened the 1690 harvest. Alternative plans, which came to nothing, were to require the members of parliament or the sheriffs to supply a quota of horses from their localities. D'Avaux lamented that the future requirements of the cavalry were compromised by the allotment of specific parts of the country to particular regiments, which led to the disorderly seizure of 4,000 horses from the stud farms which were ruined by the operation. The country people were reported to have driven their remaining horses into the mountains, as they had not been paid for those taken, but it was said that plenty of horses would become available, if horse buyers were sent into the countryside with money to purchase them. Particular difficulty seems to have been experienced by Parker's and the horseguards, probably because many of their personnel were English Jacobites who had come to Ireland without horses of their own and frequently with little money to acquire them. As late as August 1689 the horseguards were still without mounts, until eventually horses were seized in

Dublin to overcome the deficit. In 1690 carriage and brewers' horses in Dublin were taken to draw the train, with many reported stolen or substituted for inferior animals in the process. Animals suitable for cavalry mounts were seized from infantry officers, and an embargo placed on the export of horses. Lauzun thought the Irish cavalry 'better mounted than any *gendarmes* [French cavalry] I ever saw'.[25]

For the 1691 campaign the marauding Irish partisans, the rapparees, rustled horses from the Williamite quarters. Sarsfield reported in March that the army had been supplied with more than a thousand from this source, including twenty-two taken from the Williamite General Lanier's own stable and thirty belonging to Würtemburg. He thought that with a little money to distribute to the rapparees, the cavalry could be fully mounted for the coming campaign, and he made the case that every animal seized was one less for their opponents. Fumeron confirmed the rapparees' rustling activity. The Williamites heard that just before the start of the 1691 campaign, the gentlemen of Connacht were persuaded to attend at Limerick, whereupon their horses were seized as cavalry mounts. These measures probably account for the addition of three new troops to Kilmallock's cavalry regiment in 1691. Towards the end of the war the army still retained 2,000 'very fine' horses, 900 eventually accompanying it to France. They arrived in poor condition after the voyage, but the French authorities do not appear to have adversely commented on their quality, although Fumeron had warned that the best-mounted troopers had deserted with their horses after the surrender of Limerick.[26]

Cavalry drill, tactics and training

The troop, like the infantry company, was largely an administrative unit. In battle, several cavalry troops were merged into tactical units called squadrons, each 100- to 150-strong or, as d'Avaux put it, three regiments of cavalry would make eleven squadrons. In the autumn of 1689 Fumeron reported that the army had fourteen very good squadrons of cavalry and six of dragoons that he rated fairly good, but the remaining eight squadrons of cavalry and dragoons he considered very poor. The army's order of battle that autumn showed eighteen cavalry squadrons: four from Tyrconnell's, three each from Galmoy's, Sarsfield's and Parker's, two from Luttrell's and one each from the horseguards,

---

25 *Proclamations*, pp 61, 81–2, 99–100, 107–8, 124–6, 127–8, 131, 154; King, pp 129–30; *Ormonde MSS*, n.s., viii, pp 366, 369, 371; *d'Avaux*, pp 331, 343, 353, 400, 522, 567, 652; *F-I corr.*, i, p. 421; *AH*, 21, p. 149; Lenihan, *Boyne*, p. 203; 'Journal 19/5 to 18/6 1689' (Carte MS 181), ff 67, 71–2; 'A journal of what has passed since his majesty's arrival' (Carte MS 181), f. 5. **26** Story, *Continuation*, pp 85–6; *F-I corr.*, ii, pp 248, 252, 258, 279, 333, 476, 522, 526.

Abercorn's and Sutherland's. Each squadron was on average about 100-strong.[27]

Battlefield tactics had changed by the late seventeenth century. Armies had abandoned the caracole, an elaborate but largely ineffective manoeuvre conceived to enable cavalry to use firearms to disrupt and penetrate formations of infantry. It was replaced by a new French practice, whereby cavalry reverted to a shock charge by sword-carrying squadrons, drawn up in very compact formations, three ranks deep with minimal space between each and the troopers riding knee to knee. To maintain cohesion and spare the horses, the squadron initially advanced at the trot. Then, over the final fifty metres it broke into a charge to maximize shock effect as, swords in hand, it closed with the enemy. Sometimes the last phase was preceded by a discharge of firearms. While this was likely to disrupt the momentum of the advance, its purpose, like the caracole, was to disorder the enemy immediately prior to the final assault. After the charge had gone home, further combat took the form of a man-to-man *mêlée*. Other armies followed the French example, but there was much diversity even within individual armies. The official instruction manual *An abridgement of English military discipline* generally adopted the French practice, which French influence must further have reinforced in Ireland. The tight formation and charge home with sword or sabre was likely employed by the Irish cavalry at the Boyne and on the right wing at Aughrim. Generally too, where firearms had not been discharged in the advance, they could be used in the ensuing *mêlée*. It was, after all, a shot from the pistol of an Irish horseguard that dispatched Marshal Schomberg at the Boyne, and the same day King William came close to being shot by the pistol of one of his own Enniskillen cavalrymen in the confusion of his cavalry attack on Donore. Reloading in a combat situation would have been virtually impossible. A pistol once discharged could be grasped by the barrel and used as a club, before being thrown at the enemy or re-holstered, to be replaced by a sword, still the best weapon in mounted combat. A cavalry charge stood at least an even chance against enemy cavalry, but it was ineffective against disciplined infantry that maintained formation and presented a wall of pikes, bayonets or *chevaux-de-frise* (portable frames of projecting wooden spikes). Horses would shy rather than run into a line of spikes. Infantry was vulnerable to cavalry only if lacking in defensive weapons, as the Huguenot regiments were at the Boyne; if its formation was broken by ill-discipline or concentrated cannon fire; or, as with the Irish infantry at Aughrim, if it was outflanked by the defeat or withdrawal

---

27 *D'Avaux*, p. 464; *F-I corr.*, iii, pp 48, 71–2.   **28** Lynn, *Giant of the grand siècle*, pp 497–500; Childs, *Charles II*, pp 64–5; Lenihan, *Boyne*, pp 182, 197–201.

of its supporting cavalry and dragoons. In any event cavalry could still harass enemy infantry with carbine and pistol fire, and stood ready to break through and pursue a force that lacked the will, weaponry or formation to resist it.[28]

Individual cavalry training was largely a matter of developing and improving horsemanship, horse-care and weapons-handling skills. Effective use of firearms was particularly challenging on horseback. The reversion to reliance on sword or sabre required troopers to be dexterous in thrusting with the former or slashing with the latter. As a group, cavalrymen needed to be proficient in squadron formation and dispersal; in 'doublings', which was the ability to close up and open out squadron ranks and files; and in 'wheelings' by which a line pivoted on its outermost trooper. Dragoons too would have needed to be proficient in horsemanship; in arrangements for the holding or tethering of mounts when the soldiers went into combat on foot; in the handling of weapons; and in infantry deployment and its refinement in their role as skirmishers.[29]

Dragoons were generally an effective corps of the Irish army and prominent in many engagements. True, they were partly responsible for Mountcashel's defeat at Newtownbutler, but in 1690 Sir Neil O'Neill's dragoons valiantly defended the Rossnaree crossing at the Boyne although hopelessly outnumbered. Dungan's resisted the Williamites at Oldbridge, only falling back after their colonel was killed. Clare's did poorly, defending only briefly against William's crossing at Drybridge/Mill Ford, but possibly the regiment participated, perhaps with other dragoons, in the heavy fighting at Donore and Platin that saved the retiring infantry of the Jacobite right wing from annihilation. In the defence of Limerick in 1690, dragoons formed part of Sarsfield's force in the successful raid on the Williamite siege train, and Maxwell's regiment was prominent in the city garrison. In another incident, dragoons, advancing boldly and afoot in an effort to recover a redoubt outside the city's east watergate, 'did much execution among the enemy's horse' before 'they retired in very good order, still firing as they gave way'. In 1691 Maxwell's men were again to the fore in the defence of Athlone. The dragoons had few casualties at Aughrim, but the loss of nearly a third of their weapons by the rank and file suggests panic and flight, probably associated with the low morale that by 1691 seems to have infected the mounted corps of the army.[30]

---

29 Chandler, *Art of war*, pp 47–9; Carlton, *Going to the wars*, pp 135–6. 30 *JN*, pp 100, 103, 114; *d'Avaux*, pp 377, 385; *James II*, ii, pp 395–6; *Stevens*, p. 173; Story, *Continuation*, p. 102; *A particular and full account of … Aghrim*, p. 4; *F-I corr.*, ii, pp 106, 405.

CHAPTER 6

Artillery and engineering

The new professions

ARTILLERY AND THE SYSTEM OF fortification developed to resist it, the *trace Italienne*, transformed early modern warfare, and made the new professions of artillerists and engineers, with their weapons, equipment and techniques, an important component of late seventeenth-century European armies. The English compared badly with the French and Dutch, who were at the forefront of contemporary European artillery and military-engineering innovation and practice. Marshal Schomberg, whom William appointed master general of the English ordnance, formed a low opinion of its capability. Sinecurists outnumbered the small cadre of artillerists, whose skills in any case did not impress him, and he found their guns to be in poor condition. In 1689 the Williamite train in Ireland was English, but thereafter in 1690–1 most of the guns and the key personnel were Dutch, the train in those years of more than seventy guns 'being such an one as never had been seen before in that kingdom'. Engineers were an integral part of artillery trains. Many of the Williamite engineers were Huguenots, whose performance, based on continental experience, attracted little criticism. The Jacobite artillery never matched its opponent in firepower. At the outset the army lacked artillerists and engineers, but in time the input of proficient French personnel improved its capability in both fields, and its firepower was strengthened by the addition of a train of French field guns.[1]

ARTILLERY

Organization and command

In England the provision and organization of artillery was the responsibility of the board of ordnance. It was a department of state under its own master general and completely separate from the army. This division was common throughout contemporary Europe, although less marked in France where the

---

[1] Parker, *History of warfare*, pp 106–17; Rogers, *Military revolution debate*, pp 306–8 and passim; Duffy, *Fortress*, passim; Story, *Continuation*, p. 80; *CSPD 1689–90*, pp 36, 231, 368, 490.

control over the land forces exerted by Louvois, the powerful war minister, ensured that the office of *grand-maître* of artillery was largely honorific. Ireland had its own ordnance board, but from 1674 this body was subordinate to its English counterpart on whom it was dependent for key personnel, weapons and ammunition. For example, in 1687 the English master general was ordered to send six mortars, each with 100 shells, to Ireland. From 1684 the master general of the Irish ordnance was Viscount Mountjoy, who, despite being a Protestant, was retained in the office by James II, being deemed 'very industrious in the king's service'. Mountjoy's control only ended in March 1689, when Tyrconnell sent him on a spurious mission to France, where he was imprisoned. Prior to that, some of the ordnance personnel, such as the clerk, Robert Aillway, and the lieutenant, John Giles, who was also a captain in Justin MacCarthy's foot, had resigned their commissions because they were Protestants.[2]

After James II came to Ireland, he appointed Lieutenant General Justin MacCarthy, soon to be Viscount Mountcashel, as master general in succession to Mountjoy, with Lieutenant Colonel William Mansell Barker of the footguards as ordnance lieutenant. Henceforth, the Irish grand master was no longer subordinate to his English counterpart. Mountcashel was one of the most experienced soldiers in the Irish army, but his many responsibilities meant that he took little interest in the artillery, an arm in which he had no particular expertise. Rosen, the French general, wrote of him as negligent and remiss, complaining that a month after his appointment he had yet to visit the Dublin arsenal. It was the king himself who ordered siege cannon to be sent to Derry, but their departure was delayed as they first had to be mounted on carriages, and there was a dearth of trenching tools for battery construction. Melfort, the unpopular secretary of state, also took an active interest in the organization of artillery while he was in Ireland, although he was careful to respect Mountcashel's position. Mountcashel's role effectively ended with his capture at the battle of Newtownbutler at the end of July 1689 and his subsequent departure for France in 1690 at the head of the Irish brigade. There is no record of a successor being appointed to the office of master general. An unnamed controller general of artillery is mentioned in early 1690, perhaps Boisseleau or Barker.[3]

In any case, management of the Jacobite artillery had by then passed to the French. In 1689 the principal French artillerist was the baron de Pointis, a

---

[2] Childs, *Charles II*, p. 109; Lynn, *Giant of the grand siècle*, p. 509; *Clarendon*, i, p. 249; *CSPD 1687–9*, p. 4; *CP*, ix, pp 350–1; 'Longford letters', pp 55, 58. [3] *D'Avaux*, pp 143, 357; *Lib. mun.*, ii, p. 103; *AH*, 21, p. 110; 'A Journal of what has passed since his majesty's arrival' (Carte MS 181), ff 7–8; *F-I corr.*, i, p. 257.

naval gunnery officer who had won distinction in the bombardment of Algiers. He was sent to Ireland at the beginning of 1689 and prepared the report, which was the foundation of the French decision to intervene. Inter-service rivalry made him most reluctant to come under army command, and instead he sought appointment as master general, which would have left him answerable only to James II. It was not until mid-May that he could be persuaded to take charge of the artillery at the siege of Derry, where he was responsible for the construction of the boom across the Foyle that proved ineffectual to prevent the city's relief. Soon after his arrival he was badly wounded, and his successor, the engineer de Massé, was killed while directing a battery. The train that accompanied James II to Dundalk in the autumn of 1689 was under the command of Major General Boisseleau, who was not an artillerist at all and reported to be very ignorant of gunnery. The departure of Pointis in November ended naval involvement in the artillery. Tyrconnell told Queen Mary that James was 'very well pleased' with Pointis 'and has reason to be, for he has served him here very well'. Pointis won later fame as the leader of the French expedition that in 1697 captured the Spanish-American port of Cartagena with a large amount of treasure. As early as July 1689 King James had requested an artillery train and gunners from France. In 1690 a small train accompanied Lauzun to Ireland. It was under the command of Jean-Baptiste Laisné who reported to Louvois. He was given the rank of brigadier general by James II and commanded both the French and Irish guns until his departure in the autumn of 1690. Little is known for certain about the management of the train in 1691, but Saint-Ruth's artillery was probably led by le sieur Turgot des Fontaines, the senior of four French artillery *commissaires* to accompany him to Ireland.[4]

Personnel

Artillery was a dangerous science, and its practitioners needed to be literate and professional if they were to understand and master its manuals and intricacies. They have been called the military bourgeoisie. Before the war the full establishment of the Irish ordnance, excluding the master, was fifty-eight, of whom forty-six were gunners and matrosses (gunners' mates). It is unlikely that they were any more expert artillerists than their English counterparts, who had so failed to impress Schomberg. In any case, being all Protestants, they fled to England at the time of the revolution, leaving the Irish army bereft

---

4 Loeber, 'Engineers', p. 284; Black, *Kings in conflict*, p. 91; *d'Avaux*, pp 9, 63, 73, 114–15, 161, 322, 355, 470; *F-I corr.*, i, p. 90; iii, pp 67, 117, 123; 'Talbot letter-book', p. 102.

of artillery personnel. Irish Catholics had little tradition of gunnery or mathematical education, and Mountjoy's pre-war tenure of the ordnance ensured that they were ignorant of artillery when hostilities commenced. The supply and administration of the artillery was organized by French *commissaires*, two of whom, Denise and La Croix who had landed at Bantry in 1689, chose to remain on in Ireland after most of the French departed in the autumn of 1690. Gunners were recruited in Ireland, but little is known of their number, organization or antecedents. Ideally two gunners and six matrosses were reckoned to be necessary to serve a gun, but in practice somewhat fewer may have sufficed. (The train of thirty guns that Schomberg brought to Ireland was served by 147 gunners and 200 carters.) Gunners often had a civilian background, with additional personnel taken from the infantry as required. The artillery train would have included officers, artisans and drivers, with an escort/support company of 100 fusiliers or pioneers which was added in June 1689.[5]

In 1689 the Irish artillery officers were described as lazy, uncouth and ignorant, and the gunners as so maladroit that they 'could not hit a house'. At Derry their performance was very poor: for example, only one shot from the Jacobite shore batteries struck the Williamite ships as they moved up the Foyle in a light breeze to relieve the city. The gunners were said to have lost Ireland that day through their neglect of duty, because they were drunk with brandy. The Williamites supplied their gunners with barrels of beer, and it may be conjectured that gunnery was so hazardous a role that a liberal supply of alcohol was a necessary concomitant of artillery deployment. Pointis was originally intended to have had about a hundred French artillery personnel, but in practice he seems to have commanded about half that number. All were naval gunners, without experience of land warfare. By the end of the siege of Derry, only five of his thirty-six gunners were fit for service, the rest being sick or dead. Three were cut in half by a bursting cannon. Le Sieur de Saint-Martin, a French naval artillery *commissaire*, was killed at the battle of Newtownbutler, where he had been sent to direct the Jacobite artillery. Macary, another naval *commissaire*, was killed in a duel. A third *commissaire*, Lavau, was killed in a dispute with another French officer. The Irish gunners must have suffered casualties proportionate to those of the French. For the autumn expedition against Schomberg, a dearth of artillery officers and capable gunners was noted.[6]

5 Childs, *Charles II*, p. 110; *CSPD 1687–8*, p. 397; *James II*, ii, p. 328; *d'Avaux*, p. 209; *F-I corr.*, ii, p. 130; iii, p. 73; Duncan, *Royal artillery*, i, p. 59; 'Journal 1/6 to 18/7 1689' (Carte MS 181), f. 11. 6 *AH* 21, pp 128, 136; *d'Avaux*, pp 76, 334, 355, 399, 470, 638; *JN*, p. 84; S[imms], 'From Ginkel's accounts', p. 191; *F-I. corr.*, iii, p. 86.

In 1690 Laisné was accompanied to Ireland by sixty French artillery personnel. The party included eight *commissaires*, four aiming officers and eight gunners. The rest were carters and artisans, such as smiths, turners and wheelwrights, that were needed to keep the guns serviceable and mobile. It was clearly intended to supplement the small number of artillerists with additional personnel, either drafted from the French infantry regiments or recruited from the Irish. The train that set out for the Boyne numbered 460. Nearly all the French artillery personnel survived the 1690 campaign to return home in the autumn. There were certainly Irish gunners in 1690: Laisné refers to Jacobite *commissaires* and other artillery officers at the Boyne. The gunners mentioned in the terms of surrender of Charlemont in May 1690 must have been Irish, as were those who served the cannon used in the defence of Athlone, 'plagued' the Williamites at Limerick and fired on Marlborough's fleet as it approached Cork. However, their competence did not impress Berwick who blamed his failure to take Birr Castle in September 1690 on his gunners' lack of skill.[7]

In 1691 the only French artillerists sent to Ireland were four *commissaires*. Most of the artillery personnel at that stage must have been Irish. The total number with the field train was estimated to be 132, comprising the commander, six *commissaires*, three gun-aimers, three transport captains, three overseers of transport, twenty gunners, twenty workmen, eighty carters, a surgeon and a chaplain. The garrisons of Limerick, Galway, Athlone and Sligo accounted for a further 156 personnel. The largest number was in Limerick and comprised an artillery commander, five officials, thirty-eight gunners and seventy-three workers, including wheelwrights, carpenters, blacksmiths and gunsmiths. Experience and French training seem to have improved Irish gunnery skills: at Athlone their fire forced Williamite regiments camped near the river to withdraw; at Aughrim they 'maintained a heavy artillery fire'; at Galway 'they fired both great and small shot from the walls'; and at Limerick they were described as firing 'briskly' and 'furiously'. Evidence of their effectiveness during the final campaign is the number of important Williamite officers who were killed by the Irish guns, with, presumably, a proportionately greater number of lesser ranks.[8]

Weapons

The basic seventeenth-century artillery weapon was a muzzle-loaded cannon, cast from iron or bronze. Iron guns were prone to corrosion, and tended to

---

7 *F-I corr.*, i, p. 19; iii, p. 124; *Ormonde MSS*, n.s., viii, p. 385; Story, pp 60, 101–2, 118, 137, 140–1; Murtagh, 'Jacobite Offaly', pp 326–7. 8 *F-I corr.*, i, p. 90; ii, pp 341–2; Jordan, 'Aughrim', p. 4;

burst after discharging about 1,200 shots. Bronze, which contemporaries often termed brass, was somewhat lighter and more durable, but also three times more expensive to manufacture. Cannon were usually classified by the weight of their cannonball, so that, for example, a 4-pounder fired a 4-pound ball. The more traditional ornithological names, such as 'falcon' (for a 2-pounder), 'saker' (for a 6-pounder) and 'culverin' (for an 18-pounder), although still employed, were beginning to drop out of use. Drakes were smaller, lighter versions of the standard cannon, which used a reduced charge of powder. A second type of artillery piece was the mortar, a heavy short-barrelled weapon, mounted on a fixed bed at a 45-degree angle of elevation. Mortars were generally classified by the internal diameter of the barrel or bore (18-inch etc.). The Dutch pioneered the howitzer, a mobile version of the mortar, which fired at an elevation of about fifteen degrees. The Williamites deployed howitzers at the Boyne, but the Jacobites had no equivalent weapon.[9]

Light, mobile cannon, typically 4-, 6- and 8-pounders, provided an army's field artillery. Field guns could be quickly deployed to defend their own lines of infantry and cavalry by trying to break up and demoralize enemy formations and dismount their guns. In the Dutch army, small field guns accompanied the infantry regiments. A similar practice was adopted in England in 1686 when seven infantry battalions were each equipped with a pair of 3-pounders. By then, this arrangement had ceased to be the practice in France where the artillery was gathered in parks and organized as a train. In Ireland, at the start of the war, the infantry regiments of the standing army may have been equipped with field guns, such as those deployed by Mountcashel's forces, which included his own regiment, in suppressing the Munster Protestants and on his ill-fated Newtownbutler campaign. Thereafter, the French system seems to have been adopted.[10]

The use of battering cannon, 16-pounders and larger, and large mortars was confined to siege warfare. The battering cannon were used to breach the fortifications preparatory to an assault. Their power was immense: in his *Mémoires d'artillerie* (1702) Saint-Rémy, the French authority, stated that a well-served 24-pounder, firing at a range of 150 metres, could penetrate almost twelve metres into a stone-faced bastion of packed earth. Mortars lobbed projectiles across the ramparts to demolish and set fire to buildings within a

---

Story, *Continuation*, pp 163, 209, 227.   **9** Duffy, *Fire and stone*, pp 111–24; Blackmore, *Arms and armour*, pp 82–91; Wilkinson-Latham, *Discovering artillery*, pp 6–16; Guilmartin, 'Gunpowder revolution', pp 541–7; Lynn, *Giant of the grand siècle*, pp 500–12; *Danish force*, p. 62; *James II*, ii, p. 395.   **10** *CSPD 1686–7*, pp 231, 234; Lynn, *Giant of the grand siècle*, p. 502; Chandler, *Art of war*, pp 177–80; Graham, *Mountcashel*, p. 81; Hamilton, *Inniskillingmen*, p. 42.

fortress, harass the defenders and terrorize the civilian population. Field guns were used during a siege to pick off the defenders and drive off any attacks on the besiegers' lines either from within the fortress or by a relief force. The artillery of the defenders of a fortress was deployed to smash up the besiegers' batteries, dismount their cannon, rake their trenches and punish their troops if they attempted an assault or were otherwise exposed without cover.[11]

The casting of cannon was a highly skilled and expensive operation, which was largely controlled by governments because of its cost and security implications. Guns had been made in Ireland in the first half of the seventeenth century, but their manufacture was not resumed after the restoration or during the Jacobite war. England, France and the Dutch Republic all possessed artillery-manufacturing capability, and the latter two had an immense output. French commentators advocated a proportion of one cannon for every 1,000 soldiers. In the nine years war of 1688–97 Louis XIV deployed some 13,000 fortress, siege and field guns. A great variety was in existence, even in France, which had adopted a policy of standardizing the number of calibres to six. Cannon of a given calibre might be 'bastards', 'legitimates' or 'doubly-fortified', according to the thickness of the bore wall: the thicker the metal the larger the powder charge that could be safely used. French artillery systems were further complicated by the introduction of cannon *de nouvelle invention*, designed with a more efficient spherical powder chamber, which allowed for lighter and shorter guns than the traditional *de vieille invention* weapons, although the latter still remained in use. All cannon were individually cast, so that even those of the same calibre often took different shot sizes. Further variety was added by captured guns and those from earlier periods which remained in service: two old French cannon, 'caste in Cardinal Richelieu's time', helped to defend Limerick. An added complication was the fact that the French *livre* was slightly heavier than the equivalent English pound (1 livre: 1.079 pounds). Cannon and mortars were fitted with lifting lugs, traditionally in the form of two dolphins, located at the point of balance on top of the barrel. Cannon barrels were often elaborately decorated with castings of royal monograms, mottos and the name of the master general or *grand-maître* of artillery at the time of their manufacture.[12]

A good rate of fire was about one shot every three minutes, with periodic pauses to allow the guns to cool, during which water was poured down the barrel and wet sheepskins were laid on the breech. After each shot, to assist the

---

11 Chandler, *Art of war*, p. 183; Duffy, *Fire and stone*, pp 111–12, 123–4.   **12** Loeber & Parker, 'Military revolution in Ireland', pp 70, 74–5; Lenihan, *Confederate Catholics*, pp 56–7; Chandler, *Art of war*, p. 178; Lynn, *Giant of the grand siècle*, pp 503–6; *F-I corr.*, i, p. 244.

cooling process and quench any embers of flame, a gunner dipped a sponge in water and scoured the chamber. To reload, a ladle was filled with powder, about two-thirds the weight of the ball, from a barrel or sack. The charge was then inserted down the barrel into the chamber, where it was compressed by a ramrod. A wad of turf, straw, rushes, or even earth or dung was next inserted and rammed home, followed by the ball. The gun was then aligned, by using crowbars to lever it into position. To fire, the gunner primed a vent in the breech with powder from his flask, which he then ignited by the application of a glowing match attached to a linstock. This was a pole surmounted by a distinctive two-branched clamp to hold the match. For safety, until it was needed, it stood planted in the ground somewhat to the rear of the gun. The shock of the discharge typically caused a 4-pounder to recoil about a metre, obliging the gunners to reposition it after each shot. Every thirty rounds or so, the barrel was scraped out with an instrument called a worm (*tireboure*) to remove the crusted ash deposits. At full elevation a cannon could fire a ball a considerable distance – 2,500 metres according to the great French engineer, Vauban – but with no accuracy. In reality the weapons were only really effective at point-blank range (barrel parallel to the ground), which was about 800 metres for a heavy siege gun and perhaps half that for a 6-pounder. Thereafter, the shot became increasingly inaccurate, and the speed of the ball diminished so rapidly that it was possible for a human target to see it coming and take avoiding action. 'Field glasses' and 'multiplying glasses' (telescopes) were employed for artillery observation by the Jacobites at the Boyne and Limerick.[13]

Proportionate to the projectiles they fired, guns, whether of iron or bronze, were immensely heavy. The barrel of an English 16-pounder was of the order of 2,000 kilograms, and a long-barrelled French 4-pounder *de vielle invention*, the type sent to Ireland, weighed over 700 kilograms, about twice its *de nouvelle invention* equivalent. The barrel of such a weapon was 2.58m long, but the bore diameter was only 84mm (about 4½ inches). Cannon of all sizes were mounted on wooden carriages. Gun-carriage construction was a skilled and complicated process, with different sorts of wood suited to different parts of the vehicle. Field and siege guns required mobile carriages. These were all similar in design, but proportionate in size and strength to the barrel weight. Cylinder-shaped projections, called trunnions, were cast just forward of the centre of gravity on either side of the barrel. The trunnions rested in semi-circular slots cut into the heavy wooden side-pieces, or 'cheeks', of the carriage.

---

13 Duffy, *Fire and stone*, p. 116; Chandler, *Art of war*, pp 180, 206–7; *Stevens*, p. 168; Payen de la Fouleresse, p. 21.

The cheeks were of elm, each approximately the thickness of the bore diameter of the weapon they were designed to support. The carriage was completed by a wooden axle of oak between two large, spoked, iron-shod wooden wheels, half the length of the gun barrel in diameter, fitted just forward of the trunnions. The rear of the cheeks descended to the ground to form a trail, which helped absorb the recoil of the gun, partly through sliding friction and partly through digging into the ground. The cheeks were held together by the axle tree and a number of cross struts along their length, with stress points reinforced by iron bands and plates screwed to the carriage. For greater strength and stability, the wheels were angled and 'dished', that is their spokes were set at a concave angle. The gun could be elevated or depressed by being pivoted on its trunnions, and then secured at the desired angle by a wedge placed under the breech. Gun carriages had to be heavily built to withstand the shock of detonation, absorb the subsequent recoil and endure bumpy roads and cross-country deployment. The carriage of a French 4-pounder was approximately 3.6m long, and typically weighed 65–85 per cent of the barrel weight, bringing the total weight of the gun and carriage to 1,200 kilograms or more (approximately 1 ton). The severe wear and tear on gun carriages necessitated a supply of spare carriages to keep the guns operational, the usual ratio in France being one spare for every four guns, although in Ireland in 1690 the ratio was 1:2. The manufacture of gun carriages was mooted in 1689, and some were evidently made to mount the guns sent to Derry. Fortress guns were mounted like ships' cannon on low carriages with four small wheels or possibly two front wheels and rear slides, the better to lessen recoil.[14]

In 1689 all the Jacobite cannon and mortars came from resources within Ireland. An inventory of available guns that year listed 188 cannon mounted, 79 not mounted, and 6 mortars. The bulk of the serviceable cannon were relatively immobile fortress guns of numerous sizes and calibres, mainly deployed at coastal locations. No pre-war train had existed, and at most only twelve field guns and two small mortars were available to join the field army in Ulster. Indeed, some accounts put the number of mobile guns as low as eight. Gun carriages were difficult to obtain. When battering cannon were needed for the siege of Derry, it proved impossible to bring fortress guns from Charlemont because of lack of carriages, and an attempt to bring two guns from Carrickfergus ended in failure when the carriage of one broke and the other fell into a ditch. Eventually an 18-pounder and a 24-pounder, together

14 Lynn, *Giant of the grand siècle*, pp 504–6; Chandler, *Art of war*, pp 180, 186–7; Wilkinson-Latham, *Discovering artillery*, pp 10–12; *F-I corr.*, iii, p. 94; Duffy, *Fire and stone*, p. 83; *The great guns like thunder*, p. 12.

with a heavy mortar, were sent from Dublin, but only after considerable delay while their carriages were constructed, the Protestant artisans employed 'going unwillingly about their business'. In suppressing Protestant resistance in County Cork, Mountcashel deployed three field guns against Castlemartyr and probably again at Bandon. In his July campaign in the Erne valley, no doubt exercising his power as master general, he deployed a sizeable train, reported as eight cannon, comprising four brass guns, one of iron for battery and three brass field pieces. In the autumn a train of eleven guns, an assortment of 4-, 6-, 7- and 12-pounders, was assembled in Dublin to resist Schomberg, although only nine pieces were ultimately deployed: a single 6-pounder, three 4-pounders and five 1-pounders. D'Avaux reported that the latter were only small-calibre battalion guns. Rosen judged the whole train as virtually worthless. A footnote to the Jacobite artillery capability in 1689 was Galmoy's deployment against Crom Castle on the Erne of 'two cannon made of tin, near a yard long in the chase, and about eight inches wide, strongly bound with small cord and covered with a sort of buckram'. Such weapons owed their inspiration to the innovations of Gustavus Adolphus and may have been related to the Scottish leather guns used by the Williamites at the battle of Killiecrankie. The Crom guns were a failure: an attempt to fire one, using a wooden bullet, burst the breech and 'spoiled the gunner'.[15]

In early 1690 Fumeron was told by the controller general of artillery that the magazines were in a bad state, and the cannon mounted on rotten carriages and unserviceable due to a want of powder, shot and match. However, the situation soon improved with the arrival of a train of French field guns, comprising twelve long-barrelled 4-pounders *de vieille invention*, each stamped with Louis XIV's arms. They impressed the Williamites who rated the French train as excellent. Laisné would evidently have preferred weapons *de nouvelle invention*, as he made the complaint that the guns sent were too heavy. He also observed that they were badly cast, a criticism that was borne out when several split, although only exposed to relatively light use. Others were damaged by Williamite fire, leaving only five fit for service at the end of the campaign. Some Jacobite guns were added to Laisné's train. According to one report they numbered five or six, but only four can definitely be accounted for at the Boyne, of which one was lost. After the Boyne, Laisné succeeded in drawing

---

15 Macpherson, *Original papers*, p. 180; 'A journal of what has passed since his majesty's arrival' (Carte MS 181), ff 8, 29; *James II*, ii, p. 328; *JN*, p. 65; *F-I corr.*, iii, pp 37, 67, 73; *d'Avaux*, pp 81, 357, 397, 470; *Ireland's lamentation* (London, 1689), pp 22–3; *Great news of a bloody fight in Newtown*; Hamilton, *Inniskillingmen*, p. 10; Hodges, 'Cannon', pp 74–5; Stevenson & Caldwell, 'Leather guns', pp 300–17.

off the French cannon to Limerick. From there they were taken to Galway and accompanied Lauzun's expedition back to France. In 1691 the French decision to renew assistance to the Jacobites resulted in the five serviceable 4-pounders from 1690, with a 5-pounder, being shipped back to Ireland with Saint-Ruth. With the addition of some Jacobite guns, probably those brought off from the Boyne, the Jacobite train comprised nine field pieces for the 1691 campaign. Described as 'brass cannon', all were captured by the Williamites at Aughrim.[16]

Transport

A limber or *avant-train* was used to draw a field gun from place to place. It consisted of a pair of wheels, an axle and a pole or shafts. In the centre of the axle beam was an upright post, which fitted into a hole bored in the transom that separated the two ends of the gun's trail. To move off, the rear of the trail was dropped onto this post, allowing the limber to serve as a pivoting front axle for the gun. A team of three or four horses was then hitched in line to the limber to draw a 4-pounder, supplemented by more animals if the quality of the team was poor or the guns were of greater calibre. Mortars were transported on carts, from which they had to be unloaded before being positioned and fired. The artillery required a large quantity of material and munitions for its own use: powder packed in barrels, shot of various types, usually about a hundred rounds per gun; match; and such equipment as ladels, sponges, powder horns, priming irons, linstocks, rammers, sledges, wedges, ropes, hides, baskets, hatchets, crowbars, forges and equipment for smiths, spare harness, and hand weapons, and tents and beds for the artillery personnel. The army's engineering tools, ammunition supply, spare weapons, hand grenades and other equipment were also transported with the train. St Rémy's model for a train of fifty cannon with 220 wagons and carts needed a total of 1,225 horses, exclusive of officers' mounts. Proportionately, on this model Laisné's twelve-gun train in 1690 would have required over fifty wagons and carts and 300 horses for the artillery alone. The procurement of draught horses and forage, the drawing of immensely heavy loads on bad roads and the frequent breakdowns all combined to make the pace of movement of artillery trains frustratingly slow.[17]

The French trains that came to Ireland were equipped with carriages and limbers, including spares, but no other transport. In Ireland there were scarcely any wagons, and the available carts could carry no more than four hundred-

---

16 *F-I corr.*, i, pp 187, 257, 337; ii, p. 59; iii, pp 118, 208; Story, *Continuation*, p. 136.
17 Chandler, *Art of war*, pp 171, 173-4, 186-7.

weight. There was an acute shortage of draught horses: those employed in 1689 were small and old, mostly more fit for riding rather than drawing. The shortage was due at least in part to the failure to pay for horses seized by the army, with the result that the country people hid them in remote locations. The train for Derry was forced to move in relays because only fifty old saddle horses could be found to draw it. When the siege was raised, although the guns were saved, their equipment had to be abandoned for lack of transport. Soon afterwards d'Avaux reported on the artillery deficiencies. There was a lack of equipment, new ammunition wagons were of such crude construction that four horses were needed to pull each, and King James was reluctant to spend any money on purchasing horses, although they were readily available. Eventually, however, the king grudgingly agreed to purchase 300. A party of fusiliers under a French captain, Jean Dully, formed the escort for the train in 1689. Although described as a company, an order for 150 flintlocks placed by the ordnance with Colonel John Browne, suggests that the unit may have been of two-company strength. The train horses from 1689 were reported to have died of neglect during the ensuing winter, with the result that in 1690 it took six weeks to assemble 320 horses and oxen to draw the French guns to Dublin after they were unloaded at Cork. The carriage and brewers' horses in Dublin were seized to draw the train on campaign. It included spare gun carriages and limbers, and thirty carts and sledges of equipment. Some harness was to have been sent in 1690. If it was ever shipped, it was insufficient, as there are reports of the harness used being made from straw. Horse collars, harnesses, canvas covers, backrests, bridles and traces were sent for the artillery in 1691.[18]

A wagon master and twenty carters had come from France in 1690, but the other carters were Irish. Four companies of French infantry provided the escort. A sergeant and ten men with shovels preceded the train to carry out necessary road repairs. Next came twenty men under a captain to set the pace at a speed that allowed all vehicles to keep up. The bulk of the escort guarded the train and kept it in good order by marching in columns on either side. Twenty men brought up the rear to deal with breakdowns. The train averaged a commendable fourteen kilometres per day on the journey to Dublin, despite wet weather. All the coaches in Dublin were commandeered to supplement the transport for the Boyne campaign, with carriage and brewers' horses from the city and its environs replacing the worst of the draft animals that had come up from Cork. According to Lauzun, half the horses seized were either stolen

---

18 *F-I corr.*, i, pp 219, 270, 349–50, 402, 388, 421; ii, pp 60, 148; 'A journal of what has passed since his majesty's arrival' (Carte MS 181), f. 5; 'Journal 1/6 to 18/7 1689' (ibid.), f. 11; Westport papers, MS 40,899/5(6); *d'Avaux*, pp 353, 396–7.

or substituted for inferior animals that were then supplied to the train. In 1691 rapparees supplied 260 horses for the train in a single day with more to come, and a further 150 were drawn from the cavalry and dragoons, one from each troop.[19]

Ammunition

Cannon primarily fired solid cast-iron round shot, occasionally red hot, and canister, which was a container of musket balls with the destructive potential of a huge shotgun blast at short range. Chain shot (two balls linked by a piece of chain) was used at Derry against the defences at Butcher's Gate. Mortars fired stones, carcasses (incendiaries) and bombs (hollow balls filled with gunpowder and fitted with a fuse, which was lit just before firing). All were discharged by an explosion of gunpowder, a compound, according to a French ordinance of 1686, of 75 parts saltpetre (potassium nitrate), 12.5 parts sulphur and 12.5 parts charcoal. The same substance was used to fire muskets. In 1689, when James II landed, stocks of ammunition were very low, with less than 400 barrels of powder and only 789 cannonballs reported in the magazines. At Charlemont, a front-line fortress, there were no more than twenty-six balls for nine guns, and throughout the siege of Derry ammunition was in constant short supply. However, in each of the years 1689 and 1691 100,000 pounds of powder and extensive quantities of match were sent from France, and probably similar amounts in 1690. The French artillery 'consumed' 2,500 pounds of powder that year, together with most of its 1,400 cannonballs. However, the French guns saw so little action that they can hardly have fired off this amount of ammunition. Powder and cannonballs may have been given to the Irish, and possibly some balls were abandoned on the retreat from the Boyne. 3,000 cannonballs were supplied from France in 1691.[20]

A fledgling Jacobite munitions industry helped to meet the artillery's needs. Colonel John Browne supplied cannonballs from his Knappagh ironworks in Mayo. A saltpetre works, established at Limerick in 1689 under the sieur de La Croix, one of the French artillery *commissaires*, was soon producing over 200 pounds per week. A powder mill was also planned and possibly established. Early in 1690 *Commissaire* Fumeron recommended the further development of the Limerick operation. He reported the presence of good forges in the locality, and judged that if the Protestants who owned them were paid, their reluctance to work would be overcome, and they would

---

19 *F-I corr.*, i, pp 390, 396, 409, 421; ii, p. 333; iii, pp 112, 118; *JN*, pp 254–6.   **20** *F-I corr.*, i, p. xlii; iii, pp 37, 187–8, 204; Macpherson, *Original papers*, i, p. 180; *d'Avaux*, p. 82.

manufacture cannonballs, if supplied with moulds and calibre details. Gun carriages were made at Dublin in 1689. However, overall output from these various operations was small. In the summer of 1690 powder was in short supply at Limerick, and Laisné complained that his order for 4,000 cannonballs was unfulfilled. One further artillery-related manufacturing process was the minting of 'gun-money'. The term is a later invention, but it relates to the melting down in Dublin of bronze cannon to provide some of the raw material for the emergency coinage on which the Jacobite regime was financially dependent.[21]

Deployment

The major occasion on which the Jacobites deployed siege artillery was at Derry. The two 'battering cannon' and six field guns used against the fortifications made no impression, as they 'played only upon great days, and that with much moderation, ammunition being scarce and the charge of carrying it so far great'. The large mortar, until it cracked, and two or three smaller companions fired almost 600 bombs into Derry. This was a better performance, with several houses reported destroyed; but it was a heavy drain on powder, and its impact on weakening the resolution of the defenders appears to have been minimal. Galmoy's tin guns failed to bluff the defenders of Crom Castle into capitulation, and the guns brought against that stronghold by Mountcashel were of too small a calibre to have any effect. However, a few months earlier, the three field pieces he brought against Castlemartyr contributed to its speedy surrender and possibly also to Bandon's capitulation; and in January 1690 a show of field pieces persuaded the spirited Lady Newcomen to surrender Mosstown House, an isolated Williamite stronghold in County Longford. The following September seven pieces of cannon including an 18-pounder did 'some damage' to Birr Castle, firing off forty to fifty rounds in a single day, but failed to reduce the stronghold before relief arrived. A reminder of the siege is the cannonball (perhaps a later insertion) still lodged in the east flanking tower of Birr Castle.[22]

The first field train formed by the Jacobites comprised three guns brought to Ulster by Richard Hamilton for his campaign in the spring of 1689. By April this had increased to two 4-pounders and three 12-pounders which were present at Coleraine. The number of Jacobite field guns eventually rose to

---

21 Westport papers, MS 40,899/5(10–14); *F-I corr.*, i, pp 244, 255; iii, p. 123; *d'Avaux*, p. 81; Stevenson, 'Irish emergency coinages', pp 169–75. 22 *Stevens*, p. 71; *JN*, pp 65, 67; Milligan, *Londonderry*, pp 81, 183, 214–15; Story, pp 52, 137; *CSPD 1690–1*, p. 125.

about a dozen at the siege of Derry where, besides those used in the bombardment, six or more were deployed at intervals along the Foyle to sustain the blockade from the sea. During the siege, guns seem to have been transferred between blockade and bombardment. The Williamites claimed to have captured seven brass guns, together with an iron piece used to batter Crom, when Mountcashel was defeated at Newtownbutler. On that occasion Jacobite fire initially halted the advance of the Enniskillen horse, until the guns were outflanked and overrun by the Enniskillen infantry who killed the gunners. The French ambassador rated the train assembled against Schomberg in the autumn as being in the worst order of anything on the expedition. However, it impressed the Williamites, who took note of the 'very handsome field train' that paraded with the Jacobites outside Dundalk. Whatever its shortcomings, this train apparently played its part in dissuading the cautious Schomberg from continuing his offensive.[23]

The French guns that came in 1690 first saw action in May at modern Dún Laoghaire against two English frigates that sailed into Dublin Bay, although to no effect. At the Boyne, the artillery was initially posted in the vicinity of Tullyallen, north of the river, but was withdrawn to the south bank on 29 June when the guns crossed the ford at Oldbridge, a hazardous operation that appears to have passed off without incident. Next day, as the Williamites were seen to occupy the north bank, Lieutenant General La Hoguette, with the approval of James II and Lauzun, ordered Laisné to move five guns forward to a ploughed field near Oldbridge. From there, before noon, they commenced firing across the river with considerable accuracy and effect: their first shot killed two horses and a man; the second ricocheted off the riverbank into a reconnaissance party led by William III, grazing his shoulder. Subsequent shots caused further casualties, obliging the Williamite cavalry to withdraw to the security of higher ground. The Williamites responded when their own field guns and mortars (or perhaps howitzers) came up in the mid-afternoon, and thereafter both sides maintained a cannonade until dusk, with one of the Jacobite guns being dismounted in the exchange and others splitting. The Williamite fire eventually forced the Jacobites to remove the ammunition from their artillery park.[24]

In the evening Laisné erected two batteries to cover the Oldbridge crossings on sites selected by La Hoguette. Three guns were deployed in the right-hand battery and five in the left. Early on the morning of 1 July Laisné,

---

23 'A journal of what has passed since his majesty's arrival' (Carte MS 181), f. 8; *d'Avaux*, pp 76, 386, 470; *JN*, p. 64; *Great news of a bloody fight in Newton*; Story, p. 22.   24 *F-I corr.*, i, pp 414–15; ii, p. 74; iii, pp 123–4; *Ormonde MSS*, n.s., viii, p. 383; Story, pp 74–6; *Danish force*, pp 62–3.

on orders from King James, detached two of the remaining French guns and all four Jacobite cannon to reinforce the left wing. They were sent off under the command of le sieur de Montgrizy, a French *commissaire*, who was accompanied by all the Irish artillery officers. As soon as the Williamite attack commenced, James ordered the withdrawal of the guns from the Oldbridge batteries. As this was the moment when they could have been used to most telling effect, Laisné queried the order. When it was confirmed, he yoked up the serviceable guns, placed the damaged pieces on carts and moved off the battlefield. Meanwhile, on the left wing, the French infantry succeeded in bringing off five cannon from Montgrizy's battery, losing only one of the Irish guns, abandoned after it became bogged down. A claim by the Danish envoy that the Williamites captured seven guns is not substantiated elsewhere, nor does the number accord with those that can be accounted for. At Duleek, when the French turned to cover the Jacobite retreat, Montgrizy's guns, posted between the infantry battalions, were deployed and fired, before resuming their journey to Dublin, where they were reunited with the rest of Laisné's train, which then comprised fifteen cannon. From Dublin they went to Limerick. Laisné's conduct throughout was widely praised. He expressed satisfaction to Louvois at having brought off all the French guns safely, adding that all the powder was also saved, with the portable forge the only significant loss. He commended his *commissaires*, officers and gunners for their devotion to duty, particularly Montgrizy for preserving the two French guns on the left wing. The Jacobite artillery was probably saved from capture by its early withdrawal; however, it contributed nothing to the Jacobite defence at the Boyne, beyond helping to cover the retreat. Had the French guns and gunners at Oldbridge been left in place, they would surely have greatly troubled the Williamite infantry. Laisné was subsequently accused of submitting false returns about the state of the train and its personnel, which he strongly rejected. He was threatened with the Bastille for his rudeness to *Intendant* d'Esgrigny, but the good reports of his conduct at the Boyne appear to have preserved him from this fate.[25]

At Aughrim, in 1691, the nine Jacobite field pieces were heavily outgunned by the thirty cannon the Williamites deployed. Saint-Ruth positioned batteries 'to the best advantage' on either flank of his infantry. The largest battery covered the approach from Urraghry, and two guns covered the causeway leading to Aughrim village. The Urraghry battery maintained a heavy fire and played its part in repulsing the advance of the Williamite left

---

25 *F-I corr.*, i, pp 80, 450–1; ii, pp 74, 77; iii, pp 118, 124–5, 131, 144–5; *James II*, ii, p. 401; Payen de la Fouleresse, p. 23.

wing. Saint-Ruth himself had directed the aim of the second battery just before he was killed. Its fire helped to prevent the advance of the Williamite right wing until a dozen guns were brought up to silence it. In the rout, all nine Jacobite guns were captured with the rest of the train. A French *commissaire* was reported missing; the fate of the other gunners is unknown.[26]

Most of the guns available to the Irish army were fortress cannon, which started and ended the war in the same location. At Carrickfergus, the first garrison to be besieged, the garrison artillery put up some resistance, despite a shortage of powder, but all the guns were lost when the Jacobites capitulated after a week. A Williamite source claimed the capture of seventeen guns and a heavy mortar when Charlemont surrendered in May 1690. The guns were mostly of bronze, and the haul included eighty-three barrels of powder. A French report put the loss at twelve. The discrepancy may arise from the exclusion by the latter of guns such as the mortar that had been removed to Charlemont after the siege of Derry. The capitulation of Dublin and the Jacobite garrisons of south Leinster and Munster through the ensuing summer and autumn resulted in the loss of large numbers of fortress cannon: seven 4-pounders in Drogheda; seventeen guns 'in bad condition' in Waterford; fifty-six in Duncannon; an unknown number in Cork; and at Kinsale, forty-six in James Fort and ninety-four, a third of them bronze, in Charles Fort. Many garrisons surrendered without offering any resistance, but artillery was used in the defence of Cork and also at James Fort until a major powder explosion crippled the resistance. To defend Athlone in 1690 Colonel Richard Grace deployed four guns on the riverside and further artillery in the castle, subsequently listed as a total of six cannon and three mortars, which were all lost when the town was stormed a year later. Two guns, described as Turkish pieces mounted on old cartwheels, were taken at Ballymore. Forty guns were captured at Galway, after the garrison had been allowed to draw off six to Limerick, using teams of horses supplied by the Williamites. A further 'two or three very fine brass guns' were found among a number of unmounted cannon in the city. A dozen guns were surrendered on Inshbofin and sixteen at Sligo.[27]

Undoubtedly the most effective use of fortress artillery by the Jacobites was at Limerick, during the sieges of 1690 and 1691. Three dozen iron fortress cannon were available for the city's defence, including a 63-pounder, two 24-pounders and four 12-pounders, with a number of smaller guns. For the siege of 1690 there were ample supplies of powder and match, but only 2,200

---

26 *Stevens*, p. 214; Story, *Continuation*, plan facing p.135, pp 133, 136; *Rawdon*, p. 352; Jordan, 'Aughrim', p. 4.   **27** Story, *Continuation*, pp 7, 161, 173, 201, 235; Story, pp 64, 100–2; *F-I corr.*, i, p. 396; ii, pp 226, 376; *James II*, ii, p. 415; *Danish force*, pp 49, 66, 86–7, 89.

cannon balls. Boisseleau, who had commanded the artillery for a time in 1689, was the city's governor, and to organize the artillery defences he had the services of Laisné until he was withdrawn to Galway. Initially the guns were positioned on the castle and the Irishtown bastions from which they kept up a brisk fire. During the siege, the Jacobites added a battery outside the wall on the King's Island from which two guns enfiladed the Williamite trenches and covered the Irishtown counterscarp. This battery proved effective against the Williamites when they attempted to storm the breach on 27 August. On that occasion the assault troops were also subjected to rounds of cartridge shot from a two-gun battery inside the town, positioned opposite the breach. In 1691 the Williamites were again much troubled by the Jacobite artillery when they invested Limerick. The city's artillery was supplemented by seventeen guns recovered from a French vessel that had foundered in the river. Under the treaty which ended the war, all the Limerick guns were surrendered, apart from six cannon and two mortars which the Jacobites were allowed to take to France, no doubt to compensate Louis XIV for the guns lost at Aughrim.[28]

The Irish artillery was weak, poorly managed and badly served in 1689. Except for fortress cannon and gun barrels, almost everything that was needed in terms of transport, expert personnel and adequate supplies of ammunition was absent or in short supply. Its performance, notably at the siege of Derry, was correspondingly bad. In 1690 the French input ensured an adequate field train supported the army. At the Boyne, after a promising performance on the eve of the engagement, the precipitate withdrawal of the artillery, in accordance with James II's half-hearted commitment to battle, denied it the opportunity to be effective. However, signs of an improvement in Irish gunnery, probably as a result of French instruction, were evident at the first siege of Limerick and elsewhere. The small field train of 1691 seems to have performed reasonably well at Aughrim, and the fortress cannon were competently served at Athlone and Limerick. Artillery was vital for certain military tasks and therefore an essential part of any army. The muzzles of Louis XIV's guns carried the motto *ultima ratio regum* ('the last argument of kings'), an eloquent reminder that in a dangerous age artillery was a cornerstone of state power and prestige. The Jacobite army, without its modest artillery capability, would have been a less effective or credible military force.

---

28 *F-I corr.*, i, p. 254; ii, pp 224, 254; *Stevens*, pp 168–80; *Story*, pp 124–8, 130; *Danish force*, p. 72; *Stevens*, p. 180; *JN*, pp 115, 307; Story, *Continuation*, pp 190–2, 209, 224, 227.

ENGINEERING

Organization and personnel

The primary function of military engineers in the late seventeenth century was to design and build fortresses and the works needed to besiege them, and to supervise their attack and defence. They also helped to facilitate the movement of armies and the provision of their logistical support by building and improving roads and bridges, sounding estuaries and ports for shipping and reporting on the navigational possibilities of rivers for the transport of goods by inland navigation.[29] The new importance of positional warfare was reflected in the great reputations of its most skilled European practitioners: the engineers Sébastien le Prestre de Vauban in France and Menno van Coehoorn in Holland. In 1683 there were about 190 military engineers in France; by 1696 the number had risen to 274. Engineers formed part of the train, sharing such similar mathematical skills with the artillerists that their roles were still generally regarded as interchangeable, although growing specialization was making this binary function increasingly inapt. In pre-war Ireland, as in England, engineers formed part of the ordnance under the control of the master general. The principal engineer was the surveyor general of fortifications and buildings, an office within the ordnance. William Robinson and William Molyneux held the office jointly until 1687, when they were dismissed by Tyrconnell. Their successor was Captain Francis Povey, the former commander of the ordnance at Tangier. He appears to have played no role during the war, probably vacating office at the revolution. A pointer to his allegiance is his dedication to Prince George, Queen Anne's consort, of his 1703 publication, *The gunner's companion*.[30]

Irish Catholic engineers were non-existent; none emerged during the war, and Jacobite military-engineering requirements were largely met by officers from the French corps of engineers, sent to Ireland by Louis XIV. Three engineers, accompanied by a draftsman and three ex-cadets, initially came in 1689. The senior officer, le sieur de Massé, rated by d'Avaux as 'a man of merit', was appointed engineer general, only to be killed by a cannonball at the siege of Derry. Earlier, he had sought promotion to brigadier, but was rebuffed by James II who told him the rank was not given to engineers. Other officers seem to have been accorded the rank of captain. Their pay was 100 *livres* per month. One complained that his salary was insufficient for his support, citing

---

29 *F-I corr.*, iii, pp 111–12. **30** Duffy, *Fortress*, pp 6–33 and passim; Lynn, *Giant of the grand siècle*, pp 590–1; Loeber, 'Engineers', pp 247–8, 289–98; Hoppen, *Common scientist*, pp 149–50; *DIB*, vol. 6, pp 568–72; *IALKC*, p. 145; *CSPD 1686–7*, p. 397.

the high cost of living in Ireland and the lack of travelling allowances when he went on tours of inspection. Most commentators regarded the second engineer, le chevalier de Tangis, as a fool who should never have been sent to Ireland. It was suggested that a headwound may have affected his sanity. There were complaints of his bad behaviour at Derry, and in the autumn, when he was in charge of the fortifications at Ardee, his incompetence led to his removal from the post and temporary arrest. In November, to make matters worse, he killed another French officer in a duel in Dublin. This prevented his return to France, and he remained in Ireland until the end of the war, his fate uncertain. However, his performance seems to have improved in the latter part of the war: he played a part in the defence of Athlone in 1690, for which he was promoted to colonel, and won praise for his plans for the improvement of the fortifications of Limerick in December. The third engineer, Loziers d'Astier, was young and lacking in experience, although there was general praise for his application and enthusiasm, and he was eventually promoted to the rank of lieutenant colonel. His criticism of the weakness of the Derry boom was ignored. He hoped to succeed de Massé, but in 1690 Louis sent the sieur de La Vigne to be chief engineer of the French troops in Ireland. A second engineer also accompanied the French expedition. Both La Vigne and Lozieres d'Astier returned to France with Lauzun in the autumn of 1690.[31]

The primary role of the French engineers was to strengthen fortifications, but they were also involved in the siege operations at Derry, the repair of roads and the surveying of rivers and harbours. In 1689 de Boisonge, a naval captain, and de Monteguy, an engineer, were sent with the specific task of taking soundings and preparing a chart of Galway Bay. Lambety, a French frigate captain, charted the Shannon estuary. Other Frenchmen mentioned in 1689–90 in an engineering role were Brigadier d'Amanzé, who had 'a smattering of knowledge about fortification', Goulet who was a draughtsman, and three former cadets: de Goutaille, de Belligny and Bernard. The ex-cadets were dismissed by Lozieres as ignorant and lazy, although Fumeron thought Bernard had some knowledge of fortifications. Also mentioned are Lhermite who came to Ireland in August 1689 and Valleri, an assistant engineer. The latter two, with Tangis, remained in Ireland after the departure of most of the French in October 1690.[32]

---

31 Mulloy, 'French engineers', pp 222–32; 'Journal 19/5 to 18/6 1689' (Carte MS 181), f. 71; *AH*, 21, p. 160; *d'Avaux*, pp 234, 355, 571; *F-I corr.*, i, pp 19, 22; ii, p. 521, iii, pp 44, 89, 99, 168, 195–6; *AH*, 21, pp 38–9. **32** *D'Avaux*, pp 576, 637; *F-I corr.*, i, p. 247; ii, pp 130, 251; iii, pp 84, 87, 196; Conroy, 'Galway Bay', pp 36–48.

Four French engineers were sent to Ireland in early 1691, with the specific task of improving the fortifications of the principal garrisons. The senior among them appears to have been Noblesse, although he is not explicitly named as such. The others were Robert, Lacombe and Sevin. Noblesse and Sevin supervised the works at Limerick and Lacombe those at Galway. Initially Robert was the resident at Athlone. He was a fiery individual, suspected of Huguenot sympathies. He clashed with Noblesse, whom he accused of being ignorant about fortification, and drew his sword in the course of an altercation with Major General Wauchope. Saint-Ruth sent him back to France after this incident. Lacombe then took over at Athlone. Noblesse and Lacombe were praised for their bravery during the siege of Athlone and again for their work during the final defence of Limerick, where Noblesse continued to serve despite being wounded in the arm. At the end of the war, Lacombe was one of those sent to France with news of the Irish capitulation.[33]

Two non-French engineers with the Jacobite army were le sieur Canneti, a Neapolitan who served in Ireland in 1689–90 and Richard Burton, an Englishman. Early in 1688 Burton had been sent by James to the emperor's army in Hungary

> to observe their method of marching, encamping, embattling, exercising, ordering their trains of artillery, their manner of approaching, besieging, attacking any town, their mines, batteries, lines of circumvallation, and contravallation, their way of fortification, their foundries, instruments of war and engines.

He came to Ireland via France in the spring of 1689, serving with the rank of lieutenant colonel until his death at Ballymore in 1691, caused by the loss of his hand, a typical artillerist's injury possibly incurred while serving one of the garrison cannon. He had previously worked on the fortifications of Sligo. Lozieres d'Astier thought both Cannetti and Burton inexperienced, and was also critical of an unnamed Scottish engineer who worked at Kinsale in 1689. Colonel Edward Wilson was a veteran of the Anglo-Dutch brigade and dabbled in engineering. He was briefly in charge of the fortifications at Galway where he was governor for a time in 1691. He made no secret of his contempt for the French and clashed with Lacombe, the resident French engineer.[34]

---

33 *F-I corr.*, i, p. 86; ii, pp 150, 206, 229, 259, 355, 364, 376, 513, 521, 543. 34 *F-I corr.*, ii, p. 281; iii, pp 133, 196, 198; Childs, *James II*, p. 41; King, appendix, p. 90; *CSPD 1687–9*, p. 151; Story, *Continuation*, p. 90.

The earthworks involved in the improvement of fortifications were very labour intensive, and required the employment of significant numbers of soldiers and civilians. Shortages of money and food disrupted progress, but by the end of May 1691, 1,500 men were engaged for twelve hours daily to improve the fortifications of Limerick. At Athlone 400 soldiers with forty peasants and townsmen were at work and at Galway 8–900 men. After Aughrim, a thousand armed men and three regiments of unarmed soldiers were at work on the fortifications of Galway and a further eight regiments on those of Limerick. As in France, soldiers who built fortifications received extra pay. The money came from French funds, but the workforce, supported by Tyrconnell, was reluctant to accede to the French practice of payment according to the task, rather than by the day as was customary in Ireland. Fumeron was sharply reprimanded by Louvois for paying by the day, and found it difficult to attract labour when he reverted to the French system, although this was eventually accepted. As funds ran short, his attempt to cut the daily wage met with a hostile reception from the workers and caused Stevens, who had been acting as an interpreter at the works at Limerick, to resign in protest.[35]

Shovels, spades, pickaxes, billhooks, axes and wheelbarrows, the basic tools of seventeenth-century engineering workers, were in short supply in Ireland. Boisseleau could find only 400 shovels, 100 spades and 140 pickaxes in the stores in Dublin when preparing the train in August 1689. The French engineers complained of a shortage of tools to fortify Limerick in 1690, and of the impossibility of obtaining them in sufficient quantity in Ireland. Some tools were made in Dublin in the winter of 1689–90. Sleds, wheelbarrows and baskets were made at Limerick in 1691. The fortification work at Athlone required 2,000 back baskets and 200 wheelbarrows to be made. In January 1691 8,000 assorted tools and 1,000 back baskets were sent from France. These measures enabled considerable improvements, under French direction, to the fortifications of Limerick, Athlone and Galway.[36]

Fortress warfare

The principal function of the engineers in 1689–91 related to improving fortifications, although occasionally they were also involved in their demolition, as at Bandon in 1689. Fortress warfare was central to Louis XIV's

---

35 *F-I corr.*, i, p. 126; ii, pp 217, 259, 260, 264, 266, 270, 284, 315, 329, 380; *Stevens*, p. 195.
36 *F-I corr.*, ii, pp 93–4, 147, 210, 237, 264, 277, 290, 380; *d'Avaux*, pp 83, 450; Mulloy, 'French engineers', p. 231.

reign, and he was fortunate to have in his service its greatest master, Sébastien le Prestre de Vauban, whose eventual promotion to marshal of France recognized the new status of military engineering. Fortresses and fortress lines defended territory, provided gateways into enemy territory and guarded supply routes. They accommodated soldiers and magazines, and were slow and costly to overcome. The high profiles and thin vertical walls of medieval fortifications were vulnerable to artillery bombardment, and their design afforded attackers the security of considerable areas of 'dead' ground. A new system that overcame these defects evolved in sixteenth-century Italy, from where it spread to northern Europe. The dominant characteristic of the *trace italienne* (meaning the Italian fortress plan, but the term is commonly used for the whole system) was the bastion, an arrowhead-shaped artillery tower projecting from the main rampart, from which cannon and hand-guns could sweep the dead ground beneath the walls. In the analysis of Christopher Duffy, the new system reworked fortification in three important respects:

(a) fortress walls crouched lower and lower until they became massive banks of earth, lined on their outer side by masonry retaining walls ... The new ramparts gave enhanced protection against view and cannon shot, while providing defenders with a wide and solid platform for their own artillery.
(b) novel outworks endowed the bastioned fortress with the very desirable attribute of defence in depth. The most important of these defences were the 'ravelin' (a free-standing, diamond-shaped fortification) and the 'covered way' (an infantry position running along the outer rim of the ditch).
(c) the overall plan assumed a characteristic star shape, and the lines of all the works were geometrically interrelated so as to bring a lethal cross-fire to bear along the ditches or over the ground outside the fortress.

The impact of the *trace italienne* was enormous, and it was one of the key factors behind the so-called military revolution that transformed warfare in early-modern Europe. With the backing of Louis XIV and Louvois, Vauban and his engineers brought the science of fortress building to new levels of sophistication, and built or reconstructed an immense range of fortresses and fortress lines to secure the frontiers of France. It was part of Vauban's genius that as fully as he embraced and developed the geometry of the *trace italienne*, he also believed that theory should defer to common sense in such matters as adaptation to terrain. Parallel to his fortress building, he developed a corresponding system of fortresses reduction, based on elaborate trench designs, for which he boldly claimed: 'I guarantee an infallible success without a day's extra delay, if you will defer to my opinion and follow faithfully the rules I lay down'.[37]

The *trace italienne* was introduced to Ireland in the sixteenth century. Thereafter medieval town fortifications were frequently strengthened by the addition of bastions, artillery platforms, gun embrasures and citadels. New artillery forts were erected in Ulster, and at seaports, estuaries and other strategic points. The mid-seventeenth-century war brought renewed activity to fortification building, but limitations in the design and degree of sophistication of the new defence works are suggested by the comparative ease with which they were captured. At Belfast, for example, a bastioned enceinte, built in 1643 and mounted with cannon, was captured three times in the next six years, and only at Limerick, 'the strongest fortress in Ireland', did the Cromwellians feel it necessary to conduct a formal siege with an extensive circumvallation, two new redoubts and a substantial train of artillery. Galway, on whose fortifications considerable sums had been expended, was invested by Sir Charles Coote's commonwealth force for nine months before its surrender in 1652. The strength of the defences may have discouraged a formal siege and enabled the citizens to surrender on reasonably favourable terms. The major restoration fortification was Charles Fort Kinsale, a structure sufficiently Vaubanesque in appearance and proportions to impress the French in 1690, although they were critical of its location beneath a hill. In 1684–5 the English ordnance engineer, Thomas Phillips, surveyed the Irish fortifications and concluded that only four or five locations were capable of resisting a considerable army. He proposed an ambitious scheme for improving their fortifications, but the estimated cost of £554,000 deterred the government from doing anything to implement it.[38]

The reports of the French officers and engineers who inspected the Irish fortifications in 1689–90 indicate that they were generally unimpressed by what they found. Cork was overlooked by hills; its walls were weak and lacked a backing of earth. The surrounding ditch dried out at low tide, and the citadel was in poor condition, with ruinous parapets and dismounted cannon. Limerick had been the biggest obstacle to the New Model army in 1651, but in 1690 the walls lacked an earth backing and were so dilapidated that Lauzun is said to have remarked that the city could be taken with roasted apples.

[37] Duffy, *Fortress*, p. 1; Parker, *Military revolution*, passim; Lynn, *Giant of the grand siècle*, p. 571.
[38] Kerrigan, *Fortifications*, chapter 2 and pp 114–21; Müller & Williamson, 'Fortification of Belfast', pp 306–12; Loeber & Parker, 'Military revolution in Ireland', pp 78–81; Lenihan, *Confederate Catholics*, pp 157–8; Kerrigan, 'Charles Fort Kinsale', pp 323–38; Mulloy, 'French engineers', p. 230; *Ormonde MSS*, ii, pp 309–35; Phillips maps; *F-I corr.*, i, pp 271, 346–7.

Stevens described Limerick's defences as 'no other but an old stone wall made against bows and arrows'. The fortifications of Carrickfergus were very bad, and the castle of no value to the town defences, as its only battery faced seawards. The fort at Duncannon, which guarded the entrance to Waterford, was most extraordinary and irregular in plan. Improvements were required at Athlone, where the east town was defended by a stone wall, which was without an embankment of earth and could be taken without difficulty. Riverside defences were necessary in the west town, which also suffered from the defect of being overlooked by high ground. Reports on Galway were mixed: Lozieres d'Astier considered the fortifications to be weak, and this was also the opinion of Rosen and Lauzun. However, in 1691 Fumeron took the view that the city's defences were in pretty good condition, especially on the landward side, where there was a double wall of good masonry. Laisné thought Charlemont needed very little further expenditure to make it defensible, although in the autumn of 1689 some earthworks were added under the supervision of M. Bernard, one of the French ex-cadets. In the 1640s earthworks with at least eighteen bastions had enclosed Dublin, but these were apparently gone by the 1680s. The French did not consider Dublin defensible, and this view prevailed in 1690, when the Jacobites abandoned the city the after the Boyne.[39]

The French generals believed that the Shannon offered the best line of natural defence in Ireland. Provided the major towns and river crossings were fortified, the resources of the west of Ireland, supplemented from the frontier territory, were adequate to support the army, while communications with France could be maintained through Limerick and Galway. In the autumn of 1689 Lozieres d'Astier was sent to Athlone with tools to improve the fortifications. He was probably responsible for the redoubts and defensive works constructed on the west-side river bank near the bridge, and for other fortifications to the north of the town, which played a part in its successful resistance of the Williamites in 1690. At Limerick, little was done to improve the fortifications until after the Boyne, when a covered way was hurriedly added to the counterscarp of the Irishtown ditch. However, it was not the strength of the Limerick fortifications, but the weakness of the Williamite artillery, coupled with the spirit of the garrison, that enabled the city to be successfully defended. Subsequently in France, Tyrconnell stressed the need to better fortify Limerick, Galway, Athlone and Sligo for the 1691 campaign. A

---

39 *F-I corr.*, i, pp 216, 243–4, 264, 267; ii, pp 28, 82, 97, 263; iii, pp 9, 84, 122, 142; MacGeoghegan, *History*, p. 594; *Stevens*, p. 193; Mulloy, 'French engineers', p. 231; Murtagh, 'Town-wall fortifications of Athlone', pp 101–5; Mulloy, 'Galway', pp 10–16; Loeber & Parker, 'Military revolution in Ireland', pp 78–9; Simms, *Jacobite Ireland*, p. 125.

sum of 80,000 *livres* was allotted to improve the fortifications of the first three, and Fumeron was instructed to ensure that the works undertaken were cost-effective and achievable in the available time. Louis XIV was closely interested in positional warfare and throughout the war copies of plans, elevations and costings of Irish fortifications were regularly sent to France.[40]

Noblesse and Sevin worked at Limerick, where by the summer bastions, storm-poles and a covered way had been added to the Irishtown, other works constructed on the King's Island and a traverse built to protect Ball's Bridge. Comparison of the French plans with William Webb's plan of 1651 suggests that some of the work done by the French, including most of the bastions on the south and west sides of the Irishtown wall and the works on the King's Island, were a refurbishment of earlier defence works. Noblesse also prepared plans for the fortification of Athlone where Robert was the resident engineer. The two were soon in fundamental disagreement. Noblesse's scheme was to abandon the east town and turn the west town into a fortress. Robert contended that the town on both sides of the river should be fortified because the east-town wall was reasonably strong, while the west town was overlooked by high ground that made it vulnerable should the enemy cross the river which was easily fordable in the summer. After Robert's departure Lacombe was brought over from Galway to complete the works. Reflecting Noblesse's view, little was done to improve the fortifications of the east town. On the west side existing half-bastions beside the river were made into full bastions and linked by a rampart which extended along the waterfront. A ravelin to cover the west gate, a covered way, traverses, storm-poles and palisades were added to the perimeter. During the siege of Athlone, Noblesse advised Saint-Ruth against the demolition of the west-town fortifications, with the unfortunate consequence that when the Williamites took the west town, the newly strengthened defences prevented a Jacobite counterattack.[41]

At Galway a number of works were erected to strengthen the southern angle of the fortifications, including a counterguard and a covered way, with a ravelin and other works on a neighbouring hill. Lack of subsistence and pay delayed the work, which was only completed under d'Usson's direction as the Williamites approached the city in July. Sligo had been extensively fortified under Burton's direction in 1689, with earthen ramparts around the town linked to an existing earth fort ('the Green Fort') to the north-east. Burton

---

40 *F-I corr.*, i, pp 86, 89; ii, p. 82; iii, pp 84, 184, 198; Story, *Impartial history*, pp 101–2. 41 *F-I corr.*, ii, frontispiece, pp 277, 290–1, 314–15, 355, 379–80; Kerrigan, *Fortifications*, p. 92; Lenihan, *Limerick*, facing p. 258; Murtagh, 'Town-wall fortifications of Athlone', pp 101–5; Story, *Continuation*, facing p. 107; Mulloy, 'French engineers', following p. 231; *JN*, p. 136.

was almost certainly also responsible for the fortification of Ballymore in County Westmeath prior to the 1691 campaign. The fortifications comprised 'a ditch twenty foot broad and ten foot deep, being also pallisado'd around', and some earthen bastions. Engineers actively participated when an army attacked or defended fortifications and were frequently casualties. De Massé was killed at the siege of Derry. Burton died at Ballymore. In 1691 Noblesse and Lacombe were praised for their courage and diligence during the sieges of Athlone and Limerick, where Noblesse was wounded, and for their work on strengthening Limerick's fortifications.[42]

The number of engineers serving with the Jacobite army was small, but the growth of positional warfare ensured that their presence was regarded as important. Their role in the early years of the war was largely limited to inspections and reporting. Their importance grew as the Jacobite army was forced onto the defensive. They played their part in the successful defence of Athlone and Limerick in 1690. In 1691, with limited time and resources, they did what they could to strengthen the key strong points of 'fortress Connacht'. Their contribution was most effective in Limerick and possibly Galway, but less so at Athlone due to disagreements over policy. It is likely that they were competent to conducted a formal siege, but the absence of resources, especially heavy artillery, ensured that neither at Derry or elsewhere did the opportunity arise.

Figure 6. Baron de Pointis, French artillerist

42 *F-I corr.*, ii, pp 232, 263, 274, 279, 376, 380, 382, 508–9; Mulloy, 'Galway', pp 11–12; Story, *Continuation*, p. 88, facing p. 272; Wood-Martin, *Sligo*, p. 134; Simms, 'Sligo', p. 130.

CHAPTER 7

Command and staff

King and council

AS MONARCH, King James was the commander-in-chief of the Irish army. He had a close interest in military affairs. In his younger days he had experience as a soldier on the Continent under both Turenne and Condé. Subsequently he served as lord high admiral of England, personally commanding the fleet against the Dutch at the battle of Lowestoft in 1665 (where Viscount Muskerry, Mountcashel's elder brother, was killed at his side). During his sixteen months in Ireland from March 1689 to July 1690 he actively fulfilled this leadership role by being the central figure in decision making about the army's organization, deployment and strategy. He also took personal command during its major engagements, briefly and controversially at the siege of Derry, proactively to halt Schomberg's advance at Dundalk, and incompetently at the Boyne. But these bouts of activity were interspersed with lengthy periods of inertia, during which he took little interest in public or military affairs, preferring to devote himself to prayer and hunting, possibly due to melancholia. While he was capable of exercising authority, he seldom gave much attention to detail, and d'Avaux found him changeable, irresolute, over-inclined to occupy himself with small matters and reluctant to face realities that ran contrary to his desires. He viewed Ireland as a stepping stone for his return to Britain, but by 1690, as hope of this faded, he grew increasingly disenchanted with Ireland and the Irish, and his generalship at the Boyne seems to have been scarcely more than perfunctory.[1]

In 1689 a small council met secretly each evening to take strategic decisions. It comprised King James, Ambassador d'Avaux, Lord Deputy Tyrconnell and the earl of Melfort, the Scot who was James's secretary of state. Rosen and the other generals were included when military operations were being considered. For example, James held a council of war in the autumn of 1689 to consider the merits of fortifying Ardee. So sharp were the divisions between Tyrconnell and Melfort that for an extended period Tyrconnell

---

[1] Turner, *James II*, pp 38–59, 71–82; d'Avaux, introduction, pp 6, 120–1; Simms, *Jacobite Ireland*, pp 125–6, 133–4.

withdrew from affairs to his official Chapelizod residence on the grounds of ill-health. By 1690 Lauzun had replaced d'Avaux and the able Irish lawyer, Sir Richard Nagle, had succeeded Melfort, with Tyrconnell once more fully involved. The inner council that year comprised the king, Tyrconnell, Lauzun and probably Nagle. By late June a council of generals had been established. Lauzun pressed for it to include the French *intendant*, d'Esgrigny, and reported how glad he was to have the advice of the French generals, La Hoguette and Famechon, at it. On the eve of the Boyne, Lauzun with the French generals, Léry-Girardin, La Hoguette and Famechon, counselled James. It is likely that Tyrconnell also took part in these deliberations, and possibly other generals. In the latter stages of the battle Lauzun again counselled James. In the autumn of 1690, before departing for France, Tyrconnell left the young duke of Berwick in command of military affairs, but to be advised by a council of senior officers, apparently consisting of Sheldon, Maxwell, John Hamilton and Sarsfield. This arrangement was unacceptable to the senior Irish officers, who compelled a reluctant Berwick to accept a council of all the general officers for the direction of the war. This body does not appear to have functioned in any formal way, but the eventual outcome was to place Sarsfield in the position of *de facto* military commander, leaving Berwick with little more than nominal authority. Tyrconnell resumed command on his return in January 1691, only to be replaced in May by the French general, Saint-Ruth. The latter seems to have relied on his French lieutenant generals, if anyone, for advice, and certainly on neither Tyrconnell nor Sarsfield. He did, however, hold a council of war to discuss strategy after the fall of Athlone, but chose to ignore the 'general opinion' of the senior officers that were present by resolving to give battle at Aughrim.[2]

Tyrconnell's position

In the absence of the sovereign, command of the Irish army was generally vested in the lord lieutenant or lord deputy. Clarendon was excluded from this role during his viceroyalty in 1685–7, when Tyrconnell, who had been made colonel of Arran's cavalry regiment in 1685, was appointed lieutenant general of the army in Ireland in April 1686. Command of the army was reunited to the viceroyalty in 1687 with Tyrconnell's appointment as lord deputy. After James arrived in Ireland, he made Tyrconnell a duke and subsequently promoted him to captain general. As such, he seems to have had authority to

2 *D'Avaux*, pp 54, 148, 226, 313; *F-I corr.*, i, p. 448; ii, pp 110, 380; iii, pp 69, 105, 130; O'Kelly, pp 72, 83–9, 95–6, 105, 129–31; Berwick, *Memoirs*, i, pp 78–83; 'Lauzun's reports', p. 103; Faulkner, 'An Irish diary of 1689', p. 28.

make appointments to every rank up to his own. However, in 1691 when Saint-Ruth was given overall command of the army, King James's memoirs state that 'Tyrconnell who before could have made a lieutenant general had not power now to make a colonel'. He successfully implemented the pre-war Catholicization of the army and then managed its wartime expansion. His involvement in the reduction of regiments and companies after James's arrival in 1689, despite his efforts to ameliorate its impact, generated great and lasting resentment. As army leader, he shared the blame for the Boyne defeat, and his credibility was further seriously undermined by his subsequent defeatism and advocacy of surrender to William, although by 1691 he had adopted a more bellicose stance. His manner was brusque, but d'Avaux praised his sincerity, frankness of speech and openness to reasoned argument, noting with approval his commitment both to his king and his country, as well as his amenability to the wishes not only of the Irish but of the French. Tyrconnell was intelligent, cunning and forceful, a combination of qualities that might have secured a better outcome in the Limerick surrender articles, had he lived to negotiate them.[3]

The Jacobite order of battle in 1689 placed Tyrconnell in command of the right wing – the senior position – and this indeed was where he was stationed at the Boyne in 1690. In Berwick's judgement 'he had not a military genius, but had much courage'. He showed it at the Boyne, where at sixty years of age, overweight and in poor health, he bravely charged the Williamites with his own cavalry regiment, although it is unlikely that he engaged in personal combat. By then, it was thirty years since he had been an active soldier, and in truth he was much more of an army administrator than a field commander, a role for which he had no pre-war experience. At the Boyne it is likely that he delegated the tactical direction of the Jacobite right wing to military professionals such as Sheldon, Berwick and Richard Hamilton. Berwick observed: 'from the battle of the Boyne he sank prodigiously, becoming as irresolute in his mind as unwieldy in his person'. With James's departure, he resumed the role of commander-in-chief, but left the young duke of Berwick in command of the army during the four months of his absence in France. By then, many of the leading officers held the view that Tyrconnell's age, infirmity, lack of command experience and defeatism rendered him unfit for military command. Sarsfield was the apparent leader of this disaffected group, but behind him and making most of the running were Henry Luttrell, Nicholas Purcell and Thomas Maxwell, supported by many others. The dissidents sent

---

3 Lenihan, *Last cavalier*, pp 183–9; *James II*, ii, p. 452; *d'Avaux*, pp 292–3, 382; Story, *Continuation*, p. 30.

a deputation to France to demand Tyrconnell's removal, and for the 1691 campaign they got their way when James delegated full authority in military affairs to Saint-Ruth, the French general sent to command in Ireland. Tyrconnell's subsequent arrival at the army camp met with hostility. Leading officers circulated a petition to remove him, and he finally departed after a threat was made to cut the guy ropes of his tent. These animosities ran deep, and the disunity they caused was damaging to authority and discipline. Even Tyrconnell's supporters conceded he knew nothing about waging war. After Saint-Ruth's death, Tyrconnell re-assumed his former authority, and took active steps to organize continued resistance until his own death only a month later.[4]

During the war Tyrconnell displayed considerable strategic sense. He had been against offering battle at the Boyne: 'if you venture the battle and lose it, you are ever lost to all intents ... whereas if you can prevent the small army from being beaten, you have a hundred chances for you'. Nevertheless, he also accepted that there was a case for defending Dublin and Leinster. He was credited with the dissemination of the order that brought the dispersed Jacobite army behind the Shannon after the Boyne defeat, and he shared the French view that the great river and its watery hinterland offered the best line of defence. According to Berwick, it was Tyrconnell who dispatched Sarsfield on the Ballyneety raid against the Williamite train. In 1691 he advocated the removal of the west-side fortifications of Athlone, which would probably have enabled the Jacobites to recover the town. After the fall of Athlone, Tyrconnell suggested putting the infantry into Limerick and sending the cavalry to raid the Williamite bases and supply lines east of the Shannon to force Ginkel to withdraw from Connacht, a strategy he had previously rejected. This was now supported by most of the senior officers, and after initial hesitation Saint-Ruth had apparently come round to accepting it, but the battle of Aughrim prevented its implementation. Tyrconnell was capable of energetic action too, as in 1689 when he rose from his sickbed at Chapelizod to advocate and organize the Jacobite resistance that halted Schomberg at Dundalk, and in his final days when he strove to maintain the army's will to resist after the Aughrim defeat.[5]

Marshal Rosen

In 1689 Conrad von Rosen, a French general of Baltic-German origin, was senior among the officers sent by Louis XIV to inject a measure of French

---

4 *F-I corr.*, ii, pp 212, 267; iii, facing p. 49; Berwick, *Memoirs*, i, p. 95; O'Kelly, p. 72; *James II*, ii, pp 422–3, 459–62.   5 *AH*, 4, pp 129–30, 133; Lenihan, *Last cavalier*, pp 143, 172; Berwick, *Memoirs*, i, pp 57–8, 66, 72–3; *JN*, pp 131–2, 137; *d'Avaux*, p. 479; O'Kelly, pp 130–1.

professionalism into the Irish army. He had forty years of service in France, where he had attained the rank of lieutenant general, the accepted qualification for an independent command. He accompanied King James to Ireland (although on a different ship). The office of marshal was revived to give him the customary step in promotion. Only King James and Tyrconnell outranked him, and in practice for much of 1689 he was the army's everyday commander. He was a capable soldier, but his service had been confined to the cavalry. In other respects also, his appointment was unsuitable, for his rough manner, blunt speech, irascibility and constant criticism of Jacobite mismanagement soon antagonized James. A major break in relations occurred when the king supported Richard Hamilton who had countermanded Rosen's order to herd local Protestants into Derry with the intention of increasing pressure on the defenders' food supplies. This was contrary to the protections given in James's name to the Protestants who lived in the neighbouring countryside, and the king was furious, calling Rosen 'a barbarous Muscovite'. From then on, his relationship with James deteriorated, and he grew increasingly disaffected. Fumeron reported that Rosen's constant ill-humour made him unbearable, and that he pushed people to intolerable lengths. Rosen told Louvois that the Irish were lazy savages, whose only inclinations were to pillage and rob. Their officers had neither intelligence or understanding, and the 'pitiful' government had put everything in a sorry state. James's failure to reform it made him doubt that the king had any desire to be restored. James, he complained, detested him, treated him rudely, disregarded his views and turned his back when Rosen proffered advice. He accused Melfort of laziness and incompetence, thereby ensuring the secretary of state's enmity and encouragement of James's animosity to the marshal.[6]

Rosen called service in Ireland a 'purgatory', from which he sought to be recalled. With the campaign ended, he finally resigned in November after James made public his forthcoming replacement by Lauzun. Berwick thought Rosen over-cautious to hold an independent command, adding that he was 'subject to passion, even to a degree of madness, and at those times he was even incapable of listening to any representations'. Rosen's interventions at Derry were unproductive, and his caution made him urge withdrawal to the Shannon rather than oppose Schomberg's autumn offensive, although he did take part in the autumn campaign. D'Avaux claimed that Rosen was popular with the army, but it seems more likely, as Berwick recalled, that the officers could not endure him, and that his departure was 'to their great satisfaction'.

6 *F-I corr.*, iii, pp 27, 47, 67–8; *AH*, 21, pp 98, 108, 167, 200–2; *d'Avaux*, pp 142, 259; *James II*, ii, pp 366–7, 387; Leslie, p. 100.

Nevertheless, his harsh methods and critical approach probably injected much-needed professionalism and organization into the army, which he claimed, with some truth, to have left in a better position to perform well than he had found it. He died a marshal of France, but it is probably significant that he only attained that prestigious rank on his retirement.[7]

Comte de Lauzun

The senior French officer in Ireland in 1690 was the comte de Lauzun, who held the appointment of captain general of the French. He did not exercise direct authority over the Irish army, except insofar as he was a close adviser to James, participating in the war councils and decision making. He was a favourite of Mary of Modena, having organized her escape with her infant son from England in 1688, and she and James had nominated him to Louis for the Irish command. Most people were amazed at the appointment, and Berwick's verdict is probably apt: 'if he ever had any knowledge of the military profession, he had by that time totally forgotten it ... In Ireland he showed neither capacity nor resolution'. None was more opposed to Lauzun than Louvois, and fear of the great minister's wrath, should he disobey his instructions to avoid battle in Ireland and play for time, influenced Lauzun's cautious approach to strategy and preference for a defensive war. In the event, he largely confined himself to diplomacy, and left the handling of the French troops to his deputy, the marquis de La Hoguette, a professional soldier, who was promoted to lieutenant general when he came to Ireland. Lauzun relied heavily on the professional generals for military advice.[8]

Marquis de Saint-Ruth

The commander of the Irish army in the 1691 campaign was Charles Chalmont, marquis de Saint-Ruth. He was a forty-year-old professional soldier, who held the rank of lieutenant general in France. It is likely that his appointment was on the recommendation of Mountcashel, whose regiment, with that of O'Brien, had campaigned successfully under his command in Savoy in 1690. In Ireland, he held the rank of general, and James gave him supreme authority over the army in place of Tyrconnell. Saint-Ruth disembarked at Limerick as late as May 1691, but quickly displayed great energy in preparing the army for the coming campaign. He had considerable

---

7 *F-I corr.*, iii, pp 82–3, 98, 103–4; *d'Avaux*, pp 394, 515, 556; *James II*, ii, pp 373, 376; Berwick, *Memoirs*, i, pp 58–9.   8 Berwick, *Memoirs*, i, p. 76; *F-I corr.*, i, pp xxvi–xxvii, 430.

leadership qualities and charisma, and unlike most of the French officers sent to Ireland, he treated the Irish with respect, winning their confidence and raising the soldiers' morale. His death at Aughrim was accounted disastrous for the Irish cause. With him, lamented O'Kelly, 'died all the hope and good fortune of Ireland: for from that hour they never thrived, or attempted anything that was great or glorious'. Saint-Ruth, in contrast to Rosen or indeed Tyrconnell, had the advantage of being supreme commander. His army was a more professional and better-armed force than had been the case during the first two years of the war. It was securely positioned behind the Shannon barrier, and by its successes at Athlone, Limerick, Ballyneety and in the 1690 mid-winter campaign, it had shown itself a match for its opponents. Yet, within six weeks of his arrival, the line of the Shannon was lost, the Irish army was heavily defeated and he himself was dead. It was on the face of it an unimpressive performance.[9]

Athlone was lost because of Saint-Ruth's over-confidence. He failed to demolish the west-town fortifications that prevented a Jacobite counter-attack should the Williamites cross the river. Convinced that the Williamites were lifting the siege, he ignored a representation from Maxwell that they were preparing an assault. Contrary to advice, he insisted on a changeover of battalions in the garrison 'to accustom his new-raised troops to fire and discipline', which contributed to an inadequate defence of the west town at the moment of crisis. Although undoubtedly 'piqued' by the loss of Athlone, probably the principal reason for his decision to fight Ginkel in a pitched battle was the army's dependence on Connacht for its quarters and support. The location he chose was a strong defensive position at Aughrim, west of Ballinasloe. Small rivers, a marsh and flanking bogs obstructed a Williamite attack, and the only approaches were along two narrow causeways on either extremity of the Irish position. Small field boundaries were skilfully converted by the Jacobites into a series of defensive breastworks. Although Saint-Ruth's dispositions were good, his position had at least two weaknesses. One was that the topography was equally obstructive to any possible Jacobite counterattack. The other was that Limerick, the key Jacobite stronghold, lay to the south-west, which made the defence of the Jacobite right wing imperative. When Ginkel concentrated his initial attack there, Saint-Ruth was obliged to strengthen the defence with forces moved across from his left, thereby weakening his position in the vicinity of Aughrim village, which was exactly where the battle was lost. Nevertheless, he came close to victory, being denied it probably only by his own death, which occurred as he rode over to stiffen the

---

9 O'Callaghan, *Irish brigades*, pp 54–6; *James II*, ii, p. 452; *F-I corr.*, i, pp xxviii–xxx, xxxviii.

defence of his embattled left wing. Despite his defects and failure, he was probably the ablest French general sent to Ireland, and certainly the most popular and much lamented.[10]

Patrick Sarsfield

Although never more than a major general, Patrick Sarsfield played a key leadership role in the Jacobite army especially after the battle of the Boyne. The Williamites regarded him as their ablest and most intransigent opponent. He had served with the Irish regiment in France in the 1670s and subsequently in the English horseguards under James II, being one of the very few army officers to offer resistance to the invading Williamites at Wincanton in November 1688. He escaped to France and accompanied James to Ireland, where he was promoted to brigadier and given command of one of the peacetime cavalry regiments. In 1689 he had campaigned with mixed fortunes in the north-west, first capturing Sligo, then vacating it before recapturing it again in the autumn. However, it was in 1690 that he came into his own, leading the 'cabal' of Irish officers who were determined to resist William after the Boyne defeat, scoring a spectacular success with the Ballyneety raid that destroyed William's train *en route* to besiege Limerick and then successfully directing the campaign to thwart the Williamite mid-winter offensive on the Jacobite quarters as well as firmly suppressing the Jacobite peace party. At this period, although nominally subordinate to the duke of Berwick, he was the effective leader of Jacobite resistance. He extended the Jacobite quarters into the no-man's-land beyond the Shannon, and encouraged the rapparees to rustle Williamite horses in large numbers to mount the cavalry for the coming 1691 campaign, for which he was optimistic of success. Created earl of Lucan and confirmed as major general by James, he remained hostile to Tyrconnell even after Saint-Ruth took command of the army. He opposed the decision to fight a pitched battle at Aughrim, at which he commanded the cavalry and dragoons on the embattled right wing of the Jacobite army, where the initial Williamite attack stalled. Later he did his best to cover the Jacobite retreat. With Saint-Ruth dead, soon to be followed by Tyrconnell, Sarsfield resumed his central role in continued Jacobite resistance, although outranked by the two remaining French lieutenant generals. Aware of his intransigence, it came as a pleasant surprise to the Williamites, and a shock to the more resolute Jacobites, when in 'a sudden, unexpected, prodigious change' he asked for terms

---

10 *James II*, ii, p. 455; Parker, p. 29; Berwick, *Memoirs*, i, pp 89–91; *Poema*, pp 372–3; *JN*, pp 137–43; O'Kelly, p. 134.

during the second siege of Limerick. Probably he was principally motivated by the prospect of an imminent subsistence crisis in the city with the failure of the promised French supply fleet to materialize. He must also have been conscious of the cavalry's low morale. There was also the need to preserve what he could of the Jacobite army by bringing it to France, where he could continue his own military career. His detractors said that he had little brains and was manipulated by others, but this is belied by his surviving letters, which suggest he was well in charge of events. D'Avaux judged him a good commander, both brave and able, and with a greater reputation in Ireland than anyone else. No less an authority than Marshal Luxembourg told Louis XIV that he had 'particularly noticed the valour and fearlessness of which ... [Sarsfield] has given proofs in Ireland. I can assure your majesty that he is a very good and a very able officer'.[11]

Subordinate generals

Beneath the commanding generals, military leadership was provided by a range of subordinate general officers: in descending order, lieutenant generals, major generals and brigadier generals. The army's pre-war establishment of generals consisted of Tyrconnell as lieutenant general, Justin MacCarthy as major general, and Richard Hamilton, Viscount Mountjoy and Sir Thomas Newcomen as brigadiers. At the start of 1687 Hamilton vacated his Irish command for colonelship of a cavalry regiment in England, where he was promoted major general in 1688. On his return to Ireland in 1689, he and MacCarthy were promoted lieutenant generals by Tyrconnell. This occurred before James's arrival and seems to have surprised the king, as such appointments would normally have required his prior approval, and Tyrconnell, although viceroy, was still only a lieutenant general himself! However, the appointments were not disputed, and James elevated MacCarthy to the peerage as Viscount Mountcashel. He also promoted Tyrconnell to captain general. Newcomen – a Protestant – was dismissed at the insistence of the French, while Mountjoy was imprisoned in France. The expansion of the army, coupled with the arrival of senior English, French and Scottish officers, led to the appointment of a number of new generals. Among them, as lieutenant generals, were James's son, the young duke of Berwick, Henry Jermyn Lord Dover and the marquis de Léry-Girardin. Subsequently, as promotions, casualties, surrenders, resignations and recalls took their toll,

[11] Dalton, i, pp 207, 209; ii, pp 58, 75; *d'Avaux*, pp 519–20; Berwick, *Memoirs*, p. 96; *James II*, ii, p. 424; *F-I corr.*, ii, pp 230–4, 257–8; O'Kelly, pp 154–5; *JN*, p. 147; Wauchope, *Sarsfield*, passim; Simms, *Jacobite Ireland*, passim.

numerous personnel changes occurred. In all forty-seven officers appear to have achieved general's rank during the war. In nationality, nineteen were Irish, eighteen were French, five were English and five Scottish. To this number can be added the five French generals commanding the French expedition of 1690. The proportion of Irish generals increased as the war went on. The roles of subordinate generals were more flexible than in modern armies, and battlefield commands depended on availability, rank and seniority, as much as on the tasks to be fulfilled. The principal sector commanders at the Boyne were lieutenant generals, whereas at Aughrim all were major generals. Except on the battlefield, when all available generals were expected to be present, their duties were normally allotted by rotation: thus, at the siege of Athlone Maxwell was noted as being major general on the day of the final assault, whose tour of duty was 'to command at that time'.[12]

Order of battle

The surviving order of battle from September 1689, employed most of the available combat generals. It shows the army drawn up conventionally in two lines, supported by a small reserve. The cavalry and dragoons are posted on the wings with the infantry in the centre. With King James as overall commander, Tyrconnell, now captain general, commanded on the right wing – the senior position – assisted by Lieutenant General le comte de Gassé. The left wing was commanded by Marshal Rosen, assisted by Lieutenant General le comte de Léry-Girardin. In the centre, the first line of infantry was commanded by Lieutenant General Richard Hamilton and the second line by Lieutenant General the duke of Berwick. Three major generals served with the infantry, le marquis de Boisseleau and Thomas Buchan with Hamilton and le marquis d'Escots with Berwick. Twelve brigadiers each commanded four infantry battalions or three to five squadrons of cavalry or companies of dragoons. On the right, Dominic Sheldon commanded the front-line cavalry and the marquis d'Estrade the dragoons. The three squadrons of cavalry that made up the second line were commanded by Patrick Sarsfield. In the centre, the front-line brigadiers were William Dorrington, le marquis d'Amanzé and John Wauchope, with Sir Charles Carney, le marquis de Saint-Pater and Thomas Maxwell in the second line. On the left wing, Viscount Galmoy commanded the front-line cavalry brigade and le comte d'Hocquincourt the dragoons. No brigadier was available to command the three cavalry squadrons of the second

---

12 *CSPD 1686–7*, pp 52, 98–9, 376, 378; Dalton, ii, p. 200; *James II*, ii, pp 327, 330; 'Longford letters', p. 65; *DIB*, vol. 9, p. 82; Berwick, *Memoirs*, ii, p. 90; *d'Avaux*, p. 359; *F-I corr.*, i, p. 354.

line, so their command devolved on John Parker, their regimental colonel. The reserve was commanded by Brigadier General Hugh Sutherland. Pointis commanded the artillery.[13]

This line of battle excluded Lieutenant General le marquis de Maumont and Major General le marquis de Pusignan, both killed earlier at Derry. Also absent were Lieutenant General Viscount Mountcashel, captured at Newtownbutler; Lieutenant General the earl of Dover, who was on a mission to France; and Major General Anthony Hamilton, somewhat discredited by his defeat at Lisnaskea and subsequent court martial, who was governor of Dublin. Thus, at this stage of the war, apart from King James himself, the army had in service a captain general, a marshal, four lieutenant generals, five major generals and twelve brigadiers. Including the artillery commander, the generals totalled twenty-four: eleven French, five Irish, five Scottish and three English. In the line of battle, each general officer was assisted by one or two generals of one rank beneath his own. It is noticeable that the highest-ranking officers commanded the wings. The infantry in the centre was under two lieutenants general. This practice was followed through with the other generals. The more senior were posted in the front line, and within each section those of the same rank took precedence from right to left, according to seniority. Thus, Richard Hamilton commanded the front line of the infantry, with Berwick, who was of the same rank but a later appointment, in command of the second line, while Dorrington, as senior brigadier, commanded on the right of the front line. Each general appears to have had a military secretary who drafted orders. Saint-Ruth's secretary was among the casualties at Aughrim. Orders were carried by aides-de-camp. King James had several ADCs at the Boyne. Calan, one of Maumont's French ADCs, was killed with him at Derry and another, Le sieur de Montmejan, was badly wounded. Lauzun mentions two of his ADCs, implying that he also had others. In 1691 d'Usson's nephew served as his ADC. La Tour de Monfort's nephew, killed by a bomb while they were at dinner in Limerick in 1691, was probably also serving as his uncle's ADC.[14]

For the 1690 campaign there were a number of changes. Of the French generals, Rosen, d'Amanzé and Pointis had departed, and d'Escots had died. They were not replaced from France. However, five French generals were sent to Ireland in command of the French expeditionary force: Lauzun, as captain general, Lieutenant General le marquis de La Hoguette, Major General le comte de Chemerault and Brigadier Generals le comte de Zurlauben and le

---

13 *F-I corr.*, iii, facing p. 49, pp 71–3.   **14** *D'Avaux*, pp 117, 155, 235, 312, 372, 377, 543; *F-I corr.*, i, p. 148; ii, p. 537; iii, p. 80; *JN*, pp 81–2; Story, *Continuation*, p. 123; 'Lauzun's reports', p. 121.

comte de Famechon. While in broad terms these officers would have exercised the authority of their rank and commanded in their section of the line, unlike the other French generals they did not hold commands in the Irish army. Others no longer present were Dover, who had resigned, Buchan who had been sent to command in Scotland and Mountcashel, who had escaped from captivity but then gone on to command the Irish regiments sent to France. A muster of June 1690, published by the Williamites, lists Sheldon as lieutenant general of the horse, but it does not seem that he rose above the rank of major general. The same list mentions Sarsfield as a major general, although his biographer dates his promotion to later in the year, and this would appear to be correct, as confirmation of his new rank by King James came only in 1691. The same list, perhaps more plausibly, ranks John Hamilton, younger brother of Richard and Anthony, as a brigadier.[15]

No order of battle survives for 1690 or 1691, and consequently the posting of only some generals is known at the Boyne and Aughrim. At the Boyne on the right wing, Tyrconnell continued as overall commander. Richard Hamilton commanded the infantry. Sheldon served under Berwick on the right wing. Sutherland was a brigadier on the right wing, where he was wounded. The major general of infantry in the right centre was Boisseleau, with Dorrington and d'Hocquincourt, who was killed, as brigadiers. On the left, Léry-Girardin commanded the front line of the cavalry, with Anthony Hamilton in command of the second line. Sarsfield was on this side of the battlefield, together with Maxwell, now a brigadier of dragoons. The French infantry was on the left, presumably in the front line and under their own generals. Sir Charles Carney commanded the reserve. James appointed Jean-Baptiste Laisné, sent from France with Lauzun's twelve guns, as lieutenant general and commander of the Jacobite artillery. There is no positive evidence on the deployment of the remaining generals, who presumably were posted elsewhere on the battlefield. Saint-Pater later complained that he was without a command and attached only to Tyrconnell's staff; probably this was also his situation at the Boyne. Léry-Girardin and d'Estrade accompanied James to France immediately after the defeat, and Anthony Hamilton followed with news of the raising of the siege of Limerick at the end of August. Tyrconnell, Lauzun and the remaining French generals left Ireland in September. In the autumn, shortly before he died, Lord Clare is mentioned as a major general and Denis MacGillycuddy as a brigadier.[16]

---

15 *F-I corr.*, i, p. 342; *JN*, p. 92; *d'Avaux*, p. 688; Story, *Continuation*, p. 30; *James II*, ii, pp 425; Wauchope, *Sarsfield*, p. 120; Boulger, p. 139. **16** *F-I corr.*, i, pp 373, 446, 448–9, 452; ii, pp 76–8, 102–3, 110, 113; iii, p. 131; *James II*, ii, p. 397; Berwick, *Memoirs*, i, pp 64–5; Story, *Continuation*,

Tyrconnell resumed command of the army on his return in January 1691, but in May he was displaced by the marquis de Saint-Ruth, to whom James had given full authority in military affairs with the rank and title of general. Three other French generals accompanied Saint-Ruth to Ireland: Lieutenant General le chevalier de Tessé, who was made deputy commander of the field army; Lieutenant General le marquis d'Usson, who was given overall responsibility for the defence of towns; and Major General Henri de La Tour Monfort, who was governor of Limerick. All four had received the customary step-up in rank on coming to Ireland. Only Saint-Ruth and de Tessé were present at Aughrim. According to de Tessé, Saint-Ruth, as commander, positioned himself on the army's right (probably right of centre on the high ground to the rear) giving de Tessé overall charge of the army's left. Since de Tessé was the sole lieutenant general present, major generals filled the other principal commands. Sarsfield seems to have commanded the cavalry on the right and Sheldon certainly commanded it on the left. In the centre, Major General William Dorrington commanded the front line of infantry, and Major General John Hamilton the second line. Henry Luttrell was Sheldon's brigadier, and possibly Clifford was Sarsfield's. Together with Dorrington and Hamilton, six infantry brigadiers were either killed or captured on the day: William Barker, William Tuite, Mark Talbot, Baron Bellew, Maurice Connell and Gordon O'Neill. Some sources also mention a Brigadier Henry O'Neill, otherwise unknown, as being killed. The reserve consisted of a single cavalry regiment under its colonel, Brigadier Viscount Galmoy.[17]

Absent after the fall of Athlone were Major General Thomas Maxwell, 'general of dragoons', who had been captured, Brigadier Denis McGillycuddy, who was killed, and probably Major General Wauchope, who had been injured in the town's bombardment. Patrick Plunkett and Michael Rothe were mentioned as brigadiers towards the end of the war, probably as replacements for some of the Aughrim casualties. There is no mention of Hugh Sutherland after the Boyne. However, he was styled a major general in France in 1692, while serving as an officer in James II's lifeguards, and he may have attained this rank in Ireland in 1691. Balldearg O'Donnell was made a brigadier general in February 1691, a similar rank to that he had held in Spain. Thus, of the known generals in 1691, four were French, three were English and two, or possibly three, were Scots, whereas fourteen, or possibly fifteen, were now Irish. This marked a shift in favour of the Irish from the preceding years of the war, although their appointments were largely at brigadier level. After Saint-Ruth

p. 30; King, appendix, p. 68; Wauchope, *Sarsfield*, p. 120; *Stevens*, p. 187. **17** *F-I corr.*, i, p. xxx; ii, pp 383–4; *JN*, p. 138; *A particular and full account of Aghrim*, p. 4.

was killed, command of the army reverted 'in a manner' to Tyrconnell, until his own death a month later. This left de Tessé and d'Usson as ranking lieutenant generals. Both were defeatist, and neither had the authority of Sarsfield, who although of lower rank was now more than ever the dominant figure in the Jacobite high command. Meanwhile Brigadiers Clifford and Henry Luttrell had been placed under arrest.[18]

Civilian administrators

An important civilian figure in the army's high command was the secretary for war. Much to Tyrconnell's chagrin, James initially included this position in the portfolio of his Scottish secretary of state, John Drummond, earl of Melfort, who had accompanied him to Ireland. Melfort was heartily detested by both the French and the Irish, who resented his British-leaning influence on James and criticized his administrative incompetence. Following Melfort's dismissal in August 1689, Sir Richard Nagle, a leading Irish lawyer close to Tyrconnell, took over the office of secretary of state for war, which he held until the end of hostilities, with the exception of the second half of 1690, when he was in France. Although Nagle had little knowledge of military affairs, he was generally regarded as competent even by Rosen, and his tenure was uncontroversial. During Nagle's absence, Lord Riverston, an Irish judge, temporarily held the office, but in December he was dismissed at Sarsfield's insistence because of suspected complicity in the unsuccessful Williamite winter offensive. Until Nagle's return with Tyrconnell in January, the office seems to have been held by Michael Kearney, who was married to a sister of Nagle's wife. Possibly because of the example of France, where Louvois held sway, the secretaryship had grown in importance in Britain (while never rivalling France), and this was probably paralleled in Ireland. Apart from general administrative duties, the secretary was responsible for the issue of commissions and marching orders, the distribution of horses, weapons and other *matériel*, the posting of officers, the publication of the code of discipline and the adjudication of regimental seniority, which determined each unit's place in the line of battle. The surviving papers of Melfort's under-secretary and fellow Scot, David Nairne, suggest that his office was active in these roles, even if many judged his performance unsatisfactory.[19]

---

18 *F-I corr.*, ii, pp 374, 376, 503; *James II*, ii, p. 452; *JN*, pp 149, 167, 188; Boulger, p. 291; 'O'Donnells in exile', p. 55; Wauchope, *Sarsfield*, p. 254. **19** *D'Avaux*, pp 313, 429, 507–14; *AH*, 21, pp 136, 200; *F-I corr.*, iii, pp 65, 105; *ODNB*, vol. 16, p. 969; *DIB*, vol. 6, pp 849–52; McGuire, 'Sir Richard Nagle', pp 118–31; O'Kelly, pp 102–3, 106; *Proclamations*, pp 180–2; Childs, *Charles II*, pp 104–6; Officer list (Bodl., Carte MS 181), passim.

Although there was no general staff as such, there were a number of administrative 'generals', some military and some civilian. They were individual appointments, and the officers lacked any collegiate character, each reporting to Tyrconnell, as captain general, or, at least in theory, to King James, while he was in Ireland. Much the most influential was the French '*commissaire general de guerre*', Jean François de Fumeron. *Intendants* and *commissaires* were the civilian officials, answerable to Louvois, who were responsible for much of the supply and administration of the French army. Fumeron had been a trusted *commissaire* in Alsace, prior to being sent to Ireland in response to James's request for an official to organize the supply of food and munitions to the expanded Irish army. He was to be paid 100 ecus (gold crowns) per month by James, and Louvois stipulated that if this was not done Fumeron should return to France where 'he is very necessary to the armies of the king'. He later claimed that his sojourn in Ireland cost him 10,000 *livres* of his own money. D'Avaux, conscious of his own inexperience in military matters and of the inability of the Jacobites to organize the army's administration, impatiently awaited his coming and worked closely with him after his arrival in June 1689. Although styled *commissaire general*, Fumeron in effect acted in Ireland as a higher-ranking *intendant* and was sometimes addressed as such. He was present for the 1689 and 1691 campaigns, but absent throughout most of 1690, when he returned to France for medical treatment in relation to a troublesome anal fistula. He attributed the aggravation of his condition to the amount of riding he had to do, travelling throughout Ireland to inspect, reform and report.[20]

Fumeron proved an excellent organizer, and he brought order and solutions to the chaos and confusion he found in the army on his arrival. To assist him, he had a number of subordinate *commissaires*, each with specific responsibilities. His own involvement was wide ranging, and included arrangements for the provision of food, fodder, clothing, tents, weapons and other *matériel*. He also concerned himself with recruiting, discipline, musters, pay, artillery, hospital services, transport, money, fortifications, training camps, troop movements and intelligence. He oversaw the unloading of supply ships and the sale of cargoes of captured vessels. He disposed of the effects of deceased French officers. In 1690 he made preparations for the reception of the French troops in Ireland and for the dispatch of the Irish troops sent to France. In 1691 he did his best to fulfil King Louis's instructions to rebuild Tyrconnell's authority and secure recruits for the Irish regiments in France.

20 *F-I corr.*, i, p. xxxiii; *d'Avaux*, pp 41, 183; Lynn, *Giant of the grand siècle*, pp 88–97; Rowlands, *Dynastic state*, pp 78–82, 93–9.

Throughout, he kept Louvois fully informed of events in Ireland. His reports reveal him to have been clear headed, dispassionate, industrious and efficient. He did not hesitate to condemn the poor quality of some of the weapons sent from France, the lack of forward planning, Melfort's inefficiency, or the dishonesty of Aufroy, the French army contractor, whom he recommended gaoling. In d'Avaux's judgement Fumeron had served King James well, and afterwards he rose to be one of the chief clerks at the French war ministry. Less is known of the activity of his replacement in 1690, the *intendant* René de Jouenne d'Esgrigny, but there was no criticism of his conduct, which Lauzun praised when urging his inclusion at councils of war.[21]

Another important officer was the muster-master general. He, or the controller of musters, was responsible for organizing the regular inspection parades – 'musters' – conducted by their officials to check the strength, arms and equipment of each unit. The muster-master then certified the return to the paymaster general, who issued the regiment's pay to its colonel on foot of the information in it. The overall strength of the army could be calculated from the returns, a number of which survive for 1689 and 1691. Abraham Yarner, a Protestant informant of the duke of Ormond, had been appointed muster-master general for life in succession to his father, but fled Ireland at the time of the revolution. He was replaced by Solomon Slater, an English veteran of the Anglo-Dutch brigade, who held the office by June 1690. Robert FitzGerald, a brother of the 17th earl of Kildare, had been the pre-revolution controller of musters. Although FitzGerald was still listed as such in 1690, his tenure must have ended when he was imprisoned under the Jacobite regime. It is unclear how long Slater retained his appointment or, indeed, whether it was ever much more than a sinecure. Certainly, by May 1689 French *commissaires* were performing the role, as they did in France, and Fumeron seems to have included the muster-master's function among his responsibilities. (Slater was noted as being in exile at Saint-Germain in 1699.) The paymaster general, who issued the army's pay to the regimental colonels, was Sir Michael Creagh, a Dublin merchant and the city's lord mayor in 1688–9, who was himself colonel of an infantry regiment. Presumably he was appointed because of his financial acumen. The office of receiver general, with responsibility for the receipt of revenue, was shared between the English Jacobites, Sir Henry Bond and Louis Doe, who both sat in the Jacobite parliament. However, according to Lauzun, real power lay with the

---

21 *AH*, 21, pp 112–15, 127–8, 130, 136–8, 143, 154–5, 165–6, 199–200; *F-I corr.*, i, pp 85–8, 125, 241–2, 243–4, 247–8, 255–9, 263–5, 281, 431; ii, pp 177, 207, 212–18, 220–3, 238–9, 267, 275, 285, 333, 335, 363, 365–7, 382; iii, p. 48; *d'Avaux*, p. 639.

commissioners of the treasury, whose procrastination frequently frustrated executive orders.[22]

Staff appointments

In 1689 Mountcashel was appointed master general of the ordnance in succession to Lord Mountjoy. No fresh appointment seems to have been made after his departure for France in 1690. Pointis sought appointment as master general in 1689. He took command of the artillery at Derry, where he was seriously wounded, and this ended his Irish career. Boisseleau temporarily succeeded him, but was reported to be very ignorant of gunnery. An unnamed controller of artillery is mentioned in early 1690; thereafter the management of the artillery seems to have been in the hands of French *commissaires*. Laisné in 1690 was both commander of the artillery (with the rank of brigadier general) and *commissaire*. Five French artillery *commissaires* are mentioned in 1691. Boisseleau was originally sent to Ireland as adjutant general, at that time a senior staff officer assisting the army commander. His involvement in the establishment of training camps may have been related to this role, but otherwise he was primarily a field commander. Thomas Maxwell, a Scottish Jacobite officer, was appointed quartermaster general in 1689. After his capture at Athlone, Colonel James Lacy succeeded him as quartermaster general. Le marquis d'Estrade came to Ireland to be quartermaster general of cavalry, and the chevalier de Banqué (Baines?) was appointed inspector general of infantry. He was succeeded by Colonel Edward Wilson, an English veteran of the Anglo-Dutch Brigade, noted for his antipathy towards the French. Marigny, the lieutenant colonel of Clare's infantry who was captured at Newtownbutler, was also described as inspector of troops in Ireland. The roles and occupants of the posts of advocate general, chaplain general and surgeon general are covered elsewhere.[23]

An absentee from the Jacobite army's high command was a scoutmaster general, an officer responsible for military intelligence. The position existed in England and had done so in restoration Ireland, but seems to have become dormant under James. Yet, the army was well served by good intelligence. In August 1689 the paymaster general was ordered to pay Melfort £500 'for secret service', suggesting that the secretary was a conduit for intelligence at

22 *CSPD 1689–90*, p. 149; Story, p. 30; Childs, *Charles II*, pp 104–6; *PI*, i, pp 106–8; Childs, *BD*, p. 86; Dalton, ii, p. 228; 'A journal of what has passed since his majesty's arrival' (Carte MS 181), f. 30; *CB*, iii, p. 20; 'Lauzun's reports', p. 108.   23 Story, p. 30; *d'Avaux*, pp 114–15, 142, 161, 470; *F-I corr.*, i, pp 90, 257; ii, pp 520, 541; iii, p. 129; *AH*, 21, p. 110; 'Journal 1/6 to 18/7 1689' (Carte MS 181), ff 3, 17 and passim; Berwick, *Memoirs*, i, p. 43.

that time. In September 1690 the Williamites forbade the movement of Catholics out of their parishes, in part because they were conveying intelligence to the Jacobites. The family members of Jacobite soldiers killed in rebellion were thought to be particularly active as sources of Jacobite intelligence, and the Williamite sheriffs were ordered to move them to the Jacobite quarters across the Shannon. A further proclamation ordered no Catholics to live within ten miles of the Shannon to prevent their 'constant correspondence, commerce and intercourse' with the Irish in the west. Prior to the 1691 campaign Mark Bagot, the former sergeant-at-arms in the Irish parliament, was caught in female disguise as he entered Dublin 'to do secret service' for the Irish. He was subsequently hanged as a spy. But overall, Williamite counter-intelligence measures do not seem to have had much effect. 'The industrious sagacity of his trusty spies in Dublin, who penetrated every design of the enemy', kept Sarsfield fully informed of Williamite plans for their abortive winter offensive in 1690. The rapparees, operating in the Williamite quarters and in close touch with the Catholic civilian population, were also an important intelligence source. The Williamite general, Hugh Mackay, grumbled that the Jacobites in 1691 'had full information of our movements, whereas we knew nothing of theirs'. Deserters also provided information on the Williamite forces and dispositions.[24]

Battle control

In the absence of modern communications systems, general officers needed to be close to the action. They were also expected to be brave, as indeed King William was – to the point of recklessness – at the Boyne. These requirements exposed them to risk: just as Gustavus Adolphus and Marshal Pappenheim were killed at Lützen and the great Turenne at Salzbach, in Ireland the French generals, Maumont and Pusignan, were killed at Derry, and so too was Brigadier Ramsay. Le comte d'Hocquincourt was killed at the Boyne, as was Marshal Schomberg, the senior Williamite general. Saint-Ruth was decapitated by a lucky cannon shot at Aughrim, a fatality that proved disastrous for his army. Other generals on both sides were also casualties: killed, wounded, captured or died. Nevertheless, even in the proximity of the combat zone the degree of control commanders could exercise was limited. Distances could be considerable, clouds of smoke from the discharges of black powder severely restricted vision, and the intelligence and orders transmitted

24 *IALKC*, p. 1; *CSPD 1685*, p. 44; *Stuart MSS*, i, p. 46; O'Kelly, p. 104; *JN*, p. 129; Story, pp 64, 79; MacKay, *Memoirs*, p. 137; *Proclamations*, pp 208, 211–13; *F-I corr.*, i, p. 202; ii, pp 275, 279, 281, 361.

by aides galloping backwards and forwards across the combat zone were slow moving, error prone and dependent for delivery on the couriers' accurate navigation and safe survival. At Aughrim, Saint-Ruth, like his opponent, Ginkel, was continuously on the move, riding up and down the lines as necessity required. In a general way he commanded the right or southern side of the battlefield, while Lieutenant General de Tessé commanded the left or northern side. But this division was not absolute: when Saint-Ruth was killed, he seems to have been riding over to de Tessé's wing to check the Williamite breakthrough. However closely the commanding general tried to keep in touch with proceedings, the practical obstacles to exercising microscopic control of operations necessitated the delegation of considerable autonomy to the subordinate generals, who commanded different sections of the lines. They were expected to be aware of their roles and responsibilities, and were briefed beforehand on specifics by the army commander either personally or at a council of war.[25]

There were many weaknesses in the Jacobite command structure. However, the introduction of French generals compensated for the shortage of experienced general officers. These men were aware of Louvois's misgivings about the Irish campaign, and several of them were inclined to conform to his negative view by stressing the deficiencies they found in the Irish army. This brought them into conflict with James and his advisers, which tended to undermine their role. Yet their input was invaluable in turning the army into a professional force. It was reported that the army rejoiced at the promised coming of French generals to lead it in the 1691 campaign. Equally invaluable were the French civilian officials, Fumeron, d'Esgrigny and their subordinate *commissaires*, who did much to regularize the army's staff shortcomings. They sent Louvois detailed reports, and he kept a close eye on their activities. Most of the Irish and British Jacobite generals were soldiers of experience, but few had previously held general's rank. While officers like Sarsfield were well up to a command role, others like Anthony Hamilton clearly were not. Tyrconnell's perceived incompetence was destructive of Jacobite unity, but he showed no inclination to step aside, although at the Boyne he may have deferred to the advice of the professional generals that accompanied him: Richard Hamilton, Sheldon and Berwick. Berwick, despite his youth, was already an experienced soldier at the time of the Irish campaign. As James's son he was well connected, and went on to have a successful career in the French army, achieving the rank of marshal in 1706.[26]

[25] O'Kelly, p. 132; *F-I corr.*, ii, pp 383–4; Lynn, *Giant of the grand siècle*, p. 315.   [26] *F-I corr.*, ii, pp 211, 267; *ODNB*, vol. 19, pp 881–4.

CHAPTER 8

Support services: law, medicine and chaplaincy

Law

THE KING'S TRADITIONAL prerogative to maintain and command the armed forces throughout his realms was affirmed in the 1661 militia act of Charles II's English parliament. There was no precisely equivalent Irish act, but in the same year the Irish parliament's act of recognition accepted that 'all ... rights, privileges, prerogatives and pre-eminencies royal' had passed from Charles I to Charles II. The Jacobite parliament's 1689 act of recognition explicitly stated that 'the sole and supreme power, government, command and disposition of the militia, and of all the forts by sea and land, and of all forts and places of strength, is and by the laws of this realm, and of England, ever was the undoubted right of your majesty, and of your royal predecessors, kings and queens of these dominions'. This, then, was the legal basis of King James's army. The constitutional position did not recognize a distinctive Irish army, but viewed the forces in Ireland as part of the king's army, although in many respects the Irish segment, with its own establishment, was a distinctive force, sometimes referred to as 'our army in Ireland', and at other times as 'our army of Ireland'.[1]

Discipline has been described as 'the glue that held seventeenth-century armies together'. The army's internal code of discipline was contained in the Articles of War issued under the royal prerogative. Soon after his accession King James had ordered the lords justices to put the latest version into effect in Ireland, even before its promulgation in England. In June 1689 James ordered the Articles of War to be reprinted in Dublin, after which they were to be read at the head of every regiment, and all officers were charged with their enforcement. Every officer was expected to have a copy of the Articles in his possession. A short act of the Jacobite parliament addressed the troublesome issue of the enforceability of military law by declaring that it was lawful for the king to publish Articles of War to be observed by all military

---

[1] 13 Car. II, c. 6; 13 Car. II, c. 1 (Ir.); *Acts of James II's parliament*, p. 5; Hand, 'Constitutional position', p. 331.

personnel, and to proceed against and punish offenders by court martial, even in peacetime.[2]

The Articles as promulgated were almost certainly identical to those adopted in England in 1686, and wide ranging. The first five dealt with the soldier's soul, requiring his attendance at church, prohibiting the sale of drink by the sutlers during religious services, and forbidding blasphemy, fornication and adultery. A number of articles followed relating to a soldier's duty to his sovereign. They included the oath of allegiance to be taken, and bans on traitorous words, correspondence with the enemy or any rebel, enticement of a soldier from his duty, mutiny, sedition and betrayal of the watchword. Several articles prohibited duelling and related activity. A soldier who committed the common law crimes of murder, rape or robbery was subject to military trial and punishment. Articles controlling a soldier's relations with civilians included prohibitions on free quarters, the physical abuse or intimidation of his host or his family, and the destruction of property, real or personal. Combat efficiency was supported by articles prohibiting desertion, absence without leave, flight from the enemy, abandonment of a post, surrender, disobeying the order of a superior, resisting an officer in the performance of his duty, absence from guard duty, sleeping on duty, or failing to fall in upon the colours on beat of drum or sound of trumpet, and with arms decently kept and well fixed. Several articles sought to preserve equipment, including prohibitions against a soldier gambling away his horse or equipage, losing or pawning his arms and embezzling ammunition and victuals. Other proscribed practices were the violation of safe conducts, firing of muskets in camp after the watch was set, officers and soldiers acting as victuallers to the army, and the sale of drink by sutlers between tattoo and reveille (dusk and dawn). A number of articles dealt with the relief and protection of private men, safeguarding their property and allowing them to complain to their colonel over alleged wrongs and grievances, with a right of appeal to the commander-in-chief, if the colonel took no action. But this was qualified by the proviso that if the complaint proved false, the complainant would face a court martial. Disputes between regimental personnel, whether of equal or different rank, were to be tried by regimental court martial.[3]

The Articles laid down penalties for their breach. These included dismissal from the service, cashiering or reduction to the ranks in the case of officers, riding the wooden horse (sitting for an extended period on a sharp plank),

---

[2] Lynn, *Giant of the grand siècle*, p. 400; *Ormonde MSS*, i, pp 406–7; 'Journal 19/5 to 18/6 1689' (Carte MS 181), f. 70; 'Journal 1/6 to 18/7 1689' (ibid.), f. 4; *Proclamations*, p. 144; *Acts of James II's parliament*, pp 81–2; Childs, *Charles II*, pp 78–81.   [3] Walton, *History of the British army*, pp 808–17.

detention in irons, running the gauntlet, demotion to the pioneers, tongue-piercing and sentence of death. The last, although authorized for several offences, could generally be mitigated to a lesser penalty. The imposition of penalties was to be preceded by a court martial, either a general court martial, for which there was provision for a clerk; or a regimental court martial, which required authorization by the commander-in-chief, who was also required to ratify any sentence it imposed. The court was to be composed of commissioned officers of the regiment. The advocate general was the principal administrative officer for military law. He arranged the holding of courts martial, saw to the taking of witness depositions and conducted the prosecution at the trial. Felix O'Neill, a chancery barrister from Lisburn, was appointed to the office in 1687. He became a regimental officer in the army in 1689, with command of a regiment in 1690. The responsibility for holding offenders in custody and punishing them in accordance with the sentence of the court lay with the provosts marshal, either regimental or general. The regimental provost appears in practice to have been the quartermaster, whereas the provost general was a distinctive appointment that related to the army as a whole. Darby Keefe was commissioned provost marshal of the army in June 1689 and supported by a troop of dragoons. His successor, Francis Toole, had a company of fusiliers. The Articles provided for the provost marshal's protection and support in the performance of his duties. In 1689 Fumeron felt that provincial provosts were needed to restore order in the countryside, and provosts marshal were appointed in each county.[4]

There is some evidence for the enforcement of the articles in practice. The best-known court martial occurred in the wake of the Jacobite defeat at Newtownbutler in 1689. Prior to the battle, there had been a skirmish at Lisnaskea, from which the Jacobite forces had fled. Three weeks later their commander, Major General Anthony Hamilton, and Captain Peter Lavallin of Cotter's dragoons were tried by general court martial chaired by Marshal Rosen. The defence was that there had been a mix-up over the interpretation of an order. Hamilton, who was of high rank and well connected, was acquitted, but Lavallin was sentenced to be shot. The sentence was duly carried out, despite Lavallin's protests of innocence to the end. For 'quitting his post and running shamefully away at Athlone' Lieutenant Colonel James O'Neill of Cormac O'Neill's regiment was reduced to the ranks, and five captains of the regiment were suspended. There were a number of instances of

---

[4] *Middle Temple admissions*, p. 199; *CSPD 1686–7*, pp 421, 423; Childs, *Charles II*, pp 83–4, 103–4; Walton, *History of the British army*, pp 815–17; TCD MS 670; *KJIL*, ii, p. 770; 'Journal 19/5 to 18/6 1689' (Carte MS 181), f. 73; 'Journal 1/6 to 18/7 1689' (ibid.), ff 8–10; *d'Avaux*, p. 364.

1. Richard Talbot, duke of Tyrconnell, captain general.

'He had not a military genius, but much courage' (duke of Berwick)

2. King James II.

'He would be better to spend the rest of his days praying to God in a cloister than thinking about commanding armies or governing a state' (Viscount Clare)

3. Conrad Von Rosen, marshal.

'Every day that he is in a bad mood, and he pushes things to an unbearable point for everyone' (*Commissaire* Fumeron)

4. Patrick Sarsfield, earl of Lucan, major general.

'The darling of the army' (Charles O'Kelly)

5. James FitzJames, duke of Berwick, lieutenant general.

'[At the Boyne] having his horse shot under him, was for some time among the enemy, he was rid over and ill bruised; however, by the help of a trooper got off again' (King James II)

6. Antonin-Nompar de Caumont, comte Lauzun, captain general of the French.

'He was such an extraordinary person, so eccentric in every way that the vicissitudes of his life defy imagination' (duc de Saint-Simon)

7. Anthony Hamilton, major general.
'A brave man, but unsuited for command' (Ambassador d'Avaux)

8. Justin MacCarthy, Viscount Mountcashel, lieutenant general.

'Although his short sight will prevent him from becoming a great general, nevertheless he will be very useful' (Ambassador d'Avaux)

9. Henry Luttrell, brigadier general.

'At his trial… it was impossible that he could be found guilty by men that had either honesty or honour' (earl of Westmeath)

10. Marquis d'Usson, lieutenant general.

'A small man, shaped like a pumpkin, but full of spirit, courage and talent for war' (duc de Saint-Simon)

11. Thomas Maxwell, major general.

'[At the siege of Athlone] when Major General Maxwell was called to by Cormac O'Neill's men for ammunition, he asked them whether they designed to kill larks' (Colonel Felix O'Neill)

12. Battle of Bantry Bay, 1689 (Adrian van Diest)

'The French gained their point by in landing the succours they brought' (King William III)

13. Battle of the Boyne, 1690.

'An entire book would be needed to contain all the mistakes that were committed that contributed wholly to the rout of the army' (Brigadier Zurlauben)

Irlandoise à la Riuiere de Boyne en Irlande le 1 Juillet 1690.
Roy et Gravé par Theodor Maas.

1. King William at the head of his Cavalerie followed by Prince George, the Duke of Ormond and G. Ginckel.
2. Count Solms with the first Battaillon of Guardes. 3. the Second Battaillon. 4. the third Battaillon.
5. The Earle of Portland, Count Schomberg & M. G. Overlack. 6. Mons.r de Suilvinum. 7. Mons.r Isaack
8. Collonel Geer. 9. Doctor Walker kill'd. 10. King William's Cannon.
11. the Place where Duke Schonberg was kill'd. 12. Count Nassau Regiment. 13. the Brandenburgh Regiment.
14. Col. Hanours Regiment. 15. An Irish Woman.

A. King James. B. the French an Irish Cavalerie.
C. the Enemys Cannon, which wounded King William the day before the Battaile.
D. Cannon Bullets. E. Drogheda. F. the River Boyne. G. the Irish Infanterie.
H. a little Fort. I. the Enemy running away. K. the way filled with Irish running away.

Cum privilegio Regis

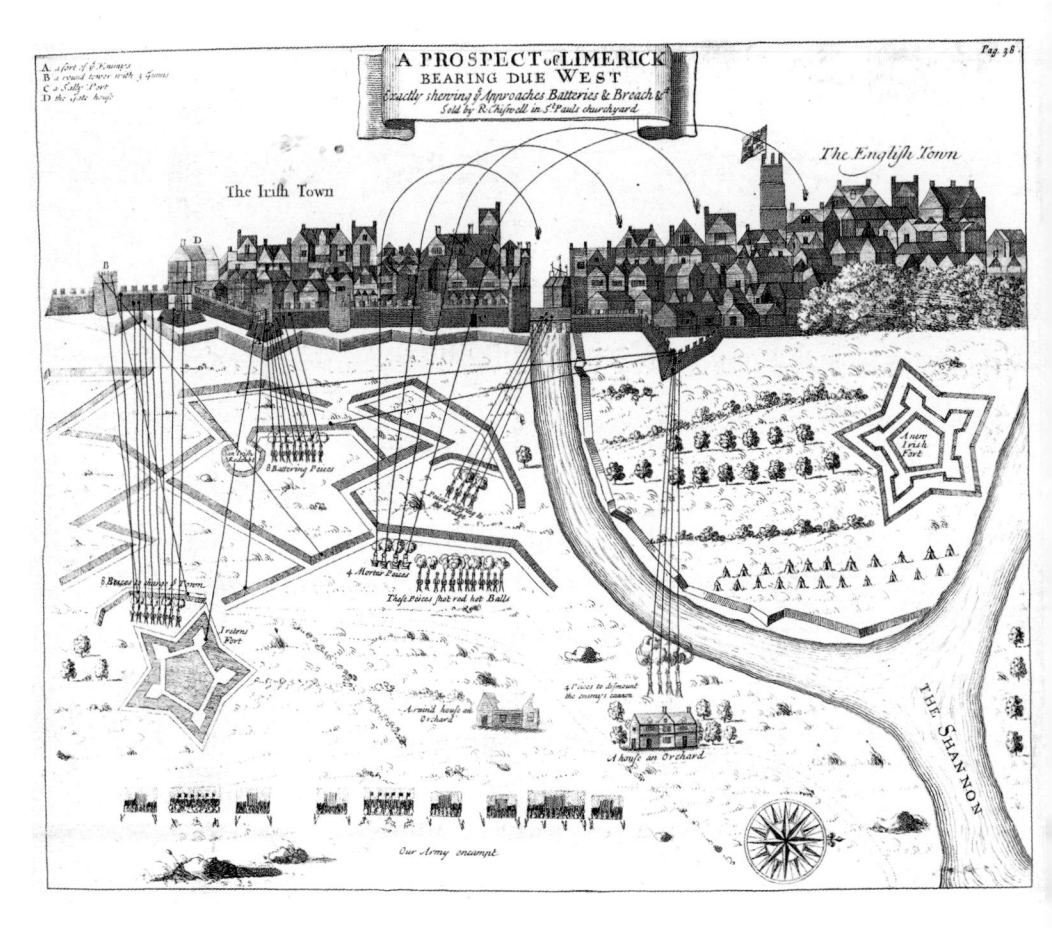

14. Siege of Limerick, 1690.

'At the breach ... the fight continued with sword in hand and the butt end of the musket' (Lieutenant John Stevens)

15. Battle of Aughrim, 1691.

'On this occasion, the Irish disputed the victory very vigorously and showed themselves to be brave soldiers. The issue was much in doubt and … nobody could be sure how the victory would go' (duke of Würtemburg)

16. Portumna Castle, Co. Galway.

The 'great, many-windowed and gabled house' of the Clanricard Burkes (Jane Fenlon)

17. Loughmoe Castle, Co. Tipperary.

Seat of Colonel Nicholas Purcell – 'a dangerous incendiary' (duke of Berwick)

soldiers being executed, presumably after a court martial. During the siege of Derry twenty-five men of Sir Neil O'Neill's dragoons, who refused to serve after their captain's death, were forced to draw lots, and his comrades were then obliged to shoot the unlucky one. In August 1689, as an example to many tempted to desert, the footguards paraded on Oxmantown Green in Dublin to witness the shooting of a soldier for leaving the colours. The following month deserters were shot in front of the troops to discourage others. A lieutenant and a soldier were hanged from a signpost in Thomas Street for the widespread offence of seizing and selling horses. For looting bread and money from bakers' shops in Dublin in early 1690, seven soldiers were hanged, although only four of them actually died. On that occasion a further seven were forced to run the gauntlet, a severe punishment in which the prisoner was stripped and forced to walk between two lines of soldiers, a company or the whole regiment, depending on the severity of the sentence, who beat him with willow rods as he passed. A sergeant preceded the victim, pressing a halberd against his chest to control his speed. The practice was for the provost to strike the first blow, and the punishment then proceeded by beat of drum. An earlier incidence of this punishment was recorded in 1686, when a soldier was obliged the run the gauntlet 'quite through the whole regiment' for speaking disrespectfully of Tyrconnell. In May 1690 two soldiers of Creagh's regiment 'being taken six or seven miles from the camp' were shot as deserters. A month later a sergeant of the grand prior's was hanged at the head of the regiment for deserting to the enemy.[5]

These examples do not disprove the general impression that discipline in the Irish army was lax. One cause was the disorder of the new levies, who were largely left to fend for themselves in the first half of 1689, with a consequent breakdown of law and order. Straggling, absenteeism and downright desertion were widespread. On one occasion when the drums beat the alarm, less than a quarter of the grand prior's regiment stood to arms, as the majority were ranging the countryside in search of provisions. Both Richard Hamilton and Wauchope included desertion among the factors preventing the army from capturing Derry. Great emphasis was placed on discipline in Louis XIV's army, and the French were shocked by the indiscipline they found in Ireland. An officer wrote that the army's behaviour was on a par with the worst-policed place on earth. He blamed the laziness and indifference of the officers, as their men were willing and would respond to direction. Rosen reported that his arrival at Derry with reinforcements was timely, as the army was in danger of

---

5 *JN*, pp 81–2, 149; *F-I corr.*, i, p. 139; ii, p. 533; iii, pp 59, 88; *AH*, 21, p. 189; *Ormonde MSS*, n.s., viii, pp 369, 371, 375; *Clarendon*, i, p. 336; *Stevens*, pp 115, 119, 212–13.

entirely melting away through desertion for want of pay. Stevens thought the Irish officers were as incapable of understanding the rules of discipline as the troops themselves. Soon after arriving in Ireland, d'Avaux expressed a wish for the presence of a single French battalion so that the Irish might see what a disciplined unit looked like. The Jacobite leadership was in agreement that some better disciplined troops than their own were needed to set an example.[6]

Enforcement of discipline was intermittent with a tendency towards leniency. A court martial of 1689 acquitted a private of Purcell's dragoons of dangerously wounding a French officer with a sword slash, accepting the prisoner's defence that he did not know his accuser was an officer, as he had never produced his commission at the head of the regiment or done guard duty. The verdict annoyed the French. D'Avaux complained to James that the officer had campaigned at both Derry and Enniskillen, paraded daily with the regiment and camped with the other officers. The court was censured by James because of its apparent partiality to a fellow Irishman, but there the matter ended. A more glaring example occurred after Aughrim, when Sarsfield arrested Brigadier Henry Luttrell after he was discovered to be in correspondence with the enemy. De Tessé thought he should have been hanged forthwith, regardless of legal process. Tyrconnell presided at the subsequent court martial and voted for Luttrell's execution, but the other judges refused to concur. Luttrell retained considerable support in the army, where Tyrconnell's credit was low. Luttrell was held in detention until the war ended, when Ginkel blocked a plan to take him to France and insisted on his release. Stevens observed that 'the soldiers were ... threatened with severe punishments for all manner of offences, but nothing at all [was] put into execution'. They 'were not easily to be curbed without some very severe examples, which were so far from being made that the men began to believe that their officers durst not punish them'.[7]

It could be argued that the lack of discipline emanated from the top. The refusal of the army leaders to accept the arrangements Tyrconnell had made for the military and civil government of Ireland in his absence, however justified in view of his decline and defeatism, was also an act of indiscipline. Berwick considered Henry Luttrell and Nicholas Purcell the 'most dangerous incendiaries'. Luttrell in particular perpetually spoke ill of Tyrconnell and inflamed opinion against him. Tyrconnell's opponents sought the viceroy's arrest until Berwick told them that such an act would be high treason and

---

6 *Stevens*, pp 63, 88; *d'Avaux*, pp 76–7; Lynn, *Giant of the grand siècle*, pp 399–400; *AH*, 21, p. 178; *F-I corr.*, iii, p. 41; Macpherson, *Original papers*, i, pp 216–17.   7 *D'Avaux*, pp 524–5; *Stevens*, p. 155; *F-I corr.*, ii, pp 414–15, 533; Macpherson, *Original papers*, i, pp 193–4; *JN*, p. 149.

ordered them to desist from their cabals. They then compelled Berwick to accept a council of officers to advise him on the conduct of the war, and to consent to an army delegation going to France to present their grievances. The delegation consisted of the Luttrell brothers, Henry and Simon, Purcell, and the bishop of Cork. Brigadier Thomas Maxwell accompanied them to tell Berwick's side of the story and communicate his recommendation that Henry Luttrell and Purcell be detained in France. According to Berwick, Luttrell and Purcell were only dissuaded from throwing Maxwell overboard by the intervention of Simon Luttrell and the bishop. Tyrconnell accused Purcell, Luttrell and Wauchope of being the leaders of the army 'mutineers', naming also Sarsfield and Dorrington. Sarsfield and the others continued to snub Tyrconnell after his return to Ireland. When he appeared at the camp at the start of the 1691 campaign, senior officers went from tent to tent with a petition for his removal. Although Saint-Ruth denied any complicity in this, Tyrconnell doubted the general's innocence, probably correctly. The outcome was that Tyrconnell 'made a noble conquest of himself' and retired to Limerick. Tyrconnell after all was lord lieutenant and captain general of the army. Whatever his shortcomings, the refusal of the most senior officers to accept his authority or even tolerate his presence was a poor example of discipline to their subordinates of all ranks.[8]

The excesses of armies were also tempered by the evolving so-called 'laws of war', which were no more than unenforceable customs of good conduct, that soldiers were generally expected to follow. The process gained currency from the excesses of the thirty years war, and the concurrent upheavals in Britain and Ireland. As a concept, it was underpinned by the work of the Dutch jurist Hugo de Grotius (1583–1645), who argued that while military violence might be justified, common humanity demanded that its impact should be limited by respect for the innocent and even those fighting on the other side. Thus prisoners, except for partisans, were to be exchanged rather than murdered; occupying armies were supposed to pay for, or at least negotiate, rather than steal supplies; defending garrisons were protected from pillage and massacre, unless the besiegers were compelled to take a fortress by storm; civilians were to be treated with compassion and their property respected. Professional soldiers were well aware of these standards, which both sides in Ireland both respected and ignored between 1689 and 1691.[9]

---

8 Berwick, *Memoirs*, i, p. 82; *F-I corr.*, ii, pp 143, 237, 257, 271, 334, 357–8, 361; *JN*, pp 133, 162–9; *AH*, 21, pp 216–17; Lenihan, *Last cavalier*, pp 162–9; Wauchope, *Sarsfield*, pp 188–95, 207–9; *Finch MSS*, ii, pp 476–8.   **9** Grotius, bk iii, 1185–1741; Childs, 'Laws of war', pp 283–300.

Medicine

The care of sick and wounded soldiers was not only humanitarian, but expedient in that it curtailed contagion and restored to the ranks men who might otherwise have died, while the awareness of its provision contributed to persuading soldiers to risk their lives in military service. These considerations, coupled with the need to remove the distressing and demoralizing sight of broken old soldiers from the streets and garrisons, lay behind the establishment of the Royal Hospital at Kilmainham, a retirement home, opened in 1684 in imitation of Louis XIV's earlier foundation *Les Invalides* in Paris.[10]

For the treatment of serving soldiers, there was a distinction between surgery and medicine. Surgery dealt with battle wounds and other injuries. Sword slashes, which were shallow, were easiest to treat and healed fairly quickly. Pike wounds were deeper, fatal if they entered the intestine or chest cavity, and otherwise prone to infection. Gunshot wounds were worst of all, tiny at entry point and leaving the bullet hard to find. Failure to extract it usually resulted in death. Gangrene and septicaemia were ever-present threats. Powder burns and broken bones were common. With the latter, if the skin was broken and the broken ends of bone exposed, the treatment was amputation. In seventeenth-century warfare, a wounded soldier had a slightly better than evens chance of survival, and an officer considerably more because of earlier treatment. Medicine dealt with the prevention, control and treatment of infectious and deficiency diseases. In winter quarters, the most common conditions were pneumonia, colds and consumption; in summer camps, dysentery, hepatitis and typhus – 'the Irish ague' – spread by lice. Fevers and even smallpox were also mentioned. Stevens referred to 'the perpetual plague of the itch' – scabies – which, he related, infected the whole island, especially the north. Poor diet, bad water, crowded quarters, careless camping practices and neglect of hygiene were contributory factors to ill-health. In 1689 the Williamite army in Ireland was decimated by disease, apparently typhus. The French regiments that joined the Jacobite army in 1690 also suffered many sick. Irish soldiers may have enjoyed a degree of immunity from common local diseases, although there is evidence that many of them also fell ill. Treatment of the various diseases was by nursing, better diet and drugs.[11]

A French report on medicinal needs in Ireland followed contemporary practice in the French army. It recommended the treatment of patients with

---

10 Craig, *Dublin 1660–1860*, pp 58–9.   11 Logan, 'Medical services 1641–52', p. 217; Carlton, *Going to the wars*, pp 209–10, 221–4; Story, p. 39; *F-I corr.*, i, pp 372, 397–8; *A true account of the present state of Ireland*, p. 13; Stevens, p. 140.

herbal teas, enemas, purgatives, ointments, exfoliants, astringents, cochlearia (a treatment for scurvy and 'other obstinate maladies'), and a compound of vitriol, sal ammoniac (ammonium chloride) and red wine to treat fevers. Elvesius powder was a recognized treatment for dysentery. The preparation of these remedies was the responsibility of apothecaries, who formed part of the hospital teams. Disease rather than combat caused most army fatalities. One modern estimate is that for every ten men that died in Louis XIV's armies, one fell in action, three died from wounds and six from disease. Others put deaths from combat at about 25 per cent. Story, after 'comparing accounts and conferring on both sides with those who have made some observations upon the matter', calculated Williamite combat casualties in Ireland to have accounted for about 30 per cent of the army's mortality rate, a figure between both estimates. As to the Jacobite army, he concluded, 'nor are we to believe that the Irish did not lose a great many by sickness also'.[12]

In the Irish army a surgeon provided a basic medical service in each regiment. He ranked as an officer and was a member of the unit's staff. His pay was 15*s.* per day in 1689, reduced to 10*s.* by 1691, which was the same as chaplains. Little is known of the regimental surgeons' backgrounds or qualifications. The surgeons of the time were not doctors in the sense of being qualified physicians, surgery being regarded as more in the nature of a trade. Charles Thomson, surgeon to the footguards and Kilmainham Hospital, and joint surgeon general, was master of the Dublin guild of barbers, surgeons and apothecaries, to which periwig-makers were added in 1687. Others who practised surgery were not necessarily members of the guild, and whether membership was a requirement for a regimental appointment is unknown. Certainly, membership did not necessarily imply any knowledge of surgery, the guild being noted in 1703 as a 'refuge for empirics, impudent quacks, women and other idle persons who quit the trades to which they were bred ... to undertake a profession whereof they are entirely ignorant'. Thompson held his appointments until 1689, when he was mentioned as a Protestant officer in London seeking employment. Because the footguards had two battalions, its staff included a surgeon's mate. Of eight surgeons that followed James II to Ireland, only one, Edmund Tully, appears to have been subsequently employed as a regimental surgeon. It seems likely that the regimental surgeons generally acquired their modest skills through a mixture of apprenticeship and inherited lore. They were capable of extracting teeth and treating minor wounds and disorders. In more serious cases, lacking antiseptics, antibiotics, anaesthetics or

---

12 *F-I corr.*, ii, p. 250; *d'Avaux*, pp 728–31; Lynn, *Giant of the grand siècle*, p. 426; Story, *Continuation*, p. 318.

scientific training, their success rate in the treatment of combat wounds and in procedures such as amputations must have been pitifully small and due as much to luck as skill. The French were not impressed by their competence, noting that at Derry no one sufficiently competent was available to treat the wounded Puisgnan who died, or Pointis who survived, probably because he refused to be treated by ignorant Irish army surgeons. Fumeron considered the Irish surgeons, doctors and apothecaries to be both unskilled and lazy, and he chose to return to France himself in preference to being operated on in Dublin for a troublesome anal fistula. In Boisseleau's opinion the lack of surgeons or medicines during the siege of Limerick meant that a man wounded was in effect dead. The new Catholic regimental surgeons had in any case no pre-war experience of combat injuries; in reality most can have been little more than medical orderlies.[13]

A small military hospital that existed in Dublin in Charles II's reign until at least 1676 may no longer have been operational. The Kilmainham veterans had been evicted from the Royal Hospital in January 1689, but only to allow the building to be used as accommodation for Jacobite soldiers, and it was the Williamites that converted it into a military hospital. Soon after his arrival, d'Avaux reported that the army had no hospitals or medicines, and Rosen complained that no doctors or surgeons accompanied the reinforcements he was bringing to the siege of Derry. He stressed their presence was necessary to treat the wounded should he come into contact with the enemy, and also its importance for morale. Fumeron set to work to remedy the situation by negotiating a contract in June with the French contractor Aufroy, who for 5s. 6d. per day per patient agreed to supply surgeons, apothecaries and medicines for hospitals, and a daily ration of white bread and meat, with a pint of beer, for the subsistence of the patients, together with kitchen furniture and utensils, sheets and blankets, hats, wood, laundry, and the general maintenance of all things apart from hospital buildings. Robert White, warden of the Dublin guild and regimental surgeon of Creagh's regiment, was appointed surgeon general. His duties were likely to have been comparable to those of his English equivalent, who oversaw the service, advised on the appointment of regimental surgeons and provided medicines. By early July a military hospital had been established at Strabane to cater for the sick and wounded of the army besieging Derry, with Charles Stapleton as surgeon major and James Lennon

[13] Story, *Continuation*, p. 30; *AH*, 21, p. 117; 'Journal 1/6 to 18/7 1689' (Carte MS 181), ff 12, 18; *AH*, 22, p. 89; *Ireland's lamentation*, p. 13; *IALKC*, pp 79, 117, 145; Dalton, iii, p. 13; MacLysaght, *Irish life*, pp 218–24; *F-I corr.*, ii, pp 219–20; iii, pp 74–5, 82, 87; King, appendix, p. 89; Officer list (Bodl., Carte MS 181), f. 15; *Patentee officers*, p. 128; *Lib. Mun.*, i, p. 101; Widdess, *College of Surgeons*, pp 4–5; *d'Avaux*, pp 136–7, 139, 308.

as physician, assisted by some regimental surgeons sent up from Dublin with surgical instruments. Fumeron, who organized the Strabane hospital, also posted four surgeons in the trenches before Derry to give immediate treatment to the wounded. These front-line surgeons were relieved at the same times as the troops, so that two were always on duty. Hardship, poor diet and bad hygiene increased the number of sick in the Irish camp, and by mid-July the hospital was catering for 6–700 patients. Fumeron's request for more surgeons resulted in only two being sent from Dublin, bringing the number in the hospital up to nine, which, he said, was insufficient for so many patients. Problems were also encountered with Aufroy, whom Fumeron judged a rogue. He overcharged, and his supply of food to the hospital was irregular, poor in quality and below the agreed weight. When the siege of Derry was raised, no transport was available to move the sick and wounded, by then reported to number 3,000. Rosen said they would have to drag themselves away as best they could, and he foresaw the mortality of a third to a half of their number.[14]

This sorry state of affairs may have been responsible for 'several good and pious persons' requesting in August a license from King James to make collections for sick and wounded soldiers. This was duly granted, with Luke Hore, a Dublin merchant, acting as collector. James invited similar initiatives in other parts of the country, but it is unlikely that charity had much impact on meeting the healthcare needs of the army. The same month Fumeron set out a blueprint on hospital needs, suggesting the establishment of a military hospital in every garrison or wherever a battalion or more of troops was posted, to be staffed by a regimental surgeon and chaplain to tend the patients. He recommended that the contracts for food, bedding and nurses should be given to local suppliers. In addition, he wanted field hospitals to be established in the towns near military camps, each with a director, physician, surgeon and assistants, apothecary, nurses and chaplain. He sought provision for surgical and apothecary instruments, cloths, lint, drugs and ointments. In addition to bread, meat and beer, eggs and broth should be fed to patients, with extra rations for officers. Little effective action was taken, and during the autumn campaign against Schomberg, Fumeron reported the hospitals to be still badly served. At that time Rosen complained that most of the many who fell ill died for lack of care. Aufroy by then appears to have been deprived of the hospital contract, but without his input the situation was even worse. D'Avaux wrote that the army hospitals were the worst in the world, with soldiers dying daily

---

14 Gruber von Arni, *Hospital care*, p. 54; *IALKC*, p. 103; *d'Avaux*, pp 139–40; *Ormonde MSS*, n.s., viii, p. 359; *Danish force*, p. 47; *AH*, 21, pp 112–13, 127, 148, 154–5, 192, 195–6; 'Journal 1/6 to 18/7 1689' (Carte MS 181), ff 9, 18; *Patentee officers*, p. 139; Childs, *Charles II*, pp 73–4.

for want of treatment. In one, which had been established near Ardee, a French inspector found 300 sick men without a physician, surgeon, cooks, bakers or anyone to provide them with meat, wine, beer or even a glass of water. There were only three loaves of bread in the whole house. In Drogheda, where there were two hospitals, one was in an old church in a ruined convent. Barely a third of the patients had beds. The rest were forced to sleep on the ground. They had been given nothing to eat since the previous mid-day and had only very bad water to drink. Soldiers were unwilling to go to such hospitals, and French officers told d'Avaux that after breaking camp at Ardee, many were left to die of cold and starvation in their huts, abandoned by their officers. While the hospital service may have fallen short of French standards, it was probably no worse than that of many armies of the time. The Williamites, for example, left their worst cases behind at Dundalk in 1689 and at Limerick in 1690, where their hospital accidentally burnt down. Nevertheless, the Irish showed little inclination to establish an effective medical service. When d'Avaux complained about the hospital situation to King James, Tyrconnell suggested that the chevalier de Saint Didier, an aide of the ambassador, be put in charge of hospitals. Saint Didier prepared a comprehensive blueprint for their operation, but d'Avaux doubted if there was anyone sufficiently concerned or competent to put it into effect, and that was indeed the outcome. Aufroy in his memorandum on Ireland, listed hospital needs as sheets, blankets, shirts, surgical instruments, copper cooking pots and transport.[15]

By 1690 White had returned to his regiment. His successor as surgeon general was Patrick Archbold, master of the Dublin guild and probably a relative of Dr Richard Archbold of Dublin, the state physician, who was a medical graduate of the university of Angers and a close associate of Tyrconnell. D'Esgrigny, the French *intendant*, reported that Archbold had well-stocked stores, and he appears to have found him helpful. Thereafter, there is no evidence that he was any more effective than White in improving the army's medical service. In 1691 Fumeron reported the hospitals, such as they were, as being devoid of mattresses, sheets and blankets. He asked for linen to cover mattresses and finer cloth for sheets to be sent from France, but thought that blankets could probably be sourced locally. He found no hospital in Galway, and that in Limerick to be completely rotten and out of service. It was probably the 400-bed hospital he had prepared in early 1690 for the French expedition that had originally been expected to disembark there. In

---

15 *Proclamations*, p. 116; Story, *Continuation*, p. 30; *F-I corr.*, i, pp 19, 235, 258; ii, p. 220; iii, p. 82, 184; *AH*, 21, pp 112–13, 127, 148; *d'Avaux*, pp 368–70, 497, 523, 547–8, 559, 711–23.

1689 Fumeron had requested surgeons to be sent from France, and in 1691 Tyrconnell asked for a dozen surgeons, together with linen and medicines. Perhaps some came, because there is a stray reference to a French surgeon attending Sarsfield in April 1691. Possibly he is identifiable with Le sieur Dascorel, an army surgeon who returned to France due to ill-health the following July. Medicines, a pharmacy box, surgical instruments and hospital utensils were certainly sent with Saint-Ruth. There are no other references to army medical services in 1691. Fumeron's silence suggests that an adequate hospital service was probably put together. By then also, experience must have made the regimental surgeons, like other army personnel, more skilled.[16]

Lauzun's French expedition brought its own medical team to Ireland in 1690, comprising twenty-seven hospital officers, surgeons and apothecaries. This had been strongly recommended by both d'Avaux and Fumeron. On arrival, hospitals were opened at Cork and Kinsale to accommodate the men who had fallen ill on the voyage. They filled up rapidly as sickness spread among the French after disembarkation, and the death rate rose alarmingly. By mid-May it was reported that 500 of the 700 who had been hospitalized had died, not counting those that had expired in their quarters. Temporary new hospitals for the French had to be opened in Limerick, Bandon, Clonmel, Kilkenny, Carlow, Waterford and Dublin. By July more than 450 were still hospitalized. Stocks of medicines were running low. There was also a growing shortage of professional staff, as most of the French medical team also fell ill. An additional problem, as the summer campaign got under way, was the recall to their regiments of the French soldiers that provided the nursing services. Irish people were considered unsuitable as replacements due to the language barrier and their alleged propensity to steal. Additional medical personnel, including a dozen nurses, were requested from France, but none was sent. Although dysentery was reported, the principal illness of the French appears to have been a chest infection and accompanying fever, likely to prove fatal within a fortnight. D'Esgrigny attributed the soldiers' ill health to the sea voyage, the wet weather encountered in Ireland and the poor quarters in which they were accommodated. He was advised that milk broth with egg yolks would be efficacious, and thought the addition of a wine canteen would improve general health. He set up a field hospital for the summer campaign, for which he had seven carts made and he bought fourteen horses to carry the hospital furniture and utensils. After the Boyne defeat, over 400 French sick personnel were successfully evacuated to Limerick, although they endured

---

16 *AH*, 21, p. 155; Brockliss & Ferté, 'Irish clerics in Paris and Toulouse', p. 102; *F-I corr.*, i, pp 132, 256, 426; ii, pp 121, 250, 257, 264, 271, 364, 369; iii, p. 184.

considerable hardship on the retreat. Medicines and pharmacy utensils were abandoned or pillaged.[17]

Chaplaincy

The Articles of War required all officers and soldiers to attend religious service and sermons, desist from blasphemy or speaking against the Christian faith, and respect churches, chaplains and church artefacts. The large number of Catholic priests in Ireland facilitated chaplaincy appointments, allowing each regiment to have at least one; a small number had two. In 1686, beginning with the footguards and two other regiments, Tyrconnell began to direct the replacement of Protestant chaplains by Catholic priests. Most of the Protestants were graduates of Trinity College Dublin, for whom military chaplaincy was not only remunerative, but also a step on the ladder of preferment: two of the displaced chaplains were afterwards Church of Ireland bishops, and a third was a dean. Catholic chaplains may have entertained similar ambitions. The chaplain general from January 1687 was Dominic Maguire, the Catholic archbishop of Armagh. He had powers of approval, inspection, censure and punishment, but not of appointment, which traditionally lay with the colonels. While the latter were their commanding officers, chaplains were also obliged to be obedient to the archbishop as their superior. Chaplains were listed as members of the regimental staff and, as in England, appear to have been formally commissioned. Certainly, this was the case with the two chaplains of Parker's horse, Edmund Hawett, an English Benedictine, and Nicholas Trappe, an English secular priest, both of whom had followed King James to Ireland. The surnames of over eighty Irish Catholic chaplains are known, but more than half lack Christian names making their identification problematic. The careers of a score of chaplains have been traced. Of these, eight were secular priests, while twelve were regulars, predominantly Dominicans and Franciscans, but with at least one Capuchin, one Jesuit and one Benedictine. The best known of the secular chaplains was Alexius Stafford, the dean of Christ Church cathedral, who served in the footguards. Another was the warden of Galway, Henry Browne, who was chaplain to the regiment of his nephew, Dominic Browne. The Dominican chaplain, Phelim/Felix MacDowell, after his capture at Ballymore, was tied to a horse's tail and forced to walk to Dublin, but afterwards managed to escape. Chaplains were also appointed to the army hospitals.[18]

17 *D'Avaux*, p. 717; *F-I corr.*, i, pp 19, 270, 348, 372, 375–6, 381–4, 386–7, 397–8, 403, 437, 455; ii, p. 88; iii, pp 87, 113, 116, 155.   **18** Walton, *History of the British army*, pp 760, 809–10; *CSPD 1686–7*, pp 254, 353, 416; *DIB*, vol. 8, p. 1109; *d'Avaux*, p. 717; 'Journal 1/6 to 18/7 1689' (Carte

A chaplaincy was a salaried appointment, paying 1s. 3d. per day, or just under £23 annually, which was the same as a regimental surgeon, and slightly below the pay of an infantry ensign. The salary, although considerably less than in peacetime, still made chaplaincy appointments attractive to impoverished priests, although not all appointees were in this category. The normal chaplaincy duties were to say Mass, administer the sacraments, comfort the wounded, sick and dying, bury the dead and uphold Christian values in their unit. Proclamations of 1688 and 1689 required them to be constantly present with their regiments, where they were to catechise and exhort the soldiers on Sundays and holy days, and hear confessions at Easter and other feast days. Soldiers were to attend churches or chapels on Sundays, with absence or misbehaviour to be severely punished. Catholic soldiers were to receive the holy sacrament at Easter and at least once a year besides, and to receive a certificate from a chaplain to this effect, which they were obliged to present to their colonel. Officers were to behave with 'religious, sober and orderly demeanour' and to support the work of the chaplains by stamping out the abuses of blasphemy, profane swearing and cursing, drunkenness, lewdness and debauchery. In 1690 the Limerick clergy offered Masses for a week for all that died in the city's defence.[19]

Many leading Jacobite families contributed members to the priesthood. No less than three of Tyrconnell's brothers were priests. In Westmeath, for example, the titular earl's elder brother was a Capuchin; Colonel Richard Nugent's brother was a priest; Captain Michael Dardis's brother 'a monk'; and Bishop Patrick Tyrrell of Meath, Tyrconnell's secretary, was a kinsman of the Tyrrells of Fartullagh, several of whom were officers. Such clerical-military interconnections were widely replicated elsewhere. Priests were among the most dedicated Jacobites and wielded great influence with the ordinary people. They stressed the need to support King James and defend the Catholic religion. They took an active role in recruitment by urging their congregations to arm themselves and to join the army, allegedly under pain of mortal sin. In 1690 parish priests were asked to inform their congregations of the advantages of joining the army as an alternative to being pressed into the French regiments. A Williamite account related that in preparation for the 1691 campaign, the priests brought men that attended Mass to the army for enlistment. They also helped to round up absentees before the campaigns. In

---

MS 181), ff 5, 12; BL, Add. MS 9763, f. 9; *PI*, iv, p. 212; Snow, *English congregation of Saint Benedict*, p. 73; 'Trappes of Nidd', pp 169–70; Fenning, 'Irish Dominicans at Rome', pp 41–2. **19** *F-I corr.*, ii, pp 219–20; iii, pp 73–5; *CTB*, 1746; *Proclamations*, pp 61, 143; *Finch MSS*, ii, p. 489.

the circumstances of the Irish war with its religious undertones, the chaplains also played an important morale-raising role. At Aughrim (which was fought on a Sunday), a Williamite soldier observed that the Irish army had all the Masses, persuasions and other encouragements that could be thought of, Saint-Ruth having 'ordered Masses and prayers to be said in all parts of the army'. It was probably true, as a Williamite report stated, that the priests assured the Irish of a most glorious victory, although the claim that they urged the men 'not to give quarter to any soul living, but to pursue every man to destruction' may have been no more than the standard anti-popery rhetoric of the time. The *Jacobite narrative* confirmed that on the morning of the battle the soldiers attended Mass, which presumably each regimental chaplain said for his regiment. A Danish account stated that the Irish chaplains urged the men to win or die, while a Williamite dragoon was quoted as saying '[the Irish] had the advantage of us in prayer'. The chaplains' role in raising the army's fighting spirit was exhibited during the battle: Dean Stafford, 'an undaunted zealot and a most pious churchman, fell at the front of the royal regiment, as he was encouraging them upon the first charge'. During the retreat, a chaplain named O'Reilly checked the Williamite pursuit by getting a drummer to beat the charge at a critical moment. According to a Williamite source, many soldiers carried protective prayers, presumably to bolster their confidence in battle. At the end of the war, the priests were active in persuading the Irish soldiers to go to France rather than suffer the 'certain damnation of joining with the heretics', and many chaplains seem to have accompanied their regiments into exile.[20]

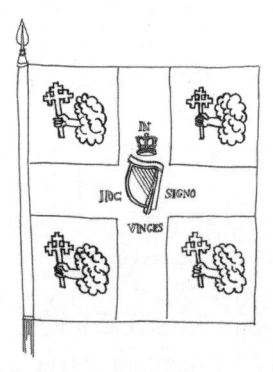

Figure 7. Colour of earl of Antrim's infantry regiment

20 *PI*, i, p. 247; 'Survey of Catholic estates', pp 101, 104; *DIB*, vol. 9, pp 547–8; Story, *Continuation*, pp 123, 125, 226, 260; *JN*, pp 139, 148; MacGeoghegan, *History*, p. 596; *Danish force*, p. 120; *CSPD 1686–7*, p. 416; *1689–90*, p. 437; *An account of the present state Ireland is in*; Simms, 'Sarsfield of Kilmallock', p. 208.

CHAPTER 9

The French dimension

French policy

LOUIS XIV AND HIS ministers recognized that the English revolution had been a significant setback to French political and military aspirations. Louis received the exiled James and his family with his usual courtesy and made the chateau of Saint-Germain-en-Laye available to them together with a generous subsidy for their support. Although the French had little faith in James's ability or judgement, they calculated that an effective counterstroke to William's coup would be an attempt to use Ireland as a springboard to restore James in Britain with the help of Irish Catholics. However, as French doubts grew about the likelihood of achieving this objective, Louis made it conditional on the occupation of a fortified English port by a substantial body of armed Jacobites, while the marquis de Louvois, the French war minister, was clear that no attempt could be made to invade England unless Ireland was firmly under control. Nevertheless, the French correctly calculated that even if the primary objective failed, a significant military effort in Ireland would sufficiently alarm William to divert him from waging an offensive war on the Continent.[1]

There was some recent history of military relations between Ireland and France. Irish regiments raised by military contractors had formed part of the French army in the thirty years war. In 1665, when France and the United Provinces were at war with England, the Dutch suggested an invasion of Ireland to Louis XIV. The proposal came to nothing at that time, nor did the subsequent suggestion of encouraging a rebellion by Irish Catholics 'who have a mortal hatred of the English' that was put forward by the French counsellor of state, Hay du Chastelet, in his influential *Traité de la guerre, ou politique militaire*, first published 1668. In the Dutch War (1672–8), a British brigade that fought in alliance with the French included an Irish Catholic regiment, to which a second was later added. These units were the training ground for many of the senior officers in the Irish Jacobite army, including Justin

---

1 Gregg, 'Exiled Stuarts', pp 11–32; Pillorget, 'Louis XIV and Ireland', pp 1–16; Childs, *Nine years war*, pp 23–4, 135–6, 156; Simms, *Jacobite Ireland*, pp 58–62; Keogh, *French support*, pp 97–8; *F-I corr.*, i, pp viii–x, xii–xiii, xx–xxi; 'Talbot letter book', pp 106, 108; *d'Avaux*, pp 112–13, 649.

MacCarthy, Patrick Sarsfield, Dominic Sheldon and Richard Hamilton. Some officers, such as Andrew Lee, remained on in the French service. Richard Hamilton and Henry Luttrell served in France until James II's accession. Remnants of the Irish regiments retained a degree of their identity as companies within German and Swiss regiments in the French army. Before the Prince of Wales was born, Tyrconnell seems to have toyed with the idea of making Ireland some sort of French dependency in the event of James dying without a Catholic heir. He enquired from the unofficial French diplomat, Bonrepaux, whether French support and military assistance would be forthcoming if he was to head up an independent Ireland. Bonrepaux, who was *intendant général* of the French navy, reported this conversation to the marquis de Seignelay, the navy minister, who replied 'in strictest secrecy' that King Louis was favourable to the suggestion, and Tyrconnell could count on considerable French help, which would be sent through Brest. The birth of the Prince of Wales put a temporary halt to the idea, but the issue arose again after the English revolution, when Tyrconnell told the French that the Irish would prefer to be placed under Louis's protection rather than submit to William of Orange. D'Avaux reported that both the nobility and the ordinary people strongly supported this idea. Not surprisingly, these dialogues ensured that Tyrconnell enjoyed the confidence of the French. The dependency idea must have been spoken about in Irish Catholic circles, which were generally Francophile, as it again resurfaced in correspondence sent to Louvois by Lord Clare after the Boyne defeat.[2]

Initial French thinking was to use James's person as a diversion, but Seignelay, whom James's memoirs describe as 'affectionate to his interest', remained well disposed towards an overseas expedition to Ireland. It would utilize the new French navy, which he had continued to foster in succession to his father, the great Colbert. By 1688 it was the largest navy in Europe, with almost 200 vessels, including 118 ships of the line and 19 frigates. The fleet had to be divided between the Mediterranean and the Atlantic, and it was short of sailors, particularly with the loss of so many Huguenots after the revocation of the edict of Nantes. Nevertheless, French naval leadership was of a high quality, and French squadrons dominated the seas. Seignelay had a favourable report from the baron de Pointis, the naval gunnery officer he sent to Ireland in early 1689 to assess the situation. The only comparable overseas

---

2 Gouhier, 'Mercenaires irlandais', pp 58–75; Atkinson, 'Charles II's regiments', pp 53–64, 128–36, 161–71; Ó Ciosáin, 'Irish soldiers in French service', pp 15–31; Childs, *BD*, pp 52, 55; 'Sheridan's narrative', pp 8–10; Pillorget, 'Louis XIV and Ireland', pp 3–4; *d'Avaux*, pp 88, 280; *F-I corr.*, iii, p. 138.

operation of Louis's reign was the French intervention in Sicily in the 1670s, which was rated a moderate success. Louvois, the forceful war minister, disapproved of diverting resources from the European mainland, as it was clear that France would be hard pressed to simultaneously hold wartime fronts in Flanders, Germany, Catalonia and Savoy. Furthermore, the policy difference between Seignelay and Louvois reflected the long-standing antagonism between their respective Colbert and Le Tellier families, which ensured Louvois's general opposition to anything that favoured the navy. Tyrconnell opined that if the great war minister could be gained or at least softened, the Jacobites would soon be masters of Ireland, but even before the decision to send French troops was implemented, Louvois was threatening to withdraw French aid. However, the war minister's influence was temporarily lessened by military setbacks in Germany. Although Louis's own interest was in land warfare, Seignelay won the support of Madame de Maintenon, the king's influential wife, and his view prevailed. Once the policy of military intervention was decided upon, it was Louvois's responsibility to organize, however reluctantly, the marshalling of men and *matériel* for transport to Ireland. In an age when everything had to be hand-crafted, to source and transport sufficient weapons and other equipment for an entire overseas army presented even the efficient French administration with a formidable challenge. Louvois gave the task his usual attention to detail, and thereafter he closely followed events in Ireland. From the outset he added the further objective to the French mission of gaining significant numbers of Irish soldiers for the French army. The death of Seignelay in November 1690 ensured Louvois's dominance of the situation until his own death the following July. Neither of their successors, the over-stretched Pontchartrain at the navy and the dissolute Barbezieux at the war ministry, were of the same calibre, although Pontchartrain oversaw the dispatch of the French supply fleets of 1691.[3]

What followed the French decision to intervene in Ireland was a sustained effort over three years, during which eight French convoys and many individual vessels brought French officers and military administrators, *matériel* and, in 1690, two brigades of infantry to Ireland. More than forty men-of-war sailed in the two principal convoys of 1689, both commanded by *lieutenants généraux des armées navales* (vice-admirals): Jean Gabaret and the comte de Châteaurenault. Fifty vessels sailed in the three convoys of 1690, of which the largest, commanded by the marquis d'Amfreville, also a *lieutenant général des*

---

3 Mulloy, 'French navy', pp 17–31; *James II*, ii, p. 432; Pearsall, 'The war at sea', pp 92–105; Powley, *Naval war*, passim; Rowlands, *Dynastic state*, pp 52, 58–9, 60–1; Bluche, *Louis XIV*, p. 299; d'Avaux, p. 282; 'Talbot letter-book', p. 101.

armées navales, arrived in March and comprised thirty-six warships, fifteen smaller vessels and twenty-five merchantmen. Sixty warships sailed in the three convoys of 1691; the first two were commanded by a *chef d'escadre* (commodore), the marquis de Nesmond, and the last, which arrived after the termination of hostilities, again by Châteaurenault. There was also considerable wartime movement of frigates or smaller corvettes between Ireland and France, with a regular sailing from Brest every two weeks. These swift vessels were important for the transmission of dispatches and information. They also carried supplies and sometimes personnel. Five to six days appear to have been the usual length of the voyage between France and Ireland, but the passage time of course was weather dependent. The French were anxious to promote commerce with Ireland, and were disappointed when James prevented the enactment of legislation in the 1689 parliament that would have banned woollen exports to England and favoured the export of wool and other commodities to France. Numerous references to commercial shipping show that merchants, mainly French but also some Irish and others, traded actively between Ireland and the Continent during the war. Their flutes carried cloth, canvas, shoes, grain, salt, hops, wine and brandy from the Continent in return for Irish wool, hides, tallow and butter in what amounted to a barter trade with France. In October 1690 the Jacobite government took control of overseas trade by banning merchants from operating independently and ordering all goods imported or designed for export to pass through its storehouses, a decree that appears to have been actively enforced. The English navy failed to seriously disrupt French communications with Ireland, which were maintained throughout the war. The revolution had left the navy somewhat disorganized, and it was further hampered by mediocre leadership and confused objectives arising from policy divisions between William and his naval advisers. Generally, the French chose as their destinations the more westerly ports of Cork, Kinsale and Bantry, and in the latter part of the war Limerick and Galway.[4]

The English fleet managed to intercept only one French convoy. That was off Bantry Bay in May 1689, when the French had the best of a rather inconclusive engagement involving, between both fleets, more than forty warships, 10,000 sailors and 2,000 cannon. It remains the largest naval battle ever fought in Irish waters. French naval superiority was confirmed in a larger battle off Beachy Head in 1690. However, the French failed to exploit fully their naval advantage, and they made no effort to disrupt British communications with either Ireland or the Continent. Tyrconnell constantly

---

4 *F-I corr.*, i, pp xlii–xliii, 220–1, 244, 261, 411; ii, pp 245, 313, 490; *d'Avaux*, pp 237–8, 296, 311;

complained of the lack of French ships in Irish waters, declaring 'would to God we had those frigates of Saint-Malo' and bemoaning 'the want of a squadron of French men-of-war in St George's Channel [which] has been our ruin'. Lauzun supported this view and sought a flotilla of ten or fifteen frigates and ten fire ships, but no immediate action followed. Instead, William's build-up of forces and *matériel* for his campaign in Ireland was allowed to proceed unimpeded. A squadron of French frigates finally arrived in July 1690, too late to achieve anything except to carry James back to France after the Boyne. This want of nerve on the part King Louis's navy to pursue a more aggressive strategy in Irish waters at this crucial juncture was surely a mistake. It was not the fault of the French admirals, but of the king and his civilian bureaucrats at Versailles who knew little of maritime matters, and directed naval policy without professional advice. Little advantage was taken of the temporary superiority enjoyed by the French navy during the war in Ireland and, after it was defeated by the combined Anglo-Dutch navies at the Barfleur/La Hogue battles in 1692, plans to invade Britain and Ireland were abandoned. Instead, France reverted to a continental strategy, in which the navy, still a formidable force, focussed on harassing enemy convoys and disrupting commerce.[5]

The 1689 convoys brought not only King James himself, accompanied by the experienced French diplomat, Jean-Antoine de Mesmes, comte d'Avaux, as Louis's ambassador extraordinary, but also a large number of James's supporters, and French officers. The latter consisted of generals to command the Irish army and regimental officers to inject professionalism into unit leadership, together with cadets, engineers and artillerists. All the officers received a step-up in rank on arrival in Ireland and frequently gained further promotion while there. There were also civilian officials, including an *intendant*, a *commissaire de guerre* and lesser *commissaires*. Such officials reported directly and in detail to Louvois and were the means by which he exercised control and management over French military affairs, including close supervision of operations in Ireland. Generals were accompanied by aides-de-camps, who were often their young relatives. The French would have been reasonably familiar with the structures, administration and tactical practices of the Irish army, as all three of Charles II's armies were modelled on that of France, and several leading officers of the Irish army had served there. Strategically, perhaps in deference to Louvois's sceptical view of the Irish campaign, the French generals were cautious in Ireland, especially after the loss of Ulster in 1689. A fundamental difference arose when Schomberg

Simms, *Jacobite Ireland*, p. 92; O'Kelly, pp 101, 406. 5 Le Fevre, 'Battle of Bantry Bay', pp 1–16; 'Talbot letter-book', pp 121, 130; Bluche, *Louis XIV*, pp 427–8.

commenced his offensive south. Rather than risk defeat and the loss of the kingdom, the French urged withdrawal to Munster or behind the Shannon, but this view was rejected by Tyrconnell and the Irish. Lauzun in 1690 was similarly inclined.[6]

The French generals, 1689–90

The complement of general officers sent to Ireland by Louis in 1689 was intended to provide much of the leadership of the Jacobite army. First in rank and importance was the veteran Conrad von Rosen, created marshal in Ireland, and effectively the army's everyday commander in 1689. His harsh methods and abrasive personality soon ruptured his relationship with James, and he was glad to return to France after nine months. In that time, however, he did much to mould the army into a more professional force. A fuller treatment of his role and conduct is given in chapter 7. The marquis de Maumont, a major general in France, was originally to have commanded the expedition to Ireland, but was subordinated to Rosen, once James agreed to go there himself. James promoted him lieutenant general on landing. Maumont was in command of the siege of Derry, where he showed considerable vigour until killed in the Pennyburn skirmish outside the city in early May. The comte de Gacé (later Matignon), promoted major general in France before his departure, arrived in Ireland in August, accompanied by nineteen other officers. He was given the rank of lieutenant general and was second-in-command of the cavalry under Tyrconnell on the right wing in the order of battle. He accompanied James to Drogheda in the autumn campaign against Schomberg. He made no secret of his low opinion of the Irish soldiers, which Fumeron considered ill-advised. He was eventually recalled and returned to France with Rosen early in 1690. He became a marshal in 1708. The comte de Léry-Girardin, a French cavalry brigadier, came to Ireland with King James, who promoted him to the rank of major general on arrival and advanced him to lieutenant general in August 1689. He was second-in-command of the left wing under Rosen in the Jacobite army's 1689 order of battle. He commanded the reserve encamped near Dublin during James's autumn campaign against Schomberg. In early 1690 he commanded the region around Drogheda and was censured for leaving his post to greet the French troops when they arrived in Cork. He took part in the Boyne campaign, commanding the front-line cavalry on the Jacobite left wing that saw little action. Afterwards he escorted James to Dublin and on his journey south, and then accompanied him back to France,

---

6 Childs, *Charles II*, p. 103; *F-I corr.*, iii, p. 69; *d'Avaux*, p. 479; 'Lauzun's reports', pp 117–18.

reluctantly, as he claimed. He was critical of Lauzun, the commander of the French expeditionary force in 1690, and blamed the Boyne defeat on the Irish. The marquis de Pusignan, an infantry brigadier promoted to major general in 1689, was mortally wounded in the Windmill Hill skirmish at Derry.[7]

The marquis de Boisseleau, a captain in the *gardes françaises*, was an experienced soldier, who was sent to Ireland with James II to be adjutant general, although it is unclear whether he ever functioned in this role. He was promoted to brigadier, and made governor of Cork, where d'Avaux reported that his patience and industry greatly improved the capability of the troops there. In the Jacobite line of battle, he was posted in the centre with the infantry. He became colonel of a new regiment that he raised and trained in the Cork area over the summer, the only French officer to hold such a command at the time. Promoted major general in August 1689, he participated in the campaign against Schomberg in the autumn and fought at the Boyne in 1690, after which he was appointed governor of Limerick. He was experienced in siege warfare and successfully defended the city against William III. He proved a brave, tough and capable professional soldier, with considerable leadership qualities. The author of the *Jacobite narrative* accused him of profligacy with his men's lives. Nevertheless, he won the respect of the Irish, although he was critical of them, declaring that he would rather carry a musket in France than remain any longer in Ireland. In the autumn of 1690 he returned to France, where his record gained him an audience with Louis XIV, who confirmed him in the rank of brigadier. The marquis d'Escots, an elderly brigadier, accompanied de Gacé to Ireland, where he was promoted to major general and included in the line of battle. He was sent to command at Drogheda, reporting pessimistically on its defensibility prior to Schomberg's autumn offensive. He died there the following March. The marquis d'Anglure volunteered for Ireland because of his religious zeal. Promoted brigadier, at Derry he led the bold attack on the Butchers' Gate, in which he was wounded in the arm. Subsequently he inspected Athlone, Galway and Limerick with the engineer Lozieres d'Astier. In February 1690 he was appointed governor of Cork, but soon after was given leave to return to France. The marquis de Saint-Pater, the marquis d'Amanzé and the comte d'Hoquincourt, three colonels sent in August 1689, were promoted to brigadier. D'Hoquincourt, shown with the left wing of the cavalry in the 1689 line of battle, was killed at the Boyne. Lauzun commended him for his service in Ireland. D'Amanzé

---

7 *D'Avaux*, pp 6 *et seq.*, 110, 117, 136, 359; *F-I corr.*, i, pp 320, 412, 447–9; iii, pp 27, 47, facing p. 49, 59, 63–4; Berwick, *Memoirs*, i, p. 43; *JN*, p. 46; King, appendix, pp 88–9.

commanded at Ardee throughout the winter of 1689–90. He was critical of the Irish officers, but claimed to have done his duty before returning to France in May 1690 on grounds of ill-health. Saint-Pater left the following autumn, complaining that he was without a command and attached only to Tyrconnell's staff. Both are shown in the centre with the infantry in the Irish line of battle. The marquis d'Estrade also came to Ireland in 1689. He was intended to be quartermaster general of cavalry, but is otherwise a shadowy figure, who was given the rank of brigadier and included in the line of battle with the cavalry on the right wing. He was at the Boyne and was one of the party that escorted King James to Waterford, subsequently accompanying him to France. The baron de Pointis was not strictly speaking a general, but he commanded the Jacobite artillery in 1689.[8]

These twelve French officers constituted half the generals in the Jacobite army in 1689. Their approach to warfare was professional, and they were frustrated by the state in which they found the Irish army. They displayed little understanding of Irish culture and mores, but complained of the misconduct and ignorance of the Irish officers, the disorder of the troops, and indeed about most things in Ireland. Virtually all of this first contingent of French generals became disillusioned by their experience and were anxious to return to France. Not one of them remained in Ireland after the departure of the French expeditionary force in the autumn of 1690. Nevertheless, while present, their contribution to the Jacobite war effort was significant. They played a major leadership role in most of the engagements of 1689 and 1690. A third of them were fatal battle casualties or died, and others were wounded. There may have been some resentment in Ireland at the appointment of so many French general officers. D'Avaux advised James to appoint more Irish officers to general's rank, and the king responded by promoting a number of colonels to brigadier in October 1689, which reportedly gave 'much satisfaction'.[9]

Regimental officers, 1689–90

In 1689 a large number of regimental officers were also sent from France. The records name approximately 130, and there may have been others. There were also about forty cadets from the Cambrai, Longwy, Tournai and Charlemont companies, who gained subalterns' commissions in Ireland. A further 103 French officers, earmarked for service in the Irish army, accompanied Lauzun's expedition in 1690, bringing the total in his estimate to 241, the deficit

8 *D'Avaux*, pp 42–3, 118–19, 130, 276, 450–1; *F-I corr.*, i, pp 246, 259, 267, 281–2, 320, 412, 448; ii, pp 102–3; iii, pp 27, 43, facing pp 49, 57, 59, 63–4, 67, 87; *AH*, 21, p. 140; *Stevens*, pp 178–9; Berwick, *Memoirs*, i, p. 43; *JN*, pp 90–1, 261–6; Wauchope, *Sarsfield*, p. 125.   9 *D'Avaux*, p. 479.

probably being accounted for by casualties and those who had already returned to France. He listed 19 lieutenant colonels, 18 majors, 138 captains, 65 lieutenants and a single ensign serving in the Irish army that year. The French government paid the officers that came in 1689 for the first six months of their service in Ireland, but from 1 October they were paid by King James. They were drawn from at least twenty-seven regiments of the French army. Louvois was reported to have sent only *de plus médiocres officiers des troupes du roi*. A Williamite source dismissed them as 'for the most part rabble of France'. Certainly, their quality appears to have been very uneven, with those that were incompetent or dissipated reportedly tarnishing the reputation of the rest. Like the generals, French regimental officers obtained a step-up in promotion in Ireland. It was intended that they should be given commissions in the Irish army, but there was strong resistance to their insertion into substantive commands at the expense of Irish officers. It was reported that the Irish gentry were discontented by the advancement of the French, and that some of the soldiers refused to follow them. D'Avaux, Rosen and Fumeron all complained of Jacobite reluctance to give the French officers substantive appointments, even when vacancies arose. Some excuse was always found, they said, and when d'Avaux complained of the failure to appoint le sieur de la Pannouse to the vacant lieutenant colonelcy of Nugent's regiment, Nagle frankly admitted that this was in accord with King James's policy.[10]

In all, only fifty-five of the French appear to have secured substantive appointments, which was less than a quarter of their total number. Most of those who did so were at field rank. Three became colonels of Irish regiments, and one was an acting colonel. Nineteen were lieutenant colonels and twelve were majors, the ranks responsible for regimental training, day-to-day administration and operations, especially where the colonel was an absentee or without military experience. Of the remainder, about twenty other French officers are known to have held substantive appointments, mostly as captains, although four were lieutenants, and there was a single ensign. Frequently the best these officers could obtain was an *en second* appointment, whereby they were subordinated to the command of an Irish officer of equal rank. All that was available for the remaining 180 or so, while ranked as captains or lieutenants, was *reformé* status, which included them in a regiment as supernumerary officers without any command. The lack of substantive appointments could perhaps have been justified in the case of the ex-cadets, who came to obtain a commission and gain experience. But this was not the

---

10 *D'Avaux*, pp 39, 206, 233, 638–9, 695 and passim; *d'Avaux suppl.*, pp 9–12; *F-I corr.*, i, pp 218, 399; ii, p. 117; iii, pp 27, 59, 83; Gregg, 'Exiled Stuarts', p. 22; *Ormonde MSS*, n.s., viii, p. 366.

case with more experienced officers. In Fumeron's view they were very badly treated and paid. He told of Irish officers forging false dates on their commissions so as to deny French officers even temporary commands of regiments to which their seniority entitled them in the absence of a colonel or lieutenant colonel. Discontent over their failure to secure substantive appointments continued to irk the French officers that remained in Ireland after October 1690. One, Santons Boullain, second-in-command of Simon Luttrell's dragoons, overturned only with difficulty an attempt to deny him temporary command of the regiment while Luttrell was absent in France. He complained that Luttrell told him that the French officers were no longer wanted by the Irish and of a subsequent attempt to deprive him of his command altogether. However, by the end of 1690 he reported that the remaining French officers were being viewed more favourably by the Irish.[11]

The contribution of the French regimental officers to the Jacobite army is hard to estimate, as little evidence survives of their role at unit level. Boisseleau claimed that he had disciplined his regiment as an example for the Irish to follow. According to Fumeron, the French and Irish did not get along, and the efforts of the French to set a good example were in vain. The language barrier reportedly made communication difficult and greatly diminished their usefulness. In 1691 interpreters had to be employed to assist the French engineers engaged on improving the Limerick fortifications. Nevertheless, the French input must have contributed to improving training, discipline and leadership. Fumeron, for example, reported that the French officers distributed among the regiments before Derry were doing what they could to instruct the Irish in musket care. The engineer Massé found the Irish to be fine fellows, well disposed to military service and easily disciplined. At the 1690 siege of Limerick, the leadership qualities of the French were very evident. Boisseleau commanded the city's successful defence, and his lieutenant colonel, Beaupré, gave his life while displaying exemplary courage and leadership in driving the Williamites back from the breach. François Boismeral, on the other hand, 'to his eternal infamy' in the opinion of John Stevens, surrendered Kilmallock, without firing a shot. In general, d'Avaux reported at first that most of the French did their duty, especially those who had been ordered to Ireland, although he judged the volunteer officers to be more careless and much given to drink. Later, in 1690, he took a more jaundiced view, telling Louvois that the Irish service had ruined the officers, who had grown idle and lazy and were contributing nothing to the Jacobite army.[12]

---

11 *JN*, pp 201–41; *AH*, 21, p. 161; *F-I corr.*, i, pp 258–9; ii, pp 124–5, 128–30; iii, pp 86, 159.
12 *F-I corr.*, i, pp 218, 376; ii, pp 27–8; *AH*, 21, pp 154, 159; *Stevens*, pp 179, 184; *d'Avaux*, p. 694.

There were occasional brawls with the Irish, who regarded the French as interlopers, although d'Avaux did his best to smooth out such disputes. Another report spoke of the natural antipathy between the two nations. Denied prospects, from October 1689 the French were paid in the 'gun-money' token currency, which left them hard up. It was found necessary to issue a proclamation in January 1690 forbidding Jacobite officers from poaching their servants. Most of the French officers who came in 1689 were glad to return home in October 1690 or, in some instances, earlier. The number embarking at Galway with Lauzun was put at 109, but there were also others who were wounded or sick. A cadre of thirty remained on to serve in the 1691 campaign. A few stayed because they were nursing wounds, or as in the case of the engineer, Tangis, and Boisseleau's new lieutenant colonel, Darpentigny, because they had killed fellow French officers in duels, for which they feared retribution if they returned to France. Others also may have had personal reasons for staying in Ireland; some even possibly out of loyalty and commitment to the Jacobite army. They were reported to be dying of hunger by early 1691. There were also other Frenchmen who turned up in Ireland and attached themselves to the army: an Irish private in Purcell's regiment accused of drawing his sword on le sieur Coverent was acquitted on the grounds that the latter held no commission at all, being only the companion of a French *reformé* officer.[13]

The French expeditionary force, 1690

In 1690 Louis honoured his commitment to send French troops to Ireland by dispatching a French expeditionary force that comprised seven infantry battalions, a small artillery train and a field hospital. It was led by the comte de Lauzun, a courtier nominated by King James and Queen Mary, but with a chequered history and no experience of high military command. The appointment met with near universal disapproval. Tyrconnell wrote to Queen Mary that all the French in Ireland were opposed to it. He feared that Lauzun would 'undo all our affairs', adding that he had the character of an ill man, known to be an enemy of Louvois 'which I fear will cost us dear'. Before his departure Louvois had warned Lauzun to restrain his martial ardour and play for time. Terrified of the minister, his former gaoler, Lauzun was in consequence most reluctant to expose the French troops to danger and disposed only to act on the defensive. He saw his main duty as the safe return

---

13 *D'Avaux*, pp 524–5, 571, 638; *F-I corr.*, i, pp 78, 241–2, 269, 348–9; ii, pp 120–1, 128–30; Macpherson, *Original papers*, i, p. 194; *Proclamations*, ii, p. 150.

of his men to France. Lauzun was both ambassador and captain general of the French. In practice he focussed most of his attention on the diplomatic side of his mission, and he was quite successful in promoting harmony among the conflicting interests and factions. He largely left military affairs to his deputy, the marquis de La Hoguette, a professional soldier promoted to lieutenant general in Ireland. Consequently, in military terms Lauzun's appointment did not prove altogether the disaster anticipated.[14]

TABLE 6 *French regiments in Ireland, 1690*

| Forest/Chemerault | Famechon | Zurlauben (2 battalions) |
| Merode | Tournasis/Brouilly | La Marche/Biron |

The arrival of the French expeditionary force initially boosted Jacobite morale. However, its only significant military contribution to the campaign was to cover the disorganized withdrawal of the Irish troops from the Boyne. Lauzun himself played no part in this, as he had already fled the scene with James. La Hoguette, like most of the French, found the Irish service disagreeable. On disembarkation he had clashed with Lord Dover over the inadequacy of the arrangements for the reception of the French troops at Cork. At the Boyne, he organized the French resistance at Duleek, although he was later at some pains to explain how he subsequently became separated from his men. Of Lauzun's six regimental commanders, le comte de Chemerault was promoted major general in Ireland and two more, Zurlauben and Famechon, were made brigadiers. Zurlauben played a central role in the orderly withdrawal of the French from the Boyne. His valour and good conduct were praised by the Jacobite officer, John Stevens. Zurlauben sent Louvois a controversial account of the battle, which criticized the other French commanders for abandoning their regiments during the retreat. Famechon had a low opinion of the Irish army, with the exception of the cavalry, although he conceded that the rank and file, if properly led, could make good troops.[15]

The total number of French personnel transported to Ireland in 1690 was 6,666. This figure included artillerists, engineers, medical staff, artisans and administrators. In addition, the soldiers were accompanied by their wives, but excluding those recently married. The infantry thus fell short of the projected number of 341 officers and 6,950 soldiers, and of those that embarked over 700 were classified as sick with fever, dysentery and other conditions. Within

14 *D'Avaux*, pp 11, 521; 'Talbot letter-book', p. 101; *F-I corr.*, i, pp xxvii, xxx, 354; Simms, *Jacobite Ireland*, pp 140–1, 145.   15 *F-I corr.*, i, pp 277, 343, 407, 410, 423, 426, 449–50; ii, pp 78–80; iii, pp 131–3; *Stevens*, pp 101, 123–4; Mulloy, 'French eye-witnesses', p. 108.

a month of their arrival almost 850 were in hospital, and by June more than 400 had died. The vacancies were filled by more than 600 Irishmen drawn from Cormac O'Neill's Ulster infantry regiment. Their signing-on bounty was two *écus* each, considerably less than recruits received in France. Irish officers, still paid by King James, were attached to the French regiments to discourage desertion by the Irish recruits. Zurlauben's regiment comprised two battalions and was composed of Germans. It included 500 Protestants, who were deserters or ex-prisoners-of-war from the forces of Louis's opponents on the Continent. The other regiments were single-battalion units. One, commanded by the comte de Merode, was composed of Walloons, who had been troublesome in France prior to embarkation. Some of the other rank and file appear to have been Irish, who deserted as soon as they arrived. In Fumeron's judgement Zurlauben's regiment was of excellent quality and Merode's good, while those of Tournesis (commanded by Brouilly), La Marche (commanded by the marquis de Biron) and Forest (commanded by Chemerault) were poor, especially their newer companies. Two of the French regiments, one being Zurlauben's, were clothed in blue and two others in white. Although their clothes and hats were observed to be old, it was reported nevertheless that they made a fine appearance when reviewed in Dublin by King James on St Stephen's Green. Stevens considered the French battalions to be 'well clothed, armed and disciplined', adding that they were 'the very flower of the foot of the army'. Their shortage of match as they covered the retreat from the Boyne suggests their muskets were matchlocks, as was still generally the case in the French army of the time, except for the grenadier companies.[16]

While the arrival of the French promised to improve significantly the army's military capability, in other respects it had a negative impact. The French soldiers were paid in silver, which contributed to the growing lack of confidence in the Jacobite 'gun-money' token currency. Quarters had to be found for them, frequently at the expense of the Irish soldiers who were forced to move to waste houses. In Cork, a drunken Irish party that included a harpist disturbed some French officers billeted next door, resulting in a row that left a French sergeant dead and some of the Irish officers severely wounded. In Dublin, a high-level quarrel over quarters led Lauzun to box the ears of Simon Luttrell, the city governor, and Dorrington, the footguards commander, to threaten his resignation. A Protestant commentator wrote of 'the barbarous rudeness of the French soldiers', whom he accused, possibly

---

16 *F-I corr.*, i, pp 15, 17–19, 184, 193, 281, 376, 410, 426; 'Lauzun's reports', p. 108; *Danish force*, p. 34; Simms, *Jacobite Ireland*, p. 140; *Stevens*, p. 101; Lynn, *Giant of the grand siècle*, pp 462–3; *Ormonde MSS*, n.s., viii, pp 381–3.

with some exaggeration, of murder, rape, robbery and extortion while quartered near the city. In May the French troops were ordered to seize nothing without paying for it on pain of cashiering or death. They were also forbidden to disturb Protestant services or churches. Lauzun stressed to Louvois the firm discipline that he maintained, and in general there were few complaints until after the Boyne, when the French were accused of treating Ireland like a country they had invaded. Reports of their looting, plundering and violations in Limerick, where they were quartered for a time, apparently caused the gates of Galway to be subsequently closed against them. O'Kelly considered that 'in lieu of assistance, they daily disheartened the people; and the irregularities they committed in their march and quarters were so exorbitant that it must alienate them from the hearts of the Irish'. Stevens thought they 'were more terrible to the country and offensive to the army than our very enemies ... from ill language, they came to worse actions, often beating even the [Irish] soldiers and forcing from them and their officers whatever they liked ... Wherever they marched they plundered the country'.[17]

Some of the disorderly conduct may have arisen because of the shortage of food, but Lauzun's decision to withdraw from Ireland greatly increased local hostility towards the French. That he persisted in doing so after the successful defence of Limerick, 'a paradox as could scarce be fathomed' according to King James's memoirs, surprised both Jacobites and Williamites alike. The disenchantment was mutual: a French view expressed their unhappiness at being among the Irish, 'the most brutish and inhuman people on earth', by whom, it was alleged, they were hated. An army plot to seize the weapons of the French before their departure from Limerick was aborted when Tyrconnell became aware of it. In late September 1690 4,649 infantry embarked for France at Galway, with 935 other personnel. Combat casualties had been minimal, but disease had killed a significant number. The victims included Colonel Merode, who died of dysentery on the voyage home. Protestants among the French rank and file were prone to desert to the enemy, and after the Boyne their Irish personnel melted away from Lauzun's battalions to avoid being shipped to France.[18]

Saint-Ruth's involvement, 1691

For the final campaign of 1691 Louis XIV sent four experienced French generals to take charge of the Irish army. News of their appointment was well

---

17 *F-I corr.*, i, p. 349; ii, p. 109; iii, p. 144; *Stevens*, pp 102–3, 156–7; *Story*, p. 116; *Ormonde MSS*, n.s., viii, pp 380–1; O'Kelly, p. 65; Mulloy, 'Galway', pp 8–9.   18 *F-I corr.*, ii, pp 88–9, 95, 117–21; *Stevens*, pp 145–6; *Story, Continuation*, pp 41–2; *James II*, ii, pp 420–1.

received in Ireland. Fumeron reported rejoicing among the troops, who expected these officers to provide better leadership than they had known in the past. The generals disembarked at Limerick in early May. The commander was Charles Chalmont, marquis de Saint-Ruth, a lieutenant general in France, who was styled general or 'marshal general' in Ireland. Units of the Mountcashel brigade had served under his command in Savoy, which seems to have given him a high degree of empathy with the Irish. Certainly, of all the French officers to come to Ireland, he was easily the most committed to the command, the most popular with the Irish and inspirational in the way that he lifted morale and prepared the army for war in a very short time. Fumeron noted that his practice of travelling round to distribute supplies greatly increased the troops' confidence in him. An Irish officer observed that he

> takes a good way to encourage the men when they do well [and] to give them money, and prefers them immediately; a private man that behaved himself gallantly the other day before him, he gave him his own wearing sword with some gold and made him a captain.

Although his loss of Athlone was somewhat careless, he was in sight of victory at the battle of Aughrim when he was killed and his army was disastrously defeated. Colonel Charles O'Kelly wrote of 'the commiseration imprinted on his generous soul for the afflicted Irish', and surely spoke for many when he lamented that 'never was a general better beloved by any army, and no captain was ever more fond of his soldiers than he … with Saint-Ruth died all the hope and good fortune of Ireland'. His role is more fully discussed in chapter 7.[19]

Saint-Ruth's lieutenants general were Jean de Bonnac, marquis d'Usson, and Philibert-Emmanuel de Froulay, chevalier de Tessé. Both were promoted to *maréchal de camp* just before they left France, and then received the customary step-up in rank to lieutenant general on arrival in Ireland. Neither possessed Saint-Ruth's charisma or leadership ability, nor were they impressed by the Irish. D'Usson, who was generally in charge of fortresses, was committed to a defensive strategy, which brought him into conflict with Saint-Ruth. D'Usson bore some of the responsibility for the loss of Athlone, and he was in Galway for that city's capitulation. He blamed the surrender on the defeatism of the defenders, which he was unable to overcome. He was treated as the senior French general after Saint-Ruth's death, but by then the initiative

---

[19] *F-I corr.*, i, pp xxviii–xxix, 109; ii, pp 284, 334; *JN*, p. 127; *Inchiquin MSS*, p. 29; O'Kelly, pp 119, 134–5.

had passed to the Irish commanders, and his role was little more than advisory. He showed no real disposition to continue the struggle, and his eye was on returning to France, bringing with him as many Irish soldiers as possible. De Tessé was Saint-Ruth's second-in-command with the field army. At Aughrim, there is little sense that he exercised effective authority after Saint-Ruth's death, probably because he himself was wounded, having taken a pistol shot in the chest and a blow to the face from a musket butt. Tyrconnell thought his injuries were slight, but they were enough to put him out of the fight. Fumeron reported that the Irish troops then lost heart without any general to command them. Although de Tessé recovered to succeed Saint-Ruth as commander of the field army, his role after Aughrim was less prominent, and he deferred to d'Usson, as the focus was on defending the remaining towns. Brigadier Henri de la Tour Monfort, promoted to major general in Ireland, was sent to be governor Limerick, the key Jacobite stronghold. Like Saint-Ruth, he appears to have had a positive attitude towards the Irish, and he displayed considerable tenacity in holding out against the Williamites in 1691. He thought that Ireland could still be saved after Aughrim, provided that sufficient supplies and *matériel* came from France. During the final siege, he narrowly escaped death when a mortar bomb landed in the room in which he was dining, killing his nephew. Apart from a small number of other officers, no French military personnel accompanied Saint-Ruth to Ireland.[20]

Technical officers

The French officers that came to Ireland during the war included engineers, artillerists, pioneers and civilian *commissaries*. Three principal engineers came from France in 1689, followed by a fourth in 1690. There was also a draftsman and three ex-cadets. Four more French engineers came in early 1691, primarily to work on fortifications. The Jacobite artillery train in 1689 was commanded by the French officers Pointis and Boisseleau. A 12-gun artillery train sent from France in 1690 was commanded by the *commissaire*, Jean-Baptiste de Laisné, and comprised 61 personnel, including gunners, carpenters, smiths and others. James gave Laisné command of all the Jacobite artillery for the campaign with the rank of lieutenant general. He was generally thought to have done well by saving most of the guns after the Boyne, and it was to his credit that he queried the order to withdraw them just as the Williamites started their advance on Oldbridge. He returned to France with his gunners and their guns in the autumn. Five French artillery *commissaires* served in

---

[20] *F-I corr.*, ii, pp 267, 380–1, 520–1; Laportaliére, 'Dusson', pp 81–7.

Ireland in 1691. They were headed by le sieur Turgot des Fontaines, who was apparently intended to be *de facto* controller of the small Jacobite field train in the summer campaign. Louis also sent fifteen civilian tradesmen: carpenters, wheelwrights, gunsmiths and a blacksmith. There is a fuller treatment of the role of the French engineers and artillerists in chapter 6.[21]

A significant input was provided by the civilian French administrative officers, styled *intendant* or *commissaire*, accustomed to reporting directly to Louvois, a practice they continued in Ireland. No one in Ireland was familiar with the organization of an army, an art perfected in France by Louvois and his father. The functions of these officials included holding regular reviews, returning unit and equipment numbers, maintaining discipline, overseeing the maintenance and improvement of fortifications, assessing the navigation potential of rivers, organizing hospitals and making arrangements for the provision of lodging and food for the troops and forage for the horses. They have been described as 'essentially inspectors charged with guarding against cheating by officers and civilian suppliers'. In Ireland they were also involved in arrangements for the exchange of troops with France. The only permanent *intendant* to serve in Ireland was d'Esgrigny. He came, at short notice, with the French expeditionary force in 1690, and was largely concerned with their needs. He was diligent and efficient, but highly contemptuous of the Irish, whom he described as an illiterate people, resembling wild beasts, and devoid of humanity or honour. He viewed them as lazy and content to live in squalor, for which he blamed their English masters. He lost all his personal baggage in the retreat from the Boyne. Next to him in seniority was Jean François Fumeron, a *commissaire ordonnateur de guerres*, whose wide-ranging authority and responsibilities in Ireland so resembled those of an *intendant* that he was sometimes referred to as such, and he seems to have achieved that status and pay at least temporarily in 1690. He served in Ireland in 1689 and 1691, having returned to France for medical treatment in March 1690, when d'Esgrigny replaced him. Fumeron was a very capable and conscientious official, who was extremely influential in the Irish army's organization. He was commissioned by James as *commissaire général des guerres* over all the forces in Ireland. D'Avaux, confronted by chaos on his arrival and inexperienced in military administration, greatly welcomed his appointment – '*c'est un homme, qui estoit absolument nécessaire en ce pays cy*' – and awaited his arrival with impatience. They worked closely together, and d'Avaux found him very dependable. Fumeron's extensive reports to Louvois and his successor, Barbezieux, are a dispassionate and informative estimation of the army's

[21] Mulloy, 'French engineers', pp 222–32; *F-I corr.*, i, p. 19; ii, pp 286–7.

strength and capability at various times. He had no wish to be in Ireland, 'where chaos, problems and difficulties abound', and resisted returning in 1691, but once there he attended to his duties with thoroughness and diligence. His orders at that time were to oversee the distribution of the food and *matériel* sent from France, but they also included the political role of encouraging support for Tyrconnell, to whom much of the army was hostile. He was also instructed to recruit more Irish soldiers for France, a delicate mission at odds with the needs of the Jacobite army.[22]

D'Esgrigny and Fumeron were supported by a number of other French civilian officials, confusingly also called *commissaires*, although they ranked well below Fumeron, and were not full-blown *commissaires de guerres*, of which the French army had comparatively few. At least one of these officials was in Ireland in 1689; five served in 1690, and three in 1691. Coubertin, one of those who came in 1690, was drowned during re-embarkation at Limerick. Des Essartz, who was appointed *commissaire* by King James in 1689, wrote to Louvois that he would rather serve in a lower position in France than remain in Ireland. Nine artillery *commissaires* accompanied the French train in 1690. An artillery *commissaire* accompanied Tyrconnell to Ireland in January 1691 and four more came with Saint-Ruth in May. Two Frenchmen, Cadet and de Bourg, who landed at Bantry in 1689, were employed by King James as *commissaires*. They remained in Ireland after Lauzun's departure, although Cadet was sent back to France in July 1691 on suspicion of being in communication with the enemy. La Croix managed the manufacture of saltpetre in Limerick, where he seems to have had the assistance of a 'saltpetre master and two journeymen' recruited in France in 1690. In 1689–90 the French treasury was represented in Ireland by a *commissaire* named Alexandre. Fumeron accused him of fraud, and he was arrested on his return to France. In 1689 Louvois sent le sieur Aufroy, a French army contractor, to organize the provision of bread to the army and oversee the hospitals. He too fell foul of Fumeron who criticized his efforts and called him a rogue, who tried to mask his chicanery behind inadequate and incomprehensible accounts. He recommended Aufroy's imprisonment on his return to France. On the other hand, des Essartz, another *commissaire*, thought Aufroy an intelligent man of business. Aufroy himself complained that he was obliged to operate under intolerable conditions, relating how his convoy was left without protection, which allowed the undisciplined Irish soldiers, including their officers, to seize his horses, manhandle his millers and steal their flour. Subsequently he

---

22 Lynn, *Giant of the grand siècle*, pp 88–97; Rowlands, *Dynastic state*, pp 78–82; *F-I corr.*, i, pp xxxii–xxxiii, 85–8, 280, 402; ii, p. 329; iii, pp 15–16, 64; *d'Avaux*, pp 39–41, 119; *AH*, 21, p. 113.

prepared an informative report on the needs of the army for the 1690 campaign. After Aufroy's departure in February 1690, responsibility for the army's food supply, as Fumeron recommended, was entrusted to an Irishman, although the French expedition in 1690 brought its own food *commissaire* in the person of le sieur Lormier. Three new French *commissaires* to assist Fumeron were sent to Ireland in 1691: Saint-Martin was stationed in Limerick, Methelet in Galway and Esmard in Athlone. They were principally involved in maintaining the food supply. After the war, Methelet was in charge of the embarkation of the Irish troops at Cork.[23]

The supply of matériel *and money*

As important to the Jacobite war effort as the personnel from France was the supply of military *matériel* sent by Louis XIV. The surviving regiments of the original Irish standing army were fully equipped and clothed in 1689, but to arm the vast number of men recruited in the army augmentation, there was immediately available only the weapons confiscated from the militia in 1685, which had been deposited in the provincial stores. This was the source of the 20,000 firearms that Tyrconnell distributed among the new regiments at the beginning of 1689. By then, the weapons were in very bad condition with only one in twenty reported serviceable. Proclamations in 1689 disarming the Dublin Protestants and ordering the surrender of all arms throughout the kingdom may have added something more. Beyond that, the Irish arms-manufacturing capacity was small, the gunsmiths being either unskilled, or uncooperative Protestants. The number of weapons requiring repair was very large, and a flow of requests for gunsmiths was sent to France. The shortage of firearms in Ireland left the Jacobite army heavily dependent on France for its weaponry. Muskets, pistols, swords, grenades, artillery, ammunition, other military equipment such as belts, bandoliers, saddles, bridles, pistol holsters and even pike heads, together with money, clothing and, increasingly as the war wore on, food all came from France. As Fumeron put it: 'here they expect everything to be provided from France'. Tyrconnell made much use of Queen Mary as an intermediary, aware perhaps of her influence with Louis, and repeatedly begged her to secure 'the wherewithal to make ... a good defence ... arms, ammunition and all things necessary to keep up the war'. The Franco-Irish correspondence is replete with requests from Ireland for military *matériel*, expressions of disappointment over the alleged paucity of the quantities shipped and complaints about the quality of what actually arrived. The amount

23 *F-I corr.*, i, pp xxxix, 19, 77, 90, 215–22, 233, 235, 244, 258, 265, 389; ii, pp 130, 251, 253, 442; *AH*, 21, p. 155; *d'Avaux*, p. 18.

sent certainly fell well below Jacobite needs, and there was a suspicion that Louvois's lack of enthusiasm 'was the true reason why these succours were dispensed with so sparing a hand'. Whatever the nature of Louvois's disposition, significant quantities of *matériel* were not so easy to source at short notice or transport to the coast. The arms came from the coastal fortresses and from Paris. Brest was the favoured port of embarkation and adjoining Brittany the main centre of operations. Bouridal, the able and conscientious provincial *commissaire ordonnateur* of the province, was the principal driving force behind the organization of support for Ireland. It was not altogether his or Louvois's fault that the storekeepers tended to dispatch their worst and not their best weapon stocks to meet the needs of the faraway Irish army.[24]

Once the decision was taken to intervene in Ireland, the original goal was to send 10,000 muskets, with appropriate quantities of match, powder and lead. However, the speedy assembly of this quantity of arms proved impossible and, in the event, the convoys, which arrived in Ireland in March and May 1689, between them brought 3,000 swords, 16,000 sabres, 1,000 pairs of pistols, 500 carbines with swivels, 500 muskets, 500 flintlocks, 100,000 lbs of powder, 1,100 pairs of pistol holsters and 19,000 belts, all at a cost to the French government of 80,000 *livres*. The conscientious Fumeron was unimpressed with the quality of the *matériel* sent, reporting to Louvois 'the more containers we open, the more [arms] we find broken, especially swords, which are all old and broken ... many of the muskets can't fire'. The sabres were of better quality. One regiment he inspected in June had only forty muskets that were effective – one in ten – despite many of their weapons having come from France. D'Avaux alleged, possibly with some exaggeration, that 8,000 pike heads sent from France lay in the Dublin stores and had never been mounted. More arms were landed in April, some at Kinsale, but the greater part at Waterford. A further 4,600 muskets arrived in August. This may have been the consignment, together with 5,000 spontoons, transported in October from Waterford to Dublin by *Commissaire* des Essartz, who reported them to be in good condition, which Fumeron confirmed. Clearly his criticism of the original consignments had had its effect. Meanwhile d'Avaux had forwarded a list of needs to Louis from James. It included 12,000 muskets, 3,000 flintlocks, 10,000 grenades, 1,000 barrels of powder with appropriate quantities of match and ball, 13,000 swords and a similar number of bandoliers. Lord Dover, a confidant of James and a lieutenant general in the Irish army, was sent to France to press the case. He succeeded in obtaining

---

24 *Proclamations*, pp 9, 18–20, 79–82; *James II*, ii, pp 328, 387; *d'Avaux*, pp 79, 334; *F-I corr.*, i, p. xxiii; ii, pp 354, 387; iii, pp 147, 183, 186–91; 'Talbot letter-book', p. 109.

2,000 muskets immediately, but the consignment was lost when English warships captured the cargo vessel carrying them to Ireland. However, 50,000 rounds of powder and ball and 20,000 matches, scheduled to be transported on the frigate that carried Dover himself back to Ireland, presumably arrived safely.[25]

Louis sent considerable *matériel* for the Irish army with Lauzun's expedition, which arrived at Cork on 22 March 1690. It included a battery of twelve 4-pounder French guns, with the equipment, including powder and ammunition, for their supporting train. However, according to Laisné, the artillery commander, the guns were of such poor quality that several split in the course of firing at the Boyne. Other arms sent included 3,000 muskets, together with powder, lead and match. It was well short of what James had requested, prompting Tyrconnell to complain that it would signify little when distributed among the sixty-one regiments of his army, where at least 20,000 firearms were needed and five times the quantity of powder sent. Furthermore, Lauzun retained 550 of the muskets, presumably to arm the Irish recruits to his battalions. Again, it was alleged that the weapons supplied were of bad quality, and it proved necessary to repair many of the firearms. The storekeeper in Limerick reported that of 499 muskets received for Viscount Kilmallock's regiment, two were beyond repair and most of the rest wanted triggers, locks or ramrods. The match needed for their discharge had to be dried in France before it could be dispatched to Ireland.[26]

Louis XIV had interviewed Tyrconnell after his arrival in France with Lauzun's returning expedition, and he also saw a rival deputation from the Irish army that had met James at Saint-Germain. Encouraged by Sarsfield's Ballyneety raid and by the successful defence of Limerick, Louis agreed to send more *matériel* to the Irish army for what proved to be its final campaign of 1691. Extensive quantities of powder, match and flints, but only a small quantity of arms, accompanied Tyrconnell on his return to Ireland in January 1691. The bulk of Louis's aid for the final campaign sailed from Belle-Île in May on Nesmond's fleet of over eighty vessels. Six cannon were sent (although only five proved serviceable), together with 3,000 cannonballs. The hand weapons supplied were 5,000 muskets, 3,000 flintlocks, 500 carbines, 500 pairs of pistols, 15,000 grenades, 3,000 swords, 500 sabres and 4,000 pike heads, together with substantial quantities of match, powder and lead. Fumeron's initial impression of the new weapons was good, but he later reported many of

---

25 *D'Avaux*, pp 7, 92, 232, 321–2, 372, 470; *AH*, 21, pp 136–7; *F-I corr.*, i, pp xlii, 179, 235; iii, pp 19, 61. **26** *F-I corr.*, i, pp 187–9, 341; iii, p. 118; 'Talbot letter-book', pp 112, 116; *James II*, ii, p. 388; Kilmallock papers, carton 5.

the firearms as unusable until repaired. A final and much awaited supply fleet of thirty ships under Châteaurenault sailed from Brest in October 1691. It carried arms and ammunition as well as other *matériel*. However, as it arrived after the conclusion of hostilities its cargo remained unloaded, and made no contribution to the Irish army.[27]

Excluding the arms carried by this final fleet, it would appear that the total number of French weapons sent to Ireland by Louis XIV over the three years of war was twelve 6-pounder cannon and a 5-pounder, 15,100 muskets, 500 bandoliers, 5,500 flintlocks, 2,000 carbines, 2,000 pairs of pistols, 16,500 sabres, 11,000 swords, 12,000 pike heads and 27,000 grenades. From the musket total should be subtracted the 2,000 captured at sea and the 550 retained by Lauzun to arm the recruits for his French regiments, although it is likely that the latter weapons remained in Ireland after his departure. Some arms were also shipped to Ireland by merchant vessels on a commercial basis. Portuguese merchants supplied 2,000 flintlocks in 1689. Their quality was so poor that only forty-seven proved serviceable. When Queen Mary pawned her jewels to buy arms and ammunition in France, Tyrconnell warned her to have the weapons first inspected by 'some skilful persons ... that understand arms well'. What quantity this yielded is unknown, but is unlikely that supplies of weaponry obtained from sources other than the king of France were very great. Overall, the total number of weapons supplied by Louis XIV appears significant, but it is much less so when account is taken of its uneven quality and its spread over a three-year period. As a consequence, the Irish army was under-armed for its first two years of campaigning, but the field army at least was probably adequately armed for its final campaign in 1691.[28]

France was the source of much other military *matériel*, together with clothing, food, hospital supplies and money. The 1690 convoys brought tents, pavilions, canvas for making tents, shirts, 6,000 pairs of shoes, waistcoats, copper and flour. Seignelay was instructed to engage merchants to supply these goods, together with salt, brandy and wine. This trade continued for most of the war; sometimes the merchant ships accompanied the convoys, but they also traded individually, taking on board wool, butter, cowhides and tallow for the return voyage. The January 1691 convoy brought flour, brandy, oats, salt, iron, steel, nails, sacks, horse collars, tools, spare handles, back baskets, straps, ropes and 11,000 shirts. 8,000 tools and 10,000 sacks came for fortification work. Fumeron complained of the poor quality of the flour. Fuses were

---

27 *James II*, ii, p. 420; *F-I corr.*, i, pp xii–xliii, 85, 88–90, 131–4; ii, pp 289, 361, 368–9, 377; iii, pp 186–92; O'Kelly, p. 91.   28 *F-I corr.*, i, p. 11; *d'Avaux*, pp 311, 665; 'Talbot letter-book', pp 112–13; *James II*, ii, p. 391.

destroyed by damp, and many of the tools were rotten. The clothes sent were reported 'so scanty and so coarse that many of the Irish regiments preferred their old ragged ones before them'. The supplies that accompanied Saint-Ruth in May included cavalry items such as 1,000 saddles, bridles, pairs of stirrups and sickles, leather slings and metal clips for carbines, with anvils and hammers for farriers, and oats to fodder the horses. There were quantities of iron, tools, steel and assorted nails to serve the farriers, gunsmiths and carpenters. 20,000 uniform coats were sent to clothe the army. The saddles were old and without saddlebags, and the coats too small, according to Fumeron. Food and drink supplies included a large consignment of 'very good quality' flour, which was vital for the army's bread supply in 1691, together with salt and biscuit, 400 barrels of wine and 1,000 barrels of brandy. A quantity of medicines was sent for the hospitals. 100,000 *livres*, allotted for the support of the Jacobite officers, was spent in France on purchasing 3,000 tents, 90,000 litres of wine, and supplies of oats and biscuit. Experience showed that wine needed to be sent in small casks and dry goods packed in bales. Fumeron was at pains to insist on proper treatment for the merchants who dealt with Ireland. He stressed that if trade ceased, 'it would be a very serious state of affairs ... because what they bring is absolutely necessary for the survival and maintenance of the troops'. James himself sent two shiploads of supplies to Galway in May 1691. The cargoes of English shipping captured by the French warships and privateers were also occasionally disposed of in Ireland.[29]

Some money came from France to support the Jacobite war effort, principally from the French government. In 1689 over a million *livres* was committed by Louis for Ireland.[30] It came in two moieties: half was given to

---

29 *F-I corr.*, i, pp 11, 12, 88–9, 131–4, 244, 247–8, 272; ii, pp 139, 145, 211–18, 241, 260, 285, 288–9, 368–72; iii, pp 18, 156–7, 173–4, 187–92; *James II*, ii, p. 388. **30** A *livre* in the late seventeenth century was a French unit of account, not a coin. It was subdivided (like the pound) into 20 *sous/sols*, each of 12 *deniers*. The coinage that represented it was the gold *Louis d'or* (or *pistole*), the *Louis d'argent*, the silver *écu* and a variety of copper coins that were multiples of sous and deniers. In 1689 the *Louis d'or* was valued at 11 *livres* and 12 *sols*, and the *Louis d'argent* at 3 *livres* and 2 *sols*. An English report by Sir Isaac Newton and others to Lord Treasurer Godolphin in 1702 stated 'the *écu* of France goes there for 3 *livres* 16 *sols*, and by the weight and assay is worth 4*s*. 6*d*. English; and thence the *livre* is worth 1*s*. 2*d*. The *Louis d'or* goes there for 14 *livres*, which [is in] amount 16*s*. 6*d*. English.' The report clearly relates to gold and silver coinage. (French paper money, denominated in *livres*, was first introduced in 1701.) Pre-war copper halfpence struck in Dublin in the 1680s were worth twelve-thirteenths of the English standard; the Dublin mint was not allowed to strike precious metals, so that gold and silver coins in circulation in Ireland were English or indeed often continental. A report from Ireland in 1689 valued a *Louis d'or* (or *pistole*) at 17*s*. 6*d*. English, but soon after his arrival King James devalued the Irish currency to 19*s*. against the *Louis*. Although exact comparisons are impossible, it is suggested that the approximate equivalent modern-purchasing power of a 1690 pound (English)

d'Avaux with instructions to pay 300,000 to the order of King James as required, and he was to retain 200,000 himself as a secret reserve for special needs. The balance travelled with Fumeron and was landed at Bantry in May. It was brought to Dublin and discreetly paid over to King James. In addition, Fumeron was supplied with a 50,000-*livres* reserve. By the summer, d'Avaux was requesting more money from France. The French expedition in 1690 brought 100,000 *écus* for James, but principally gold and silver coins to pay the French soldiers. This treasure accompanied the French regiments wherever they went. Unfortunately, much of what remained unpaid was lost by Alexandre, their treasurer, who abandoned it as he fled from the battle of the Boyne, although some was recovered. Even that was finally lost in August when a sudden gust of wind sank the boat ferrying it out to a French frigate in the Shannon estuary. Fumeron, who returned to Ireland in January 1691, was provided with 80,000 *livres* to pay for work on the fortifications preceding the summer campaign. He was reprimanded by Louvois for the '*mauvaise habitude*' of paying Irish labour at a daily rate, rather than by the task. Fumeron stressed the need for more money to support the army. Saint-Ruth apparently brought no money, but 10,000 *pistoles* arrived for him at Limerick about the time of the battle of Aughrim. Fumeron took control of this sum, confiding its existence only to the French generals. Subsequently, alleging that it came from their personal resources, they paid it over in instalments to maintain the army. King James may have supplied some funds himself. Louis gave him a generous annual allowance of 600,000 *livres* to support his court-in-exile at Saint-Germain. Some of these funds may have accompanied him to Ireland or been sent there on his orders. Queen Mary pawned her jewels to send 'a great sum of money into Ireland'. James left 50,000 *pistoles*, 'all the money he had', with the Irish on his departure in 1690. He gave Tyrconnell 15,000 *Louis d'or* to bring to Ireland in 1691, but he may have been only the conduit for this sum, which appears to have been the fulfilment of Louis's autumn promise of support to Tyrconnell and the delegation from the Irish army. Tyrconnell's requests to James for more money met with no response, possibly because they coincided with French insistence that James pay 200,000 *livres* (about 20 per cent) towards the cost of *matériel* sent to Ireland with Saint-Ruth. France was also a source of copper and brass for the Irish Jacobite 'gun-money' token coinage. Overall, the French money was intended to do no more than supplement the financial resources of the Jacobite regime in Ireland. While it

is €185, a *Louis d'or* €150, an *écu* €35 and a *livre* €12. (Shaw, *History of currency*, p. 168; Newton, 'Value of gold' (1702); *d'Avaux*, pp 45, 75; Dolley, 'Irish coinage', p. 419; Officer & Williamson, 'Purchasing power of British pounds'.)

certainly did this, the presence of French gold and silver coins, even in limited amounts, was also a factor in discrediting James's brass-token coinage, the principal means of paying his army.[31]

Irish soldiers for France

As early as January 1689 Louvois had under consideration the formation of an Irish regiment in France, with the duke of Berwick as its commander. It was to be recruited from Irish soldiers escaping from England. By February the original project was adjusted in the light of the proposal to send French troops to Ireland. Louvois insisted on the precondition that an equivalent number of Irish soldiers be exchanged for incorporation into the French army. It was a curious arrangement that afforded King James no net increase in army size and therefore offered him only limited benefit. The minister sent a letter with James, presumably with his approval, inviting Justin MacCarthy to lead the Irish regiments, and the general responded that he was 'transported with joy' at the prospect of returning to serve in France. When MacCarthy, now Viscount Mountcashel, was captured at Newtownbutler at the end of July, d'Avaux received a very frosty response from James when he asked for Sarsfield in his place. The matter was resolved by Mountcashel's escape from captivity, allowing him, as planned, to lead the Irish troops to France in 1690. The initial French proposal was for three Irishmen to be exchanged for every two Frenchmen, but later this was reduced to an exchange of equal numbers. The final outcome was that the French army received 5,387 officers and men in return for the 6,666 French personnel that accompanied Lauzun to Ireland. The Irish sailed to France on the ships that had brought Lauzun's forces to Ireland. The idea of using French officers to command the Irish troops was rejected on linguistic grounds in favour of using well-born Irishmen, especially if they had served previously in France. Few would have met the latter requirement. In practice two French majors were included.[32]

The reluctance of Irish soldiers to go to France at this stage was reflected in the difficulty in finding men to serve in the battalions of the Mountcashel brigade. D'Avaux maintained an on-going, if fractious, dialogue with King James on the matter. The original plan was to send four regiments, each of sixteen 100-man companies on the French model, but Louvois subsequently agreed to reduce the regimental strengths to ten companies, with as few as

---

31 Corp, *Court in exile*, p. 22; *d'Avaux*, pp 14, 39, 203, 223, 321; *AH*, 21, p. 80; *James II*, pp 391, 405, 422, 433–4, 451, 463; *F-I corr.*, i, pp 86, 126, 134, 189, 411, 443, 453; ii, pp 90, 213, 249, 259, 265, 353, 365–6, 382, 489, 497.   32 *AH*, 21, pp 7, 27; *d'Avaux*, pp 78, 280, 517, 519, 538–9, 583–4, 636, 688; *F-I corr.*, i, pp 19, 359, 363–70; iii, p. 5.

65 men in each, provided that the number of regiments was increased to five, which the French would arm and clothe. Differences over the selection of officers provoked sharp exchanges between James and d'Avaux. Louvois wanted aristocratic colonels with the prestige to attract recruits, and vetoed the inclusion of any of the Hamilton brothers. James angrily rejected some of the ambassador's suggested names on the grounds that the French wanted all his best officers. In the end the final choice of the colonels approximated to Louvois's requirements: all five were closely connected to the Irish peerage. Mountcashel was the son of a peer and a new peer in his own right. Arthur Dillon and Daniel O'Brien were the youthful sons of peers. Robert Fielding, although an English professional soldier, was married to Mountcashel's sister-in-law, Lady Margaret Burke, who was the only child of the marquess of Clanricard. Richard Butler was the younger brother of Viscount Galmoy. The other officers were less satisfactory to the French. Louvois wanted capable officers appointed to the ranks of lieutenant colonel and major in each regiment. James refused to release more young aristocrats, while d'Avaux rejected the king's suggestion that these field ranks could be filled by Irish officers already serving in the French army. In the end d'Avaux felt able to reassure Louvois that the field officers finally selected were generally suitable. On the other hand, the French complained of the miserable low-born captains whom they alleged were only traders or workmen, given to neglecting their duty and to drinking and socializing with their men. They were mostly chosen by their colonels, and commissioned either because they were effective at raising recruits or as substitutes for other officers who were unwilling to go to France. Their poverty inclined them towards pillaging the countryside and robbing their men. La Hoguette, when he arrived, was probably realistic when he observed that due to the great shortage of good officers in Ireland, James was understandably reluctant to part with the few that he had. There were suggestions that those who were unsuitable could be replaced after disembarking in France, but in the event Mountcashel was given the power to nominate the officers of each regiment on its arrival there, and he seems to have made little change.[33]

Raising rank and file proved difficult, with d'Avaux and Fumeron both anxious to the end that numbers would fall short. James wanted to send new recruits or at least men who had only been raised in the autumn of 1689. D'Avaux sought at least a quarter of the force to be comprised of veterans.

---

33 *D'Avaux*, pp 78, 287, 517–20, 531, 583–4, 589, 623, 634, 659, 676; *F-I corr.*, i, pp 49–53, 246, 359; iii, pp 127–8.

Lord Dover, whom the French regarded as hostile to their interests, argued that Ireland should furnish only 3,000 men directly, the balance being found from Irishmen already in France. Mountcashel's regiment had suffered heavy losses in the defeat at Newtownbutler in 1689. After his escape he won praise from d'Avaux for his success in restoring his unit to full strength, with 'very good' officers and men. He filled the ranks by the dubious method of forcefully recruiting members of the Jacobite militia in the southern counties, which left his regiment 1,530-strong on embarkation. Daniel O'Brien was colonel of one of the two O'Brien infantry regiments dating from a division of the original O'Brien regiment in 1689, but many of the officers and other ranks who went with him to France were drawn from the regiment of his younger brother, Charles, which remained in Ireland. At one point, when a dispute arose between King James and Lord Clare, officers and men declared they would not go to France at all unless led by an O'Brien. The French thought most of the regiment's officers of poor quality and sought to discharge a large proportion of the rank-and-file before embarkation because they were mere youths or riff-raff and very disorderly. Eventually the unit mustered 1,588 all ranks on embarkation. Arthur Dillon's regiment, although ostensibly a new unit, likewise drew to some extent on the existing Dillon infantry regiment in the Irish army for both officers and other ranks. It embarked with 805 officers and men. Fielding employed Colonel John Browne as his recruiting agent. D'Avaux praised his efforts, but the result was disappointing and he was unable to form even his own company. Browne's own new-raised regiment was then merged with Fielding's, despite the misgivings of some of its officers, bringing the unit to 779 officers and men at embarkation. Richard Butler's was a regular army regiment, but without arms. It was conveniently quartered at Youghal and was belatedly included to make up the numbers. The regiment's strength on embarkation was 667 officers and men. Reviews by Fumeron weeded out soldiers too old, too young or otherwise unsuitable, with the gaps being filled by detachments from the army regiments of Clancarty, O'Donovan and MacCarthy Mor, all quartered in Munster. It was reported that Mountcashel's men were shipped off 'with a great deal of howling'. On arrival in France, Fielding's and Butler's, the weakest regiments, were broken, with their rank and file consolidated into the remaining three regiments which were then incorporated into the French army. Butler may have anticipated the reduction, for he did not accompany his regiment to France. Fielding had been recommended for the lieutenant colonelcy of Mountcashel's regiment. When this failed to materialize, he retired to the Jacobite court at Saint-Germain, from where he eventually returned to England and made his peace with

William. Fifty-five junior officers, almost all from the two disbanded regiments, were sent back to Ireland. In the end Fumeron was reasonably pleased with the quality of the rank and file that embarked for France. Ragged, barefoot and penniless on arrival, once they had been clothed – in red coats and white stockings – reorganized and armed, they were deployed in Savoy under General Saint-Ruth, where their good conduct soon prompted Louvois to seek more Irishmen.[34]

Irish soldiers already serving in France provided a source of recruits for Mountcashel's regiments. In June 1690 an instruction was issued to incorporate Irishmen in the French regiments of Greder and Surbeek into his force, and a further 600 came from French regiments in Flanders. After the Boyne, when a Jacobite capitulation seemed likely, Louvois asked Lauzun to embark with his own men, and four or five good Irish regiments, together with a further 8–1,200 recruits for the Mountcashel Brigade. The successful Irish defence of Limerick thwarted this scheme, but Louvois sustained his pressure. The French frigates sailing back and forth to Ireland were ordered to bring any available recruits. When Fumeron returned to Ireland with Tyrconnell in January 1691, his orders were to find at least a thousand recruits for the Mountcashel regiments and double that number if Tyrconnell could supply them. There were also places for young men of good family to serve in French cadet companies in preparation for commissioning as officers. Tyrconnell claimed that he had only promised 200 recruits, and Fumeron observed that he seemed in no hurry to supply even that number. Tyrconnell told Louvois that the Irish soldiers, despite the misery of their situation, were reluctant to serve in France. The French suspected that Tyrconnell was motivated by animus towards Mountcashel, but the reality was that his standing with the army was low, and likely to deteriorate further if he attempted to weaken it by recruiting more soldiers for France. A sharp reaction from Louvois prompted him to renew his efforts, and he promised 1,200 men. The recently raised Prince of Wales regiment was selected to go to France, with the acquiescence of its colonel, James Lacy, who was a veteran of the French service himself. However, when the rank and file of the regiment learned of their fate, they deserted in large numbers while *en route* to Limerick. An adjusted plan to embark the remainder, supplemented with Brian O'Neill's regiment, was aborted, because the captains of the available French ships refused to carry the Irish soldiers on the grounds that they had insufficient food aboard for their

---

34 *D'Avaux*, pp 517–18, 623–4, 634–5, 646, 638–9, 676–7, 680–4, 688; *F-I corr.*, i, pp 49–53, 271, 281, 294–5, 338–9, 359, 363–70, 423; ii, p. 15; iii, pp 127–8; Kinsella, *Catholic survival*, pp 44–5; *Ormonde MSS*, n.s., viii, p. 378; Genet-Rouffiac, 'Wild geese' II, p. 35.

own sailors. Promises to find recruits by the brothers of Dillon and O'Brien yielded little or nothing. Fumeron reported that several Irish colonels had approached him offering to bring their units to France if they could be retained as a body, but this was rejected as being no solution to filling the depleted ranks of the Mountcashel brigade. Apart from French deserters and a handful of recruits, together with thirty young Irish 'gentlemen' for the French cadet companies, no more soldiers went from Ireland to France before the end of the war. The first significant reinforcement to become available to Mountcashel from Ireland was 600 men from the 15,000 or more soldiers shipped to France after the treaty of Limerick.[35]

There is no doubt that without the support given by France, the Irish army could not have sustained a three-year war against the forces amassed by King William. The money, *matériel* and personnel Louis supplied were essential to the Jacobite war effort in Ireland, and their organization and transport represented an immense effort by the French. But the French had their own interests, clearly evident in their insistence on obtaining the Mountcashel brigade and their determination to secure as many as possible of the Irish troops after the treaty of Limerick. Otherwise, Ireland was really only of interest to Louis XIV as long as it could threaten William's security in Britain and disrupt his war effort on the Continent. The withdrawal of the French infantry in 1690, and indeed their underperformance before that, revealed the limitations of French military support. The Mountcashel brigade was not returned to Ireland, and Louis got better value out of it than ever James got out of Lauzun's infantry. The French also avoided the risk of deploying their navy in the Irish Sea. Whatever trading advantages accrued to French merchants were greatly reduced after the Boyne. From the outset French officials and officers who came to Ireland found it a disillusioning experience: they reported that their treatment was unfair, French assistance was squandered, the Jacobite government was pig-headed and incompetent, the people rough, the food unappetising and the climate bad. As *Intendant* d'Esgrigny put it: 'it is impossible to state the misery and difficulty [of campaigning] in this country, where the people are ill-disposed, uncouth and lazy'. Famechon found the Irish troops ill-disciplined and prone to run away. After the Boyne defeat ended all hope of invading England, the sole wish of the French was to return home, even after the successful Jacobite defence of Limerick. Their negative attitude disappointed their Irish allies. Louis's subsequent assistance in 1691 was largely confined to *matériel*, and the small

---

35 *F-I corr.*, i, pp 19, 49–53, 65, 77, 85, 87, 123, 126, 146, 152–3; ii, pp 110, 207, 210, 242–3, 285, 312, 321, 329–30, 353, 363, 367, 372–3, 479; *AH*, 21, p. 215.

number of personnel sent consisted only of generals, technical officers and artisans. Louis's Irish intervention certainly disrupted and delayed William's involvement on the Continent and ultimately added more than 20,000 veteran troops to his military capability. French support provided the Irish Jacobites with sufficient military assistance to sustain a three-year war, but it fell short of what they needed for victory.[36]

Figure 8. 6-pounder field gun

36 *F-I corr.*, i, pp 387; iii, 132–3; *d'Avaux*, p. 83.

CHAPTER 10

Finance and logistics

The financial challenge

SOLDIERS EXPECTED TO BE paid for their service. In principle the wartime system of pay was merely a continuation of that prevailing in the peacetime army and broadly similar to that in Britain. Musters of the number of men in each regiment were returned to the army paymaster, who then issued the appropriate pay for the regiment to the colonel. A private soldier's pay, or 'subsistence', was £8 8s. per annum. In practice he received far less, for a number of deductions, known as 'off-reckonings', were made. For the support of the Royal Hospital Kilmainham (the old soldiers' home), 6d. in the pound was taken. The sum of 5s. 6d. went to three government officers involved in the process: the treasurer, the clerk of the pells (an exchequer official, who recorded monies issued) and the muster-master general. The latter two deductions were unique to Ireland and a source of grievance. Finally, 2d. in the pound went to the regimental agent, a clerk appointed by the colonel to manage the finances and clothing of the regiment. The employment of agents was prohibited from the end of 1689. As most deductions were proportionate to pay, higher ranks contributed substantially more per head. These automatic off-reckonings left the ordinary soldier with £7 16s. 11d. But even this sum was subject to further off-reckonings that went to his colonel for the hire-purchase of his uniform and equipment: £2 16s. per annum for a cavalry or dragoon private and slightly less for an infantryman. This deduction was virtually never-ending, as uniforms needed replacing every eighteen months. If a soldier was supplied with food, such as bread and meat while on campaign, and drink, he paid for them through a reduction from pay, and also contributed towards the cost of tents for his accommodation. The number of reductions was reduced and the rates laid down at the end of 1689. Whatever balance remained was then paid via the major to each captain for distribution to the soldiers in his company or troop. A common problem in most armies was that pay often fell badly into arrears. Despite the delay and deductions, and the chicanery of officers and officials who not infrequently 'did shark upon their men', in practice the soldiers had to be paid enough to subsist, without which indiscipline and misconduct were likely to become prevalent. In 1687, to forestall 'disorders and abuses' arising from the 'miserable condition of the infantry', it was decreed that privates must receive, after deductions, at least 1s. 11½d. per week. In the first six months of 1689, when the new soldiers received no pay from the government, there was widespread looting and disorder. Even when regular pay commenced for the expanded army, Fumeron, the French *commissaire*, argued that the soldiers would be hard put to survive on the amount they received, but he complained that no one in Dublin would listen. Lauzun, in 1690, stressed the need for accurate musters, proper payment of officers and men and an end to the chicanery of colonels.[1]

From 1 September 1689 the pay of the new regiments' personnel was brought up to the rates of the old establishment. The several records of wartime pay rates are not easy to reconcile, and most are in French currency. The rates quoted in Table 7 are from the papers of Lord Melfort's secretary, David Nairne. In March 1690 Captain Gafney of Colonel Edward Butler's infantry regiment paid his private soldiers exactly at the rate in Table 7, although his sergeants, corporals and drummer fared somewhat better. Colonels and lieutenant colonels also commanded a company or troop, which substantially increased their pay. This accounts for the comparatively high pay of majors, who held no other command. Adjutants, who were generally subaltern officers, gained an increase in pay while on the regimental staff. Nominally at least, the rates of pay were somewhat higher than in France, but subject in both armies to substantial off-reckonings.[2]

The annual cost of the pre-war peacetime army, including command and staff salaries, was £178,000, which (with a subvention going to support the English army) accounted for 85 per cent of the Irish revenue. The scale and rapidity of the Irish army's expansion in 1688–9 presented the Jacobite government with a major financial challenge. In the report accompanying his invitation to James to come to Ireland, Tyrconnell stressed the need for financial support: '500,000 crowns in cash, with our own industry will serve us for the present year'. Later he estimated that the government needed revenue of £100,000 per month, most of it for the army. The French estimate of £55,000 per month was somewhat lower, but it made little difference, for both sums far exceeded the government's regular income which, due to the decline in trade, had slumped to £160,000 per annum and, as the war went on, was to virtually disappear. To meet the deficit, a number of strategies were mooted or

---

[1] Childs, *Charles II*, pp 50, 57; *Clarendon, letters*, i, p. 70; Lynn, *Giant of the grand siècle*, p. 150; *Proclamations*, pp 40–2, 141–3; *AH*, 21, p. 156; 'Lauzun's reports', p. 105. [2] *Proclamations*, pp 119–20; Macpherson, *Original papers*, i, p. 309; 'Gafney', p. 166; *AH*, 21, pp 116–21.

TABLE 7 *Daily rates of pay, July 1689*

Cavalry

	shillings	pence		shillings	pence
colonel	4		captain	9	
lt colonel	3		lieutenant	4	4
major	9		cornet	3	4
adjutant	4	4	quartermaster	2	6
chaplain	1	3	corporal	1	
surgeon	1	3	private		6½

Dragoons

	shillings	pence		shillings	pence
colonel	4		captain	7	
lt colonel	3		lieutenant	4	
major	7		cornet	3	
adjutant	4		quartermaster	1	8
chaplain	1	3	corporal		10
surgeon	1	3	drummer		10
			private		5½

Infantry

	shillings	pence		shillings	pence
colonel	4		captain	6	
lt colonel	2		lieutenant	2	
major	6		ensign	1	6
adjutant	3		sergeant		8
quartermaster	1	8	corporal		6
chaplain	1	3	drummer & private		4
surgeon	1	3			

adopted. The immediate problem was addressed by requiring the new officers, in return for their commissions, to subsist their men until the summer of 1689. In France, officers at times were obliged to provide financial support to their units, and the practice occasionally occurred in England too. Many of the Irish colonels were wealthy, but the majority of the 2,500 junior officers were not. As their meagre resources of food, money and credit became exhausted, their hungry soldiers turned to desertion, marauding and pillage to survive, with adverse consequences for discipline, public order and the maintenance of food supplies.[3]

3 *CTB, 1687–8*, pp 1742–6; 'Talbot letter-book', p. 107; *d'Avaux*, pp 128, 185, 198, 217, 124; *JN*,

It was not until the end of May 1689 that the government finally took over responsibility for subsisting the new officers and men. King James had received 500,000 *livres* (about £42,000) from France, and a further 50,000 *livres* had been retained by Ambassador d'Avaux. A muster of the army was made, and these funds were used to pay officers and soldiers from May, the distribution being under French control. But it was clear that other funds were urgently needed. James rejected a suggestion by d'Avaux to raise loans internationally on the security of the properties confiscated from Williamite supporters. The Jacobite parliament, meeting in May, agreed to an act of supply for the support of the enlarged army in the form of a land tax of £20,000 per month to be levied on the counties, proportionate to their perceived wealth and to be collected by named local commissioners. In the words of King James's memoirs, 'it was a sum more agreeable to the king's necessities, and their own good will than the present abilities of the people [to pay it], considering the destruction the nation was in'. It was not scheduled to come into operation until July, but the poverty of the country coupled with the flight of gold and silver money with the Protestant *emigrés* made Fumeron doubtful that much would be collected, and ultimately indeed the measure appears to have yielded little, if anything. In the north, the pro-Williamite Protestant associates sought to seize the tax proceeds, but the reign of the collectors there was so short that their accounts were reported to amount to no great matter. There is nothing to suggest that a fresh attempt to implement the tax prior to the 1690 campaign met with any more success.[4]

The copper coinage

Faced with the immediate problem of paying the army in June 1689, the Jacobite government resorted to minting a token coinage made of copper and brass. In d'Avaux's opinion, it was the only way for King James to survive, and it became the means of paying the army for the next year. A mint operated by Quakers was established at a Dublin premises in Capel Street, using presses already available for the minting of copper halfpennies. Proclamations declared that its output of sixpence pieces, shillings and half-crowns was to pass as current money in most circumstances, with severe penalties for anyone refusing to accept it. The temporary nature of the coinage was stressed, with a commitment to exchange the coins for gold and silver once the 'present

p. 38; BL, Add. MS 28,053; *AH*, 21, p. 124; Childs, *Charles II*, pp 50–1; Rowlands, *Dynastic state*, chapter 7. **4** *D'Avaux*, pp 39, 119, 156, 185; *AH*, 21, pp 112–13; Macpherson, *Original papers*, i, pp 309–11; *James II*, ii, p. 356; *Acts of James II's parliament*, pp 6–19; *Proclamations*, p. 151; Stevens, p. 68; Leslie, p. 91.

necessity' had ceased. Each coin carried the month and year of its minting to facilitate the promised redemption process. A second mint, probably operated by French engravers, was producing coins in Limerick by early 1690. But for both mints, there was a shortage of brass and copper. Old cannon barrels were used – the origin of the sobriquet 'gun-money' for the coinage – and large supplies of copper were sent from France. Without it, Tyrconnell declared, 'we are all undone ... for it's our meat, drink and clothes'. Every suitable source of metal was sought out, including bells and cooking pots. Pewter coins were issued in 1690. The original 'gun-money' coins displayed an image of James II on their obverse with the inscription *Jacobus II Dei gratia*. The reverse bore crossed sceptres and a crown, with the concluding legend *Ma. Brit, Fran. & Hib. Rex. 1689*. The assertion that James was king of France was hardly tactful, but Ambassador d'Avaux diplomatically ignored it. Brass crowns issued in 1690 depicted James on horseback. A final issue of Limerick coins in 1691 depicted a figure of Hibernia on the reverse side and omitted James's titles, changes that were perhaps symbolic of the more nationalistic outlook by then prevalent among the Irish Jacobites. Story, the Williamite writer, heard from treasury officials that the Dublin mint's output was 'not much above £1,100,000'. A modern estimate is that coins were struck with a total value of £1.5–2 million. Nine-tenths of the output went for distribution to the paymaster general of the army, Sir Michael Creagh.[5]

Helped by the shortage of specie in Ireland, the coins were initially readily accepted as cash, which came as a great relief to James and shored up his regime. An officer was able to report that by October 1689 'the army was punctually paid, and the brass money passed as current and was of equal value with silver'. But difficulties soon arose. The injection of so much specie into a depressed market, 'where everything is lacking', inevitably led to inflation. As prices rose, confidence in the currency waned. Foreign merchants trading with Ireland would not accept it, and there was growing reluctance by Irish merchants to part with their goods for copper. By the end of September 1689, those who paid in silver were able to acquire goods much more cheaply. D'Avaux reported that by November prices in Dublin had risen three- and four-fold, primarily because of shortages and the rapacity of the merchants, but he also blamed the profusion of copper money. Fumeron recommended an increase in army pay to overcome the consequent hardship, and a small pay rise appears to have ensued in December. Another problem was forgery, which was

---

5 *Proclamations*, pp 100–1, 103–5, 165–6; *d'Avaux*, pp 219, 581, 643; Story, pp 50, 93; Stevenson, 'Irish emergency coinages', pp 170–5; 'Talbot letter-book', p. 103; *Ormonde MSS*, n.s., viii, pp 371–2; *A new history of Ireland*, iii, pp 418–19; Heslip, 'Brass money', pp 122–35; Timmins, *Gunmoney*; *An account of the present state Ireland is in*.

proclaimed high treason, and for which three forgers from the same family were hanged in 1690. The loss of confidence in the emergency coinage was reflected in its decline in value against the French *Louis d'Or*. It stood at twenty-six or twenty-seven shillings in February 1690, but by June had fallen to fifty shillings. A contributory factor by then was the arrival of the French troops, who were paid in gold and silver, despite James's well-founded anxiety that this would undermine the copper coinage. Attempts were made to fix the prices of corn, meal, wool and other commodities, but as James admitted 'things were soon sold for treble the rate they had formerly been at'.[6]

The Boyne defeat finally undermined the copper currency's credibility. William promptly devalued it: crowns and large half-crowns were to be worth a penny, shillings and sixpences a farthing and pewter pence a halfpenny. After this, although the copper currency continued to be paid to the army until the autumn of 1690, its purchasing power diminished. Officers and soldiers found it would buy very little, and 'it became so despicable ... that the commodity which might be purchased for one piece of silver, would cost twenty in brass'. The Dublin mint was lost to the Williamites, but the Limerick mint maintained a rather halting production. In the territory remaining to the Jacobites, the merchants closed their shops rather than accept the copper coins at a higher rate than the Williamite devaluation, and they were said to be little bothered by the proclamations requiring them to do so. A good shilling was reported to be worth a brass pound, or twice it where the purchase of meat, shoes, pepper and hats were concerned. Stevens, with a captain's subsistence of a crown per day, had to give £1 for a loaf of bread the size of a penny loaf in London. He paid £5 for a pair of shoes, and his tailor's bill for a new uniform, cut 'in the most frugal way', was £18.[7]

Tyrconnell formally devalued the currency on his return in early 1691. By then, the July 1690 Williamite exchange rate was considered relatively attractive, and 'by secret and cunning ways' the copper money was penetrating their quarters, where there was more to purchase. In February 1691, to counter 'this growing evil', the Williamite authorities proclaimed the copper coinage valueless. On the Jacobite side, a lack of copper forced a suspension of minting from about October 1690. An attempt to recover the coinage already in circulation in exchange for paper promises of repayment was largely unsuccessful, although some brass shillings were minted over the summer of 1691. However, it was reported that there was only metal for £60,000. The

---

6 *Stevens*, p. 83; *d'Avaux*, pp 258, 502, 551, 554–5, 557, 642; *Proclamations*, pp 158–61, 165–6; *Ormonde MSS*, n.s., viii, p. 376; *F-I corr.*, i, pp 25, 373, 419, 427–8; iii, p. 80; *James II*, ii, pp 369–70.   7 O'Kelly, p. 100; *Proclamations*, p. 197; *F-I corr.*, ii, pp 207, 213; *Stevens*, p. 192.

result was to leave the Jacobite army largely unpaid, although Fumeron gave some silver money to soldiers who worked on the Limerick fortifications. In addition, Tyrconnell brought 24,000 *Louis d'Or* sent by James from France, half of which he distributed among the officers 'who are in a wretched state'. A plan to pay the soldiers a penny per day was abandoned, and for the most part the army's subsistence in 1691 came in kind. Despite threats, merchants continued unwilling to accept such coinage as remained in circulation, especially at the prices fixed. Over the summer Fumeron was aware of growing dissatisfaction in the army over the lack of pay, so in September the French distributed 50,000 *livres* worth of coinage from a secret fund in the belief that the men would not continue to serve without it. Infantry colonels received £3 and private soldiers 1s. It was a meagre amount. John Stevens observed:

> It is really wonderful and will to after ages seem incredible that an army should be kept together above a year without any pay, or [if] of any small part of it they received any, it was … equivalent to none. And what is yet to be more admired the men never mutinied nor were they guilty of any disorders more than what do often happen in those armies that are best paid.

In an era when soldiers' pay was frequently in arrears, the Irish Jacobite army was surely one of the worst paid of all.[8]

Food supply

In his seminal study on logistics, Martin van Creveld has argued:

> What is possible [in strategy] is determined … by the hardest facts of all: those concerning requirements, supplies available and expected, organization and administration, transportation and the arteries of communication.

To sustain an army, the soldiers had to be fed, clothed, armed and accommodated. But especially, if it was without a regular supply of food for its men and fodder for its horses, an army's capability quickly diminished to the point that it was incapable of combat or other operations, due to indiscipline, disintegration or sheer physical incapacity. The logistical challenge involved to keep an army operational was immense. The reduction in size of the Irish

---

8 *F-I corr.*, ii, pp 209, 213, 218, 236, 248–9, 332, 387, 489, 493–6; *Proclamations*, pp 233–4; *James II*, ii, pp 433–4, 463; *Stevens*, p. 192.

army in April 1689 was almost certainly linked to a realistic appraisal of the size of army that could be sustained. Irish peasants were 90 per cent or more of the population and the main providers of the army's manpower. Their peacetime diet was heavily dependent on boiled or roasted meat, oaten or barley 'cakes' of bread, potatoes and milk, 'which they eat and drink above twenty several sorts of ways', preferably sour, together with eggs, peas, cabbage and, in coastal regions, fish. Stevens observed 'their drink for the most part [is] water, sometimes coloured with milk'. Plain fare it may have been, but it was also nutritious, accounting for the noticeably large physical size of Irishmen that struck such perceptive French observers as d'Avaux and d'Esgrigny. Unsurprisingly, the French were not impressed by the Irish diet. Pusignan complained 'for two days, I have eaten only very bad butter on oaten bread ... these people do not know what it is to eat, much less proffer, something that is to our taste'. D'Esgrigny's initial impression on his arrival in Cork was that the Irish peasants ate mostly potatoes, together with flour or barley diluted with water and occasionally salt meat, usually eaten raw. He blamed the illnesses of the French on the bad Irish beer and water. Tobacco-smoking was widespread among all classes and by both sexes.[9]

The diet of the better-off was more varied and sophisticated, especially in families with experience of life in London or on the Continent. Their fare included game, and imported spices, sugar products, wine, brandy and even Madeira and sherry. Going on campaign in 1689, Kilmallock requested his wife to send on oil, vinegar, sugar, pepper and cloves. In 1691 he was supplied with ten pewter dishes of several sizes, four dozen plates, three copper pots and three copper pans. The food supplies for the Jacobite army were largely sourced in Ireland, at least during the first two years of war. Grain was widely available in surplus, especially in the east and south, and butter, cheese, roots, fish and pork were found in abundance. The rich grasslands supported 'an overflowing plenty' of black cattle and sheep and also supplied adequate fodder for the numerous army horses, especially during the summer campaigning season. But after the Boyne, when the army retired to the west of Ireland, it became increasingly dependent on imports of grain and flour from France. In 1691 the Williamites noticed that much of Connacht had been ploughed and seeded for that year's harvest, but the war prevented its recovery.[10]

The standard arrangement, as in other armies of the time, was for soldiers to purchase their own food while in quarters, but on campaign to be supplied

---

9 Van Creveld, *Supplying war*, p. 1; Perjés, 'Army provisioning', passim; *Stevens*, pp 138–9; MacLysaght, *Irish life*, pp 254–6, 330–3; *F-I corr.*, i, pp 221, 348, 377; *d'Avaux*, pp 29, 82–3; Cullen, *Life in Ireland*, pp 52–3.   10 MacLysaght, *Irish life*, pp 335–9; Barnard, *Making the grand*

with a ration of bread – 'ammunition bread' – meat and salt, paid for by deductions from their pay. This basic diet could be supplemented with other food that individual soldiers could purchase from local country people, merchants and sutlers, the civilian traders that accompanied an army, selling also ale, tobacco, clothing and anything else that came to hand. Indeed, after the siege of Limerick was raised in 1690, some soldiers became sutlers themselves, trading commodities such as brandy, beer, bread, butter, tobacco, beef and mutton from market stalls in the city. This general system was subject to adjustment and change, dictated by wartime circumstances. Soldiers also supplemented their diet by looting and theft, particularly when other means of subsistence were lacking. Efforts to prevent such misconduct met with more success if the troops were adequately fed and regularly paid. In the early months of 1689, when this was not the case for the new-raised regiments, there was serious disorder throughout Ireland. Although the country people were encouraged to provision the army in the north by being promised protection and fair prices, the food-supply arrangements for the troops besieging Derry initially proved very inadequate and the surrounding countryside was soon stripped bare. Even *en route* to the city, soldiers faced starvation. The shortage of food delayed the dispatch of reinforcements to the besieging forces and was probably a factor in the high rate of desertion and ill-health of those before the city.[11]

Bread supply

Food supply improved for the army with the arrival of the capable Fumeron as senior *commissaire* and Le Sieur Aufroy, a French *munitionnaire*, who was awarded the bread-supply contract on Louvois's recommendation. He was to have the free use of the magazines in camps and garrisons. The engagement of private-enterprise *munitionnaires* to subsist the army was standard practice in France. However, officials suspected their honesty, and Fumeron soon formed the conclusion that Aufroy and his team were rogues. He had to compel the *munitionnaire* to fulfil his contract at Derry. When Aufroy's contract ceased at the end of 1689, he returned to France, evidently with the idea of securing the bread contract for the French troops expected to come to Ireland in 1690. Fumeron warned Louvois against re-employing him, alleging that he was a thieving rascal, whose accounts were a complete mess. He played

---

figure, p. 221; *JN*, p. 48; Kilmallock papers, carton 6; Simms, 'Kilmallock letters', p. 138; Story, *Continuation*, p. 196.   11 Childs, *Charles II*, p. 109; *Proclamations*, p. 96; *Ormonde MSS*, n.s., viii, p. 366; *d'Avaux*, pp 99–100; *Finch MSS*, ii, p. 478.

no further role in Ireland. Essartz, another French *commissaire*, praised Aufroy's abilities to Louvois and extolled the quality of his bread. But another source stated that his bread was very bad, and being leavened in the French manner was so disliked by the Irish soldiers as to cause a near mutiny when they were obliged to buy it at 3*d*. per loaf. Soldiers who refused it were threatened with the punishment of running the gauntlet. The Irish preference was for oaten and barley bread, with only the upper classes in the towns eating wheaten bread. According to his own account, Aufroy had experienced considerable difficulty in fulfilling his contract. He complained that it was impossible to get information from James as to the number of rations required, which kept increasing; he had been forced to build ovens in Dublin and bring in grain from other parts of the country. He managed to secure fifty horses, only to have some of them seized, together with equipment and flour, by unruly soldiers. He complained they even ejected the millers on whom he depended from their mills. By October the situation appears to have improved, partly because grain was being collected from the countryside in lieu of the money under the supply act. In the autumn of 1689 Stevens painted a rosy picture of the supply situation when the army had advanced near Dundalk to confront Schomberg:

> Whilst the army continued encamped in this place, it suffered no want of anything that was necessary … The country abounded with … corn …. The brass money … made the camp so plentiful of provisions that I have seen a good carcass of beef sold for eight shillings, and commonly for ten or twelve, good mutton for twelve or thirteen pence a quarter, geese for six or eight pence apiece, and so proportionately of all sorts of provision. At the headquarters French wines and brandy were at twelve pence the bottle, and at several sutlers throughout the camp at one shilling and six pence. The scarcest thing was ale and yet no great want of it at three pence per quart. The camp was a daily market plentifully furnished … and … good order was observed, whereby the soldiers were restrained from committing any outrages upon the people, which made them have recourse to us the more freely.[12]

The soldiers at this time had an adequate supply of ammunition bread, but this was not given to the officers. In Cork, Boisseleau accused the Protestant bakers of hiding their flour to avoid supplying his men. Unlike France, he

---

12 *AH*, 21, pp 114, 148; *d'Avaux*, p. 204; Lynn, *Giant of the grand siècle*, p. 111; *F-I corr.*, i, pp 235, 258, 265; iii, pp 58, 87; *Stuart MSS*, i, p. 44; *Stevens*, pp 83–5, 139.

wrote, no substitute bakers were to be found in the army. In October 1689 Fumeron prepared an elaborate scheme for providing the army's bread supply during the coming winter and the subsequent 1690 campaign. Whether it was ever fully implemented is doubtful, but it gives a good idea of the immense logistical challenge involved. Wheat or other cereals had to be sourced, milled into flour, transported to the baking ovens, kneaded into dough, baked, and then transported to the army and distributed in an orderly manner. The scheme was based on the premise that each soldier should enjoy a daily ration of one pound of bread. This was less than the pound and a half allowed to French soldiers, but justified on the ground that Irishmen were less dependent on bread than their French counterparts, presumably because of the availability of meat and dairy produce. It remained the standard ration for the rest of the war. On this basis, Fumeron calculated that an army of 25,000 men would require eighty-four barrels of wheat daily, or 30,240 annually. Each barrel cost eight guineas, and with the addition of milling, transport, weighing, oven-making, baking and clerical costs, together with £22,000 for the provision of fifty transport wagons and other small cars, he put a figure of £400,000 on supplying an army of this size with bread for a year, rising to £533,333 if the daily ration were to be increased to a pound-and-a-half. Forty bakers would be needed to produce a daily one-pound ration, together with *commissaires* to supervise and manage all stages of the operation, and maintain detailed records of all transactions. He recommended entrusting overall management of the bread supply to a director of provisions, chosen for his honesty and commitment to the service of the king. An intelligent and watchful man of business was needed for this position; one who knew the country well and the most convenient places to source supplies of wheat. Fumeron thought that an Irishman would be best for the job. Rowland White, a Newry barrister and MP, was appointed superintendent general of victuals in 1689, but his role appears to have been small. His only recorded activity in 1689 was in relation to the provision of forage for the horses. Described as commissary general of stores, in 1690 he was to be the recipient at Galway of 500 cattle and 900 sheep levied on County Roscommon. He was also involved in provisioning the garrison on Inishbofin off the west coast. White was outlawed by the Williamites and left Ireland after the war. Aufroy's real successor as *munitionnaire* was 'one Archbold', possibly the Dublin burgess and merchant, Michael Archbold, who held the post until August 1691, when Fumeron took over himself.[13]

13 *AH*, 21, pp 116, 142; *Stevens*, p. 87; *d'Avaux*, pp 366, 705–11; *AH*, 22, pp 35, 83; Harris, appendix, p. vi; *F-I corr.*, ii, p. 401; *Proclamations*, pp 127, 169, 177; Order to Col. Dillon, 16 August 1690 (Dillon papers).

At the commencement of the war, there was little in the way of large food magazines in Ireland, such as were the hallmark of Louvois's great supply system in France and a vital component in the supply of bread and salt meat to the French army. By the end of 1689 ten magazines had been established in different centres throughout Jacobite Ireland. To support the force facing Schomberg in Louth, Aufroy had built up stores of wheat in Drogheda and Navan, about 5,500 barrels in all, although in the other magazines only 900 barrels had been accumulated. Fumeron estimated that this amount was sufficient to sustain the army for three-and-a-half months, but it would have to be transported to Dublin. There was little grain in the city, whose merchants customarily sourced their requirements in Meath, the traditional granary of Leinster. Prices rose sharply on the army's return to Dublin, and the scarcity of bread led to the abolition of the bakers' monopoly and the opening of the trade to all persons. Disorder broke out in January 1690 when angry soldiers seized the bakers' and hucksters' bread, together with their oatmeal and other edibles, helping themselves to the bakers' money in the process. Two soldiers were hanged in the city for stealing bread, and their bodies left for forty-eight hours as a deterrent to others. Order was restored, and proclamations were issued against hoarding and fixing the price of wheat, oats and barley that were required for the army's stores. Requests for bakers to be sent from France were rebuffed by Louvois, who responded that such personnel must surely be available in Ireland. Although little is known of the arrangements for the 1690 campaign, Archbold did a good enough job for Lauzun to be able to state in May that the Irish army had bread for the next four months. However, *Intendant* d'Esgrigny judged its quality as pitiable: it was made from barley, flour, oats, rye and peas. Lauzun complained of the absence of frontier magazines in 1690. He wanted them established at Drogheda, Trim, Athlone and on the northern frontier, with Dublin as their main source of supply.[14]

Louvois made it clear to d'Avaux that when the French soldiers came to Ireland, they could not be given oaten bread, and the ambassador promised that their bread would be made from wheat mixed with bran. In fact, it was supplied by their own *munitionnaire*, and its quality was reported to be very good. The ration followed the French model of a pound-and-a-half per soldier daily, its cost being deducted from his pay. Fumeron, before returning to France, had done his best to prepare for the expected arrival of the French by gathering 40,000 biscuits, a supply of salt beef and 150 barrels of beer, as well

---

14 *Ormonde MSS*, n.s., viii, p. 375; Leslie, p. 137; *Proclamations*, pp 134–5, 158–61; 'Lauzun's reports', pp 104, 106; *d'Avaux*, p. 551; *F-I corr.*, i, pp 228, 392, 437.

as milling wheat into flour for their bread. The French also brought their own flour to Cork. It was stored in a church, where some of it was lost, probably because of dampness. It is likely that a further consignment that arrived at Cork from France in July never reached them. The Boyne defeat disrupted arrangements for their bread supply, which was reduced to half their needs, leading to 'hunger and weariness' on the retreat. Later in August Lauzun attributed the precipitate departure of the French from Limerick to a shortage of bread, and the subsistence shortage was an important factor in the deterioration of their relationship with the Irish about that time, as the hungry French soldiers simply seized what they needed wherever they could.[15]

In 1690 the soldiers defending Limerick against William were said to have had to subsist on beans and oats, eaten raw out of their pockets. Bread and other food were in very short supply during the winter of 1690–1, although Limerick remained supplied up to Christmas. The west of Ireland, to which the army was confined, was not an intensive grain-growing region. A levy of 1,000 barrels of meal was imposed on Mayo for example, but measures such as this met with only limited success, all sorts of grain being reported 'very scarce'. The situation in Limerick, the principal infantry quarters, was not helped by Berwick's destruction of the corn within ten miles of the west side of the city, which was done to impede any Williamite cavalry raid across the Shannon during the 1690 siege. Nevertheless, ammunition bread, 'made of all sorts of corn put together [and] allowed in a small quantity', was supplied for a time to the troops, but soon they were expected to bake their own bread. Officers were then issued with a daily half pint of wheat and soldiers with the same quantity of barley or oats in grain, an 'allowance ... so small that men rather starved than lived upon it'. For a time, the daily ration was reduced to three-quarters of a pound for ordinary soldiers, and later to three pounds per week. Prices were extortionate, leading to disorder which caused merchants to close their shops or abandon them when they were looted. The disorder discouraged country people from supplying the markets. Without an adequate diet, soldiers working on the Limerick fortifications grew weak. Elsewhere the situation was even worse. Efforts by Archbold and his assistants to collect grain from the countryside yielded little. By the end of March there was nothing in the stores at Athlone or Sligo. Fumeron, who had returned to Ireland in January, feared the starving garrisons would all desert. By April soldiers were reported to be dying of hunger. Some relief came in the form of French vessels trading with Ireland, and small consignments of grain and flour sent by the French government. In March seven French merchant ships were

---

15 *F-I corr.*, i, pp 247, 251, 336, 347, 356; ii, p. 5, 98; *d'Avaux*, pp 281, 295.

reported at Limerick quay, with cargoes of salt, wine, brandy, wheat and flour. Payment difficulties arose with the French captains, when their cargoes were commandeered in return for the empty currency of written promises of payment after King James was restored. Fumeron insisted that this abuse must cease in order to allow the vital trade with France to continue. There were problems too about the quality of the consignments sent from Brest by the French government. One cargo, Fumeron complained, was so old, worm-infested and dusty, that it was no more than the sweepings of the granary floor. A subsequent consignment of flour was rancid, and Archbold refused to use it, lest it harm the men's health.[16]

Archbold's own performance came in for French criticism. In Limerick his officials in charge of the bread supply were reported to lie in bed in the mornings, neglecting their duties. Their failure to mill flour left the garrison without bread for three days. They kept no proper accounts, and had only a single horse to move wheat to the mills and water to the bakery, whereas they needed at least six, which they had failed to procure. By the beginning of May Fumeron reported from Limerick that he was afraid to leave his house, as hungry soldiers followed him around the streets begging for bread. In Galway, he said, Tyrconnell didn't know where to hide, as the men were dying of starvation. Relief eventually came later in the month in the form of supplies aboard the fleet accompanying Saint-Ruth to Ireland. The delivery included 31,000 *setiers* of wheat flour mixed with rye and a large quantity of biscuit. The flour was packed in barrels and stored in churches after it was landed. This gave enough space for air to circulate between the barrels and for inspections to be made. Flour that was deteriorating could be transferred into sacks, presumably for early use.[17]

Based on the quantity of flour that had arrived, Fumeron estimated the army's bread-supply needs for the 1691 campaign. He calculated that 58,389 one-pound rations would be needed daily, a figure that excluded hospital staff, drivers and boatmen who would also have to be fed. There was a possibility also of having to supply an additional 11,368 rations to Balldearg O'Donnell's auxiliary army. The high number of rations for the army, close to twice the expected total of its personnel, is explained by the fact that officers, depending on their rank, were entitled to extra rations. Thus, in an infantry regiment, the colonel was entitled to eight rations, each captain to five, and the chaplain, surgeon and quartermaster to two. Later, in August, in the wake of the Aughrim defeat, the officers' allowances were reduced, mainly by one per day,

---

16 *James II*, ii, p. 423; *F-I corr.*, ii, pp 195, 212–18, 253, 260, 268; *Proclamations*, pp 180–2; *Stevens*, pp 191, 193; *JN*, p. 113; Clarke corr., no. 559. **17** *F-I corr.*, ii, pp 248, 279, 370–1, 409; iii, p. 190.

although colonels lost two. There was no change for the ordinary soldiers, who were already limited to a single ration. Rations also had to be found for 75 staff, 288 artillerists, 25 garrison commanders and their staffs, 124 men engaged in the supply of meat and 610 on the production and distribution of the bread itself. Fumeron made no reference to the large number of women and children that accompanied the soldiers, who also had to be fed from somewhere. An added challenge for many colonels was to meet the needs of their refugee followers and tenants.[18]

The breakdown of the 517 personnel required to maintain the bread supply to the field army is instructive. They comprised the commissary general, and twelve other *commissaires* or managers, a captain general and twenty overseers of transport, 370 drivers and carters, twenty artisans and workmen, fifteen blacksmiths and farriers, ten carpenters and wheelwrights, four masons (to build ovens) and sixty-four bakers. A further ninety-three personnel were needed to supply bread to the frontier garrisons and at the training camp at Killaloe. *Commissaires* were appointed to supervise baking and bread distribution at Limerick, Galway and Athlone. On this basis Fumeron concluded that enough flour was available to feed the army until the following November, although in September he amended this to 15 October. He was concerned at the widespread theft of bread and the lack of money to pay for security guards. An anonymous memoir expressed the view that the bread ovens were best fired by turf, which thirty grenadiers could cut and save. Suitable soldiers could be seconded from the army to bake bread, 'for there are always townsmen among the troops, who can be taught by others'. The bakers' wages should be dependent on the weight of their bread: 200 pounds of flour should yield 270 pounds of bread. It was best supplied in three-pound loaves, flatter in shape than was customary in Ireland, but easier to carry, better cooked and so healthier.[19]

The French *commissaire* Esmard complained that Fahy and Pepper, the Irish bread managers at Limerick, were helping themselves liberally to the new flour, but making only very bad bread, a situation he promised to remedy. While the army was in the field, the bread ration seems to have been baked in Limerick, and probably in Galway too, where there were sufficient mills and ovens. From there, it was transported to the troops. There is no evidence that field ovens were employed. The bread supply seems to have been adequate up to the defeat at Aughrim. After that, Fumeron took direct control of it. Archbold was dismissed on the grounds that he was serving bad bread to the troops and wasting flour, allegedly because he was defeatist and sought to

18 *F-I corr.*, ii, pp 332, 338–48.   **19** *F-I corr.*, ii, pp 340–1, 377.

apply pressure to speed up the start of peace negotiations. Thereafter the French *commissaires* maintained the bread supply until the first Irish troops embarked for France in October.[20]

Meat and dairy food

Second only to bread was the army's dependence on meat and dairy products, the other food sources for which government generally accepted responsibility. They were vital ingredients of a soldier's healthy diet. Livestock production was central to Irish economic activity, despite some contraction in the 1680s stemming from the restrictive British cattle acts, which depressed prices, although this was compensated for by an increase in butter and salt-meat production. The sheep flock expanded to meet the growing demand for Irish wool. Petty estimated the numbers of cattle in Ireland at three million and sheep at four. A French report in 1689 was that wool, cattle, tallow and hides, all livestock products, were the goods most suited for export to France. The black cattle that were predominant in Ireland were a forerunner of the Kerry breed, a hardy little animal, good for both milk and beef. Fumeron was struck by the number of sheep, noting extensive flocks around Limerick. In the early months of 1689, the unpaid soldiers appropriated or simply stole livestock on a wide scale. In many cases, as d'Avaux observed, this was purely for the resale value of their hides. During the autumn campaign, soldiers ranged beyond their camp near Dundalk, buying or stealing cattle for their food. Meat supplies in Dublin probably improved in the early months of 1690 with the abolition of the city butchers' monopoly of the trade. Soldiers were issued with a ration of salt meat and bread shortly before the battle of the Boyne.

An important source of meat and dairy products was the herds and flocks of the creaghts. These extended family groups, mainly from Ulster and itinerant by tradition or displaced by the war, had fled before the Williamites to seek protection in the Jacobite quarters, accompanied by large numbers of livestock. Although their presence had a devastating impact on the localities they occupied and challenged the forage requirements of the cavalry and dragoons, nevertheless their flocks and herds were an asset in solving the army's subsistence needs. This was especially the case in the winter of 1690–1, when the army was desperately dependent on livestock for its survival. As early as August 1690 a levy of 500 cattle and 900 sheep was placed on County Roscommon to supply the Galway garrison. The local officials were warned that failure to comply punctually with the demand would result in troops

20 *F-I corr.*, ii, pp 356, 361, 401, 403, 490, 516.

being sent into the county 'to live there at discretion, and withal to drive and bring forth double that number of beeves and weathers'. In September officials in Mayo were ordered to bring in twenty cattle out of every hundred belonging to the creaghts to be salted for the use of the army, using the support of the nearest garrison to make the seizures, if necessary. Soldiers seized the cattle of the creaghts under Balldearg O'Donnell's protection in north Connacht even, it was alleged, killing any that resisted them.[21]

After the Boyne Stevens declared that a man must either rob with the rest or starve by himself. Albeville complained that the officers and soldiers had become rapparees, stealing food, clothing and horses from the poor people and leaving behind a trail of desolation and devastation. Many colonels, he wrote, were accompanied by followers and tenants whom their regiment maintained by the cattle it robbed up and down the country. A vital extension to the grazing area for cattle and horses lay in the no-man's-land between the armies east of the Shannon and in counties Kerry and Limerick, which provided much of the army's subsistence during the winter of 1690–1. Cattle east of the Shannon were vulnerable to Williamite raids, such as the 5,000 allegedly seized in January 1691. Although the cattle herd in the Jacobite quarters was said by the end of the war to be 'extremely diminished by reason of their continual consumption', the roads from Kerry and Clare were nevertheless clogged with 'vast stocks of cattle' as the creaghts returned to the north at the war's conclusion. As far as possible the Jacobite government built up stores of beef for issue to the soldiers on the march, or during the times they were in quarters or garrisons. Soldiers cooked their own meat, not very competently according to Stevens, who maintained that their efforts led to much sickness, death and desertion during the autumn campaign 1689. After the Boyne, their meat 'kettles' were found strewn over the battlefield, having been used for brandy consumption earlier in the day.[22]

Every soldier in the army was reported to have had butchering skills, and the beef was preserved by being salted. The only limitation was the shortage of salt, due to the disruption of trade with England. This was rectified by opening up the trade to French merchants, but the first cargoes only began arriving in 1690. This may have curtailed the 1689 annual autumn cattle slaughter, for which 30–40,000 head were assembled near Dublin alone.

21 Perjés, 'Army provisioning', pp 11–14; MacLysaght, *Irish life*, pp 167–70, 244; Gillespie, *Transformation of the Irish economy*, pp 45–6; *A new history of Ireland*, iii, pp 391–6, 443–4; Petty, *Political anatomy*, pp 55–7; *F-I corr.*, i, p. 244; iii, pp 184–5; Stevens, pp 119, 161–2; *d'Avaux*, pp 85, 237; Dillon papers; *Proclamations*, p. 176; 'O'Donnells in exile', pp 55–6; *James II*, ii, p. 434.
22 *Finch MSS*, ii, p. 478; *DI*, no. 31, 21–28 April 1691; no. 40, 23–30 June 1691; *F-I corr.*, ii, p. 232; Story, *Continuation*, pp 270–1; Stevens, p. 87, 128, 191; *Rutland MSS*, ii, p. 132.

Nevertheless, Fumeron was able to gather 2,275 barrels of salt beef to subsist the French troops as they marched from their port of disembarkation. Each barrel would have held about 200 pounds. In the 1690 campaign, salt meat from the stores in Dundalk was issued to the Irish regiments. For the winter of 1690–1, as far as possible the frontier garrisons were stocked with salt beef: at Limerick, Stevens recorded that 'the garrison lived most of the winter upon the salt beef allowed out of the stores ... the allowance was half a pound a day'. Tyrconnell brought 1,500 sacks of salt, together with flour and oats, on his return to Ireland in January 1691. For the coming campaign, Fumeron argued that the salt meat should be conserved in case of a siege, and Tyrconnell agreed to substitute fresh meat for it in the soldiers' rations, which he promised could readily be done. 5,000 barrels of salt beef were subsequently stored in the principal garrisons.[23]

The fleet accompanying Saint-Ruth brought 2,724 *minots* (bushels) of salt in 1691, the monthly ration being a pound each to soldiers, with a more generous allotment to officers. During the winter, commissioners were sent out to take up cattle and provisions for the army 'with as much equality and as little burden as possible to the people'. In June, as the army took the field, instead of money the soldiers were supplied with fresh meat. 10,000 head of cattle were reported to have been supplied to the army for the campaign. Mark Talbot's regiment was allowed twelve bullocks for its meat supply, and other regiments presumably the same. The Irish cavalry, encamped outside Limerick in September 1691, was accompanied by a herd of cattle. During the final siege, Williamite forays into the Jacobite quarters procured 700 cattle, but presumably many more were preserved by the Irish. Other provisions were supplied by sutlers, country people and merchants, or simply obtained by theft. These sources provided cabbages, butter and peas, and especially potatoes, which with meat 'sustained the greatest part of our small army', often serving 'instead of bread, and the soldiers would be feeding on them all the day'. The French expedition in 1690 was advised to bring its own sutlers. The Sligo garrison survived on 'the great plenty of fish' locally available.[24]

Drink

Both Stevens and the French complained about the scarcity of good-quality drinking water, but presumably it was still commonly consumed, as was

---

23 *D'Avaux*, pp 238, 501, 504, 524, 534, 624, 665, 742; *F-I corr.*, i, pp 11, 261; ii, pp 139, 214; iii, p. 212; *Stevens*, p. 191.   **24** *D'Avaux*, pp 529, 534, 573, 624, 626, 665, 667, 742; *F-I corr.*, ii, pp 223–4, 370, 403; *Stevens*, pp 190, 200; O'Kelly, p. 116; Story, *Continuation*, pp 217, 227; *DI*, no. 6, 28 October–4 November 1690; no. 40, 23–30 June 1691.

buttermilk. Beer was easily made, but the war disrupted the supply of hops from England, although in 1690 at least one cargo of this commodity arrived at Limerick from Ostend. Consequently, much 'beer' drunk during the war was made without hops and seems to have been what the poorer peasants generally drank. Mashed bere, a coarse barley, was the main ingredient, which was heated in water and flavoured with herbs. The extracted unfermented liquid, known as wort, was served while still warm. Together with the local water, wort was blamed by the French for the high rate of illness among their troops. Some proper beer seems also to have been made. In February 1690 Fumeron accumulated almost 500 barrels of 'strong beer' (presumably not wort) at Limerick to supply the French troops when they arrived. A limited amount of ale was available at the camp near Dundalk in the autumn of 1689. It was expensive, and expected to be more so the following year because of the shortage of hops. In 1690, to prevent disturbance, a number of suttling houses in Dublin were directed to supply ale to soldiers at 2*d*. per quart ready money. Ale, which was very expensive, and beer were still being sold in Limerick in early 1691. Beer of some sort probably remained available to the Irish soldiers up to the end of the war.[25]

The growing shortage of wine and brandy in Ireland was of much concern to the French in 1689. James was persuaded to halve import duties to encourage French merchants to supply these commodities, and this measure met with some success, with cargoes arriving from the western French seaports. In 1690 the French expeditionary force brought its own supply of both. Brandy enhanced combativeness. King James ordered its distribution to the regiments prior to the battle of the Boyne. When it finally arrived, the nearby soldiers broke open the casks and imbibed so much that a thousand or more were reported to have been unfit for service on the day. The Irish cavalry, which fought so well at Oldbridge, had each been given a half pint of brandy, according to a Williamite eyewitness. In 1691 the Irish soldiers were reported to have had 'the powerful encouragement' of brandy at the battle of Aughrim. Very little wine or brandy seems to have been available in Limerick during the winter of 1690–1, although a small quantity of brandy and some tobacco, the latter 'for the most part rotten', was given to soldiers working on the fortifications. Most of both commodities, Stevens alleged, was misappropriated to enrich the regimental majors. In May 1691 the fleet that carried Saint-Ruth also brought 439 casks of brandy and 400 barrels of wine, both consignments rated good quality. Fumeron prepared a rationing scheme

25 *Stevens*, pp 45, 47, 49, 138–9, 163, 192; *Proclamations*, pp 168–9; *F-I corr.*, i, pp 261, 336, 377, 380; *d'Avaux*, pp 87, 539, 546, 588.

based on rank to make the wine and brandy last until the end of October. Cavalry and dragoon colonels were allotted a monthly ration of twenty bottles of wine and eight of brandy, with infantry colonels receiving three-quarters of this amount. Captains received half the quantity of colonels. At the other end of the spectrum cavalry troopers and NCOs were to receive three bottles of brandy per month; and their infantry counterparts two. During the subsequent siege of Limerick, a Williamite bomb destroyed thirty barrels of brandy in one of the stores, after which Fumeron posted personnel at each with water and cow hides to fight any future fires. He again rewarded with brandy those who worked on repairing the fortifications at this time. The final ration at the end of October was for the soldiers going to France: a daily pint of beer and a half naggin (*naguin*) of brandy, together with a ration of biscuit, butter and cheese for NCOs and other ranks. Officers, depending on rank, received a multiple number of rations.[26]

Although very stretched at times, especially in early 1691, these arrangements maintained the army's supply of provisions and drink, thus sustaining its operational capacity until the end of the war. Even then, a considerable quantity of undistributed French biscuit still remained in the Limerick stores. According to the author of the *Jacobite narrative*, the city had plenty of provisions, but in fact the garrison's food supply was calculated to last only to mid-October, or possibly to 25 October, Fumeron thought, after which the army's survival was dependent on further provisions promised from France. When the supply fleet had not materialized, Archbold later told George Story that the Irish were minded to negotiate before they were driven to do so from a position of weakness through lack of food. O'Kelly, the Jacobite writer, thought that anxiety about the food supply accounted for the change in attitude of the formerly diehard Sarsfield, who countersigned the explanation for the Jacobite surrender, which the French generals sent to Louis XIV. It included the justification that provisions were at an end; none could be sourced in the city or from the surrounding countryside; and a French relief fleet would be confronted by English ships off shore and by guns mounted along the riverbank on the approaches to the city. In the end, it was the diminution of food supplies and the delay in the arrival of the provisions expected from France that determined the adoption of the only strategic option left to the Jacobite army.[27]

---

26 *Stevens*, pp 128, 196; *d'Avaux*, pp 501, 554; *F-I corr.*, i, p. 208; ii, pp 370, 402–3, 528; Story, p. 85; Story, *Continuation*, pp 125, 341.   **27** *JN*, p. 170; Story, *Continuation*, p. 279; O'Kelly, pp 154–5; *F-I corr.*, ii, pp 490, 501, 514.

Transport

Adequate transport was essential to keep the army supplied with subsistence, to draw the train of artillery and ammunition, and to carry the essentials of the field hospital. A major obstacle in late seventeenth-century Ireland was the poor quality of the roads. Although passable when dry, they deteriorated in wet weather, greatly impeding the movement of wheeled vehicles. In June 1690 the governor of Cork supplied Limerick with gunpowder, carried on fifteen or sixteen wains (heavy wagons), each loaded with fourteen barrels and drawn by eight oxen. Significantly, he reported that he was unable to use carts because of the deep fords that had to be traversed on the way. Goods were frequently moved by packhorse, on small carts or even on men's backs. It was estimated that garrons could carry a burden of one and a half hundredweight. When an army was on the move, the roads were sometimes left to the wagon and artillery trains, with the cavalry riding across the country, while the infantry marched by regiment in two columns, with one or both on cross-country tracks or simply across the countryside, where there was little impediment due to the non-enclosure of pastoral land. Harbord, the Williamite paymaster, considered Ireland a very difficult country for soldiers to march in: 'there is no passing but upon the highways, with bogs on either side, and these ways are full of bridges, mostly ill-kept or broken down at the ends so that before a man can come at the bridge, he must wade at least to the knee'. After heavy rain in October 1689, Stevens found 'the ways almost impassable' near Drogheda, 'the horse road ... being broken up and quite out of repair, and the footway in the fields very boggy with abundance of ditches at that time full of water'. By French standards troop movements, certainly in 1689, lacked any proper planning and were chaotic. But despite the many obstacles, the marching speed of the Irish infantry appears to have been well up to the European average of twenty to twenty-five kilometres per day. John Stevens averaged forty kilometres per day in the retreat from the Boyne to Limerick, admittedly mounted for much of the route, although sometimes riding pillion. Later his regiment averaged about thirty kilometres per day marching over difficult terrain to relieve Athlone. In 1691, marching from Killaloe to Meelick in County Galway, the regiment averaged nineteen kilometres per day. On that occasion all the officers were on foot, and at one point Stevens felt 'quite spent with fatigue'.[28]

At the start of the war, no train existed for the movement of artillery, munitions, bread, baggage or the field hospital. An inventory in April 1689 listed only seven wagons and nine tumbrels for carrying cannonballs in

---

[28] Tyrconnell letters, nos 19, 86; *Stevens*, pp 89, 130–8, 151–4, 200–2; *CSPD 1689–90*, p. 299.

government stores. The poor quality of Irish roads meant that wagons were little used for transport, and few were available to commandeer. In the Cork locality only three could be found. Wagons had to be constructed if the army was to be kept supplied, and a supply train of wagons and carts was eventually put together. The vehicles were crudely made and their wooden axles were prone to break on the rough roads. Fumeron described the local carts as a type of wheelbarrow, but with two wheels and of such crude construction that they were constantly breaking down, slowing the movement of goods per day to under three to four *ligues* (9–12 kilometres). Such carts could only carry small loads, and this would have been equally true of wheel-less sledges, which were also used in Ireland at the time. Sledges were all that was available to transport the arms and *matériel* landed at Bantry in 1689. The following year seventy of these 'sliding cars' drew copper from Cork to the Limerick mint. The available horses were mostly small and not trained to pull vehicles, although Aufroy thought that a thorough search might procure more suitable draft animals. Harness and collars were in short supply, and he considered their local makers to be useless. Experienced carters were also needed to train the horses to pull loads. In the withdrawal from Derry, the food vehicles had to be abandoned and burned because the transport horses were needed to draw away the artillery. Some sort of new supply train was put together over the summer. Aufroy was reported to have sourced fifty horses, and he kept the army that confronted Schomberg well supplied from Dublin. Fumeron advocated the appointment of a commissary general of transport to oversee the train. He thought that three horses (as in France) should draw each wagon, with one horse per cart. There should be one driver per wagon, while a single driver could manage two carts. Every twelve wagons and every thirty carts should be under an official. Farriers, wheelwrights and harness-makers should accompany the train to keep the vehicles and horses serviceable. It was estimated that fifty wagons would be needed for the bread supply alone, together with a number of carts. Whether this amount of transport was achieved is unclear, but certainly the French *munitionnaire* secured sufficient draft horses and wagons for his provision train in 1690, and adequate transport arrangements appear to have been generally in place for the Irish army's Boyne campaign. Transport was supplemented by the use of flat-bottom, coastal boats, known as 'gabbards', to ship 'great quantities' of butter, meal and biscuits to Drogheda. Some of the cargo landed at Bantry in 1689 was carried to Cork on men's backs, and early in 1690 a hundred men brought sacks of flour and other munitions on their backs to supply Charlemont.[29]

29 *F-I corr.*, i, pp 218–19, 336, 356, 373; *d'Avaux*, pp 29, 54, 353, 367, 706, 710–11; *AH*, 21,

Most of the transport was lost at the Boyne, while Fumeron found on his return in early 1691 that such vehicles as remained had fallen into disrepair through neglect. It was easiest to supply Sligo by sea from Galway. The French investigated the possibility of using the rivers for transport, but found inland navigation poorly developed. The idea of supplying Athlone by water was initially rejected because it would first have been necessary to transport the goods overland to Killaloe, but eventually six boats were used to transport supplies on the Shannon. 250 soldiers were employed to carry by hand the tools needed for work on the Athlone fortifications. Other supplies were brought in back baskets. Some of these were made in Ireland, but a large number were sent from France. Although primarily intended for work on the fortifications, they probably also played a role in supplying the army. Fumeron advocated the use of dragoon horses to supplement the available carts in order to supply Athlone with the sacks of flour the garrison there so desperately needed. To transport the army's bread supply for the 1691 campaign, a cart-building programme was started. It was estimated that 200 vehicles would be needed to supply even a daily pound of bread to each soldier. The tradesmen were paid 'part money, part little necessaries of apparel, part fair words and part promises in which they were liberal enough'. Harness was made and draft horses sourced from the Williamite quarters by the rapparees. Additional carts may have been commandeered. By mid-May a train of 170 wagons and 400 small carts had been assembled to meet the needs of the artillery and the bread supply. The wagons can have been little more than large carts, because they proved incapable of transporting the large brandy casks that arrived from France. The bread was brought on carts from Limerick and probably Galway for distribution to the army in the field. Fumeron felt that the journey was too severe for the vehicles; he suggested that a better arrangement would be for the bread to be transported in panniers, each holding 25 to 30 loaves, carried by detachments from the mounted corps, to which Saint-Ruth consented.[30]

Fodder

The fodder requirements of a 25,000-strong army were immense. Between cavalry and dragoons, officers' mounts and remounts, the draft animals of the artillery train, the field hospital and the *munitionnaire*, 10,000 or more horses had to be fed daily, together with such other livestock as accompanied the

pp 97, 139; Macpherson, *Original papers*, i, p. 178; Tyrconnell letters, nos 86, 90; Story, p. 53; *Ormonde MSS*, n.s., viii, p. 382. **30** *F-I corr.*, i, pp 89, 92; ii, pp 145, 214, 270, 275, 333, 356, 361, 408–9; O'Kelly, pp 116–17; *James II*, ii, p. 451.

army for food and competed with its horses for pasture. Cavalry and dragoon personnel were responsible for feeding their horses, and this was reflected in the higher rates of subsistence allowance paid to each officer and soldier of the mounted corps, which were three to four times that of their infantry counterparts. Fumeron put the daily ration for cavalry and dragoon horses at fifteen pounds of hay, five pounds of straw, and a peck of oats per horse. Even if this amount of feed was available, it was clearly impossible for such quantities to be supplied on campaign. In the field, the army horses largely depended on green fodder – grass and other crops, which they grazed, or which was cut for their needs on foraging expeditions. The latter were a major chore for all cavalrymen, but it helped to preserve the meadows and cornfields from the trampling done by indiscriminate grazing, which the government sought to prevent because it would further reduce the forage and food supply. A thousand sickles sent from France in 1691 were intended to facilitate foraging. Each cavalryman could then carry a few days' supply in a sack on his horse. A modern calculation suggests that 12,000 animals would require two hundred hectares of green fodder daily. The horses of an army that halted either had to be fed with oats that it carried with it – and only a few days' supply was practicable – or by extending its daily foraging ever further afield, until eventually the fodder scarcity compelled the army to move on. Nevertheless, campaigning in Ireland held some advantages for cavalry. Grass was rich and abundant all the year round. *Intendant* d'Esgrigny considered that the immense amount of grass on the island could sustain an infinite number of livestock. The climate too was mild enough for most horses to remain outside throughout the winter, especially the hardy garrons, which were the most numerous and could be allowed to run wild. Better quality horses, such as those ridden by the cavalry, needed more care, but even they could still spend much of the winter outside, with perhaps an allowance of hay and oats to supplement their diet. It was standard practice in all armies to graze the horses on the nutritious spring grass to ensure they were in good condition immediately prior to the summer campaign. Local fodder shortages certainly arose, for example on the route to Derry in 1689, or in the vicinity of the besieged city. Later in the year, however, the force confronting Schomberg near Dundalk found plenty of local forage, despite burning much of it, a common practice intended to obstruct the enemy's advance.[31]

Despite French anxiety about fodder shortages due to the absence of magazines, by quartering the cavalry and dragoons by regiment or troop

---

31 Perjés, 'Army provisioning', p. 16; *d'Avaux*, pp 86–7, 363, 564; *Proclamations*, pp 119, 132–3, 141–2, 148, 169–70; *F-I corr.*, i, pp 349–50, 373, 401; ii, pp 228, 371; iii, pp 82–3; *Stevens*, p. 83.

throughout the territory they retained, the Jacobite cavalry horses seem to have survived the winter of 1689–90 quite well. In Dublin and elsewhere, stores of hay and oats were formed, from which each trooper drew twenty pounds daily. The exception was the artillery horses, many of which died of starvation though neglect. The enclosure of meadows was encouraged. Prior to the summer campaign of 1690 cattle were removed from the vicinity of Dublin and the deer herds in the parks of Phoenix and Rathfarnham were culled to preserve the early grass for the cavalry. Rowland White was empowered to purchase hay and oats to stock magazines that he was to form for the cavalry and dragoons. How much progress he made is unknown, but the loss of the fertile east of Ireland soon left only the poorer counties of the west and south-west for the support of the Jacobite cavalry and dragoons in the latter part of 1690 and in 1691. There, they faced competition for the available pasture from large numbers of livestock, including the flocks and herds of the refugee creaghts. Decrees were issued to preserve good winter pasture for the cavalry and dragoon horses, and for the conservation of meadows for the 1691 campaign. By burning a line of towns and houses from Macroom to Kilmallock, the Jacobites established an effective frontier between the armies, which allowed them to extend their quarters into Kerry, Limerick and west Cork. They also occupied a strip of no-man's-land east of the Shannon, stretching out as far as Nenagh, which they garrisoned, and taking in some of King's County (despite the failure of an attempt to dislodge the Williamite garrison at Birr) and south Westmeath, the latter area under the protection of a garrison at Ballymore. The dispersal of the cavalry and dragoon units throughout this broad area preserved the horses for the 1691 campaign. They could, however, be assembled in an emergency, such as confronting the brief, ill-judged mid-winter Williamite offensive. In France, Tyrconnell pressed for a supply of oats, and nearly 12,000 sacks of it were eventually sent for the 1691 campaign, which, with the new grass, resolved the immediate fodder requirements and allowed the mounted troops to muster at full strength under Saint-Ruth. By then also, hay was being cut in the meadows, which had been conserved during the winter. However, by mid-August only a fortnight's fodder remained. When the Williamites invested Limerick from the Clare side of the Shannon, the Jacobite cavalry and dragoons moved further west into County Clare, where they seem to have found sufficient forage to sustain them through the war's final weeks.[32]

---

32 *F-I corr.*, i, pp 89, 237–40, 349–50, 373; ii, pp 232–3, 269, 370, 396–7, 411, 514; iii, pp 184, 212–13; Story, *Continuation*, pp 42, 46–7; *Proclamations*, pp 169–70, 182; Westport papers, MS 40,900/1(10); *An account of the present state Ireland is in*.

Accommodation

There were no barracks in seventeenth-century Ireland, and the peacetime army was quartered in the inns and houses of the locality where troops and companies were stationed. Every infantry regiment and cavalry troop had a quartermaster responsible for overseeing the provision of accommodation. During the war, the same arrangement pertained, but on a greatly enlarged scale due to the army's expansion. Inns, houses, derelict properties and the extensive buildings of institutions, such as the Royal Hospital, Kilmainham, whose retired-soldier inmates, all Protestants, were ejected, and Trinity College, whose scholars suffered a like fate, although Father Michael Moore, the Catholic provost, and Teague MacCarthy, the librarian, saved the library from destruction at the hands of the soldiers. In the winter of 1689–90 many officers and probably other ranks also seem simply to have returned home. Conditions in assigned quarters were crowded and rough: in Limerick, for example, one or two companies were allotted a house, where the men had neither beds nor straw to lie on. Unsurprisingly, billeting could be a source of local tension. In May 1690 Lieutenant Colonel John MacNamara of Clare's dragoons described how a man demanding payment from him for billeting a trooper and his horse for five weeks, when denied the full sum that he sought, 'fell into a passion ... his abusive language was intolerable, and when I disarmed him, he threw stones at me'. Another problem was the supply of fuel for heat and cooking. In Dublin in 1689–90 the allowance of turf was less than a daily sod per soldier. Turf and timber were expensive to buy, with the result that at night the soldiers cut down trees and hedges for firing. In the winter of 1690–1 some attempt at orderly quartering in the west was made by appointing a quartermaster for each barony, with a supervisor to provide forage and provisions, and commissioners in each county to redress grievances. However, in Limerick the soldiers were reported to have 'thrust the citizens out of their beds with their wives and children ... all their houses [being] destroyed in an incredible manner, their wainscots and planks pulled up to make fire'.[33]

The field army, campaigning in the summer, utilized whatever houses and cabins were available in its vicinity, but it was largely accommodated in tents or huts. Tents had the advantage of being quick and easy to erect and move. Huts were a less flexible alternative, but drier and warmer, and so more comfortable and healthier for an extended stay, especially in bad weather. These structures seem to have been of very simple construction, using

---

[33] Chambers, *Michael Moore*, pp 46–7; *Finch MSS*, ii, pp 479–80; *Inchiquin MSS*, 25; *Proclamations*, 180; *Stevens*, pp 89–90, 102, 146, 192–3.

branches and timber for the walls, with a roof of straw or even sods of earth. In practice, while on campaign, soldiers often had to sleep on the bare ground without any shelter at all. In 1689 there was a shortage of tents. Clancarty's regiment slept in the open at Bantry in April. Rosen complained that only 300 tents arrived at Derry instead of the 500 promised. Nearly 900 tents were recorded at Drogheda for the start of the autumn campaign against Schomberg, but this was still insufficient and the soldiers built huts when encamped in Louth. D'Avaux requested canvas for tents from France at this time, and the government there encouraged French merchants to supply it. In 1690 at least one cargo of tent canvas was landed by a French merchant at Waterford. Lauzun brought tents for his own men and for the Irish army. The consignment included larger pavilions for senior officers. However, on arrival much of the canvas was found to have rotted due to dampness. Nevertheless, the field army seems to have had an adequate supply of tents for the campaign. Captains had a tent of their own and junior officers shared one; other ranks probably slept eight or nine to a tent, as in France. All the army's tents were lost in the flight from the Boyne. Subsequently, while encamped outside Limerick, the soldiers had to lie without shelter on the open ground. Stevens related that on the march to relieve Athlone 'we lay without any other covering but the canopy of heaven'. The French sent 3,000 tents for the 1691 campaign. This was less than the army needed, and Fumeron requested 1,500 more, but these, it seems, were never supplied. At Killaloe camp, Stevens's regiment had only four tents per company, one of which accommodated the officers. He thought that his unit needed to supplement their tents with at least ten huts not only to house the men, but also their women and children, who accompanied the regiment. Again, at Aughrim the tents of the Jacobite camp were lost in the defeat. The infantry was subsequently housed in Limerick and Galway. The cavalry and dragoons remained in the field. They seem to have been encamped in tents outside Limerick: possibly new supplies had arrived from France or were in the stores; alternatively, their tents may have been saved at Aughrim.[34]

Wartime industry

While the Jacobite army was heavily dependent on France for arms, *matériel*, and even some of its clothing requirements, efforts were also made to meet these needs by local manufacturing. The copper currency was minted in

---

[34] *F-I corr.*, i, pp 7–8, 11, 12, 94, 132, 272, 329; ii, pp 331, 369; iii, pp 75, 78, 119, 173; *Stevens*, pp 45, 83–7, 105–6, 120–1, 153–4, 187, 199–200; *d'Avaux*, pp 194, 529; *AH*, 21, p. 185; Lynn, *Giant of the grand siècle*, p. 442; Story, *Continuation*, pp 136, 217.

Dublin and Limerick, the metal being sourced partly in Ireland, but increasingly in France. For the most part, the army's clothing was produced in Dublin and other centres. Initially Lord Kilmallock placed his own order for regimental uniforms with tailors in the capital, but after his officers' clothes had been supplied, a central purchasing policy was introduced, and uniforms were then issued from the commissariat stores. This process was managed by the lords of the treasury: Tyrconnell, Lords Dover and Riverston, together with the exchequer officers, Bruno Talbot, the chancellor, and Sir Stephen Rice, the lord chief baron. Their workload was reported to have been so heavy that it left them able to manage little else. Inevitably they were accused of favouring some units over others, even within the same regiment. In September 1689 d'Avaux wrote that while much diligence was being shown to clothe the soldiers, progress was slow because of shortages of both workers and cloth. By the end of the first year's campaign the army's apparel was reported to be in a pitiable state: the soldiers' coats were ragged and shameful, half the men were without shoes and scarcely any had a shirt. The goal was set to have the army properly clothed by February 1690. D'Avaux reported good progress, and a Williamite source confirmed that all means were being used to produce friezes, clothes, shirts and shoes. It was believed that Dublin would be able to clothe the whole army for the 1690 campaign. Two Protestant hatters in the city were to furnish 4,000 hats. It was reported that detachments and even whole regiments were coming in daily to be clothed. However, the February deadline could not be met: it was May before the grand prior's regiment received new uniforms, and some companies were only supplied in June, if at all.[35]

From the start, work was hampered by shortages of labour and material. Although textile manufacture in Ireland was primitive, woollen cloth was widely produced. Before the war, Petty estimated that 30,000 workers were engaged in its manufacture, mostly on a domestic basis. The principal product was friezes, a cheap, coarse fabric intended for the lower end of the market, but suitable for army uniforms, especially those of the rank and file. In peacetime about a quarter of the output went for export, providing a ready surplus. In addition, a new facility to produce 'good and inexpensive cloth' for the army opened in December 1689. But output from local sources fell well short of the expanded army's demand. The scarcity of linen, which was needed to make shirts and tents, was particularly acute throughout the war, as it was mainly

---

35 Simms, 'Sarsfield of Kilmallock', p. 206; King, appendix, 67; *Stevens*, pp 106–7; Story, p. 65; *An account of the present state Ireland is in*; *F-I corr.*, i, pp 218, 409; *d'Avaux*, pp 464–5, 470, 533, 546, 615.

produced in the north, and so lost to the Jacobites in 1689. In September d'Avaux reported clothing was being made, but the following month he wrote that only a quarter of the soldiers had shirts, with no more than one apiece. Woollen cloth to dress 40,000 men, linen for 100,000 shirts and fine fabrics for officers' uniforms were sought from France in December. Tyrconnell also requested 40,000 'coarse hats'. French merchants, encouraged by their government, traded these goods with Ireland. D'Avaux wanted every town to engage in making shoes and stockings for the soldiers and to build up a reserve of these items. In Dublin, work on their manufacture went on without ceasing. In May the Williamites were told that 'all care was being taken to provide clothes for the army, by obliging the clothiers to make so many yards of cloth a month; the hatters, hats; the shoemakers shoes etc.'[36]

After the 1690 campaign, the army's clothing was again in a very ragged condition. During the ensuing winter the soldiers were reported to be nearly naked and without boots or shoes. Commercial prices in copper for clothing and shoes stood at twenty times their silver equivalent. In December the lord lieutenant of Mayo and his deputies were ordered to send to Galway all the clothiers and weavers to be found in their county with their looms and other equipment. Probably a similar order was sent to the officials in the other counties under Jacobite control. Earlier, all textile stocks were ordered to be deposited in government stores. The textile workers were employed by the commissioners for clothing the army to make trousers, stockings, shoes and bonnets (in place of 10,000 hats) for the 1691 campaign. 20,000 uniform coats and linen to make shirts were supplied from France. However, there was a shortage of leather for cavalry boots. Soon after his arrival in 1689, d'Avaux requested linen (probably hemp) to make tents. Eventually it was arranged with French merchants to supply material for their manufacture, and those used in the 1690 campaign may have been locally made. Tyrconnell sought 10,000 tents from France in autumn 1690, together with tent-makers to make them. No tent-makers came, but in 1691 3,000 army tents were supplied from France. Tents were also made that year in Connacht by Lord Athenry.[37]

Efforts were made to manufacture weapons. In early 1689 all the smiths in Fermanagh were said to have been so taken up with making skeans and half-pikes, the characteristic rapparee weapons, that it was difficult to get a horse shod. There was a shortage of gunsmiths; all but one of those in Dublin were Protestants, who were accused of sabotaging any muskets given to them for

36 'Talbot letter-book', p. 103; *A new history of Ireland*, iii, p. 396; Gillespie, *Transformation of the Irish economy*, p. 46; MacLysaght, *Irish life*, p. 180; *F-I corr.*, i, pp 10, 11; d'Avaux, pp 459, 501–4, 540, 558–9, 665.   37 *F-I corr.*, i, p. 272; ii, pp 214, 218, 253, 369; d'Avaux, pp 464–5, 574; *James II*, ii, p. 451; *Proclamations*, 178–9; Westport papers, MS 40,900/4 (1).

repair. D'Avaux requested gunsmiths from France, who could take on Irish boys as apprentices, but nothing came of this in 1689–90. However, five French gunsmiths with their equipment were sent to Ireland in 1691. Fumeron urged that the forges everywhere be used to make grenades, bombs and bullets of every calibre. The enterprising Mayo barrister and entrepreneur, Colonel John Browne, had invested heavily in the pre-war establishment of ironworks in Mayo, from which as early as May 1689 cannonballs were being supplied to the garrisons of Sligo, Cork, Kinsale, Athlone and Galway. Other disused ironworks were reopened in Wicklow and Clare. Browne established a small munitions industry in Dublin where, by early 1690, he was reportedly employing 150 men, mostly Protestants, to manufacture musket barrels. All the smiths in the city made firelocks, match being in short supply. In November 1689 Browne transferred a number of his Dublin gunsmiths, bayonet forgers, blacksmiths and sword cutlers to his Mayo works at Westport and Foxford. He contracted to supply the army with cannon and other ordnance, balls, grenade shells, spades, shovels, pickaxes, horseshoes, nails, carbines and muskets, both firelock and matchlock. The musket specification required the weapons to be '3½ [feet] in length, English bore, and to be provided with ten bullets in the pound; stocked, socked and well-fixed according to the pattern, with IR [*Jacobus rex*] and crown graved on the lock and stamped upon each barrel'. However, little steel was available, and although Tyrconnell sought ten tons from France, the first deliveries seem to have been made only in 1691. The shortage of steel and the desertion of most of his gunsmiths combined to prevent the fulfilment of Browne's firearms contracts and landed him in prison for a short time. Such production of muskets as he managed to achieve ceased with the Williamite occupation of Dublin and the transfer soon after of the remaining Mayo-based gunsmiths and blade-makers 'under guard' to Galway with their tools. In Mayo, Browne continued to produce horseshoes, tools and steel for the army until the summer of 1691. In return for the *matériel* he supplied during the war, Browne received some money payments and was also given leases of a number of confiscated Protestant estates in Connacht. Nevertheless, at the end of hostilities his finances, already perilous before the war, were in ruins. Browne seems to have been close to Sarsfield, who included him in the team to negotiate the Limerick surrender articles. He managed to secure the inclusion of a special clause imposing a levy on all restored Jacobite estate owners for the satisfaction of his pre-war creditors. However, his continued indebtedness ultimately led to the sale of most of his vast Mayo estate.[38]

38 *D'Avaux*, pp 79, 334, 388–9, 445, 471; *F-I corr.*, ii, p. 287; iii, p. 94; Hamilton, *Inniskillingmen*, p. vii; 'Talbot letter-book', pp 103, 107; Kinsella, *Catholic survival*, pp 45–51, 55–62, 147–209;

Other production ensured that sufficient quantities of lead for musket and pistol balls were locally procurable, obviating any need to strip it from church roofs. Tin guns, bound with cord and covered with leather, made for Galmoy's attack on Crom Castle proved useless. King James sought French workers to make gunpowder from saltpetre (potassium nitrate) in Ireland, a project that Fumeron strongly supported. A saltpetre master and two journeymen were duly hired, but even before that, in early 1690, a facility for the manufacture of saltpetre was established at Limerick under the direction of le sieur de Croix, a French artillery *commissaire*. It was hoped to source 'much saltpetre amongst the rubbish of old castles, pigeon houses, cellars and cabins where beasts were used to stay'. However, the Limerick output was disappointingly low, and its quality reportedly poor, so that the army remained dependent on France for most of its powder supply. A gunpowder factory was proposed, but it is not clear that it was built. Few swords were available and, according to d'Avaux, no sword cutlers, although Browne found some to employ. Only two such artisans are known to have worked in Dublin in the late 1680s, and possibly they did no more than fit hilts to imported blades. Scythes were expected to substitute for the want of pikes. Gun carriages, wagons and harness for the artillery and supply trains were made in Dublin in 1689–90, the necessary timber allegedly coming from plantations on estates near the city and from derelict buildings. In 1690 the French had to make their own wagons in Cork. Transport vehicles for the 1691 campaign were made in Limerick. France remained the primary source of weapons and *matériel*. Apart from supplying clothing and shoes, the contribution of Irish industry to the army was comparatively small, but it helped to fulfil critical needs as well as broadening the involvement of civilian society in the war effort.[39]

Figure 9. 'Gun-money' from the Limerick mint, 1691

An account of the present state Ireland is in; Westport papers, MSS 40, 899/2 (19), 40,899/3(12), 40,899/3(3), 40,899/4(13–16), 40,899/4 (19–20), 40,899/4(17), 40,899/5(2), 40,899/5(5), 40,899/5(7–8), 40,899/5(10–14), 40,900/1(4–6), 40,000/1(11–14), 40,900/2(3). **39** *D'Avaux*, p. 81; *F-I corr.*, i, pp 244, 257, 356; ii, pp 253, 268, 333; *An account of the present state Ireland is in*; Hamilton, *Inniskillingmen*, p. 10; Westropp, 'Irish gunsmiths and sword cutlers', pp 186–7; Tyrconnell letters, no. 58.

CHAPTER 11

Auxiliary forces

DURING THE WAR the Irish army had the support of three auxiliary paramilitary forces: a militia; Balldearg O'Donnell's army of Ulster and north-Connacht Gaels; and the partisans, known as rapparees. Although each force was distinctive, their identities, activities and personnel frequently overlapped. All three were distinct from the army, but each had an involvement with it.

The militia

A militia or part-time, local-defence force had been established on an *ad hoc* basis in Ireland in 1666 to support the army in the event of invasion or local disturbances during the Anglo-Dutch war. The force was organized under the authority of commissioners of array in each county, and in theory at least was exclusively Protestant, although Catholic landowners were obliged to contribute towards its cost. However, the duke of Ormond distrusted the militia, and it was embodied only on a few occasions before Tyrconnell disarmed it in 1685.[1]

In the summer of 1689, in anticipation of Schomberg's invasion, a new, countrywide Jacobite militia was raised by order of King James, following consultations with the Irish leaders. The force was to be under the authority of the lieutenant, deputy lieutenant and commissioners of array in each county (excluding serving army officers, which in practice meant virtually all the county lieutenants). They were authorized to summon all Catholic men between the ages of sixteen and sixty to arm themselves as best they could and be in readiness for militia service. In Mayo, the commission of array was held at Castlebar in early September, with a fine of 20s. imposed for non-appearance. The militia had a structure of officers and other ranks. The limited information available indicates that the officers were local gentlemen or people of note. In Meath, Alderman Edmund Reilly, a Navan merchant, and Dr Lawrence Taaffe, a physician, were among the captains, while Dominic

---

[1] Ferguson, 'Army in Ireland', pp 13–14; Loeber, 'Irish militia documents', pp 197–224; Bartlett & Jeffrey, *Military history of Ireland*, pp 212–13, 235.

Barnewall, proprietor of an 850-acre estate, was a lieutenant, as was a smallholder, James Ford. In Kilkenny city, the mayor, John Archdekin, was the captain and the force comprised a lieutenant, four sergeants, three corporals and 121 private men. The contributions of 507 local householders funded it.[2]

Traditional reasons were given for the force's establishment: to secure 'the safety of the realm ... the more effectual proceedings therein, and ... the better defence of this kingdom against the attempts of our enemies and rebels'. Another unspoken objective may have been to curtail the disorders of bands of Catholic activists who were already armed by placing them under some sort of control. If so, it was less than entirely successful, for d'Avaux blamed the near total ruin of the country on the depredations of the militia, as much as those of the army and the rapparees. A proclamation in September 1689, while acknowledging the militia's zeal, warned its personnel to behave with propriety. D'Avaux was initially dubious about the militia's military effectiveness, but he recognized that its primary purpose was to overawe pro-Williamite Protestants and crush any concerted action they might attempt while the army was committed against Schomberg in Louth. He advised: 'if we learned that the Protestants had risen in some place of the kingdom, we should generally suppress the rest'. He thought that the militia also had a role in preventing the on-going trickle of Protestant defections to the Williamite forces in Enniskillen and Derry. To counter this, he proposed patrolling the routes to the north with mounted 'archers' (police), but nothing came of this suggestion. He conceded that more than the militia's 'sticks and forks' would be needed to suppress the organized strength of the centres of Williamite resistance in the north.[3]

There is very little information on the militia's actual military activity. However, the Dublin militia rendered good service in late September 1689 in helping to successfully oppose the incursion and attempted landing at the mouth of the Liffey by a Williamite naval squadron, where d'Avaux admitted they had 'done their duty very well', and had held 'the Protestants more submissive than we could ever have believed'. In late 1689 militia were reported to be helping to guard the south-eastern coastline, but to be so lacking in arms that they would have to fight English invaders with their fists. However, the forced recruitment of Munster militiamen by Mountcashel to fill up the ranks of his regiment prior to its departure for France in 1690 spread such alarm throughout the force that the men would no longer

---

2 *Proclamations*, pp 113, 115; Westport papers, NLI MS 40,899/4 (2–3); 'Survey of Catholic estates', pp 74, 77–8, 81; Prim, 'Kilkenny militia', p. 248. **3** *D'Avaux*, pp 345–6, 372, 377, 545; *Proclamations*, pp 122–3.

assemble because of their fear of being likewise conscripted and separated from their wives and children. Lauzun considered that this loss of the militia, when it was needed in the prelude to the Boyne, was greatly prejudicial to the kingdom. The Dublin militia remained intact. D'Esgrigny put its strength at 8,000 and considered that more use could have been made of it. The militia vacated Dublin after the Boyne defeat, and subsequently some of its personnel appear to have joined the rapparees to attack Williamite garrisons in King's County. The author of the *Jacobite narrative* also took the view that the militia was under-used. He argued that 10,000 militiamen from the adjoining counties could have been employed in 1690 to bolster a Jacobite attempt to block William's egress from Ulster at strategic passes. He considered that 15,000 militiamen out of the adjacent counties of Meath, Dublin and Kildare, armed with swords, half-pikes, firearms and scythes, with skilful management, might have turned the balance at the Boyne.[4]

In August 1690 Lord Athenry, the lord lieutenant, and the commissioners of array in County Mayo were ordered to raise 'a convenient number of the ablest men in that country' to form militia companies and troops. Probably similar orders were sent at that time to the lords lieutenant of the other counties remaining under Jacobite control. After this, there is little further mention of the militia. It is very likely that many of its former personnel in Leinster and Munster became rapparees or joined the army. Indeed, as late as March 1691 the Williamites heard that Sarsfield picked out the most serviceable of the militia in north Cork to serve in the army. After Aughrim, Tyrconnell's summons to all men in the Irish quarters between the age of sixteen and sixty to enlist in the army had echoes of the original militia proclamation of 1689. Meanwhile, as the Jacobite militia declined as a force, a Williamite Protestant militia was re-formed to counteract the activities of the Irish rapparees.[5]

Balldearg O'Donnell's army

Hugh Balldearg O'Donnell, a descendant of the senior line of the famous Tyrconnell family of north-west Ulster, was a veteran soldier in the Spanish army. He had commanded one of its remaining Irish regiments until it was merged with another unit. This left him with the substantive appointment of mere cavalry captain, although he also held the rank of *maestro-de-campo* (brigadier). Balldearg was probably born in Ireland, but through long residence

---

4 *D'Avaux*, pp 476, 499–500, 622; *JN*, pp 95, 98; *F-I corr.*, i, pp 423, 453; iii, pp 127–8.
5 *Proclamations*, pp 173–4; *JN*, p. 152; Story, *Continuation*, p. 61.

abroad was noted to have acquired 'Spanish inclinations and ways'. When the war started, his request for leave to travel to Ireland was refused by the Spanish government, which was part of the alliance against France. This led him to abscond to Portugal, from which he made his way to Cork. About that time, he penned a 'manifesto' to the king of Spain, justifying his defection to Ireland:

> where legal action is being taken by force of arms, above all for the defence of religion, the just right of King James, the glory, liberty and interests of that loyal Catholic nation ... asking not only the restoration of this prince, but also the recovery from the well-known calamities which they have suffered for these causes.

He added to this 'the almost certain hope of restoring myself (if not completely) in some respectable part of my estates'. In Ireland, he claimed he had come with no other purpose but to offer his life for King James's service. Thus, his motives for returning to Ireland can be said to have been a mixture of patriotism, self-interest and opportunism.[6]

Arriving in July 1690, just after the Boyne defeat, he travelled to Kinsale where he had an interview with King James, who recommended him to Tyrconnell. He met the viceroy at Limerick, where he was asked to raise 3–4,000 men and even more, if possible, to defend the northern Shannon crossings against Williamite incursions. Balldearg championed the Gaelic Irish, and was instantly popular with them, especially those who had fled from Ulster. His sobriquet Balldearg stemmed from a red birthmark that an O'Donnell prophecy identified as the sign of the true earl of Tyrconnell, who would come from abroad to save Ireland. His followers were reported to include Gaelic gentry, friars and even some bishops, attracted, it was claimed, by his 'design of putting the kingdom into the hands of the ancient Irish, and upon an equal foot with England'. In less than a month he raised a force of 10,000 men, which was based in north Connacht. This was still its strength in a muster of June 1691. Balldearg, as head of the senior branch of the O'Donnells, claimed the Tyrconnell title and was known by it in Spain. (In fact, the title stemmed from a line of the family junior to his, and he had no right to it.) Unfortunately, his claim brought him into conflict with the duke of Tyrconnell, who had taken the title in 1685 on the assumption that it was vacant. The duke, as a Palesman, was felt to have little affinity with the Gaelic

---

6 *ODNB*, vol. 41, pp 514–15; *DIB*, vol. 7, pp 382–4; Hazard, 'Manifesto of Hugh O'Donnell', pp 133–5; 'O'Donnells in exile', p. 54; *F-I corr.*, ii, p. 545; Story, p. 124.

Irish, and to have no interest in the restoration of either their lost properties or influence. Balldearg indeed alleged that Tyrconnell sought to reduce them to servitude, and he accused the duke of circulating the view that the objectives of the Gaels were to destroy the Old English and overthrow the English government. Balldearg complained bitterly of Tyrconnell's personal hostility towards him, which even included, it was alleged, the accusation that he was a Habsburg spy. Lord Riverston later absolved him of this charge and conceded that Balldearg's treatment had been shabby. He felt that even before Balldearg's arrival, had Tyrconnell entrusted the Ulster Irish with arms and promised to restore their lands, Derry would have fallen. The author of 'The groans of Ireland', written in the 1690s, alleged that the judiciary dissuaded Tyrconnell from arming the Gaelic Irish, particularly those from Ulster. Balldearg claimed that he could have easily raised 30,000 men, if sufficient supplies of arms and ammunition were forthcoming.[7]

Balldearg was given the title of commander-in-chief of his force, and promised blank commissions for its officers, but he received no other support in 1690 and very little thereafter. Following Tyrconnell's departure, Sarsfield's intervention was necessary to extract the promised commissions from Berwick, the Jacobite army's *ad interim* commander, and then for only nine regiments, although there were as many as six more in Balldearg's force, including, it was claimed, two of dragoons. None of Balldearg's regiments was included on the army establishment until 1691, and there was always a sense that 'he was a sort of independent commander' of a force loyal to him as its chieftain, rather than to the Jacobite high command. Fumeron, perhaps influenced by Tyrconnell, considered Balldearg a doubtful ally. General Saint-Ruth, when he arrived to command the army in 1691, was more sympathetic, or perhaps had higher hopes for the military potential of Balldearg's force. By then, it numbered fourteen single-battalion infantry regiments, each of thirteen companies, supported by Lord Merrion's six-troop cavalry regiment. The latter was a new unit on the army list, possibly formed from Balldearg's mounted followers, but described as being '*en mauvais estat*'. There were also four independent infantry companies and an independent cavalry troop. It was reported that there was not a soldier in the force without a woman and children to accompany him. Balldearg praised the fighting character of the Ulster Gaels, and he made much of the Ulster character of his force. To a substantial degree it was recruited from the creaghts. These were large groups of refugees, mostly from

---

7 *JN*, pp 151, 270; 'O'Donnells in exile', p. 54; O'Kelly, pp 126, 430–1; *F-I corr.*, ii, pp 212, 338; *James II*, ii, p. 461; *Poema*, pp 242, 402–4, 440; 'The groans of Ireland', p. 131.

the north, who fled from the Williamites with their families and livestock. The intrusion of the Ulster Gaels, with their carts, livestock and temporary dwellings, was generally unwelcome to the inhabitants of the other provinces. Some at least were indistinguishable from rapparees.[8]

Balldearg and his brother, Connell, each commanded a regiment, as did Daniel O'Donnell of Castlelavan, County Donegal, who was probably their kinsman. Other colonels with Ulster surnames were Roger O'Cahan, Brian O'Neill of Tyrone, Brian Boy O'Neill and (Daniel?) O'Doherty. However, five of the colonels had north-Connacht surnames: Tiernan O'Rourke, Conor O'Rourke, Thomas Burke, O'Connor Sligo and Brian MacDermott. Conor O'Connor appears to have been from King's County. Charles Geoghegan was from King's County or Westmeath. He had raised a regiment for the army, but it was one of those never taken onto the establishment and formally disbanded on account of being composed of 'mere Irish and good for little'. Subsequently Geoghegan was alleged to have gathered together 'a huge number of loose, idle persons, commonly called rapparees, in no way concerned in the army, and had infested and laid waste as much as in him lay the country, so that he was pursued even by the Irish army and fled from them'. It seems likely that Geoghegan's disbanded regiment, his rapparees and his Balldearg O'Donnell unit largely comprised the same personnel. The junior officers in Balldearg's regiments would have been nominated by their colonels and in turn would have recruited in their own localities, suggesting that Balldearg's soldiers may have been composed as much of Connacht and west-Leinster Gaels as Ulstermen, many of the latter having been recruited into the regular army after the Boyne. In the winter Balldearg's army dispersed to their creaghts, or clusters of temporary family dwellings, where they subsisted on what they extorted locally, and on their cattle and sheep. The official view of Balldearg and his followers was expressed in King James's memoirs:

> Having got together eight regiments newly raised, with a crowd of loose men over and above. [Balldearg's followers] lived in a manner at discretion; so that these troops were in effect a rabble that destroyed the country, ruined the inhabitants and prevented the regular forces from drawing the subsistence they might otherwise have had from the people.

In September 1690 the Jacobite authorities ordered a fifth of the creaghts' cattle herds to be seized for slaughter and salting to feed the main army.

---

8 *James II*, ii, pp 434, 461; 'O'Donnells in exile', pp 54–5, 110; *F-I corr.*, ii, pp 212, 332, 337–8; *JN*, p. 270; Story, *Continuation*, pp 270–1.

Violent confrontations sometimes occurred, when army foraging parties targeted the creaghts' livestock.[9]

TABLE 8 *Balldearg O'Donnell's forces, 1691*

Infantry battalions

Balldearg O'Donnell	Tiernan O'Rourke	Daniel O'Donnell
Daniel O'Donnell	Conor O'Rourke	Connell O'Donnell
O'Doherty	Roger O'Cahan	Brian O'Neill
Thomas Burke	Brian Boy O'Neill	O'Connor Sligo
Brian MacDermott	Conor O'Connor	Charles Geoghegan

Independent companies

Gerard Moore   Patrick Burke   Henry O'Neill   Michael Cormack

Cavalry

Lord Merrion
Conor O'Connor (1 troop)

Balldearg sought arms and clothing for his force, but Tyrconnell refused him all such supplies. It was an added slight that Tyrconnell only brought back from James a brigadier general's commission for Balldearg, a rank no higher than he had already achieved in Spain. Tyrconnell was accused of fomenting opposition to Balldearg among the other Ulster Gaelic leaders, using as a counterweight Brigadier Gordon O'Neill, possessor of another iconic Ulster surname. As Tyrconnell and Fumeron began to prepare for the summer campaign in 1691, they planned to break most of Balldearg's regiments and use the personnel to fill up the ranks of the regular army and to supply the recruits that Louvois was demanding for the Irish regiments in France. Brian O'Neill's regiment was selected for the latter role, but the policy was shelved after the shipping arrangements collapsed. In any case, by August half of Balldearg's infantry regiments, namely O'Cahan's, O'Connor's, O'Doherty's, MacDermott's, the two O'Neills' and probably Burke's, while retaining their unit identities, were serving in the garrisons of Limerick and Galway. Indeed five, O'Donnell's, O'Cahan's, O'Doherty's, Conor O'Rourke's and Brian O'Neill's, had been included on army lists in early 1691. The first three, together with one of the O'Donnell regiments, were even listed by the Williamites as part of the Jacobite army before the battle of Aughrim, but this was probably true only in the general sense that they were part of the overall

---

9 *F-I corr.*, ii, p. 337–8; Simms, *Confiscation*, p. 53; *James II*, ii, p. 434; *Proclamations*, p. 176; 'O'Donnells in exile', pp 55–6, 110; Story, p. 98; Story, *Continuation*, pp 270–1.

Jacobite forces rather than present on the fatal day. Meanwhile, O'Rourke's had reverted to Balldearg's command, if indeed it had ever left it, but with this exception all seven garrison units may be regarded as being incorporated into the Jacobite army from the summer of 1691. It is possible that Balldearg's acquiescence to their transfer was secured by Saint-Ruth's release of a supply of uniforms and weapons for his own regiment, the abandonment of any immediate plan to disband the others and the inclusion of his regiments in the bread ration. In June Fumeron doubted that Balldearg's force numbered more than 6,000 men, and he allowed them only 5,684 daily bread rations. Even after their inclusion in regular Jacobite garrisons, the former Balldearg regiments remained pathetically short of weapons. In Galway, Brian Mac Art O'Neill's and O'Doherty's had nineteen firearms between them for nearly a thousand officers and men, while in Limerick less than half the men were armed, with only ninety-three firearms between the 640 men of O'Cahan's and MacDermott's, although Brian O'Neill's, O'Connor's and Burke's were somewhat better equipped.[10]

Balldearg's shortage of arms and *matériel*, coupled with the mutual distrust between him and the Jacobite high command, greatly reduced the military effectiveness of his substantial forces. In 1690 he had secured the north-Shannon crossings against potential Williamite attack. In 1691 his men were again deployed in this role, with headquarters at Jamestown, to guard against incursions from Ulster. But his force remained desperately short of powder, ball and match. He also sponsored a certain amount of rapparee activity. After the fall of Athlone in June, Balldearg offered to join the main army, or to reinforce Galway. Instead, he was ordered to retire further west with his forces to shelter the creaghts and their livestock. He was commanded to burn houses and castles as he thought necessary to deny them to the enemy. After the Irish defeat at Aughrim, the creaghts 'in the greatest consternation imaginable' fled into the remotest parts of Connacht with their herds and flocks. Balldearg by then retained only a thousand men under his command. He burned and pillaged Tuam before responding to a request from d'Usson to reinforce Galway. The Williamite army prevented any eastern approach to the city, but Balldearg controlled Cong, which allowed him to advance west of the Corrib. A Williamite force crossed the river to block his progress, and on learning that the garrison had capitulated, he withdrew to north Galway and Mayo, 'burning and destroying all the country as he marched', a Williamite pamphlet alleged. The potential threat posed by his force obliged the Williamites to

---

10 'O'Donnells in exile', p. 55; *F-I corr.*, ii, pp 212, 221, 235, 249, 332, 363, 391, 406–7; *JN*, p. 270; O'Kelly, p. 126; *Rawdon*, p. 360.

leave an infantry regiment at Athlone as their army marched towards Limerick. Lord Merrion's cavalry regiment by this time had moved to Kerry, where it was reported to be assisting rapparee activity.[11]

As the Jacobite cause disintegrated, Balldearg re-evaluated his position. His adjutant general and secretary was John Richards, a fellow officer from the Spanish army, who had accompanied him to Ireland. Richards was the Catholic son of a Cromwellian lieutenant colonel with an estate in County Wexford. His brothers were both serving with the Williamite artillery. Now, on the pretext of visiting them, he became Balldearg's go-between with Ginkel, the Williamite commander. The Williamites were concerned that Balldearg's force retained a military potential, and also at the extent of the damage being done in Connacht by his undisciplined followers. Ginkel therefore responded positively to Balldearg's overture by offering him a truce and reasonable terms to change sides. Richards returned with an assurance from Balldearg of his desire to enter William's service, but also with a number of demands. Balldearg wanted his remaining forces to be taken into Williamite pay and deployed to Flanders under his command, together with a payment of £2,000 to himself and confirmation of his claim to the earldom of Tyrconnell. Meanwhile, demonstrating that he was still a force to be reckoned with, he relieved Sligo, which was closely blockaded by a Williamite force and had been near to surrender. Premature publication of his impending defection in *Dublin Intelligence* and the *London Gazette*, and circulation of this news in the Sligo locality, forced Balldearg to call a meeting of his senior officers at which he told them their options were a fight to the death or negotiate terms. Opinions were divided: some wanted to unite with the Irish army, others to return to their homes and live there without disturbance, and still others to follow Balldearg wherever he led them. Negotiations attempting to satisfy all three views were then concluded between Balldearg and an envoy sent by Ginkel. It was agreed that a general pardon and amnesty would be granted to Balldearg's men, that his followers would be free to return to their homes or go to some other part of Ireland as they chose, to join the Irish army, or to enlist in a proposed two-regiment, 3,000-strong brigade (Balldearg's full strength at the time, according to Ginkel) that was to serve under Balldearg's command in Flanders. These demands required William's approval, and Ginkel arranged a pass for Richards to travel to the king in Flanders.[12]

---

11 'O'Donnells in exile', pp 54–5; Story, *Continuation*, pp 67, 151–2, 179, 194; O'Kelly, p. 136; *A particular relation of the surrender of Galloway*. 12 *LG*, no. 2688, 13–19 August 1691; *DI*, no. 46, 5 August 1691; Story, *Continuation*, pp 182–3; Hebbert, 'Richards brothers', pp 203–4; Clarke corr., nos 944, 970; *CSPD 1690–1*, p. 475.

Unsurprisingly, Balldearg's defection to the enemy was strongly opposed by elements within his command. It was reported that 'his interest with his brigade is very small'. Even his own 'well-armed' regiment under its lieutenant colonel, Hanlon, defected for a time, although it soon returned to his command. At one stage his regiment was threatened with disarmament by the rest. He managed to stave off a general mutiny by putting the terms agreed with Ginkel into immediate effect, including allowing those still loyal to the Jacobite cause to depart for Limerick, with a provision of cows for their maintenance. He requested a Williamite pass and bread for their journey. Charles Geoghegan's regiment was among those to take this option. It was quartered in Ennis at the end of the war, although never formally taken onto the Jacobite establishment. At the end of August, a large party of deserters from Balldearg's remaining force, estimated at 2,000, was reported near Boyle, and Balldearg's creaghts were said to stay with him only to protect their cattle. Despite the misgivings of even the men that remained, quelled only by a distribution of Williamite money, Balldearg now joined up in Mayo with Sir Albert Conyngham, the local Williamite commander, to cooperate in capturing Sligo. On a foggy morning in early September, they were surprised at Collooney by Colonel Edward Scott, Sligo's deputy governor, with 700 men. Conyngham was killed, and Balldearg narrowly escaped capture. Had he fallen into Jacobite hands, the Williamites believed, probably rightly, that he would have been hanged. Balldearg subsequently went on to capture Loughglynn, Ballymote and another strong castle. Charles O'Kelly, a fellow Gael, was generally sympathetic to Balldearg and believed he had not been well treated. However, in an encounter at this time, he failed to dissuade Balldearg from defecting and sadly concluded that by 'revolting from his natural prince, he unhappily joined with the sworn enemies of his country'. Stevens called him a traitor. A Williamite verdict was that it seemed 'incredible how the vulgar Irish flocked to him at his first coming, so that he had got in a small time seven or eight thousand rapparees and suchlike people together ... but after a while the business cooled and they were weary of one another'. Balldearg's change of allegiance was prompted by disillusionment and despair in Ireland, and presumably because he saw his own best option for the future as lying with the grand alliance against France, leading perhaps to a new career in the Williamite army or to his rehabilitation in Spain. Before defecting, he had at least done the best he could to preserve his followers and fulfil their demands. Williamite sources commended his 'zeal and forwardness' once he was enlisted in their service.[13]

13 'O'Donnells in exile', p. 107; Story, p. 124; Story, *Continuation*, p. 234; O'Kelly, pp 142–3; *Stevens*, p. 132; Clarke corr., nos 1081, 1089, 1097, 1105, 1111, 1148; Simms, 'Donegal', pp 145–6.

At the end of the war, only the regiments of Balldearg and Con O'Rourke remained embodied. O'Rourke's regiment did some service in quelling rapparee activity in Leitrim, where it was quartered, and in Roscommon. Balldearg's regiment was quartered in Mayo and Sligo. The commanders of the other remaining units, including Connell O'Donnel, surrendered their commissions and encouraged their men to enlist in the Williamite army. Balldearg's own regiment swelled to 1,300 men, and there was a suggestion to form it into two battalions, but subsequently the establishment of the whole force was reduced to 1,400 men in two regiments, one commanded by Balldearg and the other by Colonel Edward Wilson, an English Jacobite who had commanded a regiment in the Irish army in the final phase of the war. The regiments were assigned quarters, partly to prevent them becoming 'highwaymen and rapparees'. It was recommended that they be issued with tents, and furnished with drums and arms 'that they may be trained and exercised in their quarters'. Balldearg himself travelled to London in December, where he briefly enjoyed celebrity status and attended at court. He was given £1,500 and awarded an annual pension of £500 on the Irish establishment, which continued to be paid up to his death. However, there was no confirmation of his peerage and no appointment to the command in Flanders that he had expected.[14]

Meanwhile, his forces were formally disbanded in Donegal in February 1692, only to be largely reconstituted as a new force to be sent to the Continent for service under William's Catholic ally, the emperor, in eastern Europe. Eventually the unit numbered 2,200 men. Command was given to the penniless earl of Iveagh, with Balldearg as his reluctant deputy. In the end neither Balldearg nor Wilson accompanied the force. Con O'Rourke was lieutenant colonel of the unit, with his brother Michael as major. It travelled through Hamburg. The O'Rourkes' opposition to Iveagh defrauding the soldiers led to their arrest and confinement in Hungary. At Balldearg's request, George Stepney, the English envoy to Vienna, sought their release, probably successfully, after Iveagh's death in 1692. Stepney reported:

> Our poor Irish regiment has fallen to pieces though it was one of the best in the whole army ... They were put into garrison at Peterwardein (the most unwholesome place in all Hungary), where the officers by debauchery and the private soldiers by mere want have fallen into the distemper of the country and in three months' time are melted like snow ... of 1700 men, scarce 200 are upon their legs.

14 *JN*, pp 189–90; Clarke corr., nos 1233–4; *F-I corr.*, ii, p. 545; 'O'Donnells in exile', pp 107–8.

After Iveagh's own death, the regiment went out of existence, and the survivors were drafted into other corps of the imperial army. Balldearg himself, after an extended illness, travelled from England to Spanish Flanders. He was in poor financial circumstances, and at one point offered William III his services as a spy. However, he managed to mend his relations with Madrid before assembling a regiment of 400 Irish deserters from the French army in the north of Italy. It saw service, but little action, in Catalonia. Balldearg was present, or nearby, at the capture of Barcelona in 1697. Described as a general, he was appointed to a command in the army of Flanders, where he arrived in 1700, but died apparently in Spain in 1703 or 1704.[15]

Of the other colonels in his force, only Brian O'Neill, Brian MacDermott and Charles Geoghegan are known to have remained in Ireland. Their regiments were broken in January 1692, and O'Neill and MacDermott were pardoned under the terms of the Limerick articles. Geoghegan was refused a pardon on the thin legal grounds that his regiment was not on the Jacobite establishment, with the consequence that his 2,816-acre Westmeath estate remained confiscated. Nothing so far is known of the ultimate fate of Daniel O'Connor Sligo. It is possible that Daniel O'Doherty is identifiable with the officer of that name, who was listed in 1716 as a *reformé* (supernumerary) captain in the Spanish Hibernia regiment. All the other colonels went abroad, and most were duly outlawed for treason beyond the seas, which generally implied military service in France. Daniel O'Donnell brought the *Cathach*, or battlebook of the O'Donnells, with him to France, where he rose to be the rank of brevet brigadier general. Tiernan O'Rourke was said to have acquired distinction in the French army before being killed at the battle of Luzarra in 1702. Brian Boy Mac Art O'Neill alone was not outlawed, but the fact that more than 500 men from his regiment were listed as opting to go to France suggests that he too was in this category. John Richards was paid £200 for the 'good service' he had rendered in the negotiations between Ginkel and Balldearg, and from 1692 he received an annual pension of the same amount, which endured until the accession of Queen Anne. In the 1690s he served as an artillerist with his brother Jacob in the forces of Venice and Poland, before transferring to Portugal in 1703. During the war of the Spanish succession, he became a major general, achieving considerable distinction before he was killed in 1709 by an exploding mine during his stubborn defence of Alicante.[16]

15 Story, *Continuation*, p. 301; Melvin, 'Colonel Con O'Rourke', pp 67–70; *Finch MSS*, iv, p. 246; Melvin, 'Balldearg O'Donnell abroad', pp 45, 127–30; O'Neill, 'Conflicting loyalties', p. 118; O'Callaghan, *Irish brigades*, pp 180–3; *Coll. Hib.*, no. 4, p. 84.   **16** Story, *Continuation*, p. 295; *AH*, 22, pp 28, 73, 78, 79, 82, 84, 87, 96, 128; *DIB*, vol. 7, p. 384; *ODNB*, vol. 41, p. 515; O'Callaghan, *Irish brigades*, pp 113–15; Simms, *Confiscation*, p. 53; 'Irish in Spanish service' VI, p. 464; Hebbert, 'Richards brothers', pp 202–8; Ó Cochláinn, 'The Cathach', p. 167.

The rapparees

A significant strand of the lawlessness endemic in Irish society from medieval times was the small, roving, freelance bands of soldiers and robbers that existed by a mixture of theft, murder, intimidation and local support. Before the mid-seventeenth century, they were known as kerne (*ceithearn*/warband) or woodkerne, the latter from their propensity to take refuge in woods or other fastnesses. Lord Mountjoy in 1601 had written of the need to rid the kingdom of 'idle swordsmen'. Others noted the antipathy of the warrior class to any form of manual work. In the wars of the mid-century and during the restoration period these bands came to be called tories (*toraidhe*/fugitives), not essentially different in character from their predecessors, but with a more positive military function and membership, directed at waging fairly successful partisan war against the commonwealth forces. Under the restoration, they reverted to their more traditional criminal activities, but often mixed with a political role, because the groups were frequently led by aggrieved, dispossessed Catholic landowners, or their penniless younger sons, especially in Ulster. Archbishop Oliver Plunkett, who strongly opposed toryism, wrote in 1671 of certain gentlemen of leading Gaelic families that lost their properties, who took to assassination and robbery with their followers, and sheltered in Catholic houses at night. Thomas Monck in 1682 recorded 'robbers, tories and woodkernes' sheltering in woods, mountains, bogs and fastnesses, who were usually the offspring of gentlemen that had misspent or forfeited their estates. He stated that encouraged by their priests and followers they still hoped to recover their lands, and despised trade as being too mean and base an activity for gentlemen. Much of the restoration army's role was the suppression and elimination of such tory bands. Tory activity may have somewhat subsided by the time of King James's accession, but it had certainly not disappeared. The Brennans, noteworthy tories, were active in north Kilkenny at this time. In October 1686 Clarendon's secretary wrote of efforts 'to secure the country from tories and robbers, who at this season of the year when the days are short and the nights long, do always infest the country'. The army was used to suppress them in Cork, Waterford and Tipperary. The partisan activity that developed during the war of 1689–91 was in some respects a continuation of the tory tradition. But it was on a larger scale, more overtly political, and more military in its focus and direction. It bore resemblances to the irregular warfare of the Danish *Snapphanar* who had troubled the Swedes in the Northern and Scanian wars of the seventeenth century, the Catalan *Migueletes* who harassed the French army during the Spanish succession war, and the peasant *Camisard* bands of the Cévennes which had their origin in Louis XIV's persecution of the Huguenots. The wartime partisan bands in Ireland came to be called rapparees (*rapaire*/half-pike), although the term tory was still also used. While a degree of interconnection existed between the different auxiliary-army formations and there was some overlap of personnel, nonetheless the tory or rapparee bands constituted a distinctive grouping that in military terms proved much the most effective of the three Jacobite auxiliary forces. The Williamites suffered considerably from their partisan activity and found it very difficult to contain.[17]

Initially observers characterized the rapparees as countrymen who were not in the army, but who armed themselves, allegedly at the behest of their priests, with daggers and half-pikes, and sometimes scythes and muskets, to suppress rebellious Protestants, a role they used to justify robbery and plunder. In this respect there was probably not much to distinguish them from the Jacobite militia or indeed the new army levies of 1689. By early 1689 the country about Birr was 'infested by robbers and rapparees, and particularly by one Fannin, with a strong party of desperadoes, who kept the neighbourhood in perpetual alarm'. Some of the early rapparees were ex-soldiers who had been disbanded in the army reform, but many in 1689 were displaced Ulster Catholics, who were regarded as creaghts because of their transient lifestyle. It was reported that the Catholics in the north 'by the persuasion of their priests have all left their farms and betaken themselves to mountains and fastnesses, where they at present live by their cattle, where they rob, steal and exercise themselves in arms'. Andrew Hamilton, a pro-Williamite clergyman, wrote that the Fermanagh hills were daily covered with the Irish of all sorts, sexes and ages, armed with skeans and half-pikes, who threatened a new massacre of Protestants similar to that of 1641. However, the pro-Jacobite clergyman, Charles Leslie, who was a more sympathetic observer, reported that Catholics in Ulster left their homes to group together for mutual protection against the pro-Williamite Protestant associates, of whom they were 'in mortal fear'. He added that the Protestants robbed them, taxed them, forced them to work on defences and abused them with such expressions as 'bloody dogs, inhumane murderers, cut-throats and remember forty-one'. A French report called them an endless number of peasants and other Catholics under a chief, who abandoned their homes and armed themselves with anything to hand.[18]

17 Prendergast, *Restoration to revolution*, passim; Connolly, *Religion, law and power*, pp 203–7; 'Rycaut letters', p. 171; Ó Ciardha, 'Toryism', passim; Ó Ciardha, 'Irish outlaw', pp 51–69; Henry, *Military community*, pp 23–6; *Plunkett letters*, p. 160; 'Account of Co. Kildare in 1682'; *Clarendon*, ii, p. 73. **18** Story, p. 16; Hamilton, *Inniskillingmen*, p. vii; Stevens, pp 61–2; Leslie, pp 84–5; *Rosse papers*, p. 228; *The present dangerous position of Protestants under Tyrconnell* quoted in Ó Ciardha, *Ireland and the Jacobite cause*, p. 70; *F-I corr.*, ii, p. 235; Leslie, pp 84–5; *d'Avaux*, p. 545.

They formed a substantial part of Richard Hamilton's force against the Williamites of east-Ulster in 1689, although he had difficulty subsequently in keeping them under control. In the anxiety surrounding Schomberg's landing in Ulster, the government encouraged the formation of rapparee groups by ordering all Catholics between the ages of sixteen and sixty to be ready and 'as well armed as they can' to oppose the invasion. Many had posted themselves near the border between Ulster and Leinster, and a further proclamation warned them against committing any disorder or using violence against faithful subjects, but urged them instead to make incursions into the enemy quarters to seize horses, cattle, corn and other goods belonging to rebels, which they could then keep as their own. Later Rosen employed them to ruin the Ulster countryside after the siege of Derry was lifted, and they seem to have harassed the Williamite quarters in the north during the winter of 1689–90, although Schomberg's despatches are strangely silent on the topic.[19]

A turning point in the south came soon after the Boyne with William's declaration of Finglas in which he promised protection and security to 'poor labourers, common soldiers, country farmers, ploughmen and cottiers' who submitted to his authority, and forbade any violence, rapine or molestation to those who did so. This was attractive to many inhabitants of Leinster and east Munster concerned with self-preservation, and apparently also to soldiers from those localities. They duly retired to their homes expecting William's protection. William himself took care that his army was well conducted on its march to Limerick. However, the force he sent to Athlone behaved badly. Once beyond Maynooth, the soldiers marching across central Leinster plundered the Irish relentlessly. The Ulster regiments in particular were perceived as being 'very dexterous at that sport', doubtless vengeful in the light of their own experience in 1689. Douglas, the force commander, issued repeated orders against plundering and straggling, but was little inclined to impose sanctions on offenders. Leslie accused the Williamite army of having 'debauched generally all that they have left alive ... and left the marks of their wickedness as deeply imprinted on that country as of their unbridled violence, plunder, burning and destruction of Protestants, and friends as well as enemies'. This opinion was supported by the chaplain, Story, who wrote that the Williamite army looked upon Ireland 'as an enemy country, which is the reason that great spoils are made and outrages committed; nay which is worst of all no distinction is made between papist or Protestant'. Irish people who submitted to William found his protections of little use to preserve their goods from seizure or their persons from ill treatment, which occurred

---

19 *Proclamations*, pp 115, 122–3; Story, p. 4; *F-I corr.*, iii, p. 104; *d'Avaux*, p. 586.

indiscriminately. The soldiers allegedly murdered civilians in Westmeath and King's County. A similar disregard for protections was shown by the Williamite garrison at Birr in the autumn. This breach of faith drove many to turn rapparee. Their numbers continued to grow throughout the war. Stragglers from Douglas's force were already being attacked and killed on their march to rejoin William near Limerick.[20]

At Mullingar, Colonel Wolseley wrote of his unease at the disorderly conduct of his soldiers – Ulstermen from Enniskillen – 'which has been so great on our march, to all without distinction, that it is a shame to speak of it', adding that if he had had bread or money to give his soldiers, he would have 'hanged them to the last man' to halt their misconduct. A Williamite pamphlet boasted that the 'very terror of his name' was sufficient to drive the rapparees out of localities Wolseley entered. A detailed case of ill-treatment from 1691 involved Edward Geoghegan, a Catholic landowner in Westmeath who had secured a protection. He was attacked at night by Williamite soldiers, who shot and wounded him at his house near Mullingar. They killed several of his servants, stripped him and his family of their clothes, and stole all his goods and cattle. After this experience and fearing for his life, he was carried in a litter to the security of the Jacobite quarters in Connacht. Not surprisingly, despite Ginkel's concern to honour protections, such incidents undermined their credibility, and those who had taken them to no avail tended to become rapparees. As Story put it, 'many of the vulgar Irish have been abused in what they had, who thinking our soldiers in the fault, they cut their throats wherever they can get the upper hand'.[21]

In one respect the rapparees were a largely peasant reaction to the abuses of the Williamite soldiers, a form of social banditry that occurred elsewhere in seventeenth-century Europe. But they can also be viewed as an expression of popular Jacobitism, and their wartime activities had the character of a people's resistance to English Protestant domination. It is likely that many rapparees had previously served in the Jacobite militia. The Irish, it was observed, 'exalted' and were made 'very insolent' by the successful Jacobite defence of Limerick and Athlone. After this, according to the Danish commander, Würtemberg, 'the whole country' – more than 100,000 in his estimate – was up in arms. Others confirmed that the rapparees were very numerous and spread throughout the entire Williamite quarters to 'infest' the country. In 1690–1 rapparee activity was reported in at least twenty counties. Most references were to Cork and Waterford in the south, and to the midland

20 *Proclamations*, pp 195–6; *JN*, p. 104; Story, pp 99–100, 103–4, 138, 161; Story, *Continuation*, p. 32; Leslie, p. 37; Clarke corr., nos 644, 1051; *CSPD 1690–1*, p. 385.   **21** *JN*, p. 259; *A true and faithful account*; Reduction of Ireland, vii, no. 17; Story, pp 104, 160.

frontier counties of Westmeath, Tipperary and King's County, but there were incidents almost everywhere. One of the most notorious was the murder in 1691 of a party of soldiers taking refuge in Mulhuddart Church close to Dublin, in which a Catholic priest was alleged to have played a leading role. In Mayo, George Browne, the county sheriff, alleged that rapparees accused him of corresponding with the enemy and robbed him of goods worth £3,000 because he provided sanctuary for his Protestant neighbours. Würtemberg initially thought that few of the rapparees had much heart in the business. On the other hand, in County Longford, the rapparee leaders told Lord Granard that they would die before submitting to King William's government, and Colonel Wolseley reported similar sentiments in neighbouring Westmeath.[22]

Commentators remarked on the general Irish hatred of the English, and this was reflected in rapparee attitudes. For example, Munchgaar, one of the Danish colonels, observed 'the rapparees are the worst kind of fellows ... they give no quarter to English Protestants, but they spare the Danes, Dutch and French'. The bulk of the rapparees were peasants – 'the vulgar Irish' – although some, in the tory tradition, were reputed landed or ex-landed gentlemen. Fifty silver-hilted swords and fine horses were reported captured from a large party of rapparees in County Cork, suggesting to the Williamites that there must have been gentlemen among them. An 'old tory' commanded a party of 200 rapparee youths in the Bog of Allen. In December 1690 the 'trained bands' from Dublin (presumably the militia), who were 'reputed a sort of rapparees', were quartered around Ferbane in King's County. These 'gentlemen from Dublin' were well mounted and joined with the local rapparees in a raid near Birr. Possibly they were also involved in the actions of a party of sixty mounted rapparees and as many on foot, led by one O'Connor, that defeated two companies of Williamite grenadiers and then a party of dragoons, before burning Philipstown to deny it as quarters to the enemy. Like all popular rebellions, the rapparees empowered the impoverished and criminally inclined.[23]

Some in the Jacobite establishment were uncomfortable with partisan warfare and its accompanying viciousness and disorders, while at the same time glad to avail of its support when hard pressed. Fumeron initially criticized the rapparees as peasant troops that pillaged and ruined the countryside, although he later observed that they harassed the Williamites continuously by capturing men and stealing horses. King James's memoirs refer to them along

---

22 *Finch MSS*, ii, pp 390, 450; Ó Ciardha, *Ireland and the Jacobite cause*, p. 68; *Danish force*, p. 79; *CSPD 1690–1*, p. 120; Story, *Continuation*, p. 32; *Proclamations*, pp 239–40; Reduction of Ireland, v, nos 41 & 42; Kinsella, *Catholic survival*, p. 213.   **23** *Danish force*, pp 78, 96; *F-I corr.*, ii, p. 204; *James II*, ii, p. 433; *CSPD 1690–1*, p. 125; Clarke corr., no. 330; Story, pp 140, 149, 157.

similar lines, while conceding that they performed many bold actions. D'Albeville, the Jacobite secretary of state, called them 'an epidemical disease', viewing them as part of a general breakdown of order and discipline in which the strongest robbed the weakest. The poet Dáibhidh Ó Bhruadair, whose patron was the Jacobite colonel Sir John FitzGerald, probably had the creaghts as much as the rapparees in mind when he criticized 'the constant booleying (movement of cattle herds) of some of our nobility and the ceaseless disobedience of men who took to plundering'. He condemned the rapparees in bitter terms, variously calling them 'a rabble of catheads', 'muck-shovelling slovens' and 'a tribe of plebians' who robbed and plundered with impunity in a 'flood-tide of violence' that disrespected the clergy and was unchecked by the law. A similar unfavourable view of tory/rapparee activity was taken by the poet Aodh Mac Oireachtaigh in a 1690s verse dialogue with his confrere Séamas Dall Mac Cuarta. Mac Oireachtaigh called the post-war tory outlaws of County Louth criminal upstarts who were usurping the proper leadership role of the gentry, whereas Mac Cuarta praised their efforts, noted their high number of casualties (two out of three) and expressed the hope that they would succeed in maintaining their resistance until the exiled Jacobite army returned from across the sea to free Ireland. Whatever the shortcomings of the rapparees, their military value was recognized by the army. Rosen, d'Avaux and Sarsfield were all appreciative of their contribution to the war effort, and Tyrconnell overcame any reservations he may have had by actively recruiting them for the army prior to the campaign of 1691. The army became directly involved in rapparee activities especially after its withdrawal west in 1690, when a 'great part' of it was released into the Williamite quarters. In the autumn Colonel Daniel MacCarthy, a senior officer, commanded a large party of rapparees near Kinsale. During the following winter the army supplied some of the rapparees' needs, especially ammunition. Many junior officers, NCOs and soldiers were sent into Leinster and Munster to provide the rapparee bands with professional leadership. *Dublin Intelligence* makes several references to this practice, reporting for example how in June 1691 Lord Blayney, governor of Monaghan, defeated 'a party of rapparees to the number of fifty, commanded by Murphy and MacCullen, both lieutenants in the Irish army'. After the battle of Aughrim, rapparee numbers in the west were swollen by ex-soldiers and deserters. Richard Burke, an officer in the footguards, formed and led a large party of rapparees in County Galway, whom he summoned for action by blowing a horn. Sir Henry Bellasyse, the Williamite governor of Galway, called him 'a great rogue and a bloody fellow, notoriously known to have boasted what Protestant blood he has spilt in this war'.[24]

24 *F-I corr.*, ii, pp 208, 279; *Ó Bruadair*, iii, pp 171–7, 183; *DIB*, vol. 5, pp 889–90; *Finch MSS*,

The procedure, where army personnel became partisans, was for their colonel or another high-ranking officer to issue the subalterns and soldiers involved with certificates signifying their regiment, which was intended to distinguish them from rapparees and thus save their lives, if captured. For example, six rapparees were killed near Mountmellick in March 1691, but an army lieutenant accompanying them was made prisoner. In April, in the same locality an ensign and a sergeant were likewise spared, but eighteen accompanying rapparees were killed. However, this 'usual shift' was not always effective: Balldearg O'Donnell's certificates did not avail two of his officers, who were hanged as rapparees at Belturbet. Ginkel himself had no compunction about ignoring the certificate of a trooper of Galmoy's, whom he hanged with other rapparees for murdering his soldiers in 1691. In Galway, Bellasyse declared he was prepared to hang Richard Burke without ceremony, thereby disregarding his commission and certificates to this effect that were found in his pocket. However, he first sought a decision from Ginkel as to whether he should be treated as a rapparee or a prisoner of war.[25]

Rapparee bands were led by a chief, sometimes called a captain. Many of these men enjoyed considerable reputations, often laced with tales of adventure. In Galway, Richard Burke escaped from captivity in the city with the help of prominent local women, including Lady Bophin. In east Leinster the best-known rapparee leaders were the army deserters, John MacCabe and his allies, the 'White Sergeant' and one Cavenagh. They operated from the Bog of Allen and the Wicklow mountains. The 'White Sergeant' and Cavenagh were tracked down and killed. The Williamites offered a £20 reward for MacCabe, whom they eventually captured and hanged. 'Galloping' Hogan, who led a party of a hundred rapparees in west Tipperary and the adjoining counties, is traditionally credited with guiding Sarsfield's force through the Silvermine hills for the Ballyneety raid to destroy the Williamite train, an action in which his men were reported to have participated. A noble side to his character was shown by the military funeral he accorded George Story's brother after the young Williamite officer was killed in a clash with Hogan and his men near Birr. Other known rapparee leaders included Higgins, Callaghan and Grace in King's County; Jo. Meagher, 'a notorious ringleader' and Morris in Tipperary; Teige O'Donovan, O'Driscoll, Barry and Maurice Spillane in west Cork, and Captain Lew, 'one of the most famous rapparees', who was killed by the Danes near Fermoy in early 1691. A French

ii, pp 476–80; *James II*, ii, pp 386, 433; *Danish force*, p. 88; *DI*, no. 40, 23–30 June 1691; Clarke corr., nos 297, 1047, 1067, 1111; Story, *Continuation*, pp 49, 62, 73, 75–6, 137, 198; Ó Ciardha, *Ireland and the Jacobite cause*, pp 93–5. **25** Clarke corr., no. 1047; Story, *Continuation*, pp 49–50, 67, 70, 73, 221–2.

report stated that the rapparees looked upon Balldearg O'Donnel and Lord Merrion as their generals, but this appears to greatly exaggerate their role.[26]

Rapparees sometimes deployed in large bodies, frequently when allied with the Irish army. For example, 2,000 rapparees were reported to have provided from half to two-thirds of Richard Hamilton's force at the break of Dromore in 1689. Again, when Cork surrendered in 1690, 2,000 rapparees were in the garrison, a tenth of whom were scheduled for hanging, although it is not clear that these executions were carried out. At the capture of Ballymore in 1691, over 200 rapparees were among the garrison where they were treated as prisoners-of-war. There are occasional references to large parties of rapparees in the field. 'At least 3,000 of the rabble or suchlike people' assembled near Mullingar in July 1690. In September a force of allegedly 4,000 rapparees was defeated in an engagement with the Danes who were marching to Cork. Soon after, a thousand-strong force of rapparees was reported near Kinsale, and 'near 500' outside Castlehaven in November. A party of 2,000 was said to be in the Bog of Allen and to venture within twelve miles of Dublin. In 1691 the Williamites believed that Long Anthony Carroll, the Jacobite governor of Nenagh, 'could upon any alarm bring together [tories and rapparees] to the number of at least 2,000'. Another 2,000 were said to be 'hutted' at Donore, outside Mullingar. In late 1691 Richard Burke was reported to be leading 300 or more in County Galway. However, forces of this size, even if the numbers are inflated, were probably atypical, and the rapparees operated most effectively in small bands that kept in touch with each other, coming together only to mount significant operations.[27]

Taking full advantage of their local knowledge of the countryside, the rapparees hid in inaccessible areas, chiefly bogs, uplands and the remaining forests, where they lived with their families in makeshift accommodation after the manner of creaghts. According to d'Avaux, they could sleep as quietly on the ground in the rain as in good beds. They also occupied old castles, such as Carne in Westmeath and Cangort in King's County, or sheltered in local houses, whose occupants accommodated them from a mixture of fear and sympathy, despite holding Williamite protections. Story described the rapparees' methods of concealment:

> When the rapparees have no mind to show themselves upon the bogs, they commonly sink down between two or three little hills, grown over

[26] *Danish force*, p. 95; Clarke corr., no. 1106; *Proclamations*, pp 264–5; Story, p. 151; Story, *Continuation*, pp 63, 78–9, 83–4, 229, 236; Wauchope, *Sarsfield*, p. 132; *F-I corr.*, ii, p. 235; *JN*, p. 258; Claudianus, p. 147.   [27] *Danish force*, pp 78, 84; Clarke corr., nos 1067, 1111; Story, pp 4, 151, 156; Story, *Continuation*, pp 32, 50, 62, 68, 91, 175; *Ginkel corr.*, p. 320.

with long grass, so that you may as soon find a hare as one of them. They conceal their arms thus: they take off the lock and put it in their pocket, or hide it in some dry place; they stop the muzzle close with a cork and the touch hole with a small quill, then throw the piece itself into running water or a pond; you may see a hundred of them without arms, who look like the poorest humblest slaves in the world, and you may search till you are weary before you find one gun; but yet when they have a mind to do mischief, yet can all be ready in an hour's warning, for everyone knows where to go and fetch his own arms, though you do not.

In a raid in west Cork, the rapparees fastened bundles of straw on their chests as a substitute for armour, although it proved of little value against musket fire. In Westmeath a rapparee band betrayed to the Williamites had three gunsmiths working for them on a forge built in the middle of a great wood.[28]

The rapparees engaged in a variety of military activities. They had excellent intelligence, gained, the Williamites believed, from the local people who supported them in this and other ways. The Williamites were sceptical about claims that this support was secured through coercion. The rapparees seized cattle, sheep and horses from the Williamite quarters. In 1689 they drove 50–60,000 cattle into the best wheatfields and meadows in the north to ruin subsistence for Schomberg's army. It was reported that the horses stolen from Schomberg's quarters by a single rapparee band were sufficient to mount three cavalry troops in the army. In December 1690 a French officer told Louvois that the rapparees confined the Williamites to their garrisons and took many prisoners. An essential ingredient of the Irish army's preparations for the 1691 campaign was the supply of horses that the rapparees rustled from the Williamites, a process facilitated by the need to subsist the livestock by grazing during the winter. Those belonging to Würtemberg and his staff were taken from outside Waterford just before the 1691 campaign. The rapparees engaged in widespread looting and plunder. They ambushed and murdered Williamite stragglers and small parties of soldiers when given the opportunity. They attacked isolated small garrisons and burned Williamite quarters near the frontier, such as Philipstown and the villages around Mountmellick. They set upon supply convoys, inhibited foraging parties, disrupted communications, robbed sutlers, raided the posts, murdered couriers, stole weapons and stripped corpses and prisoners. In March 1691 a deserter reported 2,000 Irish soldiers

---

28 Claudianus, pp 149, 307; *d'Avaux*, pp 586; Story, pp 151–3, 156–7; Story, *Continuation*,

clothed in uniforms taken from murdered Williamites, while the quantity of stolen horses and weapons was sufficient for two regiments. They were also an important source of intelligence for the Jacobite army.[29]

This partisan warfare severely harassed the Williamite quarters and disrupted their military operations during the mid-winter offensive of 1690–1, when, as a French observer put it: 'they tormented the enemy unspeakably'. Ginkel himself wrote that the rapparees had impeded his winter offensive into Limerick and Kerry, and expressed his anxiety about their potential threat to his coming summer campaign. The Williamites admitted that one of the greatest difficulties their army faced for the 1691 campaign was to preserve its quarters from rapparee attacks. There were fears that the detachment of sufficient troops to counter the rapparees would seriously deplete the field army, although this was eventually avoided by tasking the Protestant militia, re-formed in November 1690, with their suppression. The militia grew quickly, eventually numbering 15,000. During the 1691 siege of Limerick, the rapparees contributed to the city's defence by murdering foragers and stragglers from the Williamite camp. Supplies could only be moved in well-guarded convoys. At this time Hogan successfully attacked an ill-protected Williamite supply train at Cullen, seizing seventy-one horses. In the course of the whole war, Story estimated that the rapparees 'murdered privately' 800 Williamite soldiers, which was about 4 per cent of Ginkel's army and amounted to just over a quarter of total Williamite combat casualties. The rapparees also attacked civilian Protestants and Catholics who had taken Williamite protections or who refused them assistance, burning their houses and haggards, and plundering their stock and possessions. A prominent Irish victim was Richard Fagan of Feltrim, a wealthy Dublin property owner, murdered in his home for resigning his footguards captaincy after the Boyne.[30]

The rapparees were feared and hated by the Williamites, who variously described them by such epithets as 'vermin', 'tories, robbers, thieves and bogtrotters', and viewed them as 'a permanent menace', 'cruel and barbarous', 'exceedingly troublesome', 'the worst kind of fellows', and a 'knot of rogues' that 'infested' their quarters. Their partisan warfare generated atrocities on both sides. Williamite soldiers who ventured beyond their garrisons were in ever-present danger of being captured or murdered. In 1689, near Moyry Castle in south Armagh, Story saw the body of a soldier whose head had been cut off

pp 84, 93. **29** Story, pp 139, 148; Story, *Continuation*, pp 67, 69, 77, 229; *Danish force*, pp 96, 104, 107, 110–11; *CSPD 1690–1*, pp 14, 120, 127, 231; *F-I corr.*, ii, pp 258, 333; iii, pp 104, 159, 166; Clarke corr., no. 839; Le Fleming MSS, p. 323; Reduction of Ireland, v, p. 42. **30** Story, pp 139, 148–9; Story, *Continuation*, p. 317; Ginkel corr., pp 318–20; *CSPD 1690–1*, pp 227, 365–6, 382; *Proclamations*, pp 213, 238–9; *Danish force*, p. 109; Simms, *Confiscation*, pp 35–6.

by the rapparees and placed between his legs. Near Mullingar in 1691, having murdered three Williamite stragglers, the rapparees put out the eyes of a fourth. Williamite countermeasures were equally barbarous. Captured rapparees were normally hanged, sometimes after being tortured by being broken on the wheel or having their limbs stretched. Ginkel ordered the wheel for rapparees captured near Limerick in 1691, but on being informed that torture was contrary to the laws of England, he had them hanged instead, after which their bodies were quartered and dispersed on the hedges along the highways near his camp. In this instance the executions were after a court martial, but most seem to have occurred without any legal process. There were several instances of rapparees' heads being submitted to the Williamite authorities in support of a claim for a bounty payment – 'a custom in that country and encouraged by a law, which allows so much for every head according to the quality of the offender'. The heads of executed rapparees were to be seen impaled on spikes on the walls of several towns. Williamite accounts are replete with details of the number of rapparees killed. Story's final estimate was that the army and militia killed 1,928 in combat, 112 were hanged by legal process or court martial, and 600 hanged or otherwise killed without ceremony. However, not all those included in this body count may have been actual rapparees. The Williamites, especially the Ulstermen, regarded the whole Catholic population as hostile and saw little reason to differentiate rapparees from the rest. In Colonel Wolseley's opinion, 'fair means' would never win true submissions, because 'an Irishman is to be taught his duty only by the rod'. This attitude, coupled with Williamite anger at the violence and depredations of the rapparees, meant that 'vast numbers of poor harmless natives were daily hunted up and down the fields as they were following their labour, or taken out of their beds and hanged, or shot immediately for rapparees', according to Leslie. He condemned the 'small evidence or even presumption [that] was thought sufficient to condemn men for rapparees, and what sport they made to hang up poor Irish people by dozens, almost without pains to examine them: they hardly thought them humankind'.[31]

Huts and cabins were burned to deny the rapparees accommodation. Jacobite sheriffs, such as Sir Anthony Meleady in Longford and Gerald Nugent in Westmeath, were regarded as 'torys and highwaymen', deserving of hanging if they persisted in resisting the imposition of Williamite authority in their localities. The Protestant militia supported the Williamite army by

---

31 Story, p. 28; Story, *Continuation*, pp 50, 58–9, 74–5, 78, 175, 221–2, 317; *CSPD 1690–1*, p. 227; Claudianus, p. 148; *JN*, p. 260; Leslie, p. 16.

policing their quarters to suppress rapparee activity. Local knowledge, focus of purpose and the prospect of booty gave the militia activity considerable impetus. They were reported to treat the rapparees more severely than the army and were soon killing many, including some who were betrayed by former comrades who had submitted to the Williamites. In Sligo, towards the end of the war, a Jacobite officer, Captain McSharry, who had defected to the Williamites with his fifty-strong company of 'good men, well-armed with firelocks' was employed to hunt down the numerous rapparees in the adjoining mountains. Other measures taken by the Williamites to suppress the rapparees and deny them support appear to have had little effect, and can only have been enforced sporadically. Catholics were ordered to surrender all arms, to remain in their parishes except on market days and to vacate locations within ten miles of the frontier between the armies. Horse rustling was made a capital offence. Catholic inhabitants of localities where soldiers were murdered were threatened with the loss of their protections, if they were uncooperative in the apprehension of the perpetrators. It was decreed that they must compensate Protestants whose homes were robbed or burned, and suffer the expulsion of their priests when this occurred. In May 1691, in order 'to prevent robberies, wilful burning of buildings, corn and hay, murders and insurrections', the Williamite government threatened 'the popish-Irish inhabitants' with 'the utmost severity of military execution' for failure to provide information about local rapparees or assist in their capture or destruction. It also imposed a night-time curfew.[32]

Despite the efforts to suppress them, the rapparees remained a potent force up to the end of the war and even afterwards. During the negotiations of the Limerick articles in 1691, a debate about their position was evidently disputatious, as it went on until midnight. Subsequently a clause in the military articles included them with the soldiers entitled to emigrate. An offer of pardon to rapparees, if they surrendered their arms and took the oath of allegiance to William and Mary within a month, was published in September 1691, and extended for a further month in October. Ginkel sought to encourage this process by a proclamation of his own promising all 'straggling people still in arms, whether known by the name of rapparees, volunteers, creaghts or others', safe passage to their homes, if they submitted in accordance with the lords justices' terms. Many 'in all corners of the kingdom' took up the offer: within a single week 10,000 were reported to have submitted in Kerry

---

[32] Story, *Continuation*, pp 32, 59, 68, 74–81, 158, 175, 317; Clarke corr., nos 1213, 1163, 1165; *JN*, pp 258–9; *Proclamations*, pp 201, 208–9, 212–13, 217–18, 238–9, 244–5; Ferguson, 'Army in Ireland', pp 45–6.

alone. Some sought service with the Williamite army abroad. Among those to submit were Galloping Hogan and 'the great ringleader', Richard Burke, both of whom were then employed to hunt down fellow rapparees. Hogan was subsequently murdered, the established rapparee retribution for those who betrayed them. Although rapparee activity seems quickly to have abated in the immediate aftermath of the war, the possibility of its resurgence continued to trouble the Williamites. Ginkel and the lords justices were anxious that unemployed ex-Jacobite officers might become the focus of fresh rapparee activity, and there was a move to send them to the imperial service.[33]

These fears proved well-founded. In many localities a level of rapparee activity persisted throughout the 1690s. Twenty-three grand juries made returns of named rapparees in their counties between 1694 and 1701. In Cork and Kerry, they were alleged to enjoy protection by the surviving gentry and substantial middlemen, an implication that banditry in the south-west still retained a political and military character related to the war. Government measures to curtail the post-war partisan violence included an offer of a £5 bounty for the killing or capture of several named rapparees, returns by grand juries of numerous rapparees for apprehension and trial, and orders to the justices of the peace to jail the families of tories, robbers and rapparees. Acts of parliament in 1695 and 1697 imposed financial penalties on the Catholic inhabitants of counties where tory/rapparee incidents occurred. Specifically listed offences were robberies, burglaries, burning of houses and haggards of corn, killing or maiming of cattle, and murdering, maiming and dismembering of persons. However, such quasi-political character as the remaining rapparees retained gradually declined. By the early eighteenth century those still designated tories and rapparees were little more than common highwaymen.[34]

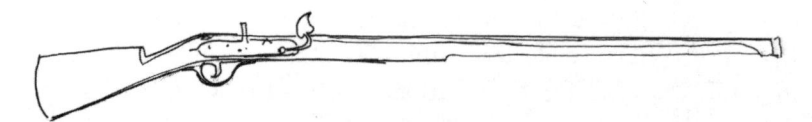

Figure 10. Matchlock musket

[33] Story, *Continuation*, pp 238, 240, 262, 268–70; *Proclamations*, pp 267–8, 271–2; *DI* no. 56, 13 October 1691; Clarke corr., no. 1225; *Danish force*, p. 138; Ginkel corr., p. 324; *CSPD 1695* [addenda 1692], p. 176; Ó Ciardha, *Ireland and the Jacobite cause*, p. 89. [34] *Proclamations*, pp 326–7, 359–61, 362–5, 379–82, 414–16, 540–3, 554–5, 556–8, 561–3, 624, 650–2; Ó Ciardha, *Ireland and the Jacobite cause*, pp 89–92; 7 Will. III, c.21 (1695); 9 Will. III, c. 9 (1697); Ferguson, 'Army in Ireland', pp 82–3.

CHAPTER 12

Backgrounds and beliefs

Composition of the officer corps

THE NAMES OF approximately 4,000 officers of the Irish army, who served in the war of 1689–91, are known, and there were at least several hundred others whose identities are no longer on record. At any one time the wartime establishment allowed for over 2,500 officers, to which can be added a substantial body of replacements, recorded and unrecorded, together with supernumerary officers who were not on the establishment of the regiment to which they were attached, but served with it as volunteers. Most of the officers, together with virtually all the army's other ranks, were drawn from Irish Catholic society, which numbered possibly a million and three-quarters people at the time. The Irish component of the officer corps was a mixture of Gaels, Old English descendants of Norman families, and a few New English settlers who were Catholics. There were instances of family members on opposing sides. These divisions were to be found at the top: after all, William and James were doubly related, while Berwick and the grand prior were nephews of Marlborough. Virtually all the Butlers were Jacobites except their kinsman, the 2nd duke of Ormond, who accompanied William at the Boyne. Families such as the Savages in County Down and the Piers and Magans in County Westmeath provided officers to both armies. Sir Drury Wray was a Jacobite officer, whereas his son Christopher fought for the Williamites. John King sat in King James's Dublin parliament and held the rank of captain, while his brother Lord Kingston organized the resistance of the Sligo Protestants to the Jacobite regime. Roger Farrell, who was killed at the siege of Derry, was a cousin of Francis Fergus Farrell, colonel of a Williamite regiment in Flanders, who subsequently made a bid to secure his estate. The Abercorn and Tyrone estates, both owned by Jacobite colonels, were saved from confiscation by the fact that their heirs were Protestants. Henry Luttrell's defection to the Williamites gained him the Luttrellstown estate of his brother Simon, perhaps a family survival strategy. An apparent arrangement between Galway and his Williamite brother-in-law, Viscount Lanesborough, to preserve Lady Galway's share of the Lane estate, regardless of which side was victorious, was enshrined in a saving clause of the Jacobite parliament's repeal of the act of settlement.

A handful of officers were veterans of the mid-century wars, and most were descendants of those who had soldiered in those conflicts but possessed no military experience themselves, as Irish Catholics were excluded from military life after 1660. However, over sixty Irish officers were professional soldiers who had gained military experience overseas. The wartime officer corps was further supplemented by about a hundred English and Scottish Jacobites, and by the French officers sent by Louis XIV. The officers' motives, with differing degrees of emphasis, ranged through King James's restoration, the recovery of Catholic property and ascendancy, hatred of the English, support for France against William of Orange and his allies, and of course career ambition, peer pressure, opportunity and prospects.[1]

BACKGROUNDS

Peers and gentry

Almost all the Irish Catholic peers were commissioned, together with many of their male relatives and connections. Other officers were drawn from those who had managed to retain or acquire significant estates or other assets despite the various confiscations. There was also a middling class of small landowners, substantial tenants and others of means, such as merchants, lawyers and public officials. The expectation was that such people could access the resources needed to support a troop, a company or even a regiment in the immediate months that followed the enlargement of the army. However, a majority of officers, including many captains and most subalterns, were from dispossessed families, or were younger family members, possessed of little or no means of their own. Even if currently propertyless or in reduced circumstances, they remained conscious of their roots in the Gaelic or Old English gentry. In local society, traditional seigneurial relationships endured to a considerable degree, maintaining respect and support for dispossessed families. In Armagh, for example, Archbishop Plunkett observed that the tenants of the new landowners continued to contribute to the support of the old leading families, even though the latter were now only tenants themselves. Plunkett's observation was confirmed by William King. Another writer described 'the commonalty … as extremely awed by their superiors'. In Westmeath, Sir Henry Piers observed in 1682 'the landlords of old were and still are great oppressors of their tenants and followers, the gentry scorning to take up any

---

1 *Savage family*, pp 133–4; *PI*, ii, pp 201–2; iii, pp 229–33; Simms, 'Parliament', p. 86; Officer list (Bodl., Carte MS 181), f. 9; Simms, *Confiscation*, pp 75–6, 89, 129–30; TCD MS 670, f. 4; Dalton, iii, p. 71; Magan, *Umma-More*, pp 128–30; *Acts of James II's parliament*, pp 43–4;

manual craft, whereby they may earn an honest livelihood ... [but] will walk from house to house ... and spend their whole age in idle wandering and coshering' (being fed and entertained by their followers). Gaelic poets such as Ó Bruadair and Ó Rathaille, who depended on the gentry class for patronage, were respectful of traditional social hierarchies, although the former was critical of the oppression of ordinary folk by their superiors. The war revived the traditional military-leadership role of the old elite and facilitated their ability to recruit, even where their wealth and property were reduced or non-existent. During the war, the paternalism inherent in the seigneurial relationship was reflected in the colonels' alleged refusal to acknowledge that any of their officers or men were responsible for the least disorder. It also burdened them with responsibility for the welfare of refugees from their localities.[2]

At the apex of the social scale were the peers, who still regarded themselves as a military caste with a special duty to rally to the sovereign's support and provide military leadership in time of war. The number of Irish peers had greatly increased in the seventeenth century both as a source of revenue and as an inexpensive means of 'making Ireland English'. Since the king bestowed their titles, it was a matter of honour that peers owed their sovereign a particular loyalty. However, for the Catholic peers – over half the total – and their progeny, the full expression of this obligation, and its attendant rewards, had been curtailed by the Tudor oath of supremacy, which denied them most public office, including the army. James's accession ended their exclusion and opened up service opportunities to them and their progeny. In addition, it held out the promise of a restoration of their fortunes where these had been destroyed or impaired by the upheavals of the preceding century. Many Catholic peers still possessed significant wealth, and even where they did not, their titles gave them a degree of prestige, allied to a leadership role in their family and locality, and in society generally. The coincidence of duty, honour, wealth, access and self-interest brought nearly all of them into the Irish army. Of the forty-three Irish Catholic peers, including seven created by James after he landed in Ireland, thirty-eight held commissions. Of these, twenty-seven were colonels, including four generals: Tyrconnell, Mountcashel, Lucan and Galmoy (the first three being new creations). At one time or another, seven peers commanded cavalry regiments, one a dragoon regiment and nineteen led infantry regiments, although the units of the impoverished Castleconnell and

---

O'Farrell, 'Downfall of the O'Ferralls', pp 206–10.   2 King, pp 35–7; Piers, 'Westmeath', pp 110, 114; Connolly, *Religion, law and power*, pp 141–2; *Finch MSS*, ii, p. 478; MacLysaght, *Irish life*, p. 87; *Ó Bruadair*, iii, pp 40–1; Ó Ciardha, *Ireland and the Jacobite cause*, p. 157.

Clanmalier were short-lived. Clanricard and his brothers, both also peers, each commanded a regiment. All five colonels chosen in 1690 for the French service were closely connected to the peerage, which was both a recruiting stimulus that acknowledged the continuing prestige and influence of the Irish nobility, as well as a concession to French social stratification.[3]

Three English Catholic peers also held commands: Berwick, an illegitimate son of King James, and Dover were both generals and commanders of lifeguard troops; Hunsdon commanded an embryonic English infantry regiment. To their number may be added Berwick's brother, Henry Fitzjames, colonel of an infantry regiment who, while not yet a peer (he was created duke of Albemarle in 1696), was dignified with the title of lord grand prior of England. Twenty-eight of the Irish peers had at least some pre-war military experience. Sixteen had served in the reformed Irish army before the war; four, together with the English peers, had served in the English army; and a further seven had gained military experience on the Continent. Antrim was a veteran of the mid-century wars in Ireland. Seven further regiments were commanded by the sons of peers and two by their younger brothers. In addition, when Ikerrin died in 1688, his brother succeeded him as commander of the mounted grenadiers. Dillon of Costello-Gallen, Brittas and Kingsale were lieutenant colonels, and a further seven peers were captains, mainly in the cavalry. Most of the latter group were generally of little or only modest means, although Costello-Gallen possessed the resources to raise two infantry regiments that were commanded by his sons. Mountgarret's alleged lack of physical and mental capacity may account for command of a regiment in which he served going to his younger half-brother, Colonel Edward Butler. Of the six peers who held no formal military appointments, Fingal and the 4th Viscount Ikerrin were minors, Fitton and Riverston were judges, while Carlingford and Mount Leinster were both present at the Boyne, where the former was killed in action as a volunteer and the latter was King James's aide-de-camp. In short, the extent of their involvement confirms the near total commitment of the Irish Catholic peerage to the Jacobite army.[4]

Next to the peers in the social hierarchy were the baronets, knights and wealthy country gentry, who provided over thirty colonels and many company and troop commanders. The small size and localized character of the Irish Jacobite elite is demonstrated by the tight-knit nature of their family relationships. For example, Sarsfield, who was not ennobled until 1691 but was

---

3 Ohlmeyer, *Making Ireland English*, pp 5, 9–11, 251–2; Officer list (Bodl., Carte MS 181), passim; TCD MS 670, passim; *JN*, pp 201–41; Story, pp 97–8; *CP*, iii, p. 225; *F-I corr.*, i, p. 355.
4 *JN*, p. 102; *CP*, v, pp 387, 391; ix, pp 354, 796–7; *PI*, ii, p. 316.

a substantial property owner in counties Dublin and Kildare, married Honora Burke, a daughter of the 6th earl of Clanricard, whose brother and half-brothers were both peers and colonels in the army, as was her sister's husband, Iveagh. After the war, when both were widowed, Honora married Berwick, while Lady Iveagh wed Colonel Thomas Butler of Kilcash. Four of their Burke cousins were married respectively to Antrim and Robert Fielding, both colonels; to Athenry, lieutenant colonel in Bophin's foot; and to Colonel Garret Moore, governor of Banagher and commander of an independent company, whose courtesy rank emanated from his earlier service abroad. Sarsfield's sister was married to Kilmallock and his mother-in-law to Captain Thomas Burke of Lord Galway's regiment, a brother of Colonel Walter Burke. The great duke of Ormond's Catholic relatives formed another overlapping group: his brother's sons, Walter and John Butler of Garryricken, were both colonels. Mountcashel, Nicholas Purcell and the three Hamilton brothers were sons of his sisters, and his grand-nephew colonels included Clancarty, Clanricard, Bophin, Galway and the aforementioned Colonel Thomas Butler. Tyrconnell's relatives and connections formed another extensive network. He was related by blood or marriage to more than a dozen Jacobite colonels and junior officers. Colonel Mark Talbot was his illegitimate son. The colonels included again Ormond's Hamilton nephews, brothers-in-law of Tyrconnell's wife, who were also generals. Many of the army's cadre of veteran officers with overseas service also belonged to the upper echelons of Jacobite society: in addition to Sarsfield, Mountcashel, Kilmallock and the Hamiltons, were such men as Mark Talbot, John Butler, Charles MacCarthy More, Oliver O'Gara, who was married to a sister of Slane, and the Luttrell brothers who were related through marriage to Tyrconnell. A military career was also seen as an appropriate outlet for illegitimate sons. King James himself set the example with the military appointments of Berwick and the lord grand prior, his sons by Arabella Churchill. Mark Talbot was another instance of this means of fostering a bastard son's career. In France after the war, Talbot's relationship with Berwick's sister, the widowed Lady Waldegrave, landed him in the Bastille. She subsequently married the exiled Galmoy. In Antrim's regiment Captain Daniel MacDonnell was an illegitimate son of the colonel, and his own two teenage sons were among the junior officers. The commissioning of illegitimate progeny was probably a common occurrence.[5]

5 *CP*, iii, p. 233; *BLGI 1912*, p. 489; *CP*, v, p. 610; *PI*, i, pp 137–8; iii, p. 417; Lenihan, *Last cavalier*, pp 181–2; *JN*, p. 68; [Kerney] Walsh, *MacDonnells*, p. 4; TCD MS 670, ff 6, 11, 15, 25, 37, 50.

Merchants, lawyers and officials

A number of officers were drawn from an emerging Catholic middle class. Over two dozen can be identified as merchants. Sir Michael Creagh, Dublin's lord mayor and a wealthy city merchant and businessman, raised a regiment, as did Galway's mayor, Dominic Browne. City businessmen were strongly represented in Creagh's regiment. In addition to merchants, his officers included an upholsterer, a goldsmith, an apothecary, a gardener, a cooper and the corporation swordbearer, together with a number of country gentlemen. Another officer, Terence MacDermott (or his son), was Creagh's successor as lord mayor. The lieutenant colonel and the major, however, were veteran officers. Thomas Hackett, Creagh's predecessor as lord mayor of Dublin, commanded a company in the footguards, as did the wealthy city property owner, Richard Fagan of Feltrim. Browne's officers were drawn from the leading Galway mercantile families, with eleven of the fourteen 'tribes' represented, although by this time many from this background, including Browne himself, were also west of Ireland landowners. His major was a French officer. A mayor's company was formed in Limerick in 1689, presumably drawing on the city for its personnel, although its commander appears to have been French.[6]

The later Stuart era had seen something of a renaissance of the Catholic bar in Ireland. At least thirty Irish entrants of the London inns of court held commissions. They were usually the sons of country gentlemen or prosperous merchants. Many had become practising barristers, often with considerable success. Both Sir Henry Lynch, a judge of the exchequer court, and John Browne, the enterprising Mayo barrister and entrepreneur, were colonels of short-lived infantry regiments. Felix O'Neill, master in chancery and advocate general, commanded a regiment from 1690 and was killed at Aughrim. Francis Toole commanded an infantry regiment throughout the 1691 campaign, and Henry Oxburgh succeeded to the command of his father's regiment probably after the latter's death. Well-known lawyer captains who commanded troops or companies included Gerald Dillon, the prime serjeant, serving in the cavalry regiment of his brother-in-law Abercorn; John Connor in Henry Luttrell's cavalry; Florence MacNamara and Rowland Savage in the dragoons; Sir Gregory Byrne in the footguards; and in other infantry regiments Terence MacDonagh, Arthur O'Keeffe and Edward Sherlock. Captain Fergus Farrell, a Protestant barrister from Longford, commanded a company in a Nugent

---

6 TCD MS 670, ff 15, 48, 50; Childs, *BD*, pp 11, 74; Harris, appendix, p. iv; *d'Avaux*, p. 570.

regiment throughout the war. Other barristers, such as John Hussey and James Eustace, held more junior appointments. At least ten officers were recorders, the barristers who provided legal services to corporations. They included Thomas Lynch, recorder of Galway, who was lieutenant colonel of Mayor Dominic Browne's regiment. James MacDonnell, a captain in Lord Clare's dragoon regiment, is said to have been the latter's attorney (and was later a post-war purchaser of part of his confiscated estate).[7]

Thirty-one heads of corporations, variously styled mayor, sovereign, provost, burgomaster or portreeve, are known to have held commissions. Most were captains, but six became colonels, some being also substantial landowners. A score of town clerks, half of them also prothonotaries or court clerks, were commissioned, generally as junior officers, although a few were captains. Captain John FitzPatrick and Ensign Richard Dease appear to have been medical doctors. Captain Micheal Morrogh of Charles MacCarthy More's regiment was a pharmacist and his lieutenant, Severus Gould, was a merchant, both from Cork. In the Jacobite parliament of 1689 two-thirds of the commons and virtually all the Catholic peers were army officers. Although some, such as Sarsfield and Galmoy, soon absented themselves to carry on the war, there was considerable criticism that others abandoned their posts for the full duration of the session – almost three months – and then embarked on the recovery of their estates, just at the time when the army was running into strong opposition in west Ulster. Many of the county commissioners appointed to administer the act of supply were also army officers, but the legislation's general ineffectualness presumably minimized its disruption of their military duties.[8]

Junior officers

Of the majority of officers, especially junior officers in the infantry, little or nothing is known of their individual lives beyond their names and rank. In contemporary European society, the army was viewed as a rite of passage for elder sons and a career prospect for their younger siblings. To serve as an officer was usually the mark of a gentleman, provoking the Williamite commentator, William King, to disdainfully observe that hundreds of Irish officers were former cowherds, horse-boys and footmen, although he held even

---

7 Story, p. 98; Maynard, 'Legal profession', passim; *Middle Temple admissions*, pp 168–222; *Gray's Inn admissions*, pp 303–39; TCD MS 670, ff, 5, 6, 10, 11, 15, 25; Officer list (Bodl., Carte MS 181), ff 17, 31, 32; Harris, appendix, pp iv–xvi; *JN*, p. 148; *F-I corr.*, ii, p. 220; *AH*, 22, p. 100; BL, Add. MS 9763, f. 9; information on James MacDonnell from M. Haugh. 8 *AH*, 22, pp 43, 51, 69, 70, 76; Harris, appendix, pp iv–xvi; Simms, 'Parliament', pp 83–8; O'Kelly, p. 34; Stevens,

these to be superior to others who had lived wild on the mountains. The English Jacobite, John Stevens, concurred, describing the background of many officers as ploughing, herding and digging potatoes. He criticized their want of military experience, poor conduct, lack of authority and even sense of honour. In his view they owed their commissions to bearing the name of a good family or having a few followers, but many of them were 'as rude, as ignorant and as far from understanding any of the rules of discipline as [the common soldiers] themselves'. He said they considered they were fit to be officers if they could march before their men and repeat by rote the common words of command, adding that the non-commissioned officers were often their relatives or foster brothers. The French were equally disparaging: the junior officers were former tailors, butchers and shoemakers, according to d'Avaux. Other French reports also stressed the lowly origins of the Irish officers, their lack of spirit or honour, their want of military instruction and their over-familiarity with their men. Nevertheless, one French observer, more perceptive than the rest, declared that there were plenty of young men of officer quality in Ireland, who could quickly assimilate the skills of command. His observation was vindicated in the eighteenth century and even in the later stages of the war in Ireland. In 1691 more than thirty young Irishmen 'with little money but coming from good families' were selected for cadetships in France. While the negative views on the Irish officers were not without validity, their authors displayed a lack of understanding of the tribulations and mores of contemporary Irish Catholic society. Poor, rustic, rough and ignorant to French and English eyes many of the Irish officers may have seemed, but most of them would have regarded themselves as gentlemen, respectful of their honour, unjustly dispossessed of their family properties, members of the warrior class and possessors still of some authority over their traditional followers, who treated them with respect and continued to give them support. They would not have seen themselves as baseborn peasants, tradesmen or labourers, although their economic status may not have been much better. The army offered them a degree of honour, income and upward mobility, together with the possibility of social and economic recovery for themselves and their society.[9]

The family relationships and occupations of untitled and junior officers are hard to trace with certainty, but sufficient examples exist to show that they too were closely inter-connected, especially with the leading families of their locality. Officers were commonly relatives or connections of their colonels.

p. 70; *JN*, pp 69–70; *Acts of James II's parliament*, pp 9–16. **9** King, p. 26; *d'Avaux*, p. 78; *F-I corr.*, i, pp 246, 336, 416; ii, pp 242–3, 321, 372–3; *Stevens*, p. 66.

Examples, among many, are Major Maurice FitzGerald, a brother of his colonel; Captain Henry Oxburgh, a son of his colonel; Captain Toby Mathew, father-in-law of his colonel; Lieutenant Colonel Walter Butler of Mountfin, stepfather of his colonel; Lieutenant Colonel John Butler, a cousin of his colonel; Captain Francis Pay, a son-in-law of his colonel; and Henry Browne, a lieutenant in the company of his father. The MacCoghlans of Dealbhna Ethra (the barony of Garrycastle in west Offaly) provide a good example of the range and interweave of family connections in the army. From Kilcolgan Castle came John MacCoghlan, a captain in Lord Galway's foot. His kinsman, Cornelius MacCoghlan of Kilnagarnagh, was his lieutenant. John's brother, Terence, commanded a company in Clifford's dragoons, with their brother-in-law, Robert Cusack, as his lieutenant. Another John MacCoghlan of the neighbouring Kincor branch of the family was a captain in Oxburgh's regiment. His mother, Maud Mooney, was a member of the nearby Doon family, which was represented in the same regiment by Captain Edmund Mooney and Lieutenant Francis Mooney, with an Edmund MacCoghlan as their ensign. Oxburgh himself was married to Clare MacCoghlan, 'a stiff bigoted papist', who seems to have been a daughter of the Kilcolgan house. Their two daughters married Jacobite officers, and most if not all of their sons served in the army. The MacCoghlans had marital connections with the Malones and MacGeoghegans of Westmeath, families that were also well represented on the army list and, in a move up the social ladder, with Lord Bellew of Duleek in whose regiment John MacCoghlan served before transferring to Oxburgh's. This network of family links was replicated throughout the army. Even where the precise details cannot be established, the correspondence of surnames is indicative that the officers of many troops and companies were related.[10]

Pre-war military experience

A valuable component of the officer corps was a small number of men with pre-war military experience gained in England or on the Continent. Excluding the French, they appear to have numbered about 160. Of over 220 new officers brought into the pre-war army by Tyrconnell, thirty-seven are known to have served outside Ireland: five solely in the English army and thirty-two on the Continent, some of whom also served in England. The new

---

10 TCD MS 670, 49; Officer list (Bodl., Carte MS 181), ff 2, 30, 35, 53; *Ormonde MSS*, i, p. 420; *JN*, p. 68; *PI*, iv, pp 41, 49; *CP*, v, p. 610; *ODNB*, vol. 24, pp 888–9; 'Brownes of Castlemacgarrett', p. 228; *DIB*, vol. 7, p. 1026; Cox, 'MacCoghlans' (2), pp 25–31; Nicholls, 'MacCoghlans', pp 452–60; Ryan, 'Kilcolgan to Ballindown', pp 112–19.

pre-war officers were overwhelmingly Irish, apart from a handful of English Catholics, such as Dorrington, Barker and Arundel in the footguards. René de Carne and René de Messandier were French, but had no record of service outside Ireland. A further cohort of experienced officers was added when the army expanded in 1689. They numbered at least 125, which is possibly an underestimate, as no returns exist for several regiments. A fifth of the wartime influx was Irish, including Patrick Sarsfield, Richard Hamilton and Robert Clifford. The rest were largely English and Scottish Catholics, who had resigned or been dismissed from the English army at the time of the revolution and subsequently accompanied or followed King James to Ireland, many landing at Bantry in May 1689. Having held James's commission in England, he favoured them by facilitating their transfer onto the establishment of the enlarged Irish army, generally lifting their rank. Of the total of 125, ten became generals, eleven were colonels, seventeen were lieutenant colonels and several more were majors. Although not always achieved, it was clearly the policy to have at least one or two experienced officers, English, French or Irish, to serve at field level in each regiment. However, there was considerable Irish opposition to this process, because it threatened to displace existing officers or disappoint expectations of an appointment or promotion of others. According to Stevens, many of the English as a consequence had to make do with supernumerary status, which he held was very much to the army's detriment. He cited as a 'pretence' the explanation that the people would not follow strangers, who would in any case not know how to manage them.[11]

The British officers also formed some new units. The new horseguard troop, initially commanded by the English peer Dover, was substantially comprised of English gentlemen, who had previously served in the horseguards there. John Lunt was excluded when it was found his service had only been in the mounted grenadiers. In Parker's cavalry regiment, for which some commissions were issued by James before he left France, twenty-nine of the officers were English. The presence of British rank and file outside the commissioned ranks seems to have been negligible. A score of apparently former English (horse?)guards came with Saint-Ruth in 1691. Hunsdon's infantry regiment had little more than nominal existence, as it consisted only of a small cadre of English officers, who were intended to provide the command structure for soldiers to be raised in England after a successful Jacobite invasion, and so it contained no other ranks. Hunsdon's attempt to

[11] *CSPD 1685–9*, passim; Officer list (Bodl., Carte MS 181); BL, MS 9763; TCD MS 670; Childs, *BD*, passim; Dalton, ii, passim; Stevens, p. 66; 'Journal 19/5 to 18/6 1689' (Carte MS 181), f. 71; *F-I corr.*, i, p. 257.

recruit 300 English and Scots that accompanied the French expedition in 1690 was thwarted by Lauzun, probably because he wanted them to fill vacancies in the French battalions. Hunsdon's officers fought as supernumeraries at the Boyne, and after the battle they went to France.[12]

The experience of most of the officers who followed James to Ireland was limited to Britain, and some had only enlisted in 1688. However, forty at least were continental veterans, who may be accounted true military professionals. Roger MacElligott, John Wauchope, Denis MacGillycuddy and several more had served in the Anglo-Dutch brigade, until they obeyed James's order recalling them from William's service in early 1688. Subsequently they formed new regiments in England, which Louis XIV secretly funded during their brief existence. Lord Clare and Thomas Maxwell were earlier veterans of the Dutch service. James Purcell, Theobald Burke and George Colgrave had served in the Tangier garrison, a British army combat zone that was a haven for Catholic soldiers. Others had served in France, where the Irish regiments in the 1670s were an important nursery for a number of prominent officers, such as Mountcashel, Anthony and Richard Hamilton, Patrick Sarsfield, William Nugent, Oliver O'Gara, Mark Talbot and James Purcell. Lawrence Dempsey, who also served in France, had previously served in Portugal. Thomas Dungan's regiment, raised in Ireland for French service in 1678, contained nearly ninety officers, more than half of whom had already served in France. The disbandment of the regiment before it left Ireland deprived the remainder, who included Galmoy, of overseas experience, but they could be said to have at least shown an early aspiration to become professional soldiers, and many subsequently served in the Irish army. Kilmallock, when a penniless young exile, had served incognito as a private in the French army, where he was promoted to sergeant on merit. He succeeded to the family peerage only on the death of a cousin in 1687. Teague O'Regan had served with a Scottish regiment in France in the 1660s. Balldearg O'Donnell and his adjutant, John Richards, had held commands in Spain. So also had such aged veterans of the mid-century civil wars as Richard Grace and Charles O'Kelly, both of whom subsequently served Charles II during his exile, as did William Tuite, Cornelius O'Driscoll and Sir Edward Scott. O'Regan, Scott, Grace and O'Driscoll were all effective as governors of Jacobite strongholds, the latter two dying at their posts. Other veterans of the mid-century wars in Ireland included Antrim, Charles Cavenagh and possibly Brian MacMahon. Alexander MacDonnell had served in the army of the bishop of Münster. In

12 Officer list (Bodl., Carte MS 181), f. 6; 'Rycaut's route'; *Kenyon MSS*, pp 239, 311; *F-I corr.*, ii, p. 450.

1686–7 Berwick, Sir Edward Vaudrey, Mark Talbot, Walter Lord Dungan, Thomas Butler and the engineer, Richard Burton, were among the officers who attended the imperial army in Hungary to observe the campaign against the Turks. One of this group, Clanricard's brother Thomas Burke, was killed at the great siege of Buda.[13]

Fourteen French officers held general's rank in Ireland in 1689–91, and five more French generals commanded the six battalions of Lauzun's 1690 expedition. In addition, excluding Lauzun's men, about 260 French regimental officers served in Ireland in 1689–90, a score remaining thereafter. Although Irish service gave French officers a step-up in rank, their career prospects in the Irish army compared badly with their British counterparts. About fifty-five, less than a quarter, secured substantive appointments, of which thirty-five were at field rank, but often *en second*, whereby the appointment was shared with an Irish officer. Three achieved colonelcies: Boisseleau raised and commanded an infantry regiment from the outset; late in the war le sieur de Bussay/Bussé succeeded to the command of Felix O'Neill's regiment following the latter's death at Aughrim; and le sieur de Sainte-Croix took command of the cavalry regiment of Henry Luttrell after the latter's arrest. A fourth officer, de Santons Bouillan, temporarily commanded Simon Luttrell's dragoons while the colonel was absent in France. But for most, the only employment was attachment to a regiment as a supernumerary, without any substantive appointment or command. Many of course were ex-cadets, glad to be commissioned, but without pre-war combat experience. There were also language difficulties and personal shortcomings, but the primary reason for the under-employment of the French, Nagle frankly admitted, was the reluctance of the Jacobite regime to give them commands, which of course would have been at the expense of Irish and British officers. Nevertheless, it was unfortunate that the French regimental officers, whose skills the army badly needed, remained an under-utilized resource.[14]

Of almost fifty general officers that led the Jacobite army through the war, only four brigadiers lacked military experience that had been gained outside Ireland, and most had served on the Continent at some stage of their careers.

---

13 *CSPD 1678*, p. 481; Dalton, i, pp 63, 209, 289; ii, pp 153, 153–6; 'O'Donnells in exile', pp 50–6; Hebbert, 'Richards brothers', pp 203–4; *PI*, i, pp 138, 212; O'Kelly, p. 12; Childs, *James II*, pp 41–2; Childs, *Charles II*, pp 244–50; Childs, *BD*, pp 4, 11, 17, 25, 27, 60, 75, 82, 107; *Ormonde MSS*, i, pp 400–7; Officer list (Bodl., Carte MS 181), ff 1, 2, 3, 6, 15, 17, 18, 19; Tyrconnell letters, no. 8; *F-I corr.*, ii, pp 14, 450; TCD MS 670, f. 64; Hayes, *BD*, p. 284; Murtagh, 'Richard Grace', pp 314–18; Garland, 'MacElligott', pp 121–2; *KJIL*, ii, p. 791; Nicholls, 'Kavanaghs', p. 733; Ó Mórdha, 'MacMahons of Monaghan', pp 191–2; de Corthuy, f. 15.   **14** *F-I corr.*, ii, pp 13, 128–30, 524; *d'Avaux*, p. 695.

Of 144 accorded the rank of colonel, fifty-six are known to have had experience in England or on the Continent (twenty-one had both). They included almost three-quarters of the cavalry and dragoon colonels, but only a quarter of those in the infantry. The discrepancy was to some extent addressed by the employment of less well-connected professional soldiers as lieutenants colonel and majors, together with French officers who often held joint appointments with Irish counterparts. Thus, in the Dublin regiment of Sir Michael Creagh, the lieutenant colonel John Power and the major Theobald Burke had both served in France in the 1670s. Burke had subsequently served in Tangier. Both were commissioned into the Irish army before the war and transferred to Creagh's regiment on its foundation in 1689. Their association with it seems to have continued throughout, and afterwards they held the same ranks in its successor, the regiment of Dublin formed by James II in France. By November 1690 a French officer, Cestan, had been added to the staff of Creagh's as second major. Some regiments had two or even three officers with pre-war military experience. Others had scarcely any, or none. Less than 20 per cent of the 224 new officers introduced into the pre-war army had previous service, but the remainder would undoubtedly have gained military experience from their commands. Most rose in rank when the army expanded, twenty-seven becoming regimental colonels. Set against this, however, were more than fifty who held the rank of colonel in the war, but seem to have been without pre-war military experience, only joining the army in 1689 and attaining their colonelcy by raising a regiment. This group included many of the short-lived units and probably most of those in Balldearg O'Donnell's force.[15]

Adding together all the officers with at least some pre-war military experience, including the French cadets, supernumeraries and those whose only service was in the peacetime Irish army, a rough figure of 500 emerges, which is approximately 20 per cent of the officer corps at any one time, or about 12 per cent of the entire wartime complement of officers. Given the very limited experience of roughly half this total, a very small professional base existed on which to quickly build an effective force.

Protestant officers

At least twenty-five pre-1685 officers remained on with their regiments in the immediate wake of the revolution. William Netterville of Mountjoy's foot, 'always a Protestant' but from a Catholic family in Meath, was one. The others

---

15 Officer list (Bodl., Carte MS 181), f. 52; *F-I corr.*, ii, p. 129; O'Callaghan, *Irish brigades*, p. 134.

must have been Protestants originally, although some, to accommodate themselves to the changing times, may have converted to Catholicism after James's accession. By the autumn of 1689 their presence in the army had dwindled to about sixteen. A handful of Irish Protestants also joined the enlarged army, such as Fergus Farrell, Harvey Morris – 'a Protestant all his life' – his nephew Redmond Morris and James Power, the last-named claiming to have been reluctantly forced into the army 'by the severity of his father', the earl of Tyrone. Sir Thomas Crosbie, who sat for Kerry in the Jacobite parliament, was commissioned a captain in three regiments in 1689, eventually settling for Cotter/Carroll's dragoons. Cormac O'Neill was said to have been a Protestant at one time, as Clancarty and Clanricard certainly were, before reverting to Catholicism after James's accession. Sir Edward Tyrrell, an elderly captain in Luttrell's dragoons and a former Cromwellian land surveyor, was described as being 'of any or no religion, sometimes a Roman Catholic, sometimes a Protestant'.[16]

Gael and Norman

Shared adversity meant that the divisions between Gael and Norman/Old English that had so undermined the mid-century confederacy were far less evident in Jacobite Ireland. Even before the divisions of the confederacy, the influential scholar Geoffrey Keating had argued that a mutual sympathy of blood, marriage and faith bound native Irish and the Old English against 'the foreign haughty swarm' of New English, and by the latter end of the century, for the most part, this was the orthodox view. The *Jacobite narrative* argued that the descendants of the 'ancient Irish noblemen and gentlemen, since they have been for several generations linked in blood to the old English of Ireland, and are of the same religion ... have the same firmness of loyalty [to the king] and the same interest'. There is no doubt that officers such as Neil O'Neill, Clare (O'Brien), Mountcashel and Clancarty (both MacCarthys), while they bore Gaelic names probably with some pride and were accepted leaders among their own people, were also comfortably integrated into Old English or indeed contemporary European society. Even Balldearg O'Donnell, who stressed his Gaelic background, had no difficulty in finding post-war acceptance at the English court. But for others of similar ethnicity, but of less sophistication or cosmopolitan exposure, the old divisions, while lessened, were not extinct. Old

---

16 *CSPD 1691–2*, p. 195; *1693*, p. 175; *1697*, p. 122; Johnston-Liik, *Parliament*, iv, p. 134; *ODNB*, vol. 35, pp 108–9; *CP*, iii, p. 233; Simms, *Confiscation*, pp 75–6, 89, 131; Leslie, p. 86; Officer list (Bodl., Carte MS 181), ff 14, 26, 29; *Clarendon*, i, p. 383.

English attitudes of superiority were met by Gaelic Irish resentment that sometimes bordered on animosity. For example, Tyrconnell, the archetypal Palesman, was accused by Sheridan, his secretary, of favouring the Old English above the Os and the Macs. This was undoubtedly Balldearg O'Donnell's experience. However, there were particular reasons in both instances. Sheridan was personally hostile to Tyrconnell, while Tyrconnell suspected O'Donnell's loyalty and resented his claim to his own Tyrconnell title. O'Kelly, a sophisticated commentator, was also of the opinion that Tyrconnell had no great love for the Old Irish, which he attributed to his desire to preserve the English interest in Ireland. Linking the peace party on the Jacobite side to the Old English, O'Kelly accused some of them of 'an inveterate hatred' towards the Old Irish, lest the latter might recover their lands.[17]

Although it is a crude measure of cultural distinction, it can be said that of 140 officers accorded the rank of colonel at some stage during the war, sixty-one had Old English surnames and fifty-seven were Gaelic, which was not an enormous difference. (Of the rest, six were New English, thirteen English or Scots and three French.) Of the five regiments disbanded by Tyrconnell in 1689 and the eleven of 'mere Irish' raised but not taken into pay in 1689–90, seven were commanded by colonels with English surnames – one of whom was New English – and nine by colonels with Gaelic surnames. The Gaelic share of the new pre-war commissions in general was only 25 per cent. In wartime, in the mounted corps it had risen to almost 40 per cent, a proportion replicated in many infantry regiments and substantially exceeded by those recruited in localities less densely settled by Old English families. For example, in Ulster all but a handful of Antrim's and Cormac O'Neill's officers had Gaelic names; this was also the case with the overwhelming majority of Heward Oxburgh's officers in south-west Leinster; and with more than half of Kenmare's and two-thirds of Nicholas Browne's in south-west Munster. Even in the Pale heartland, a third to a half of the officers of regiments such as Bellew's and William Nugent's had Gaelic names, although the proportion was smaller in other units, such as Louth's and Gormanston's. The truth was that even if Tyrconnell had wanted to do so, and the factual evidence for that is at least debatable, he could hardly have recruited such a large army without drawing on substantial Gaelic support. There was a noticeable tendency, however, for surnames from each tradition to cluster together in individual companies and troops. Family connections certainly played a part in this, but

---

17 Ó Buachalla, 'James our true king', p. 16; *JN*, pp 5, 267–72; *F-I corr.*, ii, p. 545; 'Sheridan's narrative', p. 17; O'Kelly, pp 47, 104, 146; Lenihan, 'Last cavalier', pp 119–21; Miller, 'Thomas Sheridan'; 'O'Donnells in exile', pp 54–5, 108.

a residue of cultural distinctiveness may also have been present. Furthermore, the Gaels tended to occupy the more junior appointments, in part because they lacked the means or experience for the senior positions at regimental level. Only five achieved general's rank, as against more than a dozen with Old English surnames.[18]

Insofar as their county of origin can be established, the officers of the cavalry regiments tended to come from a broad spread of counties, but with the Old English heartland of Dublin, Meath, Kilkenny, Kildare and Tipperary particularly well represented. This diversity was also true of the officers of Hamilton's dragoons, whose backgrounds lay in at least sixteen counties. However, the new dragoon regiments of 1689 were more localized, with their officers tending to come from the localities where their colonels had influence: Cotter in Cork; Clare in Clare; Maxwell in Down (where he held a command); O'Neill in Antrim, Down and Leinster; Dungan in south Leinster; Purcell in Tipperary; Simon Luttrell in Dublin and east Leinster; and O'Reilly in Cavan. Clifford was Irish-born. He was the grandson of an Elizabethan settler, but his background is otherwise obscure. Possibly he had associations with west Leinster, where several of his officers resided. In the mounted corps as a whole, most counties were represented, the exceptions being Sligo and the Ulster counties other than Antrim, Down, Cavan and Tyrone. In the infantry regiments, the footguard's officers were predominantly from Dublin and Meath, although more than a dozen other counties were represented. Most had Old English surnames, but some were Gaelic. Of the other regiments of the pre-war army, Leinster provided many of the wartime officers in the grand prior's and John Hamilton's, whereas the south of Ireland, especially Cork, was strongly represented in the MacCarthy regiments of Clancarty and Mountcashel. Only a few names can be positively associated with Ulster and Connacht. This situation changed, however, with the regiments raised in 1688 to replace those sent to England. Clanricard's officers were mainly Connachtmen and Antrim's mainly from east Ulster, while Tyrone's were from Munster, especially Waterford and Tipperary. The localized character of the numerous new infantry regiments that were subsequently raised in the army expansion was even more pronounced. Although virtually all drew their officers from more than one county, the bulk came from the county associated with their colonel: Iveagh's from Down, Barrett's from Cork, Creagh's from Dublin, Kenmare's from Kerry, Eustace's from Kildare and so on. Information for 1690–1 is fragmentary, but the

---

[18] Tyrconnell letters, no. 12; Story, p. 98; TCD MS 670, ff 21, 30, 47, 49; Officer list (Bodl., Carte MS 181), ff 27, 28, 29, 32, 60.

proportion of officers from the Jacobite quarters in western Ireland and part of the midlands possibly increased in the final phase of the war.[19]

The rank and file of the army was drawn from the large underclass of tenant farmers, artisans and labourers. The small number of surviving lists suggests their background was equally localized. Seigneurial influence, hostility to the English and a strong commitment to the Catholic faith, coupled with the pro-Jacobite stance of the influential Catholic clergy, combined to ensure that the war effort enjoyed widespread popular support. It was claimed that the numbers enlisting demonstrated the affection of the poor people to the royal cause. Pro-Jacobite sentiments persisted after the war, most obviously in the *aislings* of the Gaelic poets, but also among 'the meaner sort of Irish peasants', whom a Protestant writer judged 'may seemingly show a great respect and submission to the English ... [but] retain the same veneration for King James and the Irish gentry as ever ... for the sake of the Irish interest and the popish religion'.[20]

The official language of command in the army was English, but as Clarendon observed in 1686 the new recruits brought into the army were 'strange wretches and cannot speak, many of them, one word of English'. Practical necessity must have demanded the use of Irish within units, especially those raised from localities where little English was spoken or understood. Ó Bruadair wrote of the soldiers in the ranks talking and chatting 'in a language that soundeth not pleasant to Saxon ears' (i.e. Irish), and applauded the replacement of the military challenge 'who's there?' by the Irish '*cia súd?*' In Ireland generally, the transition from Irish- to English-speaking was a gradual and slow-moving, east-west process. In the 1680s, even in the Leinster county of Westmeath, ordinary people still communicated largely in Irish, although they were reported 'very forward to accommodate themselves to the English modes, particularly in their language, habit and surnames', while the youth of the county were learning to speak English in their 'petty schools', and the Irish language was becoming adulterated with English words. The officer corps would generally have known both Irish and English, and its upper echelons and more sophisticated personnel would also have understood French, the chief language of contemporary European culture. Probably few of the French officers understood English and certainly none knew Irish, so interpreters were needed to enable them to communicate with Irish soldiers and labourers, and probably also with the majority of Irish officers. Rosen told Louvois that the

---

19 Officer list (Bodl., Carte MS 181), passim; TCD MS 670, passim; BL, Add. MS 9763, passim; O'Kelly, p. 152. **20** *Ormonde MSS*, i, pp 416–18; Gafney, pp 162–3; Kilmallock papers, carton 2; Ó Ciardha, *Ireland and the Jacobite cause*, pp 47, 100–1.

language barrier was an obstacle to effective command by the French officers, as their orders were very often misinterpreted, particularly in the heat of battle. Stevens was one of the interpreters employed when French engineers were working on the Limerick fortifications with Irish soldiers. The soldiers employed clearly understood English, as Stevens would not have known any Irish. In eighteenth-century Ireland, the Irish language, especially its poetry, became an important medium for the secure transmission of on-going seditious Jacobite sentiments.[21]

Financial and property resources

The financial resources of the wealthier Jacobite officers lay largely in land, from which they derived a rental income in cash, kind or labour services. A survey of Jacobite-owned lands in Kildare, for example, showed almost all property to have been occupied by tenants at annual rents of from two to four shillings per acre. Some landowners chose to farm part of their property themselves. Lord Clare kept 16,000 acres around his home at Carrigaholt for his stud farm. Likewise, Captain Francis Eustace maintained a stud on part of his property in County Carlow, letting the remainder to cottiers. Some properties were simply too small to let. Among the largest remaining Catholic landowners were peers such as Clancarty (150,000 acres), Clanricard (148,000 acres), Antrim (119,000 acres), Dillon of Costello-Gallen (75,000 acres), Clare (30,000 acres), Westmeath (25,000 acres), Galmoy (16,000 acres), Mountgarret (15,000 acres), Slane (12,500 acres), Ikerrin (12,000 acres), Cahir (11,000 cares), Tyrconnell (14,000 acres), Abercorn (9,500 acres) and Gormanston (9,000 acres). Others with property holdings on a par with many of the middle-ranking peers were Nicholas Purcell of Loughmoe, County Tipperary (11,500 acres), Cúconnacht Maguire of Tempo, County Fermanagh (11,500 acres); John Barrett of Castlemore, County Cork (11,500 acres), Robert Grace of Courtstown, County Kilkenny (7,500 acres) and Walter Burke of Turlough, County Mayo (6,000 acres). Simon Luttrell's estate in County Dublin was 2,500 acres, and he owned a further 600 acres in Meath. Patrick Sarsfield's Lucan estate was about 1,400 acres, with a further 1,750 acres at Tully in County Kildare. Some peers, as a consequence of the land settlement, possessed smaller estates that were less commensurate with their status. This group included Netterville (4,000 acres), Brittas (3,000 acres), Louth (3,000 acres) and Dunsany (2,000 acres). Others, such as Iveagh,

---

21 *Clarendon*, i, p. 479; Ó Bruadair, iii, pp 129, 131; Piers, 'Westmeath', p. 108; Stevens, p. 195; *AH*, 21, p. 145; Ó Ciardha, *Ireland and the Jacobite cause*, pp 44, 47 and passim.

Castleconnell and Kilmallock, had lost virtually everything. Government pensions helped save Iveagh, Upper Ossory and Castleconnell from poverty, as well as supplementing the incomes of prominent army officers, such as Justin MacCarthy (the future Mountcashel), Sir Edward Scott, Dorrington and Sheldon. In King's County, the MacCoghlans' 3,000-acre Kilcolgan estate was valued at £400 per annum. Lower down the scale, officers like Captain John Brereton of Moore's infantry owned 830 acres in Queen's County, worth £120 annually and Captain John Dalton possessed a similar-sized estate in Westmeath, while Captain Richard Purcell of Creagh's, who was captured at the Boyne, was the tenant of 200 acres in County Meath.[22]

While acreages are a guide of sorts to wealth and influence, they do not take into account other factors, such as location, land quality, and the burdens of family settlements, mortgage interest or foreclosures, judgements, indebtedness and other encumbrances. Clanricard's estates in Connacht, for example, were diminished by mortgages and sales brought about by the extravagance of the 4th earl, the political involvements of the 5th earl and the financial entitlements of his only child, Margaret (who married three times), and the needs of his mother and his siblings. The assignment of nearly thirty impropriate rectories helped support his two younger brothers, Lords Bophin and Galway, who were both created peers by James. Galway was additionally funded through his marriage to the (underage) heiress, Lady Frances Lane. Of Clanricard's sisters, a dowry probably accompanied Lady Margaret, who married the penniless Iveagh in 1689, but none, although due, was ever paid to Lady Honora's successive husbands, Patrick Sarsfield and the duke of Berwick. After the war both her sons came to Ireland seeking it, but met with no success. Cúconnacht Maguire's Tempo estate was heavily in debt. Likewise, the estate inherited by Antrim in 1683 was described as 'much altered, impaired, mangled, and engaged in debts, mortgages, grants and otherwise'.[23]

Indebtedness also burdened the estates of many of lesser Jacobites. For example, in the barony of Delvin, County Westmeath, the estates of Colonel Richard Nugent, Cornet James Moile Nugent, and Ensign Matthew Dowdall were all mortgaged, while judgements existed against those of Captain

---

22 Ohlmeyer, *Making Ireland English*, pp 312–13, 370–1; Arnold, *Land settlement in Dublin*, p. 157; Simms, *Confiscation*, pp 177–82; 'Survey of Catholic estates', pp 70–3, 79–81, 87, 94–102, 113; Lenihan, *Last cavalier*, pp 62–3; Maguire, 'Estate of Cúchonnacht Maguire', pp 130–44; MacLysaght, *Irish life*, p. 144; 'Eustace family', no. 8, p. 377; Nolan & Whelan (eds), *Kilkenny history and society*, p. 170; *CTB 1685–9*, p. 1746.   **23** *PI*, i, pp 137–9; Melvin, *Estates in Galway*, pp 33–5; Petrie, 'Sarsfield's stepson', pp 153–4; Maguire, 'The estate of Cúchonnacht Maguire', p. 138; Ohlmeyer, *Antrim*, p. 276.

Michael Dardis and Captain John Nugent. In the same barony the earl of Westmeath had secured £1,500 by mortgaging the 400-acre property of his uncle's widow, which was presumably to revert to him on her death. The O'Farrell estate at Mornine in County Longford, home of Lieutenant Colonel Roger Farrell, was likewise heavily mortgaged, probably as a result of costly legal manoeuvring to secure its recovery after the Cromwellian confiscation. Landowners could derive additional income by exploiting other property-related assets, such as housing stock, mills, plantations, fishing weirs, and impropriate rectories and vicarages. Captain Sir John Everard, for example, besides his 1,750-acre estate, owned eighty messuages or tenements in Fethard, County Tipperary, in addition to his own stone dwelling house in the town, while Colonel William Tuite's property included two watermills and a fishing weir. In Dublin Captain Richard Fagan was the owner not alone of a 5,000-acre estate at Feltrim in the north of the county, but also of two inns and numerous houses in the city, and of Bullock Harbour on the coast to the south.[24]

It was not unusual for the former owners of confiscated land to lease some or all of their former property from the new proprietor, thereby retaining a degree of wealth and local influence. Lieutenant Peter Bath's family rented Athcarne Castle, their old home, and 900 adjoining acres in County Meath from King James, who personally owned 95,000 acres in Ireland that had been confiscated from Cromwellian regicides after the restoration, but not restored to its original owners. Captain Garrett Byrne was a tenant of 300 acres of his former property in Co. Wicklow. The MacJonnines of Mayo, a branch of the Burkes that provided four officers to Lord Kilmallock's regiment, also survived in this way, as well as by intermarriage with Galway 'tribal' families. Some rented from a wealthy relative: several Burke families in County Galway, for example, were tenants of Clanricard, while Lieutenant Garrett Fleming held 350 acres from his colonel and namesake, Lord Slane. Others were simply substantial tenants of land and buildings. Lieutenant Bartholomew Cappock rented a mill and 327 acres in Meath, Lieutenant George Noble rented 200 acres in Wicklow, while Captain Kean FitzGerald was tenant of a 140-acre estate at Stackumney in County Kildare, rented from Tyrconnell and Charles White of Leixlip Castle, the latter a fellow captain in Abercorn's cavalry regiment.[25]

---

24 Morris & O'Farrell, *Longford history & society*, pp 205–7; Conveyances of the forfeited estates, pp 356, 361, 368, 372, 381, 384, 387; 'Survey of Catholic estates', pp 101–2, 137; Simms, *Confiscation*, p. 179.   **25** *AH*, 22, p. 24; 'Survey of Catholic estates', pp 71–3, 80–1, 94–5; Simms, *Confiscation*, p. 92; Melvin, *Estates in Galway*, pp 14–19, 33–5.

Mercantile wealth is harder to estimate. Commerce was open to Catholics, who were able to benefit from the growth of the market economy. The outstanding example was Sir Patrick Trant, who had made a fortune in London through his agency for the sugar-rich, slave-worked Barbados colony, much of which he invested in the pre-war acquisition of 42,000 acres of Irish land. His son Thomas, a lieutenant colonel in the army, was closely involved in the formation of the Cotter dragoon regiment in Cork. Other Catholic merchants in Galway, Dublin, Limerick and Cork had the resources to form troops, companies, and even regiments. Lower down the scale, their business acumen also made them useful as quartermasters. Examples were David Fanning in Luttrell's horse, James White in Clare's dragoons and Laurence Dowdall in Bellew's infantry, who were all merchants. James Shee in Galmoy's horse was a rent collector for the duke of Ormond. A number of successful Catholic barristers earned substantial fees. The exclusion of the Catholic gentry from public service for most of the seventeenth century denied them the lucrative government-related appointments and also the military careers that were a particularly valuable outlet for younger sons. King James's accession in 1685 opened up public employment to Catholics, who became judges and other government officials as well as joining the army in significant numbers. This certainly improved their fortunes, but only in the few short years preceding the war. Substantial sums were paid to favourites through government pensions. Improved emoluments were also derived from Catholic ecclesiastical careers through King James's policy of leaving vacancies in the established church unfilled and using the income to subsidize the Catholic clergy, who by act of James's parliament were to receive the tithes payable by Catholics. This practice was already widespread, as was the diversion from the Church of Ireland clergy to their Catholic counterparts of fees from burials, marriages and Easter offerings. Glebelands were also seized.[26]

Jacobite houses

The homes of several Jacobite officers were in unaltered, late-medieval towerhouses such as Springfield in County Limerick, the seat of Colonel Sir John FitzGerald, Colonel Edward Butler's house at Ballyragget, the Knight of Kerry's home at Ballinruddery, County Kerry, the MacGeoghegan castles at Donore and Syonan in County Westmeath, Lieutenant Peter Bath's family home at Athcarne, County Meath, and Mornin in County Longford, the

---

26 Johnston, 'Stapleton plantations', p. 180; TCD, MS 670, ff 6, 11; Officer lists (Bodl., Carte MS 181), f. 28; Harris, appendix, pp x, xii, xvi; King, pp 223–5; *A new history of Ireland*, iii, p. 401.

family home of Lieutenant Colonel Roger Farrell. It was common also (where the owners could afford it) for a modern wing to have been added to towerhouses, which provided a horizontal living space more in keeping with seventeenth-century requirements. Examples are Patrick Sarsfield's residence at Lucan, County Dublin, Lord Clare's at Carrigaholt, County Clare, Nicholas Purcell's at Loughmoe and Thomas Butler's at Kilcash, both in County Tipperary. Some Jacobite officers from the wealthiest families lived in substantial seventeenth-century houses, such as Clanricard's at Portumna, County Galway, Lieutenant Colonel Walter Butler's at Munphin, County Wexford, Kingsland's at Turvey, County Dublin, Westmeath's at Clonyn, County Westmeath, Gormanston's in County Meath, Clancarty's at Macroom, County Cork, and Captains John and Terence MacCoghlan's family home at Kilcolgan, King's County. The Luttrells' mansion house at Luttrellstown, County Dublin, had twelve chimneys, out-offices, a malthouse, a barn and stables, all slated. The demesne included pleasure grounds, ornamental plantations, a garden, three orchards, corn and cloth mills, as well as a salmon weir on the adjoining river Liffey. Tyrconnell owned Carton, County Kildare, 'a very fine house with all manner of convenient offices and gardens'. However, it seems to have been largely lived in by his nephew, while he resided at Dublin Castle, the viceregal lodge at Chapelizod and on his 9,500-acre estate at Talbotstown, County Wicklow. Dublin had trebled in size during Charles II's reign, and merchants like Sir Michael Creagh and Richard Fagan were substantial property owners in the city. Timber or half-timber houses were common in most towns, but Thomas Phillips's prospects of Galway and Limerick show many tall, stone buildings with gable roofs, the dwellings and shops of the cities' merchant class. Town suburbs contained the cabins of the urban poor.[27]

Commentators remarked on the poverty of the ordinary Irish people, who were dependent on the vagaries of agriculture. Piers thought that if 'the poor farmer ... be able to pay his rent and live, he thinks himself happy and rich'. In Kildare the diet of the ordinary people was reported to be 'very mean and sparing, consisting of milk, roots and coarse unsavoury bread; their lodging and habit proportionable'. But levels of poverty differed: Petty estimated that as much as half the population fell below agricultural-tenant level and were no more than day labourers – 'scullogues' – with 'no pretence to land [who] live upon milk, potatoes and weeds'. Yet he acknowledged a third of the Irish cabins possessed a small horse, which was some criterion of wealth. Another

---

[27] Loeber, *Irish houses and castles,* passim; *Art and architecture of Ireland,* pp 329–44 and passim; Lenihan, *Last cavalier,* pp 69–70; Cullen, *Life in Ireland,* p. 66; Phillips maps, 28 & 36; Ó Dálaigh et al., 'Edenvale castle survey', p. 49; Ball, *Dublin* (part 4), p. 12.

observer wrote that the 'commonalty among the Irish fare very hard, and live mostly upon potatoes, parsnips, cabbage, beans, peas, barley and oat-bread, sour thick milk, or butter-milk; and rarely eat a bit of flesh, butter, eggs, or cheese'. Much of the housing of farmers and labourers was poor and often shared with their animals. In Westmeath, the ordinary people lived 'scattered in small villages, which consist mostly of poor small cottages'. These cabins were built of muddy clay or stone, with earthen floors and thatched roofs, many of the humblest lacking even chimneys or windows. In Ulster, Scottish immigration pushed the native Irish into marginal lands. There, and to a lesser extent elsewhere, there was a tradition of transhumance. In rural Munster, d'Esgrigny reported that whole families lived in congested straw-roofed huts, without a bed or chimney. But there were many gradations, with better housing for those of means. A survey of forfeited lands in Louth and Meath in 1700 showed cabins to be predominant, but it distinguished those that were 'tolerable' or 'good' from others that were 'small' or 'very bad'. There were numerous references to good farm houses, many of stone or even brick, to roofs that were slated as well as thatched, and to adjoining barns, stables, outhouses, gardens and orchards. Enclosure, regarded as a necessary improvement in the growing market economy, had started, but even in the east of the island, it was still largely limited to cornfields and meadows. As a rule, the extent of grazing rights on commonage or of ploughland share was proportionate to the amount of rent a tenant paid.[28]

BELIEFS

Motives for enlistment

Soldiers do not necessarily adopt an intellectual perspective. Nevertheless, opinions formulated by thinkers underpinned popular orthodoxy, which in turn permeated the Irish Jacobite army. The force had at its core a set of broad objectives, grounded on the hopes and principles of its leadership and personnel, of which all ranks must have had some awareness. These war aims were succinctly stated by Saint-Ruth in a speech he allegedly made to the army on the eve of the battle of Aughrim:

> You are not mercenary soldiers, you do not fight for your pay, but for your lives, your wives, your children, your liberties, your country, your

---

[28] Piers, 'Westmeath', p. 60; 'Account of Co. Kildare in 1682', p. 344; *F-I corr.*, i, pp 220, 348; *A new history of Ireland*, iii, p. 465; *Ireland's lamentation*, p. 5; Horner & Loeber, 'Landscape in transition', passim; Horner, 'Landscape of the Pale', pp 21–2.

estates; and to restore the most pious of kings to his throne, but above all for the propagation of the holy faith and the subversion of heresy.

The motivating beliefs and attitudes of the Jacobite war effort are spelled out in more depth by the acts of the Irish parliament of 1689, an assembly of which two-thirds of the commons and most of the attending peers were also army officers. Added to this are the principal Jacobite accounts of the war, three written by army officers: Charles O'Kelly, John Stevens and the Plunkett author of the *Jacobite narrative*. Lord Riverston, likely author of the fourth, was the brother and uncle of officers, while exiled army veterans in Saint-Germain probably had an input in the compilation of King James's memoirs for the period. Correspondence from the French in Ireland also throws light on Irish attitudes of the time. The several Jacobite war aims were of course closely interrelated. It must also be recognized, *pace* Saint-Ruth, that as much as for their commitment to a great cause, soldiers also enlisted for such mundane reasons as the need for a career, for pay and subsistence, for adventure, from a sense of duty, to follow a leader, to conform, to make a new life, or very probably for a variety of these reasons. Many Irish soldiers were accompanied by their families, especially after the army fell back to the west of Ireland after the Boyne, so that an added motivation was the desire to protect wives and children from molestation, privation or death. O'Kelly accounted the Irish a most warlike nation. The losses of the Catholic gentry in the century preceding the war left them with a strong sense of grievance, but they remained ready, eager and sufficiently robust to seize the opportunity for redress when it came. After James's accession, the ease with which an alternative Catholic regime emerged to run their country after decades of exclusion was remarkable. Further proof of their community's vitality and resilience was the ensuing three-year struggle they sustained against the powerful Williamite army. Of course, the Williamite outlawry of more than 2,000 prominent Jacobites compounded their opposition to the new regime.[29]

King James's legitimacy

King James's claim to reign was based on the divine right of hereditary succession, which could neither be challenged or renounced. Irish Jacobites shared with their British counterparts the belief that King James, their legitimate monarch, had been expelled on account of his Catholic religion by

---

29 Story, *Continuation*, p. 124; *F-I corr.*, ii, p. 500; O'Kelly, pp 13–14, 158; Simms, *Jacobite Ireland*, pp 283–4.

his disloyal English subjects, whose obligation of loyalty had been corrupted by their Protestantism. This view was affirmed by the Irish parliament, which declared James the legitimate sovereign of the three kingdoms 'by lawful right of descent', adding that his sovereignty came from God, and was incapable of being renounced by parliament or people. The parliament accordingly condemned William's 'horrid usurpation' and his supporters' 'unparalleled treason and perfidiousness'. The author of the *Jacobite narrative* concurred, holding that it was long established in Ireland that the king succeeded by birth and was not deposable by the people upon any cause or quarrel. It followed that the clear duty of the Irish Catholics was to take up arms, whatever the cost, for James's restoration. Their faith, he argued, imposed this obligation, regardless of injuries done to them by the king and of the king's religious belief (he had in mind the Protestant Charles II). The tenet that subjects owed a duty of loyalty to their king in temporal matters, regardless of religious difference, had become the orthodox view of Irish Catholics, including churchmen, qualified only by the requirement of not acting contrary to their faith. Old English Catholics had long subscribed to the view that it was perfectly possible for Catholics to be loyal subjects of a Protestant king. It was indeed their only *modus vivendi*, however uneasily it sat with the contemporary European orthodoxy of religious conformity. Their stated objective in 1641 had been 'to fight for our prince in defence of his crown and royal prerogatives'. The general synod of Catholic clergy, convened in Dublin in 1666, had gone so far as to explicitly reject papal authority in civil and temporal affairs. This was a gallican rather than an ultramontane position, which James's Catholicism made much easier to accept in 1689, but perhaps by then it was also linked to the French alliance and to the failure of successive popes to offer support to James, and by extension to his Irish supporters.[30]

The *Jacobite narrative* accepted James's attempt to use Ireland as a stepping stone for his restoration in Britain, although dubious as to the likelihood of its success. For Riverston, the English noblemen, who swore fresh oaths of loyalty to William in breach of those they had already sworn to James, were a 'cohort of perjurers', while the Irish took up arms for 'fixing in its place the wobbling crown'. During the seventeenth century the Gaelic Irish too had moved to a not-dissimilar conciliatory attitude towards the crown. Colonel Charles O'Kelly, spokesman for a more Gaelic point of view, opined that the Irish, who 'had always stood by the royal cause with unshaken fidelity', now committed all the power of their kingdom to restore James to his throne or perish in the

---

30 *Acts of James II's parliament*, pp 1–6; Ó Buachalla, 'James our true king', passim; *JN*, pp 37, 39–40, 183–4; Ohlmeyer (ed.), *Political thought*, pp 21–6.

attempt. Another spokesman for Gaelic Ireland, the west Munster poet Dáibhí Ó Bruadair, wrote a fulsome panegyric on the accession of James, describing him as 'the bright star of royalty that has risen under God to succour us', and underscoring his legitimacy to rule the Irish by calling him the high king who comes from the true blood of Corc (Corc mac Luigthig, legendary fourth-century king of Munster). In another poem, he offered 'a hundred thanks to God' for James's public expression of Catholicism by his attendance at Mass, for his arming of the Irish and his anticipated overthrow of the low-bred, arrogant New English settlers. Writing in the early eighteenth century, the poet Aogán Ó Rathaille still protested that the knave (William) had taken the game from the rightful king (James). For the earnest English officer, Captain Stevens, James was the best of princes, forced to flee by the most general and barbarous rebellion the world had seen. Stevens cast himself as one of 'the small remainder of King James's loyal subjects, those few thousands who had not bowed their knees to Baal, [who] either in their persons or at least in their wishes, hastened to follow ... his most sacred majesty', with no other thoughts than their duty and love of their sovereign. He conceived no greater honour than to be 'seen and known as a signal sufferer for my religion, my king, for justice and loyalty'. While many 'truly honourable gentlemen' shared his motives, he wrote that other 'libertines' followed James in the hope of disguising or reversing the misfortunes brought upon them in Britain by their indebtedness, crimes and scandalous lives. In fact, the influx of English and Scots into the Irish army were largely Catholic officers purged by William. Many were long-term professional soldiers, undoubtedly loyal to James, but also in need of rebuilding their careers. Career prospects attracted French officers to serve in Ireland. They gained a lift in rank, or for cadets a commission, the opportunity to enlarge their professional experience and to please their government. However, some who came as volunteers, rather than under orders, d'Avaux rated good-for-nothings. The ambassador was sceptical about Irish loyalty to King James, stressing that it was only maintained by the 'zeal and firmness' of Tyrconnell.[31]

Kingdom or colony

Both O'Kelly and the author of the *Jacobite narrative* share a strong sense of Irish history and identity. The constitutional issues really turned on whether Ireland was a separate kingdom or an English colony. The *Jacobite narrative*

---

[31] *JN*, p. 47; *Poema*, pp 146, 342; O'Kelly, pp 11, 18; *Ó Bruadair*, iii, pp 77–94, 95–111; Dunne, 'Gaelic response', p. 29; *Stevens*, pp 3, 27, 51, 57–8; *d'Avaux*, pp 88, 525.

had no doubt that the former was the case. Its author met the argument that Ireland was obliged to follow England, the principal kingdom, in owning or disowning the kings of the united monarchy by contending that Ireland was not ruled by the behaviour of the English, but a distinct realm, governed by a viceroy appointed by the king, and with its own parliament, laws and judiciary. In the absence of a common legitimate king, England had no more right in Ireland than France or Spain. This touched on the question of Irish independence, including the long-running issue of whether the English parliament had the right to legislate for Ireland, which had been earlier challenged by the lawyers, Patrick Darcy, Sir Richard Bolton and Sir William Domville, and was to resurface again in the late 1690s in the arguments of Domville's son-in-law, William Molyneux. The 1689 Dublin parliament firmly declared that Ireland was a distinct kingdom from England, and that no acts of the English parliament were binding in Ireland, unless also made into law by an Irish parliament. James reluctantly acquiesced to this declaratory act, which also repudiated the jurisdiction of the English courts, including the house of lords, in Ireland. However, he blocked the achievement of full legislative independence by successfully resisting a companion bill to repeal Poynings' law, which vested the king and the English privy council with the right to allow an Irish parliament to be held and to approve in advance its proposed legislation. The Irish, it was said, regarded this as 'the greatest sign and means of their subjection to England', but it did not impact on the 1689 parliament as the king was present in person.[32]

The *Jacobite narrative*'s author put forward a much more radical vision of Irish independence which, while written some years later, may well reflect ideas that were current during the war. He argued that Ireland should be made into a powerful Catholic nation that could provide the monarchy with a means of controlling the rebellious English. To this end, he argued for complete legislative independence, the restoration of confiscated estates, and the permanent appointment of Irish Catholics to the office of viceroy and to the other senior positions in government and the army. Ireland should maintain a standing army of 8,000 Catholics and a fleet of twenty-four warships, supplemented by a Catholic militia. A mint should be established in Dublin, and Irish merchants allowed full freedom of trade. Implementation of this policy would have transformed Ireland's status from being a quasi-colony to something akin to a modern British commonwealth state. A refinement of this

---

32 O'Kelly, p. 21 *et seq.*; *JN*, pp 5–8, 182–5; Simms, *Colonial nationalism*, passim; Clarke, 'Patrick Darcy', pp 35–55; 'Domville, 'That great question' (ed. Kelly), pp 17–72; Simms, 'Jacobite parliament', pp 69–71; *Acts of James II's parliament*, pp 54–7; King, p. 173; *James II*, ii, p. 461.

view was attributed to Balldearg O'Donnell, whose design, it was said, was to make Ireland a Gaelic kingdom upon an equal footing with England.[33]

Other radical views were in circulation before and during the war. Sheridan, Tyrconnell's hostile secretary, reported him as saying in 1687 that rather than suffer as slaves to England in the event of a Protestant succession, the Irish should set up a king of their own and put themselves under the protection of France, adding that he believed all the men of sense and quality were of the same view. Such ideas echoed the views of the Jesuit Conor O'Mahony, promulgated in his *Disputatio apologetica* published in 1645, which had won no support from the confederate Catholics at that time. It has been suggested that prior to Mary of Modena's pregnancy, James and some of his Catholic courtiers may have been sympathetic to future Irish independence as a means of providing a Catholic refuge from a Protestant succession. Soon after his arrival, d'Avaux reported that had Tyrconnell negotiated seriously with William or had James failed to come to Ireland, the Irish would have sought to place themselves under Louis's protection rather than submit to the new regime in England.[34]

The Boyne defeat and the king's precipitate abandonment of his army and supporters left the Irish very disillusioned with James. Lord Clare wrote to Louvois that the king should spend the rest of his days in prayer, rather than commanding armies or governing a state. He added that all Catholics of sense and spirit, save for a few lawyers, were determined to continue resistance, and maintained there was broad support for the proposal to cede the kingdom to France. While Tyrconnell was aware of this and had promised to raise the matter with James, Clare doubted his assurances of having done so. In fact, according to O'Kelly, on his arrival at Saint-Germain in late 1690 Tyrconnell won favour with the English courtiers, who were suspicious of French intentions, by stressing his own Old English background, declaring his commitment to the English interest in Ireland and affirming his opposition to any separation of Ireland from the English crown 'as the Irish would have it'. After the successful defence of Limerick, the army deputation sent to France to seek further aid and Tyrconnell's dismissal from his military command was an extension of the thinking that the regime that led the Irish Catholics into the war was of little further value to protect their interests. The deputation managed to secure an audience with King Louis, but felt inhibited by James's presence from a frank exposition of their view. The proposal that Ireland should become a French protectorate was unrealistic and does not appear to

---

33 *JN*, pp 39–40; *James II*, ii, p. 461.   34 'Sheridan's narrative', pp 8–9; Ó'hAnnracháin, 'Political ideology and Catholicism', pp 159–67; Miller, 'Tyrconnell & James II', pp 821–2; *d'Avaux*, p. 50.

have been seriously entertained by Louis. However, in the second half of the war the Irish focus shifted from the restoration of James to their own survival with French support. De Tessé reported in 1691 that by then they thought much more of making war for their own interest than for that of King James.[35]

Defence of country

The defence of their country against English invasion and conquest was a common factor in Irish thinking. Riverston wrote of Irishmen 'taking up arms to prevent their nation's (*patriae*) fall'. The *Jacobite narrative* referred to 'the old [British] design of ruining the Catholic nation of Ireland' and the 'gallant ardour' of the Irish Catholics in standing against England, Scotland, 'the violent Protestants of Ireland' and their various international allies. O'Kelly stressed his love for Ireland and his affliction at its conquest, arguing that the generality of the Irish wanted neither resolution nor courage to defend their dear country. There is plenty of evidence of the animosity the Irish Jacobites, both Gaelic Irish and Old English, bore towards the English. The 'English Protestant' author of *Ireland's lamentation* thought that the Irish would expose themselves to any misery to destroy the English, such was their 'natural aversion' for them. D'Avaux observed that the Irish were irreconcilable enemies of the English and, given the chance, would have slaughtered all the English in Ireland. Stevens too noted the suspicion and hatred of the Irish for the English. For O'Kelly, the English were the sworn enemies of the Irish, determined to reduce them to bondage or even to extirpate them 'root and branch'. Colonel Thomas Butler, the great duke of Ormond's grand-nephew, wrote that the Irish were 'quite unable to endure the yoke of the English ... who will not fail to break their word, so hostile are they to this nation'. Particular animosity was directed towards the New English settlers. Ó Bruadair expressed delight at their discomfiture under the Jacobite regime, writing that 'few of that gang have ever deserved the affection or love of my countrymen', and they were lambasted in the *Jacobite narrative* as 'a party of rascals ... murderers of harmless people ... atheists in their living ... [and] pitiful, mean men in their extraction'. Even Stevens accepted the commonly held view that the 'Oliverian English party' sought 'always to oppress and, if possible, exterminate' the Irish. De Tessé's opinion, based on conversations with Irish officers, was that their objective was to expel the English from Ireland so they would be left to enjoy its benefits alone. The Williamite lords

---

35 *F-I corr.*, ii, p. 412; iii, pp 136–9; *Ireland's lamentation*, p. 6; *d'Avaux*, p. 88; O'Kelly, pp 79, 91–5; *Poema*, pp 204 and note 6, 254.

justices thought that 'the Irish papists do every day show that they want nothing but an opportunity to be revenged upon the British inhabitants'. One of the factors reportedly encouraging the Irish to continue resistance after Aughrim was their doubt that any peace settlement would be honoured.[36]

Recovery of land

Central to the Irish Catholic interest was the restoration of their fortunes by reversing the Cromwellian confiscation and overthrowing the subsequent post-restoration land settlement. This upheaval had reduced the number of Catholic landowners by more than 5,000 to less than 1,500, and contracted their share of land from 6 million to 2.6 million acres. To some extent the impact of the settlement was mitigated at local level by tenancies and other *modi vivendi*, but nevertheless the loss, especially to the Old English, was severe and their sense of grievance correspondingly acute. The *Jacobite narrative* called the settlement 'a notorious injustice' and 'the work of iniquity'. Tyrconnell's political strength arose from his commitment to the settlement's overthrow, and the perception that his influence with James would further its accomplishment. But prior to the war, progress had been disappointingly slow. Even after James came to Ireland, his English supporters regarded repeal of the settlement as 'hugely prejudicial to his interest'. O'Kelly, Riverston and the author of the *Jacobite narrative* all agreed that the king, 'panting to grant a pardon undeserved', was over indulgent to the Protestants, who would of course be the main losers in any reversal of the settlement. However, with the summoning of parliament a reluctant James was compelled to accede to repeal, his memoirs relating that he was 'as good as told underhand that if he consented not to it, the whole [Irish Catholic] nation would desert him'. The formal statement of parliament's position was its threat to withhold consent to the act of supply intended to finance for the war. These events increased the growing disenchantment between James and his Irish supporters.[37]

Repeal of the settlement also created division among the Irish. 'New interest' men – Catholic purchasers and others in possession of confiscated land – opposed the repeal because of the threat it posed to their properties, an attitude that in time made them sympathetic to an accommodation with the Williamites, provided they could retain their acquisitions. In an effort to meet their objections, parliament made provision for their compensation from land

---

36 *Poema*, p. 156; *JN*, p. 4; O'Kelly, pp 5–6, 71, 107; *d'Avaux*, pp 50–1; *Stevens*, pp 68, 140; *Danish force*, p. 99; *F-I corr.*, ii, p. 412; *CSPD 1690–1*, p. 231; Clarke corr., nos 995–6.   37 McKenny, 'Restoration land settlement', p. 40; *JN*, pp 10, 35, 63; *Poema*, p. 204; O'Kelly, pp 33–6; *James II*,

confiscated from more than 2,000 Williamite Protestant supporters that were outlawed. Furthermore, as a Gaelic supporter of Balldearg O'Donnell observed, the act of repeal disregarded the interests of proprietors, chiefly in Ulster, who had lost their estates prior to 1641. Thus, while the repeal achieved a central objective of most Jacobite supporters, it also planted seeds of division that military setbacks brought to the surface. The ten-week parliamentary session distracted attention from the war effort against Derry and Enniskillen. Many officers deserted their commands to attend parliament or enter into occupation of their old family estates, although formal legal steps to restore properties to their original owners were deferred to the end of the war. For the 5,000 dispossessed Catholic landowners, their descendants and dependants, who stood to benefit from the repeal legislation, full legal restoration to their former estates was clearly dependent on military success. After the Boyne, the Williamite general Würtemburg reported the Irish as saying openly they were fighting not for King James, nor for the popish religion, but for their estates. Certainly, issues relating to land ownership, be they retention or recovery, were central to Irish objectives in the war.[38]

Restoration of Catholicism

The Irish Jacobites sought the restoration of the Catholic church to its former pre-eminence. The counter-reformation had won the battle for the allegiance of both the Old English and Gaelic Irish inhabitants of Ireland, whose 'indomitable constancy' to Catholicism differentiated them from the hated New English Protestants, but also subjected them to considerable disabilities. James's accession promised a better future. Jacobite writers laid great stress on the faith they shared with the king, deposed by the English 'for no fault ... but the Catholic religion'. This overcame earlier reservations surrounding the question of Catholic loyalty to a Protestant king. Riverston praised his brother, Brigadier William Nugent, for taking up arms 'to keep ... thy religion safe'. A Protestant commentator called the Irish gentry 'the most zealous Roman Catholics in the world'; a judgement echoed by Charles O'Kelly in reference to the population as a whole, which he said resolved to stand by James because he professed their religion and supported its traditional rites. He forecast that any submission to the Williamites would have the 'fatal consequence' of the suppression of Catholicism in Ireland. Ó Bruadair identified faith with national consciousness by declaring that 'everyone known as a tried and proved

---

ii, pp 360–1; *Stevens*, p. 70.   **38** *Poema*, p. 228; *d'Avaux*, pp 192–3, 215, 738–9; *Acts of James II's parliament*, pp 22, 29–31; 'O'Donnells in exile', p. 53; *Danish force*, p. 76.

Irishman' was 'in faith without question a Catholic'. He noted with approval how James's accession had brought protection and joy to the Catholic clergy, and that the soldiers were now marching to Mass. An insight into the depth and sincerity of Catholic belief is found in Lord Kilmallock's injunction to his wife, while he campaigned. She was to have 'a Mass said to the Holy Ghost daily, desiring the exaltation and maintaining of the Roman Catholic church, and our good return with victory ... I doubt not but God Almighty will help us.' In O'Kelly's view, the fear that defeat would lead to their religion being suppressed was one of the factors that sustained Irish resistance for so long. Many Jacobite officers had priests and nuns among their siblings, creating a close relationship between the Catholic clergy, secular and regular, and the Jacobite elite. The clergy were very influential: a Protestant writer asserted that 'from the highest to the lowest', Irish Catholics believed it was 'damnation to disobey the priests, and (as all other papists do) meritorious to destroy all Protestants by every sort of artifice'.[39]

The position of the 1,600 or so Irish Catholic clergy gradually improved after James's accession in 1685. Bishops and priests wore clerical dress in public, and regulars their habits. Public chapels were opened, and in some places ancient monasteries were repaired or new religious houses constructed. Riverston prayed 'that heathen error may to faith of old give way', and 'that the shrines of yore be free for former clergy'. Catholics replaced Protestants as chaplains in the army. In expectation of a full restoration of their status and wealth, the clergy were among the most enthusiastic of James's supporters. They were a unifying force, and they also played an important recruiting and morale-raising role in the army. However, James's anxiety to placate English public opinion prevented a full restoration to their pre-reformation position. As the *Jacobite narrative* put it, the king 'was infatuated with this rotten principle: provoke not your Protestant subjects'. Consequently, he resisted the substitution of a Catholic for a Protestant church establishment, although he left vacancies in Protestant bishoprics and other Church of Ireland livings unfilled and diverted their revenues to the crown. The king authorized an annual payment to twelve Catholic bishops. However, it was Protestant, not Catholic bishops that were summoned to the 1689 parliament, where the religious benefits conceded to Catholics were limited to acts for liberty of conscience and the transfer of tithes and other ecclesiastical dues paid by Catholics to the support of their own clergy. In O'Kelly's view, one of the

---

39 Ó hAnnracháin, 'Political ideology and Catholicism', pp 155–75; *Poema*, p. 414; *JN*, p. 38; O'Kelly, pp 18, 23, 66, 159; *Ireland's lamentation*, p. 6; *Ó Bruadair*, iii, pp 109, 129; Simms, 'Kilmallock letters', p. 138; *PI*, i, p. 247; 'Survey of Catholic estates', p. 101; *DIB*, vol. 9, pp 547–8.

reasons the Irish supported James was the expectation that he would restore the churches to the Catholic clergy. James prohibited this, although in practice from early in 1689 many churches were seized. The author of the *Jacobite narrative* took the view that the Irish negotiators of the Limerick surrender articles should have insisted on securing the Catholic bishops' right to exercise their authority and freedom for Catholics to practice their religion in chapels and houses. Their failure on both counts, O'Kelly wrote, was beyond his comprehension.[40]

Will to resist

Even after the Boyne, where the Jacobites felt the army had not been tested, many may have believed that although James's restoration could not be realized through Ireland, their other war aims were still achievable with the backing of France. Fumeron reported widespread disappointment when no French general or troops accompanied Tyrconnell to Ireland in early 1691. The troops, he said, then wanted Sarsfield as their commander, and had no faith in Tyrconnell as their military leader. After the Aughrim defeat, it was clear, as Fumeron put it, that the heart was gone out of the Irish; all that would persuade them to continue the struggle was the early arrival of a fleet with troops, arms and *matériel* from France. Their lack of pay was a demoralizing factor. Many now felt that their struggle to resist invasion and conquest would not succeed. Little progress had been made to restore the Catholic church to what they believed to be its proper place. Their lost estates would not be recovered and the pre-war Jacobite landowners were looking to do a deal for their own survival.[41]

Nevertheless, the army fought on, as armies will, once they are at war. When hostilities begin and soldiers become involved in the business of war, it is common to most armies for broader objectives to give way to more everyday motivating factors, such as loyalty to comrades, unit pride, personal honour, respect for commanders, self-preservation, observance of military discipline, fear of the severe penalties for desertion, and the ambition to achieve military success with its accompanying rewards, and pay. As well as the broad objectives outlined above, these mundane factors must also have been in play in the Jacobite army, sustaining its discipline and order, and bolstering its will to resist until the final days of the war.

40 O'Kelly, pp 15, 107, 159; Millett, *Survival and reorganization*, pp 30, 59–61; *JN*, pp 63, 177; *Acts of James II's parliament*, pp 19–20, 59–60; *Proclamations*, pp 138–9.   **41** *F-I corr.*, ii, pp 211–12, 385, 400, 489.

CHAPTER 13

The army's fate

THE JACOBITE ARMY'S active role in Ireland ended with the articles of Limerick, signed on 3 October 1691. However, the army was quickly reconstituted in France, nominally as King James's army, until 1698. Thereafter, although fully integrated into the French army, and later into that of Spain, the Irish regiments continued to be officered by Irishmen by birth or descent and to recruit as far as possible in Ireland. They stressed their Irish origins and character, and maintained a tradition of loyalty to the Stuarts.

The surrender terms

By early 1691, the successful Jacobite defence of 'fortress Connacht' had brought about a softening of the hardline approach of William's earlier Finglas declaration. Bentinck, William's closest adviser, and Ginkel, both Dutchmen, were particularly anxious to end the war in Ireland to enable their army's redeployment to Flanders. In February Ginkel issued a conciliatory declaration offering 'reasonable terms' to those who submitted. This was vague and met with little immediate response, but after the Jacobite defeat at Athlone, a more concrete offer was made in a proclamation of the Williamite lords justices promising pardon to officers who surrendered their garrisons or brought over a considerable portion of the troops under their command. The offer guaranteed restoration of the estates of those who submitted, and included a commitment that the sovereigns would 'endeavour ... to preserve them from any disturbance upon the account of their religion'. Its terms extended to those civilian inhabitants of Limerick and Galway who were instrumental in securing the surrender of those places. Many leading Galway citizens were supporters of the Jacobite peace party and had no appetite for further resistance. The favourable terms that Galway secured when it surrendered after Aughrim were indicative of Ginkel's anxiety to end hostilities, which was further signalled by the similar terms given to the garrison of Inishbofin off the west coast and by the extension of the Galway articles to the Sligo garrison in mid-September. The Galway articles also laid the foundation for the subsequent articles of Limerick.[1]

[1] *F-I corr.*, ii, pp 385–6, 401–2, 414, 503, 506, 522; *Proclamations*, pp 250–5; Story, *Continuation*,

It was a surprise to everyone that the leading role in the Limerick negotiations was taken by Sarsfield, for so long the principal figure in the militant Jacobite resistance party, who was considered 'the last man to hearken to a treaty'. At the outset, he made it clear that his chief concern was for the Jacobite soldiers to 'go and serve where they would' (by which he meant France). Ginkel considered the military terms to be his responsibility, even if wider than usual, and readily agreed to Sarsfield's precondition, even consenting at Fumeron's insistence to supply fifty ships for the necessary transport, and another twenty if needed. Included in the terms were the officers and soldiers in territory still under Jacobite control, together with the Sligo garrison and the rapparees. Alternatively, under the civil articles, soldiers of whatever rank from these groups could opt to remain in Ireland, peaceably retaining their pre-war estates (if they had any), provided they swore an oath of allegiance to William and Mary. This concession did not extend to those who had been killed or captured. Nor, apart from the Galway and Inishbofin garrisons, did it extend to those who had already submitted. The military terms were signed by the three remaining French generals, together with Sarsfield, Mark Talbot, Wauchope, Galmoy and Nicholas Purcell.[2]

Offers and counter-offers

Once the articles were signed, it became the policy of Sarsfield and the French generals to persuade as many of the Irish army as possible to go to France. As inevitably this would lead to their deployment with Louis XIV's forces against the grand alliance, Ginkel was equally determined to dissuade as many as he could from doing so. Sarsfield and Wauchope made speeches to the Limerick garrison, assuring them that if they went to France, they would retain their rank, receive their pay and could expect to be landed in England or Ireland as part of a large invasion force in 1692. This was backed up by sermons from the priests, blessings from the bishops and a generous issue of brandy. The regiments of the Limerick garrison, joined by the cavalry and dragoons, were then drawn up on the Clare side of Limerick (at least 14,000-strong, according to Story) where they were viewed by Ginkel and the Williamite lords justices. Colonel Henry Withers, the Williamite adjutant general, addressed them on the advantages of staying in Ireland, offering the options of serving in the Williamite army or returning home under a further protection promised by Ginkel in a simultaneous proclamation. Support for the Williamite offer came from Henry Luttrell, Robert Clifford and Edward Wilson, all freshly released

pp 53, 117–20, 220. **2** O'Kelly, p. 155; Story, *Continuation*, pp 239–51; *F-I corr.*, ii, p. 516; Simms, 'Treaty', p. 209 and passim; Kinsella, *Catholic survival*, pp 249, 255.

from captivity at Ginkel's insistence, and also from Viscount Iveagh and Nicholas Purcell, who were averse to going to France. Wilson, in a petition for payment, claimed to have brought over his own regiment and several thousand others by representing 'the difference between the benignity of English government and the slavery of France'. Of the soldiers who opted to remain in Ireland, just over a thousand were mustered after the Limerick review, although Story claimed that double that number had already departed for home, and that others deserted *en route* to the transport ships. The roads to Ulster were clogged with returning creaghts, many probably ex-combatants, accompanied by their livestock. Twenty-two Jacobite regiments with 'scarce a hundred men in each' were disbanded by the Williamites in January 1692. Some of the soldiers were recruited into Williamite regiments, until orders were given for their expulsion. The remnants of Balldearg O'Donnell's forces were sent under Iveagh to serve the emperor in Hungary, where they died in large numbers.[3]

The terms of surrender held most attraction for Jacobites with estates, the majority of whom chose to remain in Ireland. Provided they submitted to William and Mary, under the Galway and Limerick articles they were entitled to pardon and restoration if they had been outlawed; or to an amnesty and retention of their properties if not. Story describes Henry Luttrell, Clifford and 'a great many of the Irish gentry going towards Dublin' to assert their claims. Between 1692 and 1699 almost 1,300 adjudications were made, of which nearly all were favourable. Approximately 450 of the successful claimants were ex-army officers, including a dozen peers. Fumeron observed that very few people of quality or property were going to France, although a small number of leading Jacobite landowners entitled to the benefit of the surrender articles did choose to emigrate. They included Sarsfield, Galmoy, Simon Luttrell, Sir Richard Nagle, and Sir Maurice Eustace. Sarsfield's estate reverted to his niece, and Simon Luttrell's to his brother, Henry. However, the bulk of the emigrant officers were men without prospects in Ireland, either because they fell outside the Limerick and Galway articles or had no estate to which to return. Possibly financial difficulties occasioned by the war may have motivated some. The military life offered employment for those who saw no future in Williamite Ireland: after Aughrim, the colonels promoted a large number of officers probably to improve post-war career prospects as much as to fill vacancies. But less self-serving motives for choosing migration cannot be discounted. These included commitment to James's restoration, religious affiliation, hostility to the English and to the British settlers in Ireland, loyalty

---

3 Story, *Continuation*, pp 259–60, 263, 266, 270–1, 281, 295–8; *F-I corr.*, ii, p. 520; *CSPD 1691–2*,

to Sarsfield and their superior officers and a soldierly reluctance to concede defeat, especially when they were offered the opportunity to carry on the struggle elsewhere. These motives would also have influenced the rank and file. But every day, the French generals reported, officers and soldiers were changing their minds.[4]

Re-forming the army in France

A return of 8 October by Commissary Archbold of thirty-four infantry regiments listed 9,258 men who had opted to serve in France. The strongest contingents were in the footguards and the Ulster regiments. The list excluded another nine infantry regiments Archbold had not reviewed, together with all the cavalry and dragoons. The arrival of the French fleet to the mouth of the Shannon at the end of October provided transport to France for 5,600 officers and men together with more than a thousand dependants and servants. The remainder embarked from Cork in December on the ships provided by Ginkel. Sarsfield and the French *commissaire*, Methelet, supervised the Cork operation. Ginkel was hesitant about transporting dependants, but on receipt of a strong representation from Sarsfield he conceded the point. In all, perhaps 4,000 women and children embarked, although in distressing circumstances many others were left behind, especially the families of the rank and file. Louis XIV had greatly reduced the number of women accompanying his army to an average of about fifteen per regiment. The French officials were nonplussed by the number of non-combatants arriving from Ireland. Bouridal, the *commissaire ordonnateur* at Brest, complained of 'the sheer number of women, girls, children and servants; there are families of ten and twelve, of which the head is a lieutenant or supernumerary. Ordinary soldiers come with their wives and four or five children, whom their pay cannot support.' It is estimated that 42 per cent of the Jacobite refugees were women. It all added to the general disorder. Many families eventually settled in Saint-Germain or in Paris, but others followed the regiments in which their breadwinners served, as they had done in Ireland. In the 1690s more than a thousand of those who went to France were outlawed in Ireland 'for high treason ... committed in parts beyond the seas', although for most, it was of little practical consequence. A handful of exiles managed subsequently to obtain pardons and were able to return to Ireland. They included Lord Slane, Sir Michael Creagh and Richard Bellew. All three became Protestants, but Bellew alone recovered his estate.[5]

p. 196; *Finch MSS*, iv, p. 246.   **4** Simms, *Confiscation*, pp 45–54; *F-I corr.*, ii, pp 522, 544; *AH*, 22, pp 89–135, 144–5, 85.   **5** *F-I corr.*, ii, pp 445, 475, 448, 509–10, 544; O'Kelly, pp 157–8; Story, *Continuation*, p. 292; Simms, *Jacobite Ireland*, p. 259; *AH*, 22, pp 66–89; Rowlands, *Army*

A Williamite estimate put the total number who opted to go to France after the surrender of Limerick at 12,000, and this figure is replicated (and perhaps copied) by the author of the *Jacobite narrative*. Fumeron, however, who was in a better position to know and not given to exaggeration, estimated the figure at more than 15,000. This would have included Jacobite troops from outlying garrisons, not present at the Limerick review. The 14,000 personnel of James's army in France, with the addition of 600 or so supernumerary officers attached to his regiments and the 600 reinforcements sent to the Mountcashel Brigade, strongly supports Fumeron's estimate, and modern scholars tend to concur with this figure. The 15,000 soldiers of the 1691 exodus were of course in addition to the 5,387 brought to France by Mountcashel in 1690. Thus, in 1690–2, the Irish Jacobite army increased King Louis's military strength by more than 20,000 men. Those that came at the end of the war were in poor condition, ill-armed and clothed only in rags when they arrived in Brest and the other Breton ports. Many were sick. Their reception posed considerable difficulties for the authorities. Barbezieux, Louvois's son and successor as war minister, ordered them to be clothed and paid. The Irish were billeted in the towns and villages adjacent to the ports, while clothing, shoes and hats were found for them. All order had been lost in the confusion of embarkation, and discipline was poor among both officers and men. Bouridal complained they sold the shirts he had given them, sold or simply abandoned their muskets and had to be forced to vacate their billets in the towns and peasants' houses. Nevertheless, he noted their pride, and felt their morale would improve by being properly clothed. He reported the presence of a large number of fine young men and some veterans, whom he thought four months' training could form into good infantry, as well as into two good cavalry regiments. He rated the 200 horseguards the equal of the best troop in King Louis's own household cavalry. D'Usson shared this view, maintaining that the cavalry in particular had been good soldiers in Ireland and could readily be made so again. He stressed the need to respect local backgrounds in re-forming units.[6]

The three existing regiments of Mountcashel, Dillon and Clare – *les anciennes* – had been incorporated into the French army and would remain so, but reinforced by at least 600 or more recruits drawn from the pick of the new arrivals. King James appears to have had little direct involvement with these units, although the French respected their Jacobite tradition, as reflected in their colours, scarlet uniforms and largely Irish character. Indeed, Clare's

in exile, pp 5–6; *CP*, xii, pp 19–20; *DIB*, vol. 2, p. 981; Genet-Rouffiac, 'Wild geese' I, p. 20; Lyons, 'Female dependants of Irish Jacobite soldiers', pp 67–8.   **6** Story, *Continuation*, p. 292; *JN*, p. 188; *F-I corr.*, i, pp xliii, 147; ii, pp 455–6, 458–9, 463–5, 472, 478, 534; Rowlands, *Army*

regiment had mutinied when it was proposed to clothe them in standard French grey uniforms. The other regiments – *les autres* – nominally formed the army of King James, but were clothed, armed and paid by the king of France, organized as he required, obliged to swear an oath to serve wherever and against whom he directed (except against King James) and to come under the command of his generals. King James retained the right to issue (and suspend) commissions, and to maintain a military administration consisting of a secretary at war, a judge advocate general, a provost marshal, a chaplain general and a staff of physicians and surgeons. James could also nominate his own generals: the duke of Berwick was captain general of his forces from 1696. But for James's generals to hold a substantive command in accordance with their rank, they also needed to be appointed by the king of France, as was the case with Mountcashel and Berwick, both lieutenant generals, and Sarsfield who was a major general. In 1706 Berwick became a marshal of France. The existence of his army gave James a degree of status seldom available to exiled monarchs. Although he had little control over the deployment of the Irish regiments, James lobbied the French government strongly on their behalf and provided perhaps 100,000 *livres* annually for their support.[7]

The immediate task in Brittany was to form the Irish arrivals into troops and companies. This was managed by the French generals from Ireland, d'Usson, de Tessé and La Tour Monfort, who were soon joined by Andrew Lee, a senior Irish officer long in the French service, who was appointed inspector general of the Irish units. The consolidation of companies and troops into regiments was completed by King James himself when he came to Brittany in the latter part of December. He was accompanied by Nagle, who was retained as secretary of state for war as well as for Ireland. The outcome of these arrangements was the formation of seven two-battalion infantry regiments each of fourteen 100-man companies. A further single-battalion regiment of seven companies mopped up surplus personnel. The number of companies was close to the French model of fifteen or sixteen, while company strength was the standard for foreign regiments in France, although twice that of French companies. There were two troops of horseguards, each reduced to a strength of eighty, two cavalry regiments, each of twelve 50-man troops, and two regiments of dismounted dragoons, each consisting of six 100-man companies. Three experienced officers from the *gardes françaises* were sent to instruct these *autres* regiments in the principles of French drill and discipline, with the aim of preparing them for a projected invasion of England in the spring of 1692.[8]

in exile, p. 5. **7** Rowlands, *Army in exile*, pp 5–6, 12; *F-I corr.*, i, pp 158–61; O'Callaghan, *Irish brigades*, p. 144; Callow, *King in exile*, pp 189–90. **8** *F-I corr.*, i, pp 151–2; ii, pp 453–4, 462, 470–1,

This structure provided an establishment figure of 13,060 non-commissioned officers and men for *les autres*, with 4,800 for *les anciennes* of the Mountcashel Brigade. To these can be added the establishment of commissioned officers, comprising a captain, two lieutenants, a *sous lieutenant* and an ensign per infantry company, and a captain, lieutenant, cornet and quartermaster for each cavalry troop. The officer establishment per company for the two regiments of dismounted dragoons was probably the same as for the infantry. In Ireland, each troop of horseguards had an establishment of twenty-five officers. They seem to have been called lifeguards in France, where their officer establishment mirrored the French *garde du corps* with twenty officers per troop. One troop was largely English and the other Irish. The troopers were young gentlemen, and the units, like their French counterparts, likely operated as a training ground for young officers, who could expect appointment to subaltern vacancies in the main regiments. Adding in majors, adjutants and quartermasters (and allowing that, as in Ireland, colonels and lieutenant colonels also held companies or troops) a total of about 967 was the establishment of commissioned officers in the *autres* regiments, and 246 in the three regiments of *anciennes*. Thus, the full *autres* establishment was just over 14,000. The evidence suggests that this figure was initially achieved. Barbezieux foresaw it as easily attainable with the arrival of Sarsfield's contingent from Cork, and the fact that an additional seven-company regiment was added would appear to support his view. The six battalions of the Mountcashel Brigade, each apparently of sixteen companies, amounted to a further 5,000 all ranks.[9]

Unlike the Mountcashel Brigade, the *autres* regiments did not take the names of their colonels, but that of the king and queen, and of some of the celebrated engagements in Ireland: Limerick, Athlone and Charlemont, as well as Dublin and the marine. The latter took its name from the fact that its nominal colonel, Henry Fitzjames, King James's illegitimate son, titled lord grand prior in Ireland and in 1696 created duke of Albemarle by his father, was an officer in the French navy. His regiment was therefore in practice commanded by a colonel lieutenant, Nicholas FitzGerald. This was also the case with the small regiment of Clancarty, which was commanded by Sir Edward Scott, as both Clancarty and his successor, Roger MacElligott, were in prison in England, following their capture at Cork. All the *autres* colonels were veterans of the war in Ireland. Three-quarters of them were Irish, as were all the commanders of the *anciennes* regiments.[10]

476, 479; Rowlands, *Army in exile*, pp 5–6, 12–13; Lynn, *Giant of the grand siècle*, pp 466–8; 'Gaydon's memoir', iii, p. 98; vi, p. 191.   **9** *F-I corr.*, i, pp 159–61, 164–5; ii, p. 479; O'Callaghan, *Irish brigades*, pp 62, 142; Rowlands, *Army in exile*, pp 5–6, 19–20.   **10** O'Callaghan, *Irish brigades*, p. 107.

TABLE 9 *Irish regiments in France, 1692*

Irish brigade regiments[11]
Infantry
    Regiments   *commander*
        Mountcashel: Viscount Mountcashel; succeeded by Andrew Lee, 1694
        O'Brien/Clare: Daniel O'Brien (4th Viscount Clare from 1691); succeeded by Andrew Lee, 1693; succeeded by Mark Talbot, 1694; succeeded by Charles O'Brien, 5th Viscount Clare, 1696
        Dillon: Arthur Dillon

King James's army in France, 1692–8[12]
Cavalry
    Regiments
        horseguards   *commander*
        1st troop: duke of Berwick
        2nd troop: earl of Lucan; succeeded by earl of Clancarty, 1693
        king's: Dominic Sheldon
        queen's: Viscount Galmoy

Dismounted dragoons
    Regiments   *commander*
        king's: Richard Bellew; succeeded by Thomas Maxwell, 1692; succeeded by Viscount Kilmallock, 1693
        queen's: Francis Carroll; succeeded by Viscount Clare, 1693; succeeded by Oliver O'Gara, 1696

Infantry
    Regiments   *commander*
        guards: William Dorrington
        queen's: Francis Wauchope; succeeded by Sir Edward Scott, 1693; succeeded by Simon Luttrell, 1694
        marine: lord grand prior (duke of Albemarle from 1696), but actually commanded by Nicholas FitzGerald as colonel lieutenant
        Limerick: Mark Talbot; succeeded by Sir John FitzGerald, 1693
        Charlemont: Gordon O'Neill
        Dublin: Simon Luttrell; succeeded by John Power, 1693
        Athlone: Sir Maurice Eustace; succeeded by Walter Burke, 1693
        Clancarty: earl of Clancarty; succeeded by Roger MacElligott, 1693.

11 O'Callaghan, *Irish brigades*, pp 24–47.   12 Rowlands, *Army in exile*, pp 19–20.

The position of the officers

The number of officers who came from Ireland was disproportionate: 850, including eighty-nine of field rank, had sailed from Limerick with Châteaurenault alone. For many of them no appointment was immediately available in France. This was a cause of considerable dissatisfaction to men who were destitute. The anonymous Munster author of 'The groans of Ireland' was one such. Bitter at being unable to secure any appointment and consequently being forced to farm his family out to charity, he complained of the colonels' preference for officers who had served in their regiments in Ireland, although his identification of them as 'servants, storekeepers, clerks, little attorneys, apothecaries and peddling merchants' – an echo of earlier opprobriums – was little more than an embellishment to his case. His contention that Old English officers were favoured over men of Gaelic background is supported by the contemporary historian, Abbé MacGeoghegan. It was claimed in 1705 that about sixty Protestant officers – presumably English and Scottish Jacobites – were serving in the Irish regiments, a figure that would have included *reformés*. Most officers who gained commissions lost rank: colonels being reduced to captains and captains to lieutenants. Unemployed field officers were put on half pay, but Louis refused to grant *reformé* status or pay to unemployed junior officers attached to the regiments, although King James gave them an allowance of five *sols* per day. One estimate is that they numbered sixty per regiment, totalling about 600 in all. They were left with no option but to serve in the ranks. Only in 1696, after casualties had depleted their number, did the French government acknowledge their status and consent to giving them the standard half-pay allowance. The eighty-three commissioned officers in the footguards promptly jumped to 242. A similar rise took place in the other regiments. It does not seem that commissions were sold, if for no other reason than funds were lacking for their purchase. But the well-connected held a considerable advantage in securing appointments, and boy-officers were common, as the influential sought to ensure the future of their heirs. Whereas in the three *anciennes* regiments, the men received six *sols* per day, which was the normal pay of most foreign troops in France, the soldiers in King James's force – *'les autres'* – were paid only five, the same as French soldiers. Possibly this was to deny their colonels control over the funds for clothing and equipping their men.[13]

---

13 *F-I corr.*, i, p. 149; ii, pp 448, 470; Rowlands, *Army in exile*, pp 10–12; *Portland MSS*, viii, p. 182; MacGeoghegan, *History*, p. 598; O'Callaghan, *Irish brigades*, p. 31; 'The groans of Ireland', p. 132.

Deployments in the nine years war

Despite the appellation of the Irish brigade, in practice the Irish regiments seldom brigaded together in the nine years war, although there were exceptions such as Wauchope's and Maxwell's brigades in Piedmont in 1693 and Lee's on the Meuse in 1696. In 1690 the *anciennes* regiments served together in Savoy, but thereafter not necessarily in the same theatres, and none of the three was transferred to Brittany in 1692 for the planned invasion of Britain. The invasion force did, however, include all the *autres* regiments, except Athlone, and amounted to nearly a third of Marshal Bellefonds's army of Normandy. It was joined by King James, Berwick and Sarsfield. The Anglo-Dutch defeat of the French navy at Barfleur/La Hogue – the latter in full view of James and his army – ended invasion plans and James's hopes of restoration, as well as signalling that the brief era of French naval superiority was over. It was followed by the dispersal of King James's regiments to different theatres of operation, where they were engaged for the rest of the war. Possibly the regiments were scattered because the French baulked at entertaining another king with his own consolidated army on French territory, but it can also be argued that dispersal may have been dictated by the need to spread reenforcements among the different French armies, as well as helping to integrate the new units into French military culture. In 1705 the Irish units were deployed in Germany, Flanders, Italy and Spain. In subsequent wars, however, it was common for the Irish regiments to be grouped together on the battlefield. Chevalier Gaydon's memoir of the regiment of Dillon reveals a very high rate of attrition in combat situations. The loss of husbands, fathers, brothers and sons had particularly severe consequences for their dependants, often leaving them destitute, or reliant on charity, very meagre pensions and the support of family networks. In her application for a pension, for example, in the early 1720s a widow named Doyle stated that her two successive husbands and two sons had all been killed in action; she was now old, in bad health and reduced to living on the street. Surviving records show that many others were similarly distressed when their soldier husbands, or fathers, were killed or permanently maimed.[14]

Full integration into the French army

Initially the French held the Irish in very low esteem. This was the attitude in the war ministry, where both Louvois and Barbezieux regarded them with

---

14 Lenihan, 'Irish brigade', p. 48; O'Callaghan, *Irish brigades*, pp 32, 39, 165–6; 'Gaydon's memoir', iii, p. 99 and passim; *Portland MSS*, viii, p. 181; Egerton MS 1671; Lyons, 'Female dependants of Jacobite soldiers', passim.

disdain. Louvois had never wanted French intervention in Ireland, and his hostility seemed vindicated by the adverse reports that had come from French officers posted there and by the Jacobite defeats. The ragged appearance and disorderly conduct of the Irish on disembarkation re-enforced the negative sentiments of the French officials, which were compounded by the burden posed by their several thousand accompanying dependants. The low pay of *les autres* was in part a reflection of their low status. Until 1696, their place in the order of battle was generally in the less prestigious second line. However, regard for the Irish gradually increased. Marshal Vauban said they were brave troops, who had served well in the nine years war. The real shift in their prestige came in the opening stages of the war of the Spanish succession. Marshal Villeroi praised them as the best and bravest of troops and placed them in the front line in the army of Italy in 1701. The following year, much was made of the pivotal role played by two Irish regiments, Dillon's and Burke's, in the defence of Cremona against Prince Eugene. This enhanced the reputation of the Irish. Thereafter, in engagements such as Blenheim (1704), Ramillies (1706) and Malplaquet (1709) the Irish regiments were regularly in the front line alongside the elite Swiss and French guards. They now ranked among the best troops of the French army, a position consolidated by the fame of their subsequent achievements at Fontenoy (1745) and Lafelt (1747).[15]

For the *autres* regiments the division of control between between Versailles and Saint-Germain in the 1690s created a vacuum in proper supervision that led to frequent disorders, indiscipline and financial chicanery, including the old abuse of false musters. Battle casualties, disease and desertion combined to create a high level of attrition, not matched by recruitment from Ireland or of deserters from other armies, so that by 1695 the units in Italy were reported to be at less than half strength. The nine years war ended with the treaty of Rijswijk in 1697. Louis agreed to abandon his support for James and recognized William as king of England, Scotland and Ireland. Implicit in this was the disbandment of James's force, for which William's government pressed, and which took place in the spring of 1698. Formally this was the end of King James's Irish army.[16]

But in a real sense the army continued. The three *anciennes* regiments were retained in the French army, and the severity of the disbandments was tempered by the transfer of personnel to them and to five new Irish infantry regiments and one of cavalry incorporated into the French army. Four of the new infantry colonels, Dorrington, Albemarle, Galmoy and Burke, had

---

15 Rowlands, *Army in exile*, pp 9–10; Lenihan, 'Irish brigade', pp 51–3, 58; Corvisier, *Malplaquet*, pp 80, 85; Peeters (ed.), *Fontenoy*, Ó'hAnnracháin, 'Lafelt', pp 1–22. **16** Rowlands, *Army in exile*, pp 14–18.

commanded regiments in James's former army and the fifth, the duke of Berwick, a troop of horseguards. The single cavalry regiment was commanded by Dominic Sheldon. The three *anciennes* regiments retained their commanders: Lee, Dillon and Clare. All the infantry regiments, including the three *anciennes* units, were reduced to single battalions of fourteen fifty-man companies, with an establishment strength of 700 other ranks. The cavalry regiment was reduced to two squadrons, each of three troops. This amounted to a loss of more than 200 companies/troops compared to the original establishment, and left the Irish regiments with about 6,200 other ranks. This was a huge reduction on the 18,000 figure of 1692. Estimates of the number of disbanded soldiers range from 5,000 to 8,000 men. However, this may overstate the impact of the reductions, as by then the regiments were greatly under strength. The chevalier Gaydon recalled that two battalions of his own Dillon regiment plus the other ranks from the two battalions of the disbanded Limerick regiment were needed to make up a single 700-man Dillon battalion after the reform. Doubtless the same was true of other units too. Fewer and smaller companies led to a great reduction in the number of substantive appointments for commissioned officers. It was reported that at least 120 *reformé* officers were serving with each regiment in 1702, but that a hundred of them were sent to Spain to head the new levies there and another hundred to the Cevennes to head the militia against the Protestant Camisard revolt. An informant claimed that most of the officers would transfer their services to Queen Anne if given any encouragement. Possibly unemployed officers made up a disproportionate number of the hundreds of starving soldiers reported to have flocked to Saint-Germain for relief. Undoubtedly there was much distress. There were reports of banditry and lawlessness by disbanded soldiers there and in Paris. Nearly a hundred war-battered Irishmen were admitted to Les Invalides in 1698, followed by a further 151 in 1700, both major increases on preceding years. Almost half were from Munster, a quarter from Leinster a fifth from Ulster and only a small number from Connacht, which may be taken as indicative of the provincial composition of the Irish regiments as a whole. King James claimed to have relieved 'an infinite number of distressed people, ancient and wounded officers, widows and children of such as had lost their lives in his services'. He and Queen Mary sold the Stuart jewels to try to raise funds for relief, although their efforts were little appreciated. Pope Innocent XII sent 37,500 *livres*. Mary continued to pay pensions to deceased officers' families until her death in 1718, when the recipients were forced to seek other sources of support. Fortunately for the Irish, the outbreak of of the Spanish succession war in 1701 soon provided fresh avenues of employment. Many disbanded officers sought service in the armies of other powers, such as Spain, Bavaria and the Habsburg empire. The 3rd earl of Carlingford was instrumental in securing their employment in the newly formed army of the duke of Lorraine. From 1702 to 1733 the duke of Parma maintained a company of Irish guardsmen, dressed in scarlet uniforms with blue cuffs. Peter Lacy, a teenage officer in Ireland, wound up in Russia, where he rose to be a field marshal. Irish Catholic representation was particularly strong in the Habsburg army during Empress Maria Theresa's mid-eighteenth-century wars.[17]

The later lineage of the French units was that Sheldon's cavalry regiment became Nugent's and then FitzJames's until its disbandment in 1762 after its virtual annihilation in the seven years war. Albemarle's was successively Nugent's and O'Donnell's until its disbandment with Galmoy's in 1715, when its personnel were incorporated into the remaining regiments. Burke's transferred to the Spanish army at that time. A new Irish regiment of Lally, formed in 1744, was disbanded in 1762 after involvement in the French defeat in India. Lee's became Bulkeley's until the army reorganization of 1775 incorporated it into Dillon's, when Clare's also was incorporated into Berwick / Fitzjames's. Thus, three Irish regiments remained in the French army until the revolution, with Dillon's and Berwick / FitzJames's retaining their original names throughout the eighteenth century, under a succession of family colonels. The revolutionary regime discarded their Irish identity; in 1791 the latter two became respectively the 87th and 88th infantry regiments. The third regiment, Walsh's, previously Dorrington's / Rothe's / Roscommon's, became the 92nd. In numerical terms the best estimate of the combined strengths of the Franco-Irish regiments is 3,300 in 1714, 3,600 in 1741; 4,100 in 1745; 3,100 in 1764, and 2,750 in 1786. Modern scholarship suggests that just under 20,000 soldiers served in the Franco-Irish regiments between 1716 and 1791, of whom about a third were Irish. To the end, however, the officers were almost entirely of Irish birth or descent. Casualties were high. Chevalier Gaydon probably exaggerated when he claimed that by 1736 the Dillon regiment had incurred losses of 6,000 men 'and more than the proportionate number of officers'. However, at the hard-fought battle of Malplaquet in 1709 (from which the Dillon regiment was absent), the five Irish infantry regiments engaged suffered eighty-three officer casualties, killed or wounded, which implies as many as a thousand among other ranks. At Fontenoy in 1745 the

17 Lenihan, 'Irish brigade', pp 57–8; 'Gaydon's memoir', iii, p. 106; *Portland MSS*, viii, pp 181–2; Genet-Rouffiac, 'Wild geese' II, pp 37–9, 53; *James II*, ii, p. 472; Egerton MS 1671; Corp 'Irish at Jacobite court', pp 152–3; Ó hAnnracháin, 'Irish veterans at *des Invalides* (1692–1769)', p. 10; Richard-Maupillier, 'Irish regiments of Lorraine', pp 285–312; Garland, 'Parma Irishmen', pp 134–5; Ó hAnnracháin, 'Parma's Irish guards', pp 363–85; *DIB*, vol. 5, pp 263–4; Downey, 'Wild

Irish regiments had 650 casualties, and two years later at Lafelt their casualties were 1,600 other ranks and 132 officers. Charles O'Brien, 6th Viscount Clare, who commanded the Irish infantry regiments at both battles, became a marshal of France in 1757.[18]

A footnote to the story of the Franco-Irish brigade was its short-lived revival in British service in 1795–8. This was the initiative of senior *emigré* officers from France, including Vicomte Walsh de Serrant and General Daniel Charles O'Connell, who persuaded a hesitant British government to accept the concept. Six regiments were initially formed, but later only brought up to full strength by amalgamations that reduced them to three. The officers were *emigrés*, or largely so, while the rank and file were Irish Catholics. In 1797 the regiments were sent to the West Indies, a posting sufficiently distant to assuage Irish Protestant fears while still serving British military strategy. The regiments saw some military action in San Domingo and Honduras, but disease soon decimated their strength. In 1798 the survivors were brought back to Ireland and the regiments disbanded.[19]

Recruitment

Attrition rates from combat in wartime, disease in garrison and advancing years necessitated a flow of recruits, if regiments were to be kept up to strength. Little is known of recruitment in Ireland in the immediate wake of the Jacobite army's departure, but the low numbers in the regiments by 1698 indicate that whatever recruits came from Ireland, while Britain and France were at war, were insufficient to fill the vacancies. Irish poets and Protestant commentators were equally concerned with recruitment for the Irish brigades. The new Irish establishment was hostile to the concept of bodies of Irish Catholic soldiers in Europe, which it viewed as an ongoing threat. Therefore, there was opposition at official level to recruitment for the brigades in Ireland. In the 1690s Sir Robert Southwell was apprehensive that 'an employment of Irish papists [as soldiers] abroad may be rather detrimental to the Protestant interest by fitting men to be capable of leading a future rebellion in that country when time shall serve'. The outlawry of military migrants was a symptom of this concern. A generation later, Charles Forman expressed continuing Protestant anxiety about the existence of Irish brigades in France and Spain:

geese and the double-headed eagle', pp 49–54. **18** O'Callaghan, *Irish brigades*, passim; Hayes, 'Irish casualties in the French service', pp 198–201; 'Gaydon's memoir', vi, p. 191; Chambers, 'Irish in Europe', p. 574; Ó hAnnracháin, 'Lafelt', p. 3; Ó hAnnracháin, 'Fontenoy', p. 73; Ó hAnnracháin, 'Malplaquet', p. 387; Hayes, *BD*, p. 32. **19** McDonnell, 'Catholic Irish brigade', pp 150–68.

> As long as there is a body of Irish Roman Catholic troops abroad the chevalier [James III] will always make some figure in Europe by the credit they give him, and be considered as a prince that has a brave and well-disciplined army of veterans at his disposal ... they are seasoned to dangers and so perfected in the art of war that not only the sergeants and corporals, but even the private men, can make very good officers on occasion.

In 1722 the Irish parliament made it a felony to enlist recruits for foreign armies without a license, and a number of officers and agents from the French and Spanish brigades, who were recruiting in Ireland were subsequently apprehended and executed, as too were some of their recruits.[20]

Nevertheless, throughout the first half of the eighteenth century, recruits continued to come from Ireland, where popular Jacobitism was far from dead, as evidenced in the *aisling* genre of Irish poets such Aogán Ó Rathaille, Eoghan Rua Ó Súilleabháin and Seán Clárach Mac Domhnaill. Small parties or single individuals left surreptitiously, facilitated by Irish shipowners or travelling independently, in the belief that by enlisting in the brigades they were serving James III. The evocative term 'the wild geese' is frequently employed as a collective title for the military migrants and to the hope that they would return to Ireland in strength. It seems first to have been used in a revenue document in 1726, and sometime later the Munster poet, Sean Ó Cuinneagáin, referred to the exiles as '*géana*' ('geese'). However, the epithet only came into widespread use in the nineteenth century. The British government did allow limited recruitment in the late 1720s and early 1730s, when relations with France were good, but under strict conditions. The recruits were drawn from all over Ireland, with the heaviest concentrations coming from Munster and south Leinster, possibly because of proximity to ports trading with the Continent. Their number fell well below what was needed, especially after the renewal of war in 1742 when the Irish regiments incurred heavy combat casualties. Between 1716 and 1722 the Dillon regiment enlisted just over a hundred Irish-born recruits and a further forty-three born to Irish fathers in France. Thirty-three more were born in England and Scotland. However, Alsatians, Germans and other continentals formed two-thirds of the intake. The fall-off of Irish recruits intensified from the mid-century after the failure of the 1745 rising in Scotland undermined hope of a Stuart restoration. The relaxation of anti-Catholic penal laws in Ireland was

---

20 Ó Ciardha, *Ireland and the Jacobite cause*, pp 101, 139–43, 197, 251–8, 270; *AH*, 22, p. 14; Simms, 'Irish on the Continent', pp 633–4; Forman, *A letter ... for disbanding the Irish regiments*, p. 17.

another factor. Possibly too, there was a degree of disillusionment with France after the controversial execution in 1766 of Lieutenant General Lally, a popular hero in Ireland, who was scapegoated for the French defeat in India.[21]

In 1692 Irishmen constituted 82 per cent of the personnel in the Franco-Irish regiments, and they still provided two-thirds of the brigade's strength at the end of the 1730s. A *contrôle* of Fitzjames's cavalry in 1737 shows 84 per cent of its 311 troopers and NCOs as having actually been born in Ireland; most of the rest, although born in France, had Irish surnames. The troopers were largely in their twenties and thirties, with just thirty-four aged forty or over and seventeen teenagers. Another return of 1736 shows several subaltern officers to have been quite elderly. The details of Irish prisoners captured at sea *en route* for the 1745–6 Jacobite rising in Scotland confirm this picture: the vast majority were Irish-born, and most seem to have travelled to France to enlist, although some had been recruited in Ireland. There were also some deserters from the Scots-Dutch brigade and a few ex-prisoners of war and sailors captured at sea. The outbreak of British hostilities with Spain in 1739 and subsequently with France until 1748 in the Austrian succession war disrupted the supply of recruits from Ireland, permanently as it turned out. Thereafter, although there were occasional spikes in recruitment in the 1750s and early 1760s, the proportion of Irish in the rank and file of all the regiments declined. By 1748, the number of Irish-born men in Fitzjames's cavalry had fallen to 203, or just 38 per cent. Clare's regiment at Fontenoy in 1745 was 38 per cent Irish by birth or descent. By 1762 the figure for Dillon's was 23 per cent, while Berwick's by then had fallen to 20 per cent. The following year only 8 per cent of Rothe's (later Walsh's) under-strength regiment was Irish, although English and Scots brought the number of non-continentals in the unit up 24 per cent. In the final years before the revolution, recruitment from Ireland was almost non-existent. Over the three years 1786–9, Walsh's secured only half a dozen Irish recruits. A modern estimate is that of 20,000 men who enlisted in the Irish brigade between 1716 and 1791, about a third were Irish. Early measures to enlist more Irish personnel were ordnances of 1694 and 1702 requiring English, Scottish and Irish men in France to enlist in one of the Irish regiments or risk been sent to the galleys for vagrancy. Irishmen in French units were transferred to the Irish regiments. Recruiting officers from the different regiments were active at the Channel ports of Dover and Boulogne, where they competed with each other for

21 Ó Ciardha, *Ireland and the Jacobite cause*, pp 49–50, 137; Simms, 'Irish on the Continent', p. 637; Murphy, 'Wild geese', pp 23–8; Elliot-Wright, 'Officers of the Irish brigade', p. 36; Ó Conaill, '"Ruddy cheeks and strapping thighs"', p. 421; Morley, 'Irish Jacobitism', pp 27–8; Downey, 'Beneath the harp', pp 96–7.

enlistments, until Lord Clare ordered a single officer to be entrusted with the task. Deserters from British units in Flanders and Spain were another source of recruits. The Berwick infantry regiment appears to have been heavily dependent on this source for its early personnel, and in the 1780s small numbers of British soldiers deserted to Dillon's regiment, while it was posted in America and the Caribbean. The reforms of 1698, 1715 and 1775 helped to consolidate Irish representation in the remaining regiments.[22]

In all armies of the time, colonels were prepared to fill up vacancies in their units with anyone they could find, and the regiments of the Irish brigades were no exception. The Franco-Irish regiments recruited Germans, Flemings, Alsatians and men from central Europe. They numbered almost half of Clare's rank and file by the 1740s, and the heavy casualties incurred at Fontenoy and particularly Lafelt increased dependence on non-Irish recruits. A brigade officer categorized them as 'robbers and criminals from all parts of the world'. Some were Protestants, but came under pressure to convert to Catholicism. By 1789 less than a quarter of Dillon's rank and file had originated in Ireland or Britain. Men from the Low Countries and Germany made up the bulk of the remainder, but there were also Spaniards, Swiss, Portuguese, Hungarians, Poles, Russians, Swedes and even six Americans. Similarly, by then only a fifth of Berwick's regiment had originated in Ireland or Britain. The figure for the Walsh regiment was even lower: sixty out of 1,084 in 1786. However, of 206 officers serving in the brigade in 1789, only a handful, who were promoted from the ranks, were not of Irish or British origin. From 1715 French naturalization became available to all soldiers, officers and others, who had service in the French army for ten years. Even before that, Louis XIV had granted naturalization to almost 300 Irish Jacobite exiles. In 1741 Louis XV extended the same rights to naturalized Irish as French citizens enjoyed.[23]

Irish regiments in Spain

The Jacobite army also had a measure of continuity in Habsburg Spain and Naples. Following the 1698 reformation, unemployed Irish officers drifted to Spain, a traditional employer of Irish soldiers, where the succession war soon

---

22 Genet-Rouffiac, 'Wild geese' I, p. 38; Genet-Rouffiac, 'Wild geese' II, pp 45–6; Chambers, 'Irish in Europe', p. 574; Elliot-Wright, 'Officers of the Irish brigade', p. 36; Ó hAnnracháin, 'Fitzjames cavalry regiment', pp 253–76; Ó hAnnracháin, 'Fontenoy', p. 71; Kerney-Walsh, 'Wild Goose tradition', p. 15; O'Connor, *Military history of the Irish nation*, pp 392–3; Ó Conaill, '"Ruddy cheeks and strapping thighs"', pp 420–2; McDonnell, 'Documents relating to the Irish brigade', pp 7–21. **23** Genet-Rouffiac, 'Wild geese' I, pp 22–3, 38; Chambers, 'Irish in Europe', pp 574–5; Elliot-Wright, 'Officers of the Irish brigade', pp 36, 44; Ó hAnnracháin, 'Fontenoy',

offered fresh career opportunities. Regiments with Irish associations were again introduced into the Spanish army, starting with the dragoon regiments of Daniel O'Mahony, the hero of Cremona, and Henry Crofton, who had served as a dragoon captain in Ireland, dating from 1703 and 1705 respectively. Some authorities also mention a short-lived, third Irish dragoon regiment of FitzHarris. In 1709, following the withdrawal of French troops from Spain, four new Irish infantry regiments were taken onto the Spanish establishment: Castelar (actually commanded by Lieutenant Colonel Randal MacDonnell), (Dermot) McAuliffe, (Patrick) Comerford and Vandoma/Vendôme (actually commanded by Lieutenant Colonel Patrick Begg). Their officers came from the many supernumeraries serving with the Irish regiments in France. In 1715, following the contraction of the French army after the treaty of Utrecht, a fifth regiment, Walter Burke's, transferred in its entirety from the French army to that of Spain where, after Burke's death, it became Wauchope's, and was accorded seniority. From 1718 the regiments ceased to be named after their commanders, and were redesignated Edinburgh (O'Mahony's), Dublin (Crofton's), Irlanda, briefly Connacia (Wauchope's), Hibernia (Castelar's), Ultonia (McAuliffe's), Limerick (Vandoma's) and Waterford (Comerford's). A Momomia (Munster) regiment formed in 1719 was united to Limerick in 1722. Dublin was disbanded in 1722 and Edinburgh in 1766. Waterford was amalgamated with Hibernia in 1734. Limerick transferred to the service of the Neapolitan Bourbons in 1736, where it continued as the Regimiento del Rey. In the 1739 review, the officers of its 1st battalion all had Irish names, as had ten of the 2nd battalion officers.[24]

Irlanda, Ultonia and Hibernia remained in Spanish service throughout the eighteenth century. They fought with distinction in campaigns on the Peninsula, in Italy, North Africa and the Americas. The battle of Camp Santo (1743) and the defence of Velletri (1744) were two of their best-known and costliest engagements. In appreciation of their role, Philip V conferred on their colours the motto taken from Psalm 19: *In omnem terram exhivit sonus eorum* ('their sound went forth into all the earth'), together with the sobriquets *El Famoso* (the famous) to Irlanda, *La Columna* (the backbone) to Hibernia and *El Immortal* (the immortal) to Ultonia which had not actually been present at Velletri. Until 1794 the Irish regiments continued to wear the red

p. 71; Ó Conaill, '"Ruddy cheeks and strapping thighs"', p. 420; Martinez, '*Semper et ubique fidelis*', p. 140; Ó Ciardha, *Ireland and the Jacobite cause*, p. 357; information from William Runacre. **24** MacSwiney, 'First Irish regiments in Spain', pp 16–19; MacSwiney, 'Irish regiments in Spain & Naples', pp 161, 164, 170–1; MacGeoghegan, *History*, pp 598–9; Morales, *Ireland and the Spanish empire*, p. 185; Downey, 'Beneath the harp', pp 88–95; Garland, 'Irish in Neapolitan service', pp 728–9; Oman, 'Irish troops in Spain', pp 3, 6.

uniforms of the Stuart tradition and bore a gold harp on a sky-blue field on their regimental colours. From the 1740s they were linked together as *La Brigada Irlandesa*, which was dedicated to Saint Patrick, but they never served together after the Portuguese war ended in 1762. Although recruitment in Ireland continued after the initial influx, it was insufficient to maintain unit strengths. Spain drew back from negotiating a recruiting arrangement with the British government in the 1730s. From then on, despite amalgamations, the Irish component of the rank and file dwindled earlier and more sharply than in France. Numbers in the ranks could only be maintained by the recruitment of Italians, Flemings, Germans, Walloons and Spaniards. By 1791 Irish and British rank and file in the three regiments numbered only sixty-five, most of them Irish. But until the 1790s the officer corps, with an establishment of almost 200, remained almost exclusively Irish by birth or descent. As in France, after the initial influx, entry to the officer corps was via cadetships, secured through familial or other connections with the regiment, especially its senior officers. Cadets and even junior officers were often children. As late as 1808 the regimental commanders all bore Irish surnames, as did a proportion of the junior officers. It was an advantage that Irish natives had long enjoyed privileges of equality with the subjects of the Habsburg dominions, which Philip V confirmed and extended. Over 200 Irish officers were enrolled in the Spanish military orders. Several achieved distinction beyond their regiments: Daniel O'Mahony, who had gained fame in the French service at Cremona, became a lieutenant general in Spain, as did Richard Wall, afterwards a distinguished Spanish diplomat. Ambrose O'Higgins became a field marshal in South America. Alexander O'Reilly was a leading Spanish general in the mid-eighteenth century. His appointments included the important post of inspector of infantry, in which his successors included Felix O'Neill and Gonzalo O'Farrell. However, by 1818, when all three regiments were finally disbanded, little remained that was Irish about them other than their names.[25]

The 'wild geese' and the Jacobite cause

In France and Spain, the regiments were the focus of the Irish soldiers' existence. They provided a home, an identity, a respectable career, a familiar society and prospects for their children. Although some soldiers like Richard Hennessy, the brandy distiller, moved into civilian life, the regiments were a lifetime commitment for many, and the association often endured over several

---

25 Morales, *Ireland and the Spanish empire*, pp 183–234; Downey, 'Beneath the harp', pp 93–7, 105; Murphy, *Irish brigades*, pp 41–51; Rodríguez, 'Irish Brigade in Spain, 1809–11', p. 167; Oman, 'Irish troops in Spain', pp 193–4, 199, 450; Simms, 'Irish on the Continent', p. 639.

generations – over a century in the case of the Dillons. Initially intermarriage within the Irish community was the norm. Military widows frequently remarried other Irish soldiers. Margaret Dougan, for example, who died in Paris in 1741 was married to three Irish officers in succession. However, as time went on some soldiers married local women, which furthered their assimilation into continental society. While in both France and Spain Irish seems to have been spoken in the ranks, the language of command in the brigades was English, which the Irish at the Jacobite court were said to have spoken badly, perhaps because of their Irish accents or idiom. The use of English for internal command in the regiments of the brigade was confirmed in 1755 by the French war minister, the marquis d'Argenson. Of course, to communicate with other units, the war ministries or high command, French or Spanish would have been necessary. Even late in the eighteenth century some officers were unable to speak French with proficiency, evidence of the still-circumscribed character of regimental life.[26]

The message to the Jacobite soldiers who left Ireland in 1691 was that they would soon return as part of a powerful army, with the implicit expectation of restoring King James to his thrones, the Catholic religion to its proper place and their lost estates to the dispossessed Catholic elite. The hatred of the English that the French had observed in Ireland was sustained in France. In 1723 an English observer found in Andrew Lee's regiment 'an implacable hatred against all such as are not like themselves, mortal enemies to the isle of Britain and its present happy constitution'. For much of the eighteenth century, the exiled Irish soldiers continued to subscribe to these tenets, which were symbolized by their distinctive red uniforms and the motifs of their colours. Their ideology raised them above the level of mere mercenaries, even if its realization grew increasingly unlikely. By 1756 a disillusioned officer was lamenting 'our national enthusiasm is no more'. Leading officers were in close contact with James II, and maintained a relationship with his son and grandsons, even after the Stuarts had departed from France. In the 1720s James III encouraged recruiting by the brigades in Ireland. The *autres* regiments, while they existed, were of course King James's army, but even the *anciennes* regiments, over which he had no direct control, identified with the Jacobite cause. While their objective of reconquering Ireland gradually faded, it never entirely disappeared. As late as 1792 General Arthur Dillon spoke of the enslaved condition of Ireland, expressing the hope that the time was near when he would give his sword to the service of his own land. An English spy

---

26 Hayes, 'Reflections', p. 72; Elliot-Wright, 'Officers of the Irish brigade', pp 53, 71–2; Cullen, *Irish brandy houses*, pp 73–88; Swords, 'Jean Fromont files 2', p. 138.

reported that Dillon had proposed a plan for the invasion of Ireland, guaranteeing success if he were given 10,000 men. If the report was true, he was only following a series of earlier invasion plans put forward by Irish brigade officers, such as Patrick Wall in 1778, who suggested that the brigade should form the core of an invasion force. Lord Clare was involved in French plans to invade England in support of Prince Charles in 1745–6 and again in a plan for an invasion of Ireland in 1759 that included the Franco-Irish infantry. There were various other proposals for an invasion during the seven years war. Writing from Spain in the 1720s and 1730s, Colonel Charles Wogan urged James III to invade Ireland, emphasizing the political motivation of the Irish brigades. Earlier, a series of invasion plans and proposals were put forward during the Spanish succession war, including one by Colonel Gordon O'Neill. The duke of Berwick drafted an outline invasion plan in 1702, and in 1722 the seven Irish generals then in France were commissioned by James III to take command in Britain during an expected Jacobite rising, which never materialized.[27]

The Irish soldiers were involved in all the active invasion attempts. Most of the *autres* regiments were mustered at La Hogue for the abortive invasion of Britain in 1692. Leading officers, including Richard Hamilton, Sheldon, Dorrington, Galmoy, Wauchope and Nicholas FitzGerald, with detachments from the Franco-Irish regiments, accompanied James III on his abortive attempt to land in Scotland in 1708. Several officers were made prisoner when their vessel was captured by the English navy, but later exchanged. The youthful Wogan brothers, Charles and Nicholas, took part in the 1715 Rising in Northumberland before making their way to the Continent to enrol in the Irish brigade. James III's expedition to Scotland did not have the support of the French government, but nevertheless some Irish officers accompanied him, including Christopher Nugent, who as a consequence suffered deprivation of his command of the Irish cavalry regiment (but was replaced by his son). General Arthur Dillon played an active role in the planning. A supporting Spanish expedition, that included men of the Hispano-Irish regiments, was dispersed in a gale. There was major Irish involvement in Prince Charles's attempt to recover the Stuart thrones in 1745–6. Two of the seven men who landed at Moidart with the prince were Irish soldiers: Sir John MacDonnell, lieutenant colonel of Fitzjames's cavalry, and John William O'Sullivan, who had served in the French army although not in an Irish unit. Other officers

[27] Story, *Continuation*, p. 259; Hayes, *BD*, p. 62; Beresford, 'Ireland in French strategy', xii, pp 289–90; *DIB*, vol. 11, p. 1008; O'Callaghan, *Irish brigades*, pp 43–4; Simms, 'Irish on the Continent', p. 637; Ó Ciardha, *Ireland and the Jacobite cause*, pp 146–50, 221, 261, 263, 324–5; Fagan, *Stuart papers*, i, pp 31–2.

followed, together with company-size detachments ('picquets') from all six Irish brigade infantry regiments and Fitzjames's cavalry. However, the vigilance of the English navy ensured that fewer than 300 reached Scotland. The rest were captured by the British fleet, including some officers from the Spanish brigade. Energetic efforts by Lally and Clare to send further reinforcements from the Irish brigade in France were likewise thwarted by British naval supremacy, and relatively few got through the blockade. Despite their small number, the Franco-Irish soldiers instilled a stiffening of professionalism into the Jacobite army. They fought with distinction especially at Falkirk and Culloden, where their commander, Brigadier Walter Stapleton, lieutenant colonel of Berwick's, was mortally wounded and half his men were casualties. A troop of FitzJames's escorted Prince Charles from the battlefield. All the survivors were made prisoner after Culloden. Unlike the highlanders, the Irish prisoners were treated honourably by their captors and released in 1747 to return to their regiments in France.[28]

The '45 is generally regarded as marking the end of Jacobite hopes, although Prince Charles did not die until 1788 and his brother, Cardinal Henry Stuart, only in 1807. However, the Irish had not followed James III from France in 1716, or Prince Charles on his forced exile in 1748. Thereafter, the Irishmen in the Irish regiments of France and Spain, while conscious of their heritage, made their primary focus their military careers in the service of the monarchs who were providing their employment. After the revolution, many of the leading officers remained loyal to the Bourbons and left France first to serve in the army of the princes and subsequently to serve Hanoverian Britain. Their presence in Ireland proved highly unpopular. Many younger officers, more open to change and by then fully integrated into French society, chose to remain in France. When the Bourbons were restored in 1814, as many as fourteen lieutenant generals of Irish descent were to be found in the French army. But, despite requests, the Irish brigade was not re-established. Today, only the 92nd regiment survives, garrisoned at Clermont-Ferrand and providing the infantry component of the French army's 2nd armoured brigade.[29]

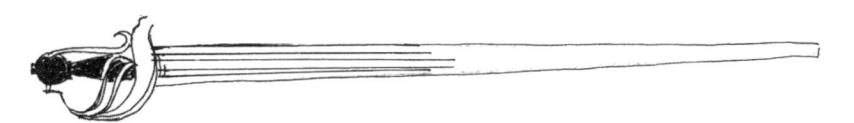

Figure 11. Seventeenth-century sword

28 O'Callaghan, *Irish brigades*, pp 256–7, 319; Hayes, *BD*, pp 60, 211; *DIB*, vol. 9, p. 1008; Hayes-McCoy, 'Irish soldiers of the '45', pp 315–34; Duffy, *The '45*, pp 523, 576–7 and passim.
29 Martinez, '"*Semper et ubique fidelis*"', p. 148; Bartlett (ed.), *Wolfe Tone*, p. 514.

Epilogue

THE IRISH JACOBITE ARMY was the largest body of Irish soldiers ever to go into battle prior to the twentieth century. Its numbers varied, but fell not far short of the 40,000 regular soldiers (drawn from a substantially larger population) who served in the Irish defence forces at the height of the second world war 'emergency'. To sustain the army of 1689–91 through three years of actual war represented an enormous effort by the Irish Catholic 'nation' of the time, not least because of its unpreparedness in terms of skilled soldiers, arms and other *matériel*.

In time, with substantial French support, many of the army's initial defects were overcome. By 1691, it was better led, armed and skilled, allowing it to face the final campaign with considerable confidence. Its combat performance that summer impressed even its opponents. Indeed, the campaign might well have gone the other way. Athlone was carelessly lost after a spirited defence; victory was close at Aughrim until the unlucky death of Saint-Ruth; Galway capitulated without a fight; Limerick was invested but never overrun; the potential of the cavalry to disrupt the Williamite rear was never utilized; division disrupted the high command; defeatism lowered morale; French aid was delayed. Better outcomes to any of these circumstances might have led to a more favourable end result. It was only after suffering a devastating defeat at Aughrim and facing, it believed, an imminent logistical crisis that the army at Limerick finally capitulated on terms that appeared reasonable. It departed from Ireland largely intact and with the promise of a possible early return. Indeed, more than one invasion involving the military exiles was subsequently planned, although in the event none materialized.

Would the outcome have been different had Derry been taken in 1689? Had William been killed at the Boyne in 1690? Had the 1691 campaign met with success? Any one of these events would have been a major setback for William and his allies. It has been said that William had more to lose in Ireland than Louis XIV had to gain. The war in Ireland was a challenge that William simply had to master. But if he had been obliged to commit even more resources to Ireland in order to stabilize his new-won crowns, his war effort on the Continent, his principal concern, would have been further weakened. The stability of his regime in England might well have been threatened: many Jacobites believed, perhaps with some truth, that his position there was less than secure. On the Irish side, no one considered the possibility of a stand-alone Irish state; nor was it realistic for Ireland to become a protectorate of France, as some mooted at the time. But, at the very least, military success would surely have enabled the Irish negotiators to secure a more favourable settlement to end the war. Modern Irish republicans are sometimes discomfited by the Jacobite army's allegiance to an English king, but they should understand that the soldiers were of their times. The cause was a popular one. Their motives were mixed and included a strong, indeed overriding strain of nationalism.

The reality, however, was that the Limerick articles masked a major defeat for Irish Catholic society, as those who remained in Ireland well recognized. The poet, Dáibhí Ó Bruadair, called it 'the shipwreck' (*'an longbhriseadh'*). Colonel Charles O'Kelly wrote of the 'conquered Irish' living in 'forced bondage', with 'nothing in prospect but contempt and poverty, chains and imprisonment, and, in a word, all the miseries that a conquered nation could rationally expect from the power and malice of implacable enemies'. Not only did the defeat dash hopes of a Catholic revival, but with the army gone, the implementation of the surrender articles was in the hands of the Williamite victors, and the Irish Protestants in particular were in no mood to be generous. The result was the enactment of extensive anti-Catholic legislation. While this impacted relatively lightly on the great mass of the population, for the elite it meant their exclusion from public life, the military and legal professions, and pressure to conform to Protestantism with a consequent diminution of remaining Catholic land ownership. The eighteenth century was the era of Protestant ascendancy. The draconian laws against the Catholic clergy were not systematically enforced, but they were occasionally harassed and continually poor.

The war in Ireland attracted considerable interest on the Continent. Dutch painters and engravers celebrated William's victory. The course of the conflict was followed in Versailles, Vienna, Brussels, Amsterdam, Copenhagen and Rome. In its wake, Irish soldiers were employed in France, Spain and elsewhere, where their prowess won considerable renown. 20,000 veteran soldiers were a considerable addition to Louis XIV's military strength. In Ireland, the deeds of the 'wild geese' were followed with interest. They inspired a heroic literary tradition among eighteenth-century Gaelic poets, such as Ó Bruadair, Ó Rathaille, Mac Domhnaill and Mac Cruithín. They linked the Irish brigades in France and Spain with a Stuart restoration and a recovery in the fortunes of Irish Catholics. Mac Cruithín actually served in the Franco-Irish brigade for a short time. Even Jonathan Swift expressed his admiration for the exiled soldiers' 'valour and conduct in so many parts of Europe, I think above all nations'. Wolfe Tone, as a republican revolutionary, had 'no great confidence in the officers of the old Irish brigade', although he was prepared to make an exception for Colonel Daniel Charles O'Connell (the Liberator's uncle and namesake), 'for I know he hates England'.[1]

In the nineteenth century the Young Irelanders, fired by their perception of an Irish nation struggling against alien bondage, rekindled interest in the Jacobite army and its continental offshoots. On a popular level, ballads such as Thomas Davis's 'Fontenoy', 'Clare's dragoons', 'The battle hymn of the brigade' and 'The surprise of Cremona' celebrated the deeds of the 'wild geese' to heroize the Irish military past. A generation later Aubrey de Vere's praise for the bravery of the Jacobite soldiers in 'A ballad of Athlone' was of much the same genre. However, this strain of cultural nationalism also generated scholarly works of enduring worth. These included Davis's own study *The Irish parliament of James II* (1843), Edward Walsh's *Reliques of Jacobite poetry* (1844) and Matthew O'Connor's *Military memoirs of the Irish* (1845). John Dalton's monumental *King James's Irish army list* (Dublin, 1855 & 1860) laid stress on the officers of the Jacobite army as 'models of honour and worth' whose heirship their descendants should be proud to claim. John Cornelius O'Callaghan, in his *History of the Irish brigades in the service of France* (Glasgow, 1870) viewed the 'gallant exiles ... as constituting for a century (and too sad a century!) the bright, as contrasted with the dark side of the national story'. Scholarship was assisted by the growing availability of important primary sources. James II's memoirs were printed in 1816, followed by the accounts of the Jacobite officers, O'Kelly, Stevens and the author of the *Jacobite narrative*. Since the 1930s much relevant material has been published by the Irish Manuscripts Commission, especially the invaluable French records.

Douglas Hyde saw the 'wild geese' as one of the bricks of Irish nationality. W.B. Yeats in his poem 'September 1913' recalled the bloodshed of 'the wild geese who spread their grey wing upon every tide'. The defence forces of the new Irish state naturally stressed the military prowess of the Jacobite army and the 'wild geese', as indeed did some, such as Rudyard Kipling, from a British perspective. Popular approbation was manifested in the naming of streets, army barracks and even pubs after Sarsfield and other Jacobite soldiers. A bronze statue of Patrick Sarsfield was erected in Limerick in 1881 and a commemorative cross on the battlefield of Aughrim in the 1970s. In 1990 the Jacobite army was fully and fairly represented in the Ulster Museum's 'Kings in conflict' exhibition marking the tercentenary of the battle of the Boyne. The Irish in Europe Project, commenced in 1997, has created a data base of thousands of Irish soldiers in early-modern France and Spain. Today, the

---

[1] Bartlett (ed.), *Wolfe Tone*; pp 513–14; Scott, *Works of Swift*, xvii, p. 395; *KJIL*, i, p. xiv; Ó Ciardha, *Ireland and the Jacobite cause*, pp 260–1; O'Callaghan, *Irish brigades*, pp vii–viii.

Jacobite army and its achievements are included in the permanent 'Soldiers and chiefs' exhibition in the National Museum of Ireland. Battle-site visitor centres have been established at the Boyne, Aughrim and Athlone Castle, and a 'wild geese' museum has opened in Limerick. The Jacobite army's war in Ireland may have ended in the pathos of defeat, but its struggle commands respect and ensures it a secure place in the canons of both Irish and European history.[2]

Figure 12. Trooper, FitzJames's cavalry, France, 1760

---

2 Yeats, *Collected poems*, p. 121; *Field Day anthology*, ii, p. 530.

Bibliography and abbreviations

Abridgement of English military discipline	*An abridgement of English military discipline* (London, 1690 edn)
Account of Aughrim (Westminster Diocesan Archives, B6, 258)	Account of battle of Aughrim in Henry Brown letter book (Westminster Diocesan Archives, B6, 258)
'Account of Co. Kildare in 1682'	'A descriptive account of the county of Kildare in 1682 by Thomas Monk' in *KASJ*, vi (1909–11), 339–46
Acts of James II's parliament	John Bergin & Andrew Lyall (eds), *The acts of James II's parliament of 1689* (Dublin, 2016)
AH	*Analecta Hibernica* (1930–)
AH, 21	Lilian Tate (ed.), *Franco-Irish correspondence December 1688–August 1691* in *AH*, 21 (1959)
AH, 22	J.G. Simms (ed.), 'Irish Jacobites; lists from TCD MS N.1.3.' in *AH*, 22 (1960), pp 11–242
A journal of the most remarkable occurrences	*A journal of the most remarkable occurrences that happened between his majesties force and the forces under the command of Mareschal de Schomberg in Ireland from the twelfth of August to the 23th of October, 1689* (Dublin, n.d., but 1689)
'A journal of what passed since his majesty's arrival' (Carte MS 181)	'A journal of what has passed since his majesty's arrival in Ireland' (Bodl., Carte MS 181)
A list of the several persons in civil affairs	*A list of the several persons in civil affairs under the late king in Ireland* (London, 1689)
An account of the present state Ireland is in	*An account of the present state Ireland is in under King James* (London, 1690)
Anc. rec. Dublin	Sir John Gilbert (ed.), *Calendar of ancient records of Dublin in the possession of the corporation*, v (Dublin, 1895)
A new history of Ireland, iii	T.W. Moody, F.X. Martin & F.J. Byrne (eds), *A new history of Ireland*, iii, *early modern Ireland 1534–1691* (Oxford, 1976)
A new history of Ireland, iv	T.W. Moody & W.E. Vaughan (eds), *A new history of Ireland*, iv, *eighteenth-century Ireland 1691–1800* (Oxford, 1986)

BIBLIOGRAPHY AND ABBREVIATIONS

Animadversions of warre	[Robert Warde], *Animadversions of warre; or, a militarie magazine of the truest rules, and ablest instructions, for the managing of warre ... by Robert Ward, gentleman and commander* (London, 1639)
A particular and full account of Aghrim	*A particular and full account of the routing of the whole Irish army at Aghrim* (Dublin, 1691)
A particular relation of the surrender of Galloway	*A particular relation of the surrender of Galloway* (London, 1691)
Arch. Hib.	*Archivium Hibernicum* (1911–)
Arnold, *Land settlement in Dublin*	L.J. Arnold, *The restoration land settlement in County Dublin, 1660–1688* (Dublin, 1993)
Art and architecture of Ireland	Rolf Loeber et al. (eds), *Art and architecture of Ireland*: vol. iv: *architecture 1600–2000* (Dublin, 2014)
Atkinson, 'Charles II's regiments'	C.T. Atkinson, 'Charles II's regiments in France, 1672–78' in *JSAHR*, xxiv (1946), pp 53–64, 128–36, 161–71
A true account of the present state of Ireland	*A true account of the present state of Ireland giving a full relation of the new establishment made by the late King James* (London, 1689)
A true and faithful account	*A true and faithful account of the present state and condition of the kingdom of Ireland* (London, 1690)
A true and impartial account of the most material passages in Ireland	*A true and impartial account of the most material passages in Ireland since December 1688* (London, 1689)
A true and perfect journal	*A true and perfect journal of the affairs in Ireland since His Majesties arrival in that kingdom, by a person of quality* (London, 1690)
Ball, *Dublin*	Francis Elrington Ball, *A history of the county Dublin* (Dublin, 1906)
Barbe, 'battle of the Boyne'	L. Barbe, 'The battle of the Boyne' in *Notes and Queries*, 5th series, viii (1877), pp 21–3 (Dispatch of J. Payen de la Fouleresse, Danish ambassador, to Christian V, 2 July 1690)
Barnard, *Anatomy of Ireland*	Toby Barnard, *A new anatomy of Ireland: the Irish Protestants, 1649–1770* (London, 2003)
Barnard, *Making the grand figure*	Toby Barnard, *Making the grand figure: lives and possessions in Ireland, 1641–1770* (London, 2004)
Bartlett (ed.), *Wolfe Tone*	Thomas Bartlett (ed.), *Life of Theobald Wolfe Tone* (Dublin, 1998)

Bartlett & Jeffrey, *Military history of Ireland*	Thomas Bartlett & Keith Jeffrey (eds), *A military history of Ireland* (Cambridge, 1996)
Beckett, *Cavalier duke*	J.C. Beckett, *The cavalier duke: the life of James Butler, 1st duke of Ormond, 1610–88* (Belfast, 1990)
Beckett, 'Irish armed forces'	J.C. Beckett, 'The Irish armed forces, 1660–1685' in John Bossy & Peter Jupp (eds), *Essays presented to Michael Roberts* (Belfast, 1976), pp 41–53
Beddard, *Revolutions*	Robert Beddard (ed.), *The revolutions of 1688* (Oxford, 1991)
Beresford, 'Ireland in French strategy'	Marcus Beresford, 'Ireland in French strategy, 1776–83' in *Ir. Sword*, xii (1975–6), pp 285–97; xiii (1977–9), pp 20–9
Berresford Ellis, *Boyne water*	Peter Berresford Ellis, *The Boyne water: the battle of the Boyne 1690* (London, 1976)
Berwick, *Memoirs*	*Memoirs of the marshal duke of Berwick written by himself* (2 vols, London, 1779)
BL	British Library
BL, Add. MS 9763	A list of King James's army in Ireland 1689 (BL, Add. MS 9763)
BL, Add. MS 28,053	Letter of Tyrconnell to James II, 29 January 1689 (BL, Add. MS 28,053)
Black, *Kings in conflict*	Eileen Black (ed.), *Kings in conflict* [Ulster Museum exhibition catalogue] (Belfast, 1990)
Blackmore, *Arms and armour*	David Blackmore, *Arms and armour of the English civil wars* (London, 1990)
Blackmore, 'British military firepower'	David J. Blackmore, 'Destructive and formidable: British military firepower, 1642–1756' (PhD, Nottingham Trent University, 2012)
BLGI 1899, 1904, 1912, 1958	*Burke's genealogical and heraldic history of the landed gentry of Ireland* (London, 1899, 1904, 1912, 1958 edns)
Bluche, *Louis XIV*	François Bluche, *Louis XIV* (London, 1990)
Boulger	Demetrius Charles Boulger, *The battle of the Boyne* (London, 1911)
BPB 1938, 1975, 1988	*Burke's peerage and baronetage* (London, 1938, 1975, 1988 edns)
Brockliss & Ferté, 'Irish clerics in Paris and Toulouse'	L.W.B. Brockliss & Patrick Ferté, 'Prosopography of Irish clerics in the universities of Paris and Toulouse, 1573–1792' in *Arch. Hib.*, 58 (2004), pp 7–166

'Brownes of Castlemacgarrett'	Lord Oranmore and Browne, 'The Brownes of Castlemacgarrett' in *JGAHS*, v (1907–8), pp 227–38
Callow, *King in exile*	John Callow, *King in exile, James II: warrior, king and saint, 1689–1701* (Stroud, 2004)
Cambridge history	Jane Ohlmeyer (ed.), *The Cambridge history of Ireland*, vol. ii
Carlton, *Going to the wars*	Charles Carlton, *Going to the wars, the experience of the British civil wars, 1638–1651* (London, 1992)
Carte, *Ormond*	[Thomas Carte], *The life of James duke of Ormond…* (6 vols, Oxford, 1851)
CB	G.E.C[okayne], *Complete baronetage* (6 vols, Exeter, 1900–9)
Chambers, 'Irish in Europe'	Liam Chambers, 'The Irish in Europe in the eighteenth century, 1691–1715' in *Cambridge history of Ireland*, iii, 569–92
Chambers, *Michael Moore*	Liam Chambers, *Michael Moore c.1639–1726, provost of Trinity, rector of Paris* (Dublin, 2005)
Chandler, *Art of war*	David Chandler, *The art of war in the age of Marlborough* (Staplehurst, 1990 edn)
Chartrand, *Louis XIV's army*	René Chartrand, *Louis XIV's army* (London, 1988)
Childs, *BD*	John Childs, *Nobles, gentlemen and the profession of arms in restoration Britain 1660–1688; a biographical dictionary of British army officers on foreign service* (London, 1987)
Childs, *Charles II*	John Childs, *The army of Charles II* (London, 1976)
Childs, *James II*	John Childs, *The army, James II and the glorious revolution* (Manchester, 1980)
Childs, 'Laws of war'	John Childs, 'The laws of war in seventeenth-century Europe and their application during the Jacobite war in Ireland, 1688–91' in David Edwards, Pádraig Lenihan & Clodagh Tait (eds), *Age of atrocity: violence and political conflict in early modern Ireland* (Dublin, 2007), pp 283–300
Childs, *Nine years war*	John Childs, *The nine years war and the British army 1688–1697* (Manchester, 1991)
Childs, *Warfare*	John Childs, *Warfare in the seventeenth century* (London, 2001)
Childs, *William III*	John Childs, *The British army of William III, 1698–1702* (Manchester, 1987)
Childs, *Williamite wars*	John Childs, *The Williamite wars in Ireland, 1689–91* (London, 2007)

Churchill, *Marlborough*	Winston Churchill, *Marlborough, his life and times* (2 vols, Chicago, 2002 repr.)
'Clann Carthaigh'	S.T. McCarthy, 'The Clann Carthaigh' in *Kerry Archaeological Magazine*, i–iv (1910–17)
Clarendon	S. Singer (ed.), *The correspondence of Henry Hyde, earl of Clarendon, and his brother Laurence Hyde, earl of Rochester …* (2 vols, London, 1828)
Clarendon, letters	*The state letters of Henry earl of Clarendon, lord lieutenant of Ireland during the reign of King James II and his lordship's diary for the years 1687, 1688, 1689 and 1690* (2 vols, Oxford, 1763)
Clarke collection	Jackie Clarke collection, Ballina, Co. Mayo
Clarke corr.	TCD, Sir George Clarke correspondence (MS 749)
Clarke, 'Patrick Darcy'	Aidan Clarke, 'Patrick Darcy and the constitutional relationship between Ireland and Britain' in Ohlmeyer (ed.), *Political thought*, pp 35–55
Claudianus	Andreas Claudianus, *The Irish mars, or, a history of the war in Ireland for two years, from notes recorded by a fellow soldier* (ed. and trans. Kjeld Hald Galster & Rasmus Wichmann) (Kingston, Ontario, 2016)
Coll. Hib.	*Collectanea Hibernica* (1958–2006)
Connolly, *Religion, law and power*	S.J. Connolly, *Religion, law and power: the making of Protestant Ireland, 1660–1760* (Oxford, 1992)
Conroy, 'Galway Bay'	Jane Conroy, 'Galway Bay, Louis XIV's navy and the "little Bougard"' in *JGAHS*, 49 (1997), pp 36–48
Conveyances of the forfeited estates	Abstracts of the conveyances of the forfeited estates and interests in Ireland in 1688 in *Fifteenth report from the commissioners appointed by his majesty to execute the measures recommended in an address of the house of commons respecting the public records of Ireland* (1825)
Cooke, *Birr*	Thomas Lalor Cooke, *The early history of the town of Birr or Parsonstown* (Dublin, 1875)
Corp, *Court in exile*	Edward Corp, *A court in exile: the Stuarts in France 1689–1718* (Cambridge, 2004)
Corp, 'Irish at Jacobite court'	Edward Corp, 'The Irish at the Jacobite court of Saint-Germain-en-Laye' in Thomas O'Connor (ed.), *The Irish in Europe, 1580–1815* (Dublin, 2001), pp 143–56

Corvisier, *Malplaquet*	André Corvisier, *La bataille de Malplaquet 1709: l'effondrement de la France évité* (Paris, 1997)
Cox, 'MacCoghlans 1/2'	Liam Cox, 'The MacCoghlans of Delvin Eathra' in *Ir. Gen.*, iv (1968–73), pp 534–46 (1); v (1974–9), pp 21–32 (2)
CP	G.E.C[okayne], *The complete peerage of England, Scotland, Ireland, Great Britain and the United Kingdom* … (13 vols, London, 1910–40)
Craig, *Dublin, 1660–1860*	Maurice Craig, *Dublin 1660–1860: a social and architectural history* (Dublin, 1969)
CSPD	*Calendar of state papers, domestic series, 1685–95* (London, 1937–72)
CTB	*Calendar of treasury books, 1685–9*, viii (London, 1923)
CTP	*Calendar of treasury papers, 1556–1696*, i (London, 1868)
Cullen, *Economic history of Ireland*	L.M. Cullen, *An economic history of Ireland since 1660* (London, 1972)
Cullen, *Irish brandy-houses*	L.M. Cullen, *The Irish brandy-houses of eighteenth-century France* (Dublin, 2000)
Cullen, *Life in Ireland*	L.M. Cullen, *Life in Ireland* (London, New York, 1978)
Dalton	Charles Dalton, *English army lists and commission registers, 1661–1714* (6 vols, London, 1892–1904)
Danish force	K. Danaher & J.G. Simms (eds), *The Danish force in Ireland, 1690–1691* (Dublin, 1962)
D'Avaux	James Hogan (ed.), *Négotiations de M. le comte d'Avaux en Irlande, 1689–90* (Dublin, 1934)
D'Avaux, suppl.	James Hogan (ed.), *Négotiations de M. le comte d'Avaux en Irlande (1689–90), supplementary volume* (Dublin, 1958)
Davis, *Patriot parliament*	Thomas Davis, *The patriot parliament of 1689* (Dublin, 1843)
De Corthuy	Narrative how basely the Baron de Corthuy has been advised by the Irish in 1689–91 (Bodl. Rawlinson MS c. 439; NLI photostat MS 908)
DI	*Dublin Intelligence*, 1690–1
'Diaries of the Boyne'	G.S., 'Two unpublished diaries connected with the battle of the Boyne' in *Ulster Journal of Archaeology*, iv (1856), pp 77–95
DIB	James Maguire & James Quinn (eds), *Dictionary of Irish biography from the earliest times to the year 2002* (9 vols, Cambridge, 2009)

Dillon papers	J.F. Ainsworth, Report on the Dillon of Clonbrock papers (NLI Report on private collections, no. 4)
Doherty, *Williamite war*	Richard Doherty, *The Williamite war in Ireland, 1688–91* (Dublin, 1998)
Dolley, 'Irish coinage'	Michael Dolley, 'The Irish coinage, 1534–1691' in *A new history of Ireland*, iii, pp 408–19
'Domville, That great question' (ed. Kelly)	'Sir William Domville: a disquisition touching that great question whether an act of parliament made in England shall bind the kingdom and people of Ireland without their allowance and acceptance of such act in the kingdom of Ireland' (ed. Patrick Kelly) in *AH*, 40 (2007), pp 19–70
Downey, 'Beneath the harp'	Declan Downey, 'Beneath the harp and Burgundian cross: Irish regiments in the Spanish Bourbon army, 1700–1818' in Hugo O'Donnell (ed.), *The Irish presence in the Spanish military – 16th to 20th centuries* (Madrid, 2014), pp 83–105
Downey, 'Wild geese and the double-headed eagle'	Declan Downey, 'Wild geese and the double-headed eagle: Irish integration in Austria *c.*1630–*c.*1918' in Paul Leifer & Eda Sagarra (eds), *Austro-Irish links through the centuries* (Vienna, 2002), pp 41–57
Duffy, *Fire and stone*	C. Duffy, *Fire and stone: the science of fortress warfare, 1660–1860* (Newton Abbot and Vancouver, 1975)
Duffy, *Fortress*	Christopher Duffy, *The fortress in the age of Vauban and Frederick the Great, 1661–1789* (London, 1985)
Duffy, 'Irish in imperial service'	Christopher Duffy, 'The Irish in the imperial service: an Englishman's comment' in *Ir. Sword*, vii (1965–6), pp 76–7
Duffy, *The '45*	Christopher Duffy, *The '45* (London, 2003)
Dumont de Bostaquet	Dianne W. Ressinger (ed. and trans.) *Memoirs of Isaac Dumont de Bostaquet, a gentleman of Normandy* (London, 2005)
Duncan, *Royal artillery*	Francis Duncan, *History of the royal regiment of artillery compiled from the original records* (London, 1872)
Dunne, 'Gaelic response'	T.J. Dunne, 'The Gaelic response to conquest and colonization: the evidence of the poetry' in *Studia Hibernica*, 20 (1980), pp 1–30
Egerton MS 1671	British Library, Egerton MS 1671, Petitions from natives of Great Britain and Ireland, chiefly Roman Catholics, resident in France, in the French service or attached to the family of the Pretender
Elliot-Wright, 'Officers of the Irish brigade'	Philipp J.C. Elliot-Wright, 'The officers of the Irish brigade and the British army, 1789–98' (PhD, Leeds, 1977)

English reports	*The English reports: house of lords* (Abingdon, 1980 reprint)
'Eustace family'	Sir Eustace F. Tickell, 'The Eustace family and their lands in Co. Kildare' in *KASJ*, xiii (1955–60), pp 307–41, 364–413
Fagan, *Stuart papers*	Patrick Fagan, *Ireland in the Stuart papers*, i, *1719–42*; ii, *1743–65* (Dublin, 1995)
Falkiner, 'Regiment of guards'	C. Litton Falkiner, 'His Majesty's regiment of guards in Ireland' in *Illustrations of Irish history and topography mainly of the seventeenth century* (London, 1904), pp 74–102
Faulkner, 'An Irish diary of 1689'	Anselm Faulkner, 'An Irish diary of the war against James II: 12 August–23 October 1689' in *Coll. Hib.*, no. 20 (1978), pp 21–9
Fenning, 'Irish Dominicans at Rome'	Hugh Fenning, 'Irish Dominicans at Rome, 1570–1699: a biographical register' in *Coll. Hib.*, no. 44/5 (2002/3), pp 13–55
Ferguson, 'Army in Ireland'	Kenneth Patrick Ferguson, 'The army in Ireland from the restoration to the act of union' (PhD, TCD, 1980)
F-I corr.	Sheila Mulloy (ed.), *Franco-Irish correspondence December 1688–February 1692* (3 vols, Dublin 1983–4)
Field Day anthology	Seamus Deane (ed.), *The Field Day anthology of Irish writing* (Derry, 1992)
Finch MSS	*Report on the manuscripts of the late Allen George Finch Esq., of Burley-on-the-Hill, Rutland* (HMC, 5 vols, 1913–2007)
Firth, *Cromwell's army*	C.H. Firth, *Cromwell's army: a history of the English soldier during the civil wars, the commonwealth and the protectorate* (London, 1992 edn)
Forman, *A letter … for disbanding the Irish regiments*	Charles Forman, *A letter to the Right Honourable Sir Robert Sutton, for disbanding the Irish regiments in the service of France and Spain* (Dublin, 1728)
Franco-Irish military connections	Nathalie Genet-Rouffiac & David Murphy (eds), *Franco-Irish military connections, 1590–1945* (Dublin, 2009)
'Gafney'	Rev. James Graves, 'Extracts from the private memorandum book of Captain George Gafney, of Kilkenny, an officer in the army of James II' in *RSAI Jn.*, iii (1854–5), pp 161–72
GAHSJ	*Galway Archaeological and Historical Society Journal* (1900–)
Garland, 'Irish in Neapolitan service'	John L. Garland, 'Irish officers in the Neapolitan service' in *Ir. Gen.*, v (1974–9), pp 728–9
Garland, 'MacElligott'	J.L. Garland, 'The regiment of MacElligott 1688–1689' in *Ir. Sword*, i (1949–53), pp 121–7

Garland, 'Parma Irishmen'	John L. Garland, 'Parma Irishmen' in *Ir. Sword*, xvii (1987–90), pp 134–5
'Gaydon's memoir'	Liam Ó Briain (ed.), 'The Chevalier Gaydon's memoir of the regiment of Dillon, 1738' in *Ir. Sword*, iii (1957–8), pp 98–106, 194–202, 273–81; iv (1959–60), pp 29–39, 121–6, 157–62, 257–63; v (1961–2), pp 88–93, 175–8, 218–22; vi (1967–8), pp 34–41, 88–93, 180–91.
Genet-Rouffiac, 'Wild geese' I	Nathalie Genet-Rouffiac, 'The wild geese in France, 1688–1715: a French perspective' in *Ir. Sword*, xxvi (2008–9), pp 11–48
Genet-Rouffiac, 'Wild Geese' II	Nathalie Genet-Rouffiac, 'The wild geese in France: a French perspective' in *Franco-Irish military connections*, pp 32–54
Gillespie, *Transformation of the Irish economy*	Raymond Gillespie, *The transformation of the Irish economy 1550–1700* (Dundalk, 1991)
Ginkel corr.	*HMC Fourth report*, appendix (Ginkel corr., de Ros MSS) (1874)
Gouhier, 'Mercenaires irlandais'	Pierre Gouhier, 'Mercenaires irlandais au service de la France (1635–64)' in *Ir. Sword*, vii (1965–6), pp 58–75
Graham, *Mountcashel*	D.P. Graham, *Lord Mountcashel: Irish general. Justin MacCarthy in the service of James II and Louis XIV, 1673–1694* (Barnsley, 2018)
Gray's Inn admissions	Joseph Foster (ed.), *The register of admissions to Gray's Inn, 1521–1889*
Great news of a bloody fight in Newton	*Great news of a bloody fight in Newton in Ireland* (London, 1689)
Gregg, 'Exiled Stuarts'	Edward Gregg, 'France, Rome and the exiled Stuarts' in Edward Corp, *A court in exile: the Stuarts in France, 1689–1718* (Cambridge, 2004), pp 11–75
Gretton, *Royal Irish regiment*	G. Le M. Gretton, *The campaigns and history of the Royal Irish regiment from 1684 to 1902* (Edinburgh & London, 1911)
Grotius	Hugo Grotius, *The rights of war and peace* (ed. Richard Tuck) (Indianapolis, 2005)
Gruber von Arni, *Hospital care*	Eric Gruber von Arni, *Hospital care and the British standing army, 1660–1714* (Aldershot, 2006)
Guilmartin, 'Gunpowder revolution'	J.F. Guilmartin, 'The gunpowder revolution, c.1300–1650' in *Encyclopaedia Britannica* (Chicago, 1994 edn), xxix, pp 541–7

Guy, 'Irish military establishment'	Alan J. Guy, 'The Irish military establishment' in Bartlett & Jeffrey, *Military history of Ireland*, pp 211–14.
Hamilton, *Inniskillingmen*	Andrew Hamilton, *A true relation of the actions of the Inniskillingmen* (London, 1690)
Hand, 'Constitutional position'	G.J. Hand, 'The constitutional position of the Irish military establishment from the restoration to the union: an introductory note' in *The Irish Jurist*, iii, n.s., part 2 (winter 1968), pp 330–5
Harris	Walter Harris, *The history of the life and reign of William-henry ... king of England ...* (Dublin, 1749)
Harris, *Revolution*	Tim Harris, *Revolution: the great crisis of the British monarchy, 1685–1720* (London, 2006)
Harris, 'Swift Nix'	Amy Louise Harris, 'The Irish career of an English highwayman: Captain Swift Nix [or Nicks] (1638–88)' in *Ir. Sword*, xxxiii (2021–2), pp 13–21
Hayes, *BD*	Richard Hayes, *Biographical dictionary of Irishmen in France* (Dublin, 1949)
Hayes, 'Irish casualties in French service'	Richard Hayes, 'Irish casualties in the French military service' in *Ir. Sword*, i (1949–53), pp 198–201
Hayes, 'Reflections'	R.J. Hayes, 'Reflections of an Irish brigade officer' in *Ir. Sword*, i (1949–53), pp 68–74
Hayes-McCoy *Irish battles*	G.A. Hayes-McCoy, *Irish battles: a military history of Ireland* (London, 1969)
Hayes-McCoy, *Irish flags*	G.A. Hayes-McCoy, *A history of Irish flags from earliest times* (Dublin, 1979)
Hayes-McCoy, 'Irish soldiers of the '45'	G.A. Hayes-McCoy, 'Irish soldiers of the '45' in Etienne Rynne (ed.), *North Munster studies* (Limerick, 1967), pp 315–34
Haynes, *History of the hautboy*	Bruce Haynes, *The eloquent oboe: a history of the hautboy, 1640–1760* (Oxford, 2001)
Hazard, 'Manifesto of Hugh O'Donnell'	Benjamin Hazard, 'The manifesto of Field Marshal Hugh O'Donnell in justification of his departure from the kingdom without leave from Charles II, king of Spain, c.1690' in *Ir. Sword*, xxvi (2008–9), pp 121–37
Healy, 'Sir Teague O'Regan'	Francis J. Healy, 'Sir Teague O'Regan of Ballynacloghy, County Cork' in *JCHAS*, xii (1906), pp 121–5
Hebbert, 'Richards brothers'	F.J. Hebbert, 'The Richards brothers' in *Ir. Sword*, xii (1975–6), pp 200–11

Henry, *Military community*	Gráinne Henry, *The Irish military community in Spanish Flanders, 1586–1621* (Dublin, 1992)
Heslip, 'Brass money'	Robert Heslip, 'Brass money' in Maguire, *Kings in conflict*, pp 122–35
HMC	Historical Manuscripts Commission
Hodges, 'Cannon'	J. Hodges, 'A cannon to beat all comers' in *New Scientist*, no. 1546 (5 February 1987), pp 74–5
Hollick, *Benburb*	Clive Hollick, *The battle of Benburb 1646* (Cork, 2011)
Holmes (ed.), *Weapon*	Richard Holmes (ed.), *Weapon: a visual history of arms and armour* (London, 2006)
Hopkins, *Glencoe*	Paul Hopkins, *Glencoe and the end of the Highland war* (Edinburgh, 1986)
Hoppen, *Common scientist*	K. Theodore Hoppen, *The common scientist in the seventeenth century* (London, 1970)
Horner, 'Landscape of the Pale'	Arnold Horner, 'Reconstructing the seventeenth-century landscape of the Pale' in *History Ireland*, xx, no. 6 (November–December 2012), pp 18–22
Horner & Loeber 'Landscape in transition'	Arnold Horner & Rolf Loeber, 'Landscape in transition: descriptions of forfeited properties in counties Meath, Louth and Cavan in 1700' in *AH*, 42 (2011), pp 61–179
IALKC	Charles Dalton (ed.), *Irish army lists of King Charles II, 1661–1685* (London, 1907; reprint Dublin, 2000)
IHS	*Irish Historical Studies* (1938–)
Inchiquin MSS	John Ainsworth (ed.), *The Inchiquin manuscripts* (Dublin, 1961)
Ireland's lamentation	*Ireland's lamentation: being a short, but perfect, full and true account of the situation, nature, constitution and product of Ireland ...* (London, 1689)
'Irish in Spanish service I, II' etc.	Richard Wall (ed.), 'Irish officers in the Spanish service. I. The dragoon regiments of Dublin and Edinburgh' in *Ir. Gen.*, v (1974–9), pp 431–4; II. 'The regiment of Limerick', pp 601–5; Hubert Gallwey (ed.), III. 'The regiment of Waterford', vi (1980–5), pp 18–21; IV. 'The regiment of Irlanda', pp 204–11; J.L Garland (ed.), V. 'The regiment of Irlanda (concluded)', pp 328–33; Hubert Gallwey and J.L. Garland (eds), VI. 'The regiment of Hibernia', pp 461–8; VII. 'The regiment of Hibernia (continued)', pp 601–5

Ir. Gen.	*The Irish Genealogist* (1937–)
Ir. Sword	*The Irish Sword* (1949–)
James II	J.S. Clarke (ed.), *The life of James II, king of England etc.* (2 vols, London, 1816)
JCHAS	*Journal of the Cork Historical and Archaeological Society* (1892–)
Jennings, *Wild geese in Spanish Flanders*	Brendan Jennings (ed.), *Wild geese in Spanish Flanders* (Dublin, 1964)
JGAHS	*Journal of the Galway Archaeological and Historical Society* (1900–)
JN	J.T. Gilbert (ed.), *A Jacobite narrative of the war in Ireland, 1688–91* (Dublin, 1892; reprint Shannon, 1971)
Johnston, 'Stapleton plantations'	J.R.V. Johnston, 'The Stapleton sugar plantations in the Leeward Islands' in *Bulletin of the John Rylands Library, Manchester* (1965), pp 175–206
Jordan, 'Aughrim'	J. Jordan (ed.), 'The battle of Aughrim: two Danish sources' in *JGAHS*, xxvi (1954–5), pp 1–13
Journal 19/5 to 18/6; 1/6 to 18/7 (Carte MS 181)	Journal 19 May to 18 June; 1 June to 18 July 1689 (Bodleian Library, Oxford, Carte MS 181)
JRSAI	*Journal of the Royal Society of Antiquaries of Ireland* (1849–)
JSAHR	*Journal of the Society for Army Historical Research* (1921–)
Kane, *Campaigns*	Richard Kane, *Campaigns of King William and Queen Anne from 1689 to 1712, also a new system of military discipline* (London, 1745)
KASJ	*Kildare Archaeological Society Journal* (1890–)
KC catg.	Eileen Black (ed.), *Kings in conflict: Ireland in the 1690s* [catalogue to Ulster Museum exhibition] (Belfast, 1690)
Kelly, 'Light to the blind'	Patrick Kelly, ' "A light to the blind": the voice of the dispossessed élite in the generation after the siege of Limerick' in *IHS*, xxiv (1984–5), pp 431–62
Kelly, *Sport in Ireland*	James Kelly, *Sport in Ireland, 1600–1840* (Dublin, 2014)
Kemp, *Weapons*	Anthony Kemp, *Weapons and equipment of the Marlborough wars* (Poole, 1980)
Kenyon MSS	*Report on the manuscripts of Lord Kenyon* (London, 1894)

Kenyon, *Sunderland*	J.P. Kenyon, *Robert Spencer earl of Sunderland, 1641–17* (London, 1958)
Keogh, 'French support'	Jonathan Keogh, 'Information and French support for Jacobite Ireland, 1689–1691' (University of Dundee, MPhil, 2013)
[Kerney] Walsh, *MacDonnells*	Micheline [Kerney] Walsh, *The MacDonnells of Antrim on the Continent* (Dublin, n.d.), pp 323–38
Kerney-Walsh, 'Wild Goose tradition'	Micheline Kerney-Walsh, 'The Wild Goose tradition' in *Ir. Sword*, xvii (1987–90), pp 4–15
Kerrigan, 'Charles Fort, Kinsale'	Paul M. Kerrigan, 'Charles Fort, Kinsale' in *Ir. Sword*, xiii (1977–9), pp 323–38
Kerrigan, *Fortifications*	Paul M. Kerrigan, *Castles and fortifications in Ireland, 1485–1945* (Cork, 1995)
Kilmallock papers	Papers of Dominic Sarsfield, 4th Viscount Kilmallock (NLI MS 17890)
King	William King, *The state of the Protestants of Ireland under the late King James's government* (Dublin, 1730 edn)
Kinsella, *Catholic survival*	Eoin Kinsella, *Catholic survival in Protestant Ireland, 1660–1711: Colonel John Browne, land ownership and the articles of Limerick* (Woodbridge, 2018)
KJIL	James D'Alton, *Illustrations of King James's Irish army list (1689)* (2 vols, Dublin, second edn, n.d., but 1860)
Laportaliére, 'Dusson'	René de Laportaliére, 'Jean Dusson de Saint Martin, lieutenant general des armées du roi (1652–1705)' in *Sociéte Ariégeoise Sciences Lettres et Arts*, xxxii (1977), pp 73–113
La Tour du Pin	*Recollections of the revolution and the empire by la marquise de la Tour du Pin* (ed. Walter Geer) (London, 1921)
'Lauzun's reports'	'Reports of the French general Comte Lauzun on the campaign of 1690' in Leopold von Ranke, *A history of England principally in the seventeenth century* (6 vols, Oxford, 1875), vi, appendix, pp 102–27
Lawson, *Uniforms*	Cecil C.P. Lawson, *A history of the uniforms of the British army*, i (London, 1969 repr.)

Le Fevre, 'Battle of Bantry Bay'	Peter Le Fevre, 'The battle of Bantry Bay, 1 May 1689' in *Ir. Sword*, xviii (1990–2), pp 1–16
Le Fleming MSS	Le Fleming MSS in *HMC Twelfth report*, appendix 7 (1890)
Lenihan, 'Boisseleau & the "battle of the breach"'	Pádraig Lenihan, '"My cabal of one": the marquis de Boisseleau and the "battle of the breach" at the first siege of Limerick, 1690' in *History Ireland*, 28:5 (September/October 2020), pp 16–19
Lenihan, *Boyne*	Pádraig Lenihan, *1690 battle of the Boyne* (Stroud, 2003)
Lenihan, *Confederate Catholics*	Pádraig Lenihan (ed.), *Confederate Catholics at war, 1641–49* (Cork, 2001)
Lenihan, *Conquest and resistance*	Pádraig Lenihan (ed.), *Conquest and resistance: war in seventeenth-century Ireland* (Leiden, 2001)
Lenihan, 'Irish brigade'	Pádraig Lenihan, 'The "Irish brigade" 1690–1715' in *Eighteenth-Century Ireland*, xxxi (2016), pp 48–74
Lenihan, *Last cavalier*	Pádraig Lenihan, *The last cavalier: Richard Talbot (1631–91)* (Dublin, 2014)
Lenihan, *Limerick*	Maurice Lenihan, *Limerick, its history and antiquities* (Dublin, 1866)
Lepage, *Vauban*	Jean-Denis Lepage, *Vauban and the French military under Louis XIV* (Jefferson, NC, 2010)
Leslie	[Leslie, Charles], *An answer to a book intituled The state of the protestants in Ireland under the late King James's government in which their carriage towards him is justified …* (London, 1692)
LG	*London Gazette*
Lib. mun.	Rowley Lascelles, *Liber munerum publicorum Hiberniae* (London, 1852)
List of 1st horseguards (SHAD, AG, A1 1241), f. 112	List of 1st horseguards (Service Historique de la Défense, Vincennes, archives de la Guerre, A1 1241), f. 112
List of 2nd horseguards (BS-G MS 3537), ff 58–61	List of 2nd horseguards (Bibliothèque Sainte-Geneviève, Paris, MS 3537), ff 58–61

Loeber, 'Engineers'	Rolf Loeber, 'Biographical dictionary of engineers in Ireland, 1600–1730' in *Ir. Sword*, xiii (1977–9) pp 30–44, 106–22, 230–55, 283–314
Loeber, *Irish houses and castles*	Rolf Loeber, *Irish houses and castles (1400–1740)* (Dublin, 2019)
Loeber, 'Irish militia documents'	Rolf Loeber, 'The reorganiziation of the Irish militia in 1678–81: documents from Birr Castle' in *Ir. Sword*, xix (1993–5), pp 197–224
Loeber & Murtagh, 'Artillery fortifications'	Rolf Loeber & Harman Murtagh, 'Artillery fortifications' in Andrew Carpenter (ed.), *Art and architecture of Ireland*, iv, Rolf Loeber et al. (eds), *Architecture 1600–2000* (Dublin, New Haven, London, 2014), pp 234–5
Loeber & Parker, 'Military revolution in Ireland'	Rolf Loeber & Geoffrey Parker, 'The military revolution in seventeenth-century Ireland' in Jane Ohlmeyer (ed.), *Ireland from independence to occupation, 1641–1660* (Cambridge, 1995)
Logan, 'Medical services, 1641–52'	Patrick Logan, 'Medical services in the armies of the confederate wars, 1641–52' in *Ir. Sword*, iv (1959–60), pp 217–27
'Longford letters'	Patrick Melvin (ed.), 'Letters of Lord Longford and others on Irish affairs 1689–1702' in *AH*, 32 (1985), pp 35–111
Lord Meath's letter	(Lord Meath's letter) in *RIA Proc.*, ix (1867), pp 534–5
Lynn, *Giant of the grand siècle*	John A. Lynn, *Giant of the grand siècle: the French army, 1610–1715* (Cambridge, 1997)
Lyons, 'Female dependants of Irish Jacobites'	Mary Ann Lyons, '"*Digne de compassion*": female dependants of Irish Jacobite soldiers in France, c.1692–c.1730' in *Eighteenth-Century Ireland*, xxiii (2008), pp 55–75
McCarmick, *Inniskillingmen*	William MacCarmick, *A further impartial account of the actions of the Inniskillingmen* (London, 1691)
McDonnell, 'Catholic Irish brigade'	Ciarán McDonnell, 'A "fair chance"? The Catholic Irish brigade in the British service, 1793–8' in *War in history*, vol. 2(2) (2016), pp 150–68
McDonnell, 'Documents relating to the Irish brigade'	Hector McDonnell, 'Some documents relating to the involvement of the Irish brigade in the rebellion of 1745' in *Ir. Sword*, xvi (1984–6), pp 3–21
McDonnell, 'Irishmen in Stuart navy'	Hector McDonnell, 'Irishmen in the Stuart navy, 1660–90' in *Ir. Sword*, xvi (1984–5), pp 87–104

McDonnell, *Wild geese*	Hector McDonnell, *The wild geese of the Antrim MacDonnells* (Dublin, 1996)
MacGeoghegan, *History*	Abbé MacGeoghegan, *A history of Ireland, ancient and modern* (trans. P. O'Kelly) (Dublin, 1844)
McGillycuddy papers	W. Maziere Brady (ed.), *The McGillycuddy papers: a selection from the family archives of the McGillycuddy of the Reeks, with an introductory memoir, being a contribution to the history of the county of Kerry* (London, 1867)
McGuire, 'Sir Richard Nagle'	James McGuire, 'A lawyer in politics: the career of Sir Richard Nagle c.1636–1699' in Judith Devlin & Howard B. Clarke (eds), *European encounters: essays in memory of Albert Lovett* (Dublin, 2003), pp 118–31
MacKay, *Memoirs*	Major General Hugh MacKay, *Memoirs of the war carried on in Scotland and Ireland, 1689–1691* (Edinburgh, 1833)
McKenny, 'Restoration land settlement'	Kevin McKenny, 'The restoration land settlement in Ireland: a statistical interpretation' in Coleman A. Dennehy, *Restoration Ireland: always settling and never settled* (London, 2020), pp 35–52
Maclean-Bristol, *Castor and Pollux*	Nicholas Maclean-Bristol, *Castor & Pollux: two Jacobite Maclean knights from the Sound of Mull at war in the Hebrides, the Highlands of Scotland, Ireland & mainland Europe 1674–1716* (Argyll, 2012)
MacLysaght, *Irish life*	Edward MacLysaght, *Irish life in the seventeenth century* (Cork, 3rd edn, 1969)
McNally, *Aughrim*	Michael McNally, *Battle of Aughrim 1691* (Stroud, 2008)
McNally, *Boyne*	Michael McNally, *Battle of the Boyne 1690: the Irish campaign for the English crown* (Oxford, 2005)
Macpherson, *Original papers*	J. Macpherson, *Original papers containing the secret history of Great Britain from the restoration to the accession of the house of Hannover* (2 vols, London, 1775)
MacSwiney, 'First Irish regiments in Spain'	The Marquess MacSwiney of Mashanaglass, 'Notes on the formation of the first two Irish regiments in the service of Spain in the eighteenth century' in *RSAI Jn.*, lviii (1927), pp 3–16
MacSwiney, 'Irish regiments in Spain & Naples'	The marquis MacSwiney of Mashanaglass, 'Notes on some Irish regiments in the service of Spain and of Naples in the eighteenth century' in *PRIA*, 37 (1924), pp 158–74

MacSwiney, 'Luzzara'	The marquis MacSwiney of Mashanaglass, 'The casualty list of the infantry regiment of Albemarle at the battle of Luzzara, 15th August 1702' in *RSAI Jn.*, lx (1930), pp 1–7
Magan, *Umma-More*	William Magan, *Umma-More: the story of an Irish family* (Shaftesbury, 1983)
Maguire, 'Estate of Cúchonnacht Maguire'	W.A. Maguire, 'The estate of Cúchonnacht Maguire of Tempo: a case history from the Williamite settlement' in *IHS*, xxvii (1990–1), pp 130–44
Maguire, *Kings in conflict*	W.A. Maguire (ed.), *Kings in conflict: the revolutionary war in Ireland and its aftermath, 1689–1750* (Belfast, 1990)
Mahaffy, *Trinity*	J.P. Mahaffy, *An epoch of Irish history: Trinity College, Dublin, its foundation and early fortunes, 1591–1660* (London, 1903)
Mangan, 'Sarsfield's defence of the Shannon'	Henry Mangan, 'Sarsfield's defence of the Shannon, 1690–91' in *Ir. Sword*, i (1949–53), pp 24–32
Marquess of Sligo, *Westport House*	The marquess of Sligo, *Westport House and the Brownes* (Ashbourne, 1981)
Martinez, '*Semper et ubique fidelis*'	George Martinez, '*Semper et ubique fidelis*' in *Franco-Irish military connections*, pp 139–49
Maynard, 'Legal profession'	Hazel Maynard, 'The Irish legal profession and the Catholic revival 1660–89' in *People, politics and power*, pp 28–50
Melvin, 'Balldearg O'Donnell abroad'	Patrick Melvin, 'Balldearg O'Donnell abroad and the French design in Catalonia, 1688–97' in *Ir. Sword*, xii (1975–6), pp 42–54, 116–29
Melvin, 'Colonel Con O'Rourke'	Patrick Melvin, 'The case of Colonel Con O'Rourke' in *Ir. Sword*, xii (1975–6), pp 67–70
Melvin, *Estates in Galway*	Patrick Melvin, *Estates and landed society in Galway* (Dublin, 2013)
Melvin, 'Irish troop movements'	Patrick Melvin, 'Irish troop movements and James II's army in 1688' in *Ir. Sword*, x (1971–2), pp 87–105
Melvin, 'Plotters'	Patrick Melvin, 'Irish soldiers and plotters in Williamite England' in *Ir. Sword*, xiii (1977–9), pp 256–67, 353–68; xiv (1980–1), pp 271–86
Melvin, 'Revolution of 1688'	Patrick Melvin, 'The Irish army and the revolution of 1688' in *Ir. Sword*, ix (1969–70), pp 288–307

Memoirs of the family of Grace	Sheffield Grace, *Memoirs of the family of Grace* (London, 1823)
Middle Temple admissions	H.A.C. Sturgess (ed.), *Register of admissions to the Honourable Society of the Middle Temple from the fifteenth century to the year 1944* (London, 1949)
Military duties of officers of cavalry	Sieur de La Fontaine, *The military duties of the officers of cavalry* (London, 1678)
Miller, 'Catholic officers'	John Miller, 'Catholic officers in the later Stuart army' in *English Historical Review*, lxxxviii, no. 346 (January 1973), pp 35–53
Miller, *James II*	John Miller, *James II: a study in kingship* (London, 1978)
Miller, 'Thomas Sheridan'	John Miller, 'Thomas Sheridan and his "Narrative"' in *IHS*, xx (September 1976–7), pp 105–28
Miller, 'Tyrconnell & James II'	John Miller, 'The earl of Tyrconnell and James II's Irish policy, 1685–1688' in *The Historical Journal*, xx (1977), pp 803–23
Millett, *Survival & reorganization*	Benignus Millett, *Survival and reorganization, 1660–95* (Dublin, 1968)
Milligan, *Londonderry*	Cecil Davis Milligan, *History of the siege of Londonderry 1689* (Belfast, 1951)
Morales, *Ireland and the Spanish empire*	Óscar Recio Morales, *Ireland and the Spanish empire, 1600–1825* (Dublin, 2010)
Morales, 'Irish émigré group strategies in Spain'	Óscar Recio Morales, 'Irish émigré group strategies of survival, adaptation and integration in seventeenth- and eighteenth-century Spain' in Thomas O'Connor & Mary Ann Lyons (eds), *Irish communities in early-modern Europe* (Dublin, 2006), pp 240–66
Morley, 'Irish Jacobitism'	Vincent Morley, 'Irish Jacobitism, 1691–1790' in *Cambridge history of Ireland*, iii, p. 47
Müller & Williamson, 'Fortification of Belfast'	G. Müller & G. Williamson, 'Fortification of Belfast' in *Ir. Sword*, xix (1993–5), pp 306–12
Mulloy (ed.), de Vault	François-Eugène de Vault, 'Mémoire ou extrait de la correspondence de la cour et des génèraux pendant la guerre en Irlande (1689–91)', ed. Sheila O'Malley (Mulloy) (PhD, NUI Galway, 1955)

Mulloy, 'French engineers'	Sheila Mulloy, 'French engineers with the Jacobite army in Ireland' in *Ir. Sword*, xv (1982–3), pp 222–32
Mulloy, 'French eye-witnesses'	Sheila Mulloy, 'French eye-witnesses of the Boyne' in *Ir. Sword*, xv (1982–3), pp 105–11
Mulloy, 'French navy'	Sheila Mulloy, 'The French navy and the Jacobite war in Ireland' in *Ir. Sword*, xviii (1990–2), pp 17–31
Mulloy, 'Galway'	Sheila Mulloy, 'Galway in the Jacobite war' in *JGAHS*, 40 (1985–6), pp 1–19
Murphy, *Irish brigades*	David Murphy, *The Irish brigades, 1685–2006; a gazetteer of Irish military service, past and present* (Dublin, 2007)
Murphy, 'Wild geese'	James H. Murphy, 'The wild geese' in *The Irish Review (Cork)*, no. 16 (1994), pp 23–8.
Murphy, *Mountcashel*	John A. Murphy, *Justin MacCarthy, Lord Mountcashel, commander of the first Irish brigade* (Cork, 1959)
Murphy, 'Captain John Stevens'	M. Murphy, 'A Jacobite antiquary in Grub Street: Captain John Stevens (*c.*1662–1726) in *Recusant History*, 24 (1998–9), pp 437–54
Murtagh, *Athlone*	Harman Murtagh, *Athlone: history and settlement to 1800* (Athlone, 2000)
Murtagh, 'Ballymore'	Harman Murtagh, 'Ballymore and the Jacobite War' in *Journal of the Old Athlone Society*, i (1974–5), pp 242–6
Murtagh, *Boyne guide*	Harman Murtagh, *The battle of the Boyne 1690: a guide to the battlefield* (Drogheda, 2006)
Murtagh, 'Richard Grace'	Harman Murtagh, 'Richard Grace (*c.*1616–91), defender of Athlone' in *Journal of the Old Athlone Society*, ii (1978–2013), pp 312–26
Murtagh, '"Some traitors amongst us"'	Harman Murtagh, '"Some traitors amongst us": what lay behind the Williamite winter offensive of December 1690?' in Terence Dooley, Mary Ann Lyons & Salvador Ryan (eds), *The historian as detective: uncovering the Irish pasts: essays in honour of Raymond Gillespie* (Dublin, 2021), pp 144–7
Murtagh, 'Thomas Phillips'	Harman Murtagh, 'Thomas Phillips's prospects of Ireland 1684–5' in *Irish Arts Review*, 24:1 (spring 2007), pp 104–9

Murtagh, 'Town-wall fortifications of Athlone'	Harman Murtagh, 'The town-wall fortifications of' Athlone in H. Murtagh (ed.), *Irish midland studies: essays in commemoration of N.W. English* (Athlone, 1980), pp 89–106
Murtagh (D.), 'Aughrim'	Diarmuid Murtagh, 'The battle of Aughrim' in G.A. Hayes-McCoy (ed.), *The Irish at war* (Cork, 1964), pp 59–69
Murtagh (D.), 'Siege of Athlone'	Diarmuid Murtagh, 'The siege of Athlone, 1691' in *RSAI Jn.*, lxxxiii (1953), pp 58–81
Newton, 'Value of gold' (1702)	I. Newton et al., 'The value of gold in proportion to silver in several parts of Europe' (1702) in Treasury papers 80, no. 105 (URL: https://www.newtonproject.ox.ac.uk//MINT 00285 accessed 25 June 2022)
Nicholls, 'Kavanaghs'	K.W. Nicholls, 'The Kavanaghs, 1400–1600, contd' in *Ir. Gen.*, v (1974–9), pp 730–4
Nicholls, 'MacCoghlans'	Kenneth Nicholls, 'The MacCoghlans' in *Ir. Gen.*, vi (1980–56), pp 445–60
Nilis, 'Irish students at Leuven'	Jeroen Nilis, 'Irish students at Leuven University, 1548–1797' in *Arch. Hib.*, 60 (2006), pp 1–304
NLI	The National Library of Ireland
Ó Bruadair	John C. MacErlean, S.J. (ed.), *Duanaire Dáibhidh Uí Bhruadair; the poems of David Ó Bruadair* (3 vols, London, 1917)
Ó Buachalla, 'James our true king'	Breandán Ó Buachalla, 'James our true king: the ideology of Irish royalism in the seventeenth century' in D. George Boyce, Robert Eccleshall & Vincent Geoghegan (eds), *Political thought in Ireland since the seventeenth century* (London & New York, 1993)
O'Callaghan *Irish brigades*	John Cornelius O'Callaghan, *History of the Irish brigades in the service of France* (Glasgow, 1870)
O'Carroll, 'Battlefield of the Boyne'	Donal O'Carroll, 'An indifferent good post: the battlefield of the Boyne' in *Ir. Sword*, xviii (190–2), pp 49–56
O'Carroll, 'Change and continuity in weapons'	Donal O'Carroll, 'Change and continuity in weapons and tactics' in Lenihan, *Conquest and resistance*, pp 211–55
Ó Ciardha, *Ireland and the Jacobite cause*	Éamon Ó Ciardha, *Ireland and the Jacobite cause, 1685–1766: a fatal attachment* (Dublin, 2002)

Ó Ciardha, 'Irish outlaw'	Éamon Ó Ciardha, 'The early modern Irish outlaw: the making of a nationalist icon' in *People, politics and power*, pp 51–69
Ó Ciardha, 'Toryism'	Éamon Ó Ciardha, 'Toryism in Cromwellian Ireland (1650–60)' in *Ir. Sword*, xix (1993–5), pp 290–305
Ó Ciosáin, 'Irish migration to France'	Éamon Ó Ciosáin, 'A hundred years of Irish migration to France, 1590–1688' in Thomas O'Connor (ed.), *The Irish in Europe, 1580–1815* (Dublin, 2001), pp 93–106
Ó Ciosáin, 'Irish soldiers in French service'	Éamon Ó Ciosáin, 'Irish soldiers and regiments in French service before 1690' in *Franco-Irish military connections*, pp 15–31
Ó Cochláinn, 'The Cathach'	Rupert S. Ó Cochláin, 'The Cathach battle book of the O'Donnells' in *Ir. Sword*, viii (1967–8), pp 157–77
Ó Conaill, '"Ruddy cheeks and strapping thighs"'	Colm Ó Conaill, '"Ruddy cheeks and strapping thighs": an analysis of the ordinary soldiers in the ranks of the Irish regiments of eighteenth-century France' in *Ir. Sword*, xxiv (2004–5), pp 411–26
O'Connor, *Military history of the Irish nation*	Matthew O'Connor, *Military history of the Irish nation, comprising a memoir of the Irish brigade in the service of France* (Dublin, 1845)
Ó Cuiv, 'James Cotter'	Brian Ó Cuiv, 'James Cotter, a seventeenth-century agent of the crown' in *RSAI Jn.*, 88 (1958), pp 135–9
Ó Dálaigh et al., 'Edenvale castle survey'	Brian Ó Dálaigh, Martin Breen & Ristéard UaCróinín, 'The Edenvale castle survey of Co. Clare 1671–79' in *North Munster Antiquarian Journal*, 45 (2004), pp 33–50
ODNB	*Oxford dictionary of national biography* (Oxford, 2004)
'O'Donnells in exile'	John O'Donovan, 'The O'Donnells in exile' in *Duffy's Hibernian Magazine* (1860), no. 2, pp 50–6; no. 3, pp 106–7
Officer list (Bodl., Carte MS 181)	A list of the commissioned officers of the forces in Ireland in the service of King James after the revolution (Nairne papers, Bodleian Library Oxford, Carte MS 181)
Officer & Williamson, 'Purchasing power of British pounds'	Lawrence H. Officer & Samuel H. Williamson, 'Purchasing power of British pounds from 1270 to present' in MeasuringWorth (URL: www.measuringworth.com/ppoweruk/ accessed 20 June 2022)

Ó hAnnracháin, 'Fitzjames cavalry regiment'	Eoghan Ó hAnnracháin, 'The Fitzjames cavalry regiment 1737' in *Ir. Sword*, xix (1993–5), pp 253–76
Ó'hAnnracháin, 'Fontenoy'	Eoghan Ó hAnnracháin, 'The Irish at Fontenoy, 11 May 1745' in Peeters (ed.), *Fontenoy*, 59–87
Ó hAnnracháin, 'Irish veterans at *des Invalides*'	Eoghan Ó hAnnracháin, 'Irish veterans at the *Hôtel Royal des Invalides* (1692–1769) in *Ir. Sword*, xxi (1998–9), pp 5–42
Ó hAnnracháin, 'Lafelt'	Eoghan Ó hAnnracháin, 'The Irish brigade at Lafelt: pyrrhic victory and aftermath' in *JCHAS*, cii (1997), pp 1–22
Ó hAnnracháin, 'Malplaquet'	Eoghan Ó hAnnracháin, 'The battle of Malplaquet, 11 September 1709' in *Ir. Sword*, xxvi (2008–9), pp 375–92
Ó hAnnracháin, 'Parma's Irish guards'	Eoghan Ó hAnnracháin, 'The duke of Parma's Irish guards, 1702–33' in *Ir. Sword*, xxix (2013–14), pp 363–85
Ó'hAnnracháin, 'Political ideology and Catholicism'	Tadhg Ó'hAnnracháin, '"Though hereticks and politicians should misinterpret their good zeale": political ideology and Catholicism in early modern Ireland' in Ohlmeyer (ed.), *Political thought*, pp 155–75
O'Heyne, *Irish Dominicans*	John O'Heyne, *The Irish Dominicans of the seventeenth century* (Dundalk, 1902)
Ohlmeyer, *Antrim*	Jane H. Ohlmeyer, *Civil war and restoration in the three kingdoms: the career of Randal MacDonnell, marquis of Antrim, 1609–1683* (Cambridge, 1993)
Ohlmeyer, *Making Ireland English*	Jane H. Ohlmeyer, *Making Ireland English: the Irish aristocracy in the seventeenth century* (London, 2012)
Ohlmeyer (ed.), *Political thought*	Jane H. Ohlmeyer (ed.), *Political thought in seventeenth-century Ireland: kingdom or colony* (Cambridge, 2000)
O'Kelly	Charles O'Kelly, *Macariae excidium, or, The destruction of Cyprus* (ed. J.C. O'Callaghan) (Dublin, 1840)
Oman, 'Irish troops in Spain'	Charles Oman, 'The Irish troops in the service of Spain, 1709–1818' in *The Journal of the Royal United Services Institution*, lxiii (1918), pp 1–8, 193–9, 450–63
Ó Mórdha, 'MacMahons of Monaghan'	Pilip Ó Mórdha, 'The MacMahons of Monaghan (1642–1654)' in *Clogher Record*, iv (1960–2), pp 190–4
Ó Murchada, 'Cork'	Diarmuid Ó Murchada, 'The siege of Cork in 1690' in *JCHAS*, xcv (1990), pp 1–19

O'Neill, 'Conflicting loyalties'	James O'Neill, 'Conflicting loyalties: Irish regiments in the imperial service 1689–1710' in *Ir. Sword*, xvii (1987–90), pp 116–19
Ormonde MSS	*Report on the manuscripts of the marquess of Ormonde preserved at the castle, Kilkenny* (HMC, London, i, 1895; ii, 1899)
Ormonde MSS, n.s.	*Calendar of the manuscripts of the marquess of Ormonde, K.P. preserved at Kilkenny Castle*, new series (HMC, 8 vols, London, 1902–20)
Parker, *History of warfare*	Geoffrey Parker (ed.), *Cambridge illustrated history of warfare* (Cambridge, 1995)
Parker, *Memoirs*	Robert Parker, *Memoirs of the most remarkable military transactions from the year 1683 to 1718 ... in Ireland and Flanders ...* (London, 1747)
Parker, *Military revolution*	Geoffrey Parker, *The military revolution: military innovation and the rise of the West, 1500–1800* (Cambridge, 1988).
Patentee officers	James L.J. Hughes (ed.), *Patentee officers in Ireland 1173–1826, including high sheriffs, 1661–1684 and 1761–1816* (Dublin, 1960)
Pearsall, 'The war at sea'	A.W.H. Pearsall, 'The war at sea' in Maguire, *Kings in conflict*, pp 92–105
Peeters (ed.), *Fontenoy*	Pierre Peeters (ed.), *11 May 1745, Fontenoy* (Tournai, 2015)
People, politics and power	James Kelly, John McCafferty & Charles Ivar McGrath (eds), *People, politics and power: essays on Irish history 1660–1850 in honour of James I. Maguire* (Dublin, 2009)
Perjés, 'Army provisioning'	G. Perjés, 'Army provisioning: logistics and strategy in the second half of the 17th century' in *Acta Historica: Academiae Scientiarum Hungaricae*, xvi, nos 1–2 (1970), pp 1–52
Petrie, 'Sarsfield's stepson'	Sir Charles Petrie, 'Patrick Sarsfield's stepson' in *Ir. Sword*, xii (1973–6), pp 153–4
Petty, *Political anatomy*	Sir William Petty, *The political anatomy of Ireland* (London, 1691)
Phillips maps	Thomas Phillips, 'Maps and report' (NLI MSS 2557, 3137)
PI	John Lodge, *The peerage of Ireland* (7 vols, Dublin, 1789 edn)
Piers, 'Westmeath'	Sir Henry Piers, 'A chorographical description of the county of Westmeath, written in 1682' in Charles Vallancey (ed.), *Collectanea de rebus Hibernicis* (Dublin, 1770), i, pp 1–126

Pillorget, 'Louis XIV and Ireland'	René Pillorget, 'Louis XIV and Ireland' in Whelan, *Great wars*, pp 1–16
Plunkett letters	John Hanly (ed.), *The letters of Saint Oliver Plunkett, 1625–1681* (Dublin, 1979)
Poema	Pádraig Lenihan & Keith Sidwell (eds), *Poema de Hibernia: a Jacobite Latin epic on the Williamite wars (Dublin City Library and Archive, Gilbert MS 141)* (Dublin, 2018)
Portland MSS	*The manuscripts of his grace the duke of Portland, preserved at Welbeck abbey* (8 vols, London, 1891)
Powley, *Naval war*	Edward B. Powley, *The naval side of King William's war* (London, 1972)
Prendergast, *Restoration to revolution*	John P. Prendergast, *Ireland from the restoration to the revolution 1660 to 1690* (London, 1887)
PRIA	*Proceedings of the Royal Irish Academy. Section C: archaeology, Celtic studies, history, linguistics, literature*
Prim, 'Kilkenny militia'	John G.A. Prim, 'Documents connected with the city of Kilkenny militia in the seventeenth and eighteenth centuries' in *RSAI Jn.*, iii (1854–5), pp 231–74
Proclamations	James Kelly & Mary Ann Lyons (eds), *The proclamations of Ireland 1660–1820. Vol. 2: James II, 1685–1691; William and Mary 1689–1701; Anne 1702–1714* (Dublin, 2014)
PRONI	Public Record Office of Northern Ireland
Rawdon	Ed. Berwick (ed.), *Rawdon papers* (London, 1820)
Reduction of Ireland	Documents on the reduction of Ireland, 1689–91 (RIA MS 24. G. 1–7)
Richard-Maupillier, 'Irish regiments of Lorraine'	Frederic Richard-Maupillier, 'The Irish regiments of Duke Leopold of Lorraine, 1698–1729' in *Arch. Hib.*, 67 (2014), pp 285–312
Riegler, 'Anglo-Irish Catholics'	Frederick Joseph Riegler, 'Anglo-Irish Catholics, the army of Ireland, and the Jacobite war' (DEd, Temple University, Philadelphia, 1983)
Riley, *Tangier*	J.C. Riley, *Catholicism and the late Stuart army: the Tangier episode*. The Royal Stuart Society, paper xliii (London, 1993)

Roberts & Tinsey, 'Matchlock musket'	Keith Roberts & John Tinsey, 'The matchlock musket' in *Military Illustrated*, no. 52 (September 1992), pp 16–20
Rodríguez, 'Irish brigade in Spain, 1809–11'	Alicia Laspra Rodríguez, 'William Parker and the re-establishment of the Irish brigade in Spain, 1809–11' in *Ir. Sword*, xxvi (2008–9), pp 150–70
Rogers, *Military revolution debate*	Clifford J. Rogers (ed.), *The military revolution debate: readings on the military transformation of early-modern Europe* (Oxford, 1995)
Rosse papers	A.P.W. Malcomson (ed.), *Calendar of the Rosse papers* (Dublin, 2008)
Rowlands, *Army in exile*	Guy Rowlands, *An army in exile; Louis XIV and the Irish forces of James II in France, 1691–1698*. The Royal Stuart Society: paper lx (London, 2001)
Rowlands, *Dynastic state*	Guy Rowlands, *The dynastic state and the army under Louis XIV: royal service and private interest 1661–1701* (Cambridge, 2002)
Rowlands, 'Foreign service in the age of absolute monarchy'	Guy Rowlands, 'Foreign service in the age of absolute monarchy' in *War and History*, xvii (2010), pp 141–65
RSAI Jn.	*Journal of the Royal Society of Antiquaries of Ireland*
Rutland MSS	*Manuscripts of his grace the duke of Rutland ... preserved at Belvoir Castle* (4 vols, London, 1888–1905)
Ryan, 'Kilcolgan to Ballindown'	Brendan Ryan, 'From Kilcolgan Court to Ballindown: tracing the lineage of Terence MacCoghlan of Kilcolgan Court through the Jacobite Oxburghs and Peys' in *Offaly Heritage* 6 (Tullamore, 2011), pp 111–27.
'Rycaut correspondence'	British Library Add. MSS 37662 (Letter book of Henry Brown, 1690–1)
'Rycaut letters'	Patrick Melvin, 'Sir Paul Rycaut's memoranda and letters from Ireland 1686–1687' in *AH*, 27, pp 125–82
'Rycaut's route'	'The route to be commanded by Coll. Rycaut' in Westminster Diocesan Archives, B6 (Letter book of Henry Browne), f. 74
Savage family	G.F.S[avage]-A[rmstrong], *The Savage family in Ulster* (London, 1906)

Scott, *Works of Swift*	Sir Walter Scott (ed.), *The works of Jonathan Swift* (London, 1884 edn)
Scouller, *Armies of Queen Anne*	R.E. Scouller, *The armies of Queen Anne* (Oxford, 1966)
'Segrave papers'	Edward MacLysaght, 'Segrave papers' in *AH*, 15 (1944), pp 384–8
Shaw, *History of currency*	William Arthur Shaw, *The history of currency, 1252 to 1896* (New York, 1896)
'Sheridan's narrative'	'An historical account of some remarkable matters concerning James II's accession, Sunderland's contrivances and corruptions, Tyrconnell's getting his government of Ireland ... written in the year 1702 [by Thomas Sheridan]' in *Stuart MSS*, vi, pp 1–75.
Simms, *Colonial nationalism*	J.G. Simms, *Colonial nationalism, 1698–1776* (Cork, 1976)
Simms, *Confiscation*	J.G. Simms, *The Williamite confiscation in Ireland, 1690–1703* (London, 1956)
Simms, 'Cork'	J.G. Simms, 'Marlborough's siege of Cork 1690' in *Ir. Sword*, ix (1969–70), pp 113–23
Simms, 'Donegal'	J.G. Simms, 'County Donegal in the Jacobite war (1689–91)' in *Donegal Annual*, vii (1967), pp 212–24
Simms, 'Eye-witnesses of the Boyne'	J.G. Simms, 'Eye-witnesses of the Boyne' in *Ir. Sword*, vi (1963–4), pp 16–27
S[imms], 'From Ginkel's accounts'	J.G. S[imms], 'From General Ginkel's accounts' in *Ir. Sword*, v (1961–2)
Simms, 'Irish on the Continent'	J.G. Simms, 'The Irish on the Continent, 1691–1800' in *A new history of Ireland*, iv, pp 629–56
Simms, *Jacobite Ireland*	J.G. Simms, *Jacobite Ireland, 1685–91* (London, 1969)
Simms, 'Kilmallock letters'	J.G. Simms, Lord Kilmallock's letters to his wife' in *RSAI Jn.*, lxxxvii (1957), pp 135–40
Simms, 'Limerick'	J.G. Simms, 'The siege of Limerick, 1690' in Etienne Rynne (ed.), *North Munster studies* (Limerick, 1967), pp 308–14
Simms, 'Parliament'	'The Jacobite parliament of 1689' in Simms, *War and politics*, pp 65–90

Simms, 'Sarsfield of Kilmallock'	J.G. Simms, 'A Jacobite colonel: Lord Sarsfield of Kilmallock' in *Ir. Sword*, ii (1954–6), pp 205–10
Simms, 'Sligo'	J.G. Simms, 'Sligo in the Jacobite war, 1689–91' in *Ir. Sword*, vii (1965–6), pp 124–35
Simms, 'Treaty'	'The treaty of Limerick' in Simms, *War and politics*, pp 203–24
Simms, *War and politics*	J.G. Simms, *War and politics in Ireland, 1649–1730* (D.W. Hayton & Gerard O'Brien, eds) (London, 1986)
Simms, 'Williamite peace tactics'	J.G. Simms, 'Williamite peace tactics, 1690–1' in *IHS*, viii (1952–3), pp 303–23
Snow, *English congregation of Saint Benedict*	T.B. Snow, *Necrology of the English congregation of Saint Benedict* (London, 1883)
Stevens	R.H. Murray (ed.), *The journal of John Stevens containing a brief account of the war in Ireland, 1689–1691* (Oxford, 1912)
Stevenson, 'Irish emergency coinages'	David Stevenson, 'The Irish emergency coinages of James II, 1689–91' in *The British Numismatic Journal*, xxxvi (1967), pp 169–75
Stevenson & Caldwell, 'Leather guns'	D. Stevenson & D.H. Caldwell, 'Leather guns and other light artillery in mid-17th-century Scotland' in *Proceedings of the Society of Antiquaries of Scotland*, 108 (1976–70), pp 300–17
Story	[George Story], *A true and impartial history of the most material occurrences in the kingdom of Ireland during the last two years* (London, 1691)
Story, *Continuation*	George Story, *A continuation of the impartial history of the wars of Ireland* (London, 1693)
Stuart MSS	*Calendar of the Stuart papers belonging to his majesty the king preserved in Windsor Castle* (9 vols, London, 1902–23)
'Survey of Catholic estates'	Rolf Loeber, Harman Murtagh & John Cronin (eds), 'Prelude to confiscation: a survey of Catholic estates in Leinster in 1690' in *RSAI Jn.*, 131 (2001), pp 61–139
Swords, 'Jean Fromont files 1/2'	Liam Swords (ed.), 'Calendar of Irish material in the files of Jean Fromont, notary at Paris, May 1701–24 Jan. 1730, in the *Archives Nationales*, Paris': part 1, 1701–15 in *Coll. Hib.*,

	nos 34/5 (1992–3), pp 77–115; part 2, 1716–1730 in ibid., nos 36/7 (1994–5), pp 85–139
Taaffe letters	Count Taaffe's letters from the imperial camp to his brother the earl of Carlingford here in London: giving an account of the most considerable actions, both before and at the raising of the siege at Vienna (London, 1684)
'Talbot letter-book'	Lilian Tate (ed.), 'Letter-book of Richard Talbot' in *AH*, 4 (1932), pp 99–138
TCD MS 670	TCD MS 670 (King James's army regiments)
Temple, *Works*	*The works of Sir William Temple, bart.* (London, 1814)
The great guns like thunder	B.G. Scott, R.R. Brown, A.G. Leacock & C.J. Salter, *The great guns like thunder: the cannon from the city of Derry* (Derry, 2008)
'The groans of Ireland'	John Gerald Barry, 'The groans of Ireland' in *Ir. Sword*, ii, (1954–6), pp 130–6
Timmins, *Gunmoney*	Philip Timmins, *Gunmoney; the emergency coinage of 1689–91 for the Irish campaign of James II* (Dublin, 2020)
'Trappes of Nid'	Richard Trappes-Lomax, 'Trappes of Nid: a family history' (ed. John Trappes Lomax) in *Recusant History*, 27 (2004–5), pp 151–216
Trimble	William Copeland Trimble, *The history of Enniskillen* (3 vols, Enniskillen, 1919–21), vol. 1
Troost, *William III*	Wout Troost, *William III, the stadholder-king: a political biography* (Aldershot, 2005)
Turner, *James II*	F.C. Turner, *James II* (London, 1948)
Tyrconnell letters	Tyrconnell letters (NLI MS 37)
Vallance, *Glorious revolution*	Edward Vallance, *The glorious revolution 1688: Britain's fight for liberty* (London, 2006)
Van Brock, 'Robert Dillon'	F.W. Van Brock, 'Lieutenant General Robert Dillon, 1754–1831' in *Ir. Sword*, xiv (1980–1), pp 172–87
Van Creveld, *Supplying war*	Martin Van Creveld, *Supplying war: logistics from Wallenstein to Patton* (Cambridge, 1977)

Walton, *History of the British army*	Clifford Walton, *History of the British standing army A.D. 1660–1700* (London, 1894)
Wauchope, *Sarsfield*	Piers Wauchope, *Patrick Sarsfield and the Williamite war* (Dublin, 1992)
Wauchope, *Londonderry*	Piers Wauchope, *The siege of Londonderry* (Dublin, 2022)
Weapon	*Weapon: a visual history of arms and armour* (London, 2006)
Westport papers	Westport estate papers, guard book papers 1689–96 (NLI MSS 40,899–40,901)
Westropp, 'Irish gunsmiths and sword cutlers'	M.S. Dudley Westropp, 'Irish gunsmiths and sword cutlers' in *Ir. Sword*, i (1949–53), pp 181–7
Whelan, *Great wars*	Bernadette Whelan (ed.), *The last of the great wars: essays on the war of the three kings in Ireland, 1688–91* (Limerick, 1995)
Widdess, *College of Surgeons*	J.D.H. Widdes, *The Royal College of Surgeons in Ireland and its medical school, 1784–1984* (Dublin, 1963)
Wilkinson-Latham, *Discovering artillery*	R.G. Wilkinson-Latham, *Discovering artillery* (London, 1987 ed.)
Wilson, *Europe's tragedy*	Peter H. Wilson, *Europe's tragedy: a history of the thirty years war* (London, 2009)
Worthington, *Central Europe*	David Worthington, *British and Irish experiences and impressions of central Europe, c.1560–1688* (Farnham, 2012)
Yeats, *Collected poems*	*Collected poems of W.B Yeats* (London, 1965)
Young, 'Scotland and Ireland'	John Young, 'Invasions: Scotland and Ireland 1641–91' in Lenihan, *Conquest and resistance*, pp 53–86

Index

Abercorn, Claud Hamilton, 4th earl of, 25, 112, 115, 120, 281, 286, 298
accommodation, 250–1
   billets/billeting, 26, 250, 318
   fuel for, 250
   houses and cabins, 250, 302–3, 278
   huts, 90, 250–1, 278
   inns, 250–1
   lack of barracks, 250
   public buildings, 250
   quartermasters' role in procuring, 75, 115–16, 250
   quarters, 26, 45, 47, 49, 59, 118, 168, 178, 181, 186, 191, 207–8, 230, 232, 237, 241, 242, 249, 271
   tents/pavilions, 44, 144, 216, 250–1, 266
      canvas for, 216, 251
An abridgement of English military discipline, 103, 109–10, 132
aides-de-camp, 171
Ailway, Robert, 135
aislings, 297
Albeville, Ignatius White, marquis d', 32, 241, 273
Alexandre, Pierre, 212, 218
Alicante, siege of (1709), 267
Alsace/Alsatians, 175, 328, 330
Amanzé, marquis d', 153, 170, 171, 201–2
American/Americans, 330, 331
Amfreville, Charles-François Davy, marquis d', 58, 197
Amsterdam, 337
Anglo-Dutch brigade, 13, 24, 31, 33, 48, 57, 154, 176, 177, 291
Anglo-Irish brigade, 327
Anglure, marquis d', 201
Anne, queen of England, 325

Antrim, Alexander MacDonnell, 3rd earl of, 35, 42, 69, 70, 79, 92, 284, 285, 291, 295, 296, 298, 299
Antrim, county of, 296
Archbold, [Michael?], 235, 236, 237, 238, 239, 244, 317
Archbold, Patrick, 190
Archbold, Richard, 190
Archdekin, John, 257
Ardee, 47, 50, 118, 153, 161, 190, 202
Ardglass, Vere Essex Cromwell, 4th earl of, 18, 20
Arlington, Henry Bennet, 1st earl of, 129
Argenson, Marc-Pierre de Voyer de Paulmy, comte d', 333
Argyle, Archibald Campbell, 9th earl of, 18
Armagh, county of, 277
armour
   cuirasses, 125–6
   morions/helmets, 101, 125
   skulls, 125
army,
   aspirations of, 303–13, 336–7
   casualties in, 1, 45, 54, 57, 65
   commissions in, 19, 35–6, 78–9
   establishments/strengths of, (1537–1684) 7; (1686–8) 13, 17, 22, 27–30, 32, 68; (1689) 36, 42–3, 44, 46, 68–9, 75–6, 85, 112, 114, 123; (1690) 50, 56, 68, 114, 123; (1691) 76, 112, 114, 123
   false musters in, 11
   fate of, 314–21
   order of battle, 170–4
   Protestants defect from, 89
   reform of, 16–27
   reorganization of, 42–4

369

army (*continued*)
  restoration, 7–11
  see also artillery; cavalry; dragoons; infantry; regiments; weapons
Arran, Richard Butler, 1st earl of, 9, 12, 162
Articles of War, 27, 180–2, 192
  lack of enforcement, 184
  penalties for breach of
    cashiering, 181, 202
    demotion, 181, 182
    detention, 182
    dismissal, 181
    execution, 182–3, 236
    riding the wooden horse, 181
    running the gauntlet, 182, 183, 234
    tongue piercing, 182
  see also discipline
artillery/ordnance, 134–51
  ammunition, 146–7
    manufacture of, 146–7
    match, 143, 144, 146
    powder, 143, 144, 146
    types of projectile
      bombs, 146, 147
      cartridge shot, 151
      carcasses, 146
      shells, 135
      shot/cannonballs, 143, 144, 146, 147, 246, 254
  arsenal, 135
  cannon
    condition of, 15, 143
    firing procedure of, 140–1
    French, 136, 140, 141, 143, 148
    manufacture of, 140, 254
    number of, 15, 142, 143–4, 148–51, 216
    range of, 141
    rate of fire of, 140
    types of, 139–40
      field, 42, 46, 139, 147
      fortress, 142, 150–1
      howitzers, 139
      mortars, 26, 135, 139, 144, 146, 147, 150
      regimental, 139
      siege/battering, 135, 139, 142, 147
      tin, 143, 147, 255
    weight of, 141
  equipment, 144
  magazines for, 143, 146
  organization of, 134–5, 139, 151
  portable forge, 149
  transport of 144–6
    gun carriages for, 135, 141–2, 143, 145, 255
    harness for, 145, 255
    horses for, 145–6
    limbers for, 144, 145
    oxen for, 145
    train, 15, 137, 138, 142, 144–6
    see also wagons
  deployment of, 51, 66, 138, 143, 146, 147–51
artillery/ordnance personnel
  armourer, 30
  carters, 138, 145
  chief engineer and fire officer, *see* engineers
  clerk, 135
  clerks of the stores, 30
  commissaires, 137, 138, 210–11
  controller, 143, 177
  cost of, 30
  French, 41, 136, 137, 138, 151, 213
  fusiliers/pioneers, 57, 145
  gunners' mates/matrosses, 30, 136–7, 138
  gun-aimers, 138
  gunners, 15, 30, 136–7, 138
  lieutenant, 30, 135
  lieutenant general & commander of, 172
  master general, 7, 15, 27, 30, 135, 177
  master gunner, 30
  master gunner's mate, 30
  ordnance board, 134–5

rations for, 239
skills of, 136–8
storekeeper, 30
surveyor/comptroller, 30
transport captains, 138
wagon master, 145
artisans, 85, 239
    bakers, 235, 236, 239
    blacksmiths/forgers/blade-makers, 211, 239, 254
    butchers, 240, 241
    carpenters, 138, 211, 217, 239
    clothiers, 94
    farriers, 117, 217, 239, 246
    gunsmiths, 15, 37, 98, 138, 211, 213, 217, 253–4, 276
    harness-makers, 246
    hatters, 253
    joiners, 37
    masons, 23
    pay of, 247
    Protestant, 98, 143, 146, 253–4
    saltpetre master, 255
    shoemakers, 253
    smiths, 138, 253, 254
    sword cutlers, 37, 102, 254, 255
    tailors, 94, 252
    textile workers, 253
    turners, 138
    weavers, 94
    wheelwrights, 138, 211, 239, 246
Arundel, Thomas, 103, 290
Athcarne Castle, Co. Meath, 300, 301
Athenry, Edward Birmingham, 13th Baron, 253, 258, 285
Athlone, Co. Westmeath, 138, 201, 213, 236, 237, 239, 254
    first siege of, 55, 83, 150, 160, 245, 270
    fortifications of, 61, 154, 158–9, 164
    second siege of, 60–1, 74, 82, 88–90, 120, 126, 133, 150, 153, 154, 160, 167, 182, 336
Aufroy, le sieur, 176, 188, 189, 190, 212–13, 233–4, 236, 246

Aughrim, battle of, 2, 61–6, 80, 90, 100, 107, 109, 110, 114, 120, 126, 132, 133, 167–8, 172, 243, 251, 262, 336; *map 3; plate 15*
Aughrim Castle, Co. Galway, 64
auxiliary forces, 256–80
Austrian succession war, 329
Avaux, Jean-Antoine de Mesmes, comte d', 36, 40, 42, 81, 85, 86, 89, 92, 98, 121, 145, 152, 175, 184, 189–90, 191, 201, 203, 204, 211, 214, 240, 251, 253, 257, 273, 275, 288
    arrives in Ireland, 41, 199
    opinion of King James, 161
    role in in formation of Mountcashel brigade, 219–20
    serves on council, 161
Aylmer, George, 78–9

Bagenal, Dudley, 70, 72, 80
Bagot, Mark, 178
Ballinasloe, Co. Galway, 62, 167
Ballinruddery, Co. Kerry, 301
Ballymore, Co. Westmeath, 91, 249
    capture of, 60, 82, 83, 90, 150, 154, 275
    fortification of, 160
Ballymote Castle, Co. Sligo, 265
Ballyneety raid, 56, 111, 114, 120, 164, 274
Ballyraggett, Co. Kilkenny, 301
Ballyshannon, Co. Donegal, 45
Banagher, Co. Offaly, 66, 285
Bandon, Co. Cork, 38, 147, 155, 191
Banqué/Baines, chevalier de, 106, 177
Bantry, Co. Cork, 137, 198, 246, 251, 290
Bantry Bay, naval battle of, 41, 198, *plate 12*
Barbados, 301
Barfleur/La Hogue, naval battle of (1692), 199, 323
Barker, William, 25, 103, 135, 173, 290
Barnewall, Dominic, 256–7
Barrett, John, 57, 70, 71, 296, 298
Barry, rapparee leader, 274
Barry, Gerat, 102

Barbezieux, Louis François Marie Le Tellier, marquis de, 197, 211, 318, 323
Bastille, la, Paris, France, 40, 285
Bath, Peter, 300, 301
battle-axe company, 7, 16
Bavaria, 326
Beachy Head, naval battle of (1690), 55, 198
Beaupré, M. de, 204
Begg, Patrick, 331
Belfast, Co. Antrim, 157
Bellasyse, Sir Henry, 273, 274
Bellefonds, Bernardin Gigault, marquis de, 323
Bellew, John, 1st Baron Duleek, 70, 72, 92, 73, 289
Bellew, Richard, 3rd Baron Duleek, 121, 295, 317, 321
Belligny, M. de, 153
Belturbet, Co. Cavan, 92, 274
Bentinck, Hans Willem, 1st earl of Portland, 314
Bernard, M., 153
Berwick, James FitzJames, 1st duke of, 80, 115, 237, 281, 284, 292, 299, 323, *plate 5*
  at the Boyne, 53, 163, 172, 179
  captain general of King James's army in France, 319
  difficulties of, when commanding Irish army, 58, 162, 184–5
  Franco-Irish regiment of, 325
  horseguard troop of, 118, 321
  in order of battle, 170–1
  lieutenant general, 169
  marshal of France, 319
  on success of recruiting, 87–8
  opinion of Tyrconnell, 163
  plan for invasion of Ireland, 334
Binns, John, 74
Biron, Armand-Charles de Gontaut, marquis de, regiment of, 206–7
Birr, Co. Offaly, 58, 269, 271, 272, 274

Blayney, Henry Blayney, 5th Baron, 19, 273
Blenheim, Germany, battle of (1704), 324
Blood, Thomas, 9
Bog of Allen, 272, 275
Boismeral, François, 204
Boisonge, M. de, 153
Boisseleau, Alexandre de Rainier, marquis de,
  at Boyne, 172
  career in Ireland, 201
  commands artillery, 135, 136, 177
  critical of Cork bakers, 234
  defence of Limerick, 56, 151, 204
  in order of battle, 170
  regiment of, 70, 72, 204, 292
  training camps organized by, 106
Bond, Sir Henry, 176
Bonrepaus François d'Usson, marquis de, 196
Bophin, John Burke, 1st Baron, 70, 72, 92, 285, 299
Bophin, Mary Burke, Lady, 274
Boulogne, France, 329
Bourg, M., 212
Bouridal, M. de, 214, 317
Boyle, Co. Roscommon, 45, 47
Boyne, battle of, 1, 49–55, 58, 73, 76, 81, 84, 87, 98, 109, 110, 111, 114, 118, 120, 123, 132, 133, 141, 161, 172, 243, 246, 258, 291, 336, *map 2*; *plate 13*
Brennan family, 268
Brereton, John, 299
Brest, France, 196, 214, 216, 318
British brigade in France, 13, 24
British brigade in Portugal, 13
Brittany, France, 214, 319, 323
Brittas, Theobald Burke, 3rd Baron, 284, 298
Brooke, George, 12
Brooke, Thomas, 12, 20
Brouilly, M., regiment of, 206–7
Browne, Dominic, 70, 286

Browne, George, 272
Browne, Henry, 192
Browne, Henry, 289
Browne, John
　financial difficulties of, 254
　ironworks of, 127, 146, 254
　munitions industry of, 254, 255
　regiment of, 71, 88, 221, 286
Browne, Nicholas, 70, 72, 295
Brussels, Belgium, 337
Buchan, Thomas, 42, 48, 170, 172
Buckingham, George Villiers, 5th duke of, 74
Buda, Hungary, siege of (1686), 25, 292
Bullock Harbour, Co. Dublin, 300
Burke, Lady Margaret, 220, 299
Burke, Michael, 73
Burke, Patrick, 73, 262
Burke, Richard, 273, 274, 275, 280
Burke, Theobald, 286, 291, 293
Burke, Thomas, 261, 262, 263, 285
Burke, Thomas, 292
Burke, Walter, 64, 71, 72, 285, 298, 321, 324, 331
Burke, William, 72, 73
Burton, Richard, 154, 159–60, 292
Bussay/Bussé, le sieur de, 292
Butler, Edward, 70, 226, 284, 301
Butler, James, 71
Butler, John, 21, 24, 34, 285
Butler, Piers, 118
Butler, Richard, 70, 71, 220
Butler, Thomas, 70, 72, 285, 292, 302
Butler, Walter, of Ballinakill, Co. Tipperary, 120
Butler, Walter, of Garryricken, Co. Kilkenny, 70
Butler, Walter of Mountfin, Co. Wexford, 289, 302
Byrne, Garrett, 300
Byrne, Sir Gregory, 286
Byrne, Toby, 123

Cadet, *Commissaire*, 212
cadets, Irish for France, 222–3, 288

Cahir/Caher, Theobald Butler, 7th Baron, 298
Callaghan, rapparee leader, 274
Camisards, 268, 325
camps
　Cork, 104, 106
　Curragh, 23, 25, 27, 104
　Drogheda, 106
　Killaloe, 107, 251
　Louglinstown, 104, 106
camp followers, 90–1; *see also* women; children; sutlers; pedlars
Campo Santo, Italy, battle of (1743), 331
Cangort Castle, Co. Offaly, 275
Cannetti, le sieur, 154
Cannon, Alexander, 48
Cappock, Bartholomew, 300
Carlingford, Francis Taaffe, 3rd earl of, 326
Carlingford, Nicholas Taaffe, 2nd earl of, 129, 284
Carlow, 191
　county of, 298
Carne Castle, Co. Westmeath, 275
Carne, René de, 290
Carney, Sir Charles, 170, 172
Carrickfergus, Co. Antrim, 42, 46, 48, 142, 150, 158
Carrigaholt, Co. Clare, 298, 302
Carroll, Long Anthony, 275
Carroll, Francis, 74, 321
Cartagena, Colombia, capture of (1697), 136
Carton, Co. Kildare, 302
Castelar, Baltasar Patiño y Rosales, 1st marqués de, 331
Castlebar, Co. Mayo, 256
Castleconnell, William Burke, 7th Baron, 71, 283, 299
Castlehaven, Co. Cork, 275
Castlemartyr, Co. Cork, 38, 147
Castlemore, Co. Cork, 298
Catalonia, Spain, 197, 267
Cathach of the O'Donnells, 267

Catholic clergy/priests,
    funding of, 301
    recruitment encouraged by, 86, 88, 193, 315
    support for war effort by, 86
    see also chaplains
Caulfield, Toby, 24
cavalry, 111–33
    battlefield formation and tactics, 111, 132
    caracole, 132
    composition of, 296–7
    inspector of, 112
    morale of, 120
    officers of, 115
        proportion of Gaelic, 115
    opinions on, 119, 131
    organization, 112–120
    proportion of army, 112
    regiments of, 112–13
    role of, 111
    social composition of, 119
    standards of, 116
    training of, 133
    see also officers; soldiers; uniforms; weapons
Cavan, battle of, 49, 88, 106
Cavenagh, rapparee leader, 274
Cavenagh, Charles, 57, 70, 71, 98, 291
Chamlay, marquis de, 110
chaplain general, *see* military-related offices
chaplains, 25, 62, 75, 115, 116, 123, 138, 192–4
    background of, 193
    Benedictine, 192
    Capuchin, 192
    Catholic priests appointed, 192
    commitment of, 193
    Dominican, 192
    duties of, 193
    Franciscan, 192
    hospital, 192
    Jesuit, 192
    morale-raising role of, 194
    pay of, 25, 193, 227
    Protestants replaced, 192
    secular, 192
Chapelizod, Co. Dublin, 162, 164, 302
Charlemont Fort, Co. Armagh, 47, 49, 90, 94, 142, 150, 158, 246
Charles I, king of England, 180
Charles II, king of England, 9, 20, 180
Charles Fort, Kinsale, Co. Cork, 15–16, 57, 150, 157
Charles Edward Stuart, Prince, 334, 335
charts, 153
Châteaurenault, François Louis de, 41, 197–8, 216, 322
Chemerault, Jean-Noël de Barbezieres, comte de, 171, 206
    regiment of, 206–7
chevaux-de-frise, 53, 132
children, 90, 239, 260, 303–4, 317
Chichester House, Dublin, 38
Churchill, Arabella, 285
Clady/Cladyford, Co. Tyrone, 42, 120
Clancarty, Donough MacCarthy, 4th earl of, 20, 57, 70, 71, 80, 285, 294, 296, 298, 302, 320, 321
Clanmalier, Maximilian O'Dempsey, 3rd Viscount, 71, 284
Clanricard, Richard Burke, 8th earl of, 35, 69, 70, 284, 285, 294, 296, 298, 299, 300, 302
Clare, county of, 66, 129, 241, 249, 254, 296, 302
Clare, Daniel O'Brien, 3rd Viscount, 35, 45, 69, 77, 86, 121, 129, 172, 196, 221, 291, 294, 296, 298, 302
Clare, 4th, Viscount, *see* O'Brien, Daniel
Clare, 5th Viscount, *see* O'Brien, Charles
Clare, Charles O'Brien, 6th Viscount, 327, 330, 334, 335
Clarendon, Henry Hyde, 2nd earl of, 11, 15, 18, 22, 23, 24, 79, 119, 129, 162, 268, 297
Claudianus, Andreas, 65, 85
Clifford, Robert, 66, 121, 122, 173, 174, 290, 296, 315, 316

Clonmel, Co. Tipperary, 191
Clonyn, Co. Westmeath, 302
clothing, *see* uniforms
club musket, 64, 102
Coehoorn, Menno van, 152
Colgrave, George, 291
Colbert, Jean-Baptiste, 196
Collier, Charles, 19
Comerford, Patrick, 331
command and staff, 161–79; *see also* military offices
commissaires, *see* France/French
commissioners of the treasury, 176–7
Condé, Louis de Bourbon, prince de, 161
Cong, Co. Mayo, 263
Connacht, province of, 87, 261, 264, 271, 296, 325
   'citadel of Ireland', 55, 61, 259, 314
Connell, Maurice, 72, 173
Connor, John, 286
convention 'parliament', 39
Conyngham, Sir Albert, 20, 265
Coote, Sir Charles, 157
Coote, Chidley, 20
Copenhagen, Denmark, 337
Cork,
   city of, 41, 157, 198, 206, 213, 234, 246, 254, 275, 317
     cannonballs sent to, 254
     capture of, 57, 58, 83, 150, 275
     fortifications of, 157
     French hospital at, 190
     governors of, 201, 245
   county of, 87, 249, 268, 296, 302
     rapparees in, 271, 272, 274, 276, 280
Cork, Richard Boyle, 3rd earl of, 128
Cormack, Michael, 73, 262
Corporation of horse breeders of Co. Down, 129
Corrib river, 263
Costello, Miles, 73
Cotter, Sir James, 121, 296
Coubertin, M., 212
council/councils of war, 161–2

Courtstown, Co. Wexford, 298
Creagh, Sir Michael, 176, 229, 302, 317
   regiment of, 70, 73, 74, 79, 87, 98, 183, 188, 286, 293, 296
creaghts, 87, 240–1, 249, 261–2, 263, 269, 273
Cremona, Italy, siege of (1702), 324, 332
Creveld, Martin van, 231
Crofton, Henry, 331
Crom Castle, Co. Fermanagh, 45, 143, 147, 255
Cromdale, Scotland, battle of (1690), 48
Crosbie, Sir Thomas, 80, 294
Coulouvray, M., 103
Coverent, le sieur, 205
Cullen, Co. Tipperary, 277
Culloden, Scotland, battle of (1746), 335
Culmore Fort, Co. Derry, 20
Curlew mountains, 45
Curragh, the, Co. Kildare, 10, 43, 128
   see also camps
Cusack, Robert, 289
Custume, Sergeant, 82, 126

Dalton, John, 299
D'Alton, John, 338
Daly, Denis, 59
D'Arcy, Nicholas, 21
Dardis, Michael, 193, 200
Darpentigny, M. de, 205
Dascorel, le sieur, 191
Davis, Thomas, 338
Dealbhna Ethra/Garrycastle, Co. Offaly, 289
Dease, Richard, 287
deer herds, 249
De Gomme, Sir Bernard, 16
Delahunty, Lawrence, 103
Delvin, Co. Westmeath, 299
Dempsey, Lawrence, 21, 24, 115, 291
Denise, M., 137
Derry/Londonderry, 39, 42, 92, 137, 248, 257
   inadequacies of army at, 44, 84, 94, 98, 135, 142, 145, 160, 233, 246

Derry/Londonderry, (*continued*)
    siege of, 44–6, 88, 89, 98, 100, 146,
        150, 153, 161, 171, 178, 189,
        201, 204, 336
Dillon, Arthur, 71, 220, 221, 321, 325, 334
Dillon, Arthur, 333
Dillon, Gerald, 286
Dillon, Henry, later 8th Viscount
    Costello Gallen, 70, 223
Dillon of Costello-Gallen, Theobald,
    7th Viscount, 284, 298
discipline, 10, 23, 33, 47, 74, 85,
    Articles of War, 180–1
    courts martial, 182, 184
    insubordination of officers, 184–5
    laxity of, 37, 42, 84, 183–4, 236, 241
    officers neglectful of, 104
    penalties and punishments, 182–3
    provosts, 75, 182, 183
Doe, Louis, 176
Donore, Co. Meath, 50, 133
Donore, Co. Westmeath, 275, 301
Dorrington, William, 20, 24, 25, 34, 58,
    65, 103, 170, 171, 172, 173, 185,
    207, 290, 299, 321, 324, 334
Dougan, Margaret, 333
Douglas, James, 83, 270, 271
Dover, England, 329
Dover, Henry Jermyn, 3rd earl of, 112,
    113, 115, 117–18, 169, 171, 172,
    206, 221, 252, 284, 290
Dowdall, Lawrence, 301
Dowdall, Matthew, 299
Down, county of, 281, 296
Downpatrick, Co. Down, 128
dragoons, 120–4
    combat deployment of, 111, 133
    guidons of, 122
    morale of, 133
    organization of, 122–3
    regiments of, 121–2
    regional links of, 123–4
    role of, 111
    training of, 133
    see also officers; soldiers; uniforms;
        weapons

drink supply, 242–4
    ale, 234, 243
    beer, 236, 243, 244
    brandy, 198, 216, 217, 232, 233, 234,
        243, 244, 315
    brandy casks, 247
    buttermilk, 243, 303
    hops, 198, 243
    Madeira, 232
    milk, 232, 302
    rationing, 243–4
    sherry, 232
    water, 232, 242, 243
    wine, 198, 232, 234, 243, 244
    wort, 243
Drogheda, Co. Louth, 45, 46, 50–1, 150,
    190, 201, 236, 246, 251
Dromore, break of, 42, 120, 275
drums/drummers/drumbeats, 75, 82–3,
    86, 122, 227, 266
drum majors, 82–3
Drybridge/Mill Ford, Co. Louth, 53, 133
Dublin,
    city of, 23, 42, 45, 46, 51, 61, 81, 87,
        94, 118, 123, 149, 150, 189, 207,
        296, 316
    bread ovens at, 234
    entry of King James to, 83
    French hospital at, 191
    governors of, 171, 207
    industries in, 252–4
    lack of defences at, 158
    militia of, 257–8, 272
    mint at, 228
    price rises lead to disorders in, 236
    Protestants in, 38
    regiment of, 293
    suttling houses in, 243
    weapon stores in, 214
    county of
        75, 296, 302
Dublin Castle, 302
Dublin Intelligence, 264, 273
Duleek, Co. Meath, 54, 149, 206
Dully, Jean, 73, 145

Duncannon, Co. Waterford, 55, 73, 150, 158
Dundalk, Co. Louth, 47, 50–1, 104, 161, 190, 242, 248
Dundee, John Graham, 1st Viscount, 48
Dungan, Thomas, 13, 291
Dungan, Walter, Lord, 35, 53, 88, 121, 123, 133, 292, 296
Dungannon, Co. Tyrone, 98
Dún Laoghaire, 148
Dunsany, Christopher Plunkett, 10th Baron, 298
Dutch Republic/Netherlands,
  army of, 31, 35, 103
  artillery of, 134, 139, 140,
  artists of, 337
  enmity with France of, 1, 13, 31
  invasion of England by, 31–2
  navy of, 195, 323
  soldiers/guards of, 2, 49, 53, 106, 272
  wars with England of, 13, 14, 161, 195
  see also Anglo-Dutch brigade

East Grinstead, Co. Sussex, England, 33
Edgeworth, Sir John, 34
engineering, 152–60
engineers
  cadet, 15
  casualties among, 160
  chief, 15, 152
  draftsman, 152, 153
  French, 41, 152–4, 157–60
  pay of, 152–3
  roles of, 152–4
  work
    on fortifications, 153–5, 158–60
    on surveying harbours and rivers, 153
Ennis, Co. Clare, 265
Enniskillen, Co. Fermanagh/Enniskilleners, 38–9, 42, 45, 257
Enniskillen, Rory/Roger Maguire, 5th Baron, 22, 71, 87
Erne, river and lakes, 45

Esmard, M., 213, 239
Escots, François-Gaston d'Hôtel, marquis d', 170, 171, 201
Esgrigny, René de Jouenne d', 85, 149, 162, 176, 179, 190, 192, 223, 236, 248, 258, 303
  role of, 211–12
Essartz. M. des, 212, 214, 234
Estrade, Louis, marquis d', 170, 172, 177, 202
Eugene of Savoy, Prince, 324
Eustace, Francis, 129, 298
Eustace, James, 287
Eustace, Sir Maurice, 70, 296, 316, 321
Eustace, Richard, 72, 74
Everard, John, 300

Fagan, Richard, 277, 286, 300, 302
Fahy, Mr, 239
Fairfax, Thomas, 20, 22
Falkirk, battle of (1745), 335
Famechon, Ignace de Belvalet, comte de, 85, 162, 172, 206, 223
Fannin, rapparee chief, 269
Fanning, David, 301
farm workers, 85
Farrell, Fergus, 286, 294
Farrell, Francis Fergus, 281
Farrell, Iriel, 70
Farrell, Roger, 130, 281, 300, 302
fascines, 100
Feltrim, Co. Dublin, 277, 300
Ferbane, Co. Offaly, 272
Fermanagh, county of, 253, 269
Fermoy, Co. Cork, 274
Fethard, Co. Tipperary, 300
Fieffe, Frederick, 15
field glasses, 141
Fielding, Sir Charles, 20
Fielding, Robert, 71, 88, 220, 221–2, 285
finance, 7, 27–30, 217–19, 225–3
  act of supply, 228, 287
  copper coinage/'gun-money', 147, 218, 228–31
  copper for, 216, 246

finance (*continued*)
  copper coinage/'gun-money',
    (*continued*)
    forgery of, 229–30
    loss of purchasing power, 230, 253
    mints in Dublin and Limerick,
      228–9, 246
    value of output, 229
  cost of army, 11, 27–30, 226, 228
  cost of bread supply, 235
  money from France, 155, 217–19,
    228, 232
  values and exchange rates, footnote,
    217–18
  see also pay
Finglas declaration, 55, 87, 89, 270, 314
Fitton of Gawsworth, Alexander Fitton,
  1st Baron, 284
FitzGerald, B., 73
FitzGerald, Edward, 72
FitzGerald, Sir John, 20, 70, 95, 273, 301
FitzGerald, Kean, 300
FitzGerald, Maurice, 289
FitzGerald, Nicholas, 72, 320, 321, 334
FitzGerald, Robert, 176
FitzGerald, Silken Thomas, 7
FitzHarris, (Myles?), 331
FitzJames, Henry, *see* grand prior
FitzPatrick, John, 287
Flanders/Flemings, 197, 264, 314, 323, 330
Fleming, Garrett, 300
fodder/forage, 232, 247–9
  foraging for, 248
  grass, 248
  hay, 248–9
  magazines for, 249
  oats, 248–9
  requirements, 247–8
  sickles to cut, 217, 248
food supply, 231–42
  magazines, 236
  diet, 232, 302–3
    beans, 237, 303
    biscuit 217, 236, 238, 244

bread/bread supply, 232–40, 302
  ammunition bread, 233, 234, 237
  bakeries, 239
  commissaires, 239
  cost of, 235, 236, 237
  distribution of, 235
  for French, 236
  flour/grain/corn/barley/oats/
    rye/wheat, 23, 216, 217,
    230, 232, 234, 236, 237,
    238, 239, 270, 303
  millers, 233
  ovens, 233, 235, 239
  peas for, 236
  personnel, 239
  rations, 233, 235, 237, 238–9
  shortage of, 237
cabbage, 232, 242, 303
eggs, 232, 303
fish, 232, 242
game, 232
geese, 234
meat and dairy food, 240–2, 303
  butter, 232, 242, 244, 303
  cattle/beef, 233, 234, 240, 241, 242, 270
    levies of, 240–1
    of creaghts, 240–1, 249
  cheese, 132, 244, 303
  meat kettles, 241
  pork, 232
  rations, 242, 244
  salt beef, 232, 236, 242
  sheep/mutton, 233, 234, 240
oil, 232
parsnips, 303
peas, 242, 303
potatoes, 232, 242, 288, 302, 303
roots, 232, 302
salt, 198, 216, 217, 242
spices, 232
sugar, 232
vinegar, 232
weeds, 302

Fontenoy, battle of (1745), 324, 326, 330
Forbes, Arthur, later 2nd earl of
    Granard, 20, 24, 25, 34
Forbes, Robert, 12
Ford, James, 257
Forman, Charles, 327–8
fortifications
    funding of, 155, 159
    labour, for 155
    positional/fortress warfare, 155–7
    sacks for, 216
    state of, 157–8
    tools for, 155, 216
    trace Italienne, 15, 156–7
    works on
        Athlone, 154–5, 158–9
        Aughrim breastworks, 62, 110
        Ballymore, 160
        Bandon, 155
        Charlemont, 158
        Galway, 154–5, 159
        Limerick, 154–5, 158–9
        Sligo, 159–60
'Forty-five' Scottish rising, 328
Foxford, Co. Mayo, 254, 329
French, Arthur, 73
fusiliers, 73, 100, 108, 137, 145
France/French, 195–294
    army of, 36, 68
        grand-maître of artillery, 135
        Irish in Franco-German
            regiments, 13, 222
        maison militaire du roi, 117
        Swiss guards, 324
    arms sent from, 40, 96, 99, 213–16
    army contractor, 212
    artillerists from, 41, 136, 137, 138
    artillery from, 51, 136, 137, 13
    artisans/tradesmen from, 211, 254
    commissaires from, 136–8, 146, 149,
        175, 176, 179, 199, 210–13, 235,
        239,
    defence of the Shannon favoured by,
        46, 50, 99–200
    expeditionary force from, 2, 50, 205–8
        at battle of the Boyne, 54, 207
        conduct of, 207–8
        departure of, 208
        hospitals for, 191–2
        Irish recruits for, 207
        number in, 206–7
        regiments of, 206
        wheat for, 236–7
        wives of soldiers, 206
    generals from, 170–2, 200–2, 208–10
    intendant from, 85, 162, 175–6, 190,
        199, 211, 223, 248
    Ireland to become a protectorate of,
        suggested, 37, 196, 308–9, 336–7
    Irish officers in, 195–6, 291, 293
    matériel from, 41, 60, 127, 146, 213–17
    money from, 217–19, 228
    munitionnaire, 236
    navy/fleets/convoys, 40, 49, 58, 196,
        197–8, 244, 317
        battle of Bantry Bay, 198
        defeat of at Barfleur/La Hogue,
            (1693), 323
        disposal of prizes, 217
        failure to exploit naval strength,
            198–9, 223
        frigates of, 196, 198, 199, 222
    objectives in Ireland, 195–7, 223–4
    officers from, 41, 58, 60, 88, 103, 184,
        199, 202–5, 223, 292, 295
        dislike of Ireland, 223
        en second, 203, 292
        obstruction to promotion of, 203–4
        reformé/supernumerary, 203, 292
        relations with Irish officers, 205
        role of, 204
        technical officers, 210–13
    opinion of James II, 195–6
    poor opinion of Irish fortifications,
        157–8
    ports used by, 198
    relations with Irish, 205, 207–8, 237
    rivalry with Dutch Republic, 1–2,
        31
    see also Irish in France; weapons

380   INDEX

Fumeron, Jean François de, 106, 143, 158, 182, 200, 209, 213, 228, 238, 240, 260, 272, 316
   reports and role of, 41, 42, 44, 72, 101, 114, 118, 119, 120, 127, 131, 146, 159, 165, 175–6, 179, 188–91, 203, 204, 207, 210, 211–12, 214, 215, 216–17, 218, 220, 221, 222, 223, 226, 229, 231, 233–4, 235, 236, 238–9, 242, 243, 244, 246, 247, 248, 251, 254, 255, 262, 263, 313, 315, 318

Gabaret, Jean, 40, 197
Gaels/Gaelic Irish, 17, 46, 71, 87, 115, 118, 259–61, 281, 282, 294–8, 322
   see also Tyrconnell, attitude to
Gafney, George, 75, 82, 83, 87, 94, 100, 101, 226
Galmoy, Piers Butler, 3rd Viscount, 20, 45, 65, 111, 112, 115, 120, 143, 147, 170, 173, 220, 255, 283, 285, 287, 291, 298, 315, 316, 321, 324, 334
Galway,
   city of, 56, 66, 73, 83, 90, 150, 157, 160, 190, 201, 217, 247, 253
      artillerists at, 138
      cannonballs sent to, 254
      civilian inhabitants of, 314
      food supply in, 213, 239
      fortifications of, 154, 158–9
      garrison of, 262
      governor of, 59, 273
      port used by French, 198, 208
      prospect of, 302
      quarters in, 251
      surrender of, 314, 315, 336
      tribal families of, 286, 300
   county of, 273, 275, 302
Galway, Frances Burke (*née* Lane), Lady, 281, 299
Galway, Ulick Burke, 3rd Viscount, 36, 59, 70, 72, 281, 285, 299
Garryricken, Co. Kilkenny, 285

Gassé/Gacé (later Matignon), Charles Goyon, comte de, 170, 200
Gaydon, Chevalier Richard, 323, 325, 326
Geoghegan, Charles, 71, 261, 262, 267
Geoghegan, Conly, 123
Geoghegan, Edward, 271
general officers, 162–74
   battle control by, 178
   French, 179, 200–2, 208–10
   mortality among, 178–9
   nationalities of, 171, 173
   place in line of battle, 170–2
   pre-war experience of, 292
   see also military-related offices
Germany/Germans, 49, 197, 323, 328, 330
Giles, John, 135
Ginkel, Godard van Reede, baron de, 56, 59, 60, 61, 62–7, 89, 120, 178, 184, 264, 271, 274, 277, 278, 314–15, 317
Gold, Severus, 287
Gormanston, Jenico Preston, 7th Viscount, 70, 72, 295, 298, 302
Gort, Co. Galway, 124
Goulet, M. de, 153
Goutaille, M. de, 153
Grace, rapparee leader, 274
Grace, John, 70, 71
Grace, Richard, 55, 59, 83, 291
Grace, Robert, 71, 72, 298
Grady, John, 58–9
Granard, Arthur Forbes, 1st earl of, 12, 18, 20, 38, 272
grand prior, Henry FitzJames, lord, later duke of Albemarle, 70, 80, 92, 94, 281, 284, 296, 320, 321, 324
'The groans of Ireland', 260, 322
Grotius, Hugo de, 185
guidons, 122
Guild of barbers, surgeons, apothecaries and periwig-makers, 187, 188
'gun-money', *see* finance
Gustavus Adolphus, king of Sweden, 143, 178

Habsburg/imperial armies, 13, 68, 103, 154, 292, 316, 326
Hackett, Thomas, 286
Hague, The, 32
Hamilton, Andrew, 269
Hamilton, Anthony, 16, 20, 24, 32, 35, 70, 172, 179, 285, 291, *plate 7*
  defeated at Lisnaskea, 45, 182
  governor of Dublin, 171
Hamilton, Sir George, 13
Hamilton, Gustavus of Monea, 20, 38
Hamilton, Gustavus, later 1st Viscount Boyne, 38
Hamilton, John, 24, 59, 65, 70, 72, 162, 172, 173, 285, 296
Hamilton, Richard, 13, 16, 24, 25, 70, 76, 121, 147, 179, 270, 275, 285, 290, 334
  at the Boyne, 53, 163, 172
  bolsters Tyrconnell's will to resist, 39
  brigadier, 18, 27, 169
  conducts siege of Derry, 44, 165, 183
  early career in France, 196, 291
  in north, 42
  in order of battle, 170–1
  lieutenant general, 39, 169
  major general, 169
  sent to negotiate in Ireland, 39
Harbord, William, 245
harpist, 20–7
hautboys, 122–3
Hawett, Edmund, 192
Hay du Chastelet, Paul, 195
Henry VIII, king of England, 7
Herbert, Arthur, 1st earl of Torrington, 41
Hibernia regiment, 267, 331
Higgins, rapparee leader, 274
Hocquincourt, Charles le Monchy, comte d', 170, 172, 178, 201
Hogan, 'Galloping', 274, 277, 280
Honduras, 327
Hore, Luke, 189

horse furniture and accoutrements
  anvils, 217
  bits, 127
  blankets, 127
  bridles, 127, 213, 217
  canvas covers, 145
  carbine buckets, *see* weapons
  collars, 216, 246
  harness, 246, 247
  horseshoes, 127, 254
  horseshoe nails, 127
  pistol holders, *see* weapons
  saddle bags, 127, 217
  saddles, 127, 213, 217
  stirrups, 127, 217
  traces, 145
horseguards, 7, 34, 35, 131, 290, 318
  at Aughrim
  at the Boyne, 53
  composition of, 118, 290
  escort troop 1685, 7, 16
  establishments, 118
  need of horses for, 130
  troops of, 112–13, 114, 117–18
  see also Irish in France; regiments
horses, 112, 119, 248, 302
  artillery, 144–6, 249
  breeding, 128–9
  brewers', 130, 131, 145
  buyers of, 138
  carriage, 131, 145
  cavalry and dragoon, 128–31
  drafts, 130, 246
  forage requirements of, 112
  for France, 129, 131
  for train, 246
  garrons, 129, 245, 248
  geldings, 129
  hobbies, 129
  neglect of, 249
  numbers in Ireland, 128
  of infantry officers, 95
  of rapparees, 272
  plough, 130
  quality of, 128, 129, 131

horses, (*continued*)
   racing, 128
   rustled by rapparees, 131, 146, 247, 270
   seizure of, 130
   stallions, 128
   stud farms, 128–9, 130, 298
   veterinary services, 117
   see also fodder
houses/homes, 301–3
Huguenots, 196, 269
Hungary/Hungarians, 330
   Irish soldiers in, 33, 266, 292, 316
Hunsdon, Robert Carey, 6th Baron, 284, 290–1
Hussey, Edward, 73
Hussey, John, 287
Hyde, Douglas, 338

Ikerrin, James Butler, 3rd Viscount, 12, 118, 298
Ikerrin, Piers Butler, 4th Viscount, 284
Inchiquin, William O'Brien, 2nd earl of, 38
independent companies/troops
   Burke (Michael), 73, 100
   Burke (Patrick), 73, 262
   Cormack, 73, 262
   Costello, 73
   Dully, 73, 145
   French, 73
   Grace, 113
   Keefe's, 73, 182
   Lacy, 73
   Limerick mayor, 73, 113
   MacMahon (Hugh), 122
   Moore, 73, 262
   O'Connor, Conor, 262
   O'Neill (Henry), 73, 262
   Toole, 73, 182
   White (Charles), 73, 113
industrial production, 251–5
   bayonets, 101
   bombs, 254
   balls/bullets, 254, 255

   bread-making, 235
   cannon, 254, 255
   cannonballs, 146–7
   carbines, 254
   copper currency, 251–2
   clothing, 252–3
   forges, 146, 254
   friezes, 252
   grenades, 254
   guncarriages, 255
   gunpowder factory proposed, 255
   half-pikes, 253
   harness, 255
   horseshoes, 254
   iron for, 101, 216, 2127
   ironworks, 254
   John Browne's munitions industry, 127, 146, 254
   lead for, 255
   looms, 253
   muskets, 254
   pistol balls, 255
   saltpetre, 146, 255
   shoes, 252, 253
   skeans, 253
   steel for, 101, 216, 217, 254
   swords, 255
   tallow, 198, 216, 240
   tents, 253
   tools, 254
   wagons, 255
   see also arms; artisans; uniforms
India, 326, 329
infantry, 68–110
   at Aughrim, 62–5, 120
   at the Boyne, 53–4
   battlefield role and formation of, 107–10
   battalion cannon of, 139
   camping, 107
   Catholics in, 22
   colonels of, 69–73
   colours of, 77–8
   desertion from, 89–90
   drill of, 102–110

establishment, (1688), 28–9; (1689), 70
inspector general of, 106, 177
instruction manuals for, 102–3
in Balldearg O'Donnell's force, 260–3
in England, 32–4
local associations of, 87
marching speed of, 245
morale of, 47, 81–2
numbers and regiments of, 7, 11, 44, 28–9, 56, 68–73, 75–6
order of battle in, 170–2
organization of, 73–6
performance of, 44–5, 49, 53–4, 56, 57, 59, 61, 64–5, 106–7, 110
personnel of, 74–85, 283–97
recruitment for, 85–9
see also Irish in France; uniforms; regiments; soldiers; weapons
Irish in France
pay of, 322, 324
pre-war service in, 195–6, 222
Irish brigade, 324–30, 335
casualties of, 325, 326–7
culture of, 332–3
dependants of, 90, 317, 323, 332–3
English and Scots in, 329
hatred of English, 333
invasion plans of, 333–4
Jacobite sentiments of, 332–5
numbers in, 325–7, 329
officers in, 322
Protestants in, 322
recruitment for, 327–30
regiments of, 326
Scottish interventions of, 334–5
'wild geese' epithet for, 328
King James's army/*les autres*, 319–22
disbandment of, 324–6
formation of, 319
indiscipline of, 318
officers of, 322
regiments of, 320–1
Mountcashel brigade/*les anciennes*, 71, 79, 88, 219–23, 318–19

formation of, 44, 220–1
numbers in, 219, 221, 320
recruits for, 221–2, 318
regiments of, 221, 321, 324–6
Inishbofin, 235, 314, 315
Innocent XII, Pope, 325
intelligence, 177–8
interpreters, 204, 297–8
invasion of Ireland, Jacobite plans for, 334
Irish Catholics
antagonism towards Protestants and English, 2
entry to the army of, 18–25
motivations of, 304–13
number of, 2
peasantry, 85
penal laws, 328
pre-war overseas military service of, 13
recovery of under King James, 2, 17, 301
Williamite restrictions on, 178, 278–9
see also Catholic clergy/priests; chaplains
Irish in Europe project, 338
Irish Manuscripts Commission, 3, 338
Irishtown, Limerick, 56
Isle of Wight, 33
Italy, 323, 331
Iveagh, Brian Magennis, 5th Viscount, 70, 266–7, 296, 298, 299, 316
Iveagh (*née* Burke), Margaret, Lady, 285, 299

Jacobite houses, 301–3
Jacobite narrative, 65, 194, 244, 258, 294, 318
James II, king of England, 11, 12, 81, 89, 98, 99, 171, 219, 281, 323, 333, *plate 2*
and Mountcashel brigade, 220
army of in France, 319–24
as commander-in-chief, 161
at battle of the Boyne, 50–4, 161
blocks promotion of French officers, 203

James II, king of England (*continued*)
  clashes with Rosen, 165
  confronts Schomberg, 46
  deposition of, 1, 31
  disillusionment of Irish with, 55, 306, 308, 312
  disillusionment with Ireland, 50, 55, 161
  disembarks at Cork, 40, 199
  entry to Dublin of, 41
  financial support from, 218, 231
  French opinion of, 195
  gives relief to disbanded Irish soldiers, 325
  Irish land of, 300
  leaves Ireland, 55
  memoirs of, 338
  nominates Lauzun for Irish command, 166, 205
  objectives of, 41, 47, 161
  recalls Anglo-Dutch brigade, 291
  reforms of, 16
  re-forms Jacobite army in France, 319
  tactics at the Boyne, 51–4, 148, 151
  urges Irish to make terms, 55
  view on Balldearg O'Donnell's force, 261
  wishes to invade Britain, 41
James III, Stuart claimant to the British and Irish thrones, 328, 333, 334
James Fort, Kinsale, 57, 150
Jamestown, 47, 263

Kearney, Michael, 174
Keefe, Darby, 73, 182
Kenmare, Valentine Browne, 1st Viscount, 70, 72, 295, 206
kerne/woodkerne, 268
Kerry, county of, 241, 249, 264, 277, 280, 294, 301
Kerry, Maurice FitzGerald, 14th knight of, 124, 301
kettledrums/kettledrummers, 28, 117
Kilcash, Co. Tipperary, 302

Kilcommadan Hill, Aughrim, Co. Galway, 62, 65
Kilcolgan Castle, Co. Offaly, 289, 302
Kildare, county of, 296, 302
  militia of, 258
  officers' estates in, 17, 285, 298, 300
Killaloe, 56, 107, 245, 247, 251
Killiecrankie, battle of (1689), 48, 143
Kilkenny,
  city of, 21
    French hospital at, 191
    militia, 257
  county of, 87, 124, 268, 296, 298
Killyleagh, break of, 42
Kilmainham holy well, Co. Dublin, 22
Kilmallock, Co. Limerick, 204, 249
Kilmallock, Anne Sarsfield, Lady, 232, 285
Kilmallock, Dominic Sarsfield, 4th Viscount, 70, 72, 80, 87, 88, 92–4, 96, 99, 113, 115, 120, 129, 252, 285, 291, 299, 321
Kilnagarnagh, Co. Offaly, 289
Kincor, Co. Offaly, 289
King, John, 281
King, William, 37, 86, 282, 287
King's County/Offaly, 249, 261, 271, 289, 299, 302
  militia of, 14
  rapparees in, 258, 269, 272, 274, 275
'Kings in conflict' exhibition, 338
Kingsland, Nicholas Barnewall, 3rd Viscount, 71, 302
Kingston, Robert King, 2nd Baron, 20, 38, 281
King William's Glen, Co. Louth, 53
Kinsale, Co. Cork, 273, 275
  cannonballs sent to, 254
  capture of, 57, 58, 72, 83, 150, 154
  French hospital at, 191
  port used by French, 198
Kingsale, Almericus de Courcy, 18th Baron, 284
Kipling, Rudyard, 338
knapsacks/haversacks, 93, 95

labourers, 65, 85, 155, 218, 270
Lacombe, chevalier de, 154, 159, 160
La Croix, le sieur de, 137, 146, 212, 255
Lacy, James, 72, 73, 74, 89, 177, 222
Lacy, Peter, 326
Lafelt, Belgium, battle of (1747), 324, 326, 330
Laisné, Jean-Baptiste, 51, 136, 138, 143, 144, 148–9, 151, 172, 177, 210
La Hogue, Normandy, France, 323, 334
La Hoguette, Charles Fortin, marquis de, 148, 162, 166, 171, 206, 220
Lally, Thomas Arthur, comte de, 326, 329, 335
Lambety, M., 153
Lanesborough, James Lane, 2nd Viscount, 281
languages, 12, 22, 41, 103–4, 204, 219, 292, 297–8, 333
Lanier, Sir John, 131
La Pannouse, le sieur de, 203
La Tour Monfort, Henri de, 171, 173, 319
  career in Ireland, 210
Lauzun, Antonin Nompar de Caumont, comte de, 145, 157, 162, 171, 176, 216, 222, 226, 237, 291, *plate 6*
  at the Boyne, 50, 54, 148, 104
  career in Ireland, 166, 205–8
  cautious strategy of, 50, 200, 205
  departs from Galway, 58, 172
  good opinion of Irish soldiers, 85
  urges Irish to make terms, 55
Lavallin, Peter, 182
Lavau, M., 137
law, 180–5; *see also* soldiers/rank and file; discipline
laws of war, 185
La Vigne, le sieur de, 153
Lee, Andrew, 196, 319, 321, 325
Leinster, province of, 50, 61, 87, 89, 258, 261, 270, 273, 296, 325, 328
Leitrim, county of, 266
Leixlip Castle, Co. Kildare, 300
Lennon, James, 188
Leopold 1st, holy Roman emperor, 266

Léry-Girardin, Claude-François de Vauvré, comte de, 51, 117, 162, 169, 170, 172, 200–1
Les Invalides, Paris, France, 186, 325
Leslie, Revd Charles, 86, 269, 270, 278
Lew, Captain, 274
Lhermite, M., 153
Limerick,
  county of, 237, 241, 249, 277, 278, 301
  city of, 69, 131, 141, 164, 167, 190, 201, 208, 245, 247
  artillerists at, 138
  civilian inhabitants of, 314
  engineering works at, 154–5
  first siege of, 55, 191 72, 73, 100, 133, 150–1, 160, *plate 14*
  food supply in, 213, 237, 238, 239
  forges near, 146
  fortifications of, 157–9
  garrison of, 73, 262
  governor of, 173, 210
  hospitals at, 190
  Jacobite headquarters at, 55, 66
  mayor of, 73
  mint, 229, 246
  port used by French, 198
  post-war review at, 315–16, 318
  prospect of, 302
  quarters in, 250–1
  saltpetre works at, 146, 212, 255
  second siege of, 66–7, 150, 154, 160, 171, 210, 277, 336
  stores at, 126, 242, 244
  surrender articles, 314–15
    adjudications under, 316
  Williamite hospital at, 190
  women of, 90
Limerick, William Dungan, 1st earl of, 35
Lisburn, Co. Antrim, 182
Lisnaskea, Co. Fermanagh, 182
living conditions of Irish, 302–3

logistics, 44, 231–55
  see also accommodation; drink;
    fodder; food supply; horses;
    industrial production; transport
London, 26, 33
London Gazette, 264
Longford, county of, 272, 300, 301
  sheriff of, 278
lords justices, 314, 315
Lormier, le sieur, 213
Lorraine, Leopold duke of, 326
Loughglynn, Co. Roscommon, 265
Loughlinstown, Co. Dublin, 104, 106
Loughmoe, Co. Tipperary, 298, 302
Low Countries, 330
Lowestoft, naval battle of (1665), 161
Lozieres d'Astier, N. de, 153, 201
Lloyd, Thomas, 20, 92
Loughmoe Castle, Co. Tipperary, 302
  plate 17
Louis XIV, king of France, 1, 32, 40,
  117, 140, 143, 151, 155, 156, 159,
  166, 169, 183, 186, 187, 201, 207,
  218, 291, 315, 318
  Irish policy of, 1, 40, 48, 58, 152, 153,
    164, 175, 195–7, 199, 200, 205,
    208, 211, 213, 215, 216, 217,
    223–4, 282, 308, 322, 324, 330,
    336, 337
Louis XV, king of France, 330
Louth, county of, 87, 273, 303
Louth, Matthew Plunkett, 7th Baron,
  70, 295, 298
Louvois, François Michel Le Tellier,
  marquis de, 40, 41, 48, 50, 58, 97,
  135, 136, 149, 155, 156, 165, 174,
  175, 176, 196, 203, 204, 206, 208,
  211, 212, 218, 220, 233–4, 236, 297,
  323
  misgivings about Irish campaign, 40,
    166, 179, 195, 197, 199, 205,
    214, 324
  receives reports from Ireland, 199, 211
  wants Irish soldiers for France, 58,
    85, 89, 197, 219–20, 222

Lucan, Co. Dublin, 298, 302
Lunt, John, 290
Luttrell, Henry, 25, 58, 66, 115, 120,
  163, 173, 174, 184, 185, 196, 204,
  281, 285, 315, 316, *plate 9*
Luttrell, Simon, 121, 185, 207, 281, 285,
  292, 296, 298, 316, 321
Luttrellstown house and demesne,
  Co. Dublin, 281, 302
Lützen, Germany, battle of (1632), 178
Luzzara, Italy, battle of (1702), 267
Luxembourg, François Henri de
  Montmorency-Bouteville, duke of,
  169
Lynch, Sir Henry, 71, 286
Lynch, Thomas, 287

MacAuliffe, Dermot, 331
MacCabe, John, 274
Macariae excidium, 71
Macary, M., 137
MacCarthy, Daniel, 273
MacCarthy, Justin, *see* Mountcashel
MacCarthy Reagh, Daniel, 71
MacCarthy More, Charles, 46, 70, 71,
  73, 85, 92, 285
MacCarthy, Owen, 46, 57, 71, 73
MacCarthy, Teague, 250
MacCoghlan, Clare, 289
MacCoghlan, Cornelius, 289
MacCoghlan, Edmund, 289
MacCoghlan, John, of Kilcolgan, 289,
  299, 302
MacCoghlan, John of Kincor, 289
MacCoghlan, Terence, 289, 302
Mac Cruithín, Aodh 'Buí', 337
Mac Cuarta, Séamas Dall, 273
MacCullen, Lieutenant, 273
MacDermott, Brian, 71, 72, 263, 267
Mac Domhnaill, Seán Clárach, 328, 337
MacDonagh, Terence, 286
MacDonnell, Alexander, 2, 261, 262I,
  24, 59, 291
MacDonnell, Charles, 115
MacDonnell, Daniel, 285

MacDonnell, James, 124, 287
MacDonnell, Sir John, 334
MacDonnell, Randal, 331
MacDowell, Felix, 192
MacElligott, Roger, 34, 70, 71, 94, 291, 320, 321
   regiment of in England, 31–3
   surrenders Cork, 57
MacGeoghegan family, 289, 301
MacGeoghegan, James, 322
magazines, 104, 146, 156, 233, 236, 249
Magennis, Daniel, 122
McGilligan, Roger, 115
MacGillycuddy, Cornelius, commission of, 78
MacGillycuddy, Denis, 33, 71, 172, 173, 291
MacJonnine family, 300
MacKay, Hugh, 178
Mackenzie, Alexander, 123
MacLean, Sir Alexander, 47
MacLean, Sir John, 48
MacMahon, Art, 47, 70
MacMahon, Brian, 70, 71, 87, 291
MacMahon, Hugh, 71, 122
MacNamara, Florence, 124, 286
MacNamara, John, 250
Mac Oireachtaigh, Aodh, 273
Macroom, Co. Cork, 249, 302
McSharry, Captain, 279
Magan family, 281
Maguire, Alexander, 72
Maguire, Cúconnacht, 71, 72, 298, 299
Maguire, Archbishop Dominic, chaplain general, 25, 27, 192
Malone family, 289
Malplaquet, battle of (1709), 324, 326
Maria Theresa, Empress, 326
Marigny, M., 177
Marlborough, John Churchill, 1st earl of, 57, 281
Mary II, princess of Orange/queen of England, 31, 39
   oath of allegiance to, 315

Mary of Modena, queen consort of England, 31, 106, 166, 205, 213, 216, 218, 319, 325
Massé, Le sieur de, 136, 152, 160, 204
Mathew, George, 33
Mathew, Toby, 289
Maumont, Jacques Fontanges, marquis de, 40, 44, 171, 178, 200
Maxwell, Thomas, 46, 121, 122, 123, 133, 162, 163, 170, 172, 173, 177, 185, 291, 296, 321, 323, *plate 11*
Maynooth, Co. Kildare, 270
Mayo, county of
   Balldearg O'Donnell in , 263, 265, 266
   cattle levy on, 241
   ironworks and arms manufacture in, 254
   lord lieutenant of, 253, 258
   MacJonnines of, 300
   meal levy on, 237
   militia of, 256, 258
   sheriff of, 272
   see also John Browne
Meagher, Jo., 274
Meagher, Philip, 24
Meath, county of, 128, 236, 237, 293, 296, 299, 300, 301, 302, 303
   militia of, 256–7, 258
Meath, Edward Brabazon, 4th earl of, 34
medicine/medical services, 186–92
   apothecaries, 189
   blueprints for hospital needs, 189, 190
   charitable collection for sick and wounded, 189
   death rate, 187
   French medical team & hospitals, 191
   field hospitals, 189, 191, 245
   French opinions of Irish medical personnel and hospitals, 188, 189–90
   hospitals, 188–90
      cooks and bakers for, 190
      directors of, 189

medicine/medical services, (*continued*)
  hospitals, (*continued*)
    garrison recommended, 189
    needs of, 190
    nurses for, 189, 191
    rations in, 189
  medicines and dressings, 187, 188, 189, 191, 217
  physicians, 189, 190
  surgeons, 75, 115, 123, 138, 187–9, 190–1, 227
  surgical instruments, 189, 190
  treatment of wounds & disease, 186–7, 191
Meelick, Co. Galway, 245
Meleady, Sir Anthony, 278
Melfort, John Drummond, 1st earl of, 41, 45, 135, 161, 165, 174, 176, 177, 226
merchants, 124, 198, 216, 217, 223, 229, 230, 231, 233, 236, 241, 242, 243, 251, 253, 286, 301, 302, 307, 322
Merode, le comte de, 208
  regiment of, 206–7
Merrion, Thomas FitzWilliam, 4th Viscount, 113, 260, 262, 264, 275
Messandier, René de, 290
Methelet, M., 213, 317
Meuse river, 323
Migueletes, 268
military-related offices, 161–79
  adjutant general, 177
  advocate general, 21, 27, 182
  brigadiers, 18, 27, 170, 173
  captain general, 17, 170, 171
  chaplain general, 25, 27, 177, 192
  chief engineer and fire officer, 15, 30, 152
  clerk of the check, 7
  clerk of the pells, 225
  commissaries of the musters, 27
  controller of musters, 176
  commissaire general de guerre/ intendant, 175–6
  general, 166, 173

inspector general of infantry, 106, 177
lieutenants general, 27, 169, 170, 171, 173
majors general, 18, 27, 170, 171, 173
marshal, 7, 165, 170
master of the ordnance, 7, 27, 30
muster-master general, 9, 11, 27, 176, 225
paymaster general, 26, 176, 177
provost marshal of the army, 182
quartermaster general, 27, 177
receiver general, 176
secretary for war, 45–6, 174
scoutmaster general, 177
surgeon general, 27
superintendent general of victuals/ commissary general of stores, 235
surgeon general, 177, 188, 190
militia
  Jacobite,
    establishment of, 256
    commissioners of array, 256, 258
    composition of, 256–7, 258
    decline of, 258
    depredations of, 257
    Dublin, 257–8, 272
    functions of, 257
    military activity of, 257–8
    numbers of, 271
    pressing of personnel of, 257–8
    rapparee connection with, 271
    under use of, 258
  restoration, 14, 18, 256
militia act, 180
military secretaries, 171
mock battles, 25, 104
Moidart, Scotland, 334
Molyneux, William, 152
Monck, Thomas, 268
Montrose, James Scott, 1st duke of, 13, 18, 103
Monteguy, M. de, 153
Montmejan, le sieur de, 171
Montgrizy, le sieur de, 149

Mooney, Edmund, 289
Mooney, Francis, 289
Mooney, Maud, 289
Moore, Charles, 70, 72
Moore, Garrett/Gerard, 73, 262, 285
Moore, Michael, 250
Mornin Castle, Co. Longford, 301
Morris, Harvey, 294
Morris, rapparee leader, 274
Morris, Redmond, 294
Morrogh, Michael, 287
Mosstown House, 49
Mountalexander, Hugh Montgomery 2nd earl of, 38, 42, 120
Mountcashel, Justin MacCarthy, 1st Viscount, 13, 24, 35, 70, 71, 74, 129, 139, 161, 166, 171, 172, 285, 294, 296, 299, 321, *plate 8*
    brigade for France of, 88, 113, 219–23, 318
    defeated, wounded and captured at Newtownbutler, 45, 133, 148
    early career in France, 195–6, 291
    fails to take Crom Castle, 147
    lieutenant general, 39, 169
    made Viscount Mountcashel, 169, 220
    major general, 18, 27, 169, 283, 319
    master general of the ordnance, 135, 177
    presses militia men, 88, 221, 257–8
    see also Irish in France (Mountcashel brigade)
    suppresses Protestant resistance in Munster, 38
mounted/horse grenadiers, 7, 28, 118
Mountgarret, Richard Butler, 5th Viscount, 284, 298
Mountjoy, Charles Blount, 8th Baron, 268
Mountjoy, William Stewart, 1st Viscount, 15–16, 18, 24, 25, 27, 38, 39–40, 70, 135, 137, 169
Mount Leinster, Edward Cheevers, 1st Viscount, 284
Mountmellick, Co. Laois, 274, 276

Moyry Castle, Co. Armagh, 277
Mulhuddart, Co. Dublin, 272
Mull, Isle of, Scotland, 48
Mullingar, Co. Westmeath, 60, 271, 275, 278
multiplying glasses (telescopes), 141
Munchgaar, Frederik, 272
munitionnaire, 233, 235, 236, 247
Munphin, Co. Wexford, 302
Munster, province of, 61, 87, 89, 258, 270, 273, 295, 303, 325, 328
Münster, bishop of, 291
Murphy, Colonel, 73
Murphy, Lieutenant, 273
Murray, Sir Charles, 27
Muskerry, Cormac MacCarthy, titular Viscount, 161

Nagle, Sir Richard, 45–6, 79, 162, 174, 203, 292, 316, 319
Nairne, Sir David, 174, 226
Nanny river, 54
Naples, Italy, 330
Navan, Co. Meath, 236
Neale, the, Co. Mayo, 54
Nenagh, Co. Tipperary, 275
Nesmond, André, marquis de, 198
Netterville of Dowth, Nicholas, 3rd Viscount, 298
Netterville, William, 293
Newcomen, Sir Thomas, 18, 20, 27, 70, 169
New English, 2, 12, 281, 295
    hostility to, 294, 306, 309–11, 316
New Model army, 92, 121, 157
Newry, Co. Down, 49, 100
Newtownards, Co. Down, 42
Newtownbutler, battle of, 45, 46, 109, 110, 120, 133, 135, 139, 148, 182, 219
nine years war, 1, 323, 324
Nix, Swift, 20, 22, 87
Noble, George, 300
Noblesse, M., 154, 159, 160
no-man's-land, 241, 249

non-commissioned officers (NCOs), 21–2, 288
  as rapparees, 273
  corporals, 75, 82, 84, 116, 118, 122, 227
  sergeants, 75, 82, 84, 93, 96, 106, 108, 118, 122, 145, 227
Normandy, France, 323
North Africa, 331
Northumberland, England, 34
Nugent, Christopher, 334
Nugent, Edmund, 71
Nugent, Gerald, 278
Nugent, James, 72
Nugent, James Moile, 299
Nugent, John, 300
Nugent, Richard, 93, 193, 299
Nugent, Walter, 121
Nugent, William, 49, 70, 88, 291, 295

oath of supremacy, 13, 16
O'Brien, Charles, later 5th Viscount Clare, 70, 72, 115, 121, 221, 223, 321
O'Brien, Daniel, later 4th Viscount Clare, 71, 121, 220, 321, 325
Ó Bruadair, Dáibhí, 83, 86, 93, 273, 283, 297, 337
O'Cahan, Roger, 71, 72, 261, 262, 263
O'Callaghan, John Cornelius, 338
O'Connell, Daniel Charles, Count, 327, 338
O'Connor, rapparee chief, 272
O'Connor, Conor, 72, 113, 261, 262, 263
O'Connor, Matthew, 338,
O'Connor, Roger, 71
O'Connor Sligo, Daniel (?), 261, 262
Ó Cuinneagáin, Seán, 328
O'Doherty, Daniel (?), 72, 162, 261, 263, 267
O'Donovan, rapparee leader, 274
O'Donovan, Daniel, 70, 93
O'Donnell, Connell, 261, 262, 266
O'Donnell, Daniel, 261, 262, 267

O'Donnell, Hugh Balldearg
  army of, 258–67, 293
    bread supply for, 238
    composition of, 259–60
    creaghts in, 87, 90, 241, 260–1
    disbanded and reconstituted, 266
    imperial service of, 316
    lack of support for, 260, 263
    numbers in, 259, 263, 264, 266
    opposition to Balldearg's defection in, 265
    rapparee activity of, 263, 274, 275
    receives uniforms and *matériel* from Saint-Ruth
    regiments of, 71–3, 113, 260–2, 266
  background of, 258–9, 291, 294
  brigadier general, 173
  defection to Williamites, 66, 89, 264
  defeat at Collooney, 265
  defence of upper Shannon, 55, 263
  fate of, 266–7
  hostility of Tyrconnell towards, 259–60, 262, 295
  manifesto of, 259
  projected Williamite force of, 266
  sponsors rapparees, 263
  views on, 261, 265
O'Donnell, Manus, 71, 72
O'Driscoll, rapparee leader, 274
O'Driscoll, Cornelius, 57, 291
O'Farrell, Gonzalo, 332
officers, 11–14, 19–21, 24–5, 281–97
  absenteeism of, 44, 81
  aides-de-camp (ADCs), 171
  allegedly low social origins of, 287–8
  as rapparees, 273
  barristers as, 286–7, 301
  commissions of, 36
    format, 78–9
    purchase of, 12, 119
  Catholic, admitted to army, 16
  composition of officer corps, 281–97
  corporation officials as, 287
  counties of origin of, 296

dissatisfaction of disbanded, 43
English, 12, 20, 25, 32, 41, 47, 115, 124, 169, 171, 173, 282, 290, 295
en second, 81
estates of, 298–300
family connections of, 284–5, 288–9
financial resources of, 298–301
French, 200–2
houses of, 301–2
inexperience of, 104, 293
in parliament, 287
insubordination of, 184–5
Irish in England, 25
leave of, 26
merchants as, 286
mobility of, 80
morale of, 66, 81, 120
motives of, 282, 316–78
New English, 12
number of, 281
Old English, 12, 115, 281, 282, 294–6, 322
opinions on,
    French, 44, 80–1, 104, 183
    King James, 81
    Protestant, 25
    Rosen, 81
    Stevens, 80–1, 104, 184
opposition to peace negotiations of, 58–9
outlawry of, 317
peers as, 283
pensions of, 299, 301
post-war fate of, 316
pride of, 288
proportion of Gaelic, 115
Protestant, 25, 293–4
rations of, 238–9
regimental, 46, 80, 115–16, 123, 202–5
    adjutants, 75, 123
    agents, 225
    captains, 76, 86, 115, 122, 145
    colonels,
        authority of, 69
        chicanery of, 226
        followers of, 239, 241
        pre-war experience of, 293
        wealth of, 74
    cornets, 115, 116, 122
    ensigns, 76–7
    lieutenants, 76, 115, 122
    lieutenant colonels, 74
    majors, 74
    provosts, 75, 182
    quartermasters, 75, 115–16, 122, 123, 301
required to subsist troops, 36–7
role in battle, 108
Scottish, 41, 47–8, 103, 169, 171, 173, 282, 290, 295
seigneurial influence of, 86–8
servants of, 91
shortcomings of, 47
supernumerary/*reformé*, 81, 113, 116, 203, 281, 290, 322
veteran, 13, 24–5, 74, 103–4, 115, 282, 289–93
see also chaplains; general officers; medicine/medical services
O'Gara, Oliver, 70, 74, 285, 291, 321
O'Higgins, Ambrose, 332
O'Keeffe, Arthur, 286
O'Kelly, Charles, soldier and author, 2, 43, 71, 167, 209, 244, 265, 291, 295, 337, 338
Oldbridge, 50–4, 106, 110, 148–9
Old English, 6, 12, 13, 17, 87, 115, 260, 281, 282, 294–6
O'Mahony, Dermot/Daniel, 72, 331, 332
O'Neill, Brian, 72, 261, 262, 263, 267
O'Neill, Brian Boy MacArt, 72, 261, 262, 263, 267
O'Neill, Cormac, 42, 294, 295
    regiment of, 46, 70, 85, 88, 207, 295
O'Neill, Sir Daniel, 121
O'Neill, Felix, 21, 27, 71, 72, 182, 286, 292
O'Neill, Felix, 332
O'Neill, Gordon, 58, 64, 70, 72, 92, 173, 262, 321, 334

O'Neill, Henry, 73, 173, 262–3
O'Neill, Henry MacTool, 71
O'Neill, James, 182
O'Neill, Sir Neil, 54, 121, 133, 294, 296
ordnance, *see* artillery
Ó Rathaille, Aogán, 283, 328, 337
O'Regan, Sir Teague, 49, 94, 291
O'Reilly, Alexander, 332
O'Reilly, Chaplain, 194
O'Reilly, Edmund, 70, 122, 296
O'Reilly, MacThomas, 71
O'Reilly, Owen/John, 122
O'Rourke, Conor, 261, 262, 266
O'Rourke, Michael, 266
O'Rourke, Tiernan, 261, 262, 267
Ormond, James Butler, 1st duke of, 9, 12, 128, 256, 285
Ormond, 2nd duke of, see Ossory
Orrery, Roger Boyle, 1st earl of, 14, 102, 128
O'Shaughnessy, Roger, 124
Ossory, James Butler, 2nd earl of, & 2nd duke of Ormond, 12, 18, 281, 301
Ó Súilleabháin, Eoghan Rua, 328
O'Sullivan, John William, 334
Oxburgh, Sir Heward, 70, 103, 289, 295
Oxburgh, Henry, 72, 286, 289
Oxmantown Green, Dublin, 183

Pale, the, 295
Pappenheim, Gottfried Heinrich von, 178
Paris, France, 317
Parker, John, 112, 113, 115, 120, 171, 290
Parker, Robert, 23, 91
Pargiter, Henry, 12
Parliament (Eng.), 121, 180
Parliament (Ire.), 130, 176, 178, 180, 198, 228, 280, 281, 287, 294, 301, 304, 305, 307, 308, 310, 311, 312, 328
    act of attainder, 311
    act concerning martial law, 180
    act to prevent the listing of his majesty's subjects as soldiers in foreign service, 328
    act of recognition, 180
    act of supply, 228
    act of repeal, 310
Parma, Francesco Farnese, 7th duke of, 326
Pay, Francis, 289
pay, 225–8,
    arrears of, 10, 44, 184, 225, 231
    deductions/'off-reckonings' from, 26, 119, 128, 225–6
    mechanism for, 11–12
    of French in Ireland, 203, 207
    rates of, 12, 26, 75, 155, 193, 225, 227, 248
    see also finance
peace party/peace negotiations, 58–9, 314
pedlars, 91
penal laws, 337
Peninsula, the, 331
Pepper, Mr., 239
Peterwardein/Petrovaradin, Serbia, 266
Petty, Sir William, 128, 240, 302
Philip V, king of Spain, 240, 331, 332
Philipstown/Daingean, Co. Offaly, 272, 276
Phillips, Thomas, 16, 157, 302
Piedmont, Italy, 323
Piers, family of, 281
Piers, Sir Henry, 282, 302
Pinkey, John, 24
pipes/pipers, 83
Platin, 53, 133
Plunkett, Archbishop Oliver, 268, 282
Plunkett, Patrick, 173
Pointis, Bernard Desjean, baron de, 171, 188
    commands artillery, 135–6, 137, 177, 202, 210
    constructs Derry boom, 136
    mission to Ireland, 40, 196
Poland/Poles, 33, 267, 330
Pontchartrain, Louis Phélypeaux, comte de, 197
popish plot, 13

population estimates, 2, 281
Portugal/Portuguese, 216, 259, 267, 291, 330
Portumna, Co. Galway, 43, 56, 302
  Castle, *plate 16*
poverty of ordinary people, 302
Povey, Francis, 152
Power, James, 72, 294
Power, John, 74, 286, 293, 321
Power, John Moone, 72
Prendergast, Edmund, 115
Price, Major, 103
privy council (Ire.), 15, 36
privy council (Eng.), 307
proclamations
  Jacobite
    against pillage and exactions, 37
    forbidding transfers to new regiments from old, 36
  Williamite
    offering amnesty, 120
    offering surrender terms, 314
    prohibiting Catholics from living near River Shannon, 178
    prohibiting movement of Catholics, 178
prostitutes, 91
Protestants
  armed associations of, 38
  fears of, 38
  in Jacobite army, 293–4
  in Williamite army, 50
  purged/resigned from army, 18–24, 38
  seizure of arms from, 38
Pudsey, Marmaduke, 24
Purcell, James, 47–8, 72, 291
Purcell, Nicholas, 58, 121, 163, 184, 185, 285, 296, 298, 302, 315, 316
Purcell, Richard, 299
Pusignan, Jean Le Camus, le marquis de, 44, 171, 178, 188, 201

Quakers, 228
Queen's County, 299

Ramillies, Belgium, battle of (1706), 324
Ramsay, Robert, 70, 178
rapparees, 1, 55, 56, 60, 90, 268–80
  area of operations of, 271–2
  army personnel with, 273–4, 275
  casualties of, 273, 278
  character of, 271
  composition of, 272
  concealment of, 275
  hatred of English by, 272
  horse rustling by, 276
  inclusion of in Limerick surrender articles, 279
  intelligence supplied by, 178, 277
  Jacobite views on, 272–3
  measures to suppress, 277–9, 280
  military activities of, 276–7
  numbers of, 271, 275
  origins of, 268–71
  post-war persistence of, 280
  submissions of, 279–80
  weaponry of, 269
  Williamite treatment of, 278
  Williamite views on, 277
Rawdon, Sir Arthur, 38
Reading, England, 33
recruits/recruitment,
  by Balldearg O'Donnell, 260, 261
  for restoration army, 9, 10
  for Jacobite army, 23, 26, 79, 83, 85–8, 104, 117, 128, 193, 213, 283, 290, 295, 297, 312
  for French regiments, 13, 207, 215, 216
  for Irish regiments in France, 58, 212, 219, 220–1, 222–3, 262, 284, 314, 324, 318, 327–30, 333
  for Irish regiments in Spain, 332
  for Scotland, 47
reduction of army, 42–4
regiments
  French in Ireland
    Famechon, 206
    Forest/Chemrault, 206, 207
    La Marche/Biron, 206, 207
    Merode, 206, 207

regiments (continued)
  French in Ireland (continued)
    Tournasis/Brouilly, 206, 207
    Zurlauben, 90, 206, 207
  Irish army
    cavalry
      Abercorn, 112, 114, 120, 132, 286, 300
      Arran/Tyrconnell, 12, 16, 20, 112, 113, 131
      horseguards, 53, 117–18
        1st troop Dover/Sarsfield, 112, 113, 114, 117–18, 119, 130, 131, 290
        2nd troop Berwick, 113, 114, 118
      Luttrell (Henry), 112, 126, 131, 286, 292, 301
      Merrion, 113, 114, 260, 262, 264
      O'Brien (Charles), 113, 114
      Ormond/Russell/Sarsfield/Kilmallock, 28, 112, 113, 114, 115, 124, 125, 131
      Ossory/Ardglass/Galmoy, 12, 18, 20, 28, 38, 112, 115, 117, 119, 125, 126, 131, 274, 301
      Parker/Westmeath, 53, 112, 113, 119, 130, 131
      Purcell, 113, 115
      Sutherland, 53, 112, 114, 115, 132
      Tyrconnell, 16, 28, 53, 112, 115, 117, 119
    dragoons
      Clifford, 121, 123, 124, 289, 296
      Cotter/Carroll, 121, 124, 182, 294, 296, 301
      Dungan/Nugent (Walter)/Bellew (Richard), 35, 53, 88, 121, 123, 124, 133, 296
      Hamilton/Butler, 12, 28, 32, 33, 123, 296
      Luttrell (Simon), 121, 124, 204, 292, 296
      Maxwell, 121, 123, 124, 127, 129, 133, 296
      O'Brien (Daniel/Charles)/Clare, 'Yellow dragoons', 45, 53, 113, 121–2, 123–4, 125, 126, 129, 133, 250, 287, 296, 301
      O'Neill (Neil/Daniel), 54, 121, 124, 129, 133, 183, 296
      O'Reilly (Edmund), 122, 124, 296
      Purcell, 113, 119, 124, 184, 205, 296
    infantry
      Antrim, 35, 69–70, 76, 79, 96, 285, 295, 296
        colours of, 76
        uniforms of, 92
      Bagenal/Power (James), 70, 72
      Barrett, 57, 70, 71, 296
      Bellew, 70, 72, 76, 289, 295, 301
        colours of, 76
        uniforms of, 92
      Boisseleau/Tuite/O'Mahony, 69, 70, 72, 73, 292
      Bophin/Burke (William), 47, 70, 72, 285
        uniforms of, 92
      Browne (Dominic), 70, 100, 192, 286, 287
      Browne (John), 71, 88, 221, 286
      Browne (Nicholas)/FitzGerald (Nicholas), 70, 72, 83, 295
      Butler (Edward), 70, 87, 226
      Butler (James), 71
      Butler (Richard), 70, 71, 73, 221
      Butler (Walter/Thomas), 70, 73, 103
      Burke (Michael), 73
      Burke (Thomas), 261, 262, 263
      Burke (Walter), 64, 68, 71, 72
      Burke (William), 73
      Castleconnell, 71

INDEX

Cavenagh, 57, 70, 71, 98
Clanmalier, 71, 70
Clanricard, 35, 51, 70, 296
Clare, 35, 70, 71, 177
Connell/Wilson, 72
Creagh, 70, 73, 74, 79, 87, 98, 183, 188, 286, 293, 296
Dillon (Arthur), 69, 71, 221
Dillon (Henry), 69, 70
Enniskillen, 71
Eustace, 70, 296
   possible colours of, 76
Fairfax/Clancarty/Prince of Wales, 20, 22, 29, 57, 69, 70, 71, 72, 74, 221, 251, 296
Farrell/O'Gara, 70, 74
Fielding, 71, 88, 221
FitzGerald (B.), 73
FitzGerald (John), 70, 74, 95
FitzGerald (Edward), 72
footguards, 9, 12, 18, 20, 26, 28, 32–3, 35, 38, 53, 69, 70, 75, 78–9, 103, 192, 286, 296, 317
   colours of, 76
   uniforms of, 92
Galway, 36, 43, 70, 72, 285, 289
Geoghegan (Charles), 71, 261, 262, 265
Gormanston/Eustace (Richard), 70, 72, 295
Grace (John/Robert), 71, 72, 73
Granard/Forbes, 20, 23, 29, 32–3, 69
Hunsdon, 284, 290
Iveagh, 70, 74, 296
Kenmare, 70, 295, 296
Kilmallock/Moone Power, 70, 72, 83, 87, 88, 94, 96, 99
   possible colours of, 76
   uniforms of, 92–3
Kingsland, 71
Lacy/Prince of Wales, 69, 72, 89, 222

Louth, 70, 76, 295
   colours of, 76
   uniforms of, 92
Lynch, 71, 286
MacCarthy, 73
MacCarthy More/the two MacCarthys/MacCarthy (Owen), 46, 57, 70, 71, 73, 85, 221, 287
   uniforms of, 92
MacCarthy Reagh, 71
MacDermott, 71, 72, 261, 262, 263
MacElligott, 34, 57, 70, 71, 76, 94
MacGillycuddy, 71
MacMahon (Brian/Art), 70–1, 74, 87
MacMahon (Hugh), 71, 74
Maguire, Cúconnacht/Alexander, 71, 72
Moore, 70
Mountcashel, 16, 24, 29, 38, 45, 69, 70, 71, 88, 166, 221, 296
Mountjoy/Hamilton (John)/Nugent (James), 23, 29, 38, 39, 69, 70, 72, 293, 296
Murphy, 73
Newcomen/Ramsay/grand prior/Talbot (Mark), 16, 22, 29, 69, 70, 72, 73, 76, 92, 94, 106, 107, 242, 251, 296
   colours of, 76
Nugent (Edmund), 71
Nugent (James), 72
Nugent (William/Richard)/'the Caps', 70, 88, 203, 286, 295
O'Brien (Charles)/Saxby, 70, 72, 221
O'Brien, Daniel, 88, 166, 221
O'Cahan, 71, 72, 261, 262, 263
O'Connor (Conor), 261, 262, 263,

regiments (*continued*)
  Irish army (*continued*)
    infantry (*continued*)
      O'Connor, (Roger), 71, 72
      O'Connor Sligo (Daniel?), 261, 262
      O'Doherty, 72, 261, 262, 263
      O'Donnell (Balldearg), 261, 262, 263, 265, 266
      O'Donnell (Connell), 261, 262
      O'Donnell (Daniel), 261, 262
      O'Donnell (Manus), 71, 72
      O'Donovan, 70, 83, 221
      O'Kelly, 43, 71
      O'Mahony, 72
      O'Neill (Brian), 72, 222, 261, 262, 263
      O'Neill (Brian Boy MacArt), 72, 261, 262, 263, 267
      O'Neill (Cormac), 46, 70, 85, 88, 100, 182, 295
      O'Neill (Felix), 69, 71, 72, 74, 286, 292
      O'Neill (Gordon), 64, 69, 70, 74, 76
        colours of, 76
        uniforms of, 92
      O'Neill (Henry MacTool), 71
      O'Reilly (Edmund), 70
      O'Reilly (MacThomas), 71
      O'Rourke (Conor), 72, 261, 262, 263, 266
      O'Rourke (Tiernan), 261, 262
      Oxburgh (Heward/Henry), 43, 70, 103, 286, 289, 295
      Prince of Wales, *see* Clancarty and Lacy
      Purcell (James)/ Sir Edward Scott, 72
      Russell/Hamilton (Anthony), 20, 29, 32–4, 69
      Skelton, 73
      Slane, 70, 73, 78
      Talbot (James), 71
      Tyrconnell/Westmeath/Toole, 70, 72, 73, 76, 286
      Tyrone, 35, 57, 69, 70, 76, 83, 296
      Wauchope, 73
  mounted grenadiers, 12, 21, 28, 38, 112, 118
Irish in France
  cavalry
    horseguards (Berwick/Lucan/Clancarty), 321
    king's (Sheldon), 321
    queen's (Galmoy), 321
    Sheldon/Nugent/FitzJames, 325, 326, 329, 334, 335
  dragoons
    king's (Bellew/Maxwell/Kilmallock), 320, 321
    queen's (Carroll/Clare/O'Gara), 321, 321
  infantry
    Athlone (Eustace/Burke), 320, 321, 324, 326; *see also* Irish regiments in Spain
    Berwick/FitzJames/88th, 325, 326, 329, 330, 335
    Clancarty/MacElligott, 321
    Charlemont (O'Neill), 320, 321
    Dillon/87th, 220, 221, 318–19, 321, 324, 325, 326, 329, 330
    Dublin (Luttrell/Power) 320, 321
    footguards/Dorrington/Rothe/Roscommon/Walsh/92nd, 321, 326, 329, 330, 335
    Galmoy, 324, 326
    Lally, 326
    Limerick (Talbot/FitzGerald), 320, 321, 325
    marine (grand prior [Albemarle]/FitzGerald/Nugent/O'Donnell), 320, 321, 326
    Mountcashel/Lee/Bulkeley, 220, 221, 318, 321, 326

O'Brien/Clare/Lee/Talbot, 220,
    221, 318, 321, 329, 330, 333
  queen's (Wauchope/Scott/
    Luttrell), 320, 32
Irish in Naples
  infantry
    Limerick/regimiento de rey,
      331; *see also* Irish in Spain
Irish in Spain
  dragoons
    Crofton/Dublin, 331
    FitzHarris, 331
    O'Mahony/Edinburgh, 331
  infantry
    Burke/Wauchope/Connacia/
      Irlanda, '*El Famoso*', 331;
      see also Irish regiments in
      France
    Castelar (MacDonnell)/
      Hibernia, '*La Columna*',
      331
    Comerford/Waterford, 331
    McAuliffe/Ultonia, '*El
      Immortal*', 331
    Momomia, 331
    Vandoma/*Vendôme* (Begg)/
      Limerick, 331; *see also*
      Irish in Naples
Reilly, Edmund, 256
Reilly, Luke, 22
Rice, Stephen, 39, 40, 252
Richard, Jacob, 267
Richards, John, 264, 267, 291
Rijswijk, treaty of (1697), 324
Riverston, Thomas Nugent, 1st Baron,
  59, 174, 252, 260, 284
Robert, M., 154, 159
Robinson, William, 152
Rome, Italy, 337
Roscommon, county of, 235, 240
Roscommon, Wentworth Dillon, 4th
  earl of, 13
Roscommon, Carey Dillon, 5th earl of, 20
Roscommon, Robert Dillon, 6th earl of,
  20

Rosen, Marshal Conrad von, 37, 40, 47,
  88, 89, 135, 161, 171, 174, 182, 189,
  203, 270, *plate 3*
  at Derry, 165, 183, 251, 273, 297
  commands left wing in order of
    battle, 170
  disillusionment of, 165
  marshal, 165, 200
  role and character of, 164–6, 200
Rossnaree, Co. Meath, 51, 54, 133
Rothe, John, 12
Rothe, Michael, 40, 173
Roughgrange, Co. Meath, 54
Royal Hospital, Kilmainham, Dublin,
  11, 19, 26, 38, 186, 225, 250
Royal Irish Regiment, 34
Russell, Theodore, 20–1
Russia/Russians, 326, 330

Sainte-Croix, le sieur de, 292
Saint-Didier, le chevalier de, 190
Saint-Germain-en-Laye, 176, 195, 221,
  317, 324, 325
Saint-Martin, le sieur de, 137, 213
Saint-Pater, Jacques le Coutelier,
  marquis de, 170, 172, 201–2
Saint-Rémy, Pierre Surirey de, 139
Saint-Ruth, Charles Chalmont, marquis
  de, 59, 60, 66, 81, 100, 136, 154,
  159, 162, 163, 168, 171, 191, 185,
  212, 218, 247, 249, 290
  abandons Ballymore, 60
  and Mountcashel brigade, 209, 222
  arrives at Limerick, 60, 166, 238
  attitude to Balldearg O'Donnell, 260,
    263
  authority of, 164, 166–8, 173
  brings arms, cannon, food and
    matériel, 127, 144, 217, 238, 242,
    243
  career in Ireland, 208–10
  conduct of battle of Aughrim, 62–5,
    120, 149–50, 167–8, 178, 179,
    194
  death of, 64, 167, 173, 178, 336

Saint-Ruth, Charles Chalmont, marquis
    de, (*continued*)
  empowered to issue commissions, 79
  empathy with Irish, 60, 167–8, 209
  loses Athlone, 61, 159, 167
  preparations for campaign, 60
  releases arms to Balldearg O'Donnell,
    263
  summarizes Irish war aims, 303–4
Salisbury, England, 33
Salkeld, Robert, 12
Salzbach, Germany, battle of (1675), 178
San Domingo, 327
Santons Boullain, le sieur de, 204, 292
Sarsfield (*née* Burke), Honora, countess
    of Lucan, 285, 299
Sarsfield, Patrick, 1st earl of Lucan, 43,
    45, 60, 61, 66, 130, 131, 184, 191,
    219, 258, 260, 273, 285, 290, 299,
    323, 338, *plate 4*
  at Aughrim, 62, 65, 111, 120, 168, 173
  Ballyneety raid, 56, 111, 133, 164,
    168, 215, 274
  brigadier, 168
  colonelcy of cavalry regiment, 112,
    113, 119, 124, 131, 168
  colonelcy of horseguard troop, 113,
    118, 321
  concern about food supply in
    Limerick, 244
  d'Avaux's estimate of, 169
  earl of Lucan, 168
  early career of, 13, 24, 25, 34, 115,
    168, 196, 291
  estate of, 298
  house and property of, 285, 302
  hostility to Tyrconnell, 58, 163, 168,
    185
  informed of Williamite plans, 178
  in order of battle, 170, 172, 173
  leadership role of, 55, 58, 66, 162,
    168–9, 174, 179, 313, 317
  leads Irish army to France post-war,
    89, 315, 316, 317, 320
  Luxembourg's estimate of, 169
  major general, 168, 283, 319
  negotiates treaty of Limerick, 168–9,
    244, 254, 315
  recaptures Sligo, Jamestown and
    Boyle, 47, 168
  role in war, 168–9, 287
  suppresses peace party, 59, 168, 174
  thwarts Williamite winter offensive,
    59, 168
  Williamite regard for, 168
Savage, family of, 281
Savage, Rowland, 286
Savoy, 166, 197, 209
Saxby, William, 72
second world war 'emergency', 336
secretary for war, *see* military-related
    offices
Schomberg, Frederick Herman, 1st duke
    of, 46–7, 49, 51, 53, 104, 132, 178,
    234, 246, 257, 270, 276
Schomberg, Meinhard, Count, 51, 54
Scotland, 41, 47–8, 334, 335
Scott, Edward, 103, 265
Scott, Sir Edward, 25, 57, 72, 74, 291,
    299, 320, 321
Seignelay, John Baptiste Colbert,
    marquis de, 40, 196–7
seven years war, 334
Sevin, M., 154, 159
Shannon river
  defensive barrier, 46, 50, 158, 178, 263
Shee, James, 301
Sheldon, Dominic, 20, 24, 25, 42, 64,
    115, 120, 162, 163, 170, 172, 173,
    179, 196, 299, 321, 325, 334
Sheridan, Thomas, 18, 295
Sherlock, Edward, 286
Sicily, 197
Skelton, James, 73
Skelton, John, 74
Slane, 51, 54
Slane, Christopher Fleming, 17th Baron,
    70, 72, 285, 298, 300, 317
Slater, Solomon, 176
Sligo, 55, 158, 266

artillerists at, 138
Balldearg O'Donnell and siege of, 264–5
cannon at, 150
cannonballs sent to, 254
evacuated by Jacobites, 45
food supply of, 237, 242
fortifications of, 159
recovered by Sarsfield, 47
Sir Teague O'Regan, governor of, 49
supplied from Galway, 247
surrender of, 66, 314, 315
Sligo, county of, 296
Protestants of, 38, 42, 281
rapparees of, 279
Snapphanar, 268
'Soldiers and chiefs' exhibition, 339
soldiers/rank and file, Jacobite, 59
background of, 85, 87, 297
butchering skills of, 241
Catholic replace Protestant, 21–3
company establishment of, 75
conduct of
at Aughrim, 84
at Ballyneety, 59
at the Boyne, 53
at Limerick, 59
against winter offensive, 59
desertion/absenteeism of, 73, 75, 84, 88, 89–90, 178, 183
disorders of, 37, 43
dragoons, 16, 28, 100, 122–3
English and Scottish, 87, 291
for Franco-Irish brigade, 219–21
grenadiers, 35, 75, 93, 99, 100, 101, 102, 107, 239
role of in battle, 11, 108
see also mounted/horse grenadiers
hunger of, 237, 238
leave, 27
morale and beliefs of, 33, 47, 60, 61, 62, 84, 86, 297
aversion to French service of, 208, 219, 222–3
hatred of English by, 86, 272

musketeers, 75, 96
exercises of, 105, 100
poor quality of musketry, 53, 55, 84
proportion to pikemen, 100–1
role in battle, 108
training of, 106
numbers that opted to go to France post-war, 315–18
number that opted to remain in Ireland post-war, 316
opinions on
Boisseleau's, 85
Clarendon's, 22–3, 24
Claudianus's, 85
d'Avaux's, 84
English, 26, 33
d'Esgrigny's, 85
French, 44
Fumeron's, 84
Wm. King's, 22–3
Lauzun's, 85
Stevens's, 75, 84–5, 87
Williamite, 85, 86
Würtemburg's, 66
physique of, 19, 84–5, 232
pikemen, 75, 101
role in battle, 108
shouting and hallowing of, 84
title, 83–4
see also arms; discipline; pay; recruits/recruitment; uniforms
Solebay, naval battle of (1672), 17
Southwell, Sir Robert, 36, 327
Spain/Spaniards, 323, 326, 329, 330
army of, 68
Irish regiments in, 330–2
Jacobite sentiments of, 334, 335
Spanish succession war, 267, 268, 325
spies; *see* intelligence
Spillane, Maurice, 274
Springfield, Co. Limerick, 301
Stackumney, Co. Kildare, 300
Stafford, Alexius, 192, 194
Stapleton, Charles, 188
Stapleton, Walter, 335

Stepney, George, 266
Stevens, John, 49, 73, 75, 80, 83, 84, 86, 87, 89, 92, 95, 100, 104, 107, 123, 158, 184, 186, 204, 207, 208, 231, 234, 243, 245, 288, 290, 298, 338
Story, George, 1, 59, 187, 244, 270, 271, 274, 275, 277, 316
Strabane, Co. Tyrone, 42, 188
St Stephen's Green, Dublin, 207
Stuart, Cardinal Henry Benedict, 335
stud farms, *see* horses
surgeons; *see* medicine/medical services
sutlers/suttling houses, 91, 233, 234, 242, 243
Sunderland, Robert Spencer, 3rd earl of, 20, 32
Sutherland, Hugh, 112, 171, 172, 173
Swedes, 330
Swift, Jonathan, 337
Swiss, 330
Syonan Castle, Co. Westmeath, 301

Taaffe, Francis, later 3rd earl of Carlingford, 129
Taaffe, Lawrence, 256
Talbot, Bruno, 252
Talbot, George, 24
Talbot, James, 71
Talbot, Mark, 72, 74, 173, 242, 285, 291, 292, 315, 321
Talbot, Richard, *see* Tyrconnell
Talbotstown, Co. Wicklow, 102
Tangier garrison, 7, 10, 13, 24, 152, 291, 293
Tangis, le chevalier de, 153, 205
Temple, Sir William, 128
Tempo, Co. Fermanagh, 298, 299
tenant farmers, 85
Tessé, Philibert-Emmanuel de Froullay, chevalier de, 65, 81, 118, 173, 174, 178, 184, 209–10, 319
test acts, 13
Thomond Bridge, Limerick, 67, 73
Thomond, Henry O'Brien, 7th earl of, 129

Thompson, Charles, 27, 187
Tilbury Fort, England, 33
Tipperary, county of, 296, 302
    rapparees in, 268, 272, 274, 296
tobacco, 232–3, 243
Toole, Francis, 70, 72, 73, 182, 286
Topham, Sir John, 21
tories, 268
Tower of London, 34, 39
transhumance, 303
transport, 245–7
    artillery train, 144–6, 245–6, 247
    back baskets, 247
    carters/drivers, 137, 138, 145, 239, 246
    carts/tumbrels, 15, 144, 145, 191, 245, 246, 247, 261
    farriers, 117, 217, 246
    gabbards, 246
    lost at Boyne, 247
    oxen, 245
    packhorses, 245
    panniers, 247
    roads, 144, 241, 245, 246, 153
    Shannon boats, 247
    sledges/sliding cars, 145, 246
    speed of, 245
    supply train, 246
    wagons, 15, 45, 144, 235, 245–6, 247, 255
Trant, Sir Patrick, 121, 301
Trant, Thomas, 121, 301
Trappe, Nicholas, 192
Trim, 236
Trinity College Dublin, 128, 192, 250
trumpets/trumpeters, 22, 116–17
Tuam, Co. Galway, 263
Tuite, William, 72, 173, 291, 300
Tully, Co. Kildare, 298
Tullyallen, Co. Louth, 50
Turenne, Henri de La Tour d'Auvergne, vicomte de, 161, 178
Turgot des Fontaines, le sieur de, 136
Turks, imperial campaigns against, 15, 24, 103
Turlough, Co. Mayo, 298

Turvey, Co. Dublin, 202
Twistleton, George, 19
Tyrconnell, Francis, duchess of, 70
Tyrconnell, Richard Talbot, 1st duke of, 13, 16, 32, 38, 59, 70, 72, 78, 82, 90, 99, 106, 120, 135, 162, 165, 222, 174, 184, 205, 213, 218, 226, 231, 242, 273, 283, 300, *plate 1*
    army reductions by, 42–3
    army reforms of, 17–24, 27–30, 92
    army enlargement by, 36
    attitude to Gaelic Irish of, 17, 21, 259–60, 295
    captain general, 41, 162, 169
    character of, 17, 163
    commands right wing in order of battle, 170, 172
    considers French dependency status for Ireland, 196
    death of, 66
    disarms Protestant militia, 18, 256
    dissatisfaction with, 163–4, 179, 184–5
    dukedom, 41
    early career of, 17, 24
    establishes militia, 35
    favours making terms, 55, 58, 163
    goes to France, 58, 172
    hostility of Sarsfield to, 58, 163, 168, 185
    hostility to Balldearg O'Donnell of, 259–60
    houses and estates of, 298, 302
    issues commissions, 19, 23, 36, 79
    lieutenant general, 18
    lord deputy, 23
    loses command of army, 60, 163, 173
    negotiations with William III, 37
    opposed to abandoning Dublin and Leinster, 46, 50
    orders general mobilization, 258
    organizes resistance to Schomberg, 164, 200
    priest siblings of, 193
    regiment of, 16, 28, 53, 112, 119, 120
    relationship with Saint-Ruth, 60
    reluctance to send reinforcements to Mountcashel brigade, 222
    response to English revolution by, 35–6
    resents Melfort, 42–3, 45, 46, 161–2
    resumes command of army, 66, 164, 173–4
    returns to Ireland, 60
    role and authority of, 162–3
    secretary of, 18, 193
    seeks supplies in France, 249
    seeks stronger French naval presence, 199
    strategic sense of, 164
Tyrone, county of, 296
Tyrone, Richard Power, 1st earl, 35, 70, 71, 281, 294, 296
Tyrrell, Sir Edward, 294
Tyrrell, Patrick, 193

Ulster, province of, 157, 263, 270, 287, 303, 311, 325
    camp followers from, 91
    creaghts from, 240, 260, 316
    Jacobite campaign in, 42, 44–6, 147, 199, 270
    rapparees from, 269, 270
    recruits from, 87
    regiments of, 46, 64, 88, 124, 207, 295, 296, 317
    Williamite quarters in, 47
    Williamite regiments from, 49, 87, 271, 278
    Williamite support in, 38, 42, 47, 48, 49
    see also O'Donnell, Hugh Balldearg
Ulster Museum, 338
uniforms/clothing, 27, 36, 60, 91–5, 124–5, 217, 225, 252–3, 262, 263, 318, 319, 324, 333
    annual allocation of, 26, 93
    baldrics, 93, 126
    belts, 93–4, 126, 213, 214
    boots, 26, 94, 125, 253
    buttons & loops, 92–4

uniforms/clothing, (*continued*)
  brogues, 95
  buckles, 26, 93
  breeches/trousers, 26, 93, 94, 95, 253
  caps/bonnets, 93, 94, 124, 253
  cloaks, 125
  coats, 9, 26, 92–4, 124–5, 252
    from France, 94, 253
    tight-fitting, 217
  condition of, 94, 252
  cost of, 92–3
  cravats, 26, 94
  drummers', 83, 93
  facings, 92, 124
  garters, 26
  gloves, 93
  gorgets, 94
  hats, 26, 93, 124–5, 252, 253, 318
  lack of, 40
  linen for, 252–3
  leather coats
  manufacture of, 252–3
  officers', 94
  sashes, 26, 93
  shirts, 26, 93, 216, 252, 253, 318
  shoes, 26, 93, 94–5, 125, 216, 252, 253, 318
  spurs, 125
  stockings, 26, 93, 95, 253
  stocks, 125
  stockpins, 125
  trousers, 253
  waistcoats, 93, 125, 216
  wigs, 94, 125
  woollen cloth for, 253
  see also armour

Upper Ossory, Barnaby/Bryan Fitzpatrick, 7th Baron, 299
Urraghry, 62, 64, 149
Usson, Jean de Bonnac, marquis d', 61, 66, 89, 118, 171, 173, 174, 263, 319, *plate 10*
  career in Ireland, 209–10
utensils, 232, 241

vagrants, 85
Valleri, M., 153
Vauban, Sébastien Le Prestre de, 40, 141, 152, 156, 324
Vaudrey, Sir Edward, 292
Velletri, siege of (1744), 331
Vandoma/Vendôme, Louis Joseph de Bourbon, duc de, 331
Venice, Italy, 267
Versailles, France, 337
Vienna, Austria, 129, 337
Villeroi, François de Neufville, duc de, 324
visitor centres, 339

Waldegrave, Henrietta, Lady, 285
Wall, Patrick, 334
Wall, Richard, 332
Wallenstein, Albrecht von, 120
Walsh de Serrant, Anthony Joseph, 2nd Count, 327
Walsh, Edward, 338
Waterford,
  city of, 55, 150, 158, 191, 214, 276
  county of, 268, 271, 296
Watson, Rowland, 103
Wauchope, Francis, 321, 331
Wauchope, John, 58, 73, 154, 170, 173, 183, 185, 291, 315, 323, 334

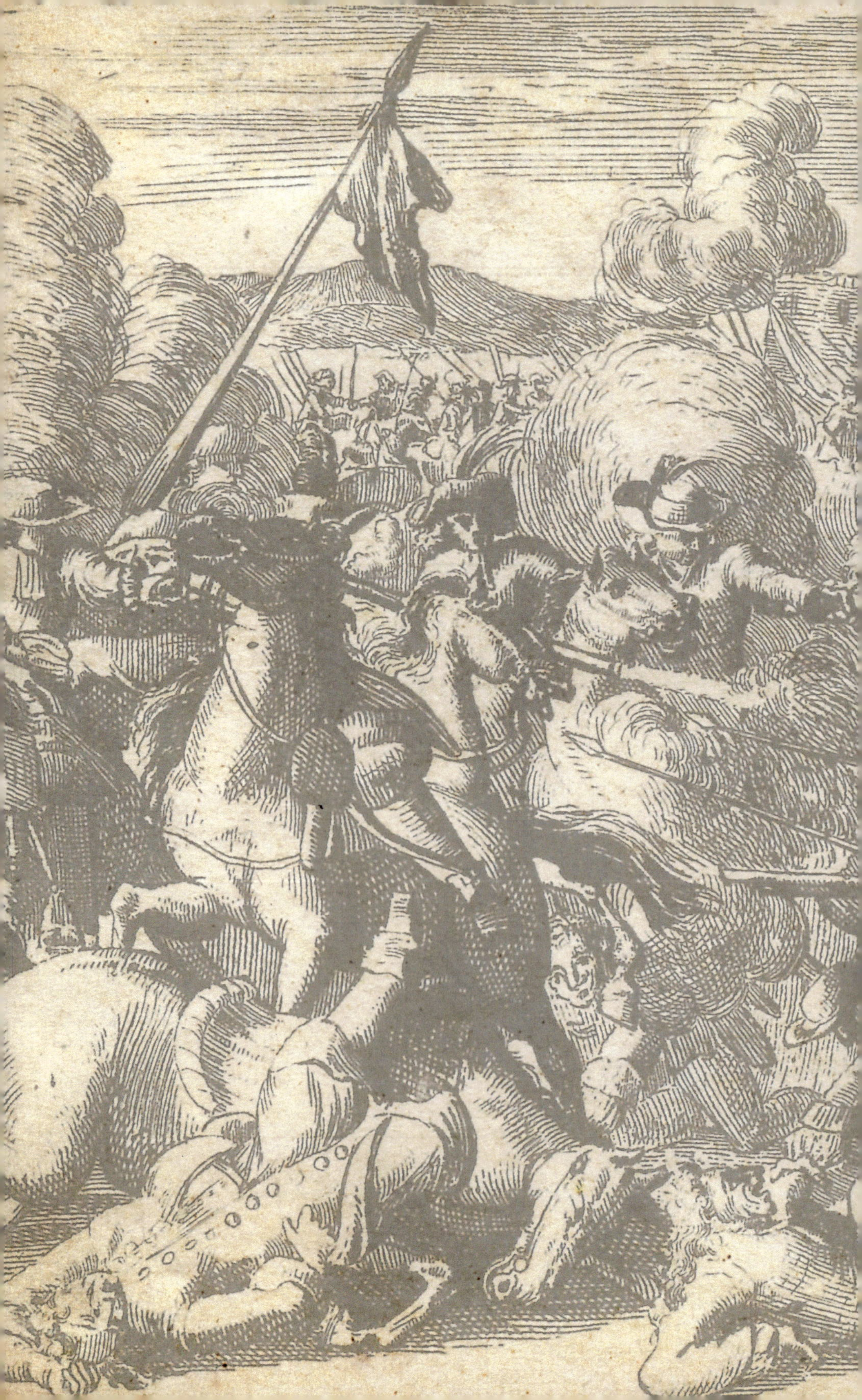